Lecture Notes in Information Systems and Organisation

Volume 33

Lecture Notes in Information Systems and Organization—LNISO—is a series of scientific books that explore the current scenario of information systems, in particular IS and organization. The focus on the relationship between IT, IS and organization is the common thread of this collection, which aspires to provide scholars across the world with a point of reference and comparison in the study and research of information systems and organization. LNISO is the publication forum for the community of scholars investigating behavioral and design aspects of IS and organization. The series offers an integrated publication platform for high-quality conferences, symposia and workshops in this field. Materials are published upon a strictly controlled double blind peer review evaluation made by selected reviewers. LNISO is abstracted/indexed in Scopus

More information about this series at http://www.springer.com/series/11237

Alessandra Lazazzara · Francesca Ricciardi ·
Stefano Za

Editors

Exploring Digital Ecosystems

Organizational and Human Challenges

 Springer

Editors
Alessandra Lazazzara
Department of Social and Political Sciences
University of Milan
Milan, Italy

Francesca Ricciardi
Department of Management
University of Turin
Turin, Italy

Stefano Za
Management and Business Administration
University of Chieti-Pescara
Pescara, Italy

ISSN 2195-4968 ISSN 2195-4976 (electronic)
Lecture Notes in Information Systems and Organisation
ISBN 978-3-030-23664-9 ISBN 978-3-030-23665-6 (eBook)
https://doi.org/10.1007/978-3-030-23665-6

This Springer imprint is published by the registered company Springer Nature Switzerland AG
The registered company address is: Gewerbestrasse 11, 6330 Cham, Switzerland

Preface

The recent surge of interest in 'digital ecosystems' highlights the impact of pervasive connectivity on firms and societies and poses several human and organizational challenges. Therefore, both scholars and practitioners are interested in better understanding and managing the key mechanisms behind their emergence and the dynamics within and between digital ecosystems. In order to disentangle such factors and explaining how digital ecosystems may benefit different stakeholders, this book contains a collection of research papers focusing on the relationships between technologies (e.g., digital platforms, AI, infrastructure) and behaviours (e.g., digital learning, knowledge sharing, decision-making), and provides critical insights about how digital ecosystems may shape value creation. The plurality of views offered makes this book particularly relevant to users, companies, scientists and governments. The content of the book is based on a selection of the best papers (original double-blind peer-reviewed contributions) presented at the annual conference of the Italian chapter of AIS which took place in Pavia, Italy in October 2018.

Milan, Italy
May 2019

Alessandra Lazazzara
Francesca Ricciardi
Stefano Za

Contents

Introduction to Digital Ecosystem 1
Alessandra Lazazzara, Francesca Ricciardi and Stefano Za

Part I Human Communities in Digital Ecosystems

Rethinking Romanian and Italian Smart Cities as Knowledge-Based
Communities 11
Ramona-Diana Leon and Mauro Romanelli

Are the Elderly Averse to Technology? 25
Jonathan Jones and Peter Bednar

Value Co-creation in Online Communities: A Preliminary
Literature Analysis 33
Stefano Za, Jessie Pallud, Rocco Agrifoglio and Concetta Metallo

Disability and Home Automation: Insights and Challenges
Within Organizational Settings 47
Luisa Varriale, Paola Briganti and Stefania Mele

Efforts Towards Openness and Transparency of Data:
A Focus on Open Science Platforms 67
Daniela Mancini, Alessandra Lardo and Massimo De Angelis

Millennials, Information Assessment, and Social Media:
An Exploratory Study on the Assessment of Critical
Thinking Habits 85
Michael Menichelli and Alessio Maria Braccini

Part II   Human Resources and Learning in Digital Ecosystems

Grasping Corporate Identity from Social Media:
Analysis of HR Consulting Companies   101
Stefano Di Lauro, Aizhan Tursunbayeva, Gilda Antonelli
and Marcello Martinez

Managing Intellectual Capital Inside Online Communities of Practice:
An Integrated Multi-step Approach   121
Chiara Meret, Michela Iannotta, Desiree Giacomelli, Mauro Gatti
and Ida Sirolli

How Do We Learn Today and How Will We Learn in the Future
Within Organizations? Digitally-Enhanced and Personalized
Learning Win   135
Leonardo Caporarello, Beatrice Manzoni, Chiara Moscardo
and Lilach Trabelsi

Understanding the Relationship Between Intellectual Capital
and Organizational Performance: The Role of e-HRM
and Performance Pay   151
Alessandra Lazazzara, Edoardo Della Torre and Raoul C. D. Nacamulli

Information and Communication Technologies Usage for Professional
Purposes, Work Changes and Job Satisfaction. Some Insights
from Europe   165
Daria Sarti, Teresina Torre and Elena Pirani

(Digital) Learning Models and Organizational Learning Mechanisms:
Should Organizations Adopt a Single Learning Model
or Multiple Ones?   179
Leonardo Caporarello, Beatrice Manzoni and Lilach Trabelsi

Part III   Processes and IS Design in Digital Ecosystems

Meta Principles of Technology Accessibility Design for Users
with Learning Disabilities: Towards Inclusion of the Differently
Enabled   195
Nabil Georges Badr and Michele Kosremelli Asmar

Business Process Analysis and Change Management: The Role
of Material Resource Planning and Discrete-Event Simulation   211
Antonio Di Leva, Emilio Sulis, Angela De Lellis
and Ilaria Angela Amantea

A Simulation-Driven Approach to Decision Support in Process
Reorganization: A Case Study in Healthcare   223
Ilaria Angela Amantea, Antonio Di Leva and Emilio Sulis

**How to Rate a Physician?—A Framework for Physician Ratings
and What They Mean**   237
Maximilian Haug and Heiko Gewald

**Last Mile Logistics in Smart Cities: An IT Platform for Vehicle
Sharing and Routing**   251
Emanuele Guerrazzi

**Digital Transformation Projects Maturity and Managerial
Competences: A Model and Its Preliminary Assessment**   261
Aurelio Ravarini, Angela Locoro and Marcello Martinez

**Reporting Some Marginal Discourses to Root a De-design
Approach in IS Development**   273
Federico Cabitza, Angela Locoro and Aurelio Ravarini

**Digital Infrastructures for Patient Centered Care:
Examining Two Strategies for Recombinability**   289
Miria Grisot, Tomas Lindroth and Anna Sigridur Islind

**Time Accounting System: Measuring Usability for Validating
the Socio-Technical Fit of E-service Exchange Solutions
in Local Communities**   301
Tunazzina Sultana

Digital Identity: A Case Study of the ProCIDA Project   315
Francesco Bellini, Fabrizio D'Ascenzo, Iana Dulskaia
and Marco Savastano

**A Monte Carlo Method for the Diffusion of Information
Between Mobile Agents**   329
Alberto Berretti and Simone Ciccarone

Part IV   Organizing in Digital Ecosystems

**Understanding the Use of Smart Working in Public Administration:
The Experience of the Presidency of the Council of Ministers**   343
Maurizio Decastri, Francesca Gagliarducci, Pietro Previtali
and Danila Scarozza

Decisions and Infrastructure (In)visibility: A Case Study   365
Roberta Cuel and Diego Ponte

**Unlocking the Value of Public Sector Personal Information
Through Coproduction**   379
Walter Castelnovo

Social Media Communication Strategies in Fashion Industry   393
F. Cabiddu, C. Dessì and M. Floris

**The Illusion of Routine as an Indicator for Job Automation
with Artificial Intelligence** 407
Jason Bissessur, Farzad Arabikhan and Peter Bednar

**IS in the Cloud and Organizational Benefits:
An Exploratory Study** 417
Emanuele Gabriel Margherita and Alessio Maria Braccini

**Organizational Change and Learning: An Explorative
Bibliometric-Based Literature Analysis** 429
Stefano Za, Cristiano Ghiringhelli and Francesco Virili

**Community-Oriented Motivations and Knowledge Sharing
as Drivers of Success Within Food Assemblies** 443
Paola De Bernardi, Alberto Bertello and Francesco Venuti

Author Index 459

Introduction to Digital Ecosystem

Alessandra Lazazzara, Francesca Ricciardi and Stefano Za

This book collects some of the best contributions presented at the XV Conference of the Italian Chapter of AIS (ItAIS) which was held at the University of Pavia, Italy, in October 2018. ItAIS is an important community of reference for scholars and researchers involved in the Information Systems domain. The participants of the itAIS conferences include national and international researchers interested in exchanging ideas and discussing the most important trends in the IS discipline. The contributions included in this volume cover a wide variety of topics related to how people, communities, and organizations address the digital age, with a specific focus on digital ecosystems.

In the first place, the concept of a digital ecosystem has been mainly used in the literature on service-oriented architectures, in order to indicate the relevant interdependencies between service providers and clients of IT services [1, 2]. However, the label of the digital ecosystem is being increasingly used also in a broader sense, to indicate the self-organizing capabilities and complex interdependencies between and across the technological and the social environment [3]. This evolution is consistent with the growing interest of all sciences in complexity, systems thinking, and sustainability concerns [4]. By choosing this theme as the common thread of this book's contributions, we intend to highlight the important role that information systems studies are called on to play in this interdisciplinary effort.

A. Lazazzara (✉)
Department of Social and Political Sciences, University of Milan, Milan, Italy
e-mail: alessandra.lazazzara@unimi.it

F. Ricciardi
Department of Management, University of Turin, Turin, Italy
e-mail: francesca.ricciardi@unito.it

S. Za
DEA—Department of Management and Business Administration,
University "G. d'Annunzio" of Chieti-Pescara, Pescara, Italy
e-mail: stefano.za@unich.it

© Springer Nature Switzerland AG 2020
A. Lazazzara et al. (eds.), *Exploring Digital Ecosystems*,
Lecture Notes in Information Systems and Organisation 33,
https://doi.org/10.1007/978-3-030-23665-6_1

All the 31 selected papers included in this volume have been evaluated and selected for publication through a standard blind review process, in order to ensure relevance and rigor. The contributions have been clustered into four sections: (a) Human communities in digital ecosystems; (b) Human resources and learning in digital ecosystems; (c) Processes and IS design in digital ecosystems; and (d) Organizing for digital ecosystems.

1 Human Communities in Digital Ecosystems

The first part of the book explores how digital ecosystems influence the options, perceptions, capabilities, and relationships within and across different types of communities.

In the paper by Leon and Romanelli, smart cities are viewed as communities of citizens. This study suggests that technological and institutional solutions to smart city challenges make sense to the extent these solutions positively influence people's values and beliefs, on the one side, and people's capabilities to translate vision into reality, on the other side. The authors adopt a knowledge management perspective to analyze six smart cities in Romania and Italy through a smart city model including six dimensions and 28 components. The resulting citizen-centered smart city view values both visionary and practical knowledge as the two key pillars of smart transformations.

Jones and Bednar conduct an empirical investigation whose results challenge common beliefs about the level of technology acceptance and use on the part of the elderly. In-depth interviews in daycare center reveal that the elderly use different technologies for different purposes and in different contexts. In addition, the study suggests that family pressure is an important factor influencing how the elderly feel about information technology and their decisions to interact with it.

Za, Pallud, Agrifoglio, and Metallo present the results of a literature analysis using bibliometric data of 246 articles debating value co-creation process within online communities. The quantitative analysis leverages social network analysis tools, which allow for the identification of interesting connections between and across research streams. The most cited and influential publications are identified and described, and the main research areas and most promising topics are highlighted.

The social inclusion of people with disabilities is at the core of the paper by Varriale, Briganti, and Mele. Based on the analysis of the literature published in the 1998–2018 period, the authors discuss whether and how the home automation solutions and devices support disabled people, and particularly their inclusion in the wider social community. The most interesting research perspectives in this field are also identified.

The study by Mancini, Lardo, and De Angelis focuses on open science. The authors argue that the literature has so far mainly addressed open access, which is only the final phase of the open science process. Moreover, they claim that a systemic shift in current practices is necessary to bring transparency in scientific research, to ensure the ongoing sustainability of the associated social and physical infrastructures, and to foster greater public trust in science. The final aim of the authors is to develop a theoretical model for assessing web interfaces of open science platforms.

Menichelli and Braccini address an issue that is of paramount importance for the role of communities in digital ecosystems: critical thinking. The authors investigate the critical thinking skills of millennials in relation to the reported intensity of use of social media and other traditional media for information acquisition. The paper is based on a quantitative analysis of an incidental sample of 424 millennials. The results show that millennials are weak regarding making inferences out of data and information, evaluating arguments, and identifying fake news. Interestingly, the study reveals no differences regarding the influence of social media on critical thinking.

2 Part II: Human Resources and Learning in Digital Ecosystems

The rise of complex digital ecosystem results in complex, intertwining changes in human resource management and learning processes. This section provides some interestingly complementary views on this issue.

Meret, Iannotta, Giacomelli, Sarti, and Sirolli investigate two online communities of practice operating within a leading Italian telecommunication company. Based on this empirical investigation, they propose a tool for assessing the dimensions of intellectual capital in online communities of practice.

Taking another perspective, the study by Di Lauro, Tursunbayeva, Antonelli, and Martinez analyses the social media profiles of 12 international HR consulting companies. In particular, it explores the platforms they use, type of content they publish, their approaches for stakeholder engagement and interaction for stronger organizational image and corporate identity.

Caporarello, Manzoni, Moscardo, and Trabelsi explore the ongoing changes in the processes through which people learn in organizations. Based on a quali-quantitative survey with 91 employees as respondents, the authors show that digitally-enhanced models and methods are constantly growing in importance (although more in terms of "expected" rather than "desired" use), together with a need for more personalized learning.

Lazazzara, Della Torre and Nacamulli leverage a survey on 168 Italian large organizations to investigate the relationship between intellectual capital and organizational performance. The results of this quantitative study are highly interesting and stimulating: in contexts of high intellectual capital, the combined presence of high level of performance pay and e-HRM nullifies the positive impact of intellectual capital on performance, whereas in contexts of low intellectual capital they lead to higher performance.

Another survey, conducted at the European level, provides further insights on the relationship between work changes and Information and Communication Technology usage for professional purposes. Sarti, Torre and Pirani leverage this large survey (with 21,540 respondents) to conduct analyses whose results enable reflections on the emerging challenges of ICT management.

Caporarelli, Manzoni, and Trabelsi investigate whether the learning models (i.e. face-to-face vs. online vs. blended) that employees use to learn have an impact on their satisfaction and enjoyment, as well as their perceptions of the organizational learning mechanisms they are confronted with. Based on a survey (67 employees) the authors highlight that the usage of multiple learning models, instead of just one, is associated to higher employee satisfaction with their learning experiences, and a more positive perception of their company's ability to put in place effective organizational learning mechanisms.

3   Part III: Processes and IS Design in Digital Ecosystems

This rich section includes papers addressing various issues relating to process design and information system design.

The paper by Badr and Kosermelli Asmar focuses on the design of accessible and inclusive technology for people with learning disabilities. Based on a literature review, the authors explore the possible guiding principles for addressing this issue and develop a set of meta-principles of technology accessibility design.

Di Leva, Sulis, De Lellis and Amantea explore the role of business process simulation to address change management projects dealing with significant organizational growth. Based on a case study, the authors illustrate how modeling, computational simulation and scenario analysis of business processes are suitable tools to support organizational change.

Simulation and modeling of business processes are also the main focus of the paper by Amantea, Di Leva, and Sulis. Their paper proposes a methodological framework to investigate risks and compliance in reorganizations by adopting a Business Process Management perspective that includes modeling and simulation of business processes. The effectiveness of the approach is illustrated by describing how it has been applied in a Blood Bank department of a large hospital.

Haug and Gewald also focus on the health care sector, and particularly on the issue of online physician ratings. Based on the literature, the authors develop a framework, which is then tested through structural equation modeling of data collected in the southern Germany context. The findings reveal that physician ratings cannot accurately predict the quality of the healthcare service but are rather a measure of how sympathetic the physician appears to the patient. Implications for design are discussed.

The evolution of last mile logistics in the e-commerce age is the core topic of the paper by Guerrazzi. The author proposes a solution based on a shared Information Technology (IT) platform that enables resource pooling to share heterogeneous vehicles in the urban network. This was achieved through the development of four software modules. The first results of this experimental approach are promising both as for cost savings and air quality.

Ravarini, Locoro, and Martinez discuss some extant technology maturity models and argue that these models while focusing on the technological aspects, tend to overlook the broader set of managerial competencies (i.e. knowledge, skill and experience) that are needed in the different phases of the digital transformation process. Therefore, the authors propose a new digital transformation maturity model and leverage a couple of pilot interviews to discuss its key features and possible future developments.

The study by Cabitza, Locoro, and Ravarini is a theoretical discussion on some main trends in IS design. The authors identify a divide between modeling and practicing, design and use, with the hegemony of the planning mind over that of the performer. However, the current convergence of networked application paradigms and the Web 2.0 infrastructure has led to agile methods, open design concepts and on the idea of a prosuming user. The authors claim that the socio-technical principles could play a pivotal role in mitigating the effects of the modernist over-design attitude, and make IS development more sustainable.

Grisot, Lindroth, and Islind focus on the challenge of designing for recombinability in digital infrastructures. The authors conduct a comparative cases study on two patient-centered digital infrastructures, thus identifying and analyzing two possible design strategies for recombinability in the health care sector.

The paper by Turnazzina presents a prototype of a time accounting system designed to support technology-based service exchange in Bangladesh. The final validation steps are described, at the level of the interface and user interaction. The heuristic-based evaluation process allows the author to identify the main usability problems to be addressed.

Bellini, D'Ascenzo, Dulskaia, and Savastano focus on a key challenge facing cloud computing: digital identity. Their paper presents the results of a project in which a digital platform has been developed in order to simplify access to different kind of digital services (public and private) using digital identity.

The study by Berretti and Ciccarone models the spread of information in random, rapidly changing mobile social networks. In these mobile social networks, users typically form small and dynamic local communities sparsely connected and without a fixed topology (e.g. a house, a company office, a residential neighborhood). The diffusion of the information is analyzed both empirically by a Monte Carlo method and analytically by mean field theory, revealing the existence of a phase transition.

4   Part IV: Organizing in Digital Ecosystems

Digital ecosystems pose unprecedented challenges in organizations of all types, as the papers in this section effectively show.

Decastri, Gagliarducci, Previtali, and Scarozza address the issue of smart working in public organizations, in the light of a recently issued law that permits and encourages smart working as an innovative approach to work, organizing, and human resource management. The study leverages the Presidency of the Council of Ministers as a case study to investigate the concrete implications of, and issues raised by, smart working.

Another recent law, the GDPR regulation issued by the EU in 2016, has significantly impacted organization and processes in the public sector. This issue is at the core of the paper by Castelnovo, who argues that people can be made more willing to consent to the processing (and possibly to the re-use) of personal information by involving them as co-producers in the processes through which the public sector organizations can support economic growth in the digital society.

The study by Cuel and Ponte takes the inter-organizational network as the level of analysis and investigates how the complex infrastructure that links different organizations is "cultivated" to enable network-level decision making. The Air Traffic Management system is taken as a case and the requirements for a decision support system are proposed.

Cabiddu, Dessì, and Floris present an analysis of the Facebook contents produced by a sample of firms in the fashion industry. Data are collected over two years (2016–2017). The results highlight the different communication strategies, time of interaction, and kind of interaction across the sample, and shed light on the role of digital ecosystems in building an organization's identity.

Bissessur, Arabikhan, and Bednar explore the concept of routineness from the perspective of the job occupants themselves. The findings reveal that jobs which are considered routine from an organizational perspective, actually require a degree of human intervention in the real-world experience. This suggests that the fear of mass unemployment at the hands of AI may be an unrealistic notion. Rather, the introduction of AI into jobs paves the way for collaborative methods of working which could augment current jobs and create new jobs.

The study by Margherita and Braccini presents the results of an exploratory comparative study analyzing 23 cases of different enterprises who run a cloud computing strategy. Using fs/QCA as a method of analysis in a multiple cases setting, the research paper investigates the organizational benefits following cloud adoption, arguing that these benefits may go beyond cost savings.

Za, Ghiringhelli and Virili leverage social network analysis to conduct a literature investigation on the organizational learning processes stemming from organizational change initiatives. The results raise many questions and identify some challenges facing this relevant research stream.

The paper by De Bernardi, Bertello and Venuti investigates the role of actors' motivations, beliefs and knowledge exchange behaviors in community-based business models. The authors collect 2115 questionnaires in an Italian alternative food network, that is, a network based on a digital platform enabling the direct trade between communities and local farmers and producers. The results confirm the influence of community-based motivations and online knowledge sharing on purchase frequency and quantity.

We are really grateful to the Authors, the Conference Chairs and Committee members, to the members of the Editorial Board, and to the Reviewers for their competence and commitment. This publication would not have been possible without their active, sustained and generous contributions.

References

1. Vargo, S. L., Maglio, P. P., & Akaka, M. A. (2008). On value and value co-creation: A service systems and service logic perspective. *European Management Journal, 26,* 145–152. https://doi.org/10.1016/j.emj.2008.04.003.
2. Lusch, R. F., & Nambisan, S. (2015). Service innovation: A service-dominant-logic perspective. *MIS Quarterly, 39,* 155–175.
3. Briscoe, G., Sadedin, S., & Paperin, G. (2007). Biology of applied digital ecosystems. In *Inaugural IEEE-IES Digital EcoSystems and Technologies Conference* (pp. 458–463).
4. McKelvey, B., Tanriverdi, H., & Yoo, Y. (2016). Call for papers: Complexity and information systems research in the emerging digital world. *MIS Quarterly,* 1–3.

Part I
Human Communities
in Digital Ecosystems

Rethinking Romanian and Italian Smart Cities as Knowledge-Based Communities

Ramona-Diana Leon⊙ and Mauro Romanelli⊙

Abstract The aim of this study is to analyse the Romanian and Italian smart cities from a knowledge management perspective, and thus 6 smart cities represent the units of analysis (Ancona, Craiova, Padova, Perugia, Sibiu, Timisoara) while a smart city model (which includes 6 dimension and 28 components) is taken into consideration. Each of these components is analysed from a knowledge management perspective due to the fact that the difference among cognitive, emotional and spiritual knowledge may influence the tools which policy-makers could use for smart city development. The results prove that smart city development is based on two pillars: the first one is represented by citizens' values and beliefs, their vision for the future while the second one reunites what they are able to do in order to transform their vision into reality. Thus, it can be stated that the smart cities model has both a visionary pillar (which incorporates spiritual knowledge) and a practical one (in which knowledge is converted into action). Beyond this, the best Romanian and Italian performers concentrate their efforts on economy, mobility and people. In other words, they focus on creating and disseminating cognitive and emotional knowledge (innovations, emotions, feelings). These findings have both theoretical and practical implications as, on the one hand, they provide the nexus between knowledge management and urban development, while on the other, they bring forward the elements on which the policy-makers should focus in order to foster smart city development.

Keywords Smart cities · Knowledge cities · Smart communities · Urban development knowledge-based

R.-D. Leon
National University of Political Studies and Public Administration, Bucharest, Romania
e-mail: ramona.leon@facultateademanagement.ro

M. Romanelli (✉)
University of Naples Parthenope, Naples, Italy
e-mail: mauro.romanelli@uniparthenope.it

© Springer Nature Switzerland AG 2020
A. Lazazzara et al. (eds.), *Exploring Digital Ecosystems*,
Lecture Notes in Information Systems and Organisation 33,
https://doi.org/10.1007/978-3-030-23665-6_2

1   Introduction

As smart communities, cities contribute to promoting economic and social development, sustaining job growth and ensuring high quality of life [1]. Technology helps cities to develop knowledge sources and human capital promoting smartness as a valuable guide for designing the future of industry, economy, living, mobility and governance while relying on skilled people and sustainable management of natural environments [2–4]. Within knowledge-based economies and open societies, cities of tomorrow should rethink the urban landscape as a smart and knowledge-based community that promotes social and economic growth while developing knowledge sources and using technology to acquire and create new knowledge, develop human capital and facilitate open innovation.

Promoting a smart approach for urban growth implies reconsidering cities that are connected to the global knowledge-based economy as knowledge-based communities that rediscover knowledge sources and management, as well as developing technological infrastructures and having skilled and well-educated people to hand [5–7]. Knowledge-based cities help connect structural and human capital merging urban development perspectives and the knowledge management approach [8, 9]. Cities of the future should become smart communities that sustain social and economic innovation and growth, encourage social interaction, develop services platforms and promote opportunities for learning and knowledge sharing ensuring better quality of life and involving both private and public actors [1, 2, 10–14]. As technology-enabled communities, cities should develop as knowledge-based cities within an urban ecosystem enabling the transformation of knowledge resources into local development as a means of sustainability [5, 6].

Cities should develop the use of smart technology as a policy and managerial innovation integrating services and capabilities while developing human capital and involving people in the smart city as part of the project and strategic vision [4, 15]. As smart communities, cities contribute to promoting economic and social development, sustaining job growth and better opportunities for employment, business and quality of life [1]. Technology helps cities to develop knowledge sources and human capital. Cities should assume the smartness as a vision and policy innovation for designing the future of industry, economy, mobility, government relying on skilled and smart people [2, 3, 16]. As communities driving for sustainable urban development, smart cities should also adopt a knowledge management perspective where values, cognitive, emotional and visionary sources contribute to transforming knowledge into other knowledge coherently with local specificity and capital identity [6, 7, 17, 18].

This research aims to analyse the Romanian and Italian smart cities via a knowledge management perspective. Thus, the research focuses on providing answers to the following questions: (i) what are the strengths and weaknesses of the Italian smart cities; (ii) what are the strengths and weaknesses of the Romanian smart cities and (iii) what type of knowledge is mostly involved in the development of the Romanian and Italian smart cities?

The paper is structured around five sections. The next section presents the literature review, and in particular, the recognition of cities as smart communities. The influences that knowledge management could have on their development is also elucidated. Section 3 sheds light on the research methodology, while in the fourth part the main results are presented. Finally, the article closes by highlighting the theoretical and practical implications of the research findings as well as discussing further research directions.

2 Developing Cities as Smart and Knowledge-Based Communities

Cities should reinvent themselves as smart, knowledge-based communities, rediscovering knowledge as a critical source and developing technological infrastructures to drive urban and sustainable growth while connecting structural and human capital [5–7, 12, 14, 17]. Developing cities as smart and knowledge-based communities relies on promoting smartness and sustaining knowledge sources to drive urban growth [3, 6, 12, 14].

2.1 Rediscovering Knowledge-Based Cities

Knowledge based urban development relies on cities embracing and strengthening smartness, technology, creativity, cultural diversity, networking, knowledge, education and connectivity to merge urban development perspectives and the knowledge management approach, acquiring and reinforcing knowledge and intellectual infrastructures to drive urban growth [5, 7–9]. "Knowledge is a fluid mix of framed experience, values, contextual information, and expert insight that provides a framework for evaluating and incorporating new experiences and information. It originates and is applied in the minds of knowers" [17]. Ideas and emotions are elements that enable service production and value creation within knowledge economies [19].

Cities as communities made of people develop and evolve relying on lives, beliefs, actions and thoughts of the individual that influence, drive and orient history, as well as values and beliefs of their cities [6]. Values and beliefs contribute to knowledge and determining what the knowers see. People see and perceive differently in the same situations and organise their knowledge because their values are different [17]. Cities live because a significant community of people organise their lives around a recognizable value system staying together. As value collectives moving from industrial to knowledge-based production, cities are evolving entities both as coproduction systems and as varying arrays of cultural, political and economic capital systems that are becoming increasingly knowledge-based value systems, driving knowledge development [6, 20].

Knowledge objects or flows are significant in relation to the value context, where goods and services produced have a symbolic value, exerting influence on the city's identity [18]. Thus, in the last 50 years, knowledge was presented as "a metaphor or fluid capable of incorporating an organised set of factual declarations, ideas and experiences, shared systematically with others by using a common communication environment" [21]. Based on its visibility, the distinction is made between explicit and tacit knowledge; the former is available at the conscious level and is shared through words, propositions and phrases, while the latter is available at the unconscious level and is shared through interactions—the only ones capable of disseminating values, emotions, beliefs and hunches. Furthermore, explicit knowledge is considered to be the "core" of a community while tacit knowledge represents the "blood" that makes individuals move in the desired direction, transforming the vision into reality [21]. Despite the fact that the nature of explicit knowledge is basically cognitive, the same cannot be claimed regarding tacit knowledge. Therefore, a distinction is made among cognitive, emotional and spiritual knowledge. Cognitive knowledge "refers to an individual's stored assumptions, hypotheses, and beliefs about thinking" and represents the result of logical thinking [22]. Emotional knowledge brings forward the importance of individual's emotions and feelings while spiritual knowledge sheds light on the values and beliefs that guide individuals' decisions and actions [23]. In other words, the former emphasises what people feel while the latter highlights why people do what they do.

2.2 Promoting Smart Cities as Communities

Cities tend to promote smartness as a value to improve competitiveness, social and human capital, mechanisms of governance, mobility as transport and ICT, the natural environment, resources and quality of life [3]. Cities using information technology tend to design smart cities as networked infrastructures that enable political efficiency, social and cultural development and inclusion, and relying on business-led urban development to promote urban growth to identify solutions for solving urban problems [15].

As smart communities, knowledge-based cities enable knowledge acquisition to support knowledge-based processes and activities, strategically using information technology to develop collaborative processes that involve private and public organisations (local government, business, education, health care institutions and the civil society) to positively transform the community and promote economic development and job growth, improving the quality of life and urban competitiveness, sustaining people's engagement in co-production of public services and leading cities in order to be entrepreneurial, pioneering, liveable and connected [1, 2, 12–14]. Cities should shape the urban development employing technology, land, people and institutions as the sources for designing the smart city as a community proceeding towards urban, social and economic growth [4, 24]. This is a transformational process utilising citizens' involvement and participation [25], legitimising the city to sustain policy and managerial innovation and rediscover a new urban identity [26, 27].

Technology, organisation and policies as knowledge sources enable people, municipal institutions, businesses, research and education centres and other organisations to adopt initiatives for driving urban growth [16]. Smart cities as communities provide ICT-enabled and digital platforms to facilitate business and life [10] to encourage public-private partnerships for innovation [11] encouraging citizens and city governments to interact for urban problem solving [24].

3 Research Methodology

The research concentrates on analysing the Romanian and Italian smart cities from a knowledge management perspective. Therefore, the following objectives are set out: to develop a comparative analysis among the Italian smart cities; to determine the strengths and weaknesses of the Italian smart cities; to develop a comparative analysis among the Romanian smart cities; to determine the strengths and weaknesses of the Romanian smart cities; to analyse smart cities' components from a knowledge management perspective. Therefore, a case study strategy is developed since this is the most appropriate one for answering the "how" and "why" questions [28] and the research focuses on determining what is possible rather than what is common [29].

Smart cities promote competitiveness, social and human capital, enhance governance and participation, develop mobility as transport and ICT, and ensure sustainable management of natural resources and quality of life [3]. City-rankings help cities to identify the better performances and policies strengthening local and identity to drive urban growth [3, 30].

The smart city model [3, 31] is used as a starting point for selecting the case study units. This presents a smart cities model which includes 6 dimensions and 28 components that emphasize both knowledge resources and processes (Table 1). Each dimension reflects a characteristic that fosters the development of a smart city while, at the same time, it incorporates several components which describe either citizens' attributes or self-decisive and independent actions that they can develop.

Thus, it is assumed that a smart city is built on a smart combination of economy, living conditions, environment, mobility, governance, and people. In order to develop a smart economy, special attention should be given to individual (citizens' innovative spirit and entrepreneurial abilities), organisational (economic image and trademarks and productivity) and national issues (flexibility of labour market, international embeddedness). These support one another as citizens' innovativeness influences company productivity and it is also reflected by the labour market's flexibility.

According to the criteria taken into account by Smart-cities.eu [32], there are 77 smart cities across Europe (Table 2); 7 are from Italy (Ancona, Padova, Perugia, Trento, Trieste, Venezia, Verona) and 3 from Romania (Craiova, Sibiu, Timisoara). Trento, Trieste, Venezia and Verona are among the first 55 smart cities while the other ones are situated at the end of the ranking. As a consequence, in order to ensure

Table 1 The smart cities model [31]

Dimension	Components
Smart economy	• Innovative spirit • Entrepreneurship • Economic image and trademarks • Productivity • Flexibility of labour market • International embeddedness
Smart living	• Cultural facilities • Health conditions • Individual security • Housing quality • Educational facilities • Touristic attractiveness • Economic welfare
Smart environment	• Environmental conditions • Air quality (no pollution) • Ecological awareness • Sustainable resource management
Smart mobility	• Local accessibility • (Inter)national accessibility • Availability of IT infrastructure • Sustainability of the transport system
Smart governance	• Participation public life • Public and social services • Transparent governance
Smart people	• Level of qualification • Lifelong learning • Ethnic plurality • Open-mindedness

Table 2 The criteria taken into account by [32]

Criteria	Value
Urban population	100,000–500,000
Universities	At least one
Catchment area	Less than 1,500,000 inhabitants
Partners in planning for energy efficient cities	Yes
Registered in the urban audit database	Yes

comparison validity and reliability, the analysis focuses on 6 cities: 3 from Italy (Ancona, Padova, Perugia) and 3 from Romania (Craiova, Sibiu, Timisoara).

After selecting the case-study units, a comparative analysis is performed in order to determine the strengths and weaknesses of the analysed smart cities. Each component is analysed from a knowledge management perspective; the difference among cognitive, emotional and spiritual knowledge is taken into account since this may influence the tools which the policy-makers could use for smart city development.

4 Main Results

4.1 A Knowledge Management Perspective on the Smart Cities Model

Cities that are in the process of becoming smart tend to develop knowledge sources and use technology in order to drive urban growth. All the elements included in the smart cities model focus on knowledge resources, and their development is fostered through knowledge acquisition, dissemination and use. Cities tend to design smartness as a vision to rediscover the city as a community by using technology for investing in knowledge sources that enable managerial, policy and organisational innovation and rely on values, beliefs and ideas of people that live the city driving urban growth and development [2–4, 6, 14, 16, 19, 24, 26, 27].

As can be noticed in Table 3, they either have their roots in cognitive knowledge or spiritual knowledge. In other words, they bring forward the fact that smart cities' development is based on two pillars: the first one is represented by individuals' values and beliefs, as well as their vision for the future while the second one reunites what they are able to do in order to transform their vision into reality. Thus, it can be stated that the smart city model has a visionary pillar (which incorporates spiritual knowledge) and a practical one (in which knowledge is converted into action).

Last but not least, only 2 out of 28 elements focus on individuals' emotions and feelings, namely: individual security and economic welfare. These emphasise the reasons for which individuals become involved in smart city development, and the desired intangible outcomes.

4.2 The Performance of the Romanian and Italian Smart Cities

According to data presented in Fig. 1, the Italian smart cities are very close to the European average in terms of (i) Smart Economy, and (ii) Smart Living. Furthermore, except for the Smart Environment dimension where Ancona is above the average, the Italian smart cities tend to range below the European average; their vulnerabilities come mainly from the (i) Smart Governance and (ii) Smart Mobility areas [33].

However, various differences appear when each city is analysed individually (Table 4). Thus, Padova's strengths rely on the Smart Economy, Smart Mobility and Smart People areas, while Ancona's strengths have their roots in the Smart Environment dimension. Within this framework, it can be stated that Padova invested

Table 3 The knowledge resources involved in the smart cities model

Factors	Cognitive knowledge	Emotional knowledge	Spiritual knowledge
Innovative spirit			X
Entrepreneurship	X		X
Economic image and trademarks	X		
Productivity	X		
Flexibility of labour market	X		X
International embeddedness	X		
Cultural facilities			X
Health conditions			X
Individual security		X	
Housing quality			X
Educational facilities	X		
Touristic attractiveness	X		
Economic welfare		X	X
Environmental conditions			X
Air quality (no pollution)			X
Ecological awareness			X
Sustainable resource management	X		
Local accessibility	X		
(Inter)national accessibility	X		
Availability of IT infrastructure	X		
Sustainability of the transport system	X		
Participation public life	X		X
Public and social services	X		
Transparent governance			X
Level of qualification	X		
Lifelong learning	X		
Ethnic plurality			X
Open-mindedness			X

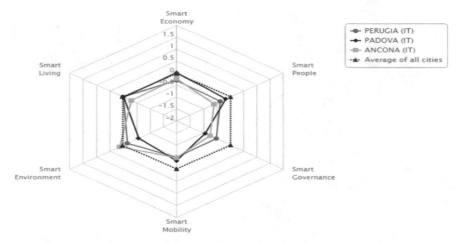

Fig. 1 Comparative analysis among the Italian smart cities [33]

Table 4 The Italian smart cities—the best and worst performer

Criteria	Best performer	Worst performer
Smart economy	Padova	Perugia
Smart living	Perugia	Ancona
Smart environment	Ancona	Padova
Smart mobility	Padova	Perugia
Smart governance	Perugia	Padova
Smart people	Padova	Ancona

in the economic and social sustainability while Ancona concentrates on the environmental side. Therefore, the former is tempted to share cognitive and emotional knowledge (innovations, emotions, feelings) while the latter focuses on spiritual knowledge (values and beliefs).

Compared with the European average, the Romanian smart cities are the worst performers (Fig. 2); their performance is below the average. However, several progresses have been made on the Smart Living, and Sibiu tends to get closer to the European average. On the other hand, it can be noticed that, in most of the cases, the Romanian cities have a similar evolution, and there are small variations among their scores in 4 out of 6 dimensions. In other words, it can be argued that the difference among the Romanian smart cities is made by the Smart Living and Smart Environment conditions.

Nevertheless, some differences appear when each city is analysed individually (Table 5). Thus, Timisoara's strengths rely on the Smart Economy, Smart Mobility and Smart People areas while Sibiu strengths have their roots in the Smart Living and Smart Environment dimension. Within this framework, it can be stated that Timisoara invested in economic and social sustainability while Sibiu concentrates on environmental sustainability. Therefore, the former is tempted to share cognitive

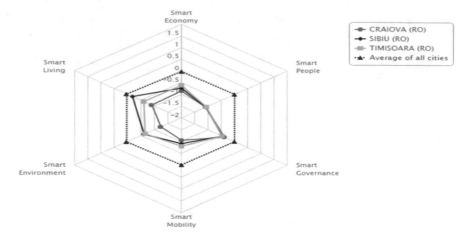

Fig. 2 Comparative analysis among the Romanian smart cities [33]

Table 5 The Romanian smart cities—the best and worst performer

Criteria	Best performer	Worst performer
Smart economy	Timisoara	Craiova
Smart living	Sibiu	Craiova
Smart environment	Sibiu	Craiova
Smart mobility	Timisoara	Craiova
Smart governance	Craiova	Timisoara
Smart people	Timisoara	Craiova

and emotional knowledge (innovations, emotions, feelings) while the latter focuses on spiritual knowledge (values and beliefs).

5   Conclusion and Further Research

As places where the majority of people reside, cities are meeting places, services providers and platforms, smart and sustainable communities where people work and live and businesses can successfully operate, dealing with economic and social gains and issues. Cities contribute to sustaining economic growth and urban development, promoting learning, education and culture, developing technology and knowledge sources, as well as driving social and economic aspects by engendering open innovation for change. Following a smart city approach is emerging as a visionary pillar and strategic perspective leading cities to invest in knowledge, financial, technical and human resources identifying a path and driving cities as communities to proceed towards sustainable development and urban growth.

Rediscovering cities as knowledge-based and oriented communities helps them to strengthen available knowledge sources adapting to local specificity and contexts and rediscovering the potential value of identity capital. Acquiring, using and disseminating knowledge is a critical resource to sustain development and growth in urban areas. Following a knowledge-based perspective for rethinking the future development of cities helps to support urban growth and the design of a sustainable and smart city as a community, developing emotional, spiritual and cognitive knowledge sources and using the potential of information technology to build cooperation and collaboration between public and private organisations, groups, individuals, other stakeholders within the community and those involved in knowledge creation processes. Promoting a knowledge-based urban development perspective for sustaining the smart city approach helps cities to design social and economic growth integrating technological, human and knowledge sources and intelligence to create environments and enabling cognitive skills and capacities to enhance knowledge and innovation following a virtuous cycle while driving cities to continuously rethink and re-plan the social and economic growth of urban areas and rediscovering strengths.

The results of the current study prove that smart city development is based on two pillars: the first one is represented by citizens' values, beliefs and their vision for the future while the second one reunites what they are able to do in order to transform their vision into reality. Thus, it can be stated that the smart cities model has a visionary pillar (which incorporates spiritual knowledge) and a practical one (in which knowledge is converted into action). Beyond this, the best Romanian and Italian performers concentrated their efforts into the aspects economy, mobility and people. In other words, they focus on creating and disseminating cognitive and emotional knowledge (innovations, emotions, feelings). These findings have both theoretical and practical implications as, on the one hand, they provide the nexus between knowledge management and urban development, and on the other, they bring forward the elements on which the policy-makers should focus in order to foster smart city' development. Thus, if the Italian policy-makers want to improve their performance and to be competitive on the European level, they should address their main vulnerabilities, namely the insurance of a Smart Governance and Smart Mobility. The former is based on cognitive and spiritual knowledge while the latter has its roots in cognitive knowledge. In other words, the development of the latter would be easier than the former since it will only require the use of tangible resources; the development of the former will involve a change in citizens' values system and attitude (they have to feel the need to be involved). Although this research provides valuable insights, its results are limited. On the one hand, it only analyses the characteristics of one smart city model, and the results could have been different if various models had been taken into account. On the other hand, only a limited number of Romanian and Italian cities were taken into consideration and the analysis was performed on a national level. Future research perspectives should further investigate how Italian and Romanian smart cities are currently planning and building knowledge-based urban developments by adopting a smart approach and relying on building and valuing knowledge sources and types.

References

1. Eger, J. M. (2005). Smart communities, universities, and globalization: Educating the workforce for tomorrow's economy. *Metropolitan Universities, 16,* 28–38.
2. Lombardi, P., Giordano, S., Farouh, H., & Yousef, W. (2012). Modelling the smart city performance. *Innovation: The European Journal of Social Science Research, 25,* 137–149.
3. Giffinger, R., Fertner, C., Kramar, H., Kalasek, R., Pilchler-Milanović, N., & Meijers, E. (2007). Smart cities: Ranking of European medium-sized cities. Vienna, Austria: Centre of Regional Science (SRF), Vienna University of Technology. Available from http://www.smart-cities.eu/download/smart_cities_final_report.pdf.
4. Nam, T., & Pardo, T.A. (2011). Conceptualizing smart city with dimensions of technology, people and institutions. In *Proceedings of the 12th Annual International Digital Government Research Conference: Digital Government Innovation in Challenging Times* (pp. 282–291). ACM.
5. Knight, R. V. (1995). Knowledge-based development: Policy and planning implications for cities. *Urban Studies, 35,* 225–260.
6. Carrillo, F. J. (2004). Capital cities: A taxonomy of capital accounts for knowledge cities. *Journal of Knowledge Management, 8,* 28–46.
7. Yigitcanlar, T., Velibeyoglu, K., & Martinez-Fernandez, C. (2008). Rising knowledge cities: The role of urban knowledge precincts. *Journal of Knowledge Management, 12,* 8–20.
8. Yigitcanlar, T., O'Connor, K., & Westerman, C. (2008). The making of knowledge cities: Melbourne's knowledge-based urban development experience. *Cities, 25,* 63–72.
9. Edvinsson, L. (2006). Aspects on the city as a knowledge tool. *Journal of Knowledge Management, 10,* 6–13.
10. Anttiroiko, A.-V., Valkam, P., & Bailey, S. J. (2014). Smart cities in the new service economy: Building platforms for smart services. *AI & Society, 29,* 323–334.
11. Deakin, M. (2014). Smart cities: The state-of-the-art and governance challenge. *Triple Helix, 1,* 1–16.
12. Lindskog, H. (2004). Smart communities initiatives. In *Proceedings of the 3rd ISOneWorld Conference* (pp. 1–16).
13. Granier, B., & Kudo, H. (2016). How are citizens involved in smart cities? Analysing citizen participation in Japanese "smart communities". *Information Polity, 21,* 61–76.
14. Begg, I. (1999). Cities and competitiveness. *Urban Studies, 36,* 795–809.
15. Albino, V., Berardi, U., & Dangelico, R. M. (2015). Smart cities: Definitions, dimensions, performance, and initiatives. *Journal of Urban Technology, 22,* 3–21.
16. Nam, T., & Pardo, T. A. (2011). Smart city as urban innovation with dimensions of technology, people and institutions. In *Proceedings of the 5th International Conference on Theory and Practice of Electronic Governance* (pp. 185–194). ACM.
17. Davenport, T. H., & Prusak, L. (1998). *Working knowledge: How organizations manage what they know*. Boston: Harvard Business School Press.
18. Fachinelli, A. C., Carrillo, F. J., & D'Arisbo, A. (2014). Capital system, creative economy and knowledge city transformation: insights from Bento Gonçalves, Brazil. *Expert Systems with Applications, 41,* 5614–5624.
19. Carrillo, F. J., & Batra, S. (2012). Understanding and measurement: Perspectives on the evolution of knowledge-based development. *International Journal of Knowledge-Based Development, 3,* 1–16.
20. Kunzmann, K. R. (2014). Smart cities: A new paradigm of urban development. *Crios, 4,* 9–20.
21. Leon, R. D., Rodriguez-Rodriguez, R., Gomez-Gasquet, P., & Mula, J. (2017). Social network analysis: A tool for evaluating and predicting future knowledge flows from an insurance organization. *Technological Forecasting and Social Change, 114,* 103–118.
22. Kluwe, R. H. (1982). Cognitive knowledge and executive control: Metacognition. *Animal Mind–Human Mind, 21,* 201–224.
23. Zohar, D., & Marshall, I. (2004). *Spiritual capital: Wealth we can live by*. San Francisco: Berrett-Koehler.

24. Dameri, R. (2013). Searching for smart city definition: A comprehensive proposal. *International Journal of Computer & Technology, 11,* 2544–2551.
25. Bencardino, M., & Greco, I. (2014). Smart communities: Social innovation at the service of the smart cities. *Tema. Journal of Land Use, Mobility and Environment, Smart City. Planning for Energy, Transportation and Sustainability of the Urban System,* Special issue (pp. 40–51).
26. Zygiaris, S. (2013). Smart city reference model: Assisting planners to conceptualize the building of smart city innovation ecosystems. *Journal of the Knowledge Economy, 4,* 217–231.
27. Vanolo, A. (2014). Smartmentality: The smart city as disciplinary strategy. *Urban Studies, 51,* 883–898.
28. Yin, R. K. (2014). *Case studies: Design and methods.* Thousand Oaks, CA: Sage.
29. Antai, I., & Olson, H. (2013). Interaction: A new focus for supply chain vs supply chain competition. *International Journal of Physical Distribution & Logistics Management, 43,* 511–528.
30. Kitchin, R., Lauriault, T. P., & McArdle, G. (2015). Knowing and governing cities through urban indicators, city benchmarking and real-time dashboards. *Regional Studies, Regional Science, 2,* 6–28.
31. Smart-cities.eu. (2014). *The smart city model.* Available from http://www.smart-cities.eu/index.php?cid=2&ver=3. Accessed April 11, 2018.
32. Smart-cities.eu. (2014). *Why smart cities?* Available from http://www.smart-cities.eu/index.php?cid=1&ver=3. Accessed April 15, 2018.
33. Smart-cities.eu. (2014). *Benchmarking.* Available from http://www.smart-cities.eu/index.php?cid=5&city=47&ver=3. Accessed May 10, 2018.

Are the Elderly Averse to Technology?

Jonathan Jones and Peter Bednar

Abstract In 2018, I interviewed seven people from the 'silent generation' to find out what they thought about information technology, whether they were averse to it, and why. Using this snap-shot image from *Hornchurch Tapestry* day care centre, this paper analyses the human activity system that frames how the elderly interact with the technology that surrounds them. It details what these interactions consist of, investigates how the participants view the purpose of the technology and explores how they 'feel' about their interactions with it. Ultimately, this paper challenges a societal assumption that elderly people are averse to information technology. The elderly use different technologies for different purposes and in different contexts. The *Tapestry* interviews highlight how critical family pressure was in determining how the elderly feel about information technology and their decisions to interact with it.

Keywords Socio-technical · Systems · Elderly · Averse · Information technology · Information systems

1 Introduction

It is a widespread societal view in the United Kingdom (UK) that the elderly are innately averse to technology. Just last year, *The Guardian* ran a story that exclaimed, "Older people can't cope with new technology—but nobody cares" [5]. This research was predicated on the view that such a societal assumption ignores how different people interact with different technologies in different ways. Moreover, Patilla-Góngora et al. research found that 74.5% of their elderly participants did not know the basic element of computer use [8]. This research further shows that over 90% did not have

J. Jones (✉) · P. Bednar
School of Computing, University of Portsmouth, Portsmouth, UK
e-mail: jonathan.jones1@hotmail.com

P. Bednar
e-mail: peter.bednar@port.ac.uk

© Springer Nature Switzerland AG 2020
A. Lazazzara et al. (eds.), *Exploring Digital Ecosystems*,
Lecture Notes in Information Systems and Organisation 33,
https://doi.org/10.1007/978-3-030-23665-6_3

the skills in databases, presentation creation, graph creation or web page creation [8]. To explore whether elderly people are averse to technology, I conducted semi-structured interviews with residents from *Hornchurch Tapestry* day care centre. The interviews sought to uncover what technologies the participants interacted with, why they did so, and how they felt about these interactions. These interviews provide this paper with a snapshot insight into the various views that elderly people hold about technology and why they might use it.

A participant's interactions with technology is characterised by purposeful action and they will interpret technology in different ways, as they interpret the world in different ways [4]. Peter Bednar states that a system is defined by interest [2]. As such, we ask what interest the elderly have towards 'information technology'.

As new information technology arrives, an elderly person may have to adapt to the new technology or at least be surrounded by a new technology. In this piece, we try to uncover what might affect an elderly person's will and ability to adapt to new technology. Eden Mumford states that there are values, attitudes and incentives for change and that some more than others may feel less threatened by change [7].

Without a boundary "we will have to take the whole planet into account, which of course we cannot do" [9]. So, when this paper talks about technology, it is of course referring to information technology. As such, we do not ask participants to talk about the steam engine, cars, or even electric toothbrushes. Instead we ask how participants interact with information processing technology like tablets, personal computers, and smart phones. By conducting semi-structured interviews, we enabled participants to reflect upon their responses and return to them if needs be. This conversational approach led the interviews to explore unforeseen ideas and themes. The interviews were semi structured for a mix of reasons, firstly, I wanted more of a conversation style, and from this conversation style hopefully we could a high level of complexity around and outside the subject area. Secondly, as the interviews were 'face-to-face' I wanted to ask follow-up questions, that could explore the topic further. From the open-end conversations new themes did arrive.

In total, seven people were interviewed in the care centre on the same day. The age of the participants ranged from 68 to 98. Due to issues of mobility and the centre's resource capacity, it was not possible to interview participants in isolation from other service users at the centre. Interviewee's varied in their receptiveness to the questions. For example, some participants wanted a short interview (seven minutes), whereas some wanted a longer interview (fifteen minutes) so they could reflect upon past examples to shape their responses. With every interview, I learned how to improve my approach to get the most out of the responses.

One of the major drives behind my decision to explore this topic is quite personal. I have family members who care for the elderly, both in professional and non-professional contexts. From their experiences of care, I have observed that there are many stereotypes about how the elderly perceive certain issues. As a group, 'the elderly' are often assumed as incapable of using information technology. Fundamentally, I argue that we should not want technology to be created or prescribed to elderly people that ignores what they think and care about as individuals.

Some scholars cite a need to address how much the elderly cost the state as a justification for their research [6]. However, this project is more concerned with exploring elderly people's perceptions of IT rather than uncovering how IT can assist the state in improving cost-effectiveness.

2 Investigation

Two weeks before the interviews took place, the participants were provided with the question 'Are you averse to technology?'. This gave them time to reflect on the question and come to possible conclusions prior to the interview. Each face-to-face interview was audio-recorded and conducted in a relaxed and familiar environment.

After giving their informed consent, participants were interviewed individually. A core issue was that there are some people at the day centre that could have dementia or Parkinson's. This was taken into consideration and before the interviews, the issue was discussed with the staff, and they selected participants.

1. What technology do you frequently use?
2. Do you have any privacy concerns with technology?

   a. If so, what concerns?

3. Is there any technology that you will not use?

   a. If so, why?

4. What technology have you liked using?
5. What technology have you disliked using?
6. Have you ever had IT lessons before?
7. Would you like to have IT lessons?
8. What do you generally think about the progression of modern technology?

The data analysis is a thematic analysis, this takes themes and ideas from the interviews. The data analysis has a 'products' and 'services' section. The intention of this is to show what the participants define technology as. This is important because they may have different ways of thinking about technology. As an example, if I asked them to talk about a specific technology, the participant may not go outside the area of the investigation. For example, if I asked a participant to talk about tablets, they may talk about the tablets, but they may not discuss their interactions with other technology, or what they think overall about technology.

3 Findings

The findings are listed in the order of the amount talked about. Not measured from the text, rather the emphasis participants put into explaining the topics. So, in order the findings are:

- Family Pressure
- Childhood
- Progression
- Apathy
- Aversion

The findings suggest that participants have a wide range of opinions and views around 'technology'. The findings, however, show some trends. The first trend is family pressure. For participant three and one, they both mentioned that they were pressured by family to get a tablet or smartphone. For example, participant three stated that there was a long struggle with their family to get a smartphone, but even when participant three got a smartphone, they weren't entirely happy with it. Participant one mentioned that her family berated her until she got a tablet. Interestingly we need to see 'why' the family pressured or encouraged the participants to adopt a technology. In multiple cases the participants were using technology to contact family abroad, perhaps families believe that information technology enables communication. And perhaps as well, families are looking to buy presents for the participants and believed they were achieving giving a present and introducing a technology at the same time. Both points, however, need more direct research; something we will investigate later.

Three of the participants directly mentioned children. This is interesting because it doesn't directly affect themselves. Participant six mentioned childhood quite a lot. They stated that children are missing out on 'childhood' and children are growing up too fast. Three of the participants really had a concern for children and their use of technology. Participant three, when asked about technology progression, said: "It's over the top too much, especially for children, they don't know how to communicate properly."

The conversations included a comparison of experience between their childhood and the current childhood of the children they observe. For example, participant two sounded very nostalgic. Participant two stated that they cannot use technology because of their upbringing, physical photos, and further commented that people are 'zombified' and distracted. A key thing to take away from participant two is that they felt powerless to change society and their interactions with technology.

Like participant two, participant six mentioned progression and stated that they felt as though: 'Times have changed'. Perhaps this means that they feel like society is changing, and this is outside of their control. However, participant four and five accept that 'progression 'is happening and sound more optimistic about it. In fact, participant four stated that "it's going to make a lot of things better". Interestingly, the question "What do you generally think about the progression of modern technology?" doesn't define what progression is, what it involves and what technology.

Reflectively, this is great because it allows for the participants to express their emotions or express how they feel about something outside of a boundary setting. If the question was more specific perhaps the participant would have stated that they didn't know or care. For example, if I asked them if the progression of online shopping was a good thing, they may have given a specific answer. But, allowing for a general answer means that they don't have to be specific. When asked what they think about societal behaviour with technology, participant two said "They'll become zombies eventually, there is nothing you can change about it. It's at the hands of the people that create all this stuff. You cannot stop progression, people will stop using their heads." One quote that sticks out is: 'Times have changed, they say it's for the better, but I sometimes think is it for the better?'

Participant one and participant five when asked some questions answered 'I don't know what I think about it' and 'I don't know, I just think it's a good thing'. Perhaps, they are either apathetic to answering questions and are not interested in the interview. However, considering the participants were told about the interview topic beforehand, perhaps these apathetic answers are more telling. Perhaps the participants do not care about technology, they may not think of it or are not interested. For example, participant five further mentioned that 'There's no one I want to phone, all my friends are here'.

This research shows how vague aversion is, and how hard it is to define it. Many of the participants said that they felt as if they didn't like technology, by their own definition. However, many participants were using technology around them. Many participants were using smartphones to phone people across the world, voice call those around, pay bills online or play board games on mobile devices. The participants can use a technology and still dislike it. It is possible that the participants see it as means to an end, a necessity to communicate, play games or search things online. You could assume that if asked 'Do you like communicating?', 'Do you like playing Scrabble?' or 'Do you like searching things online?' The participants may answer that they do, perhaps a lot of people would answer that they like communicating.

So, the devices may seem like a necessity to do these things, but this does not suggest that they like the devices they have. For example, participant six stated that technology 'drives them mad', but they further explained that it was a necessity to speak to their daughter in Australia. In this case, participant six may value speaking to their daughter enough to use the technology that they acclaimed 'drive them mad'. From this, it is urged that anyone analysing elderly interactions with technology recognise that just because an elderly person uses a technology, doesn't mean that they like it. In participant six's case, they could hate it, but find it useful. This questions what it means to say that you 'like' or 'dislike' something, which will further be explored in the discussion.

Perhaps the participants do not have an interest in technology but find the use of technology necessary. For example, in Heart et al. research 62% of the participants, when asked why they don't use computers stated that they have 'no need' or 'not interested' [6]. This questions what aversion really is, which is discussed further. From this, we can assume that we don't have to expect a person to have an opinion.

In this case, at least, some participants simply did not care for technology and didn't care to involve themselves.

4 Discussion

Bednar states that a system is defined by interest [2]. These findings support Bednar statements because systemically, the elderly have different interests in technology. For example, in this case some of the elderly participants see technology as a means of communication. Further, some of the elderly participants are interested in using technology for games. So, these different interests define the purpose of 'technology'.

Family pressure was the strongest theme. As found in the research, perhaps the reason for this family pressure is the want or need for communication. For example, many participants mentioned that they wanted a technology, so they could speak to family abroad or to distant new grandchildren. The participants mentioned distance, and the use of this technology as a tool to virtually shorten it. Research has found in between 1970 and 2000 in Europe that the propensity of an elderly person living alone had increased [10]. In Great Britain about one-half of the elderly participants in Tomassini et al. research stated that they are in contact with their children at least once a week [10]. Albeit in 2004, this research suggests that half of the elderly people in Great Britain are not in contact with their children on a weekly basis. Tomassini et al. indicate that frequency of contact can strengthen potential support for elderly people [10]. Perhaps, therefore, family members feel a need to pressure their parents or grandparents into adopting aspects of technology, to communicate and support them.

Interesting though, this family pressure has been mentioned by Asghar et al. [1] and Vacek et al. [11]. They suggest that there may be a correlation between social inclusion and technology use. These studies found that where an elderly person is socially excluded they are less likely to be taught a technology or be introduced to that technology. Perhaps, the family pressure isn't necessarily a negative thing, but just an element of social inclusion.

With a boundary setting bigger than just the participant and a technology we found the complexity of the external world. The research found, in many cases, that a participant wasn't always concerned about themselves, but they were concerned with the external, in this case, children. Within the research, we asked whether the elderly are averse to technology and assumed that if they are, it is because of things affecting them. This includes; privacy concerns, lack of education, usability, and security. Never did we wonder whether an elderly person was concerned about technology that did not directly affect them, for example, children or society. There needs to be further research on this topic.

Again, in the research design, there was no mention of concern for society, something that doesn't directly involve a participant. Some participants stated that technological and societal progression was a good thing, but most didn't. We can take from this, that not only do some participants think that society progression is good, or some think that it is bad, but that they all think it is moving or happening. Many mentioned that it was out of their control, and that time would tell. To summarise, perhaps you can be averse to something that does not directly affect you.

Contrary to the secondary research, within the primary research participants didn't have many complaints about usability. In fact, one participant mentioned that usability was an issue in the past, but not now. Cooper, a critic of poorly designed technology suggested that the technology industry was causing a software apartheid [3]. However, this research was in 2004 and this papers research was in 2018. This could suggest that usability design has improved, specifically with mobile phones and tablets. Ashgar et al. research found that most of their participants felt comfortable with using 'assistive technology' [1]. This could suggest that there has been a change in usability design between those years.

In the research, we questioned what aversion is. In addition, we questioned what it meant to feel averse to something. For example, many of the participants said that they liked playing scrabble on their tablets. If we based the research on tablets and if they said they enjoy playing games on it, we may have concluded that the participants like playing scrabble on tablets. In this context, it is purposeless. We wanted to find out how they 'felt' about something not if they use something,

The technology must have a purposeful action, for example phone calls or playing games. Contextually as mentioned earlier, a participant's interactions with technology is characterised by purposeful action and they will interpret technology in different ways, as they interpret the world in different ways [4]. As we have learnt the participants do interpret the world in different ways, and when we allowed for complexity in the open-ended conversations we found a wide interpretation of the world.

Even though Skyme et al. and Heart et al. questioned the opinions of their participants directly, other research has segmented technology use. Just because an elderly person has security concerns regarding a technology, does not mean that they dislike technology. Just because an elderly person finds some technology to be unusable, it does not mean that they dislike technology. In addition, just because they communicate with their family without the restraints of geographic location, does not mean that they like technology. Therefore, we need to question what it is to be averse.

From this discussion, there must be further research. We can gather that the elderly perceive technology as not just internal, but external. This is to suggest that the elderly care about how technology affects others, not necessarily themselves. In a society where many may be using a technology we may propagate a digital divide.

5   Conclusion

To conclude, the answer to the question "Are the elderly averse to technology?" is that the elderly includes a wide range of people, they have many different opinions and beliefs, and from the research, there are themes and trends that arrive. These themes are trends include the family pressure, children, apathy, usability, and their past interactions.

Before anything else, there needs to be more research into the family pressures that pressure the elderly into using technology. Hopefully, this research may find a mix of pressures, hidden pressure, and wrongly assumed pressure. This research would be important to find the pressures that elderly people have, and the influence of technology.

Furthermore, there needs to be more research into what the elderly think about their external world. As mentioned throughout this project, elderly people talk a lot about the external world, perhaps more than their internal world. It would be interesting to research what they care about, external to them. For example, the project found that some participants have a big concern for the impact of technology on children, and not so much themselves.

References

1. Asgha, I., Shuang, C., & Hongnian, Y. (2018). Usability evaluation of assistive technologies through qualitative research focusing on people with mild dementia. *Computers in Human Behaviour, 79,* 192–201.
2. Bednar, P. (2014). Socio-technical toolbox for business analysis in practice. In L. Caporaello, B. Di Martino, & M. Martinez (Eds.), *Smart organizations and smart artifacts*. Berlin: Springer.
3. Cooper, A. (2004). *The inmates are running the asylum, why high-tech products drive us crazy and how to restore the sanity* (2nd ed.). Carmel: Sams.
4. Checkland, P., & Scholes, J. (1990). *Soft systems methodology in action*. Chichester: Wiley.
5. Hanson, M. (2017). Older people can't cope with new technology—but nobody cares. In *The Guardian*, April 3, 2017.
6. Heart, T., & Kalderon, E. (2013). Older adults: Are they ready to adopt health-related ICT? *International Journal of Medical Informatics, 82*(11), 209–231.
7. Mumford, E. (2013). *Designing human systems for new technology: The ethics method*. Manchester: Manchester Business School.
8. Padilla-Góngora, D., López-Liria, R., Díaz-López, M. D., Aguilar-Parra, J. M., Vargas-Muñoz, M. E., & Rocamora-Pérez, P. (2017). Habits of the elderly regarding access to the new information and communication technologies. *Procedia—Social and Behavioral Sciences, 237,* 1412–1417.
9. Stowell, F. (2012). *The manager's guide to systems practice*. Chichester: Wiley.
10. Tomassini, C., Kalagirou, S., Grundy, E., Fokkema, T., Martikainen, P., Broese van Groenou, M., et al. (2004). Contacts between elderly parents and their children in four European countries: current patterns and future prospects. *European Journal of Ageing, 1*(1), 54–63.
11. Vacek, P., & Rybenska, K. (2015). Research of interest in ICT education among seniors. *Procedia—Social and Behavioral Sciences, 171*(16), 1038–1045.
12. Yusif, S., Soar, J., & Hafezz-Baid, A. (2016). Older people, assistive technologies, and the barriers to adoption: A systematic review. *International Journal of Medical Informatics, 112*(6), 112–116.

Value Co-creation in Online Communities: A Preliminary Literature Analysis

Stefano Za, Jessie Pallud, Rocco Agrifoglio and Concetta Metallo

Abstract This research-in-progress paper provides some preliminary insights to scholars who intend to investigate value co-creation process within online communities. This contribution presents the results of a literature analysis using bibliometric data of 246 articles debating this specific topic. The analysis shows the main research areas discussing value co-creation issues within online communities, selecting and describing the main cited references. Moreover, using social network analysis tools, it was possible to recognize the main connection among the most cited references (co-citation analysis) and the most used keywords and the connections among them. This quantitative bibliographic analysis represents just the starting point of a literature analysis process. Further steps will aim at conducting a systematic literature review of ongoing debate on value co-creation within online communities and to propose and test a research model for investigating the determinants of value co-creation within online communities.

Keywords Value co-creation · Online community · Citation analysis · Social network analysis

S. Za
University of Chieti-Pescara, Pescara, Italy
e-mail: stefano.za@unich.it

J. Pallud
EM Strasbourg Business School, Strasbourg, France
e-mail: jessie.pallud@em-strasbourg.eu

R. Agrifoglio (✉) · C. Metallo
University of Naples "Parthenope", Naples, Italy
e-mail: agrifoglio@uniparthenope.it

C. Metallo
e-mail: metallo@uniparthenope.it

© Springer Nature Switzerland AG 2020
A. Lazazzara et al. (eds.), *Exploring Digital Ecosystems*,
Lecture Notes in Information Systems and Organisation 33,
https://doi.org/10.1007/978-3-030-23665-6_4

1 Introduction

Co-creation was originally defined as the participation of consumers along with producers in the creation of value in the marketplace [1]. In comparison with the traditional creation paradigm where the value creation occurred inside companies only, co-creation changes the nature of the consumer-company interaction. Co-creation represents a process in which consumers take an active role—for instance, designing product/service or developing activities—and create value together with organizations [2]. As such, firms have moved the focus from the market to the interactions as the locus of value creation and value extraction [2]. Furthermore, the diffusion of ubiquitous digital ecosystems [3, 4] has facilitated the emergence of new ways for consumers to interact with organizations and to engage in their innovation processes. Conversely, digital econosystems support organizations in exploiting and better capitalizing consumers' innovative potential and knowledge [5]. At the same time, the use of digital technologies offers social and cognitive benefits to customers, thus leading to a better interaction and greater involvement during the co-creation experiences. Zwass [6] identified different prominent contributing research streams of co-creation, such as online communities (also called as internet community or virtual community), the commons, collective intelligence, and open innovation. In these scenarios online communities are the primary locus of collective contribution. Online community is a set of people who interact and exchange information within a virtual social context by using computer-mediated communication. Although there are many kinds of online communities, those active on social network platforms, which serve as community enablers for knowledge creation and sharing within a specific domain, were recognized as critical in co-creation initiatives (e.g. [6, 7]).

Prior research on online communities has mainly investigated the benefits they generate for firms in terms of economic value. However, Mein Goh et al. [8] (p. 247) pointed out that "while economic value is doubtless important, a large number of online communities are not sponsored by a particular company, nor do they have direct business implications, raising the question of how else the benefits of online communities might be conceptualized".

When co-creation initiatives occurred, market becomes a forum where the interaction with online community members contributes to co-create value not just for firms, but for individual, community and society [6]. Some scholars focus on value co-creation by extending the economic analysis of capital in the direction of sociological analysis, since online community was recognized as productive generator of social capital (e.g. [6, 8]). Nahapiet and Ghoshal [9] found that structural and relational dimensions of social capital are the most prominent in providing the opportunity to combine and exchange knowledge, as well as to anticipate value through such exchange. Other contributions, instead, focus on how the use of digital platforms affect online communities engagement and contributions [7, 10, 11]. In this regard, "online communities hold considerable promise for generating social value for participants on the platform" [8] (p. 249). Thus, the most recent research has extended the online community domain towards intellectual, social and cultural dimensions of value co-creation (e.g. [7, 8, 12]).

However, although research has focused on what types of value the online community contributes to co-create, it has neglected how value is created and leveraged and what the determinants of value co-creation are. This paper is the first part of a wider research project in which the main aim is to understand which variables affect the value co-creation within online community. Accordingly, through a bibliometric study, we firstly look at recognizing the foundations of research on value co-creation within online communities, seeking to answer to the following research questions:

- RQ1. What are the foundations of value co-creation within online communities in terms of key sources cited in articles discussing it?
- RQ2. What are the most active research areas and topics discussing value co-creation within online communities?

With this analysis, we are interested in identifying the different fields in which the value co-creation within online communities discourse is taking place, pointing out at the same time the foundations of the discourse and the main related topics.

The paper unfolds as follows. The research methodology and the literature search protocol are described in Sect. 2. The results of the analysis are provided in Sect. 3. Eventually, Sect. 4 concludes the paper summarizing findings, limitations and future steps.

2 Research Framework and Data Collection

Considering our aim to investigate the literature discussing value co-creation process in online communities in order to identify foundations and most active research areas we make use of citation analysis. Citation analysis is a form of quantitative bibliography which uses quantitative measures of number of publications and number of citations and co-citation as proxies of the influence of various sources in a research discourse [13, 14]. Citation analysis allows to investigate the evolution of knowledge production in a specific context (i.e. a discipline, a research area, a journal, a group of authors) [15, 16]. This analysis allows identifying papers considered as highly relevant for a discourse in the literature. Sources cited more frequently together tend to cluster [17] and through the analysis of these clusters the foundations of a literature discourse can be identified. Since citation analysis alone does not show the structure of ideas in a field [18], like previous studies did [16], we used social network analysis tools to obtain citation based measures of literature sources.

For bibliometric studies that involve citation/co-citation analysis literature selection is a key aspect to ensure validity and consistency. To perform the literature selection and the eventual analysis of the results we followed a sequential research protocol composed by four steps illustrated in Fig. 1.

The first step concerns the data collection and involves the identification of a suitable source for literature search. We identified ISI (Institute for Scientific Infor-

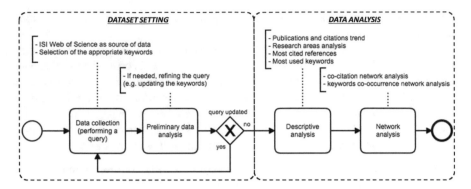

Fig. 1 Research protocol (adapted from [22])

mation) Web of Science (ISI-WoS, http://apps.webofknowledge.com) as the platform to perform the literature search and selection. Our choice is corroborated by the frequent use of ISI-WoS in other IS studies [19–21]. Moreover, the three main databases included in the platform (Science Citation Index Expanded, Social Sciences Citation Index, and Arts and Humanities Citation Index) fully cover over 12,000 major journals adding up to over 40 million searchable records.

We firstly used the following keywords: "co-creation", "co-production" and "value creation" for identify the process while "Virtual community", "Online community" and "collaborative network" as context. We perform a first query, gathering 81 contributions. We did a preliminary analysis in order to verify if some other keywords could be included in our original query. Than we took into account "Co-innovation" as one more process keyword and "social network" and "community" considered together as context keywords. Most of the keywords were stemmed and used in combination with wild cards to include both singular and plural expressions.

The last query produced 246 results corresponding to as many papers published from 1985 (starting date of the chronological ISI-WOS coverage) up to October 2017.

On this final set, following the further steps of the research protocol, we performed a descriptive analysis (Sect. 3.1) and a network analysis (Sect. 3.2).

3 Data Analysis

The examination of the 246 publications was done following two steps: (i) a descriptive analysis of our sample providing information on the evolution of number of publications and citations over the year and an overview of the most productive research areas and most cited references, and (ii) the use of SNA tools to reveal the co-citation network and the key concepts (keywords co-occurrences) that are examined in relation to our research topic, namely co-creation in online community.

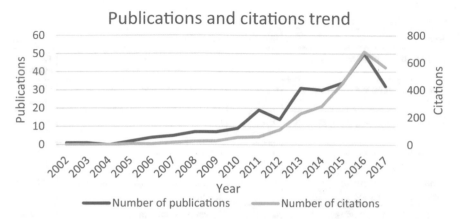

Fig. 2 The publications and citations trend over the years

3.1 Descriptive Analysis

Figure 2 reports the number of publications and citations trend per year from 2002 to October 2017. This figure shows that the topic of co-creation has received scant attention until 2005 (less than two papers per year and zero citations). Starting from 2006, more and more publications and citations were made on that topic. Co-creation in online communities is a topic that has become more prevalent with the development of Web 2.0. Indeed, this new Internet paradigm fosters creation and exchange of user generated content, thus supporting the development of online communities and co-creation projects [23]. Customers are less and less recipients of goods, but they are also co-producers of services [24]. After 2010, we even observe an exponential growth with almost the double of publications every year (10 publications in 2010, 20 publications in 2011, 30 publications in 2013 and the year 2016 reached a peak with 50 publications on that topic and 700 citations). But the number of citations has grown steadily these last past 10 years.

As indicated in Table 1, the topic of co-creation has been mainly published in academic journals from the following fields: business research, marketing, information systems, and innovation. The research area of business economics also represents 52% of the 246 articles. This indicates that the topic of co-creation in online communities is especially relevant for management researchers and business practitioner.

In Table 2, we present a set of 18 research papers corresponding to the most cited references in our 246 publications sample. These most influential sources can be grouped into three categories that are (1) determinants of participating and contributing to communities and networks; (2) processes of value co-creation through network interaction and resource exchange; and (3) research methodologies.

The first group (8 articles) refers to the reasons leading individuals to participate and to contribute to communities and networks. It focuses on 'why' people interact with each other and exchange resources within a social context. Research in that

Table 1 The most active journals and research areas

Journals	#Paper	Research areas	Freq. Nr.
Journal of business research	7	Business economics	129 (52%)
Computers in human behavior	6	Computer science	88 (36%)
Industrial marketing management	5	Engineering	42 (17%)
Technological forecasting and social change	5	Information science library science	28 (11%)
Journal of management information systems	4	Operations research management science	22 (9%)
Journal of strategic marketing	4	Telecommunications	18 (7%)
Journal of interactive marketing	4	Psychology	14 (6%)
Journal of product innovation management	3	Social sciences other topics	9 (4%)
Journal of organizational and end user computing	3	Public administration	8 (3%)
Journal of services marketing	3	Education educational research	8 (3%)
International journal of electronic commerce	3	Science technology other topics	5 (2%)
International journal of information management	3	Environmental sciences ecology	5 (2%)
Journal of service management	3	Communication	3 (1%)

category especially examines consumer participation and engagement in online brand communities. Muniz and O'Guinn [25] introduce the brand community concept such as "a specialized, non-geographically bound community, based on a structured set of social relations among admirers of a brand" (p. 412). On one hand, social factors such as group norms and social identity [29], customer relationship with the brand [34] or customer relationship with the product, the firm or with other fellow customers [32] can influence consumer participation. On the other hand, individual factors such as customer perceptions also explain why people engage in online communities. For instance, Nambisan and Baron [30] rely on the uses and gratifications approach to consider an integrated set of four perceived benefits (learning, social integrative, personal integrative and hedonic benefits) that all prove to influence customer participation in online value creation. Brodie et al. [37] develop a conceptual model illustrating the consumer engagement's cognitive, emotional and behavioural aspects and process within a virtual brand community. Other studies in that category focus more on the issue of knowledge contribution and sharing. For instance, McLure Wasko and Faraj [28] find that people contribute their knowledge in electronic networks of practice when: they perceive that it enhances their professional reputations; they have the experience to share; and they are structurally embedded in

Table 2 Most influential sources

References	Main contribution	Nr. Of Cit.	Group
Vargo and Lusch [24]	Describe the marketing evolution from a good-centered model to a service-centered model of exchange	44	G2
Muniz and O'Guinn [25]	Advance the theoretical notion of brand community and find evidence of brand community offline and online	44	G2
Prahalad and Ramaswamy [2]	Suggest the DART (Dialog, Access, Risk Assessment and Transparency) framework to implement co-creation experiences	37	G2
Kozinets [26]	Develop a new methodology based on ethnography to analyse online data	35	G3
Schau et al. [27]	Identify 12 common practices across brand communities and show how they create value-added brand community experiences	31	G2
McLure Wasko and Faraj [28]	Identify the three pre-requisites to knowledge contribution in the electronic networks of practice	27	G1
Dholakia et al. [29]	Develop a social influence model of consumer participation in virtual communities. Offer a typology to conceptualize virtual communities	26	G1
Nambisan and Baron [30]	Identify four perceived customer benefits that influence customer participation in value creation	26	G1
Payne et al. [31]	Develop a conceptual framework is based on the centrality of three main processes in co-creation: customer, supplier, and encounter	25	G2
McAlexander et al. [32]	Take into account the dynamic and multifaceted nature of brand community	25	G1
Vargo and Lusch [33]	Update their seminal paper on service-dominant logic	23	G2
Kaplan and Haenlein [23]	Provide a definition of social media and a classification according to social presence and self-presentation/self-disclosure dimensions	23	G2

(continued)

Table 2 (continued)

References	Main contribution	Nr. Of Cit.	Group
Algesheimer et al. [34]	Identify the positive consequences, such as greater community engagement, and negative consequences, such as normative community pressure and (ultimately) reactance of identification to a brand	22	G1
Von Hippel [35]	Highlight the reasons leading innovating users to share their innovations with others	22	G1
Wiertz and De Ruyter [36]	Investigate the influence of relational social capital and individual attributes on knowledge contribution of customers in firm-hosted online communities	21	G1
Brodie et al. [37]	Develop a conceptual model to capture consumer engagement's cognitive, emotional and behavioral aspects as such as process within a virtual brand community	20	G1
Fornell and Larcker [38]	Provide guidelines on how to implement and evaluate SEM approach	20	G3
Zwass [6]	Define co-creation and provide a taxonomy of web based co-creation	20	G2

the network. Von Hippel [35] investigates the user-centered innovation by focusing on the reasons leading innovating users to share their innovations with others, so creating user-innovation communities and rich intellectual commons. Wiertz and De Ruyter [36] investigate the influence of relational social capital and individual attributes on knowledge contribution of customers in firm-hosted online communities.

The second group (8 articles) refers to the processes of value co-creation through network interactions and resources exchange. Vargo and Lusch's [24] paper that is cited 44 times represents one of the seminal papers on the topic of co-creation. The authors explain how the marketing field has changed from a dominant logic (focused on exchange of goods) to a service logic, in which relationships between people and co-creation are more prevalent. As such, this paper is often cited to set the context of co-creation. Vargo and Lusch [33] analyse the major issues surrounding service-dominant logic and offer revisions to the foundational premises of their seminal article. Through the examination of different communities, Muniz and O'Guinn [25] reveal the characteristics, processes, and particularities of brand communities. Brand communities create value by amplifying consumer voices, providing information and affectual benefits. In order to clarify and optimize the processes of value co-creation, some other studies develop frameworks for value creation/extraction. For instance, Prahalad and Ramaswamy [2] offer a framework based on four building blocks of consumer-company interaction: Dialog, Access, Risk-benefits, and Transparency (DART). Another framework was developed by Payne et al. [31] to investigate how customers engage in the co-creation of value. This conceptual framework is based on the centrality of three main processes in co-creation: customer, supplier, and encounter. Zwass [6] investigates the intellectual space underlying co-creation research and then he proposes an inclusive taxonomy of Web-based co-creation, which contains co-creators, task, process and co-created value. Schau et al. [27] offer empirical evidence of value co-creation by investigating the process of collective value creation within nine brand communities using social practice theory. They also categorize value creation practices within brand communities, identifying the role of each type of practice in the value creation process, and suggesting templates for bundling practices to enhance collaborative value creation. Kaplan and Haenlein [23] investigate social media in respect of other entities such as Web 2.0 and User Generated Content. The research provides a definition and classification of social media, as well as several recommendations to decide how to utilize them.

Finally, the third group refers to methods and techniques used by researchers. Kozinets [26] develops the "netnography" method as an ethnography technique adapted to the study of online communities. "Netnography" provides information on the symbolism, meanings, and consumption patterns of online consumer groups. Since many of the studies are also conducted with the survey approach, Structural Equation Modeling (SEM) is frequently used and cited. Fornell and Larcker [38] conduct statistical tests for evaluating structural equation models (SEM) with unobservable variables and measurement error. Authors also developed a testing system based on measures of shared variance within the SEM for overcoming statistical problems when they occurred.

3.2 The Analysis of Citations and Topics Connections

Further information on the influence of different sources is shown by the network analysis of the co-citations. The results of that analysis are shown in Fig. 3. Each node in the figure is a paper cited by the articles of our sample. An arc between two papers indicates a co-citation of the two papers in one of the papers in the sample. Arcs thicker than others indicate co-citation pairs that are more frequent than others. The numbers on the arcs indicate the absolute frequency of the co-citation occurrence. The most evident co-citation triad links the papers of Vargo and Lusch [24], Muniz and O'Guinn [25] and Prahalad and Ramaswamy [2], representing the relevant building block of group G1, while Schau et al. [27] (G1) together with McAlexander et al. [32] (G1), Kozinets [26] (G3), Vargo and Lusch [33] (G2) represent connections among the three groups described in the previous paragraph.

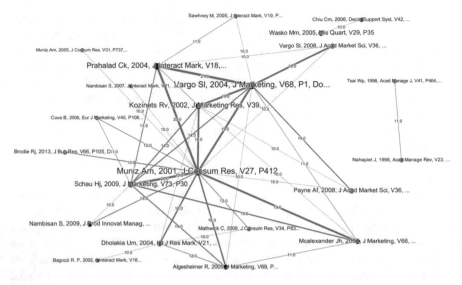

Fig. 3 Co-citations graph

The keywords analysis provides a more accurate information on the topics discussed in the 246 papers included in our dataset. We identify the most popular keywords used in the dataset, creating a graph based on their co-occurrences (Fig. 4). In the network, the keywords are the nodes and there is a tie among two of them if mentioned together in the same publication (co-occurrence); the thickness indicates the number of contributions in which the pair appears.

Figure 4 shows the 58 most frequently used keywords and their connections. The size of each node (and its label) represents the occurrence of a specific keyword within the dataset.

Considering the eleven keywords with at least 10 occurrences in the dataset, it is possible to identify the following three group of main topics: (a) co-creation; (b) social network; (c) innovation. The *co-creation* group (69 overall number of occurrences) includes the following keywords: co-creation (36), value creation (20), and value co-creation (13). The *online community* group (120 overall number of occurrences) includes online community (15), online communities (21), collaborative networks (31), social media (30), social capital (12) and netnography (11). The *innovation* group (22 overall number of occurrences) includes innovation (12) and open innovation (10).

From the observation of Fig. 4, we identify two main clusters: the first one is the sub-graph developed around the keywords "Co-creation", "Social Media" and "Online Communities", the second one is centred on "Collaborative Networks" and "Value Creation". These two clusters have direct connections "Value Creation—Online Communities" and "Collaborative Networks—Co-creation" and the keyword "co-innovation" (and in a minor manner also "Innovation") emerges as a bridge

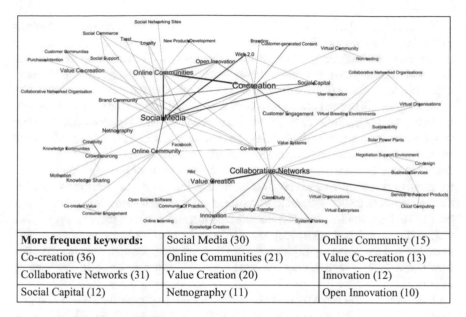

More frequent keywords:	Social Media (30)	Online Community (15)
Co-creation (36)	Online Communities (21)	Value Co-creation (13)
Collaborative Networks (31)	Value Creation (20)	Innovation (12)
Social Capital (12)	Netnography (11)	Open Innovation (10)

Fig. 4 Keywords co-occurrence graph

between the two subgraphs, underlining the relevant role of "innovation" in this context.

4 Preliminary Discussion and Future Steps

This study provides some preliminary insights to scholars and practitioners who are interested to examine issues concerning value co-creation within online communities. Regarding the first research question, this contribution offers a broad overview on the relevant literature, analyzing the most influential sources classifying them in three main categories: (1) determinants of participating and contributing to communities and networks; (2) processes of value co-creation through network interaction and resource exchange; (3) research methodologies. Through the co-citation analysis and co-citation graph it is possible to recognize the references playing the role of contact points (a sort of bridge) among these groups. Concerning the second research question, the main topics discussed by the contributions in the dataset are analyzed considering the keywords defined in each paper. The keywords analysis identified three groups of main topics: (a) co-creation; (b) social network; (c) innovation. Furthermore, the keywords co-occurrence graph offers a broad overview on the connections among the different topics (keywords), identifying two main clusters where the topic "co-innovation" seems to cover a relevant position.

The analysis of the citations and publications trends, as well as of the contributions in the dataset, indicates this topic is current and especially relevant for management researchers and business practitioners in management, IS, marketing and innovation fields. Future research could certainly be conducted with more interdisciplinary approach, for instance in order to capture both technical elements (i.e. characteristics of co-creation platforms) and human factors (i.e. individual motivations, personality traits, etc.). This study also identifies the most influential sources and the main connections among them, highlighting the main contributions that have influenced subsequent research on value co-creation within online communities. The most influential sources concern the dynamics and the determinants of participating and contributing to communities and networks, as well as the processes of value co-creation through network interaction and resource exchange, while it seems less attention was paid to strategic implications of value co-creation and research methodology. Also, it should be noted that the three most cited articles, such as Vargo and Lusch [24], Prahalad and Ramaswamy [2] Muniz and O'Guinn [25], are also the most co-cited contributions, thus representing the hard core for further research in that area of inquiry.

This research has some limitations. While our bibliographic analysis is comprehensive, it is not exhaustive. Although we performed the search on ISI-WoS using specific set of keywords, other search terms can also be used and could potentially yield different results. Despite these limitations, this paper provides a general picture of past and current research, creating a database of the academic literature on value co-creation within online communities.

Our quantitative bibliographic analysis represents just the starting point of a literature analysis process. Further steps will aim at conducting a systematic literature review of ongoing debate on value co-creation within online communities and to propose and test a research model for investigating the determinants of value co-creation within online communities.

References

1. Kambil, A., Friesen, G. B., & Sundaram, A. (1999). Co-creation: A new source of value. *Outlook Magazine, 3,* 23–29.
2. Prahalad, C. K., & Ramaswamy, V. (2004). Co-creation experiences: The next practice in value creation. *Journal of Interactive Marketing, 18,* 5–14.
3. Carillo, K., Scornavacca, E., & Za, S. (2014). An investigation of the role of dependency in predicting continuance intention to use ubiquitous media systems: Combining a media system perspective with expectation-confirmation theories. In *Proceedings of the Twenty Second European Conference on Information Systems (ECIS2014)* (pp. 1–17). Israel: Tel Aviv.
4. Carillo, K., Scornavacca, E., & Za, S. (2017). The role of media dependency in predicting continuance intention to use ubiquitous media systems. *Information & Management, 54,* 317–335.
5. Kohler, T., Fueller, J., Matzler, K., Stieger, D., & Füller, J. (2011). Co-creation in virtual worlds: The design of the user experience. *MIS Quarterly, 3516787,* 773–788.
6. Zwass, V. (2010). Co-creation: Toward a taxonomy and an integrated research perspective. *International Journal of Electronic Commerce, 15,* 11–48.

7. Barrett, M., Oborn, E., & Orlikowski, W. (2016). Creating value in online communities: The sociomaterial engagement. *Information Systems Research, 27,* 704–723.
8. Mein Goh, J., Gao, G., & Agarwal, R. (2016). The creation of social value: Can an online health community reduce rural-urban health disparities? *MIS Quarterly, 40,* 247–263.
9. Nahapiet, J., & Ghoshal, S. (1998). Social capital, intellectual capital, and the organizational advantage. *Academy of Management Review, 23,* 242.
10. Tiwana, A., Konsynski, B., & Bush, A. A. (2010). Research commentary: Platform evolution: coevolution of platform architecture, governance, and environmental dynamics. *Information Systems Research, 21,* 675–687.
11. West, J., & O'mahony, S. (2008). The role of participation architecture in growing sponsored open source communities. *Industry and Innovation, 15,* 145–168.
12. Seraj, M. (2012). We create, we connect, we respect, therefore we are: Intellectual, social, and cultural value in online communities. *Journal of Interactive Marketing, 26,* 209–222.
13. Pritchard, A. (1969). Statistical bibliography or bibliometrics? *Journal of Documentation, 24,* 348–349.
14. Culnan, M. J. (1986). The intellectual development of management information systems, 1972–1982: A co-citation analysis. *Management Science, 32,* 156–172.
15. Laine, M. (2009). Virtual communities: A bibliometric analysis. In *System Sciences. HICSS'09. 42nd Hawaii* (pp. 1–10).
16. Polites, G. L., & Watson, R. T. (2009). Using social network analysis to analyze relationships among IS journals. *Journal of the Association for Information Systems, 10,* 595–636.
17. Small, H. (1993). Macro-level changes in the structure of co-citation clusters: 1983–1989. *Scientometrics, 26,* 5–20.
18. Bernroider, E. W., Pilkington, A., & Córdoba, J.-R. (2013). Research in information systems: A study of diversity and inter-disciplinary discourse in the AIS basket journals between 1995 and 2011. *Journal of Information and Technology, 28,* 74–89.
19. Baskerville, R. L., & Myers, M. D. (2002). Information systems as a reference discipline. *MIS Quarterly, 26,* 1–14.
20. Clarke, R. (2008). An exploratory study of information systems researcher impact. *Communications of the Association for Information Systems, 22,* 1–32.
21. Ricciardi, F., & Za, S. (2015). Smart city research as an interdisciplinary crossroads: A challenge for management and organization studies. In L. Mola, F. Pennarola, & S. Za (Eds.), *From Information to Smart Society, LNISO* (Vol. 5, pp. 163–171).
22. Za, S., & Braccini, A. M. (2017). Tracing the roots of the organizational benefits of IT services. In S. Za, M. Drăgoicea, & M. Cavallari (Eds.), *LNBIP—Exploring services science* (pp. 3–11). Berlin, Heidelberg: Springer International Publishing.
23. Kaplan, A. M., & Haenlein, M. (2010). Users of the world, unite! The challenges and opportunities of social media. *Business Horizons, 53,* 59–68.
24. Vargo, S. L., & Lusch, R. F. (2004). Evolving to a new dominant logic for marketing. *Journal of Marketing, 68,* 1–17.
25. Muniz, A. M., & O'Guinn, T. (2001). Brand community. *Journal of Consumer Research, 27,* 412–432.
26. Kozinets, R. V. (2002). The field behind the screen: Using netnography for marketing research in online communities. *Journal of Marketing Research, 39,* 61–72.
27. Schau, H. J., Muñiz, A. M., & Arnould, E. J. (2009). How brand community practices create value. *Journal of Marketing, 73,* 30–51.
28. McLure Wasko, M., & Faraj, S. (2005). Why should I share? Examining social capital and knowledge contribution in electronic networks of practice. *MIS Quarterly, 29,* 35–57.
29. Dholakia, U. M., Bagozzi, R. P., & Klein Pearo, L. (2004). A social influence model of consumer participation in network-and small-group-based virtual communities. *International Journal of Research in Marketing, 21,* 241–263.
30. Nambisan, S., & Baron, R. A. (2009). Virtual customer environments: Testing a model of voluntary participation in value co-creation activities. *Journal of Product Innovation Management, 26,* 388–406.

31. Payne, A. F., Storbacka, K., & Frow, P. (2008). Managing the co-creation of value. *Journal of the Academy of Marketing Science, 36,* 83–96.
32. McAlexander, J. H., Schouten, J. W., & Koenig, H. F. (2002). Building brand community. *Journal of Marketing, 66,* 38–54.
33. Vargo, S. L., & Lusch, R. F. (2008). Service-dominant logic: Continuing the evolution. *Journal of the Academy of Marketing Science, 36,* 1–10.
34. Algesheimer, R., Dholakia, U. M., & Herrmann, A. (2005). The social influence of brand community: Evidence from European car clubs european car clubs. *Journal of Marketing, 69167987,* 19–34.
35. von Hippel, E. (2005). Democratizing innovation: The evolving phenomenon of user innovation. *Journal für Betriebswirtschaft, 55*(1), 63–78.
36. Wiertz, C., & De Ruyter, K. (2007). Beyond the call of duty: Why customers contribute to firm-hosted commercial online communities. *Organization Studies, 28,* 347–376.
37. Brodie, R. J., Ilic, A., Juric, B., & Hollebeek, L. (2013). Consumer engagement in a virtual brand community: An exploratory analysis. *Journal of Business Research, 66,* 105–114.
38. Fornell, C., & Larcker, D. (1981). Structural equation models with unobservable variables and measurement error. *Journal of Marketing Research, 18,* 39–50.

Disability and Home Automation: Insights and Challenges Within Organizational Settings

Luisa Varriale, Paola Briganti and Stefania Mele

Abstract This paper investigates the relationship between disability and new technologies, specifically home automation, evidencing how the application of new technologies can effectively promote the social inclusion of people with disability. New technologies in all their forms significantly changed the social and economic activities, recording an increasing application in any organizational settings, also allowing people with disability to be significantly involved by improving their social status and commitment in the social daily life. New technologies can facilitate and promote the social integration of disabled persons, allowing them to participate into several social daily activities, acquiring some kind of autonomy. There is an explosion of technology applications in the disabled people's daily life in different ways, but this phenomenon is still under researched in the literature. This paper aims to identify and evidence the role and function of home automation, for people with disability, specifically we aim to outline if and how the home automation solutions and devises can support people with disability improving their social inclusion. This theoretical study, conducted through a deep review of the contributions in the literature and in the practice through an online search from a 30-year period (1998–2018) on the link between technology/home automation and disability, as an interesting research starting point, contributes to systematize and clarify the main contributions on this phenomenon, also identifying new research perspectives.

Keywords Disability · Technology · Home automation · Innovation · Social inclusion

L. Varriale (✉) · P. Briganti
Department of Sport Science and Wellbeing, Parthenope University, Naples, Italy
e-mail: luisa.varriale@uniparthenope.it

P. Briganti
e-mail: paola.briganti@uniparthenope.it

S. Mele
Department of Management and Quantitative Studies, Parthenope University, Naples, Italy
e-mail: stefania.mele@uniparthenope.it

© Springer Nature Switzerland AG 2020   47
A. Lazazzara et al. (eds.), *Exploring Digital Ecosystems*,
Lecture Notes in Information Systems and Organisation 33,
https://doi.org/10.1007/978-3-030-23665-6_5

1 Introduction

New technologies are increasingly present in the daily life of each of us. Technology may assume a role really decisive in any organizational settings, from educational to manufacturing context, especially considering its recognized crucial role in promoting the process of social inclusion, enabling people in difficulties, such as people with disabilities, to carry out, independently, activities that would otherwise be precluded. We are observing, in fact, a slow and gradual realization (even from software companies) in terms of accessibility to information technologies, which are becoming more and more accessible, comfortable and used in practice to all, through the application of the principles of "design for all" [1].

Specifically, Information and Communication Technology (ICT) represents the set of digital technologies, methods and technologies that allow the transmission, reception and processing of information included. The use of technology in the management and processing of information is having an increasing strategic importance for organizations. Educational institutions, in particular, provide, through its educational project, special training courses and the use of ICT for cross several disciplines. Today, information technology (digital devices and software programs) and telecommunications (computer networks) are the two pillars on which the "society of communication" is founded.

In particular, the spread application of new technologies significantly affects the daily life of people with disability. New technologies, especially computers with their new operating systems or other devises, thanks to the powerful features provided, allow, through the easy access to information and other actions, to facilitate those people who face difficulties for their impaired position, allowing them to obtain satisfactory performance with tools that turn out to be really effective and efficient. Even more, mobile always provides a series of settings in order to easy use, and everything not present (default) can be found among the applications available and easily installed.

This attention paid to the needs of individuals, much more people with disability in any its forms (cognitive, sensory or motor disability), amplifies the use of these instruments, which often become an integral part of lives of everyone, not only from the professional point of view, but especially from a social and personal point of view, as they provide opportunities for collecting and processing information, taking useful documentation, socializing, including, through the use of social networks, more and more widespread in so many different areas, and much more for independently making the routine activities, such as eating, reading, cleaning up, and so forth.

Thus, it is interesting to analyze the characteristics of empowerment that new technologies, more specifically home automation, have shown for people with disabilities (PWD), in terms of living easily and independently and having the opportunity of expanding their network of contacts and friends beyond the restricted circles with whom you can share common problems [2–5].

New technologies in the expression of home automation or smart home consist of tools able to promote social inclusion of persons with disabilities to enable them more easily to have a job, to give them better care, to easily make their daily activities.

The technology in the human history has always influenced the way people live and, now it becomes crucial for the future of over a billion people in the world living with some forms of disability.

This conceptual study aims to investigate the role of new technologies, through the home automation form, for involving and making the active participation of people with disabilities. Indeed, this exploratory study aims to clarify and systematize the major existing contributions in the literature and practice focused on home automation and disability for evidencing and filling the gap still existing, and for identifying interesting and useful variables to investigate in the future regarding the effectiveness of home automation.

In the recent years, the significant evolution of the world, in terms of developing and adopting new technologies through home automation, has been requiring an increasing attention by scholars and practitioners especially with concern of people with disabilities.

This paper is structured as follows: Sect. 2 briefly describes the link between technology, specifically home automation, and people with disability in promoting their social integration. Section 3 provides a review through an online search of the main contributions in the literature on disability and home automation. In Sect. 4 the point of view of practitioners on the phenomenon, the link between home automation and disability, has been summarized. Finally, in Sect. 5 some final considerations are provided about the phenomenon investigated.

2 Home Automation for Supporting People with Disability

Sometimes, disability term can be inappropriately conceived, for this reason it is necessary to clearly define this concept. The idea of the disabled person is no longer conditioned by the individual's stereotype of disability seen only in a wheelchair, but it is much more extensive and includes any person who, permanently or temporarily, is having difficulty in movement (heart disease, women pregnancy, people with stroller, convalescent individuals or limb in a cast, obese, elderly, children, etc.) or sensory perceptions (the blind and visually impaired, deaf and dumb), as well as, persons with cognitive or psychological difficulties.

The concept of disability has changed from the recent definition of the International Classification of Functioning, Disability and Health (ICF) drawn up in 2001 by the World Health Organization (WHO) which identified disabilities the product of environmental factors, physical and social and inadequate or insufficient answers that the society, in general, and the company, in particular, give to people who have special needs.

The ICF framework is a revolution because it states that "any person, at any time of life, can be in health condition who become disabled, because the person is in front a context/a negative environment that limit, restrict or cancel its functional capacity and social participation" [6].

Also, at international level, it is common to talk about people with disabilities. In fact, the WHO uses the word "person", instead of adjectival forms as invalid, disabled, or handicapped nouns: this choice has the advantage without attributing the whole person an attribute that is only part of and that it leaves intact a term (person) is in itself neutral; the definition of persons with disabilities, combines the concept of person, universally accepted and considered positive, received an assignment, something that does not belong to the person, but that is imposed because disability is not derived from the psycho-physical situation, but by the failure of the society/organization to make any actions for including any people, meeting their special needs. The person who uses a wheelchair has a disability when he/she only meets overcome differences in height with ladders; the person using a white cane has a disability when it fails to orientate because he/she lacks elements (such as carefully designed flooring or sound devices, tactile, etc.) that allow him/her to safely move [6].

Therefore, disability is not caused by subjective factors but from the context or the company that have not designed thinking at all. This position allows you to abandon the concept of a person with disabilities to emphasize instead that of "non-skilled environment or un-suitable" [6].

Today, people with disabilities, through technological innovation, especially home automation, have the ability to manage their difficulties and to be successfully engaged in daily life activities, with performances ever closer to those of the able-bodied.

Assistive technologies available today not only allow you to prevent complications or aggravation of a disability, and to correct or resolve postural problems, but they also allow you to significantly reduce the gap that determines the daily life of the disabled person and the society that surrounds it.

According to most scholars [7–12], home automation, also referred to smart home concept, one relevant and spread expressions of new technologies, is not new for people because it was introduced already few decades ago. The term "home automation or smart home" has been defined in several ways. In general, this concept refers to any technology able to automate a home-based activity. For instance, electronic thermostats and motion-activated lighting, or interactive systems for controlling home activities from a central access point (a computer, personal digital assistant or remote-control device). Many ways exist for making remote control of activities in a smart home, that is for programming to control lighting, entertainment systems, appliances and thermostats. Thus, home automation concerns the ability to control electrical and electronic devices at home remotely, thus allowing ease of access to home users. Various manners can allow the application of this concept to fit the requirement of a smart home. Nowadays, many advanced tools can be used, especially including wireless technology such as Bluetooth and Internet linking, WiFi, and so forth.

For people with disabilities, hence in the overall disability community, the term home automation typically concerns the use of electronic assistive technology ("EAT"), including electronic aids to daily living ("EADL"), assistive technology for cognition ("ATC"), wireless connectivity and other tools able to provide support to people with disability in the home setting [8, 12]. This field is acquiring an increasing importance, because people with disability right fully advocate for self-determination and self-efficacy, and as the elderly population is growing and seeks to age in place. Indeed, smart homes offer the promise of increased independence and reduced need for caregiver support at home [9, 13, 14].

In this direction, interesting studies have paid their attention to the link between technology, specifically home automation and disability [9, 12–15]; in fact, home automation can allow people with disability to face their challenges and mostly to facilitate their social integration, acquiring their independence [15, 16]. Although there are significant studies, this phenomenon is still underrepresented and there is the need to systematize and clarify the state of art in the research and practice for better support the daily life of PWD.

3 Disability and Home Automation: The State of Art in the Research

This study conducted an online research to identify the prevalent contributions in the literature from a 30-year period (1988–2018) on the link between disability, psychological autonomy, smart home facilities, that is home automation. Specifically, we conducted a search on line adopting the key words "disability" and "home automation" in most freely accessible web search engines specialized in academic literature, that is Google Scholar, PubMed, Web of Science and ScienceDirect.

We used the following three criteria for selecting papers. First, they must be published in journals in the range 1988–2018. Second, the selected papers have to be in English language and contain in their abstract at least one of the word selected (disability, physical and psychological autonomy, domotics, home automation, domotic automation and smart home). Third, articles have to deal with research issues rather than specialty organizational topics, it means we selected papers from management, educational, medical, physical activity and all the issues available with connection to disability and home automation issues. We considered also journals with no high impact factor and of relatively lower ranking (e.g. Poetics, Depression and Anxiety, etc.).

The search has outlined significant elements showing an increasing attention by scholars on the issue especially since 2016, more specifically, on the existing link between disability, physical and psychological autonomy, and smart home, which has become stronger over the years (see Table 1 for a summary).

The papers resulting from the research were totally 16, and the most part consists of theoretical studies which adopt a qualitative methodology.

Starting from more recent and relevant contributions on the matter, in 2018, Esmail et al. [17] investigated the importance of technology for clothing activities in case of aging or, generally, reduction of physical and psychological autonomy linked to disability. Clothing is an important aspect of nearly all human societies from

Table 1 Summary of contributions in the literature on the topic

Year	Journal	Aim	Type of paper	Methodology
2018	BMJ open	To understand the role of technology and clothing in participation (e.g. at home, in the community, etc.) of individuals with a physical disability	Theoretical review	Qualitative-quantitative study
2017	Disability and health journal	To describe the accessibility gap still existing in both PC and smart devices for PWD, especially in the smart environment compared to PC environment	Empirical	Quantitative study
2016	Poetics	To evidence that PWD are less likely to use the Internet and are less likely to engage in a wide range of activities when online, although barriers for going online still exist, but the online world may offer a means to adapt to an inaccessible culture and society	Theoretical-empirical review	Qualitative-quantitative study
2016	International journal of medical informatics	To evidence the level of technology readiness for smart home and health monitoring technologies regarding monitoring function, cognitive and mental health in the perspective of improving the quality of life	Theoretical review	Qualitative study
2016	International journal of medical informatics	To identify the underlying factors obstacle IT use among older people and their homes	Meta-analysis review	Qualitative-quantitative study

(continued)

Table 1 (continued)

Year	Journal	Aim	Type of paper	Methodology
2016	Studies in health technology and informatics	To analyse the phenomenon of the burden of chronic disease and associated disability, that presents a major threat to financial sustainability of healthcare delivery systems	Empirical	Quantitative study
2016	JMIR mental health	To investigate the Lifeline Assistance Program as useful model designed to help eligible low-income individuals for having home phone and landline services, and help in case of emergency, and access social services and healthcare	Empirical	Quantitative study
2016	JMIR rehabilitation and assistive technologies	To assess the usage of self-management technologies on post stroke survivors while undergoing rehabilitation at home	Empirical	Quantitative study
2015	JMIR rehabilitation and assistive technologies	To develop the prototype of a smart shoe insole, a non invasive wireless insole, to respond to the needs expressed by the stakeholders (frailty monitoring and adherence improvement) for monitoring key parameters of frailty during daily life and to promote walking	Empirical	Quantitative-laboratory test study

(continued)

Table 1 (continued)

Year	Journal	Aim	Type of paper	Methodology
2015	Journal of Rehabilitation Research and Development	To test the functionality and safety of the gaze-driven powered wheelchair in the user's home environment in terms of independence and participation in disability cases	Empirical	Quantitative study
2012	Pain management nursing	To analyse technological solutions (Web-based nursing) for female patients with fibromyalgia who cope with chronic pain, emotional distress, activity avoidance and disability	Theoretical	Qualitative study
2004	Psychology in the schools	To explain the concept of physical and psychological autonomy and related technological home and social support systems for children and adolescents who have intellectual and developmental disabilities (ID/DD), including autism, considering the growing number of cases registered in last decades through epidemiological reports	Theoretical	Qualitative study

(continued)

Table 1 (continued)

Year	Journal	Aim	Type of paper	Methodology
2003	Disability and rehabilitation	To investigate Assistive Technology (AT) including specific items (structural alterations, special equipment, assistive devices, material adjustment, environmentally-based behavioural modification) and to develop a theoretical framework for developing device-specific causal models	Theoretical	Qualitative study
2003	Depression and anxiety	To describe an innovative rating scale [The Connor-Davidson Resilience scale (CD-RISC)] to assess resilience viewed as a measure of stress coping ability and, as such, could be an important target of treatment in anxiety, depression, and stress reactions	Empirical	Quantitative validation rating scale study
2003	Journal of applied research in intellectual disabilities	To analyse environmental features which, more than personal characteristics, may positively affect self-determination and autonomy functioning levels of individuals with disabilities	Empirical	Quantitative study

(continued)

Table 1 (continued)

Year	Journal	Aim	Type of paper	Methodology
1988	Journal of social issues	To investigate possible models to challenge the traditional dominance of the "functional-limitations" paradigm for the study of disability	Theoretical	Qualitative study

Source Our processing from web data scheduling

performing social and cultural functions to indicate social status, a form of protection and a way for self-expression. It can help or hinder the ability to fulfill every-day activities and social roles and with the rising industry of wearable technologies, smart textiles are adding health-monitoring functions to clothing. The influence that clothing can have on the life of someone with a physical disability is significant, and further research is needed to better understand the phenomenon. To achieve this goal, a scoping review will be performed with the aim of understanding the role of clothing in participation (e.g. at home, in the community, etc.) of individuals with a physical disability.

Then, Nam and Park [18] argued that ICT is connected with every aspect of social, cultural, economic, educational, and commercial activity. Smart devices in the contemporary world in particular have changed society and are necessary instruments for modern people. Smart device usage is rapidly growing in everyday life, also supporting the inclusion of people with disabilities. Their study investigated the effects of the smart environment on the information divide experienced by PWD, and information from the 2013 Information Divide Index Data of the National Information Society Agency were analyzed regarding three aspects, that is access, skill, and competence. The accessibility difference was investigated by comparing access to a PC or smart device in two groups, general people and PWD. The effects of a smart environment on the information device were analyzed using the General Linear Modeling (GLM), evidencing that the access rate to a PC or smart device was higher for the general group than for people with disabilities, and this difference appeared to be greater in the smart environment. Thus, disability and device access had statistically significant effects on skill and all aspects of competence.

In 2016, Dobransky and Hargittai [19] underlined that, while the digital inequality literature has considered differences in the online experiences of many population segments, relatively little work investigates how PWD have incorporated digital media into their lives. Based on a national survey of American adults, this topic was explored considering both barriers to Internet use and the possibilities that Internet offers to PWD. Findings indicated barriers for PWD, also depending on their form of disability, to access the Internet. Those with five of six types of disabilities (e.g. people with deaf or hearing impaired, blind people, etc.) are considerably less likely to be online than those who are not disabled. Hence, the findings indicated great potential for the Internet for PWD and suggested that moving more of them online holds the potential for considerable gains among this group.

Another study provides a systematic literature review [20]: (1) to determine the levels of technology readiness among older adults and (2) and to evidence for smart homes and home-based health-monitoring technologies that support aging in place for older adults who have complex needs. In fact, this study introduced and discussed about home automation and disability prevention and care, with particular reference to the role of technology for older people. Forty-eight of 1863 relevant papers were identified and analyzed, evidencing the following issues: technology-readiness level for smart homes and home health monitoring technologies is low; there is no evidence that smart homes and home health monitoring technologies help address disability prediction and health-related quality of life, or fall prevention; there are still conflicting findings about the capability of smart homes and home health monitoring technologies to address chronic obstructive pulmonary disease.

According to these perspectives focused on technology and older people health preservation and care, in 2016, Yusif et al. [21] reviewed the main barriers in adopting assistive technologies (ATs) by older adults in order to uncover issues of concern from empirical studies and to arrange these issues from the most critical to the least critical. They conducted a 4-step systematic review using empirical studies: locating and identifying relevant articles; screening of located articles; examination of full text articles for inclusion/exclusion; and particularly examining 44 articles included. Several barriers for adopting ATs were identified, that is, privacy, trust and functionality/added value, cost and ease of use and suitability for daily use, perception of "no need", stigma, and fear of dependence and lack of training.

Other scholars [22] underlined that the burden of chronic disease and associated disability present a major threat to financial sustainability of healthcare delivery systems. Thanks to the adoption of new technologies, such as the ECG monitoring system, it is possible to simplify the life of people with chronic disease with personalized home health solutions.

Jelin et al. [23] focused their research on another illness, the fibromyalgia, which implies high healthcare costs and individual social and pain disadvantages. The patients, mainly women, must simultaneously cope with chronic pain, emotional distress, activity avoidance and disability. This qualitative study explored female patients' experiences of participating in a 4-week web-based home intervention after in-house multidimensional rehabilitation, showing the positive effects in implementing ICT, such as Internet and smart phones, for text-based communications between providers and patients with chronic pain.

In 2015, Wästlund et al. [24] analysed the traditional issue of independent home mobility for disability, and tested the functionality and safety of the innovative system gaze-driven powered wheelchairs in the users' home environment. Their research described, through three users test, a novel add-on for powered wheelchairs that is composed of a gaze-driven control system and a navigation support system. The study tested the functionality and safety of the system in the user's home environment considering individuals with very high disability with no possibility of moving independently, evaluating also whether access to a gaze-driven powered wheel-chair with navigation support is perceived as meaningful in terms of independence and participation. The results show that the system has the potential to provide safe, independent indoor mobility, and that the users perceive doing so as fun, meaningful, and a way to reduce dependency on others.

Ben-Zeev' research [25] stressed the issue of growing diffusion and need of remote care of mental health disabilities, outlining that different mental health approaches are feasible, acceptable, and clinically promising for people with mental health problems. This study describes the Lifeline Assistance Program (LAP) as an useful model created in 1985 by the U.S. Federal Communications Commission (FCC). The LAP consists of a nationwide program designed to help eligible low-income individuals to obtain home phone and landline services so they can pursue employment, reach help in case of emergency, and access to social and healthcare services. In 2005, recognizing the broad shift towards mobile technology and mobile-cellular infrastructure, the FCC expanded the program to include mobile phones and data plans. Then, programs like LAP could be expanded to include mobile and wireless health (mHealth) resources that capitalize "smart" functions, such as secure/encrypted clinical texting programs and mental health monitoring and illness-management apps.

Piau et al. [26], underlining the growing aging of population around the world, evidenced the importance to take care of "frailty syndrome" of older individuals, that frequently experience reversible increasing incidence of disability. Their research, through laboratory study, aimed: to develop a technological solution designed for supporting active aging of frail older persons; to conduct a first laboratory evaluation of the device; and to design a multidimensional clinical trial for validating their solution. The results showed that the prototype smart solution, developed to respond to the needs expressed by the stakeholders (frailty monitoring and adherence improvement), was effective to monitor key parameters of frailty during daily life and to promote walking. Thanks to the first laboratory tests, the technological solution, which was a non invasive wireless insole, able to automatically measure gait parameters and to transmit information to a remote terminal via Internet connection, by showing good reliability measures and also a good acceptability by the users.

Davies et al. [27] deeply analysed the theme of smart insole, focusing on personalized self-management rehabilitation system for stroke survivors in the United Kingdom. The use of innovative technologies and the ability to effectively apply them, to promote behavior change, are paramount in meeting the current challenges. The study assessed the usage of self-management technologies on post stroke survivors while undergoing rehabilitation at home. From a methodological perspective, a realist evaluation was conducted of a personalized self-management rehabilitation system at home of 5 stroke survivors over a period of approximately two months. Using a "smart insole" it was possible to easily facilitate measurement of walking activities in a free-living, non restrictive environment. The study suggested that 4 out of the 5 participants improved their ability to heel strike on their affected limb. All participants showed improvements in their speed of gait measured in steps per minute, with an average increase of 9.8% during the rehabilitation program.

In 2004, Clark et al. [28] stressed the needs to define the concepts and principles of autonomy and self-determination and the application of those concepts and principles for working with children and adolescents who have intellectual and developmental disabilities (ID/DD), including autism, considering the growing number of cases recorded in the three decades through epidemiological reports. Self-determination concerns the ability of a person to be autonomous in his/her meaningful life choices. Specific technological practices were discussed for generating more opportunities for individuals to exercise personal control and autonomy across activities and environments in order to prevent and manage psychological problems.

Focusing always the attention on the importance of physical and psychological autonomy for PWD, Fuhrer et al. [29] analysed a key step in planning and developing assistive technology through the formulation of a conceptual model, specific to a particular type of device. Indeed, the development of device-specific causal models will be facilitated by having available an overall framework that is potentially applicable to multiple types of devices and their outcomes. The outcomes of assistive technology devices depended on the interaction among characteristics of a specific device-type, its users, and their environment.

Sometimes, disability derives from injury and accidents, not only from illness, and requires the psychological support in managing the daily life by professionals in a direct or remote way, monitoring at home too through latest validated resilience scale: the Connor-Davidson resilience scale (CD-RISC) [30]. Resilience may be viewed as a measure of stress coping ability and, as such, could be an important target of treatment in anxiety, depression, and stress reactions. In this study, sensitivity to treatment effects was examined in individuals from the PTSD clinical trials, affected by physical and/or psychological disabilities effects of traumatic events.

In 2003, other scholars [31] underlined that many people presume that physical and/or psychological disabilities means absence of self-determination of individuals, and they stressed the importance of environmental characteristics of daily life and homes. The self-determination and autonomy functioning levels of individuals with disabilities, also, depend on environmental features, beyond personal and physical characteristics; indeed, less restrictive settings help PWD to be more autonomous.

Although a "minority-group" model has emerged to challenge the traditional dominance of the "functional-limitations" paradigm for the study of disability, as intuitively showed many decades ago by adopting a sociological perspective [32], thanks to this brief review of the literature, we highlight that research still needed to be developed focusing on attitudes toward disabled people with the support and adoption of technological devises, especially home automation.

In summary, a new conceptual framework is needed in existing multidisciplinary perspective, based on the fundamental values of personal appearance and individual autonomy, considering the main positive effects of technologies for PWD helping them to improve their daily life, promoting their social inclusion and autonomy, reducing discriminations, and improving in general the life quality of people affected by disability. Thus, it has been evidenced that it is necessary to enrich the existing research, still poor, thanks to the contributions of qualified academic researchers. Investigations using this perspective might contribute to determine the attitudinal foundations of the competing models that are dividing research on disability considering and linking to new technologies, that is home automation.

Most of the items of research have as objective the analysis of the different equipment that disabled people can use to acquire more autonomy in their daily life. For instance, thanks to the relevant changes occurred in the technology and science, there are special and advanced wheelchairs, able to be empowered using mobile phone or other devises, such as wheelchairs with three wheels, two largest rear and a front smaller with a digital monitoring system.

PWD, specifically blind people or people with motor disability, thanks to the development and spread of home automation devises, can acquire an increasing autonomy in their daily life also having a stronger psychological and sociological construct.

The findings of the research outlined some challenges and critical aspects that still needed to be explored. Although the prevalent literature evidences and investigates the role played by the technology for PWD, some critical themes have been identified, such as the implementation of the technological devises making smart environment, home automation, the critical relationships between the adoption of new technologies to improve the daily life and psychological/sociological issues, the impact of technology on PWD autonomy, traditionally considered as the main challenge to face, and so forth.

This analysis allows us to recognize the importance of the application of technology for facing any challenges related to disability in its forms, in fact, thanks to the enrichment and development of innovative instruments (high quality standard devises, software monitor PWD, etc.) people with disabilities can perform their activities without high risks or any difficulties, becoming more autonomous and overcoming their daily challenges. Otherwise, the adoption of new technologies with all its forms, especially home automation, significantly affects the daily life of PWD, deeply changing their human interactions, making them more autonomous and promoting their social and cultural inclusion.

In this direction, by working together all the several organizations, academics and practitioners, that is psychologists, sociologists, researchers, engineers, and the overall community can provide affordable safe and reliable technological assistive devices, technologies for training and rehabilitation, and for making the daily world of PWD much easier and accessible.

4 Disability and Home Automation: The State of Art in the Practice

Around 80 million people in the European Union (EU), the sixth part of the over-all population, have a disability. Furthermore, according to the United Nations Convention on the Rights of Persons with Disabilities (art. 9) [33], signed by the European Commission in 2010, the accessibility is a basic right for all PWD. The purpose of accessibility is to enable PWD to live independently and to participate in all aspects of life.

Home automation has the ambition to develop a novel and revolutionary modular and adaptive multimodal human–machine interface to allow moderately and severely impaired people at interacting with intelligent devices to perform daily activities and to fully participate in society. Besides, it will develop a totally new shared-control paradigm for assistive devices that integrate information from identification of residual abilities, behaviours, emotional state, on one hand, and intentions of the user and analysis of the environment and contextual factors, on the other hand.

It is crucial in considering what a person would like to be able to do at home to take into account his/her different needs. There are numerous ways and theories to explore and many priorities, tasks and requirements. Maslow's hierarchy theory of needs sets out a pyramid beginning with a person's most basic needs at the bottom and as the persons' needs are satisfied, they move up the pyramid towards the need to develop into the person they desire to be [34]. Specifically, a good automated domestic environment wants to create a place where people with limited mobility is able to meet their needs at each stage of the pyramid in order to ultimately engage in their community as active citizens through the use of the system. The activities of daily living are essential for the existence and include fundamental tasks, such as personal care, feeding, drinking, hygiene, and mobility. However, a person requires more than their basic survival needs to get satisfaction from life. These tasks include preparing their own food or meal, shopping, light housework and managing finances. Finally, the discretionary activities are important such as leisure activities, hobbies, engaging in the community, spiritual activities, caring for people, shopping, gardening and so forth. Also, as already outlined, the ICF framework, focused on the interaction between the health condition and the contextual factors, created a checklist to support clinicians in identifying the functioning and impairment level of an individual while also considering activities, participation, environment and personal factors. This checklist is also an important tool to reflect on the important activities to people within the overall context of their living situation and environment [35].

To ensure a user centred approach a kind of road map of needs compared to devices could be developed. The road map is defined from the target end users, therapists, and caregivers input. Then, the identification of these needs is mapped against the systems specification and design solution (Table 2).

Some examples could be given as results of this process: an interesting empirical analysis could be the applied research in this field financed by the European Commission trough the 6th and 7th Framework Programs and Horizon 2020:

– SRS (Multi-Role Shadow Robotic System for Independent Living): The SRS project, funded by the European Commission under the 7th Framework Program (Call FP7-ICT-2009-4, ICT and Aging), aims to develop and to experiment with

Table 2 Summary of applications

	User requirements	Planned technical specification
Signal acquisition	**Ease of use**: The user should be able to easily establish and maintain control of the system	The user's ability to control the system will be maximised through multiple input devices that can be customised according to the unique presentation of user and their preference to interact with it
Software	**Effectiveness**: The user should be able to control the system as accurately and completely as possible with a low error rate	The adoption of the multi-level control architecture guarantees a great accuracy in task execution
Hardware	**Safety**: The system must be safe and alleviates any fear target users might have	The systems hardware could have exoskeleton and specifications aligned at achieving specific purposes

Source Our processing

a robotic aid for people assistance elderly in domestic environments, able to provide support to improve and prolong the autonomy condition. Instead of thinking of a completely autonomous device, which does not yet appear realistic in the current state of technology, they aimed at a semi-autonomous robotic solution, that is able to accomplish in autonomy only determined inalienable operations in an unstructured environment (such as, for example, circumventing obstacles encountered along the way) that for the operational functions is remote controlled by the same elderly person or remotely from a family member or a family member operator not present at that moment at home. The term "shadow robot" that is acting as a shadow of a human operator well expresses this concept. The principal target is to remotely manage emergency situations, when the family member has to leave home or even routine situations in which the elderly person can be helped in carrying out some domestic activities from a remote location;

– HEAD (Human Empowerment Aging and Disability): This project primarily aimed at defining and structuring of contextualized and individualized rehabilitative care processes with the related health and social care for chronic disability conditions caused by congenital lesions or acquired of the nervous system, with innovative use of technologies. With a telecommunication infrastructure web-based configuration, the formal organization is proposed and the activation of a neuro-rehabilitation service model in continuity between hospital and territory, using video connection for telepresence, high-tech technologies (e.g.: robotics, wireless dynamic electromyography, BCI) and low cost (e.g.: RFID, dedicated software for touch screen functions) for the recovery of cognitive and/or motor functions of the upper limbs and lower. A structured mode of service delivery of tele-neuro-rehabilitation for both motor and cognitive components will therefore be fundamental for defining direct and indirect costs, and their sustainability, compared to the real benefits detectable with rehabilitation logic in which bodily functions, activities and participation can be monitored in their own vary, and integrate into representing the state of person health;

– SMARTA (Environmental Monitoring System with Network sensors and wearable telemonitoring to support health services, prevention and security for Active Aging): The SMARTA project aims to develop an innovative system for monitoring the health picture of the elderly population over 65 age, healthy or with diseases, living in a home environment. The project aimed at supporting active aging, a concept that the European Community is promoting as a tool for control of health costs and increase in quality of life, through the development of a system of environmental sensors and personal features.

These funded projects show that technological progress has allowed the realization of disable living and rehabilitation model: the advent of smart phones (equipped with a processor, memory, wireless connection, geolocation) and their applications, have proved to be the tools most able to meet the needs of home-based rehabilitation, radically changing the management of patient care [36], and, also, to support PWD to easily manage their daily life.

Two main advantages of the automated home systems can be distinguished. First, to get the best quality of life of PWD, if monitored in conditions of absolute safety, which can more easily live their daily life. Second, to achieve economic goals and it is linked to the reduction of hospitalization.

5 Concluding Remarks

The development and adoption of new technologies in any forms and tools have significantly changed relevant aspects of the daily life, especially, for people with different forms of disability. We can observe positive or negative effects of technology, specifically home automation, such as the improvement of daily life of PWD, thanks to the innovative understanding, monitoring and evaluation digital systems introduced for enabling the normal routine activities or promoting the social integration of PWD, or the overcoming of geographic and cultural barriers. Although all these recognized benefits derived from home automation in terms of increasing autonomy of PWD, its impact is very relevant and sometimes alarming, because it contributes to change deeply the human interactions concerning the traditional daily life of these groups.

Technological innovation, mostly home automation devises, changes the nature and the way to manage the daily life of everyone, especially PWD, but this topic is still unsearched and underrepresented in the literature and in practice. Thanks to a brief review of the contributions in the literature and of the projects in the practice, this study allows to confirm that the interest in this topic is still limited and there are not specific theoretical and integrative frameworks developed to investigate how technology is deeply changing the overall daily life of PWD.

This explorative and theoretical study because of its nature have several limitations, it is still at the first step of its long development process that easily represents and describes still undeveloped ideas about the phenomenon investigated. In the future, we might conduct a meta-analysis to identify in a wide research design the main variables of the impact of home automation on disability, and also we would focus on IoT, as specific expressions of new technologies applied in any organizational settings.

References

1. Baroni, F., & Lazzari, M. (2013). Tecnologie informatiche e diritti umani per un nuovo approccio all'accessibilità. *Italian Journal of Disability Studies, 1*(1), 79–92.
2. Bundon, A., & Clarke, L. H. (2015). *Unless you go online you are on your own: blogging as a bridge in para-sport.*
3. Holmes, K. M., & O'loughlin, N. (2014). *The experiences of people with learning disabilities on social networking sites.*
4. Shpigelman, C. N., & Gill, C. J. (2014) *Facebook use by persons with disabilities.*

5. Shpigelman, C. N., & Gill, C. J. (2014). *How do adults with intellectual disabilities use Facebook?*
6. Soresi, S. (2007). *Psicologia della disabilità.* New York: Il Mulino.
7. Chan, M., Estève, D., Escriba, C., & Campo, E. (2008). A review of smart homes—Present state and future challenges. *Computer Methods and Programs in Biomedicine, 91*(1), 55–81.
8. Gentry, T. (2009). Smart homes for people with neurological disability: State of the art. *NeuroRehabilitation, 25*(3), 209–217.
9. Alam, M. R., Reaz, M. B. I., & Ali, M. A. M. (2012). A review of smart homes—Past, present, and future. *IEEE Transactions on Systems, Man, and Cybernetics, Part C (Applications and Reviews), 42*(6), 1190–1203.
10. De Silva, L. C., Morikawa, C., & Petra, I. M. (2012). State of the art of smart homes. *Engineering Applications of Artificial Intelligence, 25*(7), 1313–1321.
11. Ramlee, R. A., Tang, D. H. Z., & Ismail, M. M. (2012, September). Smart home system for disabled people via wireless bluetooth. In: *System Engineering and Technology (ICSET), 2012 International Conference* (pp. 1–4). IEEE.
12. Kamarudin, M. R., & Yusof, M. A. F. M. (2013). Low cost smart home automation via microsoft speech recognition. *International Journal of Engineering & Computer Science, 13*(3), 6–11.
13. Cofre, J. P., Moraga, G., Rusu, C., Mercado, I., Inostroza, R., & Jimenez, C. (2012, April). Developing a touchscreen-based domotic tool for users with motor disabilities. In *Information Technology: New Generations (ITNG), 2012 Ninth International Conference* (pp. 696–701). IEEE.
14. Röcker, C., Ziefle, M., & Holzinger, A. (2011). Social inclusion in ambient assisted living environments: Home automation and convenience services for elderly user. In *International Conference on Artificial Intelligence, 1* (pp. 55–99).
15. Park, K. H., Bien, Z., Lee, J. J., Kim, B. K., Lim, J. T., Kim, J. O., et al. (2007). Robotic smart house to assist people with movement disabilities. *Autonomous Robots, 22*(2), 183–198.
16. Berry, B. E., & Ignash, S. (2003). Assistive technology: Providing independence for individuals with disabilities. *Rehabilitation Nursing, 28*(1), 6–14.
17. Esmail, A., Poncet, F., Rochette, A., Auger, C., Billebaud, C., de Guise, É., et al. (2018). The role of clothing in participation of persons with a physical disability: a scoping review protocol. *British Medical Journal Open, 8*(3), e020299.
18. Nam, S. J., & Park, E. Y. (2017). The effects of the smart environment on the information divide experienced by people with disabilities. *Disability and Health Journal, 10*(2), 257–263.
19. Dobransky, K., & Hargittai, E. (2016). Unrealized potential: Exploring the digital disability divide. *Poetics, 58,* 18–28.
20. Liu, L., Stroulia, E., Nikolaidis, I., Miguel-Cruz, A., & Rincon, A. R. (2016). Smart homes and home health monitoring technologies for older adults: A systematic review. *International Journal of Medical Informatics, 91,* 44–59.
21. Yusif, S., Soar, J., & Hafeez-Baig, A. (2016). Older people, assistive technologies, and the barriers to adoption: A systematic review. *International Journal of Medical Informatics, 94,* 112–116.
22. Sladojević, S., Arsenović, M., Lončar-Turukalo, T., Sladojević, M., & Ćulibrk, D. (2016). Personalized USB Biosensor Module for Effective ECG Monitoring. *Studies in Health Technology and Informatics, 224,* 201–206.
23. Jelin, E., Granum, V., & Eide, H. (2012). Experiences of a web-based nursing intervention—Interviews with women with chronic musculoskeletal pain. *Pain Management Nursing, 13*(1), 2–10.
24. Wästlund, E., Sponseller, K., Pettersson, O., & Bared, A. (2015). Evaluating gaze-driven power wheelchair with navigation support for persons with disabilities. *Journal of Rehabilitation Research & Development, 52*(7).
25. Ben-Zeev, D. (2016). Mobile health for all: Public-private partnerships can create a new mental health landscape. *JMIR Mental Health, 3*(2), e26.
26. Piau, A., Charlon, Y., Campo, E., Vellas, B., & Nourhashemi, F. (2015). A smart insole to promote healthy aging for frail elderly individuals: specifications, design, and preliminary results. *JMIR Rehabilitation and Assistive Technologies, 2*(1), e5.

27. Davies, R. J., Parker, J., McCullagh, P., Zheng, H., Nugent, C., Black, N. D., et al. (2016). A personalized self-management rehabilitation system for stroke survivors: A quantitative gait analysis using a smart insole. *JMIR Rehabilitation and Assistive Technologies, 3*(2), e11.
28. Clark, E., Olympia, D. E., Jensen, J., Heathfield, L. T., & Jenson, W. R. (2004). Striving for autonomy in a contingency-governed world: Another challenge for individuals with developmental disabilities. *Psychology in the Schools, 41*(1), 143–153.
29. Fuhrer, M. J., Jutai, J. W., Scherer, M. J., & DeRuyter, F. (2003). A framework for the conceptual modelling of assistive technology device outcomes. *Disability and Rehabilitation., 25*(22), 1243–1251.
30. Connor, K. M., & Davidson, J. R. (2003). Development of a new resilience scale: The Connor-Davidson resilience scale (CD-RISC). *Depression and Anxiety, 18*(2), 76–82.
31. Wehmeyer, M. L., & Garner, N. W. (2003). The impact of personal characteristics of people with intellectual and developmental disability on self-determination and autonomous functioning. *Journal of Applied Research in Intellectual Disabilities, 16*(4), 255–265.
32. Hahn, H. (1988). The politics of physical differences: Disability and discrimination. *Journal of Social Issues., 44*(1), 39–47.
33. United Nations: Convention on the Rights of Persons with Disabilities (CRPD). (2006). http://www.un.org/disabilities/convention/conventionfull.shtml.
34. Harper, R. (2006). *Inside the smart home*. Berlin: Springer.
35. Mann, W. C., Belchior, P., Tomita, M. R., & Kemp, B. J. (2007, January–March). Older adults' perception and use of PDAs, home automation system, and home health monitoring system. *Topics in Geriatric Rehabilitation, 23*(1), 35–46.
36. Mann, W. C., & Milton, B. R. (2005). Home automation and smart homes to support independence. In *Smart technology for aging, disability, and independence: The state of the science* (pp. 32–66). Hoboken: Wiley.

Efforts Towards Openness and Transparency of Data: A Focus on Open Science Platforms

Daniela Mancini, Alessandra Lardo and Massimo De Angelis

Abstract Although Open Science currently enjoys widespread support across scientific and technological communities, institutional and cultural barriers remain, as does the lack of investment in knowledge to foster Open Science. Generally, open research processes are based on information system infrastructure, such as informatics platforms where efficient web interfaces should be developed to easily record and share open data. Moreover, Open Science requires a systemic shift in current practices to bring transparency across the system, to ensure the ongoing sustainability of the associated social and physical infrastructures, and to foster greater public trust in science. Until now, the literature has focused its attention more on the final phases of the research process and, in particular, on Open Access, which is only one of the final steps of the Open Science research process. From this perspective, our research focuses on Open Science infrastructure, considering the openness and transparency attributes, with the aim of identifying a theoretical model able to assess web interfaces of Open Science platforms.

Keywords Open science · Open platforms · Transparency

1 Introduction

Research and innovation have been changing rapidly in the last few years. Digital technologies are key components that make the conduct of science and innovation more collaborative, more international and more open to citizens [1, 2]. To encourage

D. Mancini · A. Lardo (✉)
Parthenope University of Naples, Naples, Italy
e-mail: alessandra.lardo@uniparthenope.it

D. Mancini
e-mail: mancini@uniparthenope.it

M. De Angelis
Italian Space Agency, Rome, Italy
e-mail: massimo.deangelis@asi.it

© Springer Nature Switzerland AG 2020
A. Lazazzara et al. (eds.), *Exploring Digital Ecosystems*,
Lecture Notes in Information Systems and Organisation 33,
https://doi.org/10.1007/978-3-030-23665-6_6

the transition from linear knowledge transfer towards more dynamic knowledge circulation, scholars [3–5], national and supranational organizations agree that it is essential to create and support an open innovation ecosystem that facilitates the transformation of knowledge into socioeconomic value.

According to this perspective, Open Science represents "a new approach to the scientific process based on cooperative work and new ways of diffusing knowledge by using digital technologies and new collaborative tools" [6: p. 33]. Open Science is a disruptive phenomenon emerging around the world and especially in Europe [7]; it brings about sociocultural and technological change, based on openness and connectivity and on how research is designed, performed, captured, and assessed [8]. Although Open Science currently enjoys widespread support across scientific and technological communities, institutional and cultural barriers remain, and the lack of investment in knowledge and infrastructure may hinder local efforts to foster Open Science.

In fact, according to many scholars [9–11], Open Science requires a systemic shift in current practices to bring transparency across the system, to ensure the ongoing sustainability of the associated social and physical infrastructures, and to foster greater public trust in science.

In practice, the discussion on broadening the science base and on novel ways to produce and spread knowledge has gradually evolved according to two global trends: Open Access and Open Source. The former refers to online, peer-reviewed scholarly outputs, which are free to read and are subject to limited or no copyright and licensing restrictions [12], while Open Source refers to software co-created without any proprietary restriction and that can be freely accessed and used [13].

In the beginning, Open Access was considered the keystone of the entire process of a particular publishing or scientific dissemination practice; instead, currently, the attention has been shifted to a broader concept that includes the general re-use of all kinds of research products. Open Science affects the entire process of research, starting from the selection of research subjects to carrying out research, as well as its use and re-use.

As we observe from the following Fig. 1, the standard process of research composed of the phases of data gathering, analysis, publication, review and conceptualization is linked to ongoing changes brought about by Open Science.

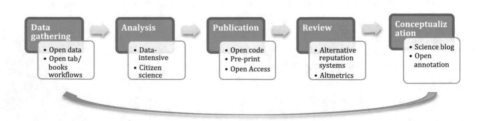

Fig. 1 Interconnected research process in the Open Science paradigm

Until now, the literature has preferentially focused on the final phases of the research process and, in particular, on Open Access, mainly because one of the most significant obstacles to openness involves the incentive structures of academic research, which can often fail to recognize, value, and reward efforts to open up the scientific process [14–16]. However, Open Access is only one of the final steps of the Open Science research process (Fig. 1).

Therefore, most of the existing literature focuses on the definition of open data and on the development and impact of Open Access, but less is written about infrastructure that allows users and other stakeholders to reach and utilize open data. In the Open Science infrastructure perspective, our work focuses on how web interfaces are built, identifying the needed requisites to efficiently pursue openness and transparency goals.

This paper aims to investigate the Open Science infrastructure, analysing the web interfaces of Open Science platforms to define, based on the literature, a model able to assess the openness and transparency of web interfaces.

The research develops in accordance with the five lines of potential policy actions to support the improvement in Open Science in Europe, identified by the European Commission in 2015, with the expectation that Open Science will lead to better science by making science more credible (addressing scientific integrity), reliable (enabling better and more transparent verification of data), efficient (avoiding duplication of resources) and more responsive to societal challenges [6]. The potential interventions are fostering and creating incentives for Open Science, removing barriers to Open Science, mainstreaming and further promoting Open Access policies, developing research infrastructure for Open Science, and embedding Open Science in society as a socioeconomic driver.

In particular, the purpose of our research is strictly linked to the fourth line of action of improving the development of a common framework for research data to create a European Open Science Cloud.

This article is structured as follows. After the introduction, Section 2 provides a literature review of the Open Science paradigm and of existing classifications of transparency of Open Science platforms. Section 3 proposes a model for assessing such platforms' transparency. Section 4 contains the discussion and primary conclusions.

2 Literature Review

2.1 Open Science Paradigm

The Open Science movement has gained visibility and influence for a number of reasons. These reasons range from scientific advances, such as recent developments in computing and communication technologies and the rise of Big Data, to political and economic factors, including the interest of European and North American governments in reinforcing the transparency and accountability of research processes to renew public trust in science-based policies [10].

Examining the relevant literature on Open Science, Fecher and Friesike [17] structure the overall changes encompassed by the term Open Science into five schools of thought: the infrastructure school, which is concerned with the technological architecture; the public school, which is concerned with the accessibility of knowledge creation; the measurement school, which is concerned with alternative impact assessment; the democratic school, which is concerned with access to knowledge; and the pragmatic school, which is concerned with collaborative research.

Focusing on the infrastructure literature [18, 19], efficient research depends on the available tools and applications. The goal is to create openly available platforms and tools and services for scientists and other stakeholders to foster collaboration. Therefore, the infrastructure school is concerned with the technical infrastructure that enables emerging research practices on the Internet, for the most part, software tools and applications, as well as computing networks. The literature on this topic is, therefore, often practice-oriented and case-specific; it focuses on the technological requirements that facilitate particular research practices (e.g., the Open Science grid).

Most Open Science practices described in terms of Internet technologies represent an unprecedented and extraordinary two-way channel of communication between producers and users of data [20, p. 1]. For this reason, the web is widely recognized as an asset capable of achieving the fundamental goal of transparency of information and of data products.

Nielsen [3] extrapolates, from current events, the rise of a scientific culture of "extreme openness", where "all information of scientific value, from raw experimental data and computer code to all the questions, ideas, folk knowledge, and speculations that are currently locked up inside the heads of individual scientists" is moved onto the network "in forms that are not just human-readable but also machine-readable, as part of a data web."

With the recent push to Open Science and, thus, to Open Data [13, 21, 22], the need for transparency and the resulting concern about reproducibility are of increasing interest to the scholarly community [23]. Reproducibility can be defined as "the calculation of quantitative scientific results by independent scientists using the original datasets and methods" [24, p. vii]. Although the two concepts are sometimes used interchangeably in the literature, reproducibility applies to the use (or re-use) of data to recreate findings, and replication applies to the broader testing of hypotheses and potentially the replication of entire studies.

The openness and transparency issues are analysed by many scholars in the field of the Open Data movement. This commitment is seen to play a central role in enabling researchers to effectively reuse existing outputs for their own purposes [25] and to foster intelligibility and reproducibility of research findings across disciplinary boundaries.

The requirements for data sharing (e.g., G8 Open Data Charter, America COMPETES Act, etc.) seem straightforward: a scientist receives funding and, therefore, is required to share his or her data with other scientists. However, the physical sciences and social sciences produce different kinds of data that are more or less easily stored.

Additionally, in some cases, researchers can (and should) put restrictions on who can view their data because of ethical concerns.

Moreover, the openness of data and code is not an all-or-nothing binary proposition; openness may be more accurately considered on a sliding scale [26]. There are different levels of openness. Such openness can help shore up transparency; therefore, the two concepts are closely linked.

2.2 Existing Classifications of Transparency of Open Science Platforms

Despite widespread recognition of the value of Open Science, proponents differ in how they interpret the norms of openness and transparency in research and in what they consider the best procedures to practice and encourage such norms [11]. As other scholars have noted, there is little consensus over what is meant by or how to practice openness and transparency in science [27–30], and consequently, there is little clarity as to how the implementation and enforcement of Open Science should occur. Policies have different terms and requirements for researchers [31], institutions have different infrastructures for repositories and databases, and scholarly communities have different commitments and goals. Such variations often mean that researchers do not know how and in what way to practice Open Science [32]. Therefore, a variety of approaches have been used in the study of data openness and transparency and the criteria that can be used to measure the quality of a database. According to the studies of various authors [30, 33, 34], we can define two main problems: first, defining the characteristics that data and databases should possess to be considered open and, therefore, transparent, and second, given that the desired characteristics have been agreed upon for a given set or category of data and databases, evaluating how well an open platform meets those standards.

The first step involves the analysis of Open Data characteristics to solve the first part of the problem. Many scholars define Open Data characteristics in the field of e-democracy and open government; e.g., Peled [34] asserts that transparency is openness to public scrutiny as defined by the rights and abilities of organizations and individuals to access government information and information about government, and Open Data represents the requirement that governments release authoritative, high-quality, complete, and timely data on the web in a downloadable, non-proprietary, and license-free format. Moreover, other authors [35] adopt the definition of the Open Knowledge Foundation [36] to identify Open Data: to be considered open, data have to be complete, primary, timely, accessible, machine-processable, non-discriminatory, non-proprietary, and license-free.

However, to facilitate transparency, it is not sufficient to simply provide a platform on which to disclose datasets or other quantitative aspects of studies [37, 38]. A review of the portal assessment literature shows that the structure and organization of portals where data are published are essential. Following this perspective, we have analysed studies defining requirements for and elements of an Open Data e-infrastructure because web portals are a tool, the ability of which to achieve transparency is affected by the content of information, the design of information delivery to users, and the functionality of the web portal.

For instance, Zuiderwijk et al. [39] state that an e-infrastructure to support the provision and use of Open Data must have specific features, organized by category. These features can be grouped into the following main categories:

(a) Data Provision;
(b) Data Retrieval and Use;
(c) Data Linking;
(d) User Rating; and
(e) User Cooperation.

Data Provision considers data and metadata acquisition, data cleansing and validation (comparison with similar datasets), data conversion and metadata enhancement. Data Retrieval and Use consist of retrieval by facets, retrieval by query, data display, the data requests module, and version management. Data Linking can be automated based on syntactic and semantic matching and mapping using enhanced metadata or be manual when users may assert that there is a linkage between two datasets (or instances of objects within those datasets). User Rating is a feature that allows for not only rating the datasets based on the user's qualitative perception but also rating users based on their participation in the platform. After the user rating, there is the quality control provided by contextual metadata about the dataset, the link (if one exists) and the person allowing the successive user to evaluate his or her own confidence in the rating provided. Finally, the last defined feature is User Cooperation, implemented through user profiles recording user preferences, responsibilities, authorities and usage history.

Glassey and Glassey [40] define proximity dimensions for e-infrastructure in the field of e-government, considering, as the main parameter, the low number of clicks. Using this parameter, platforms' openness is measured by studying the features of connectivity, actuality, navigability, accessibility, transparency and interactivity. Connectivity is defined as the low number of clicks to find the means of communicating directly with public administrations; actuality is the possibility to reach elements showing the temporal relevance of information or services or to access up-to-date information; navigability is the existence of navigation tools; accessibility is the possibility to retrieve elements guaranteeing that the portal is open to varied users; transparency concerns the identification of elements that help understand administrative services and provide feedback regarding these services; and finally, interactivity represents the possibility to find elements allowing the users to undertake administrative procedures.

Another study on Open Science describes the evolution of functions needed by a platform before and after the Web 2.0 revolution [41]. The traditional functions refer to data publication/uploading, data modelling, data searching, data visualization, and data downloading; after the advent of Web 2.0, the preceding features have been updated, considering the possibilities of grouping and interactions between users, a new way of processing data and metadata, enhanced capabilities of description of flat, contextual and detailed metadata of any metadata/vocabulary model, the possibility of expressing and receiving feedback, communicating to other users and providers about the level of quality of the datasets that the user perceives, becoming informed of the level of quality of datasets perceived by other users through their ratings and, finally, the capabilities of data and metadata linking to other ontologies in the Linked Open Data Cloud. A study carried out in Brazil [35] has identified a Digital Transparency Index based on only three dimensions: usability, accessibility, and interoperability.

Moreover, a useful comparison of more than 250 open data portals is provided by the study of Kubler et al. [42], which analyses multiple quality dimensions of portals. The cited paper develops an Open Data Portal Quality framework in the context of e-government that enables end-users to assess, rank and compare open data portals easily and in real time, integrating various data quality dimensions and end-user preferences. The model proposed by the above authors is based on a data openness indicator that focuses on evaluating the degree of openness of the published data based upon criteria consistent with the Open Government WG's [43] list of preferable characteristics for open data, a transparency indicator, consisting of two indicators, (i) Government Transparency, observed as a measure of insight into governmental tasks, processes and operations, and (ii) Data Transparency, calculated as an average of the Authenticity, Understandability and Data Reusability values, and finally, participation and collaboration indicators, where user involvement is used as an indicator.

Another relevant research item is represented by the analysis of the case study of the Open Universe Initiative carried out in the field of Astronomy and Cosmology data and proposed by the Italian Space Agency [44]. The authors present a complete definition of transparency and identify the components that contribute to transparency in Open Science, specifically naming availability, usability, and accessibility. Each factor has properties and indicators for performance measurement of transparency in Open Science data.

In conclusion, despite the growing interest in Open Science, a complete framework useful in assessing openness and transparency of Open Science platforms has not been defined clearly in the literature. Starting from this research gap, we aim to design a model based on the literature review to understand the type of properties and indicators that must be used to effectively assess and appreciate the level of openness and transparency of data and platforms.

3 Proposed Model for Assessing Platforms' Openness and Transparency

The aim of this section is to systematize the literature and extrapolate from it a model for assessing the openness and transparency of an Open Science platform usable in various scientific fields. To define more specifically how the objective of the study could be reached, elements for the model were gathered from the literature review analysis of requirements of open data e-infrastructure, by searching for journal papers, conference papers, books, governmental [6, 7, 25] and non-governmental reports [23, 36, 43, 45] and other information.

The requirements defined in the model are ordered by category and not by priority because it is difficult to prioritize requirements: one requirement may be important for one way of using data yet less important for another way of using data.

In the following Table 1, we describe the factors, related properties, items and related indicators useful in assessing openness and transparency of the platforms; for each factor, the main references analysed in order to organize the model are listed. In particular, some quantitative and, especially, some qualitative indicators to assess openness and transparency have been identified through the analysis and added to each item, developing the model to measure the degree of openness and transparency of web interfaces of Open Science platforms. Considering that the openness of data and code is not an all-or-nothing binary proposition and that openness may instead be more accurately considered on a sliding scale [26], in our model, we use a rating scale from 1 to 5 points to assess various indicators.

4   Discussion and Primary Conclusions

In this paper, we describe a model able to be a complete framework for quantifying and comparing the openness of scientific data platforms, with a particular emphasis on the transparency issue. This issue needs to be addressed to ensure that the output is a useful Open Science platform compliant with the European and international objectives for Open Science.

Presently, potential users of open public and private data are often unable to exploit the potential of open data to the fullest. Although the reuse of Open Data can be encouraged in various ways, e-infrastructure, such as open platforms, plays an important role. From this perspective, our preliminary research aims at presenting a complete set of factors that a science platform would need to achieve the desired outcome of fostering social and economic benefits arising from Open Data.

Many organizations note the importance of archiving and long-term maintenance and sustainability of such archives, given the power of datasets for generating new knowledge. These organizations proposed the promotion of the visibility of science worldwide, including for educational purposes and to the general public, and the development of more user-friendly interfaces. In fact, one of the main aspects of knowledge circulation is to ensure that scientific work corresponds to the needs of the users and that knowledge is findable, accessible, interpretable and reusable (FAIR) [49].

Implementing a completely Open Data policy on the creation of databases is the result of the application of the principles of unrestricted access to data and greatly expanded provision of software services. Such a policy's aims are to foster dialogue

Table 1 Proposed model to assess openness and transparency of web interfaces of OS platforms

Factors	Properties	Items	Indicators	Rates				
Availability [6, 7, 34–36, 39, 42, 44, 48]	Availability of Open Data	Complete	Amount of data made available not subject to valid privacy, security or privilege limitations	1	2	3	4	5
		Primary	Amount of data collected at the source, with the highest possible level of granularity, not in aggregate or modified forms	1	2	3	4	5
		Timely	Amount of data made available as quickly as necessary to preserve the value of the data	1	2	3	4	5
		Accessible	Level of quality of the metadata describing the data itself	1	2	3	4	5
		Machine-processable	Amount of data reasonably structured to allow for automated processing	1	2	3	4	5
		Non-discriminatory	Amount of data for commercial and non-commercial re-use	1	2	3	4	5
		Non-proprietary	Amount of data available in a format over which no entity has exclusive control	1	2	3	4	5
		License-free	Amount of data not subject to any copyright, patent, trademark or trade secret regulation (reasonable restrictions may be allowed)	1	2	3	4	5

(continued)

Table 1 (continued)

Factors	Properties	Items	Indicators	Rates				
				1	2	3	4	5
	Reusability	The amount of data available to be reused in a useful way	Amount of data available for reuse through retrieval by facets, retrieval by query, data requests module, and version management	1	2	3	4	5
Authenticity [39, 41, 42, 46]	Quality of uploaded data	Quality control	Existence of a section of published information about data sources at the portal	1	2	3	4	5
			Use of Uniform Resource Identifiers that help improve metadata and ensure authenticity	1	2	3	4	5
			Secure database encryption	1	2	3	4	5
			Long term storage of (and web access to) data	1	2	3	4	5
			Explanation of the methodology used to obtain results	1	2	3	4	5
		User rating	Provision of the possibility of reviewing datasets published by a specific data source	1	2	3	4	5

(continued)

Table 1 (continued)

Factors	Properties	Items	Indicators	Rates				
				1	2	3	4	5
			Data quality rating					
Usability [34, 35, 39, 40, 42, 44]	Comprehensibility	Data search and navigability	Existence of a legend to ensure that the items of a query and data are fully described, so that visitors have sufficient information to understand their strengths, weaknesses, analytical limitations, and security requirements and to understand how to use the data	1	2	3	4	5
		Data visualization and download	Possibility to consult/download a user's guide	1	2	3	4	5
		Information overload risk	(a) Amount of unnecessary information	5	4	3	2	1
			(b) Amount of redundant information	5	4	3	2	1
			(c) Amount of undefined information	5	4	3	2	1
			(d) Number of synthetic indices	5	4	3	2	1
			(e) Compact display	5	4	3	2	1
	Actuality	Observation period	Presence of elements showing the temporal relevance of information	1	2	3	4	5

(continued)

Table 1 (continued)

Factors	Properties	Items	Indicators	Rates				
		Delay period	Presence of up-to-date services and information about the period between the event and the publication of data: latest updates, newsletter, or push services	1	2	3	4	5
	Interactivity	Data linking	(a) RSS for users to receive timely updates from favourite websites or to aggregate data from many sites	1	2	3	4	5
			(b) Ability to make queries	1	2	3	4	5
			(c) Ability to save queries	1	2	3	4	5
			(d) Ability to personalize services	1	2	3	4	5
			(e) Ability to customize queries	1	2	3	4	5
			(f) Ability to be notified of mistakes or anomalies	1	2	3	4	5
		Grouping and interaction	(a) Possibility of searching for users/providers having similar interests in order to engage in knowledge exchange and cooperation	1	2	3	4	5

(continued)

Table 1 (continued)

Factors	Properties	Items	Indicators	Rates				
			(b) Possibility of forming groups with other users/providers having similar interests with us to engage in knowledge exchange and cooperation	1	2	3	4	5
			(c) Maintaining datasets/working on datasets within one group	1	2	3	4	5
Accessibility [6, 7, 40, 41, 44, 47]	Web readiness	Level of readiness	Amount of data processing necessary to re-use data	1	2	3	4	5
		Efficient drilldown or drill-up	One click or two clicks	1	2	3	4	5
	Accessibility	Users' accessibility	(a) Amount of personal information the user must release to access Open Data	1	2	3	4	5
			(b) Number of bureaucratic or administrative barriers the user has to overcome to access Open Data	1	2	3	4	5
			(c) Disabled access	1	2	3	4	5
			(d) Ubiquitous access to Open Data	1	2	3	4	5
	Openness	Feedback and collaboration	(a) Number of answers to the query or files that can be easily retrieved	1	2	3	4	5

(continued)

Table 1 (continued)

Factors	Properties	Items	Indicators	Rates				
				1	2	3	4	5
			(b) Number of types of activities available to users to download, index or search data by all commonly used web search applications	1	2	3	4	5
			(c) Unrestricted access to the data (no ownership restrictions)	1	2	3	4	5
			(d) Possibility to communicate one's own thoughts and ideas on the datasets to other users and data providers through comments on datasets	1	2	3	4	5
			(e) Availability of user comments	1	2	3	4	5
			(f) Possibility to express need for additional datasets that would be interesting and useful	1	2	3	4	5
	Discoverability	Likelihood of obtaining data	The amount of data available as output of a query compared to the amount of data available from the same query in another Open Data source	1	2	3	4	5

between data providers and networks of users and developers to enhance the studies' potential for scientific discoveries and facilitate education and inspiration among all communities from professionals to citizens of all ages. Moreover, these efforts are intended to extend to all sectors, including the science sector, in view of the current widespread desire for transparency of goods produced with public money.

Finally, an Open Data policy is expected to enhance recognition of the efforts involved in producing research components other than journal publications, which could in turn enhance impact and citations of developers of such components [50, 51] and encourage the use of high standards, such as careful data production, well-tested modelling and robust software [45], in research.

From this perspective, the practical implications of the development of a model able to assess openness and transparency of web interfaces of Open Science platforms could be not only its use to evaluate those responsible for projects that have, among other goals, the purpose of implementing and managing open platforms but also its contribution to defining standards to build open infrastructure capable of adapting to innovations in Open Knowledge practices as requested by the European Community [45]. At the same time, increasing transparency in research practices can have unintended consequences. Finding common ways to decide how sharing and transparency can be organized to be as fruitful as possible is one of the main challenges at the present.

The originality of this paper consists of highlighting the characteristics that web interfaces should possess to be considered open and, therefore, transparent, bringing in a single model of web interfaces' attributes previously unsystematically identified in the literature. This paper proposes a complete and comprehensive scheme to assess and measure transparency and openness, identifying parameters, indicators and metrics in a unique model.

While our preliminary study is a step in this direction, further work remains to be done to refine the model based on the literature through collaboration with scientists and platform managers and, then, applying this assessment model to various web interfaces of Open Science platforms to verify if it is valid and applicable and whether it could become a standard.

Acknowledgements This research is financially supported by the University "Parthenope" of Naples (Italy) within the research program 2015–17 (competitive research 2016-18). A previous version of this article was presented at the 15th Conference of Italian Chapter of AIS (Association for Information Systems) "Living in the digital ecosystem: technologies, organizations and human agency" (Pavia, October 12–13, 2018).

References

1. Friesike, S., Widenmayer, B., Gassmann, O., & Schildhauer, T. (2015). Opening science: Towards an agenda of open science in academia and industry. *The Journal of Technology Transfer, 40*(4), 581–601.

2. Carayannis, E. G., Meissner, D., & Edelkina, A. (2017). Targeted innovation policy and practice intelligence (TIP2E): Concepts and implications for theory, policy and practice. *The Journal of Technology Transfer, 42*(3), 460–484.
3. Nielsen, M. (2012). *Reinventing discovery: The new era of networked science*. Princeton University Press.
4. Stilgoe, J., Lock, S. J., & Wilsdon, J. (2014). Why should we promote public engagement with science? *Public Understanding of Science, 23*(1), 4–15.
5. Franzoni, C., & Sauermann, H. (2014). Crowd science: The organization of scientific research in open collaborative projects. *Research Policy, 43*(1), 1–20.
6. European Commission. (2016). *Open innovation, open science, open to the world. A vision for Europe*. Luxembourg: Publications Office of the European Union.
7. OECD. (2015). *Making open science a reality, OECD science, technology and industry policy papers*, No. 25. Paris: OECD Publishing. http://dx.doi.org/10.1787/5jrs2f963zs1-enOECD.
8. Vicente-Saez, R., & Martinez-Fuentes, C. (2018). Open Science now: A systematic literature review for an integrated definition. *Journal of Business Research*.
9. Friesike, S., & Schildhauer, T. (2015). Open Science: many good resolutions, very few incentives, yet. In Welpe, I. M., Wollersheim, J., Ringelhan, S., & Osterloh, M. (Eds.). *Incentives and performance*. Governance of Research Organizations. Heidelberg: Springer.
10. Leonelli, S. (2013). Why the current insistence on open access to scientific data? Big data, knowledge production, and the political economy of contemporary biology. *Bulletin of Science, Technology & Society, 33*, 6–11.
11. Levin, N., Leonelli, S., Weckowska, D., Castle, D., & Dupré, J. (2016). How do scientists define openness? Exploring the relationship between open science policies and research practice. *Bulletin of Science, Technology & Society, 36*(2), 128–141.
12. Laakso, M., Welling, P., Bukvova, H., Nyman, L., Björk, B.-C., & Hedlund, T. (2011). The development of open access journal publishing from 1993 to 2009. *PLoS ONE, 6*(6), e20961.
13. Joseph, H. (2016). The evolving U.S. policy environment for open research data. *Information Services & Use, 36*, 45–48.
14. Harnad, S. (2011). Open access to research: Changing researcher behavior through university and funder mandates. *JEDEM Journal of Democracy and Open Government*, 33–41.
15. Wilsdon, J. R., Allen, L., Belfiore, E., Campbell, P., Curry, S., Hill, S., et al. (2015). *The metric tide: Report of the independent review of the role of metrics in research assessment and management*.
16. Munafò, M. R., Nosek, B. A., Bishop, D. V., Button, K. S., Chambers, C. D., du Sert, N. P., ... & Ioannidis, J. P. (2017). A manifesto for reproducible science. *Nature Human Behaviour, 1*.
17. Fecher, B., Friesike, S. (2014). Open science: One term, five schools of thought. In *Opening science* (pp. 17–47). Cham: Springer.
18. Hey, T., & Trefethen, A. E. (2005). Cyberinfrastructure for e-Science. *Science, 308*(5723), 817–821.
19. Altunay, M., Avery, P., Blackburn, K., Bockelman, B., Ernst, M., Fraser, D., ... Livny, M. (2011). A science driven production cyberinfrastructure—The open science grid. *Journal of Grid Computing, 9*(2), 201–218.
20. Nentwich, M. (2003). *Cyberscience: Research in the age of the Internet*. Vienna: Austrian Academy of Sciences Press.
21. Ramjoué, C. (2016). Towards open science: The vision of the European Commission. *Information Services & Use, 35*(3), 167–170.
22. Williamson, K., Kennan, M. A., Johanson, G., & Weckert, J. (2016). Data sharing for the advancement of science: Over-coming barriers for citizen scientists. *Journal of the Association for Information Science and Technology, 67*(10), 2392–2403.
23. Open Science Collaboration. (2015). Estimating the reproducibility of psychological science. *Science, 349*(6251), aac4716-1–aac4716-8.
24. Stodden, V., Leisch, F., & Peng, R. D. (2014). *Implementing re-producible research*. Boca Raton: CRC Press.

25. The Royal Society. (2012). *Data sharing*. Retrieved from http://royalsocietypublishing.org/data-sharing.
26. Schopfel, J., Chaudiron, S., Jacquemin, B., Prost, H., Severo, M., & Thiault, F. (2014). Open access to research data in electronic theses and dissertations: An overview. *Library Hi Tech, 32*(4), 612–627.
27. Borgman, C. L. (2012). The conundrum of sharing research data. *Journal of the American Society for Information Science and Technology, 63,* 1059–1078.
28. Grand, A., Wilkinson, C., Bultitude, K., & Winfield, A. F. (2016). Mapping the hinterland: Data issues in open science. *Public Understanding of Science, 25,* 88–103.
29. Wallis, J. C., & Borgman, C. L. (2011). Who is responsible for data? An exploratory study of data authorship, ownership, and responsibility. *Proceedings of the American Society for Information Science and Technology, 48*(1), 1–10.
30. Wynholds, L. A., Wallis, J. C., Borgman, C. L., Sands, A., & Traweek, S. (2012). Data, data use, and scientific inquiry: Two case studies of data practices. In *Proceedings of the 12th ACM/IEEE-CS Joint Conference on Digital Libraries*, Washington, D.C.
31. Corrall, S., & Pinfield, S. (2014). Coherence of "open" initiatives in higher education and research: Framing a policy agenda. In *iConference 2014 Proceedings* (Vol. 7, pp. 293–313).
32. Ferguson, L. (2014). How and why researchers share data (and why they don't). Wiley Exchanges.
33. Nichols, D. M., & Twidale, M. B. (2017). Metrics for openness. *Journal of the American Society for Information Science and Technology, 68*(4).
34. Peled, A. (2013, May). Re-designing open data 2.0. In *Conference for E-Democracy and Open Government* (p. 243).
35. Araújo, A. C., Reis, L., & Sampaio, R. C. (2017). Do transparency and open data walk together? An analysis of initiatives in five Brazilian Capitals. *Medijske studije, 7*(14).
36. Open Knowledge Foundation. (2011). Beyond access: Open government data and the right to (re)use public information. https://papers.ssrn.com/sol3/papers.cfm?abstract_id=2586400.
37. De Angelis, M., Guerra M. (2012). Mandatory compliance in transparency of public administration. In D. Mancini, E. Vaassen, R. P. Dameri (Eds.), Accounting information systems for decision making, LNISO (Vol. 3), Heidelberg: Springer.
38. Lourenço, R. P. (2015). An analysis of open government portals: A perspective of transparency for accountability. *Government Information Quarterly, 32,* 323–332.
39. Zuiderwijk, A., Janssen, M., & Jeffery, K. (2013, May) Towards an e-infrastructure to support the provision and use of open data. In *Conference for E-Democracy and Open Government* (p. 259).
40. Glassey, O., & Glassey, O. F. (2005). A proximity indicator for e-government: The smallest number of clicks. *Journal of e-Government, 1*(4), 5–20.
41. Alexopoulos, C., Loukis, E., & Charalabidis, Y. (2014). A platform for closing the open data feedback loop based on Web2. 0 functionality. *JeDEM-eJournal of eDemocracy and Open Government, 6*(1), 62–68.
42. Kubler, S., Robert, J., Neumaier, S., Umbrich, J., & Le Traon, Y. (2017). Comparison of metadata quality in open data portals using the Analytic Hierarchy Process. *Government Information Quarterly.*
43. Open Government Working Group. (2007). *8 principles of open government data*. Retrieve from https://public.resource.org/8principles.html.
44. Giommi, P., De Angelis, M., Pollock, A. M. T., & Mancini, D. (2017). Prospects for a new era of data transparency in a shared, global and openness world. The case of open scientific data in astronomy and cosmology. In *ITAIS 2017: XIV Conference of the Italian Chapter of AIS—Organizing For Digital Economy: Societies, Communities And Individuals*, October 6th–7th, 2017, University of Milano Bicocca, Milan.
45. Nature Special 2013 Challenges in Irreproducible Research. www.nature.com/nature/focus/reproducibility/index.html.
46. Veljković, N., Bogdanović-Dinić, S., & Stoimenov, L. (2014). Benchmarking open government: An open data perspective. *Government Information Quarterly, 31*(2), 278–290.

47. Janssen, M., Charalabidis, Y., & Zuiderwijk, A. (2012). Benefits, adoption barriers and myths of open data and open government. *Information systems management, 29*(4), 258–268.
48. Solar, M., Concha, G., & Meijueiro, L. (2012, September). A model to assess open government data in public agencies. In *International Conference on Electronic Government* (pp. 210–221). Heidelberg: Springer.
49. Wilkinson, M. D., Dumontier, M., Aalbersberg, I. J., Appleton, G., Axton, M., Baak, A., & Bouwman, J. (2016). The FAIR guiding principles for scientific data management and stewardship. *Scientific Data, 3*.
50. Leonelli, S., Spichtinger, D., & Prainsack, B. (2015). Sticks and carrots encouraging open science at its source. *Geo: Geography and Environment, 2*(1), 12–16.
51. Piwowar, H. A., Day, R. S., & Fridsma, D. B. (2007). Sharing detailed research data is associated with increased citation rate. *PLoS ONE, 2*(3), e308.

Millennials, Information Assessment, and Social Media: An Exploratory Study on the Assessment of Critical Thinking Habits

Michael Menichelli and Alessio Maria Braccini

Abstract Critical thinking is as a systematic habit of being able to question information, confront different information sources seeking diversity of points of view, understanding statements, and being able to make inferences out of information. Critical thinking is an active behavior against information processing which influences in a positive way individual and organizational decision making. While we can observe different levels of critical thinking in different individuals, millennials are reputed to possess low critical thinking skills given their habit of passively receiving information through social media. In this paper, we study the critical thinking skills of millennials, and we explore the level of critical thinking shown in relation to the reported intensity of use of social media and other traditional media for information acquisition. The paper is based on a quantitative analysis of an incidental sample of 424 millennials.

Keywords Critical thinking · Digital natives · Millennials · Information assessment

1 Introduction

Digital technologies are used for information dissemination and retrieval. Digital technologies exacerbated both individual and organizational communication capabilities and offered new venues for information dissemination for individuals and organizations [1–3]. Among these technologies, social media emerged recently for their capabilities of circulating information directly among people and both inside

M. Menichelli
Università LUISS Guido Carli, Rome, Italy
e-mail: Michael.menichelli@studenti.luiss.it

A. M. Braccini (✉)
Università degli Studi della Tuscia, Viterbo, Italy
e-mail: abraccini@unitus.it

© Springer Nature Switzerland AG 2020
A. Lazazzara et al. (eds.), *Exploring Digital Ecosystems*,
Lecture Notes in Information Systems and Organisation 33,
https://doi.org/10.1007/978-3-030-23665-6_7

and outside organizations [1, 3, 4]. The dissemination potential of social media brought many opportunities for organizations and individuals [3, 5, 6]. However, they presented also challenges especially about the mass of unreliable or counterfeit material purposefully disseminated over social media to orient individuals' opinions and decision making.

In this context, we study the critical thinking skills of millennials, the generation of people born after the year 1982 [7], about their intensity of use of social media. Critical thinking is the skill to be able to critically assess information and judge its reliability [8–10]. It is a necessary skill to master the information overload and improve decision making [11]. To reach our objectives, we run an exploratory study to investigate the level of critical thinking of future members of the workforce in organizations. We distributed a survey containing both self-assessed measures of critical thinking and information analysis tasks through which we could directly assess the critical thinking level. We focused specifically on millennials as the literature suggests they are a generation of digital natives, born and immersed in a digitized world, using digital technology for communication and information dissemination [12, 13].

2 Theoretical Framework

The capability to acquire and process information is at the basis of the three fundamental organizational processes: sense making, decision making, and knowing [14]. We define critical thinking as the capability to critically evaluate pieces of information found on online sources, and to choose the most authoritative ones [8, 9, 15]. While thinking is a capability of human being, critical thinking is a specific kind of reflexive thinking, open to changing and improving the points of view of the thinker, and it is an active process on concepts and information [16].

Under a managerial perspective, critical thinking is an approach to problem setting and analysis with the potential to improve the effectiveness of decision-making processes [11]. It is an organized and systematic way of thinking that involves both the problem definition phase and the assessment of the resources available and the possible alternatives [17]. Critical thinking requires active engagement with problems and solutions avoiding—to the largest extent possible—the influence of individuals' judgments.

Critical thinking is a set of capabilities about the use of information which an individual shall possess [18]:

- Interpretation: the capability to understand and express the meaning of events, situations, data, rules, processes, judgments;
- Analysis: the capability to identify relations among declarations, statements, concepts, descriptions or other forms of representation of information used to express judgments, experiences, and opinions;
- Evaluation: the capability to evaluate credibility and reliability of statements or other sources of representations of facts which stem out of individuals' perceptions,

experience, judgments, beliefs, opinions or by the contextual conditions in which the person is to be found. The evaluation capability also extends to the possibility to assess the logic soundness among different statements, descriptions, declarations or another form of representation of information;

- Inference: the capability to identify the required elements to formulate hypotheses or consequences stemming from data, declarations, principles, tests, judgments, beliefs, opinions, concepts, descriptions or other forms of representation of information;
- Explanation: the capability to be able to explain the path followed to assert specific considerations out of specific conditions;
- Self-regulation: the capability to apply critical thinking to themselves to improve one's opinions.

2.1 Critical Thinking and Millennials

Individuals differ regarding critical thinking capabilities. Systematic habits of questioning information, looking for alternative points of view, and assessing strong and weak points in the information to be assessed can improve critical thinking [18]. All individuals depend on heuristics and routines for information processing. Cognitive biases could influence the latter, and these biases and heuristics might influence in turn the level of critical thinking [19, 20].

Millennials are suspected of possessing low critical thinking skills, due to the passive habit of receiving information in the form of words and images on digital technologies [13]. However, they are also described as a cohort competent in information browsing and searching [8], with habits and preferences in the use of digital technologies different than that of other generations [21, 22], but with significant internal differences [9].

However, millennials are born and grown up in a world permeated by digital technologies [23]. They have expectations for easy and quick access to information, and they frequently use social media to acquire and disseminate information [24]. They are constantly connected to the network, with their smartphones and have had no previous experiences of a world different than that [25]. If and how these habits of use of social media influence their critical thinking has still to be empirically studied.

3 Research Design

To explore the critical skills capabilities of millennials about their use of social media we created and distributed a survey based on existing measurement instruments to assess critical thinking. The survey is structured in four sections as follows:

- Section one: sex, age, academic degree, the intensity of use of social media, traditional media, and press for information retrieving;
- Section two: assessment of critical thinking capabilities through the Watson-Glaser Critical Thinking test;
- Section three: assessment of critical thinking capabilities through fake news detection capabilities;
- Section four: self-assessment of critical thinking capabilities.

The *Watson-Glaser Critical Thinking Appraisal* test used for section two is reputed a reliable source for the assessment of critical thinking [26]. The test encompasses five key areas, each one covered in the survey by three questions, to which respondents are required to answer with a multiple choice after having read a short text statement to which the questions are referred:

1. *Inference*: the section measures the capability to distinguish between true and false assertions;
2. *Recognize Assumptions*: the section measures the capability to identify assumptions underpinned in a specific text;
3. *Deduction*: the section measures the capability to deduce conclusions out a specific text;
4. *Interpretation*: the section measures the capability to identify acceptable conclusions out of a specific text statement;
5. *Evaluation of Arguments*: the section measures the capability to assess the validity and relevance of inductive reasoning based on a specific text statement.

We measured the capability of detecting fake news capabilities reporting two fake news circulating over the network based on plausible, but inaccurate, real-life events. Finally, we used a model from the literature to assess the behavioral traits of digital natives [13] to perform the self-assessment of critical thinking.

The survey has been administered anonymously through a public page on Facebook, and data were collected and analyzed anonymously. Participants were guided by online instructions on how to fill the survey and had the chance to opt out once started. Respondents were voluntary informed participants who agreed to share their responses with us. We collected 422 complete responses to the survey of millennials born in the period from 1982 to 2001 [12, 23, 27].

4   Data Analysis

This section describes the main results of the exploratory analysis of the data collected from the survey. The description focuses on the profile of the respondents first and the details on the answers collected by respondents using descriptive statistics.

4.1 The Profile of Respondents

Out of the 422 responses 67 were males (15.80%), and 357 were females (84.20%). Respondents age varied between 17 and 36, with an average of 22. Under this perspective, the sample is biased towards the major presence of women among respondents. Most of the respondents have a high education degree (71.23%), and one fifth a three-year bachelor's degree (21.46%). Only 7 participants (1.65%) declared only a high school degree, 22 (5.19%) a single-cycle or two-cycle degree and 2 (0.47%) a master's degree. This profile is in line with the general trend in the millennials generation, which is considered to be the most educated generation ever [28]. However, the presence of high education degrees among millennials in our sample is larger than the average of the generation: 71.23% in our sample against 54% of the millennials generation average [28].

Concerning their engagement with social media, 95.75% of respondents (n = 406) said to use WhatsApp every day, while only 2 (0.47%) never use it. Similar situation for the usage intensity of Facebook: 90.09% of the sample connects to the site every day and 6.84% more times a week, while less than 3% declared to use it seldom or not use it at all. The use of social media platforms other than WhatsApp and Facebook is instead less frequent. Only 52.12% (n = 221) of respondents declared a daily use of other social media, and a further 19.81% declared to use them several times a week.

On the other hand, as regards millennials' trend to obtain information from traditional sources, the context appears to be less homogeneous. While the use of social media in general (Facebook, WhatsApp, and other platforms) is diffused among the sample of Millennials, only 23.82% (n = 101) and 29.01% (n = 123) respectively declared to read newspaper articles (including those online) and watch TV news on a daily basis. On the other hand, the percentage of those who never resort to these information media is higher compared to that of the use of social media platforms: 6.60% (n = 28) for the former and 11.32% (n = 48) for the second. In general, we can say that about 60% of respondents tend to use these channels of information quite frequently, while about 25% use them seldom or not at all.

4.2 Critical Thinking Skills: Descriptive Statistics

The survey contained 15 questions, divided into five sections, to measure critical thinking skills with the Watson-Glaser critical thinking appraisal schema [26]. We measured the answers on the following scale: 0 points (wrong answer), 1 (correct answer). The maximum theoretical score for each section is 3. The maximum theoretical score for the 15 questions on critical thinking is 15.

In the first section, *Inference*, the average score was 1.21 (S.D. 0.94). Only 10.38% of the participants answered all the questions correctly, while 25.24% answered none.

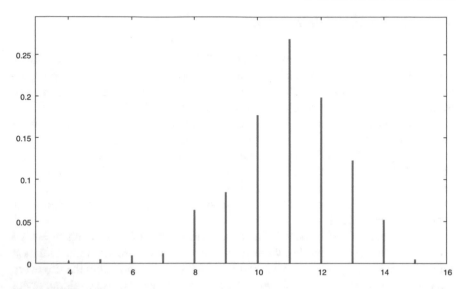

Fig. 1 Distribution of total score

The results of the second section, *Recognizing Assumptions*, are better. The average score was 2.40 (S.D. 0.68), and 50.71% of the respondents answered all the questions correctly. The scores of the third section, *Deduction*, were even higher, in which everyone answered at least one question, and 76.42% of the participants at all correctly. The average score was 2.73 (S.D. 0.52). In the fourth section, *Interpretation*, we found an average score of 2.62 (S.D. 0.63). In this case, only 0.71% of respondents could not answer the questions, while 69.81% completed them without errors. Finally, the *Evaluation of Arguments* section was completed only by 21.23% of participants, with an average score of 1.98 (S.D. 0.70).

Considering the five sections together, we note an average total score of 10.94 (S.D. 1.74) on a maximum of 15. The worst result (4) is only in one case, while two participants achieved the maximum score of 15. The modal score is 11, obtained from 26.89% of respondents (n = 114). Figure 1 shows the distribution of the total score.

To further assess the interviewees' critical thinking skills, we inserted into the survey two fake news based on events discussed by communication media during the period of administration of the survey. Concerning the first fake news, 63.92% (n = 271) recognized it as false, 28.77% said they did not know it, and only 7.31% (n = 31) believed it was real. The opposite happened for the second fake news: only 18.40% of the participants (n = 78) correctly stated it was false, while 62.74% (n = 266) considered it to be true. The remaining 18.87% could not evaluate the validity of the news.

We ask respondents to declare the reasons for their answers. Those who felt the news to be false reported to know the facts, to have other sources which proven the news fake, or reported inconsistencies in the information in the news. The respondents who declared to ignore whether the news was true or false stated they were not sufficiently informed on the topic or declared to have not been able to find the original or related sources. Finally, who believed the news to be truly stated to have already read it or heard of it from sources reputed reliable. The second news, in some cases, was considered true by the "credible and logical" information it contained.

4.3 Self-assessment of Critical Thinking Skills

In the last part of the survey (four questions), we asked respondents to self-declare their critical thinking skills. The scores for the self-assessment were taken from a validated scale available in the literature [13] and ranged from a minimum value of 1 (completely disagree) to a maximum value of 5 (completely agree). The self-assessment encompassed the following set of questions:

- I am used to selecting information sources on the Internet and to judge their relevance (average score of 4.39, S.D. 0.73);
- It is easy for me to identify and avoid unreliable information sources on the Internet (average score of 3.88, S.D. 0.88);
- I never fall into the trap of considering as reliable an unreliable information source on the internet (average score of 3.65, S. D. 0.98);
- I think I am capable of assessing the reliability of information sources on the Internet (average score of 4.10, S. D. 0.74).

The theoretical total score on the self-assessed measure ranged from 4 (min) to 20 (max). Figure 2 shows the distribution of the total score. The distribution is skewed towards the higher value of the scale.

To analyze potential differences among the average scores in the different sections of the survey, we noted that in the overall, in Sections 3–7, men obtained a higher average score in respect of that of women (respectively of 11.03 and 10.92), although this difference is not statistically significant (p-value 0.65). Men also reported a higher self-assessment score: 17.18 compared to 15.8 (p-value 5.159). While about the recognition of fake news, results show no particular inequality.

Repeating the test after dividing the participants into two groups based on ages, 17–21 years (n = 204) and 22 to 36 (n = 220), the average score obtained in the evaluation of Critical Thinking is very similar, respectively 10.90 and 10.98 (p-value 0.657), to that obtained in the self-assessment: 15.90 and 16.12 (p-value 0.388). However, the second group turned out to be better able to recognize fake news (p-value 8.596e−5).

Considering the differences regarding the degree we divided the interviewees into two groups: the first of those who have a middle school diploma or a higher school diploma (n = 309) and the second of those who have a university degree or a master (n = 115). We note that the latter obtained a higher average score in the analysis of Critical Thinking, 11.15 compared to 10.86 (p-value 0.136) and in the self-assessment, 16.27 compared to 15.93 (p-value 0.222). Moreover, they recognized the

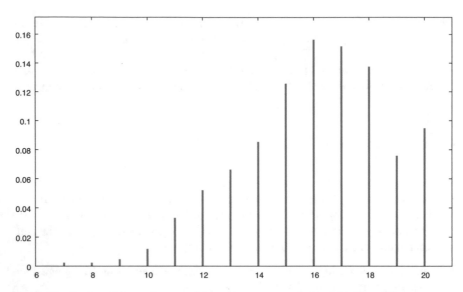

Fig. 2 Distribution of the total scores of the self-assessment of critical thinking skills

falsity of the news better (*p*-value 0.579). Through an ANOVA test, it is clear how the average score obtained in Critical Thinking increases with the increase of the qualification: 10.71 for the middle school diploma; 10.87 for the diploma; 11.11 for the three-year degree and 11.32 for the master's degree (*p*-value 0.638).

Going to analyze the differences due to the frequency of use of social media and information channels, through the ANOVA test, we note that: increasing use of Facebook is associated with an average descending score on Critical Thinking. From a maximum of 11.4 for those who do not use it (n = 5) to a minimum of 10.92 for those who use it every day (n = 382), with a non-significant *p*-value equal to 0.946. Instead, there are no particular inequalities between groups in recognizing fake news. Also, concerning the use of the others social media platforms, there are no significant differences between the various sub-groups.

Those who said they read newspapers or listen to news broadcasts more frequently (daily or several times a week) were better at recognizing fake news (*p*-value 0.13 in the first case and 0.185 in the second).

Finally, analyzing the relationship between the self-assessment of critical thinking made by the participants and the ability to recognize the falsity of the two news, we noted that those who obtained a score greater than 16/20, on average, were better than those who were attributed a score equal to or less than 16/20. The difference is not statistically significant (*p*-value 0.271).

4.4 Exploratory Analysis

Considering that almost no difference regarding averages among the groups defined over the variables in section one was statistically significant, and with the objective of further exploring the data, we run a cluster analysis to extract homogeneous groups within the dataset. The analysis was performed using a complete clustering analysis algorithm with the Wards. D2 method: Fig. 3 shows the resulting dendrogram. According to Fig. 3, and to the quality metrics we calculated, both a two and four clusters solutions are possible. We explored both and opted for a two clusters solution.

To understand the composition of the different groups, Table 1 show min and max value, the first and third quartile, median and mean of the data of the two clusters. The table is divided into two parts: the first part refers to cluster number one with 264 observations (right cluster in the dendrogram), while the second part refers to cluster number 2 with 158 observations.

The columns in Table 1 are to be interpreted as follows:

- wAp: Intensity of use of WhatsApp (min 1 − max 5)
- Fb: intensity of use of Facebook (min 1 − max 5)
- Sn: intensity of use of other Social Networking platforms (min 1 − max 5)
- Nws: intensity of use of traditional newspapers (min 1 − max 5)
- Tg: intensity of use of TV news programs (min 1 − max 5)
- Inf: Inference (min 0 − max 1)
- Asp: Assumption (min 0 − max 1)
- Ded: Deduction (min 0 − max 1)
- Int: Interpretation (min 0 − max 1)
- Arg: Arguments following (min 0 − max 1)

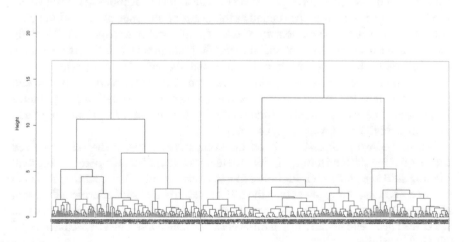

Fig. 3 Cluster dendrogram

Table 1 Description statistics of cluster data

		wAp	Fb	Sn	Nws	Tg	Inf	Asp	Ded	Int	Arg	sCri	Fake
264 obs	Min	1.00	1.00	1.00	1.00	1.00	0.00	0.00	0.33	0.00	0.00	0.35	0.67
	1Q	5.00	5.00	3.00	3.00	3.00	0.00	0.67	1.00	0.67	0.67	0.70	0.67
	Med	5.00	5.00	5.00	4.00	4.00	0.33	0.83	1.00	1.00	0.67	0.80	0.67
	Mean	4.94	4.85	3.92	3.63	3.54	0.38	0.81	0.92	0.88	0.66	0.80	0.74
	3Q	5.00	5.00	5.00	4.00	5.00	0.67	1.00	1.00	1.00	0.67	0.90	0.83
	Max	5.00	5.00	5.00	5.00	5.00	1.00	1.00	1.00	1.00	1.00	1.00	1.00
158 obs	Min	2.00	1.00	1.00	1.00	1.00	0.00	0.00	0.33	0.33	0.00	0.50	0.33
	1Q	5.00	5.00	3.00	3.00	3.00	0.33	0.67	0.67	0.67	0.67	0.75	0.33
	Med	5.00	5.00	4.00	4.00	4.00	0.33	1.00	1.00	1.00	0.67	0.80	0.50
	Mean	4.91	4.82	3.77	3.51	3.45	0.44	0.79	0.89	0.87	0.65	0.81	0.50
	3Q	5.00	5.00	5.00	4.00	4.00	0.67	1.00	1.00	1.00	0.67	0.90	0.50
	Max	5.00	5.00	5.00	5.00	5.00	1.00	1.00	1.00	1.00	1.00	1.00	0.83

- sCri: self-perception of critical thinking (min 0 − max 1)
- Fake: detection of fake news (min 0 − max 1).

The column from wAp to Tg represent behavioral data on the main sources of information used by the respondents. The columns from Inf to Arg represent the five dimensions of the Watson Glaser survey. The column sCri represent the self-assessment of critical thinking assessed with the dimension in the scale provided by [13], while the column Fake represent the capability of detecting fake news measured by the judgment formulated by respondents on the truthfulness of a two fake news.

The data on the habits of information acquisition do not show significant differences among the samples. Both groups are intense users of Facebook and WhatsApp. The first group differs from the second as the usage of other social networking platform is more diffused. The intensity of use of traditional newspaper and TV daily news is lower than the usage of social media in both groups, and this is consistent with the profile close to that of digital natives that respondents show [29].

Concerning the critical thinking skills measured by the Watson Glaser instrument, both groups show low average scores for the inference and evaluation of arguments dimensions. The average scores of the remaining dimensions are all quite high and not so differentiated between the two groups.

Where the two groups differ is on the comparison between the self-perceived critical thinking skill and the capability to detect fake news. The self-perceived critical thinking skill is equally high for both groups. Consequently, the capability to detect fake news is consistently lower than the self-perceived capability of critical thinking, still in both cases. However, groups two shows lower scores on the capability to detect fake news and marks a larger difference between the self and the actual critical thinking capability.

5 Discussion

The analysis of the data shows three aspects to discuss: critical thinking scores, differences between measured and self-assessed critical thinking, and sample homogeneity.

Concerning the results on critical thinking, the analysis potentially disputes the claims from the literature [9, 15] on the lack of critical thinking by millennials. The scores on the Watson-Glaser instrument reported by the millennials are on average not low, if not for the inference (particularly) and evaluation of arguments dimensions. Adding to this, we need to mention also the capability of detecting fake news which, though higher than one might expect, at least for the second cluster affects 50% of the millennials. This statement seems to suggest that, though millennials are capable of interpreting and deducing information, and recognizing assumptions in it, they are weak in identify true and false assertions—and the capability to detect fake news confirms that—and in assessing the validity and relevance of inductive reasoning based on information.

Concerning the differences between the measured and self-assessed critical thinking skills, the study shows that, when we measure it by the capability to detect fake news, the perceived critical thinking skills are on average greater than the actual ones in the investigated group of millennials. The statement also holds for the dimensions of inference and evaluation of arguments. In a way, this result is expected since the self-assessment of critical thinking skills might be affected by individual biases [13].

The third aspect concerns the homogeneity of the sample. The literature warns on treating millennials as a homogeneous cohort of individuals all showing the same traits [9]. Empirical sources also identified significant internal differentiation among the characteristics of the millennials [8]. However, looking at the analysis of the data sample we collected we are not in the position to confirm such statement, as the data show in our case a higher level of homogeneity. Out of the two cluster solutions found indeed, individuals belonging to them differ only by little details.

Finally, no significant evidence emerge from the adoption of social media or traditional media as the source of information of millennials as, also from this perspective, the respondents do not show differences about the usage of social media.

6 Conclusions

This paper presents the results of an exploratory analysis on a sample of 422 responses from millennials to a survey designed to assess the critical skills capabilities of respondents. The results of the exploratory study show that—among the dimensions of critical thinking—millennials are weak regarding making inferences out of data and information, evaluate arguments, and identify fake news. Given that the intensity of use of social media among the other information sources is similar for the two groups of millennials analyzed, the study revealed no differences regarding the influence of social media on critical thinking.

As mentioned in the paper, the sample analyzed is biased towards the presence of female among the group of millennials. Respondents of our sample also show a higher level of education compared to the average of millennials. As a limitation, we have to acknowledge that the differences among means in the groups could be affected by these biases. Adding to this, we also acknowledge that the use of Facebook for the formation of the incidental sample might have contributed to the lack of diversity in it. For this reason, we retain this analysis exploratory, and we make no inferences. In future research, we will collect further data balancing the representativeness of the sample from the sex point of view and use different channels for the selection of respondents.

References

1. Federici, T., & Braccini, A. M. A. M. (2012). How internet is upsetting the communication between organizations and their stakeholders: A tentative research agenda. In: De Marco, M., Te'eni, D., Albano, V., & Za, S. (Eds.), *Information systems: A crossroad for organization, management, accounting and engineering* (pp. 377–385). Heidelberg: Physica-Verlag, A Springer Company.
2. Majchrzak, A., Faraj, S., Kane, G. C., & Azad, B. (2013). The contradictory influence of social media affordances on online communal knowledge sharing. *Journal of Computer-Mediated Communication, 19,* 38–55.
3. Huang, J., Baptista, J., & Newell, S. (2015). Communicational ambidexterity as a new capability to manage social media communication within organizations. *The Journal of Strategic Information Systems, 24,* 49–64.
4. Braccini, A. M., & Federici, T. (2013). New Internet-based relationships between citizens and governments in the public space: challenges for and integrated system design. In R. Baskerville, M. De Marco, & P. Spagnoletti (Eds.), *Designing organizational systems. An interdisciplinary discourse* (pp. 157–180). Heidelberg: Springer.
5. Zheng, Y., & Yu, A. (2016). Affordances of social media in collective action: The case of free lunch for children in China. *Information Systems Journal, 26,* 289–313.
6. Vaast, E., Safadi, H., Lapointe, L., & Negoita, B. (2017). Social media affordances for connective action—An examination of microblogging use during the Gulf of Mexico oil spill. *MIS Quarterly, 41,* 1179–1205.
7. Parry, E., & Urwin, P. (2011). Generational differences in work values: A review of theory and evidence. *International Journal of Management Reviews, 13,* 79–96.
8. Hargittai, E., & Hinnant, A. (2008). Digital inequality—Differences in young adults' use of the internet. *Communication Research, 35,* 602–621.
9. Bennet, S., Maton, K., & Kervin, L. (2008). The "Digital Natives" debate: A critical review of the evidence. *British Journal of Educational Technology, 39,* 775–786.
10. Paul, R. W., Binkler, A. J. A. (1990). *Critical thinking: What every person needs to survive in a rapidly changing world.*
11. Leyden, D. P. (2011). *Critical thinking in economics.* Charlotte, North Carolina: Kona Publishing and Media Group, Higher Education Division.
12. Prensky, M. (2005). Listen to the natives. *Learn Digit Age, 63,* 8–13.
13. Braccini, A. M. A. M., & Federici, T. (2013). A measurement model for investigating digital natives and their organisational behaviour. In *Proceedings of the 2013 International Conference on Information Systems (ICIS 2013).* Milano.

14. Choo, C. W. (2006). *The knowing organisation*. New York: Oxford University Press.
15. Lorenzo, G., & Dziuban, C. (2006). Ensuring the net generation is net savvy. *Educause Learning Initiative Paper, 2,* 1–19.
16. Sarigoz, O. (2012). Assessment of the high school students' critical thinking skills. *Procedia-Social and Behavioral Sciences, 46,* 5315–5319.
17. Aa, Y., Karakaya, A., & Yilmaz, K. (2015). Relations between self—Leadership and critical thinking skills. *Procedia-Social and Behavioral Sciences, 207,* 29–41.
18. Facione, P. A. (2013). *Critical thinking: What it is and why it counts*. Insight Assessment.
19. Hammond, J. S., Keeney, R. L., & Raiffa, H. (1998). *The hidden traps in decision making*. Harv Bus Rev September.
20. Hogarth, R. M., & Soyer, E. (2015). Providing information for decision making: Contrasting description and simulation. *Journal of Applied Research in Memory and Cognition,* 221–228.
21. Metallo, C., & Agrifoglio, R. (2015). The effects of generational differences on use continuance of Twitter: An investigation of digital natives and digital immigrants. *Behaviour & Information Technology, 34,* 869–881.
22. Braccini, A. M., & Marzo, F. (2016). Digital natives and digital immigrants behaviour in trust choices: An experimental study on social trust attitudes and cognition. In: D'Ascenzo, F., Magni, M., Lazazzara, A., & Za, S. (Eds.), *Blurring the boundaries through digital innovation* (pp. 103–115). Heidelberg: Springer.
23. Howe, N., & Strauss, W. (2000). *Millennials rising: The next great generation*. New York: Vintage.
24. Oblinger, D. G. T. G., & Oblinger, J. L. (2005). Is it age or IT: First steps toward understanding the net generation. In: Oblinger, D. G., & Oblinger, J. L. (Eds.), *Educating the net generation* (pp. 2.1–2.20). North Carolina State University.
25. Taylor, A. (2012). A study of the information seeking behaviour of the millennial generation. *Information Research, 17.*
26. Goldberg, L. R., & Coufal, K. L. (2009). Reflections on service-learning, critical thinking, and cultural competence. *Journal of College Teaching and Learning, 6.*
27. Tapscott, D. (1998). *Growing up digital: The rise of the net generation*. New York: McGraw-Hill.
28. PewResearchCenter. (2010). Millennials. *A portrait of generation next.*
29. Prensky, M. (2001). Digital natives, digital immigrants. *Horiz, 9,* 1–6.

Part II
Human Resources and Learning in Digital Ecosystems

Grasping Corporate Identity from Social Media: Analysis of HR Consulting Companies

Stefano Di Lauro⑩, Aizhan Tursunbayeva⑩, Gilda Antonelli⑩ and Marcello Martinez⑩

Abstract Corporate identity is often defined as "what an organization is". This concept relates to organizational identity. However, while organizational identity has an internal employee focus, corporate identity has an external focus. As such, it is often used as a synonym to organizational image that organizations project externally. Social media have created a multitude of ways for organizations, as well as for their employees, independently, to develop and disseminate corporate identity. However, although there have already been attempts to explore the role of employees' personal social media profiles in projecting organizational identity externally, little is still known about how organizations use their social media profiles for these purposes. This empirical research, which is part of a broader doctoral research focusing on organizational identity and social media, aims to address this gap. Building on previous corporate identity and social media research, and adopting an existing framework explaining the relationship between social media and corporate identity, it analyses social media profiles of 12 international HR consulting companies. In particular, it explores the platforms they use, type of content they publish, their approaches for stakeholder engagement and interaction for building stronger organizational image/corporate identity. Diverse off-the-shelf applications were used for collecting social media data for the period between January and December 2017. We expect that the results of our analysis will help to understand how organizations

S. Di Lauro (✉)
Università degli Studi di Napoli Federico II, Naples, Italy
e-mail: stefano.dilauro@gmail.com

A. Tursunbayeva
Università degli Studi del Molise, Campobasso, Italy

University of Edinburgh, Edinburgh, UK
aizhan.tursunbayeva@gmail.com

G. Antonelli
Università degli Studi del Sannio, Benevento, Italy
e-mail: gilda.antonelli@unisannio.it

M. Martinez
Università della Campania Luigi Vanvitelli, Capua, Italy
e-mail: marcello.martinez@unicampania.it

© Springer Nature Switzerland AG 2020
A. Lazazzara et al. (eds.), *Exploring Digital Ecosystems*,
Lecture Notes in Information Systems and Organisation 33,
https://doi.org/10.1007/978-3-030-23665-6_8

(specifically HR consulting companies) use social media to project and strengthen their corporate identity, and what organizations from other sectors can learn from them.

Keywords Corporate identity · Organizational image · Social media · Human resources

1   Introduction: Corporate Identity and Social Media

The concept of corporate identity has been widely discussed and defined in the literature [1]. It is often referred to as "the mix of attributes which makes any entity distinct" [2], or in other words what organization do, how it does it, and where it is going [3]. The concept of corporate identity strictly relates to organizational identity [1]. The latter refers broadly to what members perceive, feel and think about their organizations [4] or in other words "who are we as an organization" [5]. As such organizational identity has an internal employee focus, while corporate identity is a socially constructed view on organization of external stakeholders [1]. Therefore, corporate identity is often used as a synonym to organizational image that organizations project externally [6]. This image is formed through the company's identity, which is composed by strategy, philosophy, culture and organizational design [7].

According to Kaplan and Haenlein [8], "social media is a group of Internet-based applications that build on the ideological and technological foundations of Web 2.0, and that allow the creation and exchange of User Generated Content". Social media have created a multitude of ways for organizations, as well as for their employees, independently, to develop and disseminate their identity [9]. However, although there have already been attempts to explore the role of employees' personal (public) social media profiles in projecting organizational identity externally [10], little is known about how organizations use their official social media for these purposes. This empirical research, which is part of a broader doctoral research focusing on organizational identity and social media, aims to address this important literature gap. Drawing from the existing research on corporate identity and social media, it analyses official social media pages of 12 companies belonging to the same specific industry—HR consulting companies. This is done to understand how companies from the same industry, which can also be direct competitors to each other [11], can use social media to project and strengthen their own corporate identity. The specific objectives of the research are the following:

- To understand the social media platforms HR consulting companies use;
- To understand the main content themes of the posts made by HR consulting companies on different social media platforms;
- To understand whether and how organizations (specifically HR consulting companies) use social media for stakeholder engagement and to project and strengthen their corporate identity.

In order to facilitate this research, we drew on the framework linking corporate identity and social media developed by Devereux et al. [9] which summarizes this relationship according to five stages of social media including Social media adoption, Choice of platform/s, Choice of content, Stakeholder engagement and Organization interaction.

The article is structured as follows. First, we present the latest research on corporate identity and social media. Next, the paper describes the research design methods, followed by the description and discussion of the findings. The paper closes with the conclusions that consider also limitations of the current research as well as future research areas.

2 Theoretical Framework

One of the most cited academic social media classification was developed by Kaplan and Haenlein in 2010 [8]. It defines social media as collaborative projects, blogs, content communities, social networking sites, virtual game worlds and virtual social worlds. However, as demonstrated by the updated classification published recently by Hootsuite [12] in its influential practitioners' blog, considering the rapid latest developments in the social media field, this definition is no longer fully inclusive. Hootsuite reclassified social media into 10 categories according to what users hope to accomplish by using them: 1. Social networks (e.g. Facebook, Twitter, LinkedIn); 2. Media sharing networks (e.g. YouTube, Instagram); 3. Discussion forums (e.g. Reddit, Quora); 4. Bookmarking and content curation networks (e.g. Pinterest); 5. Consumer review networks (e.g. Yelp, TripAdvisor); 6. Blogging and publishing networks (e.g. WordPress, Tumblr); 7. Social shopping networks (e.g. Etsy, Fancy); 8. Interest-based networks (e.g. Goodreads, Last.fm); 9. 'Sharing economy' networks (e.g. Airbnb, Uber); and 10. Anonymous social networks (e.g. Whisper, Ask.fm). It is worthwhile to mention that these days, however, the lines between social networks and media sharing networks are blurring. For example, Facebook and Twitter have recently added live videos and other multimedia services on their platforms.

Previous research on social media use and organizational or corporate identity relevant to this study is limited. Some existing studies focused on the ways organizations can exist on social media. These areas can include official means, employee accounts, parody accounts, and online discussions [9]. Other studies focused on examining the ways different online media channels can contribute to organizations' projected image. These reported that every social media has specific objectives and can deliver specific benefits to business. For example, social networks can be used for connecting with people and brand and they can be beneficial for market research, brand awareness or even lead generation; social media sharing networks can be used for finding and sharing photos and videos and they can help with audience engagement and brand awareness; bookmarking and content curation networks can be used to discover, share and discuss new and trending content and media, and they can help with customers engagement and website traffic [12]. Some studies also focused on the ways organizations can best present their identities on social media for different audiences. Thus Postman [13] stressed the importance of the graphic elements, such as for example logo, in order to build corporate identity. Morgan et al. [14] noticed that social media has also changed the consumers' role from passive to active participants, transforming corporate identity into a process of brand co-creation—in collaboration with the consumers on social media [15]. Kuvykaite and Piligrimiene [16] concluded that overall the way organizations present their identity on social media depends on the organizational social media strategy that can include aims of social media interaction, message theme/s, content form, social media channel. However, although as aforementioned every social media has different goals and can benefit organizations in different ways, it is believed that it is more efficient and productive for companies to migrate toward a larger-scale, integrated strategy covering all social media they use [17].

Some previous research also focused on exploring how social media affected specific organizations' corporate or organizational identity or some specific areas within organizations. Thus, for example, we know how social media affected brand image of organizations in the hospitality industry [18] or how social media influenced HR functions or the HR management practices they perform, such as recruitment or training and development (e.g. [19]). However, little is known on how HR consulting companies use social media, especially how they do it to project their corporate identity. In this study we focused on addressing this research gap. In order to do it, we draw from the framework developed by Devereux et al. [9] that links social media and corporate identity concepts, and summarizes their relationship into the specific stages of social media. These stages together with some of the specific aspects (questions) that we consider relevant to this research are presented in the Table 1.

Description of how the framework was applied to this research is described in the following research design section.

Table 1 Framework on the relationship between corporate identity and social media (adapted from Devereux et al. [9])

Social media adoption	Choice of platform/s	Choice of content	Stakeholder engagement	Organization interaction
• To use or not to use social media? • How to use it (e.g. for internal or external use)? • Who needs to look after them?	• How many platforms should be adopted? • Why are they chosen? • When are they adopted?	• Why is it created? • Who will create it? • What form will it take? • What does it contain? • When is it published?	• What is the Level/Nature of Engagement?	• How does the organization react to engagement? • How does the organization interact with other users?

3   Research Design

Twelve worldwide HR consulting companies were selected for this research. These companies are all based in Europe and in the USA and even though they differ by size, they provide similar services and products to their customers. In order to identify suitable companies, expert interview was conducted with the CEO of one of these companies located in Italy. Data for the companies that he labelled as his direct competitors were collected in this research from the official social media pages of these companies.

In order to classify different types of social media we followed social media classification of Hootsuite's [12] discussed in the aforementioned section. Being present on social media, however, was not the only criteria we considered, as such companies also had to be "active", meaning that they had to regularly update the content of their social media and/or interact with their users. The whole analysis took into consideration a twelve months period (from January to December 2017). Data were mostly collected manually, although diverse off-the-shelf applications were used where possible.

In order to reveal corporate identity of the analysed companies, following Devereux et al. [9] framework presented in Table 1 we first identified which platform/s companies used and the number of these platforms. Then we focused on understanding the content these platforms contained and tried to explore why it was created, and on analysing the stakeholder engagement, and the nature of this engagement. Finally, we considered organizations' interaction with their social media audience.

Detailed description of our approach to data collection and data analysis with regards to each social media the companies used is presented in the Table 2.

4   Results

4.1   Choice of Platform

12 HR consulting companies analysed are present only on social networks [12], including Facebook, Twitter and LinkedIn, and media sharing network [12]—YouTube. Social media platforms each HR consulting company is present on are demonstrated in Fig. 1.

As illustrated in Fig. 1, LinkedIn is the most used social network. Indeed, all analysed companies have an official LinkedIn page. However, only nine out of 12 companies are active on LinkedIn, meaning that they regularly share their updates. Twitter is the second mostly used social network platform (10 out of 12). However, it is the first, together with LinkedIn, in terms of companies' level of activity (nine out of 12 companies are active on Twitter). Facebook is the least used social network. It is actively used only by five companies, and another company which only has an official page without any recently published content. Finally, the most common

Table 2 Data collection and analysis methodology

	Facebook	LinkedIn	Twitter	YouTube
Audience	– Number of fans (number of users who like the page)[a]	– Number of followers (number of users who follow the page)[a]	– Number of followers (number of users who follow the page)[b]	– Number of subscribers (total number of channel subscribers)[a]
Aspects considered	– Call to Action Button (CTA) (There are a wide variety of CTA buttons available on Facebook to add to the company pages: book now, contact us, send message, send email, call now, use app, play game, shop now, see offers, sign up, watch video [20])[a]	– Type of page: (LinkedIn offers three types of pages: Company page, showcase page (an extension of the company page) and career page (to attract talents and to quickly and easily provide candidates with a personalized look into company, culture, and jobs)[a]	– N/A	– Featured video[a]
Content analysis	– Presence of the defined publishing calendar (the posts are planned and published regularly)[a] – Type of posts (categories: status, picture, link, video, questions, offer, music, slideshow, others [21])[b] – Internal or external content[a] – Typology of internal content[a,b] – Top posts (total reactions, comments and shares)[b]	– Presence of the publishing calendar (the posts are planned and published regularly)[a] – Internal or external content[a] – Typology of internal content[a]	– The most used hashtags[c] – Type of tweets (categories: original, reshare and reply [21])[b] – Main typologies of original tweets[a,b] – Most retweeted tweets[c] – Top mentioned content topics[b]	– Type of videos (categories were created manually based on the types of videos available on the company's YouTube channel: interviews with professionals; informative/promotional videos; company videos (stories); CEO and employees' interviews; tutorial videos; conference recordings; workshops)[a] – Main created playlists[a] – Most popular videos (the most-viewed video on the channel)[a]

(continued)

Table 2 (continued)

	Facebook	LinkedIn	Twitter	YouTube
Understanding frequency, engagement and interaction	– General level of engagement (It is the average number of likes, comments and shares per day, divided by the number of fans [21][b] – Posts per day (average number of posts per day)[b]	– Posts per month (approximate average number of post per month)[a] – Likes per post (approximate average number of post likes per month)[a]	– Twitter engagement (It is the total number of users' interactions on one day divided by the number of followers. This includes retweets and favourites [21][b] – Tweet interaction (It is the number of reactions divided by the tweets and divided by the fans [21][b] – Tweets per day (average number of tweets per day)[b]	– Video views (total number of all the video views)[a]
Other	– Related pages (pages related to the main page; e.g. branches or associated partner pages)[a]	– Related groups (LinkedIn groups provide a place for professionals in the same industry or with similar interests to share content, find answers, post and view jobs, make contacts, and establish themselves as industry experts [22][a] – Number of employees on LinkedIn[a]		

[a]Manual data collection; [b]Data collection with the help of FanPage Karma; [c]Data collection with the help of Twitonomy

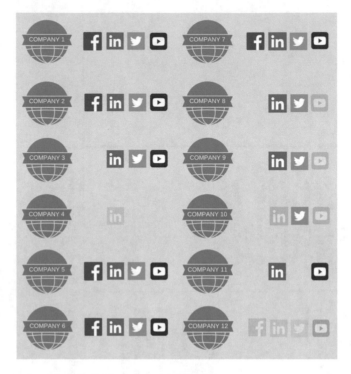

Fig. 1 Types of social media the companies analysed use

media-sharing network [23], YouTube, is actively used by seven companies. Four companies have an official channel on YouTube, but they are not using it. As "social media are all about sharing and interaction" [8] Company4 and Company12 were not included into analysis as they did not share any content on their official pages in the past 12 months. The remaining companies are all active on social media channels they use.

4.2 Choice of Content

Our analysis demonstrated that none of the companies has a fully integrated social media strategy, as none of them is a frequent and regular simultaneous publisher of the content on all of the platforms adopted. For example, none of the companies shared the same update on all of its social media simultaneously. Our analysis also demonstrated that none of the analysed companies published content on Facebook regularly implying that they do not have a pre-defined social media publishing calendar. However, we observed that some companies (Company7 and Company8) have a structured publishing plan on LinkedIn.

Typology of content companies posted differed by social media platform. Almost all companies present on Facebook (Company2, Company5, Company7) published internal content related to their employees' company life, especially pictures. These, together with employees' video interviews were the most popular in terms of total reactions, comments and shares (see Appendix 1 for details).

The content published on LinkedIn is richer, and the publishing calendar although not always well defined, looks to be more dynamic and professional. It included case studies, reports, whitepapers, insights on trends, informative and promotional tests, announcements about workshops, trainings and/or webinars, and provided some space to content related to company's values, culture and identity. This included awards and recognitions, internal testimonial interviews and blog posts from the LinkedIn publishing platform—Pulse. One company (Company8) even had a dedicated career page containing employees' and top managers' interviews and photos taken during or outside working hours (e.g. during outdoor team buildings) and demonstrating a friendly working environment (see Appendix 2 for details). It can be grasped from the content analysed that the primary aim of this career page is to attract talents.

Twitter is used by all of the active companies. Team life pictures were again the main typology of original content posted by the companies (seven out of nine companies with Twitter). Live tweeting during events and pictures for these events were also very common content tweeted by the companies. Moreover, all of the companies used hashtags related to their business activity (e.g. #HR is the most used hashtag among all companies). However while most of the companies use trending and content hastags (e.g. #assessment #leadership), three companies (Company1, Company5 and Company8) frequently used a personalized hashtag (brand hashtag) with their company name (see Appendix 3 for details).

Finally, YouTube channel is mostly used by companies to show company videos including stories about the company, to share informative/promotional videos, and to help clients with tutorial videos. The most preferred content by users included informative videos by company employees' and managers on company values and culture (see Appendix 4 for details). Only one company (Company6) had a featured or default video with a generic presentation about the company, which automatically plays when any user opens their YouTube channel.

4.3 Engagement

The level of engagement was generally low on all the social media pages analysed. Even though there are companies with slightly higher level of engagement on some specific platforms, none had the same (high) level of engagement on all the social media platforms adopted.

On Facebook, almost all of the companies shared less than a post per day. The level of engagement on Facebook was mostly inversely proportional to the number of fans. For example, Company2 has the lower number of fans (526) and the highest level of engagement (0.34%) and Company7 has the highest number of fans (25 K) and the lower level of engagement (0.0047%). Company7 also has the highest number of posts per day (7.5) (see Appendix 1 for details).

Company7 and Company8 had the highest number of followers on LinkedIn (209 and 148 K respectively). However, here, the number of followers did not affect much the total number of likes per post. Company8 has a Career page and it has the highest number of employees linked to the page (4.3 K) (see Appendix 2 for details), which potentially can also represent the total number of company employees in general. However, considering the aforementioned company's page goals and focus which as emerged from our analysis is to attract talents, it is worthwhile to assume that the company pays great attention to its employees' network. Company8 also has the highest number of followers on Twitter (20 K) and the highest number of tweets per day (9.0). The level of engagement (0.29%) of Company8 is the highest among all of the other companies (see Appendix 3 for details), showing the highest number of users interacted with the company's tweets. Company6 has the lowest level of engagement (0.0028%).

Company6 has YouTube channel with the highest number of subscribers (2.7 K) and video views (410 K). Overall, the number of subscribers on this social media channel is directly proportional to the total number of views (see Appendix 4 for details).

4.4 Interaction

The concept of interaction is related to the concept of engagement. However, interaction involves also how the companies respond to users' engagement. Similarly to the engagement, the level of interaction is overall pretty low, especially on Facebook. Our analysis revealed that the companies use social media only for information push purposes, as such as a one way interaction tool. Only one company (Company9) responded to their LinkedIn and Twitter users timely providing them requested information, but especially trying to establish a dialogue. Moreover, this company creates interaction not only through its official social media channels but also through the public (personal) social media accounts of its employees (in particular on Twitter). Here the employees retweet the company posts, reply to comments, and mention the company in their posts. Moreover, analysing the top retweets we noticed that the content related to employees' life and live corporate events generates more interaction also from the users' side. Detailed information on the user interaction findings can be found in Appendix 1. Similar high-level interaction between companies and personal (public) employee accounts on LinkedIn was notable also by Company7, Company8 and Company9, where they shared LinkedIn Pulse articles written by their employees or consultants. On Facebook we observed that most of the companies use "call now" or "send message" CTA buttons, instead of "shop now" or "see offers" buttons (see Appendix 1 for details).

5 Discussion and Conclusions

Previous research has already identified social media as a relevant and useful tool for building and managing corporate identity. In our research we aimed to explore whether and how companies from the specific HR Consulting industry actually use social media to develop and strengthen their corporate identity/organizational image.

The analysed companies used several social media platforms. This is in line with the findings of previous generic social media research [24] mentioning the adoption of several social media channels as a successful strategy for expanding the range of their organizational image. The companies, however, were present only on two typologies of social media (social networks and media sharing networks) out of 10 categories proposed by Hootsuite [12]. This finding is similar to the findings of research on social media use by other organizations, for example, by public health organizations [25], most of the non-profit organizations [26] and by Fortune 500 Companies [27] which named Facebook, Twitter, YouTube and LinkedIn as the most commonly used social media.

Overall, most of the selected companies seem to recognize the importance of using social media for sharing and demonstrating externally a positive organizational image (corporate identity). The companies do it with the help of company life pictures and video interviews of CEO and employees. This once more confirms the effectiveness of posting visual materials on social media [9]. However, companies can do more by taking advantage also of the latest types of visual materials such as infographics and gifs. Another approach to demonstrating corporate identity was observed from the use of personalized hashtag with the company's name. Indeed, marketing professionals have already referred to this as an effective strategy for promoting the brand online and achieving an extended reach for the company with the help of users [28].

Our findings demonstrate, however, that none of the companies has a fully integrated social media strategy focused on aspects that could be helpful to grasp their corporate identity. Some companies were found to be better structured on some specific social media platforms. For example, it was notable that they published posts according to a pre-defined publishing calendar. Publishing calendars, overall, are recommended to be used [29] to maintain the audience expectations and to select the best time/date to publish content. This is usually done after carefully studying social media insights and/or other analytics [29].

Moreover, the type of content companies posted differed by social media platforms. This finding is in line with Gilpin's [24] study reporting high level of message differentiation among the different communication channels, and suggesting that each social media plays a distinct role in constructing organizational image. However, we observed that the companies analysed did not link the content posted on different social media. Furthermore, the content for which it was possible to track this connection was not well adapted to each individual platform. For example some tweets were shared also on Facebook, without taking into consideration the word limits available on each platform (e.g. Twitter has a limit of 280 characters, while

Facebook post character limit is 63,206)—and the use of the hashtags, which have an essential role in Twitter, but are pointless in Facebook.

Our analysis demonstrated that having a high number of fans/followers does not always mean having a higher number of likes. This counter intuitive result can be possibly explained by the fact that the followers of these companies are not well targeted (e.g. many followers are not related to the business of the companies) or that the followers do not consider the content of a particular interest to them. An exception to this was observed on YouTube, where the number of subscribers is always more or less directly proportional to the total number of video views. Sharing too many posts per day on Facebook can also be considered a cause of having a low level of engagement on the platform (e.g. Company7), as sharing more than 1 or 2 posts per day can push the boundaries of civil participation [30].

While we observed some evidence that companies were paying attention to the content they publish and the organizational image this content can project to their followers/fans, focusing specifically on its visual representation, less attention was paid by the companies on interaction with followers. This is evident not only from the low interaction rates or from the companies' low response rates to their followers, but also from the written content posted by the companies. Very rarely companies' asked questions or tried to involve users with the content they posted by, for example, sharing followers comments or commenting on follower's posts [17]. Overall, the concept of interaction closely relates to the concept of co-creation—"it is through the interaction with the stakeholders that the identity would develop" [9]. However, the idea of co-creation with external stakeholders (e.g. clients or possible clients) seemed to be neglected in most of the companys' social media strategies observable from their social media with the exception of LinkedIn where some companies liked or shared positive content written (and published) by their employees. This type of content is generally considered more credible [31], as such employees are often nominated as ambassadors for promoting company culture and values—components of organizational identity. Employee's important role in projecting externally organizational identity on social media has indeed been empirically confirmed by a relevant recent study on organizational identity and social media [10]. Finally, also the "call now" or "send message" CTA buttons chosen frequently by the companies demonstrate that rather than only selling their product/services, companies are also eager to understand their customers' needs and try to create opportunities for dialogue.

Like any research, this study has some limitations. First of all, it does not take into consideration all of the questions proposed by Devereux et al. [9] to understand the connection between social media and corporate identity. Not included questions would have required an additional analysis (e.g. qualitative interviews) not considered in this study's research design. Future scholar might want to cover this gap and to combine their findings with the findings of this research. We used only secondary data collection approach, as in this study we focused only on external social media channels, although we understand that also internal social media can play an important role in creating or strengthening organizational identity [32]. This opens an additional avenue for the future scholars to explore.

Despite the aforementioned limitations, we believe this study could be of value for academic scholars, as using an existing theoretical/methodological framework it explains the approaches to social media use by HR consulting companies for projecting their corporate image and/or for strengthening it. This study is also of value for practitioners, as it can provide them a practical guidance on how they can analyse their or their competitors' corporate identities independently, as well as practical recommendations on how they could potentially strengthen their corporate identities on social media.

Appendix 1

Facebook analysis

Main company page	Company1	Company2	Company5	Company6	Company7
Number of fans	19 K	526	15 K	6.9 K	25 K
CTA button	Buy now	Call now	Call now	Send message	Call now
General level of engagement (%)	0.19	0.34	0.11	0.010	0.035
Post interaction (%)	0.24	1.3	0.15	0.15	0.0047
Editorial calendar	NO	NO	NO	NO	NO
Posts per day	0.8	0.3	0.7	0.07	7.5
Type of posts in ascending order	Pictures; Videos; Links; Status	Pictures; Links; Videos	Links; Pictures; Status; Videos	Links	Pictures; Links; Videos
Internal or external content	Internal content	Both internal and external	Both internal and external	External content	Internal content

(continued)

(continued)

Main company page	Company1	Company2	Company5	Company6	Company7
Main typologies of internal content	Company news; Tests Promotion; Industry news & research; Events	Team life; Job opportunities; Company news; Industry news & research; Industry articles; Tests promotion; Whitepapers	Team life; Video interviews; Events; Re-posts; Company news; Tests promotion	–	Links from the blog; Team life
Top 10 posts (total reactions, comments and shares)	Events; Company news; Industry news & research	Team life (pictures); Tests Promotion; Company news	Video-interviews; Events; Tests Promotion; Team life (pictures)	–	Links from the blog Employees' video-interviews; Team life (video interview); Team life (pictures)
Related pages	1	4	1	5	1

Appendix 2

LinkedIn analysis

Main page	Company1	Company2	Company3	Company5	Company6
Type of Page	Company page	Company page	Company page	Company page	Showcase page
Followers (K)	7.4	3.3	11.3	7.2	20.4
Posts per month	2	6	11	5	11
Likes per post	12	15	18	4	12

(continued)

(continued)

Main page	Company1	Company2	Company3	Company5	Company6
Editorial calendar	NO	NO	NO	NO	NO
Internal or external contents	Internal	Internal; External	Internal	Internal	Internal; External
Typologies of internal posts	Interviews; Promotion and offers	Interviews; Awards and recognitions; Trends; Reports; Tests promotion	Testimonial; Case studies; Awards and recognitions; Webinars; Test promotion; Conferences; Trainings and courses	Case studies; Free ebook; Tests promotion; Workshops and trainings	Webinars; Posts from the blog/website
Related groups	N.A.	1 (2.3 K members)	N.A.	1 (5.3 K members)	N.A.
Employees on LinkedIn	46	156	429	126	N.A.

Main page	Company7	Company8	Company9	Company11
Type of Page	Company page	Career page	Company page	Company page
Followers (K)	209	148	4.2	3.9
Posts per month	13	5	18	7
Likes per post	15	20	4	9
Editorial calendar	YES	YES	NO	NO
Internal or external contents	Internal External	Internal	Internal External	Internal External
Typologies of internal posts	Pulse written by managers or consultants	Whitepapers; Webinars; Workshops and trainings; Tests promotion; Pulse written by managers or consultants	Pulse written by mangers or consultants; Team testimonials; Trainings and workshops; Tests promotion	Tests promotion; Training and workshops; Case studies
Related groups		12.5 K		
Employees on LinkedIn	4.2 K	4.3 K	444	101

Appendix 3

Twitter analysis

Main page	Company1	Company2	Company3	Company5	Company6
Followers	1.4 K	992	154	18 K	6.3 K
Engagement (%)	0.013	0.11	0.096	0.029	0.0028
Tweet interaction (%)	0.061	0.18	0.34	0.034	0.020
Tweets per day	0.2	0.6	0.3	0.9	0.1
Most used hashtags	#hr #psychometrics	#hr #management #talent	#assessment #human resources #webinar	#leadership #personality #company5	#hr #leadership #talent #recruitment
Type of tweets in ascending order	Original Reshare Reply	Original Reshare	Original	Original Reshare Reply	Original
Main typologies of original tweets	Promotions and offers; Conversations with users	Team Life; Live tweeting; Links to SM and website; Promotion	Industry news & research; Informative and promotional tweets	Team life; Live tweeting; Links to interviews	Team life; Pictures; Live tweeting; Links to SM and website
10 most retweeted Tweets	Conversations with users; Promotion and offers	Links to interviews; Promotions and offers	Industry news & research	Links to Interviews; Links to SM	Pictures; Info about Events

Main page	Company7	Company8	Company9	Company10
Followers	13 K	20 K	850	320
Engagement (%)	0.012	0.29	0.059	0.056
Tweet interaction (%)	0.0092	0.032	N.A.	0.22
Tweets per day	1.3	9.0	N.A.	0.3
Most used hashtags	#digital sustainability #career #jobs	#digital sustainability #leadership #career	#hr #management #company9ta lent	#hr #assessmen tupdates #tests

(continued)

(continued)

Main page	Company7	Company8	Company9	Company10
Type of tweets in ascending order	Original Reshare Reply	Original Reshare Reply	Original Reshare Reply	Original Reshare Reply
Main typologies of original tweets	Webinars; Team life; Infographics; Promotions and offers	Conversations with users; Links to SM and website; Webinars; Team life	Live tweeting; Team life; Promotions and offers; Mentions (employees); Quotes	Quotes; Live tweeting; Team life; Promotions and offers
10 most retweeted Tweets	Webinars; Team life	Team life; Webinars	Live events (pictures); Team life;	Team life; live event (Pictures); Quotes

Appendix 4

YouTube analysis

Main channel	Company1	Company2	Company3	Company5
Subscribers	503	320	230	1.1 K
Views (K)	111	134	29	385
Main types of videos	Interviews with authors; Conferences	Informative/ promotional videos; Company videos (stories); Tutorial videos	Informative/ promotional videos; Company videos (stories)	CEO and employees' interviews; Workshops; Informative/ promotional videos; Tutorial videos
Main created playlists	Interviews with authors; Tests and tools	Client case studies; Careers at Company2; Products	Webinars; Podcasts; Client testimonials; Company3 education; Company3 culture	None

(continued)

(continued)

Main channel	Company1	Company2	Company3	Company5
Most popular videos (total views)	Interviews to authors	Tutorial videos; Company videos (stories)	Company videos (stories)	CEO interviews; Company videos (stories)

Main channel	Company6	Company7	Company11
Subscribers	2.7 K	1.2 K	70
Views (K)	410	160	N.A.
Main types of videos	Company videos (stories); Informative/ promotional videos	Company videos (stories); Informative/ promotional videos Video interviews	Workshops; Tutorial videos; Employees presentations; Conference Recordings
Main created playlists	Success stories; Company6 careers	Company7 careers; Company7 solutions; News	Trainings; Employees presentations; Conference Recordings
Most popular videos (total views)	Company videos (stories)	Company videos (stories)	Tutorial videos

References

1. Kitchen, P. J., Tourky, M. E., Dean, D., & Shaalan, A. S. (2013). Corporate identity antecedents and components: Toward a theoretical framework. *Corporate Reputation Review, 16,* 263–284. https://doi.org/10.1057/crr.2013.18.
2. Balmer, J. M. T., & Greyser, S. A. (2002). Managing the multiple identities of the corporation. *California Management Review, 44,* 72–86. https://doi.org/10.2307/41166133.
3. Balmer, J. M. T. (2008). Identity based views of the corporation: Insights from corporate identity, organisational identity, social identity, visual identity, corporate brand identity and corporate image. *European Journal of Marketing, 42,* 879–906. https://doi.org/10.1108/03090560810891055.
4. Hatch, M. J., & Schultz, M. (2002). The dynamics of organizational identity. *Human Relations, 55,* 989–1018. https://doi.org/10.1177/0018726702055008181.
5. Albert, S., & Whetten, D. A. (1985). Organizational identity. In L. L. Cummings & B. M. Staw (Eds.), *Research in organizational behavior* (pp. 263–295). Greenwich: JAI Press.
6. Cornelissen, J. P., Haslam, S. A., & Balmer, J. M. T. (2007). Social identity, organizational identity and corporate identity: Towards an integrated understanding of processes, patternings and products. *British Journal of Management, 18,* S1–S16. https://doi.org/10.1111/j.1467-8551.2007.00522.x.
7. Gray, E. R., & Balmer, J. M. T. (1998). Managing corporate image and corporate reputation. *Long Range Planning, 31,* 695–702. https://doi.org/10.1016/S0024-6301(98)00074-0.
8. Kaplan, A. M., & Haenlein, M. (2010). Users of the world, unite! The challenges and opportunities of social media. *Business Horizons, 53,* 59–68. https://doi.org/10.1016/j.bushor.2009.09.003.

9. Devereux, L., Melewar, T. C., & Foroudi, P. (2017). Corporate identity and social media: Existence and extension of the organization. *International Studies of Management & Organization, 47,* 110–134. https://doi.org/10.1080/00208825.2017.1256161.
10. Di Lauro, S., Antonelli, G., & Martinez, M. (2018). Understanding employees' perspectives on organizational identity change from their LinkedIn accounts. In: Cabitza, F., Lazazzara, A., Magni, M., & Za, S. (Eds.), *Organizing for digital economy: Societies, communities and individuals.* LUISS University Press.
11. Hatch, M. J., & Schultz, M. (1997). Relations between organizational culture, identity and image. *European Journal of Marketing, 31,* 356–365. https://doi.org/10.1108/eb060636.
12. Foreman, C. (2017). 10 types of social media and how each can benefit your business. In *Hootsuite Social Blog.* https://blog.hootsuite.com/types-of-social-media/.
13. Postman, J. (2008). *SocialCorp: Social media goes corporate.* Indianapolis, USA: New Riders Publishing.
14. Morgan, N., Jones, G., & Hodges, A. (2011). *The complete guide to social media from the social media guys.*
15. Bruce, M., & Solomon, M. R. (2013). Managing for media anarchy: A corporate marketing perspective. *Journal of Marketing Theory and Practice, 21,* 307–318. https://doi.org/10.2753/MTP1069-6679210305.
16. Kuvykaitė, R., & Piligrimienė, Ž. (2013). *Communication in social media for company's image formation.*
17. Wilson, H. J., Guinan, P. J., Parise, S., & Weinberg, B. (2011). What's your social media strategy? *Harvard Business Review, 89,* 23–25.
18. Perera, G. R., & Perera, I. (2016). Influence of social media marketing on the brand image of organizations in the hospitality industry of Sri Lanka. *International Journal of Asian Business and Information Management, 7,* 30–41. https://doi.org/10.4018/IJABIM.2016010103.
19. McFarland, L. A., & Ployhart, R. E. (2015). Social media: A contextual framework to guide research and practice. *Journal of Applied Psychology, 100,* 1653–1677.
20. (2014) New for Facebook pages: Calls to action. In *Facebook business.* https://it-it.facebook.com/business/news/call-to-action-button.
21. Fanpage Karma. (2018).
22. LinkedIn Help. (2018). *LinkedIn groups—Overview.* https://www.linkedin.com/help/linkedin/answer/1164/linkedin-groups-overview?lang=en.
23. We Are Social, Hootsuite. (2018). *Global Digital Report 2018.*
24. Gilpin, D. (2010). Organizational image construction in a fragmented online media environment. *Journal of Public Relations Research, 22,* 265–287. https://doi.org/10.1080/10627261003614393.
25. Tursunbayeva, A., Franco, M., & Pagliari, C. (2017). Use of social media for e-Government in the public health sector: A systematic review of published studies. *Government Information Quarterly, 34,* 270–282. https://doi.org/10.1016/j.giq.2017.04.001.
26. Nah, S., & Saxton, G. D. (2013). Modeling the adoption and use of social media by nonprofit organizations. *New Media and Society, 15,* 294–313. https://doi.org/10.1177/1461444812452411.
27. Nanji, A. (2017). Social media and blog usage by Fortune 500 companies in 2017. In: *Marketing Profs.* https://www.marketingprofs.com/charts/2017/33156/social-media-and-blog-usage-by-fortune-500-companies-in-2017.
28. Wishpond. (2013). *3 key hashtag strategies: How to market your business & content.* https://blog.wishpond.com/post/62253333766/3-key-hashtag-strategies-how-to-market-your-business.
29. Killian, G., & McManus, K. (2015). A marketing communications approach for the digital era: Managerial guidelines for social media integration. *Business Horizons, 58,* 539–549. https://doi.org/10.1016/j.bushor.2015.05.006.
30. Hutchinson, A. (2018). Facebook now lists page posting frequency in search results. In *SocialMediaToday.* https://www.socialmediatoday.com/news/facebooks-now-listing-page-posting-frequency-in-search-results/513906/.

31. Dreher, S. (2014). Social media and the world of work. A strategic approach to employees' participation in social media. *Corporate Communications: An International Journal, 19,* 344–356. https://doi.org/10.1108/CCIJ-10-2013-0087.
32. Madsen, V. T. (2016). Constructing organizational identity on internal social media: A case study of coworker communication in Jyske Bank. *International Journal of Business Communication, 53,* 220–223. https://doi.org/10.1177/2329488415627272.

Managing Intellectual Capital Inside Online Communities of Practice: An Integrated Multi-step Approach

Chiara Meret, Michela Iannotta, Desiree Giacomelli, Mauro Gatti
and Ida Sirolli

Abstract The increasingly use of social online services has contributed to raising interest in studying a renewed active contribution of individuals to business development processes and value creation. As in knowledge-based organizations the phenomenon of value creation refers to intangible assets, in this study we apply a validated refined framework for intellectual capital (IC) analysis. Accordingly, IC can be grouped into three dimensions: (a) human capital (HC); (b) structural capital (SC); and (c) relational capital (RC). Because of their characterizations, Communities represent a privileged place for IC analysis on an individual and collective level. The unit of analysis of our integrated step-by-step methodology are two online communities of practice (CoPs), operating within one of the most important Italian telecommunication company (TIM S.p.A.). As a result of their empirical investigation, this integrated approach is able to provide both academics and practitioners with an effective tool for assessing intellectual capital and its related dimensions.

Keywords Online communities of practice · Intellectual capital assessment · Multi-step approach

C. Meret (✉) · M. Iannotta · D. Giacomelli · M. Gatti
Department of Management, Sapienza University of Rome,
Via del Castro Laurenziano, 9, 00161 Rome, Italy
e-mail: chiara.meret@uniroma1.it

M. Iannotta
e-mail: michela.iannotta@uniroma1.it

D. Giacomelli
e-mail: desiree.giacomelli@uniroma1.it

M. Gatti
e-mail: mauro.gatti@uniroma1.it

I. Sirolli
TIM S.p.A., Corso d'Italia, 41, 00198 Rome, Italy
e-mail: ida.sirolli@telecomitalia.it

© Springer Nature Switzerland AG 2020   121
A. Lazazzara et al. (eds.), *Exploring Digital Ecosystems*,
Lecture Notes in Information Systems and Organisation 33,
https://doi.org/10.1007/978-3-030-23665-6_9

1 Introduction

Online communities are increasingly widespread in organizations. They allow their members to communicate, collaborate and share their expertise. However, a crucial issue remains the way in which members evaluate their work, and how this affects their decisions to participate actively (and even proactively) in these communities.

Communities of practice (CoPs) depend on two central premises: (1) an activity-based nature of knowledge, and (2) a group-based character of the organizational activity [1, 2]. Thus, it is possible to define the learning value of CoPs as the ability to develop a shared commitment among its participants [3]. Moreover, CoPs consist of four main features: (1) a stock of shared knowledge, (2) shared values and attitudes, (3) common group identity, and (4) a flow of relationships and interrelations between the abovementioned variables [4]. These features emphasize interdependent contribution over devotion to duty, based on a common purpose toward which employees work together [5, 6].

IC in CoPs have been recently analyzed by both researchers and practitioners [7, 8], although there are still insufficient empirical contributions, due both to a non-univocal conception of the meaning, and to different contexts in which it has been applied. Furthermore, there is still a necessity of in-depth exploring and empirically assessing the impact of IC components to the contribution of CoPs to the value creation process.

To fulfill this gap, different methods can be combined [9–14] to define a comprehensive methodology to analyze IC and its components by including members, sponsors, internal and external leaders of CoPs [10, 11]. In this field we place our research. Our basic assumption relies on the possibility to identify a common path of conceptual foundations for both IC and Knowledge Management, such as the resource-based view, the dynamic capabilities, and the knowledge-based view of the firm, according to which the organizational ability to develop, use, and benefit from its IC supports the building of a sustainable competitive advantage [3, 12, 15–17]. The sections that follow present the theoretical background and the methodology of the research; in the last two sections we discuss our findings with a look to further insights.

2 Theoretical Background

2.1 Communities of Practice

CoPs represent an "interdependent process management" [5: 2] in which people orient their interests and actions beyond physical or vertical organizational boundaries and share identity around a set of topics [3, 5]. The sustainability of CoPs strongly depends on the possibility that its members want to be part of it, and that they are consistent with this intent during its existence. Previous studies focused on motivation to join online CoPs, factors that affect members' satisfaction, different kind of interactions and relationships, knowledge management, different typologies of community members, etc. [18–20]. Thus, while some online CoPs are successful, others are abandoned.

Still, regardless of their nature, CoPs are implemented in the learning organizations to lead change and complexity by fostering informal relations and encouraging a free, horizontal flow of knowledge, both inside and outside their borders [11]. This explains the attributed meaning of value creation of online CoPs, at the heart of our investigation.

2.2　Intellectual Capital

In line with the extant literature, IC can be seen as a set of intangible assets generally grouped into three dimensions: (1) Human Capital (HC), as the set of intangible resources associated to the individual, such as employees' values and attitudes, know-how, competences and skills; (2) Structural Capital (SC), which represents the organizational internalized knowledge, culture, procedures, systems and intellectual property; and (3) Relational Capital (RC), as the valuable internal and external relationships with stakeholders [11–26].

Several authors suggest assessing the firm value creation by making use of IC concept and its characterizing factors [10–12, 27–30]. However, measuring intangible assets is difficult [31] and traditional measures are inadequate. Brooking attributes it to new massive intangible benefits of Information Technology (IT) [32]. Her Technology Broker IC audit assumes the four components of market assets, intellectual property assets, human-centered assets and infrastructure assets and combine both qualitative and quantitative measures of IC. Skandia was the first company introducing a dynamic IC report, by highlighting hidden factors of human and structural capital [22, 31]. Here, IC is the multiplication of an overall IC value and its coefficient of efficiency. By reducing the number of indices, Edvnisson and Malone [22] stress cross-references between measures. Roos et al. [33] derive an IC-Index to overcome previous anchoring to monetary measurements and accounting both for the underlying relationships between measures and dynamics of IC. Bontis et al. [34] suggest the necessity to develop a process model for selecting the correct indicators, based on the sources of company value coming from IC, key success factors, identity, strategy and long term-goals. Finally, Sveiby's [35] Intangible Assets Monitor model states that by correctly leveraging IC, financial capital will follow. Despite previous efforts, a methodology capable of capturing all the aspects related to the new paradigm is still hard to be found. Additionally, given the twofold nature of CoPs (formal and informal), it is necessary that decision makers participate directly in assessing and managing the value creation process together with members.

The concept of CoPs was originally developed by Lave and Wenger [27] as a system of relationships between people, activities, and the rest of the world and vital places of negotiation, learning, meaning, and identity. CoPs, therefore, have a horizontal and informal membership, where members use each other's experience of practice around a topic as a learning resource, enhancing the level of IC in all of its articulations [3, 29]. In line with Seraj [19: 213], "By adding comments and opinions to the disclosed message or visual item, others also contribute to the generated content and the totality becomes an asset or "artifact" of the online community". As in knowledge-based organizations the phenomenon of value creation refers to intangible assets, IC elements should be assessed as important catalysts for product and process innovation success [9, 12].

3   A Four-Step Methodology

The assessment of the strategic impact to the value creation process requires combined methods and a focus on people's opinions besides the specificity of the context [36]. Starting from this necessity, we implement a four-step methodology to assess the factual contribution of IC elements of two online CoPs, for defining their value creation and development strategies. The methodology consists of a sequence of steps firstly implemented for the MindSh@re project [10–13] and requires combined analysis of outcomes. Then, hermeneutics is applied for interpreting qualitative data in light of the whole aim of developing two value creation models. Combining different interpretations several times allows the researchers to support the results of analytical steps and validate the aggregated results [19]. The research project is the result of 14 preliminary meetings between the researchers and 3 managers of TIM S.p.A. These meetings drove the project group to the identification of two online CoPs for the start of a one-year pilot project. The main criteria used to identify the two CoPs (among the 12 ongoing TIM communities) were: (1) at least two years of development and activity; (b) the commitment of the governance to this project; (c) the quality of output produced and shared; and (d) the community impact in innovation/re-engineering process. Thus, the CoP *Process and Procedures Design* (from now on Community A) supports idea and know-how sharing, through the comparison and the sharing of knowledge and professional experience of colleagues operating in the Process and Procedures Design Functions throughout the company as well as among colleagues, experts of Lean Six Sigma or EFQM. The Community provides and shares with its members: (a) teaching materials, digital learning and best practice; (b) planning and monitoring process mapping and re-engineering; and (c) all the news about reference contest and system. The CoP *Pioneers* (from now on Community B) is one of the actors of the Learning & Developing Ecosystem of the Company Academy. It is composed by senior professional members, representative of the whole internal organisation. It is involved in: (a) scouting the capabilities useful to guarantee medium and long-term competitiveness to the company; (b) contribution to the skill innovation process and in building and speeding up the learning offer; ad (c) updating of the Internal Professional Job System.

A total number of 12 Subject Matter Experts (SMEs) was selected for the community A, while a number of 13 SMEs were selected for the second designated online

CoP. The selection criteria were: (a) participation to discussion; (b) promotion of topics; and (c) previous knowledge with Network Leaders. The samples consisted of both managerial and professional staff, contacted via email. After processing the contents and materials, the project operatively started in November 2017.

The first step consists in the identification of the IC components. For this process to be possible it is necessary to understand the company's strategic direction and goals. It involves both the members of the CoPs and its governance. The associated sub-steps are: (a) definition of the CoPs' strategic objectives in relation to the company's strategy, with the project group proposed by the company; (b) definition of Intellectual Capital Factors (ICF). Their identification is derived by using the Nominal Group Technique (digital version), involving the total number of 25 selected SMEs [37, 38]. The content for the selection was previously differentiated and validated through preliminary meetings with the CoPs' representatives; (c) identification of a number ranging from 3 to 5 Value Drivers (VD), defined as a homogeneous set of ICF [10, 39, 40], together with the Network Leaders of the CoPs. This sub-step and the following three ones were defined within the same focus group (one per CoP); (d) clustering of the identified VD into the strategic objectives of the CoPs, to verify their consistency with the company's strategic goals; (e) assemblage into homogeneous groups of ICF in a minimum of 3 and a maximum of 5 VD, based on pertinence, in turn assigned to the three dimensions of HC, SC, RC; (f) definition of each VD; and (e) assemblage into a comprehensive model for intellectual capital and value creation, to be subsequently shared with and evaluated by the SMEs.

Step 2 consists in the evaluation of the strategic impact (SI) of VD. It represents the relevance of ICF for achieving the goals of the CoPs. Step 2 is divided into: (a) assigning a score from 1 to 5 (low-medium-high impact) to each ICF by the SMEs. This evaluation measures the influence of each of the VD; (b) the Impact Score of each VD is obtained by averaging its scores assigned to the ICF; (c) the strategic impact (SI) of each VD (low-medium-high scale) denotes the interval in which the Impact Score falls. This step and the following one were entirely developed within a one-day focus group (one per CoP), moderated by the project promoters. The focus groups were fully recorded, transcribed and analyzed by one of the researchers. The meetings took place in separate times and places for the two communities, and only the involved SMEs, one of the researchers and two members of the project team could access it.

Step 3 consists in evaluating the Performances (*stocks* variables) pertaining to each VD and Cross-Relationships (CR) between them (*flows* variables). Its sub-steps are: (a) VD Performance Analysis and assignment of a value ranging from 1 to 9 by the SMEs (from 1 = min to 9 = max); (b) CR Analysis to assess the influence that each VD has on the others. Participants are called upon to express a judgment on the nature of the influence of each VD on the remaining, whether direct or indirect; (c) calculation of the average value of each row that provides the Performance Score of each VD; (d) calculation of the Performance Level of each VD, based on a qualitative evaluation low-medium-high; (e) assignment of a value of 0.5 for indirect and 1 for direct influences identified, with the goal of identifying the number of relationships;

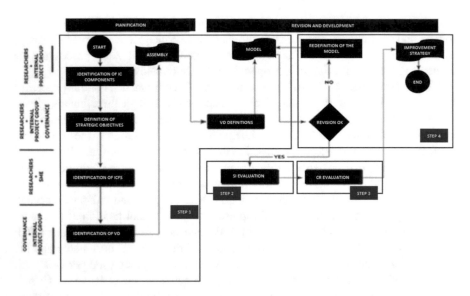

Fig. 1 Project flowchart. Own elaboration

(f) calculation of the CR level of each VD, based on a low-medium-high qualitative assessment.

In step 4, relevant information from previous stages is elaborated for data analysis, with the aim of identifying actions and priorities to be included in the Improvement Strategy. It is articulated as follows: (a) processing of the "SI-Performance" Matrix; (b) processing of the "CR-Performance" Matrix. The comparison between them makes it possible to identify critical VD. It also allows to identify VD initially considered critical, but showing no impact on performance. Placement within the matrix paves the way for formulating corrective actions and implementation strategies for achieving strategic goals; (c) development of the IC Report to be shared with the Hubs of knowledge; d) definition of the Improvement Strategy, corrective actions and priorities (1 = max, 2 = med, 3 = low); e) sharing a final report with all participants; f) online publication and diffusion of the resulting value creation models.

We are aware of the density of information just provided to the reader; thus, we deepen each step in the section that follows, together with associated findings. However, Fig. 1 represents the flowchart that synthetizes the steps.

4 Discussion of Findings

4.1 The Nominal Group Technique

As part of the project, a total of 54 ICFs have been submitted to the 25 SMEs' judgment. The list is the result of a mixture of ICF from: (a) academic and managerial literature, (b) data emerging from direct analysis on the field, and (c) documental analysis of reports. Thus, they have been previously differentiated per community. Each participant was contacted by email and had one week to select 27 out of the 54 ICF presented, and assign a unique score from 1 to 27, based on their relevance to the community (1 = min-27 = max). Once the contributions were received, one of the authors proceeded to weight and order all the answers, as shown in Tables 1 and 2.

4.2 The Focus Groups with the Governance

Since the process of value creation largely depends on how the IC components interact, the authors selected several VD, representing the categories with the highest frequency of occurrence in recent publications and company practices. These were subsequently reclassified into 15 macro-categories following the criterion of non-intersection, to make them as exclusive and exhaustive as possible and presented to the governance of the two communities for analysis. They are shown in Table 3.

Table 1 Ordered list of ICF of Community A

Problem solving	Team working
Competence growth	Emotional intelligence
Internal collaboration	Trust
Development of a shared technical culture within the group	On job training
Previous experience	Social net interaction
Motivation	Proactivity
Shared values	Influence and weight of the community
Information management	Sense of belonging to the company
Knowledge sharing procedures	Community building
Diversity of skills	Consistency with company strategy
Organizational identity	Customer relations
Best practice	Informal relations
Lateral thinking	Members' satisfaction
Flexibility	

Table 2 Ordered list of ICF of Community B

Motivation	Development of a shared technical culture within the group
Proactivity	Knowledge sharing procedures
Trend analysis	Shared values
Members' creativity	Influence and weight of the community
Management support	Sense of belonging to the company
Competence growth	Experience
Scouting and evaluation of technology	Professional seniority of members
Consistency with company strategy	Best practice
Diversity of skills	Members' satisfaction
Lateral thinking	Relations with universities and institutions
Team working	Social net interaction
Cross fertilization	Selection criteria for members
Customer relations	Empowerment
Internal collaboration	

Table 3 List of VDs

Knowledge skills	Customer relations
Management skills	Inter-firm relations
Creativity and innovation	Intra-firm relations
Work attitude	Supplier relations
Education and training	Financial relations
Intangible infrastructural assets	Institution relations
Information technology	Brand and image
Intellectual property	

As part of two focus groups, participants were asked to: (1) define the strategic objectives of their CoP; (2) identify own (and customized) Communities' proper VD for each category of HC, SC and RC; (3) grouping in homogeneous sets of ICFs; (4) develop a definition for each VD; and (5) elaborate the community IC creation model.

4.3   The Focus Groups with the Members

The focus groups with the SMEs were led by one of the authors with the purpose of obtaining the three evaluations of: (a) strategic impact; (b) cross-relationships; and (c) performance, on the different components of the first models identified by the governance. Therefore, using a bottom-up approach, the members had the opportunity to discuss the contents. For reasons of space, it is not possible to include all nine tables relating to the three abovementioned evaluations. Figures 2 and 3 compare the results of the SI-Performance and CR-Performance matrices of both the communities.

Each VD is positioned basing on the respective SI and Performance values. The positioning leads us to reflect on possible corrective actions for improvement strategies. The blue dots represent the VD of the HC, the pink ones the VD of the ST and the yellow ones the VD of the RC. Without entering the merits of the specifics, a profound difference between the two communities immediately catches the eye. Community A has strong critical points, which can also be found in the subsequent matrix. Overall, two of the VD hypothesized as fundamental by the governance, are not at all consistent with the perceived and the operations of the SMEs, who does not recognize either the definitions, nor the contents. In both cases we found a greater impact associated with drivers of relational capital, followed by those of HC.

These matrices represent the synthesis between CR and Performance. Their graphical representation allows recognizing critical and influential VD. The final objective is to understand which VD need investments, before establishing strategic actions. Even in this comparison, A presents greater criticalities, compared to B. Factors that

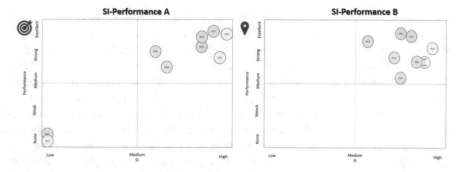

Fig. 2 SI-performance matrices. Own elaboration

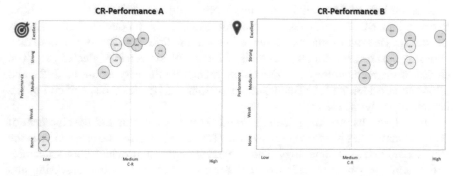

Fig. 3 CR-performance matrices. Own elaboration

previously seemed to have greater strategic impact, de facto seem have no direct influences on other VD. This provides a first important result for the discussion of implementation actions. It is important to highlight that for both Communities, the two most influential VD are: (a) Information Technology and (b) Creativity and Innovation. This result suggests the need to intervene in the strengthening both of the VD, in order to have a positive effect on all the other VDs.

4.4 Corrective Actions and the Improvement Strategy

The formulation of the final Improvement Strategies is synthetized in Table 4. Together, the results from previous sub-steps are reported. These are the result of two preliminary focus groups with the governance, subsequently discussed in the final workshop together with the SMEs.

5 Conclusions and Further Insights

Adopting a systemic-dynamic approach, this project aims to identify the factual contribution of each constituent element of IC and its direct and indirect influence on the creation of value of the online communities under investigation. To achieve this goal, it is necessary to identify the IC value drivers (VD), and the ICF that compose it. This methodological approach also allows implementing a strategic guide to their management, in relation to the strategic objectives of the online community. This research project is an integral part of a pilot and wider project for the evaluation of intellectual capital generated by two selected online CoPs of TIM S.p.A. Its purpose is to provide an integrated methodology to evaluate strategic IC components of online CoPs, grounded in theory to ensure relevance, and data-oriented (directly derived by involving relevant stakeholders) to provide validity and reliability. In reviewing and applying different measures to two online CoPs, we have not left any relevant dimensions behind. The creation of value is presented as an effect of the connections between HC, SC and RC. Their interaction can only be productive if their bonds are strong. This means that managing online communities involves much more than choosing the correct technological tools, if human dimension is neglected [41]. The choice of the methodology is, in fact, consistent with the very nature of CoPs, and allows to consider the relevant stakeholders opinions besides the specificity of the context of analysis [11, 13].

Overall, results provide guidelines to efficient management and development of online communities inside the organization. The first strength of the project lies in the use of a multi-step methodology. The integrated approach provides both academics and practitioners with an effective tool for proactively promoting, assessing and managing the creation of value of CoPs. Its application is not only able to value the stock and flow variables of IC, but also to analyze its factual contributions in order to

Table 4 Improvement strategies

B			SI	CR	Perf	Actions	Priority
VD 1	H C	Information Technology and Big Data	High	Med	High	New communication of the definition; follow-up within a year to evaluate changes and results	1
		Work Attitude	Med	High	High	New communication of selection criteria and re-evaluation of partici-pants based on contributions	1
VD 2		Creativity & Innovation	High	Med	High	No Actions	NA
		Creativity & Innovation	High	High	High	Feedback collection on: a) Industrial Plan and impact on new skills and jobs; b) 15 top trends in technology	1
VD 3		Knowledge Skills	High	Med	High	Training for best per-formers; engage the community to suggest self-candidatures for 2 Network Supporters; participation to events	1
		Knowledge Skills	High	High	High	Increasing the devel-opment of and transver-sal skills; reflection, exchange and reciprocal contamination on: a) innovation drivers; b) co-construction of train-ing courses for the corporate university (CU); c) testimonies in the training modules; d) insertion the CU as trainers; e) participation in valuable training for the most active SMEs	2
VD 4		Information Technology	Med	Med	High	Clarification of the importance of the tool	1
		Intellectual Property	High	Med	Med	No Actions	NA
VD 5	S C	Supplier Relations	NA	NA	NA	Elimination	NA
		Organiza-tional Cul-ture	High	High	High	Communication and dissemination of com-munity activities through videos, news on the intranet, etc.	2
VD 6		Intangible Assets	Med	Med	Med	Net learning; News intranet/ Smart Corner webinar on the recogni-tion of best practices developed by the com-munity	2
		Intangible Infrastruc-tural Assets	High	Med	Med	No Actions	NA
VD 7		Customer Relations	NA	NA	NA	Elimination	NA
		Customer Relations	High	High	High	No Actions	NA
VD 8	R C	Inter-Firm Relations	High	Med	High	New communication of the definition; strength-ening the role of the Network Supporter	3
		Inter-Firm Relations	High	High	High	Participation to work-shop events	2
VD 9		Manage-ment Rela-tions	High	Med	High	No Actions	NA
		Intra-Firm Relations	High	High	High	No Actions	NA

propose action plans for its effective functioning, furthermore contributing to theory by broadening the definition proposed by Brown and Duguid [4, 10, 11]. Accordingly, this multi-step approach has several implications for researchers in guiding future projects for IC analysis. This will allow for a further exploration in the assessment of the strategic impact to the value creation process of online communities [5]. We are aware of the limits related to the presentation of a first pilot project. However, the easy replicability of the steps does not make this a *taylor made* work. The analysis can produce results with a strong impact for the investigation and management of all the online communities within the organization.

References

1. Hislop, D. (2003). The complex relations between communities of practice and the implementation of technological innovations. *International Journal of Innovation Management, 7*(2), 163–188.
2. Hislop, D. (2009). *Knowledge management in organizations. A critical introduction* (2nd ed.). Oxford: Oxford University Press.
3. Wenger, E., Trayner, B., & de Laat, M. (2011). *Promoting and assessing value creation in communities and networks: A conceptual framework*. Rapport 18, Ruud de Moor Centrum.
4. Brown, J. S., & Duguid, P. (2001). Knowledge and organization: A social-practice perspective. *Organization Science, 12*(2), 198–213.
5. Adler, C., & Hecksher, B. (2007). *The firm as a collaborative community. Reconstructing trust in the knowledge economy*. Oxford University Press (2007).
6. Barnes, J. (1997). Methods of measuring community characteristics. *Child Psychology & Psychiatry Review, 2*(4), 163–169.
7. Alcaniz, L., Gomez-Bezares, F., & Roeslender, R. (2011). Theoretical perspectives on intellectual capital: A backward look and a proposal for going forward. *Accounting Forum, 35*(2), 104–117.
8. Purani, K., & Satish, N. (2007). Knowledge community: Integrating ICT into social development in developing economies. *AI & Society, 21*(3), 329–345.
9. Costa, R. V., & Ramos, A. P. (2015). Designing an AHP methodology to prioritize critical elements for product innovation: An intellectual capital perspective. *International Journal of Business Science and Applied Management, 10*(1), 15–34.
10. Grimaldi, M., Cricelli, L., & Rogo, F. (2013). A theoretical framework for assessing managing and indexing the intellectual capital. *Journal of Intellectual Capital, 14*(4), 501–521.
11. Grimaldi, M., Cricelli, L., & Rogo, F. (2012). A methodology to assess value creation in communities of innovation. *Journal of Intellectual Capital, 13*(3), 305–330.
12. Grimaldi, M., Cricelli, L., Rogo, F., & Iannarelli, A. (2012). Assessing and managing intellectual capital to support open innovation paradigm. *World Academy of Science, Engineering and Technology, 6*(1), 93–103.
13. Binder, M., & Clegg, B. (2007). Enterprise management: A new frontier for organisations. *International Journal of Production Economics, 106*(2), 409–430.
14. Zheng, S., Zhang, W., & Du, J. (2001). Knowledge-based dynamic capabilities and innovation in networked environments. *Journal of Knowledge Management, 15*(6), 1035–1051.
15. Seleim, A. A. S., & Khalil, O. E. M. (2011). Understanding the knowledge management intellectual capital relationship: A two-way analysis. *Journal of Intellectual Capital, 12*(4), 586–614.
16. Lin, C., Liu, A., Hsu, M. L., & Wu, J. C. (2008). Pursuing excellence in firm core knowledge through intelligent group decision support system. *Industrial Management & Data Systems, 108*(3), 277–296.

17. Spender, J. C. (1996). Making knowledge the basis of a dynamic theory of the firm. *Strategic Management Journal, 17,* 45–62.
18. Yao, C.-Y., Tsai, C-C., & Fang, Y.-C. (2014). Understanding social capital, team learning, members' e-loyalty and knowledge sharing in virtual communities. *Total Quality Management & Business Excellence, 26*(5,6), 619–631. https://doi.org/10.1080/14783363.2013.865918.
19. Seraj, M. (2012). We create, we connect, we respect, therefore we are: Intellectual, social, and cultural value in online communities. *Journal of Interactive Management, 26*(4), 209–222, https://doi.org/10.1016/j.intmar.2012.03.002.
20. Bagozzi, R. P., & Dholakia, U. M. (2002). Intentional social action in virtual communities. *Journal of Interactive Management, 16*(2), 2–21. https://doi.org/10.1002/dir.10006.
21. Bontis, N., Chua, W., & Richardson, S. (2000). Intellectual capital and the nature of business in Malaysia. *Journal of Intellectual Capital, 1*(1), 85–100.
22. Edvinsson, L., & Malone, M. S. (1997). *Intellectual capital: Realizing your company's true value by finding its hidden brainpower.* New York, NY: Harper Business.
23. Sveiby, K. E. (1997). *The new organizational wealth: Managing and measuring knowledge-based assets.* San Francisco, CA: Berrett-Koehler Publishers.
24. Kaplan, R. S., & Norton, D. P. (1992). The balanced scorecard—Measures that drives performance. *Harvard Business Review, 70*(1), 71–79.
25. Marr, B. (2008). *Impacting future value: How to manage your intellectual capital.* Canada: The Society of Management Accountants of Canada, the American Institute of Certified Public Accountants and the Chartered Institute of Management Accountants.
26. Roos, G., Bainbridge, A., & Jacobsen, K. (2001). Intellectual capital analysis as a strategic tool. *Strategy and Leadership, 29*(4), 21–26.
27. Lave, J., & Wenger, E. (1991). *Situated learning: Legitimate peripheral participation.* Cambridge: Cambridge University Press.
28. Amin, A., & Roberts, J. (2008). *Communities of practice? Varieties of situated learning.* EU Network of Excellence Dynamics of Institutions and Markets in Europe (DIME).
29. Lesser, E. L., & Prusak, L. (2000). Communities of practice, social capital and organizational knowledge. In E. L. Lesser, M. A. Fontaine, & J. A. Slusher (Eds.), *Knowledge and communities* (pp. 123–131). Boston: Butterworth Heinemann.
30. Marr, B., & Spender, J. C. (2004). Measuring knowledge assets–implications of the knowledge economy for performance measurement. *Measuring Business Excellence, 8*(1), 18–27.
31. Bontis, N. (2001). Assessing knowledge assets: A review of the models used to measure intellectual capital. *International Journal of Management Reviews, 3*(1), 41–60.
32. Brooking, A. (1996). *Intellectual capital: Core assets for the third millennium enterprise.* London: Thomson Business Press.
33. Roos, J., Roos, G., Dragonetti, N. C., & Edvinsson, L. (1997). *Intellectual capital: Navigating in the new business landcape.* London: Mcmillan.
34. Bontis, N. (1999). *Managing an organizational learning system by aligning stocks and flows of knowledge: An empirical examination of intellectual capital, knowledge management and business performance.* London, Canada: University of Western Ontario.
35. Sveiby, K. E. (1997). *The new organizational wealth: Managing and measuring knowledge-based assets.* San-Francisco: Barrett-Kohler.
36. Binder, M., & Clegg, B. (2007). Enterprise management: A new frontier for organisations. *International Journal of Production Economics, 106*(2), 409–430.
37. Delbecq, A. L., & van de Ven, A. H. (1971). A group process model for problem identification and program planning. *The Journal of Applied Behavioral Science, 7*(4), 466–492.
38. Randall, B. D. (2006). *Nominal group technique: A user's guide.* University of Wisconsin. http://instruction.bus.wisc.edu/obdemo/readings/ngt.html.
39. Andreou, A. N., Green, A., & Stankosky, M. (2007). A framework of intangible valuation areas and antecedents. *Journal of Intellectual Capital, 8*(1), 52–75.

40. Chu, P. Y., Lin, Y. L., Hsiung, H. H., & Liu, T. Y. (2006). Intellectual capital: An empirical study of ITRI. *Technological Forecasting and Social Change, 73,* 886–902.
41. Meret, C., Iannotta, M., & Gatti, M. (in print). The power of web 2.0 storytelling to overcome knowledge sharing barriers. In: Harfouche, A., & Cavallari, M. (Eds.) *ICT for a better life and a better world.* Berlin: Springer.

How Do We Learn Today and How Will We Learn in the Future Within Organizations? Digitally-Enhanced and Personalized Learning Win

Leonardo Caporarello, Beatrice Manzoni, Chiara Moscardo and Lilach Trabelsi

Abstract In a fast-changing environment, learning—the individual and organizational process of knowledge creation—can assist employees as well as their organizations in remaining competitive. Reflecting on what learning is and how it occurs should therefore be on the agenda of any organization. In this paper, we explore how learning is evolving, its meaning, and the most used learning models and learning methods, describing the present but also imagining the future. We collected data from 91 employees who answered an online quali-quantitative survey. Results show that digitally-enhanced models and methods are constantly growing in importance (more in terms of "expected" use than "desired" use), together with a need for more personalized learning.

Keywords Future of learning · Learning models · Learning methods · Digitally-enhanced learning · Personalized learning

1 Introduction

Over recent decades, the labor market has experienced economic, social, and cultural changes [19]. In such environments, learning—the individual and organizational process of knowledge creation—can assist employees, as well as their organizations, in adapting to changing demands, keeping skills updated, managing organizational

L. Caporarello (✉) · B. Manzoni
SDA Bocconi School of Management, Bocconi University, Milan, Italy
e-mail: leonardo.caporarello@unibocconi.it

B. Manzoni
e-mail: beatrice.manzoni@unibocconi.it

C. Moscardo · L. Trabelsi
Bocconi University, Milan, Italy
e-mail: chiara.moscardo@unibocconi.it

L. Trabelsi
e-mail: lilach.trabelsi@unibocconi.it

© Springer Nature Switzerland AG 2020
A. Lazazzara et al. (eds.), *Exploring Digital Ecosystems*,
Lecture Notes in Information Systems and Organisation 33,
https://doi.org/10.1007/978-3-030-23665-6_10

agendas, and handling uncertainty [7, 8, 11, 29]. For firms, 'learning and development' is also one of the top drivers of employee attraction and retention [35]. Hence, for firms, reflecting on what learning is and how we learn today, as well as anticipating what learning will be like in the future, is critical for sustaining both a short- and a long-term competitive advantage.

Research on learning is constantly growing [9]. One of the most debated topics refers to how we learn today and how we have learnt so far in terms of models and methods. However, we still know little about what learning will look like in the future. In this article, we take on the challenge of systematizing the present and imagining the future in terms of the meaning of learning and the different learning models and methods. In particular, using employee surveys, we seek to answer the following questions: (i) what does learning look like today?, (ii) what will learning look like in the future?, and (iii) what are the differences, if any, between the way in which employees learn today and the way in which they expect to learn in the future?.

In this paper, in addition to analyzing responses to open-ended questions about learning today and in the future, we compare the past and expected use of face-to-face, online, and blended learning models, and a variety of learning methods. The various models and methods represent both digital and non-digital learning means, and have different possible degrees of interaction and personalization.

The article is organized as follows. In the next section, we review the main research streams in the literature on learning within organizations, focusing on the employees' experience. Then we present our research methods and discuss results comparing current trends and future trends. We conclude with implications for research and practice.

2   Research on Learning Within Organizations: "Why", "Who", and "How"

Existing research approaches learning within organizations using different lenses of analysis. We have research about "why" we learn or should learn, looking at the positive returns from learning investments; "who" learns, looking at the target of learning and development initiatives; and "how" we learn in terms of models, modes, and methods.

First, regarding the "why", we know that learning is beneficial at the individual as well as at the organizational level [1, 28]. At the organizational level, learning facilitates continuous improvement [23], product and service enhancement [20], knowledge sharing [12], and ultimately helps generate increased performance and profits [25]. At the individual level, learning helps increase job performance [27], develop skills [18], and enhance innovation [6]. It also drives satisfaction [27] and contributes to turnover and absenteeism reduction [14].

Secondly, regarding the "who", we know that learning can take place at the individual or team level [3], but also at the organizational one, with discussions around "organizational learning" [e.g. 5] and the "learning organization" [e.g. 36] taking place.

Finally, regarding "how" employees learn, we have recently seen an increasing variety of conceptualizations and interpretations of learning, reflecting scholarly research interests and what employees use within their organizations. According to a recent comprehensive content review, learning can be categorized into models, modes, and methods [9].

Choosing a learning model implies a choice between online, blended, and traditional learning [e.g. 2]. Learning modes may be, for example, synchronous versus asynchronous [37], individual versus team-based [22], active versus passive [21], personalized versus standardized [30], include face-to-face versus distance learning [4, 24], and be formal versus informal [19, 29]. Learning methods can be, for example, lecture-based [34], case-based [16], game-based [33], problem-based [17], project-based [10], and cooperative [15].

Recently, the research stream focusing on how learning occurs has been amongst the most debated ones, as organizations are increasingly reflecting on improving the effectiveness of employees' learning experience both in terms of returns at the individual level and in terms of impact on the business [31].

However, existing research has a predominant focus on the past (how did learning evolve over the years?) and on the present (how does learning occur today?). Despite the need for further investigation and the existence of some more practice-oriented contributions [e.g. 26, 32], we have not yet put enough effort into anticipating the future and forecasting future learning trends in academic research.

3 Methods

This study is part of a broader research project on how we learn today and how we will learn within organizations in the future. Using an online survey, we asked open-ended and closed questions about employees' learning experience with different learning models and methods, their perception of organizational learning mechanisms, and their expectations for the future of learning.

For the purposes of this study, we used three open-ended questions about what learning looks like. We collected a sample of 91 employee responses for the first question ("*What do you think learning looks like today?*"), 87 for the second one ("*What do you think learning will look like in 2025?*"), and 83 for the third one ("*How would you like learning to be in 2025?*"). We also used closed questions to ask about how much respondents use different learning models (72 responses collected) and methods (66 responses collected) today versus how much they expect to use them in the future.

The analysis of the open-ended responses followed Gioia et al.'s [13] coding process. The initial coding, resulting in first-order terms, was open and more informant-centric, while the second-order themes were more researcher-centered and suggest concepts able to describe and explain phenomena (see Table 1). Overall, we assigned

487 codes to words/short pieces of sentences: 208 to the 91 responses to the first question, 136 to the 87 responses to the second question, and 143 to the 83 responses to the third question. As an example of the coding we used, the quotation "*We will learn more and more with gamified experiences outside the organizations. These games will however need to be transferred within the organizations afterwards. E-learning and interactive platforms will replace face-to-face learning.*" was assigned the codes multimedia learning, e-learning, and gaming, resulting in 'digitally-enhanced learning' as a second-order coding.

When analyzing the data for the closed questions regarding the three learning models and the various learning methods, we used only the data from fully-completed surveys (54 in total). We divided and aggregated respondents' answers according to various meaningful cut-off points to create different respondent categories. For example, we have created three categories for the usage intensity (i.e. low, medium, high) of the learning models and methods. We compared between the percentages of responses in the various categories pertaining to questions about past usage with those obtained for the questions about future usage.

The sample's respondents are predominantly Italian (90% of the sample), and work in Italy (also 90% of the sample). In terms of age and work experience, around 60% of respondents are 35 years old or younger and have at the most 10 years of experience, while 40% of respondents are more than 35 years old and have more than 10 years of work experience. Most of the responses were obtained from female employees (65% of the sample). Finally, around 40% of respondents work for SMEs, while around 60% of respondents work for large firms (i.e. firms with more than 250 employees).

4 Results

4.1 The Meaning of Learning: Present Versus Future

Based on the coding of the open-ended answers, learning emerges as a complex and multifaceted concept that cannot be coded in just one single way. We coded each answer in multiple ways, with an average of 2.3 codes per answer. This is because learning often requires a mix of models and methods. For example, respondents often stress the need to combine learning on the job with formally-designed class-based training or to personalize learning using digital tools.

Figure 1 and Table 2 compare the distribution of second-order concepts that emerged from responses given to the three open-ended questions. What we see is that, while learning today is predominantly done "on the job", with a strong emphasis on the individual experience in making learning happen, in the future learning will take place much more "in class", and will be more digitally-enhanced. The process of "in class" learning refers to the concept of direct learning, or in other words to the possibility of attending a learning program that is managed and led by an edu-

Table 1 Data structure of the open-ended responses about what learning looks like

First-order concepts	Second-order concepts	Aggregate dimensions
Training on the job Learning by doing Learning is a day-to-day work Leveraging on personal experience Learning through job rotation assignments Learning thanks to cross functional/special projects	Individual learning, experience- based	Learning "on the job" (indirect learning)
Mentoring Feedback from boss and colleagues Cross-generational exchange of experiences Sharing/networking among peers Social learning	Social learning, experience-based	
Custom programs Training courses with external providers/trainers Training courses with internal faculty Face-to-face class	Class-based learning	Learning "in class" (direct learning)
One-on-one learning Open and easily accessible learning Personalized learning Continuous learning/"as you go" Modular and flexible learning	Personalized learning	
E-learning Online learning Gaming Blended learning Digital learning Mobile learning Multimedia learning Artificial Intelligence	Digitally-enhanced learning	

cational institution. The digital presence is something that employees expect but do not really desire. In terms of aspirations, personalized learning is in fact as important as digitally-enhanced learning and is given greater importance than it is being given today.

Specifically, looking at the present ("*What do you think learning looks like today?*"), respondents focus in particular on learning on the job, which counts for 67% of total codes assigned, and stress the relevance of individual day-to-day work

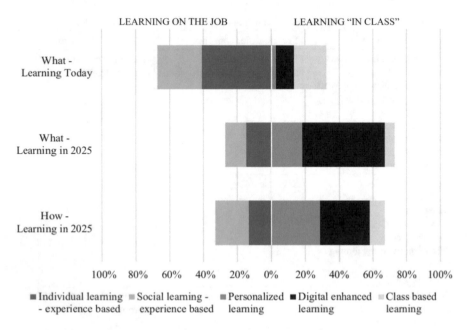

Fig. 1 Frequency of second-order concepts in the three open-ended questions

Table 2 Percentages of the frequency of second-order concepts in three open-ended questions

	Learning "on the job"		Learning "in class"		
	Individual learning, experience-based (%)	Social learning, experience-based (%)	Personalized learning (%)	Digitally-enhanced learning (%)	Class-based learning (%)
What do you think learning looks like today?	41	26	3	11	19
What do you think learning will look like in 2025?	15	13	18	49	6
How would you like learning to be in 2025?	13	20	29	29	9

Table 3 Exemplary quotes—*"What do you think learning looks like today?"*

Second-order concepts	Exemplary quotes (# of respondent)
Individual learning, experience-based	"On the job mainly, being involved in stimulating projects and thanks to the exchange of ideas with competent people." (#16) "There is not much time for trainings. You need to learn fast. You need to face the problem and "investigate" for a solution." (#26) "We learn from managing projects in a responsible way, with the proper delegation and trust." (#42)
Social learning, experience-based	"A boss or a colleague who is also mentoring/coaching you is key. Having a community or a network to share ideas is also important, together with getting continuous stimuli from the organization." (#79) "Learning is mainly possible thanks to knowledge sharing among peers. This knowledge sharing can also be structured and institutionalized." (#84) "If you are lucky, you learn from your boss, but also from training courses, networking, cross-functional groups, and asking questions, being curious and open to cross-fertilization even outside the organization." (#54)
Class-based learning	"I learn thanks to the other functions, but also joining training courses, conferences, and reading specialized magazines." (#7) "Today we learn with short and frequent trainings, which are organized so that they provide a great variety of topics." (#65) "Lectures, e-learning, and paper-based training materials." (#85)
Personalized learning	"One-on-one training course." (#4)
Digitally-enhanced learning	"Global connectivity and new social media are crucial drivers which are reshaping the working environment, and how people learn and develop the skills to work in the future." (#39) "E-learning mainly, which is poorly personalized based on individual needs." (#57) "Learning has become more digital and multidisciplinary." (#80)

in creating learning opportunities (see Table 3 for exemplary quotes). Both the personal experience (41%) and the experience of colleagues within the organization (26%) matter. Respondents mention traditional training on the job, but also job rotation assignments and special cross-functional projects. They also say that they learn significantly from internal networking and knowledge-sharing with peers, which can be formally or informally organized.

When asked about learning tomorrow (i.e. in 2025), respondents were asked two separate questions. The first one was *"What do you think learning will look like in*

2025?" aimed at exploring the expected trends. The second one, *"How would you like learning to be in 2025?"*, aimed at intercepting respondents' needs or aspirations with the intention of understanding whether employees believe that learning is going in the desired direction or not.

In both cases, we see a shift in importance from learning on the job to learning in class. The second-order concept personalized learning, which was almost not present in the answers to the question about learning today (it counted for only 3% of the codes), emerged as very important. It counts for 18% of the codes in the answers to the question about the expected future, and for 29% of the codes in the answers to the question about the desired future.

With regard to the question *"What do you think learning will look like in 2025?"* (see Table 4 for exemplary quotes) we notice that experience-based learning still makes up 28% of the codes (down from 67%), and that digitally-enhanced learning increases to make up 49% of the codes (up from 11%).

With regard to the second question about the future (*"How would you like learning to be in 2025?"*), personalized learning together with digitally-enhanced learning are the two equally most important elements (each accounting for 29% of the codes). We also see a focus on mixed learning, combining learning-by-doing and formal training (see Table 5 for exemplary quotes).

4.2   Learning Models: Present Versus Future

When comparing responses (present vs. future) regarding the three learning models (face-to-face, online learning, and blended learning), interesting insights emerge. Figure 2 shows whether respondents say that they would like to increase or decrease their low/medium/high use of each learning model in the future compared to the present.

We observe that respondents wish to learn less using the face-to-face model, and that they wish to learn more using blended learning. Responses for the use of online learning are similar in relation to the present and to the future. These observations seem coherent with the idea that effective learning occurs when we combine multiple learning models. It is in the nature of blended learning to combine online and face-to-face experiences.

In the past 12 months, the face-to-face learning model has been used in at least 50% of the learning experiences of 68% of the respondents, while only 40% of the respondents wish for this to be the case in the future. With regard to online learning, we see a moderate increase from 19 to 28% of respondents saying that they have used/will use this learning model in the future at least 50% of the time. The use of blended learning is expected to increase. Whereas only 4% of respondents said that blended learning has been used in at least 50% of their learning experiences in the past year, 26% of respondents said that they would like this model to be used in at least 50% of their learning experiences in the future.

Table 4 Exemplary quotes—*"What do you think learning will look like in 2025?"*

Second-order concepts	Exemplary quotes (# of respondent)
Individual learning, experience-based	"Training on the job will remain, while using more technology for training courses." (#16) "We will learn from day-to-day experience with a short/medium-term perspective." (#40) "We will increasingly use new methods, games, outdoor experiences, to be linked with the organizational life." (#17)
Social learning, experience-based	"Flat communities with no hierarchy, openness to communication, sharing of best practices." (#27) "We will learn by having useful information available and interacting with colleagues who are involved in the organizational processes." (#18) "Platforms allowing for knowledge-sharing will become more and more diffused. [...] Professional communities will have clearer goals and will be less self-referential." (#75)
Class-based learning	"Meeting with other people in person, in class, is as important as the taught content, if not even more important." (#34) "A face-to-face relation with the others is key especially for developing soft skills. I am not necessarily thinking about class-based training. I mean the ability to involve people and make people enthusiastic about learning, thanks to gamified experiences, outdoor activities, digitalization." (#58)
Personalized learning	"The work will be even more dynamic. Therefore, learning processes will require constant self-paced learning." (#11) "I think it will definitely be a faster process, due to the availability of information and ways of sharing it, and a "by doing" process." (#37) "Learning will become more fluid, ongoing, and pervasive. Platforms will provide microlearning contents on specific business situations which are relevant for and suggested by the professional communities." (#30)
Digitally-enhanced learning	"More technology-driven, boundaries between artificial intelligence and human intelligence will be more blurred, interacting with technologies will be almost as rewarding and educational as interacting with people." (#5) "Webinar and online courses." (#6) "Face-to-face learning will be replaced by e-learning or interactive platforms." (#17) "Basically, everyone will learn by picking up their phone. Not sure it's a good thing—quite the opposite, in fact—but everything seems to go through one's iPhone nowadays." (#23)

Table 5 Exemplary quotes—*"How would you like learning to be in 2025?"*

Second-order concepts	Exemplary quotes (# of respondent)
Individual learning, experience-based	"Learning by doing." (#12) "Attending very short face to face seminars. Learning by doing in a safe virtual environment." (#41)
Social learning, experience-based	"We need the human interaction. We need mentors to observe and replicate behaviors. This is more important than any theory." (#51) "We are evolving towards professional networking, either face-to-face or virtual, to share best practices." (#39)
Class-based learning	"I would like to keep the idea of the class group. We learn the most from other people. Platforms make us lose this interaction." (#16) "I hope that learning will occur thanks to physical interaction among professionals." (#34) "I would like that, notwithstanding the technological evolution and the organizational change, we keep using face-to-face interactions." (#77)
Personalized learning	"We will be able to learn from anywhere thanks to e-learning, with personalized courses which will be targeted based on individual needs. They will be less standardized, and more tailor-made." (#4) "Participants will be able to pick their buddies/trainers on online apps devoted to specific topics. They will be able to interact and acquire key information in a short time span. Interaction should occur on a one-on-one basis through video calls. They will be offered the opportunity to fully personalize their learning." (#29) "More focus on the individual and on individual skills, more engaging and interactive." (#22) "Easy, fast, and continuous." (#44)
Digitally-enhanced learning	"New technologies will be able to identify individual needs even remotely. Yet I don't want to lose the personal human contact. People make the difference in teaching." (#2) "Technology-driven for the standard content, allowing more meaningful and rich human interactions for non-standard content." (#5) "Online training sessions, both function-specific and cross-functional, not only for the onboarding but for the entire time spent in a company. Learning is ongoing." (#40)

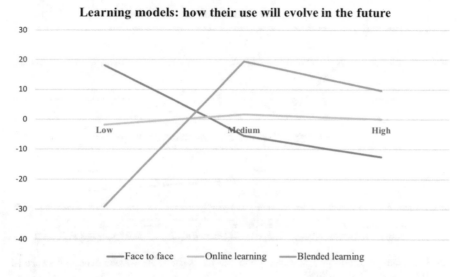

Fig. 2 Learning models: present versus future (low use is below 30%, medium use is between 30 and 70%, high use is above 70%)

When we split the sample according to age (respondents who are 35 years old or younger vs. those who are more than 35 years old), and firm size (respondents working for SMEs vs. those working for large firms), results remain qualitatively similar. We see that, generally, respondents are interested in reducing the time spent learning using the face-to-face model, with slightly stronger interest from respondents who work for SMEs versus those who work for large firms. With reference to online learning, we see that older respondents and those from large firms are relatively more interested than younger respondents and those from smaller firms in using more online learning in the future. All groups are similarly interested in more blended learning.

4.3 Learning Methods: Present Versus Future

Looking at the responses relating to the various learning methods (see Fig. 3), we observe that, overall, respondents wish to learn less using instructor-led lectures, even if this method has often been the most used one in the past. Instead, they want to learn more using, in particular, guest speakers and interactive class activities. This is a trend that is aligned with the need for more personalized and hands-on experiences, as well as digitally-enhanced ones.

In particular, 66% of respondents said that learning using instructor-led lectures has represented at least 20% of their learning experiences in the past year, versus 54.5% of respondents who would like this to be the case in the future. On the contrary,

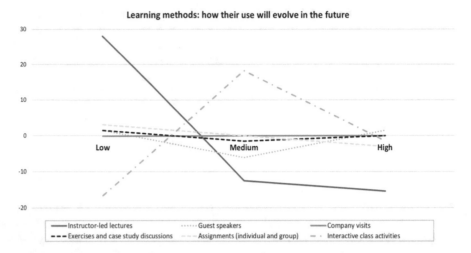

Fig. 3 Learning methods: present versus future (low use is below 30%, medium use is between 30 and 70%, high use is above 70%)

36% of respondents said that learning using guest speakers has represented at least 20% of their learning experiences in the past year, versus 47% of respondents who would like this to be the case in the future. A similar trend is recognizable for company visits (from 20 to 44%), exercises and case discussions (from 23 to 51.5%), and interactive class activities (from 20 to 48.5%). Responses concerning the use of assignments remain stable (30%).

Again, when we split the sample according to age (respondents who are 35 years old or younger vs. those who are over 35 years old), and firm size (respondents working for SMEs vs. those working for large firms), results remain qualitatively similar. Some interesting differences between the groups are the following: (i) respondents from large firms feel more strongly about a future reduction in instructor-led lectures than those from SMEs, (ii) there is an especially strong interest from SME respondents to attend more guest lectures in the future, (iii) younger respondents are more interested than older respondents in less instructor-led lectures, more guest lectures, company visits, and interactive means, whereas older respondents are more keen on exercises and case studies.

5 Conclusions

With this paper, we aim to provide both a research-oriented contribution and a practice-oriented one to the field of learning within organizations.

From a research perspective, we collected the points of view of 91 employees to get a snapshot of how they have been learning recently, and their perceptions of the future of learning. Employees have noticed that, currently, learning happens mainly on the job, while in the future they would like to benefit more from occasions of formal educational paths where learning is organized and led by educational institutions. Moreover, learning in the future is expected to be supported, and not substituted, by digital technologies. Employees have to deal with a continuous dynamic environment, so it will be even more important for them to access learning programs that are characterized by a high level of personalization, and that do not include much self-paced study. Employees may not be experts in designing the learning process that is most effective for their goals, so being guided in their learning journey will be a success factor in future learning processes.

From a practice perspective, we provide organizations, HR, and instructors with insights about what employees expect and prefer, in particular in terms of learning models and methods.

Future research could further explore the preferences for "being effective learners in the future", including the generational perspective of both learners and instructors. Another direction for research is looking at how academic institutions are preparing themselves to respond to changing learning demands in order to be able to meet and anticipate organizational needs.

References

1. Aguinis, H., & Kraiger, K. (2009). Benefits of training and development for individuals and teams, organizations, and society. *Annual Review of Psychology, 60,* 451–474.
2. Al-Qahtani, A. A., & Higgins, S. E. (2013). Effects of traditional, blended and e-learning on students' achievement in higher education. *Journal of Computer Assisted Learning, 29,* 220–234.
3. Arbaugh, J. B., & Benbunan-Finch, R. (2006). An investigation of epistemological and social dimensions of teaching in online learning environments. *Academy of Management Learning & Education, 5*(4), 435–447.
4. Artino, A. R. (2010). Online or face-to-face learning? Exploring the personal factors that predict students' choice of instructional format. *The Internet and Higher Education, 13,* 272–276.
5. Bapuji, H., & Crossan, M. (2004). From questions to answers: Reviewing organizational learning research. *Management Learning, 35,* 397–417.
6. Barber, J. (2004). Skill upgrading within informal training: Lessons from the Indian auto mechanic. *International Journal of Training and Development, 8,* 128–139.
7. Becker, W. S., & Burke, M. J. (2014). Instructional staff rides for management learning and education. *Academy of Management Learning & Education, 13*(4), 510–524.
8. Bell, B. S., & Kozlowski, S. W. (2008). Active learning: Effects of core training design elements on self-regulatory processes, learning, and adaptability. *Journal of Applied Psychology, 93*(2), 296–316.
9. Caporarello, L., Giovanazzi, A., & Manzoni, B. (2017). Reimagine E-learning: A proposal for a 21st learning framework. *EAI Endorsed Transactions on e-Learning, 4*(16), 1–9.
10. DeFillippi, R. J. (2001). Introduction: Project-based learning, reflective practices and learning. *Management Learning, 32,* 5–10.
11. Dragoni, L., Tesluk, P. E., Russell, J. E., & Oh, I. S. (2009). Understanding managerial development: Integrating developmental assignments, learning orientation, and access to developmental opportunities in predicting managerial competencies. *Academy of Management Journal, 52*(4), 731–743.

12. Gerpott, F. H., Lehmann-Willenbrock, N., & Voelpel, S. C. (2017). A phase model of intergenerational learning in organizations. *Academy of Management Learning & Education, 16*(2), 193–216.
13. Gioia, D. A., Corley, K. G., & Hamilton, A. L. (2013). Seeking qualitative rigor in inductive research notes on the Gioia methodology. *Organizational Research Methods, 16*(1), 15–31.
14. Islam, T., ur Rehman Khan, S., Bahru, J., Ahmad, U. Bahru, J., et al. (2013). Organizational learning culture and leader-member exchange quality. The way to enhance organizational commitment and reduce turnover intentions. *The Learning Organization, 20*(4/5), 322–337.
15. Johnson, D. W., Johnson, R. T., & Stanne, M. B. (2000). *Cooperative learning methods: A meta-analysis*. Minneapolis: University of Minnesota.
16. Kolodner, J. L., Camp, P. L., Crismond, D., Fasse, B., Gray, J., Holbrook, J., et al. (2003). Problem-based learning meets case-based reasoning in the middle-school science classroom: Putting learning by design™ into practice. *The Journal of the Learning Sciences, 12*(4), 495–547.
17. Kong, L. N., Qin, B., Zhou, Y. Q., Mou, S. Y., & Gao, H. M. (2014). The effectiveness of problem-based learning on development of nursing students' critical thinking: A systematic review and meta-analysis. *International Journal of Nursing Studies, 51,* 458–469.
18. London, M., & Hall, M.J. (2011). Unlocking the value of Web 2.0 technologies for training and development: The shift from instructor-controlled, adaptive learning to learner-driven, generative learning. *Human Resource Management, 50*(6), 757–775.
19. Manuti, A., Pastore, S., Scardigno, A. F., Giancaspro, M. L., & Morciano, D. (2015). Formal and informal learning in the workplace: A research review. *International Journal of Training and Development, 19*(1), 1–17.
20. Matthing, J., Sandén, B., & Edvardsson, B. (2004). New service development: Learning from and with customers. *International Journal of Service Industry Management, 15*(5), 479–498.
21. Michael, J. (2006). Where's the evidence that active learning works? *Advances in Physiology Education, 30,* 159–167.
22. Michaelsen, L. K., & Sweet, M. (2008). The essential elements of team-based learning. *New Directions for Teaching and Learning, 116,* 7–27.
23. Mitki, Y., Shani, A. B., & Meiri, Z. (1997). Organizational learning mechanisms and continuous improvement: A longitudinal study. *Journal of Organizational Change Management, 10*(5), 426–446.
24. Moore, M. G., & Kearsley, G. (2011). Distance education: A systems view of online learning. *Cengage Learning.*
25. Perez Lopez, S., Montes Peon, J. M., & Vazquez Ordas, C. J. (2007). Human resource practices, organizational learning and business performance. *Human Resource Development International, 8*(2), 147–164.
26. Puri, I. K. (2018). Why learning from experience is the educational wave of the future. *The Conversation.* Online at http://theconversation.com/why-learning-from-experience-is-the-educational-wave-of-the-future-92399. Retrieved June 1, 2018.
27. Rose, R. C., Kumar, N., & Pak, O. G. (2009). The effect of organizational learning on organizational commitment, job satisfaction and work performance. *Journal of Applied Business Research, 25*(6), 55–65.
28. Sessa V. I., & London M. (2015). *Continuous learning in organizations*. Psychology Press. Taylor & Francis Group.
29. Sinha, A. (2012). The learning continuum: Formal and informal learning experiences–enabling learning and creation of new knowledge in an organization. *International Journal of Advanced Corporate Learning, 5*(2), 10–14.
30. Song, Y., Wong, L. H., & Looi, C. K. (2012). Fostering personalized learning in science inquiry supported by mobile technologies. *Educational Technology Research and Development, 60,* 679–701.
31. Spar, B., & Dye, C. (2018). Workplace learning report. *LinkedIn Learning.*
32. The Open University: Trends in Learning Report 2017. (2017). Online at http://www.open.ac.uk/business/apprenticeships/blog/trends-learning-report-2017. Retrieved June 1, 2018.

33. Tobias, S., Fletcher, J. D., & Wind, A. P. (2014). Game-based learning. In *Handbook of Research on Educational Communications and Technology* (pp. 485–503). Heidelberg: Springer.
34. Wijnia, L., Loyens, S. M., & Derous, E. (2011). Investigating effects of problem-based versus lecture-based learning environments on student motivation. *Contemporary Educational Psychology, 36*(2), 101–113.
35. Willis Towers Watson's 2017 Global Talent Management and Rewards, and Global Workforce Studies. (2017).
36. Yeo, R. K. (2005). Revisiting the roots of learning organization: A synthesis of the learning organization literature. *The Learning Organization, 12*(4), 368–382.
37. Young, T. P., Bailey, C. J., Guptill, M., Thorp, A. W., & Thomas, T. L. (2014). The flipped classroom: A modality for mixed asynchronous and synchronous learning in a residency program. *Western Journal of Emergency Medicine, 15*(7), 938–944.

Understanding the Relationship Between Intellectual Capital and Organizational Performance: The Role of e-HRM and Performance Pay

Alessandra Lazazzara, Edoardo Della Torre and Raoul C. D. Nacamulli

Abstract While the bulk of the literature on intellectual capital focuses on its role as a source of competitive advantage, fewer studies have analyzed the mechanisms through which human, social and organizational capital translate into high organizational performance. Drawing on the resource-based view and intellectual capital research, this paper aims to analyze how the adoption of e-HRM tools and performance pay affects the contribution of intellectual capital to organizational performance. The analysis performed on a sample of 168 Italian large organizations from the CRANET survey (2015) shows that, while intellectual capital is positively related to organizational performance, such relationship is weakened in presence of high levels of e-HRM. Moreover, in contexts of high intellectual capital, the combined presence of high level of performance pay and e-HRM nullifies the positive impact of intellectual capital on performance, whereas in contexts of low intellectual capital they lead to higher performance. Implications of these findings for theory and practice are discussed.

Keywords Intellectual capital · e-HRM · Performance pay · Organizational performance · Resource-based view · Italy

A. Lazazzara (✉)
Department of Social and Political Sciences, University of Milan, Milan, Italy
e-mail: alessandra.lazazzara@unimi.it

E. D. Torre
Department of Management, Economics and Quantitative Methods,
University of Bergamo, Bergamo, Italy
e-mail: edoardo.dellatorre@unibg.it

R. C. D. Nacamulli
Department of Educational Human Sciences, University of Milano-Bicocca, Milan, Italy
e-mail: raoul.nacamulli@unimib.it

© Springer Nature Switzerland AG 2020   151
A. Lazazzara et al. (eds.), *Exploring Digital Ecosystems*,
Lecture Notes in Information Systems and Organisation 33,
https://doi.org/10.1007/978-3-030-23665-6_11

1 Introduction

In the current knowledge-based economy intellectual capital represents one of the main sources for companies success [26]. It can be defined as "the sum of all knowledge firms utilized for competitive advantage" [26, p. 451] and has been categorized into three components: (a) human capital refers to knowledge, skills, and capabilities of individual employees; (b) social capital involves the knowledge embedded relationships and interactions among individuals; (c) organizational capital is the institutionalized knowledge stored in databases, manuals, culture, systems, structures, and processes. Adopting a resource-based perspective [1, 18], it can be argued that the three dimensions of intellectual capital (i.e., human, social and organizational capital) are often location-specific, involve tacit learning, and are socially complex and causally ambiguous [4, 20, 27]. The influence of intellectual capital on firms' outcomes has been widely investigated by existing literature and, although some contrasting findings emerged, it can be generally maintained that intellectual capital has a positive relationship with firms' outcomes [6, 29].

While the bulk of the literature on intellectual capital focuses on its role as a source of competitive advantage, fewer studies have analyzed the mechanisms through which human, social and organizational capital translate into high organizational performance. In this paper, we contribute to this stream of the literature by analyzing how electronic-HRM (e-HRM) and performance-pay affect the relationship between intellectual capital and firm performance. Indeed, the adoption of "integration mechanisms and contents between HRM and IT, aimed at creating value for targeted employees and managers" [2, p. 507] is one of the most significant changes that has characterized the HR function in the last decade. Similarly, performance-related pay has been often indicated as one of the main tools that HR managers can adopt in order to increase employees motivation and performance. Thus, a better understanding of how these practices (e-HRM and performance-pay) impact on the intellectual capital of a firm is of paramount importance for advancing the HRM field and depicting relevant implications for HR professionals.

Drawing on the resource-based view and intellectual capital research, this paper aims to analyze how the adoption of e-HRM tools and performance pay affect the contribution of intellectual capital to organizational performance. The analysis is based on 168 Italian organizations and the data come from the CRANET survey (2015). In the next section, the theoretical approach is presented and the hypotheses are developed. Then we present the empirical analysis and the results. We conclude by discussing the contribution and implications of the main findings of the study.

2 Theoretical Framework and Hypotheses

2.1 Intellectual Capital and Organizational Performance in the RBV Perspective

Over the last years, many researchers have applied the resource-based view (RBV) to identify the kind of resources most likely to influence competitive advantage and performance. In so doing, many have converged on companies' intellectual capital as one of the most universally valuable resources (see [6, 23]).

According to the RBV, firms are bundles of tangible and intangible resources and capabilities which can create a competitive advantage [1]. Indeed, RBV assumes that the primary driver of the firm's durable competitive advantage and economic performance is a collection of resources which are valuable, rare, inimitable and organized (VRIO; [1]). According to the VRIO framework resources are valuable when are a significant source of profitability; should be rare in the sense that there is a scarcity of such resources; those resources should be hard to imitate and organizations should be fully organized in order to effectively exploit them. Therefore, this perspective "explains an important route to achieving competitive advantage and corporate success in a modern economic system in which firms rely far less on homogenous factors of production such as labor and capital and much more on differentiated resources such as human expertise, organizational routines, reputation, and complex linkages with customers and suppliers" [3].

More specifically, the RBV relies on two main assumptions which derive from the pioneering work of Penrose [18]: resource heterogeneity and resource immobility. Resource heterogeneity refers to the idea that performance differences may be related to the heterogeneous distribution of valuable resources—such as intellectual capital—among firms. The value of such resources increases as they are bundled together to create idiosyncratic combinations which are able to solve firm-specific problems that are peculiar of the firm's unique competitive context [18, 23]. Moreover, when such idiosyncratic combinations are so complex that others cannot easily duplicate or substitute for, those companies will outperform competitors lacking such resources [1, 19].

Theoretically, a distinct branch of the RBV—the intellectual-based view—has argued that intangible assets that firms acquire, develop and accumulate over time such as knowledge, skills, and behaviors of employees may generate outperforming results and thus create value for the company [22]. Therefore, intellectual capital may be seen as an intangible asset which has the potential to create value. However, such result is related to the company's capability to implement specific sets of practices which leverage intellectual capital and allow to achieve a better incremental and radical innovative performance [7, 8, 26].

2.2   The Moderating Role of e-HRM and Performance Pay

The literature on e-HRM usage in organizations has been growing rapidly together with a specific interest in advantages and opportunities that such systems are expected to confer on organizations [16]. However, research looking at weather e-HRM is related to specific strategic outcomes such as organizational performance is lacking [11] and empirical evidence for the actual attainment of expected benefits is scarce [17].

According to Strohmeier [25], the resource-based view may be applied as theoretical foundation explaining the relationship between e-HRM and its consequences. In this perspective, e-HRM can be seen as a means to obtain human resources which are valuable, rare, difficult to imitate and non-substitutable [1]. Moreover, e-HRM may contribute to the effective management and development of these valuable resources.

Therefore, organizations characterized by a high level of intellectual capital may gain higher performance by successfully applying e-HRM because it allows a better exploiting of human resources with such strategic characteristics. It follows that the outcome of intellectual capital depends on the extent to which IT is viewed as useful and strategic by the organization. Youndt and Snell [28] predict that (and found support for) a positive relationship between the adoption of an accessible, user-friendly and integrated information technology HR configuration and organizational capital. In this view, hard IT infrastructures and soft HR management systems both help organizations to institutionalize tacit knowledge. Thus we expect that e-HRM positively interact with intellectual capital in influencing organizational performance. In formal terms, we predict that:

H1: The adoption of an e-HRM system moderates the positive relationship between intellectual capital and organizational performance, so that the relationship is stronger at higher level of e-HRM system adoption compared to lower.

Similarly to e-HRM, an increasing number of organizations, predominantly in the private sector, embrace pay schemes linking pay to the employee or firm performance [5]. Organizations can implement three distinct types of pay for performance (PRP), namely individual-based performance pay, group (collective)-based performance pay and/or company-based performance pay (profit sharing and stock options) [12]. These three forms of pay may have different logics and effects [14] and the debate about the effectiveness of PRP programs is not yet resolved. However, it is generally argued that PRP is beneficial to employee performance [9], and that variable (bonus) pay is more effective in influencing future employee performance than permanent (merit pay) [15]. At the organizational level, these systems would likely to ensure higher skill levels in the workforce by attracting employees who had already achieved higher performance levels from outside and by retaining the best performers within [10]. These incentive and sorting effects of individual PRP should, in turn, increase the level of human capital of the organization. Highly skilled employees are more likely to be motivated when their pay is linked to their performance compared to more traditional (i.e., fixed) pay systems. Moreover, when PRP is based on group or company performance, employees are more likely to share their knowledge and to support each other, thus making the relationship between social and intellectual capital and performance stronger than in traditional pay settings. Thus, we predict that:

H2: The adoption of performance-based pay moderates the positive relationship between intellectual capital and organizational performance, so that the relationship is stronger at higher level of adoption of performance-based pay compared to lower.

Despite the positive moderating effect that e-HRM and performance pay may have on the relationship between intellectual capital and organizational performance, the situation may become more nuanced when considering the context in which they are implemented. We argue that the joint effect of e-HRM and performance pay systems depends on contextual features and more specifically on the extent of intellectual capital characterizing the organization. More specifically, these elements working together may be perceived as either an opportunity to enhance value for the organization or having the opposite effect. Herremans et al. [8] found evidence that an organizational design combining technology infrastructures with results-based control system is associated with reduced perceived uncertainty. All organizations face uncertainty and reducing the amount of uncertainty associated with decision-making processes is one of the main organizational aims. However, uncertainty can be either positive or negative according to the context. For example, Rastogi [21] proposed that intellectual capital is primarily deployed in environments that are dynamic or in rapid flux, so contexts in which people have to continuously foresight, assess problems, find solutions, learn and change strategies and action plans. Therefore, the very nature of intellectual capital suggests a higher degree of uncertainty as a driver to the development of intellectual capital capabilities [8]. In this perspective, since the adoption of e-HRM and performance pay directs employees' behaviors, those individuals operating in organizations characterized by high intellectual capital may perceive the reduced uncertainty due to the joint adoption of technology and results-based control systems as a threat to the development of intellectual capital capabilities thus resulting in lower performance. In formal terms, we predict that

H3: The combined influence of e-HRM and performance-based pay on the relationship between intellectual capital and organizational performance will be stronger for firms with lower level of intellectual capital.

3 Methodology and Results

3.1 Sample and Procedure

This study is based on data from the CRANET survey (2015) and the sample consisted of 168 Italian organizations. The survey provides comprehensive information about the HRM practices of organizations with over 200 employees. The key informants were the participating companies' HR directors.

Thirty-four percent of these companies operated in the manufacturing sector, 42% in the services sector and 24% in the advanced service sector. Companies were mainly private (66%) and operating on the domestic market (54%). Fifty-two percent had over 25% highly educated workers, and on average 75% of them reported providing some degree of flexible work arrangements. Forty percent of the firms involved in the study had over 2000 employees.

3.2 Variables

Organizational performance. It is measured by four variables (Service quality, level of productivity, profitability, rate of innovation) measuring perception of performance. A principal component analysis with Varimax rotation was conducted using SPSS, to identify emergent factor solutions for organizational performance. Factorability of the correlation matrix, as assessed via the Keyser-Meyer-Olkin test (KMO $= 0.17$) and Bartlett's test of sphericity ($\chi^2 = 155.832$, df $= 6, p < 0.000$), was supported. The analysis yielded a one-factor solution. Percentage variance explained $= 59\%$. Cronbach's $\alpha = 0.76$

Intellectual capital. We used the scale developed by Youndt et al. [29] and later used by Subramaniam and Youndt [26] to assess HR directors' perceptions of organizational intellectual capital. After an introductory statement referring to the extent the respondent agreed with the following items describing his/her organization's intellectual capital, fourteen items on a Likert scale from 0 (total disagreement) to 4 (total agreement) measuring the three types of intellectual capital (i.e., human, social and organizational) were provided (e.g., "Our employees develop new ideas and knowledge", "Our employees share information and learn from one another", "Our organization embeds much of its knowledge and information in structures, systems, and processes"). The three scales were combined to form one single factor measuring intellectual capital as the sum of all knowledge firms utilize for competitive advantage [13, 29]. Cronbach's $\alpha = 0.87$.

e-HRM. For determining the amount of e-HRM adoption a set of binary categorical variables were employed. It was calculated by adding seven categorical (yes/no) questions from the CRANET questionnaire: (a) Human resource information system or electronic HRM systems for HRM activities (HRIS); (b) manager self-service for HRM activities (manager self-service); and (c) employee self-service for HRM activities (employee self-service); (d) the vacancy page on the company website as a recruitment method (e-recruitment); (e) online selection tests as the selection method (e-selection); (f) bottom-up or top-down electronic communication (e-communication); and (g) the use of computer-based packages/e-learning for career management (e-learning). Therefore, e-HRM is a formative measure of e-HRM adoption with a minimum of 0 and a maximum of 7.

Performance pay. The amount of performance pay adoption was calculated by adding a set of binary categorical variables representing different types of payment schemes. The categorical variables from the CRANET questionnaire were: (a) employee share schemes; (b) profit sharing; (c) stock options; (d) flexible benefits; (e) individual performance related pay; (f) bonus based on individual goals/performance; (g) bonus based on team goals/performance; and (h) bonus based on organizational goals/performance. Each company rated the adoption of the above payment schemes for both professionals and clericals/manuals. Therefore, performance pay is a formative measure with a minimum of 0 and a maximum of 16.

Control variables. Organizational size is a single indicator measuring the log of the total number of employees of the organization. Organizational age is a single indicator measuring the log of years since firm's foundation. We also controlled for sector (1 = private company 0 = not private company) and industry membership (three categories: manufacturing, services, advanced services (ref.)). We asked respondents to rate the growth of the market currently served by their organization (5-point scale ranging from 1-"Declining to a great extent" to 5-"Growing to a great extent"). A six-point scale was adopted to measure the proportion of the workforce with a higher education/university qualification and the proportion of young employees (1 = "0%", 2 = "1–10%", 3 = "11–25%", 4 = "26–50%", 5 = "51–75%", 6 = "76–100%").

3.3 Analysis and Results

We first validated the measurement model and then tested the moderation hypothesis. Numerical predictor variables were centered on the grand mean. Descriptive statistics and correlations are reported in Table 1. The results of the hierarchical multiple regression analyses are reported in Table 2.

In terms of main effects, results of the full model (Model 4) showed that intellectual capital and performance pay were positively and significantly related to organizational performance. With regard to the two-way interactions between performance pay and e-HRM, performance pay and intellectual capital, e-HRM and intellectual capital, results show that e-HRM has a negative impact on the relationship between intellectual capital and organizational performance, while the interaction between intellectual capital and performance-pay is non-significant. Hence, Hypothesis 1 and Hypothesis 2 were not supported by our analysis. Interestingly, results showed that the three-way interaction term was negative and significant, thus supporting Hypothesis 3. In order to better understand the pattern of the interactions, the results were plotted in Figs. 1 and 2.

As Fig. 1 illustrates, when intellectual capital is high, low-e-HRM adoption results in better organizational performance than high e-HRM performance ($p < 0.01$). Furthermore, Fig. 2a indicates that in organizational contexts where intellectual capital is low, the relationship between performance pay and organizational performance is significantly stronger at high e-HRM levels ($p < 0.001$), while it is non-significant at

Table 1 Descriptive statistics and correlations

	Mean	St. dev.	1.	2.	3.	4.	5.	6.	7.	8.	9.
1. Organizational performance	3.68	0.63									
2. Performance pay	5.43	2.87	0.309**								
3. e-HRM	4.29	1.62	0.230**	0.469**							
4. Intellectual capital	2.31	0.57	0.271**	0.279**	0.283**						
5. Org. size	2.22	1.22	0.065	0.108	0.351**	0.234**					
6. Org. age	690.08	880.95	−0.128	−0.176*	0.028	0.108	0.195*				
7. Manufacturing	0.34	0.47	−0.010	0.055	0.057	0.205**	−0.037	−0.006			
8. Services	0.42	0.49	−0.137	−0.127	−0.189*	−0.199***	0.016	−0.146	−0.606**		
9. Market trend	2.88	0.80	0.297**	0.124	0.098	0.079	−0.002	−0.065	−0.020	−0.066	
10. Higher education	3.50	1.13	0.242**	0.187*	0.209**	0.174*	0.074	0.042	−0.259**	−0.024	0.161*

Notes *p < 0.05, **p < 0.01

Table 2 Hierarchical multiple regression results for organizational performance

	Model 1		Model 2		Model 3		Model 4	
	B	s.e.	B	s.e.	B	s.e.	B	s.e.
Org. size	0.15[†]	0.08	0.05	0.088	0.05	0.09	0.03	0.09
Org. age	−0.37***	0.10	−0.32**	0.100	−0.31**	0.10	−0.30**	0.10
Industry[a]								
Manuf.	0.06	0.23	−0.03	0.221	−0.04	0.22	−0.01	0.22
Services	−0.19	0.23	−0.19	0.221	−0.18	0.22	−0.191	0.21
Market trend	0.34**	0.10	0.30**	0.093	0.30**	0.10	0.29**	0.09
Higher education	0.14	00.07	0.06	0.074	0.08	0.07	0.07	0.07
Performance pay			0.07[†]	0.034	0.08*	0.03	0.09**	0.04
e-HRM			06	0.066	0.03	0.07	0.04	0.07
Intellectual capital			0.26	162	0.33*	0.17	0.57**	0.19
Performance pay * e-HRM					−0.01	0.02	−0.01	0.02
Performance pay * Intellectual capital					−0.02	0.07	−0.02	0.07
e-HRM * Intellectual capital					−0.17	0.11	−0.25*	0.11
Performance pay * e-HRM * Intellectual capital							−0.09*	0.04
Adj. R^2	0.25		0.31		0.32		0.35	
F change	7.1***		6.4***		5.4***		5.6***	

Note $†p < 0.10$, $*p < 0.05$, $**p < 0.01$, $***<0.001$. Ref. category: [a]Advanced services

low levels of e-HRM. Conversely, in organizational contexts where intellectual capital is high (Fig. 2b), the relationship between performance pay and organizational performance is significantly stronger at low e-HRM levels ($p < 0.001$), while it is non- significant at high levels of e-HRM.

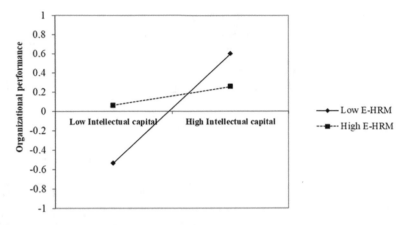

Fig. 1 Interaction between Intellectual capital and e-HRM on organizational performance

4 Discussion and Conclusion

Though preliminary, the findings reported above offer interesting evidence about how e-HRM and performance pay interact with intellectual capital in influencing organizational performance. First, consistently with existing studies, we found that intellectual capital is positively related to organizational performance. This confirms that companies that want to remain competitive in modern markets should invest on the quality of their human resources by attracting high-skilled employees, developing a cooperative and supportive social context, and providing adequate organizational practices to institutionalize the existing knowledge.

Surprisingly, our findings also show that when a company combines investments in intellectual capital with the adoption of an advanced e-HRM system the positive effect of intellectual capital is reduced. This finding can be interpreted in three ways. First, it may be the case that in presence of high levels of intellectual capital an e-HRM system may be perceived as a form of control rather than as a mechanism to leverage on for further developing the human, social and organizational capital. Skilled and knowledgeable employees may be less positive toward pervasive e-HRM tools as these may reduce their perception of autonomy and freedom [24]. Second, e-HRM systems may have negative effects on some specific dimensions of intellectual capital, and specifically on social capital. Indeed, the digitalization of the workplace can also imply a reduction (or disruption) of social interactions at work [24], thus reducing the social capital of the organization. Given that the three dimensions of intellectual capital complement each other, the result is a reduction of the impact of intellectual capital on organizational performance. Third, it could be that e-HRM adoption is not the result of a strategic choice on the part of the HR function. Rather, e-HRM adoption could be seen by companies in our sample more as a transactional way to automate administrative HR tasks and saving costs. Therefore, understanding

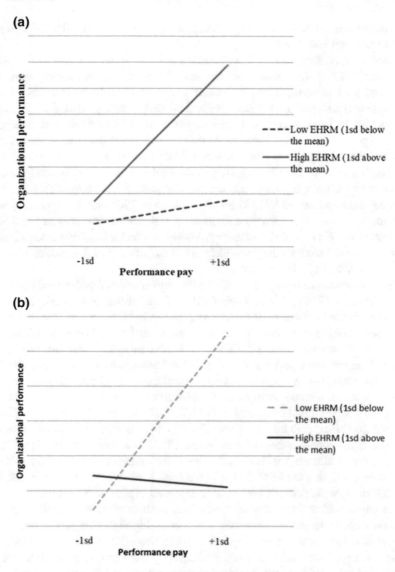

Fig. 2 Relationship between performance pay and organizational performance for different levels of e-HRM and intellectual capital. **a** Low intellectual capital. **b** High intellectual capital

the broader context and the strategic intent behind e-HRM adoption is critical in order to fully explain its effect.

Concerning performance pay, the results show that it has a positive relationship with organizational performance, but the interaction with intellectual capital is non-significant (and negative). Thus, while PRP per se seems able to contribute to organizational performance by the incentive and sorting effects predicted by economic theories [10], it also seems unable to increase the potential contribution of intellectual capital to performance. This latter effect may be explained with the increased sense of control the employee may perceive when PRP schemes are in place. Indeed, firms with a high level of intellectual capital generally rely on the creativity and innovative behaviors of their employees as a source of competitive advantage. This organizational culture contrasts with HRM practices, such as PRP, that foster employees to adopt more conservative behaviors focused on task accomplishment rather than on the exploration of a new idea. Indeed, exploiting intellectual capital through innovation and creativity requires the possibility to fail and make mistakes, which is usually not contemplated in PRP programs.

This interpretation is consistent with the findings showing that the combined effect of high levels e-HRM and high levels PRP on the relationship between intellectual capital and organizational performance is positive in situations of low intellectual capital and is negative in situations of high intellectual capital (Fig. 2). When firms do not rely on intellectual capital for competitive advantage, having pay strictly related to performance and a strong e-HRM infrastructure that increases the level clarity and transparency in performance requirements motivates employees to be productive and to increase their level of effort to reach the assigned objectives. On the contrary, when intellectual capital is high, such systems demotivate employees to fully exploit their potential. Surprisingly, Fig. 2b also shows that in the context of high intellectual capital when e-HRM is low, PRP has a strong positive moderating effect on the relationship with organizational performance. Consistently with our predictions (H3), this confirms that it is only the joint effect of high e-HRM, high PRP that reduces the positive impact of intellectual capital on performance.

The paper suffers from several limitations such as cross-sectional design and common-method variance. However, the results highlight important managerial implications. Indeed, the joint adoption of these two HRM tools (i.e., e-HRM and performance pay) should be carefully evaluated by managers by taking into account the role that they assign to intellectual capital as a source of competitive advantage. Moreover, our findings highlight also the risk of an excess of techno-optimism in the adoption of e-HRM and question the appropriateness of a deterministic view of e-HRM as causing organizational positive outcomes [25]. Therefore, future research could usefully explore more in-depth the contextual HRM conditions that allow (or prevent) organizations to (from) fully exploiting the performance potential of intellectual capital. More specifically, we suggest further research to better analyze how the reduction of perceived internal uncertainty impacts knowledge-intensive organizations.

References

1. Barney, J. (1991). Firms resources and sustained competitive advantage. *Journal of Management, 17*(1), 99–120.
2. Bondarouk, T., & Ruel, H. (2009). Electronic human resource management: Challenges in the digital era. *International Journal of Human Resource Management, 20*(3), 505–514.
3. Chinsholm, A. M., & Nielsen, K. (2009). Social capital and the resource-based view of the firm. *International Studies of Management and Organization, 39*(2), 7–32.
4. CIPD. (2017). *Human capital theory: Assessing the evidence for the value and importance of people to organizational success* (Technical report).
5. Cohen, K. (2006). *The pulse of the profession: 2006–2007 salary budget survey.* Workspan, Sept 23–26.
6. Crook, T. R., Todd, S. Y., Combs, J. G., Woehr, D. J., & Ketchen, D. J. (2011). Does human capital matter? A meta-analysis of the relationship between human capital and firm performance. *Journal of Applied Psychology, 96*(3), 443–456.
7. Donate, M. J., Peña, I., & Sánchez de Pablo, J. D. (2016). HRM practices for human and social capital development: Effects on innovation capabilities. *The International Journal of Human Resource Management, 27*(9), 928–953.
8. Herremans, I. M., Isaac, R. G., Kline, T. J. B., & Nazari, J. A. (2011). Intellectual capital and uncertainty of knowledge: Control by design of the management system. *Journal of Business Ethics, 98*(4), 627–640.
9. Jenkins, G. D. Jr., Mitra, A., Gupta, N., & Shaw, J. D. (1998). Are financial incentives related to performance? A meta-analytic review of empirical research. *Journal of Applied Psychology, 83*(5), 777–787.
10. Lazear, E. P. (2000). Performance pay and productivity. *American Economic Review, 90,* 1346–1361.
11. Marler, J. H., & Fisher, S. L. (2013). An evidence-based review of e-HRM and strategic human resource management. *Human Resource Management Review, 23*(1), 18–36.
12. Milkovich, G., Newman, J., & Gerhart, B. (2011). *Compensation* (10th ed.). Irwin: McGraw-Hill.
13. Nahapiet, J., & Ghoshal, S. (1998). Social capital, intellectual capital, and the organisational advantage. *Academy of Management Review, 23*(2), 242–266.
14. Nyberg, A. J., Maltarich, M. A., Abdulsalam, D. D., Essman, S. M., & Cragun, O. (2018). Collective pay for performance: A cross-disciplinary review and meta-analysis. *Journal of Management, 44*(6), 2433–2472.
15. Nyberg, A. J., Pieper, J. R., & Trevor, C. O. (2016). Pay-for-performance effect on future employee performance integrating psychological and economic principles toward a contingency perspective. *Journal of Management, 42*(7), 1753–1783.
16. Obeidat, S. M. (2016). The link between e-HRM use and HRM effectiveness: An empirical study. *Personnel Review, 45*(6), 1281–1301.
17. Parry, E., & Tyson, S. (2011). Desired goals and actual outcomes of e-HRM. *Human Resource Management Journal, 21*(3), 335–354.
18. Penrose, E. T. (1959). *The theory of the growth of the firm.* Oxford: Oxford University Press.
19. Peteraf, M. A. (1993). The cornerstones of competitive advantage: A resource-based view. *Strategic Management Journal, 12,* 95–117.
20. Ployhart, R. E., Nyberg, A. J., Reilly, G., & Maltarich, M.a. (2014). Human capital is dead; long live human capital resources! *Journal of Management, 40*(2), 371–398.
21. Rastogi, P. N. (2003). The nature and role of ic: Rethinking the process of value creation and sustained enterprise growth. *Journal of Intellectual Capital, 4*(2), 227–248.
22. Reed, K. K., Lubatkin, M., & Srinivasan, N. (2006). Proposing and testing an intellectual capital-based view of the firm. *Journal of Management Studies, 43*(4), 867–893.
23. Spender, J. C., & Grant, R. M. (1996). Knowledge and the firm: Overview. *Strategic Management Journal, 17,* 5–9.

24. Stone, D. L., & Lukaszewski, K. M. (2006). An expanded model of the factors affecting the acceptance and effectiveness of electronic human resource management systems. *Human Resource Management Review, 19*(2), 134–143.
25. Strohmeier, S. (2007). Research in e-HRM: Review and implications'. *Human Resource Management Review, 17,* 19–37.
26. Subramaniam, M., & Youndt, M. A. (2005). The influence of intellectual capital on the types of innovation capabilities. *Academy of Management Journal, 48*(3), 450–463.
27. Wright, P. M., Coff, R., & Moliterno, T. P. (2014). Strategic human capital: Crossing the great divide. *Journal of Management, 40*(2), 353–370.
28. Youndt, M. A., & Snell, S. A. (2004). Human resource configurations, intellectual capital, and organizational performance. *Journal of Managerial Issues, 16*(3), 337–360.
29. Youndt, M., Subramaniam, M., & Snell, S. (2004). Intellectual capital profiles: An examination of investments and returns. *Journal of Management Studies, 41*(2), 335–361.

Information and Communication Technologies Usage for Professional Purposes, Work Changes and Job Satisfaction. Some Insights from Europe

Daria Sarti, Teresina Torre and Elena Pirani

Abstract This paper aims at investigating the relationship between work changes and Information and Communication Technology usage for professional purposes. These two major concepts are at the heart in current research on working environment and its conditions for fostering job satisfaction, an important and well recognized outcome. In order to pursue our goal, the paper is organized in the following way. In the first part, a brief overview of work changes is provided, together with a review of recent literature linking current contributions within the two chosen areas of study, and hypothesis to test are suggested. In the second part, results of the analysis —carried out on a sample of European employees (N = 21,540) taken from the Sixth European Working Conditions Survey (EWCS 2015) is described. Finally, first interesting counter-intuitive evidence is discussed and concluding remarks on managerial implications of our enquiry about a 'good' management of ICTs are reported.

Keywords Work change · ICT usage · PC usage · Job satisfaction · Job resources · Europe

1 Introduction

In the last decades, Information and Communication Technologies (ICTs) usage for professional purposes has represented a largely debated issue in economics and in organizational field. Coherently with the prophetical forecast by Kiester and col-

D. Sarti
Department of Economics and Management, University of Florence, Florence, Italy
e-mail: daria.sarti@unifi.it

T. Torre (✉)
Department of Economics and Business Studies, University of Genoa, Genoa, Italy
e-mail: teresina.torre@economia.unige.it

E. Pirani
Department of Statistics, Computer Science, Applications "G. Parenti",
University of Florence, Florence, Italy
e-mail: elena.pirani@unifi.it

© Springer Nature Switzerland AG 2020
A. Lazazzara et al. (eds.), *Exploring Digital Ecosystems*,
Lecture Notes in Information Systems and Organisation 33,
https://doi.org/10.1007/978-3-030-23665-6_12

165

leagues—who wrote that 'computers are transforming work and, in some cases, lives' [1: 1123]—the technological revolution is still deeply modifying labour and the way in which it is performed.

If a number of studies has already been conducted with attention to the implications of this evolution, research is still needed in order to effectively understand the relevance of ICTs in the work organization and in its change processes, which involve work and which could influence employees' behaviour [2].

According to authors, as technology changes at a rapid pace, organizations increasingly incorporate technologies into their work places and methods, thus leading to continuous adaptations and, in turn, to alterations in work design [3, 4].

However, and independently from the antecedents (that is the source of stimuli) of the work changes and job redesign (such as for example, technology rapid change, market and labour competition, etc.), the individuals' strategy of adaptation to the new working conditions—defined by the organizations as interventions of job redesign—may lead them to rethink their own working routines, also considering a different use (for other activities, i.e. for communicating) or a larger one (i.e., in terms of hours) of technological instruments. The basic idea is that work changes enable a higher use of the ICT tools, introducing a counter-intuitive suggestion, which seems to us a good explanation for the enlargement in use of technologies. Indeed, researches show an increasing in the pervasiveness of technologies, so that it can be imagined a connection, which is interesting to deepen.

Starting form this premise, the aim of the present work is to analyse the relationship between work changes and the ICTs usage in the work context, with specific reference to the PC usage.

At the same time, it is observed that literature pays a particular attention on the role of employees' positive outcomes in organizational context. A number of works investigate their antecedents and consequences, considering the importance of job satisfaction (JS), the influence of which is determinant to get 'quality' work, on its turn at the basis of the success of a company. JS has been classically defined as affective orientation towards the role a person is occupying [5]. Armstrong [6] suggests that JS refers to the aptitude and the sentiments an individual has about his/her work. It is closely related to all the characteristics of the job. Coherently, it is presented as a multifaceted psychological construct that measures the degree to which an employee is satisfied and happy with his/her job [7, 8]. In any case, the relevance of JS is established and the conditions able to favour it are worthy to be deepened.

Therefore, the mediating role of ICT usage in the relationship between work changes and JS is investigated. It is our opinion that this issue can offer interesting stimuli to better understand the role played by ICTs in employee's work conditions and to offer suggestions for management in order to improve these processes. In detail, the research assesses the impact of some job characteristics—which are strictly connected to the important role that ICT may have on work organization and in its changes—on JS.

For the purpose to develop our ideas, the paper is organised in the following manner. In the second paragraph, the theoretical background is offered and the hypotheses are presented. In the third, the analysis and the most relevant results are presented. Finally, some preliminary suggestions in relationship to the research questions and to their counter-intuitive evidence towards some managerial implications are introduced and considerations useful for future research activities are proposed.

2 Theoretical Background

2.1 Work Change and Job Satisfaction

Since the Seventies, work design has been recognized as the most important strategy for improving both productivity and the quality of the work experience in organizations [9]. In this sense, job design and job re-design might indeed represent a fundamental focus of motivation for employees [9–11], also increasing organizational productivity and improving the quality of working experience for employees [12].

Recently, it was proved that work redesign directly affect positively employees' attitudes—reinforcing their psychological balance—since work re-design interventions are perceived as a signal of organizational investments in job and working conditions improvements [13–15].

Thus, we posit that changes in work routine may have a positive impact on JS:

- HP1. There is a positive and significant relationship between work change and JS.

2.2 The Mediating Role of ICT Usage

Starting from the evidence that, according to most studies, change is nowadays essentially technology-driven and that this produces deep effects on the way people work [16, 17], we think that work changes may bring about an intensification in the usage of technological instruments for professional purposes—e.g., PC usage. Indeed, when changes in work design arise—for example through the improvement of tasks and responsibilities—as a consequence, employees may experience an increase in the need for new instruments to cope with the new configuration of their works. These instruments may be new technology tools. At the same time, the changes in employees working routines may increase the employees' perception of the actual utility of ICT instruments already in use in their organization, thus leading them to increase the intensity of their usage [18]. Coherently, the Unified Theory of Acceptance Model had underlined that both performance expectancy (that is the degree, to which a worker believes that the use of ICTs helps his performance) and effort expectancy (that is the degree of ease in the use of technologies) have a positive effect on the use of technologies [19]. PC is indeed the principal tool for working activities, but also it is the essential tool for relationships with the members of own team, with the boss and to support the change itself.

Coherently, we state that:

- HP2. There is a positive and significant relationship between work changes and PC usage for professional purposes.

According to recent reviews, the use of ICT in the workplace can have both positive and negative effects on employees' work experiences [20, 21]. Some authors highlight the positive impact of new technologies on the increase of individuals' overall JS. In particular, it has been shown that ICT usage favours a growth in the rate of communications among employees [22, 23]. Other streams of literature suggest that in modern workplaces ICT usage can increase job demands due to increasing expectations and employee accessibility to the workplace [21]—which in turn can have a negative impact on employees' health and well-being [24] and on family-to-work conflict [25]. Other studies suggest that ICTs can improve employees' working conditions thus favoring their positive attitudes and behaviors. Hendriks [26] for example demonstrated that ICTs can enhance knowledge sharing by lowering temporal and spatial barriers between knowledge workers and improving access to information and sources of knowledge.

However, if we start from the pivotal study of Barnard [27] and from his idea of the organization as a 'cooperative' system—in which the satisfaction of both the organizational goals and individuals' needs have to be pursued—we can approach ICTs as an 'instrument' for the achievement of the above mentioned twofold goals. Thus, we believe that a conscious use of such instruments are pursued within a context in which the social nature of the organization as a 'cooperative system' is a constitutional element. In this vein, we posit that:

- HP3. There is a positive and significant relationship between PC usage and JS, and the use of PC for professional purposes do mediate the relationship between work changes and JS.

2.3   The Job Resources' Moderation Effect

The use of technology at work, which is nowadays so essential and which leads employees to the experience of better working conditions, and in turn to JS, may have a number of interacting elements—especially job and organizational characteristics—favouring (or not) its positive impact on final and overall JS.

According to the Job Demand-Resource model [28, 29], working conditions—considering characteristics of work, referring to physical, social and organizational aspects of the job—favour the positive attitudes of workers whilst they may reduce counter-productive behaviours.

In this vein, we believe that a number of job and organizational conditions, pre-existing in the working environment, may play an interaction effect on PC use in its relationship with JS, when work changes are involved.

So, we aim at demonstrating that:

- HP4. Job resources (JRs) moderate the relationship between PC usage and JS.

In Fig. 1, a brief path diagram representing the relationships among the factors examined in our analysis is shown. The hypotheses are depicted in the figure by the causal arrows, meaning that we hypothesize that work changes affect JS in a positive and significant manner (HP1), that is the main effect to verify. Also, work changes affect PC usage (HP2), which in turn affects JS also having a mediation effect (HP3). Moreover, it is hypothesized that JRs may have a moderation effect on the relationship between PC usage and JS (HP4), so that when PC usage is implemented, due to work changes, the overall impact on JS would also be 'facilitated' (or 'hindered') by JRs.

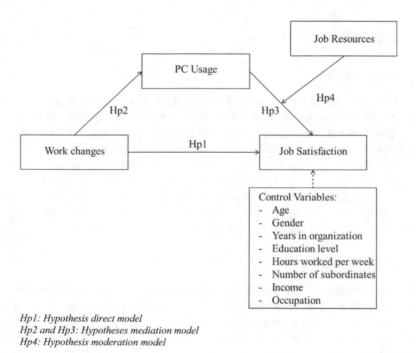

Hp1: Hypothesis direct model
Hp2 and Hp3: Hypotheses mediation model
Hp4: Hypothesis moderation model

Fig. 1 The model of analysis

3 Empirical Analysis

3.1 Method

The empirical research was based on data gathered from the database of the sixth European Working Conditions Survey (EWCS) conducted in 2015 on a large sample of workers from the EU35 and which is the most recent at disposal. Only people who declared their status of employed were included in the analysis since the purpose of our analysis. Final sample results composed by 21,540 individuals belonging to EU 27.

3.2 Analysis

Dependent Variable

The chosen dependent variable is JS. It is measured with a one-item question taken from the EWCS questionnaire: "On the whole, are you very satisfied, satisfied, not very satisfied or not at all satisfied with working conditions in your main paid job?". The range of response was based on a four-point scale ranging from 1 = 'Not at all satisfied' to 4 = 'Very satisfied'. Despite some authors suggest for caution in using single-item scales in empirical research [30], others express approval for this solution (e.g., [31]). Indeed, as it has been demonstrated that "single-item measures of overall JS correlated highly with multiple-item measures of overall JS" [31: 77], the same solution might be used in special circumstances [30] so that in the present case.

Independent Variables

ICT usage is measured with one single questions available in the questionnaire. The question is: "Does your main paid job involve... working with computers, laptops, smartphones etc.?". The responses were based on a seven-point-scale ranging from 7 to 1; in detail: 7 = 'Never'; 6 = 'Almost never'; 5 = 'Around ¼ of the time'; 4 = 'Around half the time'; 3 = 'Around ¾ of the time'; 2 = 'Almost all the time; 1 = All of the time. The scale was reversed for the purpose of this study.

Work change is measured with four questions present in the questionnaire. One example of these questions is: "In the last 12 months work changed in the amount of influence you have over your work?". The range of response was based on a five-point scale ranging from 1 = 'decreased a lot' to 5 = 'increased a lot'. The scale reliability coefficient, Cronbach's alpha, is 0.657.

Job resources. Seven JRs for this study are computed (using the mean) considering items of the questionnaire which were coherent with those presented in previous scales of measure validated in current literature (see for example: [32–34]). In the following table, these JRs are presented (Table 1).

Table 1 The JRs used in this study: name, number of items, example of question and Cronbach's alpha

Variable	Number of items in the scale	Example of item	Alpha Cronbach
Supervisor support	6	'Your immediate boss gives you praise and recognition when you do a good job'	0.894
Organizational support	6	'How much do you agree with the following sentence: The management trusts the employees to do their work well?'	0.861
Participation	6	'How often are you consulted before objectives are set for your work?'	0.798
Work-life balance	6	'How often have you kept worrying about work when you were not working?'	0.773
Job clarity	3	'You know what is expected of you at work?'	0.707
Time strain	3	'Does your job involve working at very high speed?'	0.693
Social support	2	'Your colleagues help and support you?'	0.700

Note All items were assessed based on a 5-point scale of response ranging from 1 = 'always/completely agree' to '5 = never/completely disagree'

For the purpose of this analysis, the scale of response for ICTs usage and JS were reversed, so that a higher score in response was the maximum and the lower score the minimum.

Control Variables

These are: *age* (continuous, in year); *gender* (1 = male; 2 = female); *years in the organization* (continuous); *education level* (ranging from 1 = no formal education to 7 = tertiary education, advanced level); *hours worked per week* (continuous), *number of workers subordinates to the respondent in the job* (continuous), *income* (aggregated into categories but considered as a continuous variable in the model), *occupational classification* (ISCO classification in 8 categories).

Table 2 Results from the structural equation model predicting JS, total effects (N = 21,506)

	Coef.	Std. err.	P > z
Job satisfaction <==			
Gender (rif.: male)			
Female	−0.015	0.010	0.125
Age	−0.001	0.000	0.108
Size organization	−0.062	0.006	0.000
Years working in the organization	0.001	0.001	0.328
Hours worked	−0.007	0.000	0.000
Education	0.004	0.003	0.226
N. of subordinates	0.022	0.005	0.000
Income	0.032	0.002	0.000
Occupation classification (rif.: technicians and associate professionals)			
Managers	0.073	0.023	0.002
Professionals	0.043	0.016	0.008
Clerical support workers	−0.021	0.018	0.250
Service and sales workers	−0.060	0.017	0.000
Skilled agricultural, forestry and fish	−0.088	0.051	0.084
Craft and related trades workers	−0.096	0.020	0.000
Plant and machine operators, and assemb.	−0.141	0.022	0.000
Elementary occupations	−0.144	0.022	0.000
Armed forces occupations	0.150	0.064	0.019
Work changes	0.074	0.010	0.000
PC usage	0.012	0.002	0.000
PC usage <==			
Work changes	0.819	0.035	0.000

3.3   Results

A structural equation model was implemented in order to test the mediation hypothesis presented in the second paragraph. All analyses have been performed using the statistical package STATA. Table 2 shows the total effects of the different key and control variables on JS, together with the total effect of work change on the use of technological instruments, whereas Fig. 2 shows the path diagram of direct and indirect effects of work changes on JS. Please note that the higher the value of the variable work change, the higher the increase of the various aspects linked to changes in job used to build the indicator (e.g., hours worked, salary, tasks and responsibilities).

While for control variables JS is lower for women and decreases as far as the dimension of the firm increases or the number of hours worked increases. Conversely,

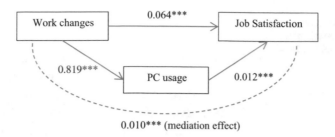

Fig. 2 Direct (continuous lines) and indirect (dashed line) effects of work change on JS, mediated by ICTs usage

JS is positively associated with the time passed in the organization, and for highly educated workers. Having high professional positions is positively related to JS, as proved by the coefficients of the variables referring to the number of subordinates who depend on the respondent worker and his/her income, and the occupational position. For the latter, specifically, managers and professionals are on average more satisfied with their job relative to technicians and associate professionals, whereas all the other positions seem to be less satisfying (or not significantly different). Finally, once controlled for the job characteristics, age and gender are not significantly associated with JS.

As for our key variable, results prove a significant association between work changes and the dependent variable, which is JS ($\beta = 0.074$; $p < 0.001$): the higher the level of work changes (in the sense of an increasing), the higher the level of JS, thus supporting HP1. Moreover, also HP2 is supported: increasing level of work changes are associated with an increasing use of ICT instruments at work ($\beta = 0.819$; $p < 0.001$).

The total effect of work change on JS presented in Table 2 can be indeed splitted into a direct and an indirect effect, through ICTs usage (Fig. 2). Our results proved a small but significant indirect (or mediation) effect of work change on JS trough ICTs usage ($b = 0.010$; $p < 0.001$). Thus, HP3 is supported, meaning that the ICTs usage do have an impact in affecting the relationship between work change and JS. It is worthwhile noting that, once the model is accounted for the job characteristics, both the total and the mediation effect of work changes on JS reduce (results not shown but available upon request), but they remain significant, denoting that the relationship may change depending on the type of occupation and its responsibilities.

Additionally, various types of JRs was investigated in order to test their potential moderator effect in the relationship between ICTs usage and JS. Specifically, we considered: boss support, organizational support, participation, work-life balance, job clarity, time strain, social support. We estimated seven separate models considering time by time a single type of job resource, and interacting it with ICTs usage. Table 3 reports the main and the interaction effects estimated. The principal effects estimated show that all aspects linked to JRs are positively associated with JS, as expected. Nevertheless, our analyses proved the existence of a significant and pos-

Table 3 Main and interaction effects between different types of JRs and PC usage

		Coef.	Std. err.	$P > z$
Mod. 1	PC usage	0.014	0.008	0.602
	Boss support	0.313	0.009	0.000
	Interaction term	0.001	0.002	0.660
Mod. 2	PC usage	−0.008	0.009	0.346
	Organizational support	0.387	0.010	0.000
	Interaction term	0.005	0.002	0.012
Mod. 3	PC usage	−0.035	0.006	0.000
	Participation	0.186	0.008	0.000
	Interaction term	0.011	0.002	0.000
Mod. 4	PC usage	−0.015	0.010	0.130
	Work life balance	0.295	0.012	0.000
	Interaction term	0.008	0.002	0.001
Mod. 5	PC usage	−0.056	0.012	0.000
	Job clarity	0.230	0.012	0.000
	Interaction term	0.015	0.003	0.000
Mod. 6	PC usage	0.018	0.005	0.001
	Time strain	0.110	0.006	0.000
	Interaction term	−0.000	0.001	0.981
Mod. 7	PC usage	−0.027	0.008	0.001
	Social support	0.188	0.008	0.000
	Interaction term	0.009	0.002	0.000

Results from structural equation models predicting JS, models controlled for variables listed in Table 2 (N = 21,506)

itive moderating effect for all the elements tested except for boss support and time strain. Overall, it is worthwhile noting that controlling for the moderating effect of participation, job clarity or social support reverse the positive effect of pc usage on JS, whereas the moderating effect of boss and organizational support and work-life balance seems to explain the association, coherently with HP4.

Further analyses should be conducted in order to understand if these elements overlap and which of them prevail.

4 Conclusions, Limitations and Further Research

This paper is based on the stream of research, which considers ICTs usage and its improvements as functional to the success of any process of organizational change.

In particular, it wishes to examine the need for a correct management of all organizational levers (technology and JRs, especially) in order to grant the implementation of overall positive employees' attitudes at work related to an organizational change.

In specific, our analysis has been carried out aimed at demonstrating that changes in work practices—i.e. work re-design—are positively associated with JS and this relationship is mediated by ICTs usage; also, interacting effect of JRs on PC usage was demonstrated in affecting JS.

The study leads to three main considerations, which might represent useful stimuli for current debate as well as points of departure for future investigations.

First, coherently with what suggested by previous fundamental motivational studies [9, 12] which date back to the Seventies, work changes in terms of job re-design do affect in a positive and significant way employees' attitudes and behaviours at work. In this vein, this paper aims at restoring the centrality of the relationship between the two variables—i.e. job re-design and JS—in current debate on organizational contexts, which are even more conditioned by continuous organizational changes.

Second, this study supports the evidence that work changes may affect ICTs use for professional purpose, so that proposing a counterintuitive causality effect on which to reflect. Indeed, while we do not reject the causal effect of ICTs affecting organizational change, we rather consider that even the other way round condition might be as well feasible in organizations thus leading to the importance of managing if with awareness.

Third, and in the end, an important result leads to consider that an interaction effect may exist between ICTs usage, here considered in terms of pc use, and JRs in predicting employees' satisfaction at work so that pushing to consider the ICTs as an instrument to be integrated into the organizational work system.

At the state of the art of our research, we think that it is important to underline how relevant it is to manage all these variables. Further analyses should be conducted in order to understand if these elements overlap and which of them prevail, so enriching our knowledge on how they work and offering a more detailed support for managers engaged in developing changes in working context.

In conclusion, we think that our research contributes to get evidence on an always more interesting topic, which is intended to maintain a central role in research just for its implication in organizational context, especially when change processes are underway and people have to face them.

The present study has some limitations, we are aware of. Foremost, it is based on secondary data. This means that the population studied and the measures undertaken may not be exactly those that we would chosen to collect for the specific topic we are interested in studying. Nevertheless, the use of a database such as EWCS presents the advantage of having a very large sample—which offers the statistical power required to obtain significant interactions. Also, the use of a single-item measure for JS represents a potential weakness. Moreover, other JRs could be considered to examine in a more complete and detailed way their moderating role in the relationship between PC use and JS and to analyze how they can be appropriately managed.

References

1. Kiesler, S., Siegel, J., & McGuire, T. W. (1984). Social psychological aspects of computer-mediated communication. *American Psychologist, 39*(10), 1123–1134.
2. Bissola, R., & Imperatori, B. (2010). Generation Y at work: The role of e-HRM in building positive work attitudes. In S. Strohmeier & A. Diederichsen (Eds.), *Evidence-based e-HRM? On the way to rigorous and relevant research, Proceedings of the Third European Academic Workshop on electronic Human Resource Management, Bamberg, Germany, May 20–21.*
3. Tsung-Hsien, K., Li-An, H., Chinho, L., & Kuei-Kuei, L. (2010). Employee empowerment in a technology advanced work environment. *Industrial Management & Data Systems, 110*(1), 24–42.
4. Shamsuzzoha, A., Kyllönen, S., & Helo, P. (2009). Collaborative customized product development framework. *Industrial Management & Data Systems, 109*(5), 718–735.
5. Vroom, V. H. (1964). *Work and motivation.* New York, NYC: Wiley.
6. Armstrong, M. (2006). *A handbook of human resource management practice.* London, UK: Kogan Page Publishing.
7. Christen, M., Iyer, G., & Soberman, D. (2006). Job satisfaction, job performance, and effort: A reexamination using agency theory. *Journal of Marketing, 70*(1), 137–150.
8. Dawal, S. Z., Taha, Z., & Ismail, Z. (2009). Effect of job organization on job satisfaction among shop floor employees in Automotive Industries in Malaysia. *International Journal of Industrial Ergonomics, 39*(1), 1–6.
9. Hackman, J. R., & Oldham, G. R. (1976). Motivation through the design of work: Test of a theory. *Organizational Behavior and Human Performance, 16*(2), 250–279.
10. Hackman, J. R., & Oldham, G. R. (1975). Development of the job diagnostic survey. *Journal of Applied Psychology, 60*(2), 159–170.
11. Tyagi, P. K. (1985). Relative importance of key job dimensions and leadership behaviors in motivating salesperson work performance. *The Journal of Marketing, 49*(3), 76–86.
12. Hackman, J. R. (1980). Work redesign and motivation. *Professional Psychology, 11*(3), 445–455.
13. Chaudhry, A., Coyle-Shapiro, J. A. M., & Wayne, S. J. (2011). A longitudinal study of the impact of organizational change on transactional, relational, and balanced psychological contracts. *Journal of Leadership & Organizational Studies, 18*(2), 247–259.
14. Kickul, J., Lester, S. W., & Finkl, J. (2002). Promise breaking during radical organizational change: Do justice interventions make a difference? *Journal of Organizational Behavior, 23*(4), 469–488.
15. Holman, D., & Axtell, C. (2016). Can job redesign interventions influence a broad range of employee outcomes by changing multiple job characteristics? A quasi-experimental study. *Journal of Occupational Health Psychology, 21*(3), 284–295.
16. Ramirez, R., Meliville, N., & Lawler, E. (2010). Information technology infrastructure, organizational process redesign and business value. *An empirical analysis, Decision Support System, 49*(4), 417–429.
17. Brynjolffson, E., & McAfee, A. (2014). *The second machine age: Work, progress, and prosperity in a time of brilliant technologies.* New York, NYC: WW Norton.
18. Eason, K. D. (2014). *Information technology and organisational change.* Boca Raton, FL: CRC Press.
19. Venkatesh, V., Morris, M. G., Davis, G. B., & Davis, F. D. (2003). User acceptance of information technology: Toward a unified view. *MIS Quarterly, 27*(3), 425–478.
20. Day, A., Scott, N., & Kelloway, E. K. (2010). Information and communication technology: Implications for job stress and employee well-being. In P. Perrewe & D. Ganster (Eds.), *New developments in theoretical and conceptual approaches to job stress* (Vol. 8, pp. 17–350). Bingley, UK: Emerald Group Publishing Limited.
21. O'Driscoll, M. P., Brough, P., Timms, C., & Sawang, S. (2010). Engagement with information and communication technology and psychological well-being. In *New developments in theoretical and conceptual approaches to job stress* (Vol. 8, pp. 269–316). Bingley, UK: Emerald Group Publishing Limited.

22. Morgan, K., Morgan, M., & Hall, J. (2000). Psychological developments in high technology teaching and learning environments. *British Journal of Educational Technology, 31*(1), 71–79.
23. Moomal, A., & Masrom, M. (2015). ICT development and its impact on e-business and HRM strategies in the organizations of Pakistan. *Journal of Advanced Management Science, 3*(4), 344–349.
24. Coovert, M. D., Foster Thompson, L.: Technology and workplace health. In J. C. Quick, L. E. Tetrick (Eds.), *Handbook of occupational health psychology.*
25. Golden, T. D., Veiga, J. F., & Simsek, Z. (2006). Telecommuting's differential impact on work-family conflict: is there no place like home? *The Journal of Applied Psychology, 91*(6), 1340–1350.
26. Hendriks, P. (1999). Why share knowledge? The influence of ICT on the motivation for knowledge sharing. *Knowledge and Process Management, 6*(2), 91–100.
27. Barnard, C. I. (1938). *The functions of the executive* (pp. 221–242). Cambridge, MA: Harvard University. Washington, DC: American Psychological Association (2003).
28. Schaufeli, W. B., Bakker, A. B., & Van Rhenen, W. (2009). How changes in job demands and resources predict burnout, work engagement, and sickness absenteeism. *Journal of Organizational Behavior, 30*(7), 893–917.
29. Schaufeli, W. B., & Taris, T. W. (2014). A critical review of the job demands-resources model: implications for improving work and health. In G. F. Bauer & O. Hamming (Eds.), *Bridging occupational, organizational and public health* (pp. 43–68). Netherlands: Springer.
30. Nagy, M. S. (2002). Using a single-item approach to measure facet job satisfaction. *Journal of Occupational and Organizational Psychology, 75*(1), 77–86.
31. Diamantopoulos, A., Sarstedt, M., Fuchs, C., Wilczynski, P., & Kaiser, S. (2012). Guidelines for choosing between multi-item and single-item scales for construct measurement: a predictive validity perspective. *Journal of the Academy of Marketing Science, 40*(3), 434–449.
32. Agervold, M., & Mikkelsen, E. G. (2004). Relationships between bullying, psychosocial work environment and individual stress reactions. *Work & Stress, 18*(4), 336–351.
33. Karasek, R. A., Triantis, K. P., & Chaudhry, S. S. (1982). Coworker and supervisor support as moderators of associations between task characteristics and mental strain. *Journal of Organizational Behavior, 3*(2), 181–200.
34. Karasek, R., Brisson, C., Kawakami, N., Houtman, I., Bongers, P., & Amick, B. (1998). The Job Content Questionnaire (JCQ): An instrument for internationally comparative assessments of psychosocial job characteristics. *Journal of Occupational Health Psychology, 3*(4), 322–355.

(Digital) Learning Models and Organizational Learning Mechanisms: Should Organizations Adopt a Single Learning Model or Multiple Ones?

Leonardo Caporarello, Beatrice Manzoni and Lilach Trabelsi

Abstract Creating effective learning experiences matters for both employees and employing organizations as these experiences generate positive outcomes (e.g. improved performance). Organizations can create effective learning experiences by designing and implementing organizational learning mechanisms (OLMs). Yet, in many cases, they fail to do so. In this paper, we explore how employees perceive learning and their company's efforts in providing OLMs. We also investigate whether the learning models (i.e. face-to-face vs. online vs. blended) that employees use to learn have an impact on their satisfaction and enjoyment, as well as their perceptions of the OLMs. We surveyed 67 employees and discovered that respondents that learn using multiple learning models, instead of just one, tend to be more satisfied with their learning experiences, and have a more positive perception of their company's ability to put in place effective OLMs.

Keywords Organizational learning mechanisms · Employee perceptions · Digital learning · Learning models

1 Introduction

Researchers [e.g. 10, 14, 23] and practitioners [e.g. 22] alike widely recognize that it is important to create learning experiences that matter for employees and their organizations. Scholars are interested in exploring how organizations can enable their organizational members' learning so as to create positive outcomes such as

L. Caporarello (✉) · B. Manzoni
Bocconi University, Milan, Italy
e-mail: leonardo.caporarello@unibocconi.it

B. Manzoni
e-mail: beatrice.manzoni@unibocconi.it

L. Trabelsi
SDA Bocconi School of Management, Milan, Italy
e-mail: lilach.trabelsi@unibocconi.it

© Springer Nature Switzerland AG 2020   179
A. Lazazzara et al. (eds.), *Exploring Digital Ecosystems*,
Lecture Notes in Information Systems and Organisation 33,
https://doi.org/10.1007/978-3-030-23665-6_13

higher satisfaction and efficiency, increased innovation, improved performance, and, ultimately, a competitive advantage.

Organizations do not always manage to provide meaningful learning experiences. This is evident when we listen to the voices of employees and top management [22]. Often, organizations fail to align learning and business needs, and to provide the proper organizational support needed to connect learning to employees' role responsibilities and career plans [22]. They also sometimes fail to create a supportive learning-oriented culture [e.g. 4]. Existing literature grouped these issues under the concept of organizational learning mechanisms (OLMs) [e.g. 1], intended as a set of organizational values, processes, and systems that support and facilitate individual and organizational learning.

Over the years, scholars have studied and categorized the different types of OLMs, as well as their impact, in terms of individual and organizational outcomes. However, we still know little about how employees perceive and evaluate their company's efforts in creating and implementing these mechanisms. In particular, there is a need for research on the extent to which digital and tech-based models help boost the learning experience and create a better perception of OLMs. Does digital learning reinforce the employees' perception of the effectiveness of OLMs? This question is extremely relevant if we consider that the use of digital and tech-based learning models and learning methods has increasingly grown over the past years [5], yet the effectiveness of these models and methods is often debated.

Indeed, the great majority of studies point out that technology facilitates learning in multiple ways, but that it also presents a set of potential drawbacks [e.g. 7, 16]. This is one of the reasons why, recently, several studies suggested that effective learning occurs when we rely on a combination of multiple learning models, methods, and modes [e.g. 5].

In this article, we aim to compare employees' perceptions of OLMs based on how much they rely upon digital and non-digital learning models, and on the extent to which they use a single learning model versus a combination of multiple learning models. Are employees more satisfied and do they value more their company's effort when (a) they learn in a traditional or in a digital way? (b) they use only one learning model or more than one learning model at the same time?

The article is organized as follows. In the next sections, we introduce the concept of OLMs and we review the different learning models according to the literature. Then, we present our research methods and discuss results, which suggest that while employees tend to perceive OLMs similarly notwithstanding how much they learn using a face-to-face versus an online versus a blended model, differences in perception occur when we compare employees who rely on a single learning model (regardless of the specific model) versus those who rely on a combination of multiple models (i.e. a mix of all three models). Implications for research and practice follow.

2 Organizational Learning Mechanisms (OLMs)

Organizations can—and have the responsibility to—support and facilitate employees' learning. It is not new that "in the absence of explicit intention and appropriate mechanisms, the learning potential may be lost" [13: p. 432]. Organizations can enhance employees' learning by adopting a set of OLMs, which are those organizational processes and structures that can create or improve learning opportunities [2] and help organizational members gather and apply knowledge-related resources effectively [20, 21].

Given this, it is undoubtedly clear that OLMs play a fundamental role in organizations [3]. For example, they generate positive outcomes related to knowledge creation [8], continuous improvement [19], the fostering of a creative climate [9], and organizational performance [11].

Existing literature has categorized OLMs into cultural and structural facets [1, 12, 20, 21]. Cultural facets (or cognitive mechanisms [9]) enable the development of a learning culture. These include having shared vision, values, norms, assumptions, beliefs, roles, and behaviors. Structural facets (which include also procedural mechanisms [9]) are people development processes, as well as elements that ensure that learning activities are supported and realized within the workplace. For example, they include leadership, management (including performance and change management), communication, information and knowledge systems, and technology.

Taken together, existing studies posit OLMs as extremely relevant for sustaining an organizational competitive advantage. While research often explores 'why' having OLMs in place within an organization is important, and 'what' precisely OLMs are, we still know little about how organizational members perceive their implementation within the employing organization. We also know little about whether a positive perception of existing OLMs drives learning satisfaction and enjoyment.

3 Learning Models

Employees increasingly learn in multiple ways within organizations, using different learning models [5]. By learning models, we refer to the set of general principles that an entire learning experience is built upon [5]. According to the literature, choosing a learning model implies a choice between traditional, online, and blended learning.

Traditional learning is typically associated with face-to-face learning, where learners and instructors are physically present in the same place at the same time [2].

Online learning is a form of distance learning where technology mediates the learning process and teaching is delivered completely online. Learners and instructors are not required to be present in the same place at the same time [15].

Blended learning provides a learning experience through the integration of different learning methodologies, including face-to-face with a technology-enabled environment [6].

Until now, traditional learning has been predominant, even as the use of online and blended learning has been increasing, given the general increase in the use of tech-based learning [5]. Despite these trends, we still do not know whether any of the models is more or less successful in generating positive employee perceptions of OLMs.

This study therefore seeks to compare the perceptions that employees have of OLMs and their learning satisfaction and enjoyment depending on whether they use face-to-face, online, or blended learning, but also on whether they almost exclusively learn using one of these three models or a mix of models.

4   Methods

This study is part of a broader research project on how we learn today and how we will learn within organizations in the future. In the broader study, respondents replied to both open-ended and closed questions about their view on learning, their expectations, their experiences with learning models and methods, as well as their perceptions of organizational learning mechanisms and learning outcomes.

The sample in this paper consists of 67 employees, 70% of which are female, 60% of which are 35 years old or younger, 93% of which are Italian or working in Italy, 47% of which are non-HR employees (i.e. they either work in administration, accounting, or finance positions, technical or R&D positions, marketing or sales positions, general management positions, or operations, production, and logistics positions), and 55% of which work for large firms (i.e. firms with more than 250 employees).

With the exception of Lyons et al.'s [18] scale on work values, we measured the responses to the scales below by asking respondents to rate the extent to which they agree with each statement (with 1 = strongly disagree and 5 = strongly agree, including a N/A or I don't know option, where applicable).

Learning as a work value. Adapting Lyons et al.'s [18] scale on work values, we asked respondents how important it is for them to have "*the opportunity to continuously learn and develop new knowledge*" (i) when deciding to accept a potential job, (ii) when staying in a job, (iii) for being engaged in their job. The scale ranged from 1 to 5, with 1 equaling not at all important, and 5 equaling absolutely essential.

Mission-linked learning. We used a 10-item scale [1]. A sample item is "*Learning and development plans are linked to my organization's vision, mission, and goals*".

Facilitative learning environment. We used two 5-item scales [1]. A sample item is "*The continuing commitment of top management to developing people is communicated to all employees*".

Learning identification satisfaction. We used two scales [1]. One is a 5-item scale considering the section/work unit. A sample item is "*My section/work unit has a sound process for prioritizing my learning and development needs*". The other one is a 9-item scale considering the immediate supervisor. A sample item is "*My immediate supervisor uses a constructive approach to discuss my learning and development needs with me".*

Learning and development need (organizational support). We used a 7-item scale [1]. A sample item is *"I am usually able to undertake training programs that meet my training needs".*

Learning application. We used three scales [1]. The first one measures suitability using 3 items (sample item: *"I am usually asked to evaluate the suitability of my completed learning and development activities for my co-workers"*). The second one measures effectiveness using 2 items (sample item: *"Learning and development activities within my organization are cost effective"*). The third one measures immediate supervisor support and feedback using 5 items (sample item: *"My immediate supervisor helps me to put my learning into practice in the workplace"*).

Learning satisfaction. We used two 5-item scales [1]. A sample item is *"The learning programs I have undertaken in the last 12 months usually meet my learning needs".*

Learning enjoyment. We used a 3-item scale adapted from Lin et al. [17]. A sample item is *"While learning I feel happy and satisfied".*

For all these measures, Cronbach's alpha values are above 0.7, with a few exceptions that are highlighted in the tables in the rest of the paper.

5 Results

5.1 Learning Is a Key Driver for Attraction, Retention, and Engagement

The opportunity to continuously learn and develop knowledge within an organization is a key driver for potential and existing employees. It is critical for attraction, retention, and engagement.

When asked about the importance of having the opportunity to continuously learn and develop new knowledge, 83% of respondents said that it is very important or absolutely essential for them to have the opportunity to continuously learn and develop new knowledge when deciding to accept a job, or when deciding to stay in a job. Similarly, 81% of respondents felt this way with regards to being engaged in their job.

Given this, organizations need to invest in providing adequate solutions that enable employees to make the most out of their learning experiences. This is the focus of the next sections, where we analyze how employees learn (looking at learning models), and how they think their organization is doing in terms of making learning relevant and aligning it with the company's mission, as well as in terms of providing support for the exploitation of learning opportunities, and for making them relevant for daily work.

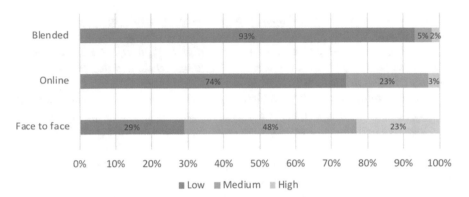

Fig. 1 Use of learning models (*Note* low category = percentage of use chosen by respondents is between 0 and 30; medium category = percentage of use chosen by respondents is between 31 and 70; high category = percentage of use chosen by respondents is between 71 and 100)

5.2   The Use of Learning Models

Despite growing attention to the use of blended learning in practice and in academic literature, in reality, employees still make ample use of the traditional, face-to-face, learning model. In our sample, 23 and 48% of respondents make up the high and medium use categories, respectively. The use of digital models, instead, is still scarce in the great majority of cases. In particular, the high use of blended learning is very limited (2% of the cases), while 93% of respondents said that they either do not use it, or use it only to a very limited extent (see Fig. 1).

5.3   Face-to-Face Versus Online Versus Blended Learning Models: Differences with Regards to Satisfaction, Enjoyment, and OLMs

When comparing the learning satisfaction and enjoyment of employees who declare a low versus medium versus high use of the three learning models, the most interesting findings are the following (see Fig. 2).

In general, overall satisfaction levels are lower than enjoyment levels. Respondents are most satisfied with low face-to-face use and are least satisfied with high online and blended use. These results confirm the idea that online learning is not yet fully exploited and properly designed. Moreover, they highlight the importance of providing employees with a range of learning models to be combined.

Respondents who indicated a low use of the face-to-face model are more satisfied relative to those who indicated medium and high use of the face-to-face model, while they enjoy learning less than those who chose medium and high face-to-face

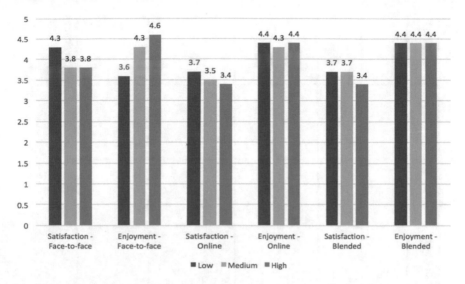

Fig. 2 Learning satisfaction and enjoyment means across sub-samples of face-to-face, online, and blended learning models (*Note* low category = percentage of use chosen by respondents is between 0 and 30; medium category = percentage of use chosen by respondents is between 31 and 70; high category = percentage of use chosen by respondents is between 71 and 100)

use levels. At medium and high levels, enjoyment levels are higher than satisfaction levels.

Respondents who indicated lower levels of use of online and blended learning models are more satisfied overall relative to those who indicated that they use these models to a higher extent. Overall, respondents using online/blended learning models report higher levels of enjoyment than satisfaction. This raises a reflection about whether digitally-based learning is just "fun" or also effective in making learning happen.

Next, the overarching trend in the data shows that employees' perceptions and evaluations of OLMs are similar across the three learning models (see Table 1).

5.4 Single Learning Model Versus Multiple Learning Models: Differences with Regards to Satisfaction, Enjoyment, and OLMs

In this section, we explore whether respondents using a mix of face-to-face, online, and blended learning models perceive higher levels of OLM effectiveness, as well as have higher learning satisfaction and enjoyment levels, compared to those who rely on a single learning model (either face-to-face, online, or blended).

Table 1 Perceptions of OLMs when using face-to-face, online, and blended learning models

	Face-to-face low	Face-to-face medium	Face-to-face high	Online low	Online medium	Online high	Blended low	Blended medium	Blended high
Mission-linked learning	3.5	3.8	3.5	3.6	3.6	3.4	3.6	3.6	3.4
Facilitative learning environment	3.6	3.9	3.6	3.7	3.7	3.6	3.7	3.5	3.6
Learning identification satisfaction—section/work unit	3.4	3.7	3.5	3.5	3.3	3.3*	3.5	3.1	3.3
Learning identification satisfaction—immediate supervisor	3.6	4.0	3.9	3.8	3.6	3.9	3.8	3.5	3.9
Learning and development need—organizational support	3.6	3.6	3.6	3.6	3.4	3.5	3.6	3.2	3.5

(continued)

Table 1 (continued)

	Face-to-face low	Face-to-face medium	Face-to-face high	Online low	Online medium	Online high	Blended low	Blended medium	Blended high
Learning application—suitability	3.8	3.6	3.9	3.9	3.4*	3.9	3.7	3.8	3.9
Learning application—effectiveness	3.6	3.6	3.9	3.7	3.1	2.8*	3.6	4.0	2.8
Learning application—immediate supervisor support and feedback	3.3	3.7	3.8	3.6	3.1	3.7	3.5	3.4	3.7

Note *Means that Cronbach's alpha values are below 0.7 or NA

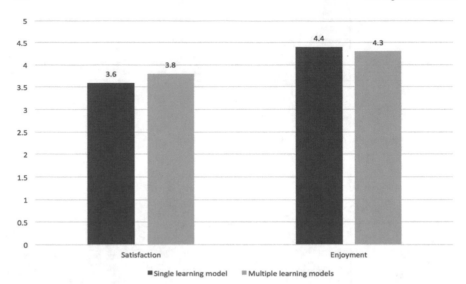

Fig. 3 Learning satisfaction and enjoyment means when using single versus multiple learning models

We perceive opposite results for satisfaction and enjoyment, even though the difference is small. Satisfaction is higher when respondents use multiple learning models, while enjoyment is slightly lower (see Fig. 3). We may assume that employees perceive a multiple learning model experience as more complex (and less "fun") but also as more effective, leading therefore to greater satisfaction.

With regards to OLMs, respondents who use multiple learning models give higher scores to all of the OLMs with the exception of learning application—effectiveness (see Table 2). This might confirm that there is no single winning learning model, because learning can occur better when an appropriate mix of different learning models is used.

6   Conclusions

In this paper, we reflect on whether digitally-based learning (including online, but also blended learning) is more or less effective in providing a learning experience that is perceived to be aligned with business and individuals' needs, and its effect on the evaluation of company OLMs.

Relying upon evidence from 67 employees' responses to an online survey, we suggest that, more than a matter of blended versus online versus face-to-face learning, it is a matter of adopting multiple learning models versus a single one to create an enriched learning experience. This implies that digitally-based learning, despite being a trend, is not always good, or at least not on its own. At the same time,

Table 2 Perceptions of OLMs when using a single learning model versus multiple learning models

	Single learning model	Multiple learning models
Mission-linked learning	3.5	3.8
Facilitative learning environment	3.6	3.9
Learning identification satisfaction—section/work unit	3.4	3.7
Learning identification satisfaction—immediate supervisor	3.6	4.0
Learning and development need—organizational support	3.5	3.7
Learning application—suitability	3.8	3.7*
Learning application—effectiveness	3.6	3.6
Learning application—immediate supervisor support and feedback	3.5	3.7

Note *Means that Cronbach's alpha values are below 0.7 or NA

traditional, or face-to-face learning, is still effective, but even more so when combined with online and blended learning models.

In fact, blended learning already implies multiple learning models, because it combines face-to-face and tech-enabled experiences, even if its current use is very limited. This means that organizations already have the "solution" to make learning more effective and improve employees' perceptions of OLMs. It is "only" a matter of making blended learning the most diffused learning model.

Given this, from a practice point of view, we recommend organizations and instructional designers to better explain and communicate what blended learning is, what the potential benefits are for employees, and how it can be used effectively. Moreover, they should carefully design learning experiences using a mix of learning models, and help employees choose and integrate them into their personal learning, in line with their learning needs.

Future research could expand on the data collection by enlarging the sample, and also explore whether additional differences emerge among groups that differ in terms of age, seniority, role, exposure to training and development, topics that they have received training on, as well as the size of the companies that respondents work for.

Moreover, future studies could include measures for learning effectiveness. In this paper, we focused on learning enjoyment and satisfaction. These measures, however, do not necessarily reflect how much employees actually learn. Alternatively, a two-stage study could be designed, where respondents answer surveys prior to and after going through learning experiences designed using a single learning model versus multiple learning models. Including a third-party evaluation (e.g. by a superior or colleagues) of learning effectiveness could also be interesting, and help avoid reliance on self-evaluation only.

References

1. Armstrong, A., & Foley, P. (2003). Foundations for a learning organization: Organization learning mechanisms. *The Learning Organization, 10*(2), 74–82.
2. Artino, A. R. (2010). Online or face-to-face learning? Exploring the personal factors that predict students' choice of instructional format. *Internet High Education, 13,* 272–276.
3. Beer, M. (2011). Developing an effective organization: Intervention method, empirical evidence, and theory. *Research in Organizational Change and Development, 19,* 1–54.
4. Cannon, M. D., & Edmondson, A. C. (2005). Failing to learn and learning to fail (intelligently): How great organizations put failure to work to innovate and improve. *Long Range Planning, 38*(3), 299–319.
5. Caporarello, L., Giovanazzi, A., & Manzoni, B. (2017). Reimagine E-learning: A proposal for a 21st learning framework. *EAI Endorsed Transactions on E-Learning, 4*(16), 1–9.
6. Caporarello, L., & Inesta, A. (2016). Blended learning approach: How is the learning educational paradigm changing? Reflections and a proposed framework. In F. D'Ascenzo, et al. (Eds.), *Blurring the boundaries through digital innovation* (pp. 49–58). Cham: Springer.
7. Caporarello, L., Manzoni, B., & Bigi, M. (2018). E-learning effectiveness from a students' perspective: An empirical study. In C. Rossignoli, F. Virili, & S. Za (Eds.), *Digital Technology and Organizational Change* (pp. 163–172). Cham: Springer.
8. Chou, S., & Wang, S. (2003). Quantifying 'ba': An investigation of the variables that are pertinent to knowledge creation. *Journal of Information Science, 29,* 167–180.
9. Cirella, S., Canterino, F., Guerci, M., & Shani, A. B. (2016). Organizational learning mechanisms and creative climate: Insights from an Italian fashion design company. *Creativity and Innovation Management, 25*(2), 211–222.
10. Fink, L. D. (2013). *Creating significant learning experiences: An integrated approach to designing college courses.* Hoboken: Wiley.
11. Fredberg, T., Norrgren, F., & Shani, A. B. (2011). Developing and sustaining change capability via learning mechanisms: A longitudinal perspective on transformation. In R. Woodman, W. Pasmore, & A. B. Shani (Eds.), *Research in organizational change and development* (pp. 117–161). Bingley: Emerald Group Publishing Limited.
12. Gephart, M. A., Marsick, V. J., Van Buren, M. E., Spiro, M. S., & Senge, P. (1996). Learning organizations come alive. *Training & Development, 50*(12), 34–46.
13. Ghoshal, S. (1987). Global strategy: An organizing framework. *Strategic Management Journal, 5,* 425–440.
14. Huysman, M. (1999). Balancing biases: A critical review of the literature on organizational learning. In M. Easterby-Smith, J. Burgoyne, & L. Araujo (Eds.), *Organizational learning and the learning organization: Developments in theory and practice* (pp. 59–74). London: Sage.
15. Joksimović, S., Kovanović, V., Skrypnyk, O., Gašević, D., Dawson, S., & Siemens, G. (2015). The history and state of online learning. *Preparing for the Digital University, 93–122.*
16. Kirkwood, A., & Price, L. (2014). Technology-enhanced learning and teaching in higher education: What is 'enhanced' and how do we know? A critical literature review. *Learning, Media and Technology, 39*(1), 6–36.
17. Lin, A., Gregor, S., & Ewing, M. (2008). Developing a scale to measure the enjoyment of web experiences. *Journal of Interactive Marketing, 22*(4), 40–57.
18. Lyons, S., Higgins, C., & Duxbury, L. (2010). Work values: Development of a new 3-dimensional structure based on confirmatory smallest space analysis. *Journal of Organizational Behavior, 31,* 969–1002.
19. Oliver, J. (2009). Continuous improvement: Role of organizational learning mechanisms. *International Journal of Quality and Reliability Management, 26,* 546–563.
20. Popper, M., & Lipshitz, R. (2000). Organizational learning: Mechanisms, culture, and feasibility. *Management Learning, 31,* 181–196.
21. Popper, M., & Lipshitz, R. (1998). Organizational learning mechanisms: A cultural and structural approach to organizational learning. *The Journal of Applied Behavioral Science, 34,* 161–179.

22. Spar, B., Dye, C., Lefkowitz, R., & Pate, D. (2018) Workplace Learning Report. LinkedIn Learning.
23. Yoon, S. W. (2003). In search of meaningful online experiences. *New Directions for Adult & Continuing Education, 100,* 19–30.

Part III
Processes and IS Design in Digital Ecosystems

Meta Principles of Technology Accessibility Design for Users with Learning Disabilities: Towards Inclusion of the Differently Enabled

Nabil Georges Badr⬛ and Michele Kosremelli Asmar⬛

Abstract People with learning disabilities are often in isolation from the rest of society. This affects their development, their health and their full participation in society. Technologies are an indispensable answer to the problem of this marginalization and not only allows to promote their inclusion in societies but also to raise awareness of society while connecting them to the services and resources available. This paper aims at exploring guiding principles to cater for the needs for inclusive technology accessibility. We review the state of the literature and identify extant concepts in search for a set of Meta principles of technology accessibility design for users with learning disabilities.

Keywords Learning disability · Human computer interaction · User interface design · User centered design · Assistive technologies

1 Introduction

Learning disabilities (LD) are generally neurologically based processing problems. These processing problems can interfere with learning basic skills such as reading, writing and/or math. LD could also be the result of visual acuity, hearing issues, or motor handicaps; of intellectual disability; of emotional disturbance; or of environmental, cultural or economic disadvantages [1]. Children and young adults with a learning disability may struggle in society, school, and family. In adult life, LD can interfere with higher-level skills such as organization, time planning, abstract reasoning, long or short-term memory and attention, thus, influencing their life beyond academics and can have serious societal impact.

People with LD may experience barriers at the level of simple essential activities such as using traditional telephones [2], operating a digital TV [3], interfacing with

N. G. Badr (✉) · M. K. Asmar
Higher Institute for Public Health, USJ, Beirut, Lebanon
e-mail: nabil@itvaluepartner.com

M. K. Asmar
e-mail: michele.asmar@usj.edu.lb

© Springer Nature Switzerland AG 2020
A. Lazazzara et al. (eds.), *Exploring Digital Ecosystems*,
Lecture Notes in Information Systems and Organisation 33,
https://doi.org/10.1007/978-3-030-23665-6_14

automated teller machine, or even voting [4]. In the US, a 2017 study by the National Center for Learning Disabilities, found that 19% of students with LD drop out of high school and 46% of adults between 18 and 65 cannot enter the labor force due to LD related conditions.[1] In 2016, in the UK, a survey has shown that only 7% of people with LD have a job. They are 58 times more likely to die before the age of 50, and 4 times more likely to have a preventable cause of death due to lack of good healthcare. One in 4 people with LD spend less than one hour outside their home each day and 93% of those interviewed by the Foundation for People with LD in 2012 said they felt lonely and isolated.[2] According to the United Nations (UNDP), 80% of people with disabilities live in developing countries, where the issue gest even more critical as most schools (91%) tend to be ill equipped with technology aids to care for the needs of students with special needs.[3]

1.1 Motivation

Historically, finding accessibility solutions for LD have concerned communities [5], employers [6], policy makers [7]. Nevertheless, persons with disabilities are often underserved. Schooling can be can be discriminatory [8], often presenting parallel education systems. Once formal schooling is over, accessibility solutions for supporting adults with disabilities are still scarce [9]. Decades ago and since, most reviews of issues in LD in the non-medical literature examine use cases and obstacles, successes and failures, adoption and abandonment of related assistive technologies [10]. Human Computer Interaction (HCI) design principles were defined for ease of use and often applied using user-centered design approaches (UCD). Users began taking center stage in the needs analysis, design and testing of the application, until there was a need for more inclusive designs to improve the usability of assistive technology (AT) products [11] and broaden their application to different user groups. Technology publications boast the existence of standards and guidelines for inclusive designs without directly addressing the needs of people with LD in the depth required [12]. *What is the state of research on accessible designs for people with LD? What principles of HCI design exist for users with disabilities? What Meta principles for accessibility of users with LD can be instantiated towards the inclusion of differently enabled users?*

---

[1] https://www.ncld.org/.

[2] https://www.mencap.org.uk/about-learning-disability/about-learning-disability/facts-about-learning-disability.

[3] InfoPro Survey in Lebanon 2014.

2 Approach

In line with the pivotal work of [13, 14] in HCI design, our paper seeks to underscore Meta principles (higher order guiding principles) for accessible designs for people with LD. Our aim is not to present an exhaustive set of principles, but rather to underscore essential higher order guiding principles for technology accessibility design for users with LD. Our approach consists of four basic steps:

First, we provide a background on the context of people with LD followed by an overview of related assistive technology, interfaces, and accessibility/usability concepts for the foundation of our paper's objective.

Then we conduct a thorough review of the literature on suggested rules and guidelines for accessible designs for inclusion. We search for papers written in the English language and including keywords of "information technology"; "information technologies"; "human computer interaction"; "user interface design"; "user centered design"; "assistive technology"; "assistive technologies" in the context of LD. We pay attention to include all possible permutations in plural and singular form of the keywords.

Next, in an attempt to deepen the exploration on the main topic of the paper within its stated scope, we conduct a search for empirical case studies in peer reviewed journals written in English, with the keywords "case studies" AND "learning disability" AND "accessible design". No date limits were applied and no journals were excluded in the search. Case studies are investigated as they reflect an in-depth, and detailed examination of a subject of study [15]. The search on Google Scholar found only 124 articles in journals on education, assistive technology, human computer interaction and disability informatics including medico-social journals, practitioner publications and policy periodicals. The papers were read in full, checked for relevance, excluding patents and citations, removing duplicates, and restricting the review to papers relevant to our study. Consequently, 32 papers were singled out for our work as they relate directly to technology designs for people with LD or related disabilities as opposed the remaining studies that pivoted around classroom settings, landscape, environment, or access for the physically disabled. Findings from these papers are presented in Sects. 4.1 and 4.2.

Lastly, we categorize the extant case studies under themes to guide the discussion around accessibility design guiding principles for users with LD.

3 Background

Though scarce, most of the literature in the context of people with LD focus on use cases for technologies, interfaces, and present concepts of usability and guidelines for accessible designs.

3.1   Context of People with LD

The term "Learning Disabilities" is an "umbrella" term describing a number of other, more specific LD, that affect a person's ability to understand numbers and learn math facts (Dyscalculia); or a person's reading ability and related language-based processing skills (Dyslexia); or a person's handwriting ability and fine motor skills (Dysgraphia). Most people with LD (85%) have a reading disability, or dyslexia [16].

LD could derive from or induce other behavioral disorders such as ADHD (Attention Deficit, Hyperactivity Disorder), a condition that would make learning extremely challenging. Such is in the case of Visual Perceptual/Visual Motor Deficits affect the understanding of information that a person sees, or the ability to draw or copy. Other non-verbal LD, such as trouble interpreting nonverbal cues like facial expressions or body language and may have poor coordination, which may induce learning difficulties. Although not a learning disability, Dyspraxia (a developmental disorder of the brain in childhood causing difficulty in activities requiring coordination and movement) often exists along with dyslexia, dyscalculia or ADHD and affects the ability of executive functioning (processes such as planning, organization, strategizing, paying attention to and remembering details, and managing time and space). LD related physical disabilities such as Auditory Processing Disorders (APD) affect how sound that travels unimpeded through the ear is processed and interpreted by the brain may also impede learning abilities, precisely in the case of Language Processing Disorder (LPD), a specific type of (APD) that affects attaching meaning to sound groups that form words, sentences and stories.

3.2   Technologies, Interfaces, Usability and Inclusion

The notion of assistive technology (AT) refers to devices used to compensate for disabilities. The US Technology-Related Assistance Act of 1988 defines an assistive technology as *"any item, piece of equipment, or product system acquired commercially off-the-shelf, modified, or customized, that is used to increase, maintain or improve the functional capabilities of individuals with disabilities"*. Persons with LD have deficits in the ways they process information. AT would then provide a means of modifying the way they receive or express information in a manner that accentuates their strengths and helps them work around their difficulties in potentially achieving job independence, satisfaction, and success to their use of technology [17]. The selection of an appropriate technology will depend on the individual's strengths and weaknesses in areas such as reading, writing, math, spelling, listening, memory, and organization as well as on the individual's prior experience with and interest in using AT [18].

AT for persons with LD can include, but is not limited to, recorded books, computers with speech recognition, tape recorders, readers/tablets, spellers/spellcheckers, calculators and organizers, word processors with optical character recognition (OCR) systems (as an aid for dyslexia and reading disabilities). AT tools for auditory processing disorders can include listening devices, audio recorders captions and text-to-speech apps. Software solutions include speech recognition, text-to-speech and typing tutors, ideal for those with dyslexia, dysgraphia (voice recognition software, word processing with OCR, etc.) and dyscalculia (software that assists with mathematical function using graphics, simplifications and breaking down complex functions into simpler ones [19].

In the early understanding of AT, researchers report that developers have sought ways to adapt mainstream technologies and modify them for the use of people who have disabilities [20]. However, acceptance of AT among users is impacted by its utility and usability [21]. In the last few years, technology standards have explored ways to transform AT that can result in new forms of social inclusion, transforming the thinking of technology developers to build technology for people, not disabilities [22].

Inclusive and accessible user interface standards (as opposed to assistive) are proposed as part of new implementations [23]. Technology feature and functionality standards for LD have transitioned focus from which technology to use to what interface to use for the technology. Adapting interfaces of existing platforms to include persons with LD (inclusive) instead of developing specific AT that assists persons with LD (assistive). Touch to see, tactile learning, 3D technologies bring a sense of inclusion [24], with features of haptic feedback [25]. Such features are leading this inclusion transition.

Workers with mental deficiencies have advocated tactile interaction for learning of real tasks using devices and equipment that support tactile interfaces as opposed to computer mouse or keyboard as a means of data entry [26]. Their colleagues who have no impairment could reach the same outcome, benefit equally and share the experience. Wearable computing [27], internet of things (IoT), artificial intelligence (AI), and cloud computing are becoming integrated into a trend to achieve the claim of inclusion [28].

3.3 Legislation for Accessibility of Web-Based Interfaces

International legislations (US[4] (1973 with an amendment to section 508 in 2017); AU[5] (1996); UK[6] (2012); Canada[7] (2012) and the EU[8] (2016), have precipitated to set guidelines for accessibility of web-based interfaces [12].

In summary, section 508 technical standards for features of accessibility at the interface level, software applications and operating systems discussing accessibility

---

[4]https://www.access-board.gov/attachments/article/1877/ict-rule.pdf.

[5]http://webguide.gov.au/accessibility-usability/accessibility/.

[6]https://www.out-law.com/page-330.

[7]Canadian Treasury Board Secretariat Standard on Web Accessibility. Tbs-sct.gc.ca. 2011-08-01.

[8]Council of the European Union Inter-institutional File: 2012/0340 (COD).

Table 1 Web content accessibility guidelines (WCAG 2.0)

Principle	Guidelines
Perceivable—ability to perceive information being presented (even if it can't be invisible to all of the users senses)	• Provide text alternatives for non-text content • Provide captions and other alternatives for multimedia • Create content presentable in different ways without losing meaning • Make it easier for users to see and hear content
Operable—Ability to operate the interface (cannot require interaction that a user cannot perform)	• Make all functionality available from touch, keyboard or mouse • Help users navigate and find content • Give users enough time to read and use content
Understandable—Ability to understand information as well as operation of the user interface	• Make text readable and understandable • Make content appear and operate in predictable ways • Help users avoid and correct mistakes
Robust—Ability to access the content as user capabilities evolve and technologies advance	• Maximize compatibility with current and future user tools

related to standardized ports, and mechanically operated controls such as keyboards and touch screens. The definition of the specification assures accessibility to web content, e.g., text description for any visuals such that users of with a disability or users that need AT such as screen readers and refreshable Braille displays, can access the content.

At a macro level, section 508 technical standards echo guidelines of Web Accessibility Initiative (WAI), developed by the World Wide Web Consortium (W3C) covering web authoring tools, content and browsers and media players, including some aspects of AT.[9] Web Content Accessibility Guidelines version 2.0 (WCAG 2.0), published by the Web Accessibility Initiative (WAI) have defined 12 guidelines for inclusion organized under four principles (websites must be perceivable, operable, understandable, and robust) (Table 1).

4 Findings and Discussion

4.1 Principles and Guidelines for Accessible Designs

Principles of HCI Design for Users with Disabilities. Though scarce, research has recognized the value of accessible web design [29] and identified principles for HCI design for users with disabilities. Our literature review reveals a wide consensus that

---

[9]https://www.w3.org/WAI/intro/components.php.

Table 2 HCI Design for users with disabilities[a]

Focus	Guidance
Layout	• Use bigger graphic elements i.e. fonts, buttons, icons etc. • Use very few colors, clearly distinct from one another • Use sound (sparingly) to reinforce the visual information
Content	• Avoid lengthy written information • Minimize information that must be remembered from one screen to the next • Use familiarity and imagery for what must be remembered • Reduce the normally suggested number of maximum elements on a screen
Navigation aids	• Direct users' attention by structuring and grouping elements • Avoid simultaneous tasks • Offer a narrow and shallow decision structure with few choices for options • Avoid situations when the user feels 'trapped' in a screen—triggering severe frustration
Motor & Sensory Aids	• Find alternatives to using the mouse or part of the keyboard. Minimize the number of gross motor movements e.g. back and forth between mouse and keyboard and transitions between gross and fine motor movements

[a]Consolidation from the literature [20, 21, 24, 25, 30–37]

an approach of principles for simplicity (in layout, navigation and content) that has produced a positive outcome for target user groups in different contexts, cultures and social settings based on user centered design practices (Table 2).

4.2 State of the Research on Accessible Designs for People with LD

We have found that research on this subject has focused on advocating the Web Accessibility initiative, noting the lack of awareness about the needs of the disabled and addressing suggestions to improve the quality of services.

"Accessibility *in learning shouldn't be viewed as a compliance activity, rather it should be embraced as a means of ensuring good design*" [38; p. 62]. The state of the art in web accessibility research, development and practice shows timid progress in this domain [39, 40]. Empirical investigation exploring the use of accessibility standards for people with LD is scarce. Our literature search has identified four main directions of research. The first direction presents case studies that advocate the use of Web Accessibility Standards [41–44], identify shortcomings [45] and suggest ways to refine the related guidelines [46].

Another stream of studies recommends approaches to promote awareness on the need for diversity [47], identifies accessibility needs, requirements, and preferences

[48, 49], and provides guidance to develop accessible e-learning practice [50]. In a third direction, empirical studies have concluded strong support for extending user centered design principles [51] that engage persons with disabilities in all the phases of the technology design [52]. Finally, we have identified a recent trend in the literature promoting inclusion for differently enabled users especially in quality of services for learning [40, 42, 53–55].

Table 3 summarizes these findings into four suggested Meta principles of Technology accessibility design for users with LD.

4.3   Accessibility Design Principles for Users with LD

Refining Web Accessibility Principles and Guidelines. Colwell et al. [40] describe the need for a diverse solution for access to laboratory work for students unable to attend conventional lab setting due to visually, physical or hearing impairment [40]. This brings up the conversation that different people can have different but related views of accessibility [41]. Case studies in distance learning for students and teachers with general disabilities have recognized positive experience enhancements in the adoption of universal design and universal access principles [46] with the implementation of web accessibility standards [42]. Most studies found advocate the use of reference principles from the Web Accessibility Initiative in a general context [42–44]. Shortcomings are related to evaluation benchmarks and indicators [45], lack of policies required, integration tools available and additional tools needed [42].

Building Awareness on the Need for Diversity. Awareness at the policy making level has been set for more than a decade [56]. Yet, case studies still find significant obstacles. Addressing accessibility needs for secondary adolescent with disabilities, Savi et al. [48] evaluate acceptable use outcomes for a website that adhere to accessibility standards. Library programs and service providers lack awareness about the needs of the disabled among the leaders and trainers in the library profession [47], giving rise to case studies offering suggestions to improve the quality of library services for students with disabilities [55]. Studies involving people with cognitive disabilities [44] confirm the scale of diversity in the need for accessibility with specific requirements and preferences. For individuals with LD, synchronous discussion is not very conducive as it is synonymous with the rapid delivery and execution of thoughts and ideas. Pedagogical approaches must be aware of these specific disabilities to be able to plan for an alternate method of communication [54].

Extending the Application of User Centered Design Principles. Deep awareness is required in order to develop accessible e-learning practice that would provide an inclusive accessibility for a large scope of individuals with LD. For instance, accessibility features in technology may not be sufficient in the case of the visually impaired demanding a certain dependence on support by a seeing person for their learning experience [51]. In their case study, Kennedy and Leung [52] have advocated user centered design principles that considering the needs of intellectually disabled communities might be beneficial for effective digital experience design. The diver-

Table 3 Meta Principles of Technology Accessibility Design for Users with LD

Meta principles	Study findings [Ref]	Use case (Related disability)
Refining web accessibility principles and guidelines	Advocate the web accessibility initiative in a general context [41]	Access to laboratory work for students unable to attend conventional setting (visual/physical/hearing)
	Recognize the value of web accessibility designs [42]	Distance learning (students and teachers with general disabilities)
	Web accessibility design standards—shortcomings: evaluation benchmarks, policies, tools [45]	Distance learning (students and teachers with general disabilities)
	Suggested accessibility indicators for distance learning [46]	Distance learning (students and teachers with general disabilities)
	Advocate the Web Accessibility initiative in a general context [43]	Evaluate outcome for website that adhere to accessibility standards (Secondary adolescent)
	Advocate the web accessibility initiative in a general context [44]	Using accessible web 2.0 (students with disabilities)
Building awareness on the need for diversity	Lack of awareness about the needs of the disabled [47]	Access to library programs and services (general disabilities)
	Deep awareness is required in order to develop accessible e-learning practice [50]	Different people can have different but related views of accessibility (general disabilities)
	Confirms diversity of the accessibility needs, requirements, and preferences [48]	Synthesize measures for accessibility to electronic communication (people with cognitive disabilities)
	Awareness of disabilities is needed to plan for an alternate method of communication [49]	Synchronous discussion is not very conducive to this type of learning (learning disability)
Extending user centered design principles	Advocate extending user centered design principles [51]	Needs identification considered beneficial to digital experience designers (intellectual disability)
	Framework for assessing the potential effectiveness of emerging experiential media platforms [52]	Including persons with disabilities in building media prototypes... (differently enabled users)

(continued)

Table 3 (continued)

Meta principles	Study findings [Ref]	Use case (Related disability)
Inclusion of differently enabled users—quality of services	Suggestions to improve quality of library services for students with disabilities [53]	Library programs and services (general disabilities)
	Accessibility is not sufficient—dependence on support by a seeing person [54]	Accessible education for blind learners (visually impaired/Blind)
	Universal design and universal access in distance learning [40]	Distance learning (students and teachers with general disabilities)
	Lack of governmental governance for equally accessible systems for education [55]	Serious discrimination persists in some societies (general disabilities)
	Recommendation to use graphical content to counteract the negative impact of dyslexia [42]	Accessibility study of dyslexia and information retrieval (learning disability/dyslexia)

sity of LD challenges the usability (fit for use) and accessibility (fit for purpose) of devices by multiple user groups, generating a need for complex customizations [57]. Increasingly, developers of application for people with LD have found better success by integrating user centered design (UCD) processes to improve accessibility and usability (visibility, legibility and language) of systems by users with impaired functions [58]. Users with special needs [59], perceptual impairments [34], visual impairments [60], cognitive impairments [61], and reading disabilities [32] participate in defining, testing and adjusting application interface and functionalities to inform inclusive designs [62].

Towards the Inclusion of Differently Enabled Users. Since more than a decade, closer to the practitioner's circle, inclusive design guidelines have stipulated adequate design principles of user interfaces that have a high impact on the social lives of users with disabilities [63]. The intention is to inform design thinking in the context of providing a comparable experience for all, suitably in different situations, to people regardless of their circumstances [ibidem]. Designers have looked at ways to provide information, tools, services and structures that is readable, understandable and usable for the biggest possible user group [23]. In their study on accessibility study related to information retrieval, Dyslexia had a negative effect on search performance in systems with a low tolerance for errors [53]. Berget et al. [53] recommend using graphical content to counteract the negative impact of dyslexia. Emerging experiential media platforms, using augmented and virtual reality. These platforms advance accessible AT in the direction of inclusion of differently enabled users [43].

5 Conclusion

The paper explores the present LD literature to outline the principles capable to support the present transition from assistive technologies to inclusive technologies (i.e. that can be used both by impaired and non-impaired people). We have reviewed guidance indicated for HCI for users with disabilities (with a special attention to LD), user centered design approaches recommended for enhancing the usability of AT and interfaces, legislations driving the need for accessible designs at the policy level and inclusive design guidelines used by practitioners. Following these guidelines, and associated techniques, the World Wide Web Consortium (W3C) claims to make content accessible to a wider range of people with disabilities, including blindness and low vision, deafness and hearing loss, learning disabilities, cognitive limitations, limited movement, speech disabilities, photosensitivity and combinations of these.

From our review, it is evident that interest in the subject of this paper is growing. With less than 10 papers found dating prior to the turn of the millennium, we found a steady increase in publications since. The period between 2001 and 2016 has seen an average of 5–6 papers published per year, whereas our search shows twice as many (12 papers) in 2017 alone. These publications address obstacles and shortcomings [42, 44, 47, 54], sometimes provide suggestions for improvements [43, 45, 53, 55] and largely advocate the use of web accessibility standards and UCD [40, 42, 46, 48, 50, 52].

That said, we recognize that there has been a clear focus on improved reading capabilities for people with cognitive disabilities in the case of WCAG 2.0. However, adherence to accessibility guidelines is weak as concluded by Jaeger and Xie [64], possibly induced by the constant change of technology platforms and implementations [65].

Extant contributions from the literature postulate how to make content accessible ubiquitously, interfaces usable to all user agents, primarily for people with disabilities. Nevertheless, a consensus is yet to be reached in areas of access to technology for people with cognitive difficulties [66].

We have not yet found a formalized set of principles that can be essential in the complete usability experience of people with learning disabilities! For instance, internet access technologies for individuals with deaf-blindness are still in the early stages of development and are targeted towards specific functions of the internet. This signals that inclusive design principles have not yet reached the breadth required for effective inclusion [37]. Therefore, we conclude that research has yet a significant challenge ahead to provide a more pragmatic evidence for theory and practice in the direction of inclusive AT.

The authors are aware that a set of design principles for inclusion may be costly and arduous to implement but still helpful to orient practitioners' work and further development. Awareness of ethical-technical implications of IT/IS design is increasing so that writing and conversation and elaboration of these concepts are of importance. Furthermore, learning disabilities also affect the elderly, a part of the world population which is steadily increasing and looking for support through the development of inclusive ITs.

In closing, we borrow from MacIver [67; p. 1708) and reckon that "*Inclusion is influenced by the physical environment, attitudes, expectations and opportunities, in addition to a learner's skills and abilities*". Through this paper we encourage broader and deeper studies on inclusion for people with LD in order to enrich the literature and heighten the awareness on the subject. Requirements for inclusion could be costly and complicated hindering its realization in contexts where accessibility to information is mostly necessary [68].

Still, "it is necessary to move beyond guidelines that focus on one-way transfer of information and to develop guidelines for multidirectional communication" [69; p. 55). Practitioners and technology developers are invited to use this paper to hone their approaches towards inclusive platforms. Platforms that combine HCI simplicity principles discussed in the paper, refine guidance from WCAG 2.0 with benchmarks and indicators, broaden the application of UCD principles with clear awareness for the need for diversity, serving the sustainable agenda,[10] towards the inclusion of differently enabled users in the digital ecosystem.

References

1. Gerber, P. J. (2001). Learning disabilities: A life-span approach. In *Research and global perspectives in learning disabilities* (pp. 173–186). London: Routledge.
2. Mann, W. C., Belchior, P., Tomita, M. R., & Kemp, B. J. (2005). Barriers to the use of traditional telephones by older adults with chronic health conditions. *OTJR: Occupation, Participation and Health, 25*(4), 160–166.
3. Pedlow, R. (2008). How will the changeover to digital broadcasting in 2009 influence the accessibility of TV for Americans with disabilities? *Disability Studies Quarterly, 28*(4).
4. Summers, K., & Langford, J. (2015). The impact of literacy on usable and accessible electronic voting. In International Conference on UAHCI (pp. 248–257). Springer, Cham.
5. Onyett, S., Pillinger, T., & Muijen, M. (1995). *Making community mental health teams work.* London: Sainsbury Centre for Mental Health.
6. Bruyere, S. M., Erickson, W., & Horne, R. L. (2002). Survey of the federal government on supervisor practices in employment of people with disabilities. *Employment and Disability Institute Collection, 65.*
7. Bruyere, S. M., Erickson, W., & Horne, R. L. (2002). Disability employment policies and practices in US Federal Government agencies: EEO/HR and supervisor perspectives.
8. Maisak, R. (2015). Accessibility of Thai university websites: Awareness, barriers and drivers for accessible practice.
9. Hoppestad, B. S. (2013). Current perspective regarding adults with intellectual and developmental disabilities accessing computer technology. *Disability and Rehabilitation: Assistive Technology, 8*(3), 190–194.
10. Butler, D. L. (2004). Adults with learning disabilities. In *Learning about learning disabilities* (3rd ed., pp. 565–598).
11. Campbell, P. H., Milbourne, S., Dugan, L. M., & Wilcox, M. J. (2006). A review of evidence on practices for teaching young children to use assistive technology devices. *Topics in Early Childhood Special Education, 26*(1), 3–13.

---

[10]https://www.un.org/sustainabledevelopment/sustainable-development-goals/.

12. Anderson, S., Bohman, P., Burmeister, O., & Sampson-Wild, G. (2004). User needs and e-government accessibility: The future impact of WCAG 2.0. UI4All 2004, LNCS 3196 (pp. 289–304). Berlin: Springer.
13. Cockton, G.: Getting there: Six Meta-principles and interaction design. In: CHI 2008 (ACM Conference on Human Factors in Computing Systems), Boston. USA, April 4–9, 2009.
14. Cockton, G. (2010). Design situations and methodological innovation in interaction design. In CHI'10 Extended Abstracts on Human Factors in Computing Systems (pp. 2745–2754). ACM (2010).
15. Benbasat, I., Goldstein, D. K., & Mead, M. (1987). The case research strategy in studies of information systems. MIS quarterly, 369–386.
16. Shaywitz, S. E., & Shaywitz, B. A. (2007). The neurobiology of reading and dyslexia. *The ASHA Leader, 12*(12), 20–21.
17. Yeager, P., Kaye, H. S., Reed, M., & Doe, T. M. (2006). Assistive technology and employment: Experiences of Californians with disabilities. *Work, 27*(4), 333–344.
18. Gillespie, A., Best, C., & O'Neill, B. (2012). Cognitive function and assistive technology for cognition: A systematic review. *Journal of the International Neuropsychological Society, 18*(1), 1–19.
19. Groba, B., Pousada, T., & Nieto, L. (2010) Assistive technologies, tools and resources for the access and use of ICT by people with disabilities. In *Handbook of research on personal autonomy technologies and disability informatics* (Vol. 1) (2010).
20. Brodwin, M. G., Star, T., & Cardoso, E. (2004). Computer assistive technology for people who have disabilities: Computer adaptations and modifications. *Journal of Rehabilitation, 70*(3), 28.
21. Alper, S., & Raharinirina, S. (2006). Assistive technology for individuals with disabilities: A review and synthesis of the literature. *JSET, 21*(2), 47–64.
22. Foley, A., & Ferri, B. A. (2012). Technology for people, not disabilities: ensuring access and inclusion. *Journal of Research in Special Educational Needs, 12*(4), 192–200.
23. Giakoumis, D., Kaklanis, N., Votis, K., & Tzovaras, D. (2014). Enabling user interface developers to experience accessibility limitations through visual, hearing, physical and cognitive impairment simulation. *Universal Access in the Information Society, 13*(2), 227–248.
24. Knochel, A. D., Hsiao, W. H., & Pittenger, A. (2018). Touching to see: Tactile learning, assistive technologies, and 3-D printing. *Art Education, 71*(3), 7–13.
25. Sorgini, F., Caliò, R., Carrozza, M. C., & Oddo, C. M. (2018). Haptic-assistive technologies for audition and vision sensory disabilities. *Disability and Rehabilitation: Assistive Technology, 13*(4), 394–421.
26. Loup-Escande, E., Christmann, O., Damiano, R., Hernoux, F., & Richir, S. (2012). Virtual reality learning software for individuals with intellectual disabilities: comparison between touchscreen and mouse interactions. In *ICDVRAT* (9; 2012; Laval) (pp. 295–303). The University of Reading.
27. de Oliveira Neto, J. S., Silva, A. L. M., Nakano, F., Pérez-Álcazar, J. J., & Kofuji, S. T. (2018). When wearable computing meets smart cities: Assistive technology empowering persons with disabilities. In Examining developments and applications of wearable devices in modern society (pp. 58–85). IGI Global.
28. Vanderheiden, G. C., Chourasia, A., Tobias, J., & Githens, S. (2014, June). The library GPII system. In International Conference on UAHCI (pp. 494–505). Springer, Cham. .
29. Thoms, E. L. (2004). Accessible solutions: The value of accessible web design.
30. Raskind, M. H., & Higgins, E. L. (1998). Assistive technology for postsecondary students with learning disabilities: An overview. *Journal of Learning Disabilities, 31*(1), 27–40.
31. Evett, L., & Brown, D. (2005). Text formats and web design for visually impaired and dyslexic readers—Clear text for all. *Interacting with Computers, 17*(4), 453–472.
32. Pareto, L., & Snis, U. L. (2006). Understanding users with reading disabilities or reduced vision: Toward a universal design of an auditory, location-aware museum guide. *International Journal on Disability and Human Development, 5*(2), 147–154.

33. Aspinall, A., & Barnard, S. (2007). Assistive technology and telecare to support adults with learning disabilities: key findings from the TATE Project. *Journal of Assis. Tech., 1*(1), 53–57.
34. Jacko, J. A., Leonard, V. K., & Scott, I. U. (2009). Perceptual impairments: New advancements promoting technological access. Human-Computer Interaction: Designing for Diverse Users and Domains, 93–110 (2009).
35. Jaeger, P. T. (2006). Assessing Section 508 compliance on federal e-government web sites: A multi-method, user-centered evaluation of accessibility for persons with disabilities. *Government Information Quarterly, 23*(2), 169–190.
36. Shokuhi Targhi, S. A study of mobile accessibility for users of IOS VoiceOver.
37. Perfect, E., Jaiswal, A., & Davies, T. C. (2018). Systematic review: Investigating the effectiveness of assistive technology to enable internet access for individuals with deaf blindness. *Assistive Technology* (2017).
38. Jagger, P. (2018). Good by Design. *ITNOW, 60*(1), 62–63.
39. Miesenberger, K., & Petz, A. (2014). "Easy-to-Read on the Web": State of the Art and Needed Research. In ICCHP (pp. 161–168). Springer, Cham. (2014).
40. Colwell, C., Scanlon, E., & Cooper, M. (2002). Using remote laboratories to extend access to science and engineering. *Computers & Education, 38*(1–3), 65–76.
41. Seale, J. (2006). The rainbow bridge metaphor as a tool for developing accessible e-learning practices in higher education. *CJLT, 32*(2).
42. Burgstahler, S., Corrigan, B., & McCarter, J. (2004). Making distance learning courses accessible to students and instructors with disabilities: A case study. *The Internet and Higher Education, 7*(3), 233–246.
43. Pavlik, J. V. (2017). Experiential media and disabilities in education: Enabling Learning through Immersive, Interactive, Customizable, and Multi-sensorial Digital Platforms. *Ubiquitous Learning: An International Journal, 10*(1).
44. Borg, J., Lantz, A., & Gulliksen, J. (2015). Accessibility to electronic communication for people with cognitive disabilities: A systematic search and review of empirical evidence. *Universal Access in the Information Society, 14*(4), 547–562.
45. Burgstahler, S. (2006). The development of accessibility indicators for distance learning programs. *ALT-J, 14*(1), 79–102.
46. Burgstahler, Sheryl. (2002). Distance learning: Universal design, universal access. *AACE Journal, 10*(1), 32–61.
47. Schmetzke, A. (2001). Web accessibility at university libraries and library schools. *Library hi tech, 19*(1), 35–49.
48. Savi, C. O., Savenye, W., & Rowland, C. (2008). The effects of implementing web accessibility standards on the success of secondary adolescents. *JEMH (AACE), 17*(3), 387.
49. Maisak, R. (2015). Accessibility of Thai university websites: Awareness, barriers and drivers for accessible practice.
50. Ellis, K. (2011). Embracing learners with disability: Web 2.0, access and insight. *Telecommunications Journal of Australia, 61*(2).
51. Kinash, S., & Paszuk, A. (2007). Accessible education for blind learners: Kindergarten through postsecondary. IAP. (2007).
52. Kennedy, H., & Leung, L. (2008). Lessons from web Accessibility and Intellectual disability. *Digital Experience Design: Ideas, Industries, Interaction, 69* (2008).
53. Berget, G., Caldwell, B., Cooper, M., & Guarino Reid, L. (2016). Search and find? An accessibility study of dyslexia and information retrieval WCAG 2.0. University of Wisconsin-Madison (2016).
54. Newland, B., Pavey, J., & Boyd, V. (2018) *Disabled students and VLEs—Introduction*. Durham University (2018).
55. Hernon, P., & Calvert, P. J. (Eds.). Improving the quality of library services for students with disabilities. Libraries Unlimited. (2006).
56. Jaeger, P. T. (2006). Telecommunications policy and individuals with disabilities: Issues of accessibility and social inclusion in the policy and research agenda. *Telecommunications Policy, 30*(2), 112–124.

57. Petz, A., & Tronbacke, B. (2008). People with specific learning difficulties: Easy to read and HCI. In ICCHP (pp. 690–692). Berlin: Springer.
58. Selker, T., Rosenzweig, E., & Pandolfo, A. (2006). A methodology for testing voting systems. *Journal of usability studies, 2*(1), 7–21.
59. Hagelkruys, D., Motschnig, R., Böhm, C., Vojtova, V., Kotasová, M., & Jurkova, K.: Human-centered design in action: Designing and performing testing sessions with users with special needs. In EdMedia (pp. 499–508). (2015) AACE.
60. Huang, P. H., & Chiu, M. C. (2016). Integrating user centered design, universal design and goal, operation, method and selection rules to improve the usability of DAISY player for persons with visual impairments. *Appl. Ergon., 52,* 29–42.
61. Jokisuu, E., Langdon, P. M., & Clarkson, P. J.: A framework for studying cognitive impairment to inform inclusive design. In Designing inclusive systems (pp. 115–124). Berlin: Springer.
62. Hagelkruys, D., & Motschnig, R. (2017). The LITERACY-portal as the subject of a case study on a human-centered design solution supporting users with special needs. *International Journal on E-Learning, 16*(2), 129–147 (Waynesville, NC USA (2017): AACE).
63. Abascal, J., & Nicolle, C. (2005). Moving towards inclusive design guidelines for socially and ethically aware HCI. *Interacting with Computers, 17*(5), 484–505.
64. Harper, S., & Chen, A. Q. (2012). Web accessibility guidelines. *World Wide Web, 15*(1), 61–88.
65. Harper, S., & Yesilada, Y.: Web accessibility: Current trends. In *Handbook of research on personal autonomy technologies and disability informatics* (Vol. 1, pp. 172–190).
66. Easton, C. (2010). The web content accessibility guidelines 2.0: An analysis of industry self-regulation. *International Journal of Law and Information Technology, 19*(1), 74–93.
67. Maciver, D., Hunter, C., Adamson, A., Grayson, Z., Forsyth, K., & McLeod, I. (2018). Supporting successful inclusive practices for learners with disabilities in high schools: A multisite, mixed method collective case study. *Disability and Rehabilitation, 40*(14), 1708–1717.
68. Yi, Y. J. (2015). Compliance of Section 508 in public library systems with the largest percentage of underserved populations. *Government Information Quarterly, 32*(1), 75–81.
69. Jaeger, P. T., & Xie, B. (2009). Developing online community accessibility guidelines for persons with disabilities and older adults. *Journal of Disability Policy Studies, 20*(1), 55–63.

Business Process Analysis and Change Management: The Role of Material Resource Planning and Discrete-Event Simulation

Antonio Di Leva, Emilio Sulis, Angela De Lellis and Ilaria Angela Amantea

Abstract This contribution explores the role of business process simulation to address change management projects dealing with organizational growth. In particular, we consider the adoption of new ICT applications in the context of a growing Small Medium Enterprise based in northern Italy. As income doubled in few years, managers exploited the opportunity to implement a more efficient material resource planning together with an accurate business process analysis. First, the organization was modeled by adopting standard notation BPMN 2.0. Second, data analysis explores organization details as orders arrival, duration of activities, staff working hours. Finally, discrete-event simulation of business processes offers interesting suggestions by varying incoming transactions as well as different parameters in the model. The approach clearly shows how modeling, computational simulation and scenario analysis of business processes are suitable tools to support organizational change.

Keywords Business process management · Discrete-event simulation · Change management · Scenario analysis

1 Introduction and Related Work

Industrial organizations are often involved in the reorganization of their business processes, mostly to adapt their processes to new market perspectives. In particular, companies with increasing incomes and experimenting organizational growth

A. Di Leva · E. Sulis (✉) · A. De Lellis · I. A. Amantea
University of Turin, 185 Corso Svizzera, 10149 Turin, Italy
e-mail: sulis@di.unito.it

A. Di Leva
e-mail: dileva@di.unito.it

A. De Lellis
e-mail: delellis@di.unito.it

I. A. Amantea
e-mail: amantea@di.unito.it

© Springer Nature Switzerland AG 2020   211
A. Lazazzara et al. (eds.), *Exploring Digital Ecosystems*,
Lecture Notes in Information Systems and Organisation 33,
https://doi.org/10.1007/978-3-030-23665-6_15

in terms of profit or revenues, have to decide if and how to face new opportunities by changing the internal organization. New business processes imply an improvement of industrial performance [11]. In the context of Business Process Management (BPM) [7, 19], computational simulation is an useful management instrument playing a key role in the definition of processes re-engineering [20]. Several modeling techniques have been developed in the analysis of the actual (As-Is) situation to describe organization's processes, as well as in the re-engineering phase leading to restructured (To-Be) processes [5]. Among the existing techniques, computer-based Discrete Event Simulation (DES) [13] is relevant for planning and decision-making in the enterprise. In fact, managers can greatly benefit from the analysis of the outcomes of simulated scenarios. Simulation results allow to detect inefficiencies, bottlenecks, constraints, and risks [2] as well as to estimate the performance of the system when some modification has been applied.

To evaluate the impact of ICT on organizational processes and stress the relevance of the adoption of computational simulation, we focus on the real-case of a medium-sized enterprise (SME). The company produces excellent plastic decorations for high fashion stylists, rapidly increasing in recent years by almost doubling profits as well as their production. From January 2017 the Company adopted a Material Requirements Planning (MRP) to improve the production management. Such innovation introduces considerable benefits in organizational efficiency [14, 16]. In our approach, we explore the industrial organization changes by adopting a methodological framework based on three phases: Context and Data Analysis, Process Engineering, and Scenario Analysis.

In this paper we explore a design science [3] perspective to investigate business processes and change management [10] for improve, re-engineer and automate an organization [11]. Design science is a recent paradigm in the Information Systems (IS) research community, emerged as an alternative paradigm different from the Management Information Systems tradition. While the last mostly concerns analytical efforts in studying organisations to better understand cause and effect, design science adopt a more inclusive vision of IS research, also focusing on the design and building of different kinds of IS artefacts. In the Design Science Research Process proposed by [15], we mostly focus on the entry points of Design and demonstration of artifacts and Demonstration activities, by studying the adoption of MRP, as well as modeling and simulating business process.

Process modeling techniques support changes at different levels, e.g. human resources, warehouse management, third parties applications [4]. Such techniques include specific languages. In this work we adopted the standard language Business Process Modeling and Notation (BPMN) [1]. Among the existing simulation software we adopt in our methodological framework iGrafx Process [12]. The tool supports BPMN and implements Discrete Event Simulation (DES) [13]. In addition, other common simulation modeling methods are System Dynamics (SD) [8] and Agent-Based Modeling (ABM) [9, 18]. Scenario analysis explores different options by applying changes at computational level, before intervening on an existing process [4, 6].

The remainder of this paper is structured as follows. Section 2 presents the methodological framework, which is used in Sect. 3 to discuss the case study. Section 4 describes the outcome of scenario analysis, while some remarks and future works conclude the paper in Sect. 5.

2 The Methodological Framework

This section introduces our proposed methodological framework consisting of three main phases:

1. *Context and Data Analysis.* The context analysis step aims: i) to set the overall strategic scenario of the company, and ii) to determine the organizational components (units) that will be investigated in relation to the process under examination. The data analysis involves the collection for each unit of the more relevant information for the process, i.e. data concerning duration activities, destinations of products, transformation rules, involvement of other enterprises/stakeholders.

2. *Process Engineering.* The purpose of this phase is the determination of activities carried out in each unit involved in the process. The outcome of this phase investigates the causal relationships existing between units, resources and each activity. The process is then reconstructed from external input/output events and objects. A visualization effort rely on process diagram (i.e. process map or flowchart). The process model must be verified and validated with all the main actors involved in order to finally obtain the so-called As-Is model. This phase provides managers and engineers with accurate Company specifications in their current form. Simulation results obtained by business process modeling allow for detection and understanding of inefficiencies, bottlenecks, constraints and risks.

3. *Scenario analysis and Process Reorganization.* This phase manage problems eventually highlighted in the previous phase, including solutions adopted to restructure the As-Is model by generating the new To-Be version. Starting from the baseline scenario (related to the Company's current As-Is situation), the What-if analysis explores different scenarios both at medium and long term. This step provides indications and guidelines for restructuring of the process. The analysis is carried out by modifying the initial setting and parameters of the model, verifying the validating these changes by the evaluation of the new values of key indicators, through a set of simulation experiment.

The Process Model used in our work is based on the specification of the process flows by means of BPMN language. In the process diagram we added descriptions of how each activity react to a transaction path, representing an order in a manufacturing line (or maybe a patient that follows a clinical procedure, or a customer in an information office). In the flows through the process we define how much time the activity takes and what are the necessary resources. The new aspects characterizing the process will be better illustrate in the following section.

3 The Case Study

Our case study concerns a medium-sized Company in northern Italy.[1] In particular, we focus on processes that directly affect the production unit, which includes daily delivery of products to and from several other companies describing a large network of companies [17]. According to first phase of our methodology, after several interviews with manager and operators, we documented the core aspects of the process in a high level functional diagram as illustrated in Fig. 1. The diagram includes the following organizational units:

Scheduling: in this unit, orders from clients are processed in the Management Resource Planning (MRP) system, which checks the stock situation and prepares for each order:

- a production order;
- one or more contractor orders. A product may be requested as raw or must undergo further processing (such as painting) that are done by external companies (Contractors);
- a shipping order that prepares the final shipment to the customer of the requested products.

Molding: concerns the activities of setting the presses, molding and manual cutting of the pieces.

Quality: concerns every controls of products coming from suppliers and contractors.

Warehouse: concerns the general management of materials, semi-finished and finished products used in the production sector.

Administration: concerns the management of invoices and other administrative documents.

We analyse the resources needed for the production process by considering 60 workers organized into two main working hours. Working hours consist of production schedule (henceforth PS, with two shifts from 6 am to 10 pm) and standard schedule (henceforth SS, from 8.30 am to 5.30 pm). Finally, we identify five main roles of workers:

- warehouse operators (4 workers for each shift, in schedule PS): they deal with the management of materials and products, for packaging and shipping orders to clients;
- administrative employees (2, SS): they manage invoices and other office documents;
- cutting operators (6, PS): they manually cut the pieces coming out of the molding. Usually they are 6 but can vary depending on the workload;
- quality operators (2, SS): they control quality and quantity of products and materials;
- production operators (3 workers for each shift, PS): they take care of the various machines, in particular their settings.

---

[1]The Company, which prefers to remain anonymous, produces artistic decorations (stones, rhinestones and studs) used by famous fashion designers in their products.

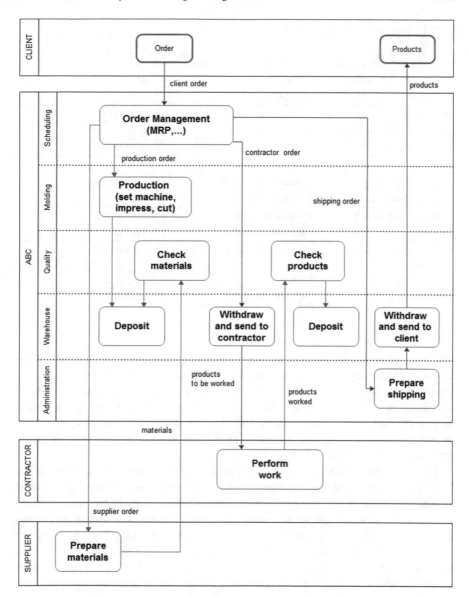

Fig. 1 High level diagram of the company

The Company's main machines are presses for molding parts, scheduled to operate in the production schedule PS. There are three types: (1) Medium Tonnage (MT) 11 presses, (2) Low Tonnage (LT) 8 presses, and (3) Plastic-Clad Silica (PCS) 3 presses. Interviewing the operators and analyzing their tasks, we model the activities of the whole production process. Table 1 shows the tasks with their duration

Table 1 Activities of the production process

Activities	Resources	Duration (min)
Set machine (MT-LT-PCS)	Production operator, presse	Variable
Impress (MT-LT-PCS)	Press	Variable
Manual cutting products	Cutting operator	Variable
Deposit raw product	Warehouse worker	From 2 to 60
Check purchased materials	Quality operator	Variable
Deposit material	Warehouse worker	From 2 to 60
Check products	Quality operator	Variable
Deposit products	Warehouse worker	From 2 to 120
Prepare shipping to contractors	Warehouse worker	From 5 to 40
Withdraw from warehouse	Warehouse worker	From 2 to 120
Prepare shipping to client	Warehouse worker	From 5 to 40
Withdraw product from warehouse	Warehouse worker	From 2 to 120
Prepare invoice	Employee	From 3 to 20
Send shipping	Warehouse worker	From 5 to 20

and the resources involved in their execution. It should be noted that, for activities with variable timing, the actual estimated duration in the simulation effort directly depend on the workload (for example, the number of pieces to be produced or to be shipped). According to the phase 2 of our methodological framework, we analyzed all the activities, events and decision points of the production process, as well as the relationships existing among them. The process diagram is illustrated in Fig. 2, designed with the BPMN 2.0. language.

The simulation environment includes the following features in addition to the diagram: (a) the description of resources and their use in the activities, (b) the time required by the activities, and (c) the generators of transactions to be entered during the simulation. Transaction types correspond to the different start events in the process diagram of Fig. 2, as orders and administrative notes describing the materials and products processed. In our case, the Company information system provided data corresponding to six months of work in 2017. The As-Is model built in this manner can be simulated to verify that it represents the system in a reasonable way. This validation step is performed by comparing the results provided by the simulation for a set of critical indicators with the values of the same indicators detectable in the real world. Table 2 shows the simulation results for the different activities of the Company process before (2016) and after (2017) the introduction of MRP.

The Company organization has certainly improved after the introduction of MRP, as it has encouraged the aggregation of a greater number of orders and therefore fewer shipments in terms of transport. For this reason our attention has been given to the results of 2017 (see Table 3) that were presented to managers and operators in the Company who judged reasonable these simulated times, based on their experi-

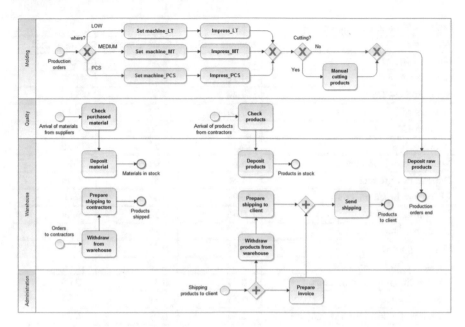

Fig. 2 As-Is diagram of the company

Table 2 Simulation results 2016/2017 (h)

Activities	Average cycle		Average work		Average wait	
	2016	2017	2016	2017	2016	2017
Set machine-MT	298.63	111.48	2.77	2.63	295.87	108.86
Set machine-LT	319.64	84.10	3.11	3.03	316.53	81.07
Set machine-PCS	549.24	147.40	2.44	2.37	546.80	145.03
Impress-MT	38.31	37.34	17.96	17.21	20.35	20.13
Impress-LT	10.37	8.35	4.42	3.70	5.95	4.65
Impress-PCS	24.31	19.49	10.66	9.23	13.65	10.26
Manual cutting products	23.10	18.87	3.27	3.01	19.83	15.86
Deposit raw product	1.46	1.36	0.52	0.52	0.94	0.84
Check purchased materials	17.22	40.27	0.51	0.48	16.71	39.80
Deposit material	0.33	0.45	0.12	0.12	0.20	0.34
Check products	29.15	8.16	2.00	1.86	27.15	6.03
Deposit products	0.50	0.45	0.40	0.37	0.11	0.08
Withdraw from warehouse	20.32	1.89	0.19	0.19	20.13	1.70
Prepare shipping to contractors	0.58	0.37	0.38	0.37	0.20	0.00
Prepare invoice	7.58	1.51	0.19	0.19	7.39	1.32
Withdraw products from warehouse	16.29	6.82	0.08	0.08	16.20	6.74
Prepare shipping to client	0.29	0.32	0.21	0.21	0.08	0.11
Send shipping	26.21	12.85	0.21	0.21	26.01	12.64

Table 3 Simulation results (h) BS

Activities	Average cycle	Average work	Average wait
Set machine-MT	111.48	2.63	108.86
Set machine-LT	84.10	3.03	81.07
Set machine-PCS	147.40	2.37	145.03
Impress-MT	37.34	17.21	20.13
Impress-LT	8.35	3.70	4.65
Impress-PCS	19.49	9.23	10.26
Manual cutting products	18.87	3.01	15.86
Deposit raw product	1.36	0.52	0.84
Check purchased materials	40.27	0.48	39.80
Deposit material	0.45	0.12	0.34
Check products	8.16	1.86	6.03
Deposit products	0.45	0.37	0.08
Withdraw from warehouse	1.89	0.19	1.70
Prepare shipping to contractors	0.37	0.37	0.00
Prepare invoice	1.51	0.19	1.32
Withdraw products from warehouse	6.82	0.08	6.74
Prepare shipping to client	0.32	0.21	0.11
Send shipping	12.85	0.21	12.64

ence and an assessment with real data (controlled over a short period of work). The comparison between simulated and actual times concludes the validation step for the As-Is model which is then ready for the analysis of different scenarios.

4 Scenario Analysis

A scenario is as a description of a possible future situation. It is not intended to be a complete specification of the future, but rather the description of the basic elements of a "possible" future in order to draw analysts' attention to the key factors that can help to effectively improve the process. Scenario analysis allows managers to process various parameter configurations to investigate different results besides a baseline scenario. In our approach the specification of the scenarios to be analyzed depends on changes to be made to the As-Is model parameters. The above mentioned scenarios can be compared on the basis of three indicators: Average cycle, Average work, and Average wait time for each activity. According to Company management, two different types of scenarios have been considered for our case study, which will then be compared with the baseline scenario provided by the As-Is model (Base Scenario—BS). (1) Improve molding schedule (S1): in this scenario, all molding presses are allowed to work with a continuous program, so even at night and on weekends. Such a scenario may be necessary to deal with some very heavy orders that do not require a particular urgency. (2) Full time schedules (S2): in this scenario, all the operators (warehouse, cutting, production and quality) and the presses work with a continuous schedule, i.e. for 24 h a day and five days a week. Clearly, this scenario concerns a situation in which there is a strong increase in the demand for products to be satisfied as soon as possible.

4.1 Improve Molding Schedule (S1)

By performing the simulation of the new scenario S1 with the same workload of the base scenario, we obtain the results shown in Table 4. Times are drastically reduced with regard to average cycle times and waiting times in production. In particular the activities related to setting machines decreased by 80%, while impress activities had an average loss of about a half. This means that production orders have been completely satisfied, while in the base scenario compared to 1642 production orders about one hundred have not yet been satisfied at the end of the simulation.

The greater number of orders to be cut and deposited justifies the increase in average times for cutting and deposit activities. Since only the presses work with a continuous program, without the intervention of any operator, it has been considered that this scenario S1 could be useful to satisfy orders that do not have an immediate expiry date.

4.2 Full Time Schedules (S2)

As in the previous case, the simulation of the new S2 scenario provided the results shown in Table 5.

Table 4 Simulation results S1 (h)

Activities	Average cycle		Average work		Average wait	
	BS	S1	BS	S1	BS	S1
Set machine-MT	111.48	24.12	2.63	2.68	108.86	21.45
Set machine-LT	84.10	20.99	3.03	3.03	81.07	17.96
Set machine-PCS	147.40	34.98	2.37	2.39	145.03	32.59
Impress-MT	37.34	23.87	17.21	23.85	20.13	0.02
Impress-LT	8.35	3.77	3.70	3.77	4.65	<0.01
Impress-PCS	19.49	9.32	9.23	9.32	10.26	<0.01
Manual cutting products	18.87	25.51	3.01	3.26	15.86	22.25
Deposit raw product	1.36	9.42	0.52	0.52	0.84	8.90

Table 5 Simulation results S2 (h)

Activities	Average cycle		Average work		Average wait	
	BS	S2	BS	S2	BS	S2
Set machine-MT	111.48	37.61	2.63	2.68	108.86	34.94
Set machine-LT	84.10	26.59	3.03	3.03	81.07	23.56
Set machine-PCS	147.40	48.24	2.37	2.39	145.03	45.86
Impress-MT	37.34	28.91	17.21	21.13	20.13	7.78
Impress-LT	8.35	5.22	3.70	3.69	4.65	1.52
Impress-PCS	19.49	12.40	9.23	9.32	10.26	3.08
Manual cutting products	18.87	4.82	3.01	3.53	15.86	1.29
Deposit raw product	1.36	1.02	0.52	0.52	0.84	0.50

In this case concluding suggestions are similar to those seen for the previous case. The average cycle and waiting times have significantly dropped in comparison with those of BS. This requires a greater use of resources and for this reason this scenario can be taken into consideration in case of immediate need of some products. The demand for products in a short time does not frequently occur, otherwise it would became a problem both for the company in terms of costs and for resources in terms of time.

5 Conclusions

In this paper we described an industrial application of business process modeling and simulation for change management. The combination of techniques and tools support managers for decision-making. In our case study, we finally describe the utility of computational simulation for a Small Medium Enterprise increasing income to evaluate and forecast their business model as well as planning the organizational change. The methodological framework presented in the paper includes three steps to model, validate and analyze business processes, and an extended process model that combines the simulation of the actual (As-Is) process with a What-if analysis of different scenarios to describe possible evolution of the actual process. The possibilities offered by this framework was illustrated through the industrial case study of a real medium Company, with several scenario related to production process. In this way managers obtained useful suggestions for deciding on the most appropriate restructuring actions to improve the process efficiency. Applications from Industry 4.0 can be tested in simulated scenarios before applying in the organization. In the near future, different analysis will be treated to assist the Company in its reorganization activities. We plan to improve our work with a study of logistics by georeferencing orders, customers, contractors. Furthermore we intend to study the extension of the methodology to take into consideration the analysis of the risks connected to the production activities.

References

1. Allweyer, T. (2016). BPMN 2.0: Introduction to the standard for business process modeling. BoD–Books on Demand.
2. Amantea, I. A., Leva, A. D., & Sulis, E. (2018). A simulation-driven approach in risk-aware business process management: A case study in healthcare. In *Proceedings of 8th International Conference on Simulation and Modeling Methodologies, Technologies and Applications (SIMULTECH)* (Vol. 1, pp. 98–105). INSTICC. SciTePress.10.5220/0006842100980105.
3. Bichler, M. (2006). Design science in information systems research. *Wirtschaftsinformatik*, 48(2), 133–135.
4. Chang, J. F. (2016). *Business process management systems: Strategy and implementation*. Boca Raton: CRC Press.
5. Di Leva, A., & Sulis, E. (2017). Process analysis for a hospital emergency department. *International Journal of Economics and Management System*, 2(1), 34–41.
6. Di Leva, A., Sulis, E., & Vinai, M. (2017). Business process analysis and simulation: The contact center of a public health and social information office. *Intelligent Information Management*, 9(05), 189.
7. Dumas, M., Rosa, M. L., Mendling, J., & Reijers, H. A. (2013). *Fundamentals of business process management*. Berlin: Springer.
8. Forrester, J. W. (1997). Industrial dynamics. *Journal of the Operational Research Society*, 48(10), 1037–1041.
9. Gilbert, G. N. (2008). *Agent-based models* (No. 153). London: Sage.
10. Hammer, M. (2015). What is business process management? In:*Handbook on business process management 1* (pp. 3–16). Berlin: Springer.
11. Harmon, P. (2014). *Business process change*. Morgan Kaufmann.
12. iGrafx: iGrafxProcess 2015. http://www.igrafx.com (2015)
13. Johnson, M. W., Christensen, C. M., & Kagermann, H. (2008). Reinventing your business model. *Harvard Business Review*, 86(12), 57–68.
14. Leon, A. (2014). *Enterprise resource planning*. New York: McGraw-Hill Education.
15. Peffers, K., Tuunanen, T., Gengler, C., Rossi, M., Hui, W., Virtanen, V., et al. (2006). The design science research process: A model for producing and presenting information systems research. In DESRIST International Conference on Design Science Research in Information Systems and Technology, Claremont, CA, USA (pp. 83–106), February 24–25, 2006.
16. Ptak, C.A., & Schragenheim, E. (2016). *ERP: Tools, techniques, and applications for integrating the supply chain*. Boca Raton: CRC Press.
17. Sulis, E., & De Lellis, A. (2018). The impact of information system: A network analysis perspective. In 2018 Fifth International Conference on Social Networks Analysis, Management and Security (SNAMS) (pp. 215–219). IEEE.
18. Sulis, E., & Di Leva, A. (2017). An agent-based model of a business process: The use case of a hospital emergency department. In: Business Process Management Workshops. Lecture Notes in Business Information Processing (Vol. 308, pp. 124–132). Berlin: Springer.
19. Van Der Aalst, W. M. (2013). Business process management: A comprehensive survey. *ISRN Software Engineering*.
20. Van der Aalst, W. M., Nakatumba, J., Rozinat, A., & Russell, N. (2010). Business process simulation. In *Handbook on BPM 1* (pp. 313–338). Berlin: Springer.

A Simulation-Driven Approach to Decision Support in Process Reorganization: A Case Study in Healthcare

Ilaria Angela Amantea, Antonio Di Leva and Emilio Sulis⊙

Abstract Companies are currently forced to update their technologies to store and analyze data in order to remain competitive in a rapidly changing market. Digitalization and dematerialization of documents are increasingly needed especially for companies with a large amount of data to manage or store. The efficiency of the process must be balanced to risk management which is a key factor of success for organization as risks are part of every business activity. Compliance is an integral part of risk management with not only economic implications but also on the legal and liability level. This paper proposes a methodological framework to investigate risks and compliance in reorganizations by adopting a Business Process Management perspective that includes modeling and simulation of business processes. We applied our methodology to processes in a Blood Bank department of a large hospital. Our results show that a simulation-driven approach is an effective way to provide a decision support to guide department's managers to the reorganization and verify, before implementation, the balance between efficiency of the reorganization of activities, risk management and compliance. In addition, digitalization in the health sector would facilitate the self-reporting of errors (methodology encouraged by the Joint Commission for accreditation and certification in Healthcare), that increase transparency. Reporting such incidents can provide a variety of information about successful error management practices as well as weaknesses.

Keywords Risk management · Business process simulation · Healthcare

I. A. Amantea · A. Di Leva · E. Sulis (✉)
Computer Science Department, University of Torino, 185 Corso Svizzera, Torino, Italy
e-mail: sulis@di.unito.it
URL: http://di.unito.it

I. A. Amantea
e-mail: amantea@di.unito.it

A. Di Leva
e-mail: dileva@di.unito.it

1 Introduction and Related Work

One of the main issue of Business Process Management (BPM) [1, 14, 30] is change management. The adoption of process-centric approach relying on a process-aware information system [15] allows the redesign of business processes in an organization. A simulation-driven approach is a versatile tool to produce results that are relatively easy to interpret by comparing different scenarios to evaluate process changes (**What-if analysis**). A **scenario** can be considered as a description of a possible future situation. It is not a complete description of the future, but rather a way to consider the basic elements of a possible future and to draw analysts' attention to the key factors that can help to effectively improve the actual process (As-is model) [12].

Risk is part of every business activity and therefore part of every business process [19, 29]. If a risk occurs it may cause loss of quality, increased costs, time delays, complaints and legal problems [4] as well as, in healthcare, serious and permanent damages up to death. Thus, risks need to be managed by the applications of principles, frameworks and activities in the context of Risk Management [18, 23, 26]. The discipline introduces a whole range of new regulation [5, 11] facing two sets of problems: on one side the process have to be compliant to law; from the other side new reorganizations must be implemented with the introduction of new procedures [20], i.e. for privacy control. In healthcare studies on business process analysis are relevant for the direct and indirect consequences of errors [9, 12, 16, 33]. It is possible to find several studies on compliance with laws, rules or regulations in the case of processes related to patient health [3, 7, 25, 31].

The adoption of digital innovations makes physical products programmable, communicable, memorable, traceable [17]. Digitalization furthermore requires an organization to revisit its management logic and its use of corporate Information Technology (IT) infrastructures [34]. The intensive use of ICT solutions to collect, share and digitize data of a health process, makes it necessary to prepare tools able to identify any possible risk scenario related to the use of computer systems and lack of awareness on the agents, as well as to facilitate the adoption of appropriate countermeasures. Previous research on IT in healthcare explored digitalization challenges for organization [10]. Traditional approaches stress enforcement styles [24, 32] as well as reconsidering project implementations [21]. Following a different strategy from common business analysis [8, 13], we applied an approach oriented towards the understanding of cases of success [6], as a way to address other departments of the same organization in process optimization. Our case study refers to an Italian Hospital.[1] In particular, we selected a well-performing department (accordingly with the Risk Manager office of the hospital) such as the Blood Bank (BB) department. The department's laboratory performs tests necessary for production of blood components (immunohematology, blood-borne infectious diseases) as well as for diagnostic, pre-transfusion testing and prevention of hemolytic disease of the newborn. The compliance model is the starting point for the minimum requirements. This

[1] This research was conducted at *Città della Salute e della Scienza* of Turin (Italy) within the project "CANP - CAsa Nel Parco" of Regione Piemonte - POR FESR PIEMONTE 2014-2020.

model satisfied the minimum level of checks protecting from legal risk. It would also be a very streamlined process, even if a large amount of errors are not detected. For this reason, and to solve this problem, a large amount of corrective actions have been carried out by workers in current real model. Actually the process is very efficient in detecting errors even if it suffers of a lack of staff (which would imply higher costs), mainly involved in repetitive manual checks that implies elongation of times. With the corporate restructuring with the new single management and scanning documents you would maintain the efficiency of the process in the detection of errors, streamlining the process in terms of number of tasks, so staff and timing and consequently costs. Furthermore, current process FMEA analysis reveals that the causes with greater risk index are precisely those which would be torn down thanks to the new type of process. In the next section we describe our methodological framework, while Sect. 3 includes the case study which includes modeling, compliance and business process analysis.

2   The Methodological Framework

This section introduces our methodological framework which is based on a Risk-aware Business Process Management (RBPM) [28].

2.1   The RBPM Methodology

Our methodology consists of four phases:

- *Context Analysis and Compliance Verification* - this phase aims: (a) to fix the overall strategic scenario of the enterprise, (b) to determine the organizational components that are related to the process under analysis, and (c) to collect the laws and regulations related to the process and analyze them in order to identify which controls are mandatory or simply suggested.
- *Process Engineering* - the initial purpose of this phase is the determination of the activities performed in the functions involved in the process and the causal relationships existing between them. The process is then reconstructed from facts external to the system, events and objects in input/output: this provides the Process diagram (sometimes referred to as process map or flowchart) that will be specified using the Business Process Model and Notation (BPMN) language [2]. The process model must be validated with the stakeholders involved in the process, using animation and simulation of BPMN specification, obtaining the so called *As-is model*.

– *Compliance checking and Risk Analysis* - the purpose of this phase is to verify the compliance of the current process to underline which rules and controls must be present in the new optimized process.
  In the risk analysis phase the possible causes of error must be analyzed to decide which corrective actions must be introduced.
– *Reengineering Process* - this phase creates a new optimized version of the As-is model, the To-be model that includes the necessary rules and corrective actions as well as other restructuring actions such as, e.g., the digitization of paper forms.

2.2 Optimization, Compliance and Risk in Healthcare Processes

Methods and systems for the optimization of business processes, the compliance with laws and regulations, and the management of risks and vulnerabilities are of particular importance in the medical field. For this reason, it is essential that the methodology that will be developed will see the integration and development of these three factors at the same time. Optimizing patient-centered clinical processes helps improve clinical performance, reduce costs and resource, labor, and supply requirements, and provides an integrated approach to care management.

Within a framework of continuous development, hospital management must regularly evaluate the risk management system in care pathways to increase the safety of patients and those involved in their care. A risk control procedure should include:

– *Risk identification*: to perform risk identification the hospital can take into account notifications from reporting errors (usually stored into an incident reporting data base), such as events that caused problems to patients and complaints. Even results of inspections and audits can provide useful indications.
– *Risk analysis*: the goal of this step is to determine the causes of risks and factors that favor errors as well as their effects on the safety of patients.
– *Risk assessment*: decision-makers must determine what kind of risks should be treated with priority.
– *Risk treatment*: a risk can be treated by introducing preventive measures and/or accepting risk with or without supervision.

Compliance refers to an organization's ability to meet the obligations set by laws and regulations. It must become part of the organization's culture and integrate into its processes. The risk of compliance may be characterized by the likelihood of occurring and by the consequences of non-compliance with the obligations during patient treatment. A compliance framework must establish organizational procedures to implement, monitor and continuously improve compliance management across the organization.

3   The Blood Bank Case Study

The blood banking system is the process that takes place in the hospital to make sure that blood products are safe before being used in blood transfusions and other medical procedures. The blood banking system includes blood typing and infectious disease testing. Whole blood is now rarely used for transfusion because most patients require only a specific blood component, such as red blood cells or platelets.

The hospital BB unit consists of three functional departments: Acceptance, Laboratory and Distribution. In Acceptance, requests from other hospital departments (e.g. the Emergency Room) are checked: for example, staff should confirm if the data on the tube label and on the transfusion request form are identical. In case of any discrepancy or doubt, a new blood sample should be obtained. Then, the request and the test tube with the patient's blood are sent to the Laboratory. When a patient's blood sample is received, the Laboratory performs the required tests and, if necessary, a pack with the correct blood is prepared (rather a lot of requests only concern the execution of some tests). In Distribution, the required pack of blood (or a component) is sent to the requesting department through appropriate personnel.

In our RBPM methodology the process diagram is integrated with a description of how each activity treats a transaction (in our case a request), how long it takes and what resources are needed to perform it. Furthermore, it is necessary to specify how the transactions are introduced in the model and how long the simulation must last. The integrated As-is model can be simulated by means of a design and simulation environment, the RBPMTool, which is based on the iGrafx Process tool [22]. In this paper we decided to show only the Acceptance (sub)process for lack of space, but the same analysis was carried out for all three (Acceptance, Laboratory and Distribution) processes and results are provided. In particular, for the Acceptance process, we will consider a workload that includes about 350 requests a day, distributed according to the timetable in Fig. 1, for a total of approximately 84,000 requests received by the Blood Bank during the initial 8 months of the 2017.

Fig. 1 The Blood Bank daily workload

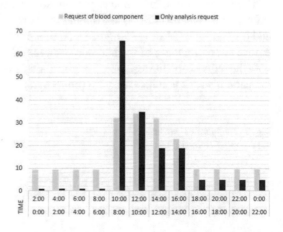

3.1   Acceptance Process: Compliance Analysis

At the beginning of the analysis of the BB case the Working Group was set up which subsequently carried on the project. The Working Group was composed of members of the Department of Computer Science (authors of this article), and of doctors, biologists, technicians and administrative employees of the Blood Bank. In the Acceptance process, the Italian law only imposes to check that the surname, name and date of birth of the patient reported on the request are the same as reported on the test tube. The Working Group discussed a reasonable possible implementation of the Acceptance process with this rule and the result is shown in Fig. 2. The RBPMTool allows to introduce a counter C in the process diagram that counts the requests that flow along an arc of the diagram, in this case C shows the number of incorrect requests at the end of the simulation. The simulation of the compliance model with the workload shown in Fig. 1 provides as a result 440 intercepted errors.

3.2   Acceptance Process: The As-is Model

The number of errors that can be detected with the compliance model is very low and, over the years, the BB staff has introduced many other checks, the so called Corrective Actions, to discover the largest possible number of errors. The application of the Process Engineering phase of the RBPM methodology results in the As-is model illustrated in Fig. 3. In this process the requests (a test tube and a paper request) are received (**Receive Request**), and the staff makes a first set of generic checks:

– the test tube is empty,
– the test tube has not the label,
– the patient's data on the tube label and on the paper request are different,
– there is a lack of data or signatures on the paper request.

   If no errors are found, another person adds the request in the Local Management Information System (LMIS) and applies an identifying barcode on the paper request and the test tube (**Manage Request**). At this point, the request is further checked to ensure the correctness of the barcodes (**Check, Double Check, Verify validity**) on both the request and the test tube. Since the "decision to transfuse" is a critical step for the patient's safety in his care path (unnecessary transfusions are common), the BB

Fig. 2 Acceptance process: the compliance model

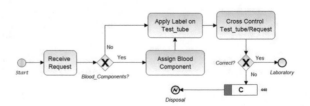

Fig. 3 Acceptance process: the As-is model

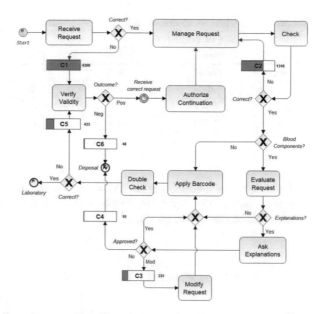

doctor can discuss (**Ask explanation**) with the requesting department about adequacy of the request and, if necessary, refuse it. If all these controls are positive, the request with the test tube is sent to the Laboratory (event *Laboratory*), otherwise the request is rejected (event *Disposal*). The C1–C6 counters are positioned on the process to count the number of errors intercepted during simulation at different control points. Simulating the As-is process with the same workload as above, we obtain a total number of intercepted errors equal to 6356 (sum of all counters). The result obtained was discussed (and validated) with the Working Group, and it is certainly interesting because it shows how the simple application of controls deriving from the current law can provide very poor results. Similar results were obtained for the Laboratory and Distribution departments, and are shown in Table 1 in which the first column (**As-is**) reports the errors intercepted with the As-is model, the second column (**Compl**) those intercepted with the compliant model, the third column (**Not-int**) shows the percentage of errors that would not be intercepted with the compliant model. Finally, in the fourth column are reported the Complaints arrived at the BB in the considered period (January–August 2017), i.e. errors detected in the requesting departments that have been reported to the BB and stored in its LMIS.

The case analysis suggests some interesting considerations:

– the number of errors detected must be compared with the total number of requests processed in the BB, which is about 84,000. Errors not detected in the final phase of the blood distribution process (7940) represent a very small percentage of the total number of requests, and this shows how the whole BB process is very effective in detecting errors. However, since the consequences of errors in the distribution could be very serious, it is important to continuously improve the whole process;

Table 1 Comparison between As-is and compliant processes

	Errors			Complaints
	As-is	Compl	Not-Int (%)	
Acceptance	6448	440	93	10
Laboratory	1031	725	30	4
Distribution	461	235	49	12
BB Process	7940	1400	82	26

- the limited number of complaints confirms the efficiency of the process. It should also be noted that, in the last 20 years, only in two cases the hospital has been reported for damage to patients.

3.3 Acceptance Process: Risks Analysis

Although the Acceptance process is very efficient, the consequences of certain errors can be very serious, so there is always a need to improve the process. The BB provided us with a database reporting the error causes with the relative number of errors, and the Working Group decided to perform a risk analysis using the FMEA (Failure Mode and Effects Analysis) technique.

The method is based on the assignment, for each cause (and the related effect) of a severity score (S), an occurrence score (O) and a detection score (D):

- S shows the severity of the effects eventually happening. It can range from 1 (very moderate problems) to 10 (death),
- O estimates the frequency with which an effect will occur. May vary from 1 (unlikely to occur) to 10 (almost certain to occur),
- D refers to the possibility of the operators and the control measures to detect error before the effects occur. It can range from 1 (the system will always detect error) to 10 (detection is not possible).

The scores S, O and D were estimated with the Working Group and validated with the analysis of the detailed data for a limited number of days. To calculate the Risk Priority Number (RPN) the 3 scores were multiplied (each RPN index has a range between 1 and 1000). In this way, the FMEA matrix shown in Table 2 is obtained.

Looking at Table 2, the most relevant RPN indices were highlighted in the Table and were the subject of an in-depth discussion in the Working Group.

- (F1) Inaccurate request and (F2) Delivery delay request: concern errors committed in the requesting departments and therefore will not be considered further (they will be treated in the hospital risk management),
- (F3) Incomplete data and (F4) Insert error: concerns errors made by the staff in entering the patient and the request data in the LMIS,

Table 2 FMEA matrix for the acceptance process

Causes	Occurrence (O)	Detection (D)	Severity (S)	RPN
Incoming from the outside				
Improper sample	1	1	5	5
Inaccurate request	1	3	5	15
Delivery delay request	2	6	6	72
Other	1	1	1	1
Internal acceptance				
Incomplete data	2	2	5	20
Switching errors	1	1	7	7
Insert errors	2	5	5	50
Other	1	1	1	1
Internal check in acceptance				
Cross check (request-tube) missing	1	1	7	7
Signature check missing	1	1	3	3
Doctor check missing	1	2	5	10
Inappropriate request				
Data: inappropriate/reconsidered	1	1	7	7
Quantity: inap./recons.	1	1	7	7
Urgency: inap./recons.	1	1	7	7

– (F5) Doctor check missing: concerns the lack of final doctor's control.

The causes of error (F3) and (F4) will be taken into consideration in the following optimization phase.

3.4 Acceptance Process: Optimization

The optimization step in the RBPM methodology determines a set of possible restructuring actions on the As-is process in order to improve the efficiency and effectiveness of the process with respect to a certain set of critical indicators. The verification of the validity of these actions takes place by introducing the appropriate modifications on the As-is model (generating a candidate To-be model) and comparing the new values of the indicators, obtained through the simulation, with the previous values. In our case, the Acceptance process must continue to comply with the strict error control requirements previously seen. On the To-be model it is therefore useful to introduce actions that can remove some possible causes of errors, in particular those identified by the FMEA analysis. A new web-based version of the LMIS management system, currently under development, has been proposed to address the problems that

Fig. 4 To-be model of the
acceptance process

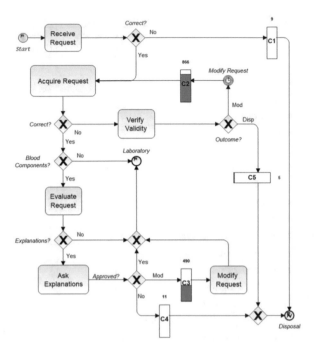

emerged during the risk analysis. The new system (local) will be integrated with the central management system of the hospital and the process will be developed with the following requirements:

- the requesting department prepares the label with the patient's data and the barcode, places it on the test tube and loads, with the same barcode, the request (which will be dematerialized) on the central system,
- in the Acceptance department the test tube arrives and, through the barcode, with the new local system the request is retrieved (the control will be much faster).

The new scenario was discussed with the Working Group and the candidate To-be model was modeled producing the diagram in Fig. 4, which is very simplified. The optimization mainly concerns the Acceptance sub-process (while the other two, Laboratory and Distribution, will remain almost the same). In fact, the integration of local and general management systems involves the introduction of patient and request data only once, avoiding rewriting errors and eliminating the need for controls. The digitization allows to remove the causes of error (F3) and (F4) detected with the FMEA analysis.

To compare the models As-is and To-be, it is necessary to define the set of indicators for which to make the measurements. In our case, we will consider the following set: the *number of incoming and rejected requests*, the *average cycle time*, the *average working time* and the *average waiting time* for requests that pass through the Acceptance process (between the initial event *start* and the final event *Laboratory*).

Table 3 Comparison between the As-is and the To-be model of the acceptance process

	As-is	To-be	Earn
Total request in input	86,160	86,160	–
Disposal request	58	25	33
Average cycle time	35.22	2.61	32.61
Average work time	5.46	2.20	3.26
Average waiting time	29.75	0.41	29.34

In the RBPMTool the measurement of these indicators is carried out with the help of a *monitor* which is placed in the process diagram between the *start* event and the *Laboratory* event. A monitor collect the statistical data related to the set of requests that travel the path between these two points. The simulation of As-is and To-be models with the same workload allows the comparison between the two processes and the results are shown in Table 3 (times are expressed in minutes).

Table 3 shows how the digitization of the request and the integration of hospital and BB management systems leads to a drastic reduction in waiting times when processing requests. This is particularly important at peak times of requests, between 8 and 12 am (see Fig. 1). In fact, urgent and very urgent requests require a rapid delivery of blood: between 15 and 20 min for very urgent requests, within 1 h for urgent requests.

4 Conclusions

In this paper we described a simulation-based approach to address the challenge of corporate reorganization and digitization while maintaining a global vision that also includes risk management and compliance. The proposed framework includes a methodology to model and analyze the current process (As-is model), to verify its compliance with current laws, to highlight the risks that may occur during its execution, and to evaluate some future scenarios which describe its possible evolutions so as to select the most appropriate restructuring actions (To-be model). The possibilities offered by the methodology have been illustrated through a complex case study describing the behavior of the BB that provides for the storage and distribution of blood for patients in a large hospital. This case study has shown that it is possible to construct an accurate model of the process, able to be validated and analyzed from different points of view (risk and compliance analysis) using a powerful discrete event simulator. We plan to adopt an agent-based modeling approach [27], to include cognitive aspects of personnel. Simulation allows to easily study a number of possible operational scenarios, thus providing the analysts with useful information to evaluate the restructuring actions on the process. Moreover, for the purpose of transparency and safety of care, that including prevention and management of risk related to the provision of health services, one of the techniques used to date and encouraged by most States in the world is the reporting of adverse events and Sentinel events[2]; digitization could favor this signaling.

References

1. Abo-Hamad, W., & Arisha, A. (2013). Simulation-based framework to improve patient experience in an emergency department. *European Journal of Operational Research, 224*(1), 154–166.
2. Allweyer, T. (2016). BPMN 2.0: Introduction to the standard for business process modeling. In *BoD–Books on Demand*.
3. Amantea, I. A., Leva, A. D., & Sulis, E. (2018). A simulation-driven approach in risk-aware business process management: A case study in healthcare. In *Proceedings of 8th International Conference on Simulation and Modeling Methodologies, Technologies and Applications—Vol. 1: SIMULTECH* (pp. 98–105). INSTICC, SciTePress. https://doi.org/10.5220/0006842100980105.
4. Betz, S., Hickl, S., & Oberweis, A. (2011). Risk-aware business process modeling and simulation using xml nets. In: *2011 IEEE 13th Conference on Commerce and Enterprise Computing (CEC)* (pp. 349–356). IEEE.
5. Blake, J., & McTaggart, K. (2016). Using simulation for strategic blood supply chain design in the Canadian prairies. In *2016 6th International Conference on Simulation and Modeling Methodologies, Technologies and Applications (SIMULTECH)* (pp. 1–8). IEEE.
6. Braithwaite, J., Westbrook, J., Coiera, E., Runciman, W., Day, R., Hillman, K., et al. (2017). A systems science perspective on the capacity for change in public hospitals. *Israel Journal of Health Policy Research, 6*(1), 16.
7. Buddle, J. J., Burke, B. S., Perkins, R. A., Roday, L. E., Tartaglia, R., & Vermiglio, I. A. (2005). *System and method for compliance management* (US Patent 6,912,502).
8. Chang, J. F. (2016). *Business process management systems: Strategy and implementation.* CRC Press.
9. Chartier, Y. (2014). *Safe management of wastes from health-care activities.* World Health Organization.
10. Cresswell, K., & Sheikh, A. (2013). Organizational issues in the implementation and adoption of health information technology innovations: An interpretative review. *International Journal of Medical Informatics, 82*(5), e73–e86.
11. DeRosier, J., Stalhandske, E., Bagian, J. P., & Nudell, T. (2002). Using health care failure mode and effect analysis: The VA national center for patient safetys prospective risk analysis system. *The Joint Commission Journal on Quality Improvement, 28*(5), 248–267.
12. Di Leva, A., & Sulis, E. (2017). Process analysis for a hospital emergency department. *International Journal of Economics and Management Systems, 2*(1), 34–41.
13. Di Leva, A., Sulis, E., & Vinai, M. (2017). Business process analysis and simulation: The contact center of a public health and social information office. *Intelligent Information Management, 9*(05), 189–205.
14. Dumas, M., Rosa, M. L., Mendling, J., & Reijers, H. A. (2013). *Fundamentals of business process management.* Springer.
15. Dumas, M., Van der Aalst, W. M., & Ter Hofstede, A. H. (2005). *Process-aware information systems: bridging people and software through process technology.* Wiley
16. Fishman, G. (2013). *Discrete-event simulation: Modeling, programming, and analysis.* Springer.

---

[2]https://www.jointcommission.org/sentinel_event_policy_and_procedures/.

17. Fitzpatrick, G., & Ellingsen, G. (2013). A review of 25 years of cscw research in healthcare: Contributions, challenges and future agendas. *Computer Supported Cooperative Work (CSCW)*, *22*(4–6), 609–665.
18. Haimes, Y. Y. (2015). *Risk modeling, assessment, and management*. Wiley.
19. Hashmi, M., Governatori, G., & Wynn, M. T. (2016). Normative requirements for regulatory compliance: An abstract formal framework. *Information Systems Frontiers*, *18*(3), 429–455.
20. Hayes, J. (2014). *The theory and practice of change management*. Palgrave Macmillan.
21. Hornstein, H. A. (2015). The integration of project management and organizational change management is now a necessity. *International Journal of Project Management*, *33*(2), 291–298.
22. iGrafx: iGrafxProcess. (2015). http://www.igrafx.com.
23. McNeil, A. J., Frey, R., & Embrechts, P. (2015). *Quantitative risk management: Concepts, techniques and tools*. Princeton University Press.
24. Parker, C., & Nielsen, V. L.. (2011). Explaining compliance: Business responses to regulation. Edward Elgar Publishing.
25. Racz, N., Weippl, E., & Seufert, A. (2010). A process model for integrated it governance, risk, and compliance management. In *Proceedings of the Ninth Baltic Conference on Databases and Information Systems (DB&IS 2010)* (pp. 155–170). Citeseer.
26. Sadgrove, K. (2016). *The complete guide to business risk management*. Routledge.
27. Sulis, E., & Di Leva, A. (2017). An agent-based model of a business process: The use case of a hospital emergency department. In *Business Process Management Workshops. Lecture Notes in Business Information Processing* (Vol. 308, pp. 124–132). Springer.
28. Suriadi, S., Weiß, B., Winkelmann, A., ter Hofstede, A. H., Adams, M., Conforti, R., et al. (2014). Current research in risk-aware business process management: Overview, comparison, and gap analysis. *Communications of the Association for Information Systems*, *34*(1), 933–984.
29. Van Der Aalst, W. M. (2013). *Business process management: A comprehensive survey*. ISRN Software Engineering.
30. Van der Aalst, W. M., Nakatumba, J., Rozinat, A., & Russell, N. (2010). Business process simulation. In: *Handbook on BPM* (Vol. 1, pp. 313–338). Springer.
31. Vincent, C. (2017). *Patient safety*. Wiley.
32. Vincent, C., Taylor-Adams, S., & Stanhope, N. (1998). Framework for analysing risk and safety in clinical medicine. *BMJ: British Medical Journal,316*(7138), 1154.
33. Vincent, C., Taylor-Adams, S., Chapman, E. J., Hewett, D., Prior, S., Strange, P., & Tizzard, A. (2000). How to investigate and analyse clinical incidents: Clinical risk unit and association of litigation and risk management protocol. *BMJ: British Medical Journal,320*(7237), 777.
34. Yoo, Y., Henfridsson, O., & Lyytinen, K. (2010). Research commentary the new organizing logic of digital innovation: An agenda for information systems research. *Information systems research,21*(4), 724–735.

How to Rate a Physician?—A Framework for Physician Ratings and What They Mean

Maximilian Haug and Heiko Gewald

Abstract With the possibility to exchange consumption information over the internet, rating websites have emerged in large quantity. Also, healthcare evaluations, especially physician ratings, are part of this trend. The volume of physician rating websites shows the same quantity of different rating criteria on which patients can evaluate their physician and healthcare service. We adapted patient satisfaction literature to generate a framework how these ratings constitute. A quantitative study in southern Germany was conducted to evaluate the research model using structural equation modelling. Our findings show several implications on how a rating framework should look like and also how patients should interpret physician ratings in terms of their information value. In essence, physician ratings cannot accurately predict the quality of the healthcare service, but are rather a measure how sympathetic the physician appears to the patient.

Keywords Physician rating · Patient satisfaction · eWOM

1 Introduction

In the age of ubiquitous communication, consumers have online access to information about literally every good and service. Information and assessments of products are provided by the producing companies, by professional testers and/or by fellow consumers. The traditional interpersonal word-of-mouth (WOM) is nowadays complemented by its digital companion, the electronic word-of-mouth (eWOM) via multiple internet-enabled channels like Facebook, YouTube etc.

Due to the characteristic that services can show little physical evidence, it is difficult to evaluate them. Especially in the context of physician ratings, patients

M. Haug (✉) · H. Gewald
University of Applied Sciences Neu-Ulm, 89231 Neu-Ulm, Germany
e-mail: maximilian.haug@hs-neu-ulm.de

H. Gewald
e-mail: heiko.gewald@hs-neu-ulm.de

© Springer Nature Switzerland AG 2020
A. Lazazzara et al. (eds.), *Exploring Digital Ecosystems*,
Lecture Notes in Information Systems and Organisation 33,
https://doi.org/10.1007/978-3-030-23665-6_17

237

usually do not hold the same knowledge as a doctor in terms of medical skills [1]. It is difficult for patients to evaluate doctors as they cannot assess the quality of the medical service, even after consumption. Symptoms may disappear, but there can be malicious long-time effects, patients do not know about. Objectively spoken it is literally impossible for patients to rate the medical treatment based on common peoples' knowledge. Regardless of this, patients actually do evaluate physicians and rating websites increase in popularity. From 2005 to 2010 the number of ratings on U.S. platforms rose by a factor of more than 100 [2]. In Germany studies showed that 29–74% of the patients are aware of physician rating websites [3]. In 2017 Jameda.de, one of the biggest German physician rating platforms has six million users per month and holds around 480.000 doctor addresses with more than 1.5 million narrative reviews [4].

Helping other people, revenge on the service provider, digital literacy and the effort to submit reviews have been found as determining factors to participate in eWOM [5]. The heterogeneity amongst criteria to rate physicians is as large as the number of rating websites and no commonly accepted framework has yet emerged in the online world. Doctor interaction, treatment, staff, office, waiting times and office times were previously identified as influential towards the rating [6]. However, a research model providing a coherent overview of influential factors of the rating is still missing. Thus, the research question arises: which factors influence the (subjective) rating patients assign to physicians?

A quantitative data collection has been conducted with patients before and after visiting the doctor. The findings show that factors involving human interaction, which are not necessarily medical treatment related, tend to influence the rating the most. Also, the physicians' office and its organizational structure show an impact on the final rating. The paper is structured as follows. Related research is discussed, followed by an explication of the research model and the underlying hypotheses. Subsequently, the research method is described, results presented and implications discussed. Finally, limitations and further research are addressed and the paper closes with a conclusion.

2 Literature Review

2.1 Factors Influencing Patient Satisfaction

Patient satisfaction is described as the personal evaluation of a health care consumer towards the health care services received [7]. It is the patient's personal rating of a physician.

Literature shows that there are multiple influences which are not directly connected to the medical treatment. Möller-Leimkühler et al. [8] found that the relationship between doctor and patient plays a vital role in the patient satisfaction. The authors show that verbal and non-verbal communication between patient and doctor shape the relationship. Hall et al. [9] investigated the liking of the patient towards the doctor and how it influences the patient's perception of the quality of medical treatment. Ware et al. [7] use the term interpersonal manner to describe how patients perceive their physicians based on their interaction.

The technical quality, which is described as the competency and skills of the physician by Ware et al. [7], was found to contribute to patient satisfaction. A negative perception of the professionals' skills leads to patients' dissatisfaction. Even though it can be argued that the physician has more competency and knowledge regarding medical treatment and diagnosis, so that patients are not able to rate the technical quality, Fitton and Acheson [10] found that patients are able to judge the seriousness of their health condition. Also, Stimsom [11] argues that physicians do not have absolute knowledge about every condition.

Accessibility and availability of medical treatment shape patients' satisfaction [7]. Time and effort spent to gain medical treatment involving the wait times and the location influence how patients perceive their medical experience. Waiting time was found to be a key component of patient satisfaction [12, 13].

The assessment of the outcomes of medical treatment is a long term measurement. Jackson et al. [14] investigated patients' satisfaction over a 3 month time-window after the treatment. Similar to physical goods patients need time to evaluate how successful the medical treatment eventually was. Furthermore, the research shows that patients who were asked right after the treatment value human interaction with doctor and staff more, whereas the long-term outcomes gained influence, when patients were asked 3 months later.

The immediate environment, in which medical care is delivered, i.e. the physician's office rooms, showed a strong influence on patient satisfaction [7, 15]. Patients perceive the environment subjectively on how pleasing and comfortable they experience the framework in which treatment is delivered. This influence can reach from the general atmosphere, the degree of cleanliness of the facility to the judgement about whether the right medical equipment is available based on personal perception.

Möller-Leimkühler et al. [8] show moral support from nurses affects satisfaction as well as the doctor-patient relationship. Interaction not only with the physician, but also with the staff on a personal, but also technical level has shown to influence the satisfaction. The evaluation of the staff happens on the same level as the evaluation on the physician. The perceived technical quality as well as the sympathy shows differences in how the patient experiences the medical treatment service. This is in line with Hendriks et al. [16] who evaluated the impact of the atmosphere among nurses as well as their expertise with their impact on patient satisfaction.

An investigation on physician rating websites by Reimann and Strech [6] suggests that there is a distinction between directly doctor related influences and factors which influence the organizational and administrative part of the treatment. The distinction can also be found in the article of Permwonguswa et al. [17] and Camacho et al. [18].

2.2 Physician Rating Websites

On physician rating websites patients can share medical treatment experiences and rate doctors. For the U.S., Kadry et al. [12] and Lagu et al. [19] have shown that 2 out of 3 patient reviews are in favor of the doctors. Also, 82% of U.S. patients seek information on the internet before their first appointment [20]. Emmert et al. [21] showed that one third of the participants of their study in Germany were aware of the existence of dedicated rating platforms for doctors. In addition to that 11% of the respondents already reviewed a doctor on such websites.

Abramova et al. [1] investigated German PRWs and found that rating websites have more female than male users. Also, users of PRW have a positive feeling about the internet and in general a better digital literacy. The study revealed that especially young people in Germany use PRWs.

The research of Reimann and Strech [6] presents different English and German PRWs and the criteria on which patients can rate their physicians. In total 21 physician rating websites in English and German language were analyzed. The results show that each physician rating website has a unique set of criteria to rate a doctor. They conclude that there is no common rating framework.

3 Research Model

Figure 1 depicts the research model. The influences were adapted from patient satisfaction literature and implications from physician rating website research. The structure of the model is based on Permwonguswa et al. [17], who showed how a framework on rating criteria in the context of medical care should look like.

Overall satisfaction mirrors the patient's satisfaction, which is defined by Ware et al. [7] as the personal evaluation of health care services and providers. Satisfaction ratings are subjective and capture the personal evaluation of care the patient received. Williams and Calnan [22] call it general satisfaction with general practice. Patient satisfaction is a multidimensional concept [7] with several heterogeneous influences such as the satisfaction with the physician and the satisfaction with the administration [17, 18]. Thus, we postulate two influences on the overall satisfaction:

H1: *The higher the satisfaction with the physician, the higher (more positive) the overall satisfaction.*

H2: *The higher the satisfaction with the administration, the higher (more positive) the overall satisfaction.*

Satisfaction with the physician is defined as how satisfied patients are with the physician and the medical care delivered by her/him. The construct is shaped by the characteristics of the doctor in terms of perceived technical quality and the doctor-patient relationship [8].

Doctor-patient relationship focuses mainly on how patients perceive their doctor on a personal level, without considering medical aspects. The balance of power

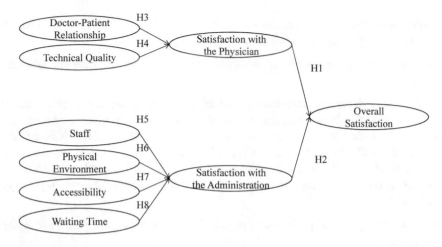

Fig. 1 Research model

between patient and doctor has not been found as influential in the doctor-patient relationship [11]. LaCrosse [23] found that non-verbal communication transmits emotions and attitudes, which are rarely spoken out loud. Leaning forward and nodding while communicating with the patient seem to have an influence on the patient satisfaction. Patients see their doctors warmer and more attractive. The liking of the patient towards their doctor has been found to positively correlate towards the satisfaction with the treatment and the doctor [9, 22]. Thus:

H3: *A high level of doctor-patient relationship positively influences the satisfaction with the physician.*

Technical quality is defined as how patients perceive the competence of the providers and their adherence to high standards [7]. As examples the accuracy of the diagnosis, taking unnecessary risks and medical mistakes are mentioned. Patients usually do not have the same medical knowledge as physicians have. The status of the doctor is not only carried by his social status, but also by his knowledge and perceived competence. Patient satisfaction will suffer greatly if patients have a negative perception concerning the competence of the doctor [24]. Thus:

H4: *A high level of perceived technical quality positively influences the satisfaction with the physician.*

Satisfaction with the administration features the organization in which the medical care is delivered, mainly with respect to the doctor's office and the staff interaction. Accessibility, staff and the physical environment have been shown as influences for patient satisfaction [7, 25]. Waiting times are also often researched in the case of how satisfied patients are with their medical care experience [16].

Staff describes how patients perceive the staff personnel in the office and how helpful they interact, when there are questions or uncertainties but also the atmosphere between individual staff members. Staff behavior and nursing care have been found to be an element of patient satisfaction [16, 25, 26]. Thus:

H5: *A positive staff attitude positively influences the satisfaction with the administration.*

Physical environment is the setting in which the medical care is delivered. Examples are orderly facilities and equipment, clarity of signs and directions. This construct evaluates how the patient perceives the doctor's office in terms of the facility itself without the staff or the practitioners [7, 25]. Therefore, no personnel are involved in the evaluation of the physical environment. Unclean facilities and bad comfort in the waiting rooms have been found to yield a high level of dissatisfaction to patients [22]. Thus:

H6: *A positive physical environment positively influences the satisfaction with the administration.*

Accessibility expresses how easy or how much effort is needed for the patient to receive medical care, in terms of appointment times and office hours. Ware, Snyder [7] defined it as factors involved in arranging to receive medical care. Williams and Calnan [22] describe this influence on patient satisfaction with the accessibility and availability of the health care services. Thus:

H7: *A high level of accessibility positively influences the satisfaction with the administration.*

Waiting time is defined by how long patients have to wait in the physicians' facility to receive treatment and how satisfied they are with the duration and the general appointment time. The waiting time includes the time in the waiting room, in the exam room. The satisfaction with the appointment time is the subjective content with the date of the examination [13, 22]. Thus:

H8: *A high level of satisfaction with waiting time positively influences the satisfaction with the administration.*

4 Research Method

A quantitative survey was conducted in the south of Germany. Based on the available literature and reflecting the research model presented above, a structured questionnaire was developed. Every construct was measured reflectively by three items. Existing measures have been used wherever possible. Items have been adapted and altered to fit the context. All items were translated to German and measured using a five-point Likert-scale.

The questionnaire was delivered in person by the research team to the patient. The physicians allowed the research team to approach patients while these were waiting for their appointment in the waiting area (some physicians provided a separate

Table 1 Sample demographics (n = 115)

Variable	Categories	Sample	Distribution (%)
Gender	Male	49	42.61
	Female	66	57.39
Age	<31	32	27.83
	31–45	30	26.09
	46–60	28	24.35
	>60	25	21.74

room for the interview). The patients were interviewed before the appointment took place and directly after seeing the doctor before leaving the premises. The questions after the treatment aimed towards the satisfaction with the physician and the overall satisfaction.

Data collection took place in the first half of 2017 and 115 completed questionnaires could be gathered.

The characteristics of the sample are given in Table 1. The distribution of responses amongst physicians was: general practitioner 24 (22.22%); otolaryngologists 47 (43.52%); orthopedists 44 (40.74%). The distribution is relatively even among the professions and also among age.

5 Results

Structural equation modelling (SEM) technique using partial least squares (PLS) was used with SmartPLS version 3.2.6 [27]. Even though the sample size of 115 is relatively small, it is sufficient to assess the model based on the rule of ten [28], as the research model would require a minimum of 40 questionnaires. In order to assess the quality of the measurement instrument, tests concerning convergent validity and discriminant validity were performed.

Convergent validity is represented by the loadings of the items to their respective construct. All loadings were significant at the 0.001 level and exceeded the recommended value of 0.7. Construct reliability was tested by examining the composite reliability (CR) and the average variance extracted (AVE). The values exceeded the threshold of 0.6 for CR and 0.5 for AVE.

Discriminant validity has been assessed by observing the cross-loadings of the items. Every item correlates with their respective construct the most. In addition, the Fornell-Larcker criterion shows the highest value for the respective construct and therefore supports discriminant validity. In the next step, the path coefficients have been examined which represent each hypothesis.

The results of the SEM calculation are depicted in Fig. 2.

The path coefficients of satisfaction with the physician ($\beta = 0.459$, $p < 0.001$) and satisfaction with the administration ($\beta = 0.480$, $p < 0.001$) towards the overall

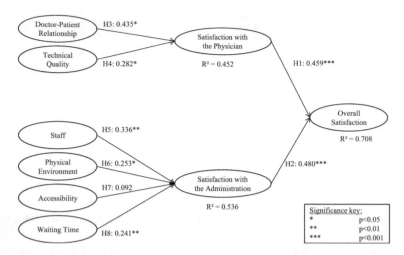

Fig. 2 Research model results

satisfaction are significant with comparatively strong influence on the dependent variable, supporting H1 and H2. Doctor-patient relationship ($\beta = 0.435, p < 0.05$) and technical quality ($\beta = 0.282, p < 0.05$) have been found significant for the satisfaction with the physician, which supports H3 and H4 with a bigger influence of the doctor-patient relationship. Staff ($\beta = 0.336, p < 0.01$), physical environment ($\beta = 0.253, p < 0.05$) and waiting time ($\beta = 0.241, p < 0.01$) have a significant influence on the satisfaction with the administration, with staff as the biggest influence. Therefore, H5, H6 and H7 are supported. Accessibility ($\beta = 0.092$, n.s.) has not been found as a significant influence on the satisfaction with the administration. Therefore, H8 was not supported. The explanatory power of the model has been assessed by the squared multiple correlations (R^2). The explained variance of patient satisfaction ($R^2 = 0.708$) is substantial.

6 Discussion and Implications

6.1 Empirical Findings

The empirical results show evidence that doctor-patient relationship has strong impact on the rating which is in line with the findings of Möller-Leimkühler et al. [8]. Communication and empathy are shown to have great influence on how patients perceive their treatment. Technical quality as an influence shows a weaker influence on the direct satisfaction with the physician. For the satisfaction with the administration, the same characteristics as for the satisfaction with the physician can be found. Interpersonal aspects such as the communication and treatment by the staff have the highest influence. Physical environment and waiting time show an equally strong impact on the satisfaction with the administration. This is in line with the research of Medway et al. [13] and Ware et al. [7]. However, accessibility has not been found as an influence on the satisfaction with the administration of the office. In literature accessibility for general practitioners is also not mentioned among the most powerful influences [24]. The physicians involved in the study mostly had their offices in rural areas. Patients mentioned that they do not want to reach out to a physician who is a long distance away from their hometown. This suggests that choosing the right physician comes down to convenience if there is no need to see a rare specialist.

6.2 Theoretical Implications

This research complements the literature examining how patients' ratings constitute. Patient satisfaction is a well-researched area, without the existence of physician rating platforms. The existing literature of patient satisfaction did not explicitly focus on an overall rating of the doctor in case of recommending the physician to others. This research establishes a link between patients' satisfaction and rating on physicians in the context of rating physicians in a public context like PRWs. Since patients rate their physician mostly positive, the scarce of negative ratings on PRWs can be explained. Patients seem to be biased in the way that they mostly visit doctors with whom they already have good experiences with. Kadry et al. [12] support the finding on patients' rating being favorable on physician rating websites. The strong impact of the doctor-patient relationship on the satisfaction with the physician shows in relation to the technical quality that patients focus more on how they like the doctor instead of how competent they think physicians are. It is also an indicator that physician ratings do not reflect the true quality of the medical treatment, since patients are not able to evaluate the competency of the physician or the medical treatment itself due to the knowledge gap between patient and doctor. Furthermore, the high cross-loadings between the constructs of the doctor-patient relationship and the technical quality show evidence that patients are not able to distinguish between their sympathy towards their doctor and the perceived competency. The data suggests that patients who like their physician automatically are biased in a way that they think the physician is competent enough to decide for the right treatment. It is also an indicator that patients may be more forgiving in case of bad treatment, when they sympathize with their physician. Therefore, additionally to the knowledge gap between doctor and patient, the evaluation of the technical quality is also biased due to the doctor-patient relationship.

6.3 Practical Implications

The results provide important insights for physicians to improve their online ratings and for potential patients how to use PRWs. Physicians can improve their reputation and therefore, rating with their patients. The research suggests that physicians should focus on their relationship with their patients. Communication and sympathy have been shown as a key element of patients' ratings. Keeping in touch with patients in the office, but also online on a personal level should increase patients' satisfaction and the reputation of the physician.

Even though PRWs suggest that only doctors are rated, reality shows that the whole office is part of the rating. Staff influences the patients' rating by the same criteria: human interaction. A good atmosphere among the staff and the patients already show great impact on patients' satisfaction. This has to be kept in mind to achieve a good patient rating and online reputation. The doctor alone cannot influence the rating as a whole, since the whole staff is involved. The model shows that patients are able to distinguish these separate influences way better than the single influences.

Comparing the influences of the satisfaction with the physician and the satisfaction with the administration, this research provides evidence, that both are equally relevant for the overall satisfaction. Even though staff has a greater influence than physical environment and waiting time, physicians should consider to get feedback about how patients feel about the appearance of the office and if waiting times are perceived as too long. However, changing the office surrounding and encountering waiting times will imply additional cost for physicians' offices. On a good note, the strongest influence to improve online ratings, the direct human interaction, can be implemented immediately.

The study also has shown that ratings are already overwhelmingly positive. Therefore, physicians should enforce patients to participate on physician rating websites. Past research has shown that physicians are rather skeptical about rating websites [1]. Also, physicians in the study articulated their skepticism on these rating websites, which can be the reason for a more conservative encounter with PRWs. For a better representation of how patients feel and a better online reputation, physicians should find ways to motivate patients to rate online.

For people who are looking for a physician, this research has a clear yet inconvenient message: Laymen who rate physicians' online predominantly rate their subjectively perceived well-being when interacting with the physician. In other words: users of PRWs looking for the technical best specialist will get recommended the most empathic etc. physician but not the best medical expert. As such the whole system of PRWs needs to be taken for what it is: Medical laymen providing their subjective feelings towards the behavior of the physician they met. Unless specific information on the (long term) treatment success is given, the evaluation of the medical quality of the services provided remains doubtful.

7 Limitations and Further Research

This study only focused on patients and physicians situated in a metropolitan area in southern Germany (convenience sampling). The location was of special interest to contribute to the knowledge basis of physician rating platforms in the context of German patients. For further research, the sample size needs to be increased for better results and the items for the patient satisfaction should be altered to make up for the favorable bias of patients towards their doctor to achieve a better fitting model. A suggestion would be to identify a group of patients who were clearly not satisfied with their doctor visit. Another way to overcome the positive bias of patients can be the focus on specialized physicians who are only visited once by the patient. This would exclude general practitioners who are visited more often or even regularly by the same patient.

To fully understand the ratings and what constitutes the perception of the physician, the outcome of the treatment should be considered in further research. The study focused on the short-term satisfaction of the patient immediately after the treatment, at which point the patient is not able to judge whether the treatment will improve the personal condition. Further research should ask patients 2 weeks and 6 weeks after the treatment, to investigate how much the impact of the outcome changes the rating.

8 Conclusion

The main influences of patients' ratings have been examined. The results show that that patient satisfaction and physician rating criteria can be observed on the same level. The direct rating on the physician and the rating of the organizational part have an equally big impact on the final rating. The study has shown that doctor-patient relationship, physician's competency, staff interaction, physical environment and waiting time play key roles in the patient's rating. The emphasis on human interaction as a main role of patients' satisfaction shows potential for further research.

Appendix

See Table 2.

Table 2 Questionnaire

Construct	Indicator
Overall satisfaction	I am satisfied with my doctor and office
	I always visit the same doctors' office
	I would recommend my doctor and office to my friends and family
Satisfaction with the physician	I am satisfied with the medical treatment
	I always visit the same doctor, if I have a problem
	I would recommend my doctor to my friends and family
Satisfaction with the administration	I am satisfied with the procedure until I saw the doctor
	I am satisfied with the organization of the office
	I would recommend my doctors' office to my friends and family due to the good organization
Interpersonal manner	The doctor treats me with respect
	The doctor lets me tell him/her everything that I think is important
	The doctor listens, when I have uncertainties
Technical quality	The doctor is very careful to check everything when he/she is examining me The doctor always explains the side effects of the medicine he/she prescribes The doctor never exposes me to unnecessary risk
Doctor-patient relationship	I like my doctor as a person
	I feel understood by the doctor
	The doctor is interested in my problem
Staff	The atmosphere among the staff is good
	The staff helped me when I had questions
	I was treated with respect by the staff
Physical environment	The office is modern and up to date
	The waiting area was comfortable
	The treatment area was clean and sanity
Accessibility	It's hard to get an appointment (−)
	Office hours when you can get medical care are good
	If I have a medical question, I can reach someone for help without any problem
Waiting time	I am satisfied with my appointment time
	I am satisfied with the waiting time in the waiting room
	It takes too long to see the doctor (−)

References

1. Abramova, O., et al. (2016). Physician-rating platforms: How does your doctor feel? In *Americas Conference on Information Systems*.
2. Gao, G. G., et al. (2012). A changing landscape of physician quality reporting: Analysis of patients? Online ratings of their physicians over a 5-year period. *Journal of Medical Internet Research, 14*(1), e38.
3. Trehan, S. K., & Daluiski, A. (2016). Online patient ratings: Why they matter and what they mean. *The Journal of Hand Surgery, 41*(2), 316–319.
4. Jameda. (2017). *Jameda Factsheet*. https://www.jameda.de/jameda/jameda/jameda-Factsheet.pdf.
5. Hennig-Thurau, T., et al. (2004). Electronic word-of-mouth via consumer-opinion platforms: What motivates consumers to articulate themselves on the Internet? *Journal of Interactive Marketing, 18*(1), 38–52.
6. Reimann, S., & Strech, D. (2010). The representation of patient experience and satisfaction in physician rating sites. A criteria-based analysis of English- and German-language sites. *BMC Health Services Research, 10*(1), 332.
7. Ware, J. E., et al. (1983). Defining and measuring patient satisfaction with medical care. *Evaluation and Program Planning, 6*(3), 247–263.
8. Möller-Leimkühler, A. M., et al. (2002). Is patient satisfaction a unidimensional construct? *European Archives of Psychiatry and Clinical Neuroscience, 252*(1), 19–23.
9. Hall, J. A., et al. (2002). Liking in the physician–patient relationship. *Patient Education and Counseling, 48*(1), 69–77.
10. Fitton, F., & Acheson, H. W. K. (1979). *The doctor/patient relationship: A study in general practice*.
11. Stimsom, G. (1975). *Going to see the doctor: The consultation process in practice*.
12. Kadry, B., et al. (2011). Analysis of 4999 online physician ratings indicates that most patients give physicians a favorable rating. *Journal of Medical Internet Research, 13*(4), e95.
13. Medway, A. M., et al. (2016). Why patients should arrive late: The impact of arrival time on patient satisfaction in an academic clinic. *Healthcare, 4*(3), 188–191.
14. Jackson, J. L., Chamberlin, J., & Kroenke, K. (2001). Predictors of patient satisfaction. *Social Science and Medicine, 52*(4), 609–620.
15. Bos, A., et al. (2005). Patient compliance: a determinant of patient satisfaction? *The Angle Orthodontist, 75*(4), 526–531.
16. Hendriks, A. A. J., et al. (2001). Improving the assessment of (in)patients' satisfaction with hospital care. *Medical Care, 39*(3), 270–283.
17. Permwonguswa, S., et al. (2016). Development of a doctor rating criteria for a medical tourism portal. In *European Conference on Information Systems*.
18. Camacho, F. T., et al. (2009). Validation and reliability of 2 specialty care satisfaction scales. *American Journal of Medical Quality, 24*(1), 12–18.
19. Lagu, T., et al. (2010). Patients' evaluations of health care providers in the era of social networking: An analysis of physician-rating websites. *Journal of General Internal Medicine, 25*(9), 942–946.
20. Hay, M. C., et al. (2008). Why patients go online: multiple sclerosis, the internet, and physician-patient communication. *The Neurologist, 14*(6), 374–381.
21. Emmert, M., et al. (2013). Physician choice making and characteristics associated with using physician-rating websites: Cross-sectional study. *Journal of Medical Internet Research, 15*(8), 16.
22. Williams, S. J., & Calnan, M. (1991). Convergence and divergence: Assessing criteria of consumer satisfaction across general practice, dental and hospital care settings. *Social Science and Medicine, 33*(6), 707–716.
23. LaCrosse, M. B. (1975). Nonverbal behavior and perceived counselor attractiveness and persuasiveness. *Journal of Counseling Psychology, 22*(6), 563.

24. Sitzia, J., & Wood, N. (1997). Patient satisfaction: A review of issues and concepts. *Social Science and Medicine, 45*(12), 1829–1843.
25. Abramowitz, S., Coté, A. A., & Berry, E. (1987). Analyzing patient satisfaction: A multianalytic approach. *QRB. Quality Review Bulletin, 13*(4), 122–130.
26. Pascoe, G. C., & Attkisson, C. C. (1983). The evaluation ranking scale: A new methodology for assessing satisfaction. *Evaluation and Program Planning, 6*(3–4), 335–347.
27. Ringle, C., S. Wende, & Becker, J.-M. (2015). *SmartPLS 3*. http://www.smartpls.com.
28. Hair, J. F., Ringle, C. M., & Sarstedt, M. (2011). PLS-SEM: Indeed a silver bullet. *Journal of Marketing theory and Practice, 19*(2), 139–152.

Last Mile Logistics in Smart Cities: An IT Platform for Vehicle Sharing and Routing

Emanuele Guerrazzi

Abstract Due to the current remarkable growth of e-commerce, the *last mile* logistics has become a relevant problem. In this paper, the main issues of the *last* mile logistics in a smart city context are introduced. We propose a solution based on a shared Information Technology (IT) platform that needs no material investments. The principle of resource pooling is applied to the sharing of heterogeneous vehicles in the urban network. In particular, an IT platform powered by an optimization algorithm is proposed to allow couriers to make their deliveries more efficiently, that is, to reduce the total distance covered by the vehicles. This was achieved through the development of four software modules: an ETL, an optimizer, a web application and a map displayer. First results are promising, but further investigations should be done in order to evaluate more accurately the expected benefits and the possible positive externalities such as improvement of air quality in the city.

Keywords Last mile delivery · Logistics · Smart city · Vehicle sharing

1 Introduction

In the recent years, business practices worldwide have been shaped by the remarkable rise of e-commerce. The rapid e-commerce growth has resulted in the steady increase of parcel delivery and returns volumes, which has accentuated the pressure on last mile delivery actor and has created a demand for new solutions [1].

Globalization and the web market have led to exponential growth in transport, allowing the development of an open market: products can be purchased anywhere; goods travel around the world; and most of the goods are delivered to cities. The topic of the last mile delivery is dealt with innovative modes thanks to the development of Information and Communication Technologies (ICT), Information Transport Systems (ITS), Industry 4.0 and new transport vehicles [2].

E. Guerrazzi (✉)
University of Pisa, 56121 Pisa, PI, Italy
e-mail: emanuele.guerrazzi@gmail.com

© Springer Nature Switzerland AG 2020 251
A. Lazazzara et al. (eds.), *Exploring Digital Ecosystems*,
Lecture Notes in Information Systems and Organisation 33,
https://doi.org/10.1007/978-3-030-23665-6_18

In this context, a *Smart City* is defined as "A ICT enabled development which extensively uses information as a way to improve quality of life for its citizens and population at large" [3]. It is well known that transportation is one of the main contributors of CO_2 emissions [4]. Thus, public authorities are encouraging companies to collaborate in order to increase sustainability. They not only aim at reduced emissions of harmful substances, but also on reduced road congestion, and noise pollution.

Urban areas require a massive quantity of goods, services and resources, which are causing many problems for citizens. Transportation systems are often influenced by unexpected conditions that affect their performance, with inconveniences for citizens due to the lack of interoperability among the various transport operators [5]. Studies indicate that freight vehicles represent no more than 15% of total traffic flow in urban areas [6], but due to their size and frequent stops for deliveries have a more significant impact than passenger vehicles.

Sii-Mobility Project, co-founded by Italian Ministry of Education, University and Research, aims to create an ICT platform for the introduction of smart solutions for urban mobility, the optimization in the use of public and private resources and the reduction of traffic and pollution impacts in urban areas, improving the concept of *"smart city"* as a solution to face the increasing problems related to traffic and pollution and the growing demand for sustainable mobility and quality of services [7]. In this context, we focus on a typical city logistic scenario, where there are a certain number of *couriers* and a much bigger number of *last-mile operators* (aka *"masters"*) that are accountable for delivering and picking up small packages in the urban and extra-urban environment. These operators have exclusive agreements with couriers, and they are responsible for picking up packages at the logistic centres and for visiting the final addressees. This transportistic organization leads to a redundant presence of vehicles of different couriers, even at the same addresses or in the same areas in the same day, resulting in an increase of urban traffic, an increase of delayed deliveries and an increase of pollutant emissions, as well as all the indirect consequences.

The main objective of this work is to provide couriers with a tool that allows them to organize more efficiently their last mile distribution, through the shared use of vehicles and Information Technology (IT) platform in a *smart city* context. The core of the designed IT platform is powered by an optimization algorithm in order to make the distribution of goods in the last-mile delivery more efficient.

This article is organised as it follows. In Sect. 2 the state of the art about last mile delivery and vehicle sharing is presented. Section 3 shows more in detail the objectives and the methodology used for this work. In Sect. 4 preliminary results are shown. Finally, the discussion and conclusions, including future developments, are presented in Sect. 5.

2 State of the Art and Empirical Background

Ranieri et al. [2] provides a review of the last mile logistics innovations in an externalities cost reduction vision, classifying the innovative contributions into five categories:

(1) Innovative vehicles
(2) Proximity stations or points
(3) Collaborative and cooperative urban logistics
(4) Optimization of transport management and routing
(5) Innovations in public policies and infrastructures.

Particularly, this work deals with issues 3 and 4.

The cooperative urban logistics concept is based on the sharing of the resource and the revenue in the last mile delivery. An interesting application can be found in [8], in which the delivery of small- and medium-sized packages is carried out using public transport means. Liakos and Delis [9] propose an interactive freight-pooling service using a *trustee* (i.e. a city authority) to orchestrate the process by specifying constraints (i.e. changing time windows). In this work a *cluster-first route-second* heuristic has been used in order to optimize the cost of the last-mile delivery, supposing that the cost depends on the time the freight remains engaged to a hired carrier and suggesting a fair pricing policy that encourages the participation of couriers.

We mention also Juan et al. [10] that discuss a backhaul-based cooperation among couriers, comparing cooperative and non-cooperative scenarios. Results show that cooperation leads to a lower distance overall covered, even if the technique is limited only to the backhaul route.

For what it concerns the optimization of transport management and routing we cite the work of Kin et al. [11], where a mathematical model is developed to calculate the costs of alternative distribution set-ups for the last mile transportation in urban areas. This work suggests four different set-ups (direct, cross-dock, direct with small vehicles, urban consolidation centre) depending on the volume of transported items and distances covered.

Zhou et al. [12] introduce a city logistics problem in the last mile distribution involving two levels of routing problems (depots-satellites, satellites-customers), proposing a hybrid multi-population genetic algorithm.

Actually, routing problems in logistics are modelled as variants of the VRP, and they are often solved by heuristics [13], especially when applied to the real-world.

As concerning the empirical background, in the EU area, a number of innovative experiences about city logistics have been implemented in the last decades. The most important are reported here following (for a more detailed description see [14]):

– On street package collection and delivery stations (Germany)
– Coventry's zero-emission postal service (UK)
– Delivering goods by cargo tram in Amsterdam (Netherlands)
– Electronic vehicles for companies in Stavanger (Norway)
– Utrecht's sustainable freight transport (Netherlands)

- Smart packaging solutions for cleaner urban freight in Berlin (Germany)
- Padova Cityporto: a success model for urban logistics (Italy)
- Distripolis: a new city logistics solution in Paris (France).

3   Objectives and Methodology

3.1   Objectives

The main objective of this Sii-Mobility solution is to allow multiple couriers to optimize their last-mile delivery using a shared pool of vehicles. In order to achieve this purpose, it is necessary to accomplish the following objectives:

(1) Allow data integration and sharing among all couriers and masters. In particular, couriers have to share their transportistic requests and masters have to share the information about their vehicle fleet.
(2) Make the overall distribution more efficient, in terms of:

   a. Reducing couriers' logistics costs
   b. Reducing air pollution in the urban context
   c. Reducing traffic jam

(3) Show the route to drivers, using a suitable displayer.

   Main benefits expected from such a solution are:

- sharing the logistics resources for pickup and delivery
- optimizing the use of the available resource in order to reduce cost
- reducing urban mileage and consequently reducing pollution and traffic
- improving the quality of services.

3.2   Methodology

The proposed solution is IT platform that enables the centralization and processing of info from several couriers and *masters* in order to optimize the pickup and delivery processes of goods.

An overall vision of the IT platform is reported in Fig. 1.

In the following, each part of the system will be described.

ETL Module This module implements ETL processes in order to retrieve information from external and heterogeneous sources and to store them on a shared Data Warehouse (DW).

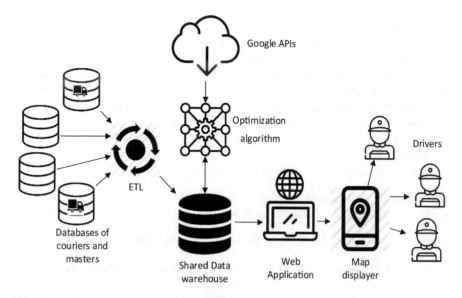

Fig. 1 Representation of the proposed IT platform

These ETL processes have two objectives:

1. To acquire and manage static data provided by couriers and *masters*, (i.e. the capacity of the vehicles)
2. To acquire and manage dynamic data provided by couriers, in particular data about the deliveries/pickups.

This is achieved by implementing the following phases:

– *Phase 1*: extracting data from outside sources (Ingestion phase). This phase includes data retrieval, the processing, the selection and the internal storage of data, interacting (in different ways) with external sources.
– *Phase 2*: transforming data to fit operational needs which may include improvements of quality levels (Data Quality Improvement phase). This phase allows to preliminary analyse data in order to identify attributes of interest, how they are made and, if necessary, acting to improve their quality. For example, a "name" could be trimmed, an "email" could be checked, an "address" could be uppercased and so on.
– *Phase 3*: loading data into the data warehouse (or another end target such as a database or a data mart).

Optimization Module This module is the core of the entire algorithm and it solves a variant of the popular *Vehicle Routing Problem* (VRP) called *Multi-Depot Pickup and Delivery Heterogeneous Capacitated VRP with Time Windows* (MDPDHCVRPTW) that can be stated as it follows: given a certain number of heterogenous vehicles that are at disposal of various depots, we have to make the optimal assignment of packages in order to satisfy the transportation requests of customers within their required arrival time, minimizing the overall distance covered by the vehicles.

This is a generalization of the VRP, that is already a NP-hard problem [15].

We decide to specify the objective function as it follows: to reduce the total distance covered by vehicles through a coordinated and optimized management of the vehicle pool and of the transportation requests (pickups or deliveries).

Indeed, this typically would lead to the benefits cited in 3.1.

Besides, the use of more ecological vehicles is more appreciated than old trucks, and the module takes in account this.

More operatively, this module has to provide:

– The optimal allocation of packages to the vehicles
– The optimization of the route of each vehicle.

in order to reduce the total distance covered by the vehicles.

An implementation of the *Tabu Search* metaheuristic has been developed, the details of its mechanism are reported in Appendix.

This module reads data from the DW and write into an appropriate table the resulted solution, that consists in the assignment of packages to the selected vehicles, indicating the sequence of the visit to each customer and to each courier's warehouse.

The module integrates data from Google APIs, in particular it gets geographical coordinates, distance matrix and time matrix from it.

These data are essential in order to make the algorithm work correctly.

Web Application Module This module is a Web application that has to show for each vehicle:

1. The *warehouse pickup* list, that states which packages the vehicle has to pick up at which courier's depot (it could be more than one)
2. The *pickup and delivery* list Which packages the vehicle has to deliver or pickup at customers' addresses.

This module gets data from the Optimization Module in order to show the required outputs. Every next modification can be requested by couriers or *masters* through this module.

This web application arranges a user interface to access:

– Static data about couriers, *masters*, vehicles, drivers and depots
– The *warehouse pickup* and *pickup and delivery* list
– Info about the delivery status of the packages.

In this way both couriers and *masters* can customize the assignments suggested by the algorithm according to their necessities (i.e., reassigning a package from a vehicle to another one). Once the manual reassignment has been done, it is possible to ask again the algorithm a new optimized solution, without changing the packages that have been manually reassigned.

Map Displayer Module This module is an APP developed in order to display on the map the info about the warehouse pickup and pickup and delivery lists.

It also provides an interface that allows the drivers to point out all the info useful to track the package (i.e., delivery status, interruption on the itinerary).

4 Preliminary Results

In order to validate the system, a local *master* of the city of Pisa has been contacted and 3 real instances have been tested.

Note that in this case an instance consists in a set of transportation requests that have to be accomplished in a specified day. Every transportation request includes the customer's address, the weight of the item, the requested arrival time, the type of transport (pickup or delivery) and all the info about the origin of the item.

Besides, as it would not be possible to use all the features of the algorithm with the original data of the *master,* these have been slightly modified in order to test the full potentiality of the algorithm and its main applications.

Results are shown in the following table:

Instance type	CD_m (km)	CD (km)	S (%)	C	P	ET (s)
MDPDHCVRPTW	267	201	24.7	68	72	38
PDHCVRPTW	200	148	26.0	66	69	34
MDHCVRPTW	268	243	9.3	107	123	126

where:

- CD_m is the covered distance (km) by *master* solution
- CD is the covered distance (km) found by our algorithm
- C is the number of customers (i.e., the number of distinct addresses visited by the vehicles)
- P is the total number of packages
- ET is the total execution time of the algorithm (s)
- S is the saving percentage in distance, computed as: $S\,(\%) = \frac{CD_p - CD}{CD_P} \cdot 100.$

5 Discussion and Conclusions

The problem of the last-mile distribution has been faced, and a tool that allows couriers to manage more efficiently their deliveries has been designed, using an optimization algorithm that relies on the resource pooling principle and that is based on a modified version of the tabu-search metaheuristic.

First results show that there is a possibility for couriers to have the daily total distance covered by their trucks reduced.

Besides, there are some limitations that must be taken in account:

- It could be impossible to couriers to share their information due to privacy and perceived risk/issues.
- Google APIs restrict the algorithm's capacity to handle a large number of customers because there is a limit on the free daily queries [16].

Further investigations should be conduct in order to study possible positive externalities such as:

- The improvement of air quality
- The effective reduction in the transportation costs of the couriers
- The time saving of the planner

Also, a complete instance involving real data from more than one courier should be used to further test the proposed solution.

In the context of smart-city, such a shared IT platform could enable a disruptive change in the business model of couriers and masters. As an addition, it could provide local authority with a tool to support environmental policies.

Finally, we remind that the modular nature of the algorithm allows future adjustments to the algorithm itself can be done (i.e., considering the fairness among vehicles).

Acknowledgements This work has been supported by a yearly research contract between T.I.M.E. S.r.L. and the University of Pisa, Department of Computer Science. This work is part of the Sii-Mobility project, which is funded by MIUR.

The author desires to thank prof. Antonio Frangioni and prof. Laura Galli, both of the Department of Computer Science of the University of Pisa, for their precious contribution to the development of the optimization algorithm.

The author thanks also Mirco Manciulli, Alice Carminati and Daniela Landucci, of T.I.M.E. S.r.L., for the suggestions received during the year.

Appendix: Optimization Algorithm Details

In this appendix is reported more in detail how the algorithm works.

The optimization algorithm is a modified implementation of the popular *tabu-search* technique, and it can be divided in four phases:

(1) *Clustering of the customers*: through the geographical coordinates of the customers, is it possible to apply a simple K-Means algorithm in order to get the desired K clusters. K is an integer computed through the cost of the Minimum Spanning Tree of all the nodes (customers and courier's depots). Every cluster is then ordered, or rather, every customer of the cluster is sorted in an ascending manner according to a distance-time function that takes in account both the

geographical distance from a customer to another one and its requested arrival time.

(2) *Choice of vehicles and assignment of packages*: once the K clusters are obtained and ordered, K vehicles are chosen from the pool. The algorithm chooses first the most ecological vehicles, then those ones that have larger capacity. Once the vehicles are selected, all the packages are sequentially assigned to one of the vehicles according to the same distance-time function of step 1), that is a package is assigned to the nearest vehicle. If no vehicle is available, or one or more constraints are violated, (i.e., overload of the truck, customer not served in time) then another vehicle is chosen from the pool.

(3) *Local search*: once a first constructive solution is obtained, five local search moves are applied sequentially so that only improvements to the current solution are allowed. Some of these moves are well-known moves used for the Travelling Salesman Problem, such as 2-opt or Or-opt, while others are a modification of classical moves.

(4) *Tabu search*: after the local search, a tabu search based on the same moves is started. It is possible to choose how many iterations of the tabu search the algorithm has to run. We remind that this technique is used in order to escape eventual local minima found in 3.

References

1. Vakulenko, Y., Hellström, D., & Hjort, K. (2018). What's in the parcel locker? Exploring customer value in e-commerce last mile delivery. *Journal of Business Research, 88,* 421–427.
2. Ranieri, L., Digiesi, S., Silvestri, B., & Roccotelli, M. (2018). A review of last mile logistics innovations in an externalities cost reduction vision. *Suistanibility, 10,* 782.
3. Mamkaitis, A., Bezbradica, M., & Helfert, M. (2016). Urban enterprise: A review of smart city frameworks from an enterprise architecture perspective. In: IEEE International Smart Cities Conference (ISC2) (pp. 1–5). Trento, Italy: IEEE. September 12–15, 2016.
4. Ballot, E., & Fontane, F. (2010). Reducing transportation CO_2 emissions through pooling of supply networks: Perspectives from a case study in French retail chains. *Production Planning & Control, 21*(6), 640–650.
5. http://www.sii-mobility.org/index.php/il-progetto.
6. European Commission: Study on Urban Freight Transport. Technical Report, April 2012.
7. Nesi, P., Po, L., Viqueira, J. R. R., & Trillo-Lado, R. (2018). An integrated smart city platform, IKC 2017. *LNCS, 10546,* 171–176.
8. Chatterjee, R., Freulich, C., Edelkamp, S. (2016). Optimizing last mile delivery using public transport with multi-agent based control. In Proceedings of the 2016 IEEE 41st Conference on Local Computer Workshop. Dubai, United Arab Emirates, November 7–10, 2016.
9. Liakos P., Delis A. (2015). An interactive freight-pooling service for efficient last-mile delivery. In 16th IEEE International Conference on Mobile Data Management.
10. Juan, A. A., Faulin, J., Pérez-Bernabeu, E., & Jozefowiez, N. (2014). Horizontal cooperation in vehicle routing problems with backhauling and environmental criteria. *Procedia—Social and Behavioral Sciences, 111,* 1133–1141.
11. Kin, B., Spoor, J., Verlinde, S., Macharis, C., & Van Woensel, T. (2018). Modelling alternative distribution set-ups for fragmented last mile transport: Towards more efficient and sustainable urban freight transport. *Cases Studies on Transport Policy, 6,* 125–132.

12. Zhou, L., Baldacci, R., Vigo, D., & Wang, X. (2018). A multi-depot two-echelon vehicle routing problem with delivery options arising in the last mile distribution. *European Journal of Operational Research, 265,* 765–778.
13. Crainic, T. G., & Sgalambro, A. (2014). Service network design models for two-tier city logistics. *Optimization Letters, 8*(4), 1375–1387.
14. http://www.eltis.org/discover/case-studies.
15. Dantzig, B., & Ramser, J. H. (1959). The truck dispatching problem. *Management Science, 6,* 80–91.
16. https://developers.google.com/maps/documentation/javascript/usage.

Digital Transformation Projects Maturity and Managerial Competences: A Model and Its Preliminary Assessment

Aurelio Ravarini, Angela Locoro and Marcello Martinez

Abstract This paper sheds light on an overlooked aspect of Digital Transformation processes and projects: the managerial competences necessary to make them happen, evolve and be achieved. Many technology maturity models are discussed in the literature, but little or no mention is done regarding how to model and assess the broader set of managerial competences (i.e., knowledge, skill and experience) besides the technical ones, which managerial roles should exhibit in each phase of the maturity models proposed. This paper discusses some of these maturity models and motivates a new one focused on Digital Transformation maturity in the direction of filling this gap. The model is then presented in its conceptual design as well as in its empirical assessment. A couple of pilot interviews to Italian companies are also discussed as a preliminary test of the main feelings about it and as a ground for our final refinements and future works upon it.

Keywords Digital business transformation · Maturity model · Managerial competences · Qualitative model assessment

1 Introduction and Motivations

Digital Business Transformation has been defined[1] as "the profound and accelerating transformation of business activities, processes, competencies and models to fully

A. Ravarini · A. Locoro (✉)
Università Carlo Cattaneo—LIUC, Castellanza, VA, Italy
e-mail: alocoro@liuc.it

A. Ravarini
e-mail: aravarini@liuc.it

M. Martinez
Università della Campania Luigi Vanvitelli, Caserta, Italy
e-mail: marcello.martinez@unicampania.it

[1]The definition is available at https://www.i-scoop.eu/digital-transformation/, last accessed 28th May 2018.

© Springer Nature Switzerland AG 2020   261
A. Lazazzara et al. (eds.), *Exploring Digital Ecosystems*,
Lecture Notes in Information Systems and Organisation 33,
https://doi.org/10.1007/978-3-030-23665-6_19

leverage the changes and opportunities of digital technologies and their impact across society in a strategic and prioritized way, with present and future shifts in mind." Today, Digital Transformation is able to challenge traditional business strategies and management roles to the point of no return. Adapting to rapidly changing scenarios where technologies are sovereign seems an imperative to survive in the global economy. But what is it really at stake when it is time for an enterprise to align to the main digital transformation drivers? Does this transformation mean only a technical transformation or also a social one?

For [1, p. 6] its all quite a matter of *leadership*. In defining the key points for which enterprises fall short of expectations when going digital, Fitzgerald and their colleagues declared that both "management temperament and relevant experience" are key drivers to success, as "todays emerging technologies, like social media, mobile, analytics and embedded devices, demand different mindsets and skill sets than previous waves of transformative technology". The problem of vagueness around the Chief Information Officer (CIO) and CxO roles in relation to the management of "information and technology for competitive differentiation and the maturity of [organizational] information leadership capabilities" [2] is well known in IS research. Diverse idealtypes has been characterized for CIOs roles in regard to business and IT alignment [3–6]. However, digital business transformation projects are a relatively new scenario of analysis of the top management roles.

In a previous work [blinded reference], we tried to trace the main characteristics of the CIO and Chief Digital Officer (CDO) in regard to their roles, in order to understand in which aspects these managerial roles differed or were analogous, what were their relation with the new waves of technology, and how their interplay had sense to create a synergy towards the successful digital business transformation of enterprises. In this paper, we partly ground on our previous analyses, but we shift our focus on a set of characteristics named managerial competences. Competences has been defined as any "knowledge, skill, trait, motive, attitude, value or other personal characteristic essential to perform a job" [7, p. 843]. Among managerial competencies there are "such characteristics as communication skills, problem solving, customer focus and the ability to work within a team".[2] We structure competence types under the three concepts of knowledge, skill, and experience. In this way, we set them apart from roles, activities, responsibilities and purposes of managerial figures, so as to be better scrutinized and well outlined in their traits, and we propose a conceptual justification of the term competence first. Then, we contextualize these concepts in digital transformation projects maturity.

---

[2]The definition is available at https://bizfluent.com/info-8216837-managerial-competencies-mean. html, last accessed 28th May 2018.

1.1 About Competences

The definition of competence and managerial competence justify an in-depth digression about the origin of the conceptual structure surrounding the terms that we proposed above, namely: "knowledge, skill and experience". We deem this detour as a useful tool for readers to better understand what we intend with competences and our interpretation of them. This digression may justify why we prefer to keep competences well separated from roles, responsibilities, tasks, and so on; why we consider them all necessary tiles of the managerial equipment; what their mutual relations and interplay may be, and so on.

We owe the first conceptualization of the virtues of our rationality[3] to Aristotle, who defined the dual nature of our "rational soul": that of being thoughtful and practical, and kept "alive" by its main driver, the pursue of "goodness". The principle of our action is deliberation, and this in its turn is based on rational thought and rational practice. To pursue the "right" choices, we as humans reasons about goals and means to reach them, and we do this through our "dispositions", i.e., our tendencies towards goodness. Aristotle named such dispositions as:

- science[4] ("episteme" in Greek) or the formal methods we apply to know what can be considered as "necessary and enduring" (i.e. true);
- intellect[5] ("nous" in Greek) or the intuitive understanding, the engine of our formal reasoning about truth;
- "sophia",[6] which is composed of science and intellect, that we translated into the term *knowledge*;
- art[7] ("techne" in Greek) or "rational disposition to production", ability to "create and design" (virtual or material) objects. We translated this term into *skill*;
- wisdom[8] ("phronesis" in Greek) or the proper disposition to action, i.e., practical judgment to "deliberate and act for the best", which we translated with the term *experience*.

We argue that the umbrella term competence is a contemporary way to define all of those "personal dispositions" necessary to act in the world, managing problems and pursuing goals with our best efforts. However, despite the above systematization, it is clear how all of these elements are difficult to be separated into rigid definitions and isolated from each other. For example, knowledge is related to experience in that it partly drives it and aids to take the most suitable actions; skills are not action, but a specialized knowledge (i.e., technical knowledge) that allows the production

---

[3] We refer here to our synthesis of the discourse about dianoetic virtues – i.e., virtues of our reason – in the translation from the original Greek in Italian of Nichomachean Ethics: Book VI (E.N.,B:VI from now on), available at http://www.filosofico.net/eticaanicomaco6.htm.

[4] E.N.,B:VI, part 3.

[5] E.N.,B:VI, part 6.

[6] E.N.,B:VI, part 7.

[7] E.N.,B:VI, part 4.

[8] E.N.,B:VI, part 5.

of objects and services and / or the manipulation of people and processes. This production is then related to action (knowing how to ride a bike is manifested when riding a bike). Wisdom is impossible without knowledge (and intellect in particular) but it is not knowledge of something, rather it extends to "practice" as the rationality applied to situational and contingent events, with the aim of acting for the best.

Although a too rigid classification of competences is unrealistic, we keep at least the conceptual structure of the terms composing competence, with the aim of identifying those that should all be part and parcel of management background and character in Digital Transformation projects. In particular, our aim is that of exploring the varying degrees and combinations of competences triggering the maturity steps under exam of a digital transformation project.

1.2   Research Questions

In general, technology maturity models show stepwise evolution in the adoption of a technology or in the making of a digitalization project up to the best possible levels of efficiency and effectiveness for the enterprise. Starting from this assumption, our goal is to create a model that identifies the competences (knowledge, skill and experience) of the managerial roles (CIO, CDO, and the like) who are responsible of the digital transformation in an enterprise. This managerial features should be analyzed in the different phases of an organizational transformation. In particular, the following research questions aims at filling a gap in the current literature, where the competences outlined for the CIO and CDO specific roles seems to be forced into rigid and static abilities:

– should the managerial role responsible for digital transformation projects be unique?
– should an activity be mapped one to one to a specific role (e.g., in a tayloristic perspective), or is there room for a more flexible and partial overlapping when not even redundancy of roles?
– should the role or roles involved in a digital transformation project be static or may they evolve along with the organizational transformation?

The paper is organized as follows: Sect. 2 is an overview of enterprise technology maturity models. In Sect. 3 we present our model of digital transformation maturity and managerial competences through the lenses of its conceptual design and pilot assessment. Section 4 concludes and sketches our future work.

2 Background

2.1 Technology Maturity Models Compared

The problem with the current technology-driven models of organizational maturity and the like is that they mainly focus on different aspects of (technical) transformation *per se*, and leave the social concern in participating to the transformation implicit or underdeveloped. As the socio-technical perspective is well established in acknowledging the importance of both aspects and how deeply they are intertwined, the lack of clarity or the lower level of investigation on the human side of organizational transformation may fail short of providing a crystal clear interpretation of the phenomenon and, as a consequence, the absence of adequate tools for intervention. The following review is performed on organizational models of "maturity" and aims at revealing their strength and weaknesses in the direction of orienting our work towards the detection of a more balanced construct for understanding digital transformation maturity levels in connection with managerial competences. In what follows, we take into consideration models of technological analysis and concern in organizations.

One of the first models implemented in this direction is the "Capability Maturity Model" (CMM), which was laid down by Nolan first [8] in respect to IT evaluation adoption, and then evolved by other authors while it became a standard of software development and process modelling. This model presents organizational evolution starting from a chaotic state, where processes are left running in a primeval condition where no formalization and control is possible, into a higher stage of maximum clearness, efficiency, and optimization. This transformation has been modelled in five levels, where the more technology is used to support processes and their optimization, the more maturity is achieved and ascribed to the organizational business and IT strategies. In this model, no alternatives are foreseen, but a straight and strictly increasing technological advancement towards an organizational goal. No perspective is taken regarding the human competences to reach this goal, nor this model delves into the organizational complexities and dynamics that are at play while reaching the proposed goals.

Among the revised versions of the CMM the one from Galliers and Sutherland [9] extended the stages detection and description with the factors influencing the maturity of different aspects of an organization. Each factor is either present or not in a particular stage, so as to better describe and understand where an organization is positioned according to the model. These factors ranges from strategies to infrastructures and operators, and also specifies operative roles and general skills that are necessary in each phase of maturity. Starting from technology adoption, this model shows how also strategic and organizational considerations are relevant, and how to translate them into influencing factors of maturity. These factors are then instantiated in each phase of the model and each of them contributes with a different intensity to each organization maturity phase. Many models originated from CMM, for example in the healthcare domain (see [10] for an overview). However, for these set of models, it may suffices to note how social actors are left aside, and the use of an adequate digital recording of clinical data and a networked infrastructure seem sufficient to lead to the level of desired maturity.

A model related to the healthcare domain, but more focused on data analysis processes for business intelligence (BI) projects is the one designed by Brooks and colleagues [11]. This model borrows its structure from the Design Science Research Methodology (DSRM) framework [12], a methodology composed of six steps that are exploited to represent the phases of maturity for a BI project. The difference with respect to the previous models lays in the higher level of details regarding the specific steps and activities to be taken in each phase of the BI project. In a separated section of the study, the authors describe the main factors affecting the success for these kind of projects: among them, "People skills (analytic, business and IT)", "Supporting technology" and "Quality evaluation of the results" [11, p. 338]. Although these factors are more adhering to our idea of organizational effort for more specific tasks and phases, these factors are just left separate from the BI model, so that it was not feasible for us to figure out a possible mapping between a specific phase or activity of the model and the related skills or competences. In the same study, a comparative analysis of maturity models is also carried out in order to demonstrate the lack of previous focus in the literature on the complexities of data analysis management.

Another model we took into consideration in our analysis is the one by Schumacher [13]. This model takes into exam the Industry 4.0 readiness of manufacturing industries. In so doing, a model of nine dimensions with sixty-two maturity items spread out among them is presented and discussed in the study. In particular, dimensions such as Leadership, Culture, People, Governance and Technology are deemed relevant for framing the maturity of organizational capabilities in the manufacturing domain for Industry 4.0 projects. The list of dimensions is sustained by a corresponding list of items, whose importance was assessed by interviews and a structured questionnaire with Likert scale values for each of the maturity items of the model. Some of the highest scores were assigned by the respondents to the items belonging to the dimensions of People, Culture and Government. However, as no further details are given in the study about the items and the scores of the single items inside each dimension of the model, we could not go deeper into it.

A maturity model specifically designed for the digital transformation of the supply chain in manufacturing industry was developed by Kotzler and colleagues [14]. This model is focused on a specific goal of digital transformation, i.e. the production and application of "smart products", i.e. products with an added value embedded in them: the continuous and knowledgeable exploitation of data-driven services, which transform these products into innovative "service systems" [14, p. 4215]. A new mindset is advocated for this new production paradigm, up to the level of a "data-driven enterprise" [ibidem]. To reach the latest level, the model envisages five levels and nine dimensions characterizing them and allowing the definition, measurement and evaluation of each level. Among the dimensions defined, there is a distinction between the "Smart product" dimension and the "Complementary IT dimension", and an emphasis is given to the social and competency dimensions, by including in the matrix also "Collaboration", "Structual" and "Process" organization, "Competences" and "Innovation Culture". In paricular, the "Competences" dimensions is stated for each level in terms of technical competence on each piece of technology adopted during each phase of the production and application models. No emphasis is given in this study to other competences rather than technical, such as for example the soft skills and other knowledge and experience of the participants involved in the smart product management. Concerning the dimension of "Innovation Culture", the authors hints at general characteristics of the top management such as openness, service and digital thinking, and understanding of the innovation phenomenon of data availability.

2.2 CIO and CDO Roles, Responsibilities, Tasks and Goals: What About Competencies?

Roles, responsibilities, tasks and goals for CIO/CDO figures can be defined off the table. The necessary competences (besides the technical ones) to accomplish them are partly ineffable and needs a subtler intuition as they are a quite subjective aspect of CIO/CDO background and "personalities", as we have just outlined in Sect. 1.1. This is one of the reasons why they are often disregarded or considered only in their technical aspects when modelling organizational activities, projects and strategies. However, we believe that starting from an outline of the roles that CIO and CDO are called to cover, together with their main responsibilities, tasks, and goals, may help frame competences as being in relations with them, rather than identifying competences with them.

The traditional goal of a *CIO* is the productivity improvement through the adequate exploitation of IT enterprise infrastructures. CIOs are recently called to play a leading role in the Digital Transformation [2]. In this role, they should drift from the management of technology to the management of information, having a global and strategic vision of the organization, rather than a limited functional and operative orientation.

In the literature, there is no mention of how a CIO's background may influence his corresponding attitudes and behaviors. The only question under analysis is the kind of background of a CIO, being a "soft skill" background or a "hard skills" one and the related correlation between these kinds of skills and the stronger or weaker influence exerted by the CIO vs the other Top Executives [3]. A second trait of the CIOs capabilities is outlined in [15] where the CIO is considered as the main enabler of an IT innovation strategy in enterprises. Among the characteristics and their definitions that CIO should possess for enabling IT innovarion there are:

- political savvy: capability to influence, negotiate and persuade;
- communicative ability: capability to communicate with an appropriate business jargon, and in a clear and persuasive way;
- relationship building ability: capability to strengthen reputation and authority among peers;

- strategic business knowledge: capability to comprehend people, business strategy and the competitive forces in an organization;
- strategic IT knowledge: capability to understand the emergent technologies, their potential, their relevance for the organization and catch the "kairotic" moment when investing on them.

Regarding the *CDO*, this role is almost new in the organizational landscape. About this role, it is claimed[9] that today it is one of the roles with the higest increasing rate of employment during the last years and a global phenomenon. On the other hand, it is also claimed that among the top-ranked companies in the world, only 6% of them has a CDO in its hierarchy.[10]

According to [16] the CDO is a role responsible for:

- defining a digital strategy shared by the whole organization so that a unifying vision could lead the organizational awareness of the Digital Transformation at hand;
- coordinating the digital harmonization of activities;
- exploiting the opportunities of digital business offered by markets;
- driving an organization through the digital transformation of its business.

In regard to "Digital Transformation", Hess [17] focused on the responsibility of a CDO to continuously monitoring the internal and external organizational contexts, so as to get the opportunities offered by the "Digital Disruption",[11] and yielding the highest benefits from it.

For Ariker and colleagues[12] the CDO competences should partly overlap with the ones of the "Chief Marketing Officer" in having a strong focus on KPIs and big data, as well as a clear vision of the business strategy; on the other hand, the CDO should also have competences that make this role getting closer to the CIO [18], such as, for example, the capability to exploit the technology infrastructure to increase the revenue, a deep knowledge of the technological trends, project management skills, and data analytics skills [19].

None of these studies proposes a systematization of competences in the strand of what we deem necessary to map them with project phases and maturity steps like the one required by Digital Transformation.

---

[9] See for example http://cdoclub.com/first-look-chief-digital-officer-and-chief-data-officer-talent-map-2016/.

[10] https://www.strategyand.pwc.com/reports/chief-digital-officer-study.

[11] Digital disruption is the change that occurs when new digital technologies and business models affect the value proposition of existing goods and services. Source: https://searchcio.techtarget.com/definition/digital-disruption.

[12] Article available at: https://www.mckinsey.com/business-functions/digital-mckinsey/our-insights/getting-the-cmo-and-cio-to-work-as-partners.

3   A Digital Business Transformation Project Maturity Model for Managerial Competences

Our method of enquiry of the above literature strictly followed the main principles and coding tasks devised within the Grounded Theory framework [20]. From the analysis and synthesis of the literature, we derived a sequence of steps for our Digital Transformation Project Maturity Model and a set of Competences that should belong to the management roles in charge of activating, governing and bringing each phase of the Digital Transformation project to success.

The resulting schema is depicted in Table 1, where we show the main phases of a Digital Transformation Project, the Competences that we deemed necessary in each phase of the project, and references to the literature from which we borrowed some terms and model structures. In particular, the model phases were borrowed from the work of Brooks et al. [11] with the exception of the "Demonstration" phase, whereas the specific competences described in column 2 of the Table were mainly inspired by works on maturity models and others (which are properly cited in the Table at each phase level).

3.1   Model Outline

The six phases of the model are explained and justified in what follows.

Identify: this phase is an explorative one, where the goal is twofold: the monitoring of digital opportunities and technological trends; the analysis of the inner and outer

Table 1   The digital transformation project maturity model with a focus on managerial competences

Phase [11]	Competence
Identify [11, 14, 15, 21]	Knowledge of: - Business strategy skills in: - Digital & technology trends Experience of: - Inner & outer contextual analysis to identify problems and opportunities
Define [1, 2, 6, 15]	Knowledge of: - Organizational processes skills in: - Project management (resource allocation) experience of: - Relationship building - Leadership
Design [1, 2, 10, 14, 15]	Knowledge of: - Business & IT alignment strategies skills in: - Project management (planing, scheduling, etc.) Experience of: - Business & IT integration projects design
Develop [2, 6, 15, 19]	Skills in: - Project management (coordination, problem solving, re-alignment, etc.) Experience of: - Leadership - Change management
Evaluate [10, 11]	Skills in: - Data analytics experience of: - Data-driven decision-making
Communicate [2, 6, 15]	Skills in: - Communication - Persuasion experience of: - Leadership

scenarios to compare them and evaluate the possibility (or the necessity) to start a digital transformation process. The competences required in this phase should span from the ability to monitor, analyze and comprehend the potentials and the benefits of technological trends, to the deep knowledge of the organizational business structures, processes, strategies, in order to disclose possible convergences among the two.

Define: this phase includes the setting of the necessary resources and tools for starting the digital transformation process. Indeed, in this phase the main competences required should be at the organizational level (resource management, and so on), and at motivational level, so that a common vision of the process of transformation could be effectively communicated and shared among both supporters and opponents, and opponents could be persuaded to change their mind. In this context, some "soft skills" such as leadership are strongly required.

Design: this is the phase where the digital transformation borns, and where all the technological aspects are taken into consideration for development. Also organizational aspects such as technology deployment and adoption are pursued. Technical IT competences for integration purposes, as well as business process design competences for process re-design are both necessary. Project management skills are highly recommended in this phase, and make or buy analysis experience is also a requirement.

Develop: this is the "Go Live" of the digital transformation project, where the whole organization is involved. Project management competences are highly required in this phase, for the organizational and coordination aspects of the project at hand. Leadership and change management competences should be functional to managing the impacts of the projects for all the people involved and for maintaining the right dose of attention and popularity among the stakeholders.

Evaluate: in this phase data analysis capabilities are fundamental in order to evaluate the risks and impact of the project, which is by its nature characterized by a high volume of data that should be gathered, elaborated, interpreted, and communicated.

Communicate: the communication to the stakeholders subsumes a set of competences related to leadership, communication skills, persuasion techniques and the ability to gain approval for the project results. The communication phase is a delicate one, as a correct or wrong attitude may shift the balance of the stakeholder opinions about the project itself.

3.2   Pilot Assessment

The pilot assessment of our model was shaped as the administration of five semi-structured interviews among the top management of an Italian fashion company that has started a digital business transformation process impacting its retail sales strategy. The roles who were interviewed are: the CEO, the IT Manager, the Planning and Allocation Manager of the company, and the CTO of one of its external IT consulting companies. The main considerations emerged from the content analysis of these interviews are related to specific considerations about competences in the Design phase that cannot be left out of the scope of a digital transformation project, i.e., user-oriented technologies and as well as a special gaze and sensitivity for socio-technical aspects of digital transformation. A second point is related to a deep knowledge of technological trends and the like. This knowledge should not necessarily be an internal one, rather it can be acquired from outside partners. A third consideration is related to the importance given to soft skills and marketing assets, which should be practiced since the beginning of a digital transformation project. Another important consideration emerged from the interviews: the recommendation of not adhering to too rigid labels, rather by focusing on the competences practiced by whomever is covering them, without any constraints based on roles. The main limitations in current oranizational roles are due to the "one role, one task" restriction and to the lack of collaborative paradigms and effective ways to promote them in enterprises.

4 Conclusions

In this paper, we presented a digital transformation maturity model and the related managerial competences that cannot be left anymore out of consideration when taking digital transformation seriously. Our future work will focus on refining our model through the method of multi-case studies and on possibly unveiling new organizational models for the management of multiple and multifaceted organizational roles co-responsible of the same digital transformation project. In particular, we will launch an online survey gathered around four main questions: for each phase in the model and competences we ask the degree of importance of each of them, the motivations behind this evaluation, whether these competences are present in the company and, in case yes, by whom they were practiced. Our goal is to extend this model by considering each step taken and each competence as a pivotal structure that can be filled with meaningful content based on the assessments in the field.

References

1. Fitzgerald, M., Kruschwitz, N., Bonnet, D., & Welch, M. (2014). Embracing digital technology: A new strategic imperative. *MIT sloan management review, 55*(2),
2. Peppard, J., Edwards, C., & Lambert, R. (2011). Clarifying the ambiguous role of the cio. *MIS Quarterly Executive, 10*(1),
3. Carter, M., Grover, V., & Thatcher, J. B. (2011). The emerging cio role of business technology strategist. *MIS Quarterly Executive, 10*(1),
4. Li, Y., & Tan, C. H. (2013). Matching business strategy and cio characteristics: The impact on organizational performance. *Journal of Business Research, 66*(2), 248–259.
5. Guillemette, M. G., & Paré, G. (2012). Toward a new theory of the contribution of the it function in organizations. *Management Information Systems Quarterly, 36*(2), 529–551.
6. Al-Taie, M.Z., Lane, M., & Cater-Steel, A. (2014). The rel.between organisational strategic it vision and cio roles: One size does not fit all. *Australasian Journal of Information Systems, 18*(2)

7. Abraham, S. E., Karns, L. A., Shaw, K., & Mena, M. A. (2001). Managerial competencies and the managerial performance appraisal process. *Journal of Management Development, 20*(10), 842–852.
8. Nolan, R. L. (1973). Managing the computer resource: A stage hypothesis. *Commun. ACM, 16*(7), 399–405.
9. Galliers, R. D., & Sutherland, A. (1991). Information systems management and strategy formulation: The stages of growthmodel revisited. *Information Systems Journal, 1*(2), 89–114.
10. Rocha, Á. (2013). Evolution of information systems and technologies maturity in healthcare. Healthcare Information Technology Innovation and Sustainability: Frontiers and Adoption: Frontiers and Adoption, p. 238
11. Brooks, P., El-Gayar, O., & Sarnikar, S. (2015). A framework for developing a domain specific business intelligence maturity model: Application to healthcare. *International Journal of Information Management, 35*(3), 337–345.
12. Peffers, K., Tuunanen, T., Rothenberger, M., & Chatterjee, S. (2007). A design science research methodology for information systems research. *Journal of Management Information Systems, 24*(3), 45–77.
13. Schumacher, A., Erol, S., & Sihn, W. (2016). A maturity model for assessing industry 4.0 readiness and maturity of manufacturing enterprises. *Procedia CIRP, 52*, 161–166.
14. Klötzer, C. & Pflaum, A. (2017) Toward the development of a maturity model for digitalization within the manufacturing industrys supply chain. In T. Bui & R. Sprague (Eds.), *Procs of the 50th HICSS.*
15. Liu, B., Luan, S., & Li, D. (2014). It-enabled business innovation: Does cio capability matter? A perspective from institutional entrepreneurship theory. In *PACIS* p. 10
16. Westerman, G., Bonnet, D., & McAfee, A. (2014). Leading digital: Turning technology into business transformation. Harvard Business Review Press
17. Matt, C., Hess, T., & Benlian, A. (2015). Digital transformation strategies. *Business & Information Systems Engineering, 57*(5), 339–343.
18. Milovich, M., Jr. (2015). Moving technology leaders up the influence curve. *MIS Q Exe, 14*(1)
19. Laufer, A., Hoffman, E. J., Russell, J. S., & Cameron, W. S. (2015). What successful project managers do. *MIT Sloan Management Review, 56*(3), 43.
20. Wolfswinkel, J. F., Furtmueller, E., & Wilderom, C. P. (2013). Using grounded theory as a method for rigorously reviewing literature. *EJIS, 22*(1), 45–55.
21. Shao, Z., Wang, T., & Feng, Y. (2016). Impact of chief information officers strategic knowledge and structural power on enterprise systems success. *Ind Manag & Data Sys, 116*(1), 43–64.

Reporting Some Marginal Discourses to Root a De-design Approach in IS Development

Federico Cabitza, Angela Locoro and Aurelio Ravarini

Abstract In this work, we challenge the concept of design in the development of information systems. Information systems are usually considered to be so complex systems that they simply cannot be developed outside of a specific activity of planning. However, in the specialized literature, some voices have also been raised saying that it is this situated and contingent complexity that always prevents information systems from having been really effectively designed. These voices have so far criticized the formal and methodical approaches in IS design, and not design itself, thus exonerating the role of the modernist designer from the current rate of failure and user dissatisfaction in IT projects. The current idea of designer has reinforced over time a divide between modeling and practicing, design and use, and the hegemony of the planning mind over that of the performer. The current convergence of networked application paradigms and the Web 2.0 infrastructure has led to agile methods, open design concepts and on the idea of a prosuming user. This paper outlines some discourses in IS research that could challenge the more traditional ones in current IT design, and argues about the importance to revamp some of the most important socio-technical principles for maintaining a critical gaze on positivistic and automation stances, mitigating the effects of the modernist over-design attitude, and make IS development more sustainable.

Keywords De-design · Socio-technical artifact · ST artifact · IT artifact · Undesign · Meta-design

F. Cabitza
Università degli Studi di Milano-Bicocca, Milan, Italy
e-mail: federico.cabitza@disco.unimib.it

A. Locoro (✉) · A. Ravarini
Università Carlo Cattaneo—LIUC, Castellanza, VA, Italy
e-mail: alocoro@liuc.it

A. Ravarini
e-mail: aravarini@liuc.it

© Springer Nature Switzerland AG 2020
A. Lazazzara et al. (eds.), *Exploring Digital Ecosystems*,
Lecture Notes in Information Systems and Organisation 33,
https://doi.org/10.1007/978-3-030-23665-6_20

1   Introduction

As widely known, Information Systems (IS) research is concerned with "the design, development, implementation and use of socio-technical systems in organizational contexts" [1]. In this discipline, design as a topic of concern has been largely discussed [2]. We also will focus on design in this paper. However, as rightly noted by Fallman, design is a term that is intrinsically difficult to define, since "it can denote many different things to different people: including design as a profession, as an activity, and—when design is used as a noun—as an artifact." [3]. For instance, in an influential contribution for the IS community, Hevner states that "the design process is a sequence of *expert* activities that *produces* an innovative product." [2] (our emphasis).

This vision is mainly grounded on the rich conceptualization of Simon [4], who understood design to encompass all of the conscious activities in which artifacts are created and "existing conditions" are transformed "into preferred ones" [5]. That notwithstanding, for our aims we will follow Baskerville et al. to differentiate the actual construction of any new (IT) artifact[1] from the "working out [of its] form" [3] "the purposeful organization of resources [to build it]" [2] and "formulating hypotheses [on it]" [6], that is from its "design".[2]

Indeed, we need to create some room between the concept of design, intended as "creation of artifacts", which is so preeminent in IS research [4] and especially in the "design science" branch of it [2], and the *situated* use of those artifacts by the so called end users, which conversely is the current main object of investigation of the HCI field [7] and increasingly so of the "behavioral science" branch of IS [2], in order to accept the idea that IT artifacts are not "given" to their users but rather evolve in interaction with an organizational context.

This does not mean to simply acknowledge that design is a never-ending activity that occurs in "the long now" [8, 9] and that artifacts are "perpetually in the making" [10]. Rather, the point is to recognize the active role of users in the necessary transformation of the artifact they use over time; or, at least, of the situated ways they appropriate and accommodate the artifact [11] and work with it. These "ways" and practices are part and parcel of the Socio-Technical (ST) artifact, which should substitute that of IT artifact in IS research [12].

This work in particular focuses on the extreme consequences that can be drawn from those ST-Design (STD) principles that were originally denoted as "Minimal Critical Specification" and "Incompletion"; in so doing, we aim to build on the work where Garud et al. argue that "designing for incompleteness" is far from being an

---

[1] In this paper we equate the IT artifact with the software applications constituting an Information System (IS), that is the technical component(s) of an IS, and of the related ST system. For simplicity's sake then, the IT artifact definition we refer to is close to the one proposed by Hevner et al. [2], which "include[s] not only instantiations [... of] the IT artifact but also the constructs, models, and methods applied in the development and use of information systems, [while it does not include] people or elements of organizations [...] nor [...] the process by which such artifacts evolve over time" (p. 82).

[2] After all, OED defines design as "action of producing a plan" (2002).

oxymoron, and propose to the readers a provocative question (even in the title of a section) that they clearly left without an answer: "to design or not to design?" [10].

2 Opposing Stories of Modernist Design

This paper aims to shed light on the phenomenon of the *erosion* of a certain discourse on design, and the contextual emergence of some alternative voices. This phenomenon, on one hand, is becoming increasingly more apparent, likely due to the diffusion of the Web 2.0 and the social media; on the other hand, it has become simply more perceivable by researchers that now look with renovated attention to what happens after that a technology has been designed and built, and has been instantiated into an organizational setting, a sensitivity that has also been dubbed as the "turn to the users" [13].

To frame this phenomenon we have first to claim *what* discourse on design we refer to. We acknowledge the existence of multiple perspectives toward IT design: Johansson-Sköldberg et al. enumerate the main ones in IS research [4]. That notwithstanding, if we focus not on what differentiate these perspectives, but rather on what all these discourse have *in common*, we recognize like a common fil rouge tying these together. We then call this heterogeneous bundle the "grand narrative of the modernist design". We choose the term "modernist" after Berman, who relates that condition to "a socially progressive trend of thought that affirms the power of human beings to *create, improve and reshape their environment*" [14].

With the development of modern industrial societies, when modernism stabilized in philosophy, figurative arts and architecture, we observed the remarkable success of Taylorism in the dawning mass production industry, with its core ideas: "standardization, […] the setting of precisely defined tasks, the emphasis on efficiency and productivity, […] the sharp and permanent split between planning and doing, [the related] irreversible and complete handover of all planning, control and decision making from the workmen to the new class of scientific managers" [15] and the "scientific approach to design [itself, which] was done by specific individuals [such as industrial engineers] but not by those engaged in ongoing operations whose job was to 'do and not to think'" [10].

The same pattern can be recognized 50 years later when the discipline of software engineering was established [16] to cope with what at that time was perceived as "the software crisis" [17]. Professionals whose name (i.e., software engineers, requirement engineers, software architects, software and interaction designers) was chosen in the mold of the building industries and their successful methodologies began to spread over until this day. In this age, many accounts of the conflicting relationship between designers and users (the so called designer/user divide) in organizational context, and how the intentional design plans of the formers become thwarted by the latter ones make and *gain* sense (e.g. [13, 18–20]).

In the next section then, we will collect some of the most important approaches to design that more or less consciously challenge the main assumptions underlying the grand narrative of modernist design. After Lyotard [21], we will collect these (still) minor discourses into a paralogy,[3] the *paralogy of de-design*. Such an idea undermines the legitimacy of the modernist design in the first place, but also the prominence of the designer as the "high priest" [22] "at the top of the solution hierarchy" [23], of which Le Corbusier represents a sort of archetype.[4] Similarly to anti-design approach [24], which programmatically conceived products not "intended as finished or closed forms", also de-design denotes a departure from the idea of design as detailed planning and envisioning of future objects and situations, to embrace the more extreme consequences of the "open design" age, which Atkinson associates with many related phenomena, among which the advent of the "cult of the amateur" (which opposes the connoisseur's one, cf. Keen), the diffusion of the Do-It-Yourself rhetorics (e.g., the scripting programming,[5] the "maker age", Arduino and the 3D Printing Industry), and the shift from "co-creation or co-design to a position where users take on the responsibility for creative and productive acts in their entirety", and also build products from scratch and tinker them until they fit their needs almost totally, since amateurs are "those who know themselves what is best for them" [26]. This loop cuts out the designer, and challenges also the need to "conceive ideas" explicitly and to "form a representation of those ideas", to build models, which are the main cognitive tasks that Cross associates inextricably to the very notion of design lying at the basis of design research [9]. To this respect the first anticipatory ideas within the Information Systems field (at large) at the basis of the de-design paralogy can be recognized in those (few) works that have so far questioned the importance and reliability of explicit representations and formal models of work and use in technology design [1, 25, 27–29].[6]

---

[3]In this context, a paralogy is an alternative discourse (or "little narrative") that is developed in opposition to an established way of reasoning ("grand narrative", or metanarrative).

[4]In 1923 Le Corbusier stated that houses were to be conceived (and hence designed) as "machines for living" ("une maison est une machine-à-habiter"). This resonates with the Tayloristic image of the "organisation as a machine" (actually by a Taylor's follower, Gantt). See also Evenson, N. (1969). "Le Corbusier: The Machine and the Grand Design" Studio Vista, and Morgan, G. (1997). Images of organization. SAGE Publications.

[5]As noted in [25] open design and open software development can be paralleled but present also stark contrasts: in open design instead of collectively making single uniform products, there is a collection of outputs that are built by single makers to fit their needs, possibly by exploiting (by either adoption or adaptation) products or contents of the others.

[6]In those works what it is usually questioned is either the ostensive (i.e., prescriptive) or descriptive power of models [30], while their function as an aid for introspection, reflection on practice and, most notably, communication is rightly often recognized (e.g., [31, 32]), even where IS design methodologies are depicted as a "necessary fiction to present an image of control or to provide a symbolic status" [33] in the essentially political process of IT design [34].

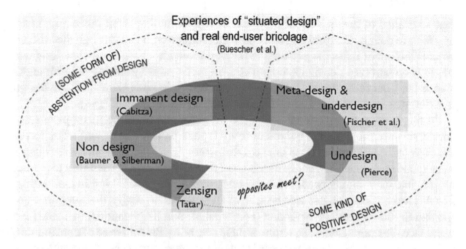

Fig. 1 The spectrum of the various stances in the de-design paralogy

3 The De-design Paralogy

The paralogy of de-design encompasses a spectrum of approaches that differ for few but important aspects and have in common the more or less explicit questioning of the grand narrative of modern(ist) design. We articulate this spectrum (see Fig. 1) in terms of the extent traditional designers and methods are still involved in the organization of activities of de-design, paradoxically as it might sound, to reduce the impact of professional design on the final artifact, or to change the nature of the relationship between the phases of problem framing, solution defining, decision making and eventually planning, and those of resource instantiation and continuous refinement of the artifact.

Thus, one extreme of this spectrum is represented by more or less programmatic stances that advocate various forms of *abstention from design*, on the basis of an explicit will to (self)-limit the scope and ambit of intervention of the designer.

3.1 Zen-Sign

The most elegant example of this stance has been suggestively denoted as "zensign": an understated attitude to design that has been proposed as a way to solve *design tensions* that may "arise in the construction of a system in relationship to a socio-technical situation" [35], for instance when the designer is stuck in-between two equally feasible but essentially irreconcilable design solutions, or even ways to frame the problem itself. This term, which Tatar has purposely avoided to explain too precisely, evokes the idea that omitting and leaving out features from a design is just as critical to the success of a system as it is including them positively: since any feature does both afford and constrain interactions with and through the artifact, what is left out of it has the potential to be even more important than what designers put in it on purpose. Zensign is not an anti-theoretic or programmatically mindless stance [36], but rather highly "disciplined and principled omission" [37]: "a design inaction that is intentional, thoughtful, purposeful, and impactful" [38].

In this viewpoint, functional omissions do not come from the incompetence or carelessness of the designer, but rather result from a precise strategy of reduction of the risks of the unintended consequences that would (also) derive from the designer's inadequate knowledge and comprehension of the setting, and impossibility to predict all possible uses, interdependencies and effects of the designed thing in that setting. For this reason, Zensign can also be seen as an approach to design that support argumentation and meaning construction (i.e., "design" à la Krippendorff, [4]), and help users face the unpredictable in virtue of their flexibility for "absence of constraints", informed by a humble stance in regard to how to frame, comprehend and support an ever-changing context [39].

The decision "not to design" can also result from an analysis of the pros and cons that deploying a new IT artifact into a specific setting would entail. In this second case, a more proactive de-design attitude can be related to what Baumer and Silberman call implication "not to design" [40] and Pierce as "foreclosure of a potential future technology" in his review of how technology can be *undesigned* [41]. This is the case where professionals decide *not to* intervene on the basis of an analysis that recognizes that a computing technology, although being perfectly feasible and applicable, could be inappropriate or socio-technically unsuitable for a specific setting, or just potentially worse than a "equally viable low tech or no-tech" solution [40]. This resolution can be taken either on the basis of reports of earlier experiences undertaken in similar settings; on the analysis of the unintended consequences that can be traced back to the deployment of similar systems (considering whether "a technological intervention results in more trouble or harm than the situation it's meant to address"); or according to an activity of introspection by which the "critical designer" [42] comes either to "question the need for such a system in the first place", or recognizes that the "technology would solve a computationally tractable transformation of a problem rather than the problem itself". Thus the "no design" solutions that we find at one extreme of the de-design paralogy can also be seen as one of the options, indeed the most radical one, of a fully coherent Critical Design activity, that is a "design that asks carefully crafted questions and makes us think" [43] and thus opposes traditional "modern" design, which conversely focuses on solving problems and on finding (often remunerative) answers.

3.2   Immanent Design

Another form of abstention from conceptual design is advocated in [28] where we proposed an approach now dubbed as "immanent design". This proposal started from a reflection upon the deep affinity we found between computation and human work as essentially distributed and co-ordinated "manipulations of signs" [44], on the nature of design specifications and how they "specify" the construction of new artifacts while deeply ingrained with symbolic and ritualistic content [22, 25, 34]. By affirming the legacy and link of any invention with the past (its nature of *dis*-covering, etymologically speaking), in immanent design specifications are programmatically recognized as *immanent* to the object to be digitized and automated, that is *already there*, as tangible reality of a stratified process of coevolution with practice so far, thus integrally inherent to and intimately indwelling the material "web of things" [45]. Immanent design affirms that design specifications do not need to be reconceptualized linguistically, while artifacts to be only transformed, or better yet, trans-*format*-ed, rather than recreated from scratch and "reengineered" (as in the construction of "black boxes" aimed at supporting work by "affording" [46] the routine patterns of sign manipulation that can be observed in the traditional, pre-digitization, usually paper-based artifacts). In this case, then de-design as a general principle is reached by abstaining from designing the task "around" the artifact (and hence also the social reorganization the new artifact entails [47]), but rather limiting the designer role to that of facilitating the change of format (e.g., from paper-based to electronic) in which signs-representations are handled and triggering the related local transformations of the artifact that acts as a "mere" scaffolding of practice [48].

3.3 Meta-Design and Underdesign

Walking through the above mentioned spectrum from the more radical instances of de-design to the more softer and almost blurred with traditional professional design,[7] we find what Fischer and colleagues have richly characterized and widely advocated in the last 15 years as meta-design [50–52]. Meta-design was proposed as a framework to develop Socio-Technical Systems and extend the "traditional notion of system design beyond the original development of a system to include an ongoing process in which [end users] become co-designers" but, differently from Participatory Design, not exclusively "at design time" but rather "at use time, throughout the whole existence of the system" [52]. This idea was clearly influenced by the socio-technical argument by Henderson and Kyng that "design as a process is tightly coupled to use and continues during the use of the system." [53]. Accordingly, meta-design builds on the recognition that real design problems are often wicked problems [54], that is problems that cannot be (entirely) delegated to professionals because

---

[7]The careful reader looking at Fig. 1 will have noticed a sort of leap between these stances, which is denoted as "situated design" [49], something we could not reflect upon for obvious page limit constraints. In very short terms it is when end users do the job of professional designers and design their own artifacts. In the process something is obviously left behind but the attitude will be more bent on the left (of the spectrum depicted in Fig. 1) or on the right, according to how conscious and purposeful end users are in their letting things "out" of the design scope (the more conscious, the more on the left, of course).

only end users as "domain experts" and "owners of the problems" have the necessary knowledge (if not skills) to "incrementally refine" their formulation and contribute local solutions over time. To this aim, the meta-design also encompasses a prescriptive model for the development of "large evolving systems" where periods of activity and unplanned evolutions, carried out mainly by end users, alternate with periods of deliberate restructuring and enhancement, which professional designers govern in more traditional manners.

Within the more general framework of meta-design, Fischer and colleagues also introduced the (indeed less articulated) concept of *underdesign*. As we said above, meta-design regards not only a painstaking design of methods, environments and communication campaigns to involve users in the construction of their tools, but also a contextual (and convergent) de-design of the resulting artifact. Accordingly, underdesign regards the intentional design of systems where some non-critical parts are left unimplemented to stimulate end-user participation and appropriation [11]: more precisely, only the structures and processes of an STS that are indispensable to meet legal norms, security requirements, and basic economic needs are specified so that the resulting system presents a "loose fit" and the necessary "slack" [55] so that unexpected uses of the artifact can be accommodated at use time [11, 53].

3.4 Undesign

At the other extreme of the de-design spectrum that we are outlining in this paper we find a framework presenting some affinities with our intent. In [41] and most recently in [38], Pierce reasons about "the intentional and explicit negation of technology, i.e., the *undesign* of technology". In the undesign theory, Pierce enumerates four kinds of "intentional actions that are each concerned with the intentional negation of technology: [...] inhibiting, displacing, erasing, and foreclosing".

The first three strategies regard an increasing effectiveness in *getting rid of* some technology. Inhibition refers to design "that aims to hinder or prevent the use of technology in particular ways and contexts": this can refer to the design of technologies that hinder *other* technologies from working properly (like Web browsers or social applications in corporate LANs, or mobile phones in restaurants and theaters, or speed bumps on urban streets); or also to a sort of "design for non-use" of technologies [7, 56] that purposely try to convince *their* users "to do without them" either in particular situations or in the indeterminate future (e.g., the meetup application, cigarette packs).

Displacement regards the physical removal of technology from its typical or currently occupied position. Erasure: the "complete elimination of a technology from existence". In these latter cases, Pierce also mentions "replacement and restoration" as a design "that aims to undesign a technology by [either] replacing it with some other technology [or] (re)introducing a displaced or foreclosed technology [respectively]". The first case regards, for instance, "replacing a product with a service, like car-sharing services that replace personally owned vehicles; the second, promoting farmers' market in an endeavor of undesigning industrial processed food". Negative and positive interventions are often coupled in the undesign framework: similarly, foreclosure is mentioned as an undesign activity that entails the (positive) "design of public policies and services [and of] communication campaigns" convincing the target population that, e.g., certain foreclosed technologies are undesirable or detrimental.[8] In analogy with an oft-cited definition of design, undesign regards "the ability to understand that-which-currently-exists, to make it disappear in concrete form as a new, purposeful subtraction from the real world" [38]. Lastly, "foreclosing (a technology)" is a kind of "degenerate case" of undesign (in the light of its positive definition), and for this reason has been subsumed earlier in the opposite extreme of the de-design paralogy: as it is to abstain from designing a technology, which nevertheless has been conceived.

Although both the de-design paralogy and the undesign theory refer to a set of common sources, we conceive the discourse on de-design as encompassing "undesign thinking". Indeed, this latter regards an *intentional* act of design that is explicitly aimed at limiting the technology's scope, scale and reach: as stated clearly in [41] undesign regards the negation of technology, not of design itself.

It builds on the Fry's notion of "elimination design", which is a design approach aimed at identifying and eliminating the unsustainable [57], and on the dyad "creative destruction and disruptive innovation" therein proposed and so undesign remains an intentional intervention *on* the world that is recognized to have both a positive (i.e., constructive) effect and a negative (i.e., destructive) one. The de-design paralogy instead, overlaps with this kind of negative design, and also encompasses more radical stances that deny both "artifact design" (i.e., meta-design, underdesign and partly zensign) *and design itself* as a professional practice: zensign again, the sort of anti-representational development of "immanent design" [28], end-user bricolage [58], situated design [49], "open design" and the "non design" by Baumer and Silberman.[9]

---

[8]To this respect much of the work of a requirement analyst concerns the systematic undesign of the solutions suggested by the client in the first place, and their substitution with more feasible or cost-effective solutions (personal communication with the author).

[9]To this respect, we consider refraining from designing a technology as a form of designerly action only if this results from an activity involving experts denoted as "designers" engaged in and accountable for the "conception and planning of the artificial" [54]. Pierce also makes an insightful point on the impact of design inaction (like in non-design and zensign), sustaining that such a practice must be "continually articulated in some manner [and] materialized, to be acknowledged and recognized" as such, to convince the reader that undesign is necessary also for the most extreme cases of de-design to be impactful in the long run. However, the paradoxes he calls attention to ("How do you literally sell nothing in a commercial context? Or get paid to design nothing? How does an interaction designer "undesign interaction" without actually designing an interactive technology?") are such only within a modernist grand narrative of design. If we let expectations about design finally go [59], or "if design is something else" [8], we will have gone a step further in deconstructing the modernist idea of design and in making an alternative discourse (de-designed, so to say) conceivable and, therefore, debatable.

4 Discussion

In this paper we have outlined some approaches to design that we have put under the rubric of de-design in order to stress their potential to undermine the main assumptions of the modernist idea of design mentioned in Sect. 2 and that we recognize to be still mainstream in professional practice and IS research. At this point, one could come to ask: what can the paralogy of de-design add to the strand of STD? [60] Rather than being taken in just for its provocative and iconoclastic message, reflecting on de-design can contribute to revamp the deeply democratic stances of the ST approach: not only by going beyond the models of participatory design in which users are involved in tasks of (still modernist) design (usually gamified to some extent like in card sorting and comic scenario drawing), and so to say temporarily accommodated in the "ivory tower"; but rather by taking a conscious and sensible "backward step" to leave room for the users' viewpoints and initiatives.

In particular, de-design discourses can contribute to sensitize on the importance of the principles of "minimal critical specification" and "intrinsic incompletion" defined in the STD framework [10, 60]. To this regard, also Trist noted the importance in ST theory of these principles [61], which regard that "only the essentials are decided a priori [and] as much as possible is left open to be decided [by workers] at later stages as operating experience is gained"; in so doing, he added, "the barriers between planners and implementors are reduced [and] design and operations are seen as a continuous process" (p. 41). More recently, also Kallinikos et al. [62] recognize that any technical systems is intrinsically if not necessarily incomplete and perpetually in the making, if it is embedded in the real world [63].

4.1 From Formal IS Development to Effective IS Design

This vision and the de-design discourse point both to a de-emphasis of the importance of formal, accurate and consistent a priori models and descriptions of the IT artifact, not to hinder its "growth" and evolution [64] on the basis of an *informed wariness of the capacity of the expert called designer to envision, specify and create effective solutions for someone else* (the needy). This stance is probably grounded on two main assumptions: first, "the efficacy of autonomous work groups", in its turn grounded on "the cybernetic concept of self-regulation" [61] (p. 34); second, the primacy of *performativity* in IS development.

The first assumption conceives work groups as "nonhierarchical social formations" and "learning systems" that become more and more proficient in "setting their own machines" over time by facing "day-to-day issues" (p. 34). To this respect design is relegated to posing "boundary conditions in the group's environment so that the group itself may be freed to manage its own activities" (p. 34). The latter assumption aims "to challenge the representationalist belief in the power of words to represent preexisting (and prospective) things" [65] and invites to conceive ISs as resulting from the "socio-technical entanglement of IT artifacts, work practices, users, and the developers" involved [66] instead of being highly complicated and resource-consuming machines designed to support a neo-tayloristic program aimed at "providing [timely and] appropriate intelligence for managers at all levels, [helping them] develop [forms of] budgetary control [and enact over detailed] performance indicators and measurements of work performance" [67] on the basis of the "big data" available.

Intended to overcome the limitations and minimize the shortcomings of those closed systems that designers traditionally give to passive end users hoping in behavioral compliance and process "normality", de-design discourses rely on the idea that social creativity and collective intelligence (if not crowd wisdom) can be effectively and efficiently promoted, harvested and leveraged in organizations in face of important socio-technical challenges.

4.2 Social Implications of De-design

These regard both the technical and the social dimension. In the former case the challenge to, on one hand, devise and experiment new and more user-friendly and engaging visual tools that could exhibit a mild learning curve but nevertheless allow for even complex customizations and extensions in both the information structures and the activity flows of the organizational application [68, 69]; and on the other hand, to exploit the full potential of technologies currently available, like the Web 2.0 infrastructure (e.g., github.com, superuser.com, stackoverflow.com, myriads of geek blogs and specialized forums), the visual programming languages and design environments (e.g. Google Blockly, SketchUp), the collective repositories (e.g., Google Warehouse) to enable and empower end users in taking a more proactive attitude towards the improvement and evolution of their tools.

And the social dimension as well, where further research must address, e.g., how to tap in social and human capital in *coopetitive* settings and communities of practice; how to foster the willingness of users to engage in additional learning to become active "developers" (and acquire the related mindset), and engage in really participatory activities of co-development; how to conciliate the progressive end-user empowerment with new figures of professional IT "designers", like those of facilitators, gardeners [64], maieuta-designers [70], and community managers, just to mention a few; and also how to factor in IT consumerization, i.e., the use of privately-owned IT resources for business purposes in addition to their original private ones.

De-design narratives could support approaches to IS development where people are invited not only to open up the "black boxes"[10] with which they work and

---

[10]Future work could be aimed at understanding de-design as an activity of purposeful de-covering of the concealment and black boxing of traditional design: as a sort of de-de-sign, as noted recently by Storni [71], to build more appropriable artifacts.

through which they interact, and in so doing undertake more *tinkering* than conceptual thinking [72, 63]; but also to try and assemble new "glassy boxes" [69] in genuinely bottom-up and incremental manners, in order to create user-generated information systems [73]. To this aim, they could just assemble at interface level "building boxes", i.e., components and simpler services (e.g., mashup) connected to the organizational IS infrastructure as well as to external services in the cloud, which they could either define by themselves [68], or find among those provided by professional meta-designers and made freely available by peer developers, as advocated by the "open design" movement [26].

5 Conclusions

That said, what "de-designing the IT artifact" exactly means is a matter of interpretations and idiosyncratic stances on IS design and development methodologies. Surely the paralogy of de-design is not "yet another approach to IT design", lacking the necessary coherence for such a role. A paralogy, we recall, is just a collection of minority voices, in this case on IT design, that we gathered in this paper for their potential to influence the mainstream discourse, especially in the STS design arena.[11]

However, we claim that efforts in de-designing the IT artifact should be paid to create "some room" between the "IT" and the "artifact" so that the ST artifact "including" both could evolve and "grow" in a less constrained and controlled manner.

While in this contribution we focused on the de-design of IT artifacts in STSs, future work could also be aimed at framing the de-design of the "social" component of a STS (e.g., going beyond job descriptions, organigrams and the related hierarchies, as well as the institutional and "formal" definition of standard operating procedures). This would probably lead to join the performative project of the Critical Management Studies [75] to investigate phenomena like the thriving of "real" bossless organizations (like Valve and GE Aviation in the US, Semco in Brazil, Mondragon Corporation in Spain) and the bottom-up self-organization of communities of peers, like in open source development, open design and citizen science initiatives and projects, in an attempt to deconstruct the "intelligent design" myth in IS design research [76].

This new attitude can improve the resilience of socio-technical systems to the ever-changing context in which people live and work, as well as the overall capability of the "system" to cope with the unexpected. In these systems the ST artifact will be called to support—or just not hinder—the ingenuous efforts of the people, which

---

[11] For this reason we did not adhere to any particular methodology of literature review. Our aim is not to either "fill or address gaps in the literature", but rather to problematize modern(ist) IT design and challenge the assumptions of most of current literature [74] to advocate some STS design tenets. To this aim, recalling the most relevant works from our serendipitous readings in the last 10 years was considered sufficient to draw the spectrum in Fig. 1. In doing so, we are aware that many other voices have been probably left out of the picture, arbitrarily but unintentionally, which will be enriched in future similar works.

are tacit, deeply embodied, and situated in the wrinkles of the territory of practice, which the modelling "rational" mind will never know, both for its efficient snubbing of the irrelevant details, and the atavistic fear of the unintended consequences [12] that hide in these details even too well.

References

1. Riemer, K., Johnston, R. B., Hovorka, D. S., & Indulska, J. (2013) Challenging the philosophical foundations of modeling organizational reality: The case of process modeling. In ICIS 2013 p. 18. Association for Information Systems.
2. Hevner, A. R., March, S. T., Park, J., & Ram, S. (2004). Design science in information systems research. *MIS Quarterly, 28,* 75–105.
3. Fallman, D. (2007). Why research-oriented design isn't design-oriented research: On the tensions between design and research in an implicit design discipline. *Knowledge, Technology & Policy, 20,* 193–200.
4. Johansson-Sköldberg, U., Woodilla, J., & Çetinkaya, M. (2013). Design thinking: past, present and possible futures. *Creativity and Innovation Management, 22,* 121–146.
5. Simon, H. A. (1981). *The sciences of the artificial.* Cambridge, USA: MIT Press.
6. Baskerville, R., Pries-Heje, J., & Venable, J. (2009). Soft design science methodology. In *Proceedings of the 4th International Conference on Design Science Research in Information Systems and Technology* (pp. 9:1–9:11). New York, NY, USA: ACM.
7. Satchell, C., & Dourish, P. (2009). Beyond the user: Use and non-use in HCI. In *Proceedings of the 21st Annual Conference of the Australian Computer-Human Interaction Special Interest Group: Design: Open 24/7* (pp. 9–16). ACM.
8. Aanestad, M. (2012). What if design is something else: The challenges of dealing with interdependencies. In *Nordic Contributions in IS Research* (pp. 95–108). Springer.
9. Cross, N. (2007). From a design science to a design discipline: Understanding designerly ways of knowing and thinking. In *Design research now* (pp. 41–54).
10. Garud, R., Jain, S., & Tuertscher, P. (2009). Incomplete by design and designing for incompleteness. In *Design Requirements Engineering: A 10-Year Perspective* (pp. 137–156). Springer.
11. Dix, A. (2007). Designing for appropriation. In *Proceedings of the 21st British HCI Group Annual Conference on People and Computers: HCI… but not as we know it* (pp. 27–30). UK: British Computer Society, Swinton.
12. Silver, M. S., & Markus, M. L. (2013). Conceptualizing the SocioTechnical (ST) artifact. *Systems, Signs & Actions, 7,* 82–89.
13. Oudshoorn, N., & Pinch, T. (2008). User-Technology Relationships: Some Recent Developments. In O. Amsterdamska (Ed.), *The handbook of science and technology studies* (pp. 543–565). Cambridge, MA, USA: MIT Press.
14. Berman, M. (1983). All that is solid melts into air: The experience of modernity. *Verso.*
15. Kanigel, R. (1997). *The one best way: Frederick winslow taylor and the enigma of efficiency.* New York: Viking.
16. Haigh, T. (2011). Inventing information systems: The systems men and the computer, 1950–1968. *Business History Review, 75,* 15–61.
17. Haigh, T. (2010). *Crisis what crisis? Reconsidering the software crisis of the 1960s and the origins of software engineering.* Milwaukee, USA: University of Wisconsin.
18. Obradovich, J. H., & Woods, D. D. (1996). Users as designers: how people cope with poor HCI design in computer-based medical devices. *Human Factors, 38,* 574–592.
19. Ciborra, C. U., Braa, K., Cordella, A., Dahlbom, B., Failla, A., & Hanseth, O. (2000). *From control to drift.* Oxford University Press.

20. Aanestad, M., Henriksen, D., & Pors, J. (2004). Systems development in the wild: User-led exploration and transformation of organizing visions. In: *Information Systems Research* (pp. 615–630). USA: Springer.
21. Lyotard, J.-F. (1986). *The postmodern condition: a report on knowledge*. Manchester, UK: Manchester University Press.
22. Hirschheim, R., & Newman, M. (1991). Symbolism and information systems development: Myth, metaphor and magic. *Information Systems Research, 2*, 29–62.
23. Spinuzzi, C. (2003). *Tracing genres through organizations: a sociocultural approach to information design*. Cambridge, Mass: MIT Press.
24. Mazé, R., & Redström, J. (2007). Difficult forms: Critical practices of design and research. *IASDR, 2007*, 1–18.
25. Robinson, M., & Bannon, L. (1991). Questioning representations. In *ECSCW'91*. Amsterdam, The Netherlands.
26. Van Abel, B., Evers, L., Troxler, P., & Klaassen, R. (2014). *Open design now: Why design cannot remain exclusive*. BIS Publishers.
27. Berg, M., & Toussaint, P. (2002). The mantra of modeling and the forgotten powers of paper: A sociotechnical view on the development of process-oriented ICT in health care. *Journal of Medical Informatics, 69*, 223–234.
28. Cabitza, F. (2011). "Remain Faithful to the Earth!": Reporting experiences of artifact-centered design in healthcare. *Computer Supported Cooperative Work CSCW, 20*, 231–263.
29. Button, G. (1993). *Technology in working order: Studies of work, interaction, and technology*. New York, NY, USA: Routledge.
30. Poltrock, S., & Handel, M. (2010). Models of collaboration as the foundation for collaboration technologies. *Journal of Management Information Systems, 27*, 97–122.
31. Wagner, I., Schmidt, K., & Jacucci, G. (2008). Herding cats: Or model-based alignment of heterogeneous practices. In *MCIS* (p. 28). AISeL.
32. Cabitza, F., Colombo, G., & Simone, C. (2013). Leveraging underspecification in knowledge artifacts to foster collaborative activities in professional communities. *International Journal of Human-Computer Studies, 71*, 24–45.
33. Nandhakumar, J., & Avison, D. E. (1999). The fiction of methodological development: a field study of information systems development. *Information Technology & People, 12*, 176–191.
34. Robey, D., & Markus, M. L. (1984). Rituals in information system design. *MIS Quarterly, 8*, 5–15.
35. Tatar, D. (2007). The design tensions framework. *Hum-Comput Interact, 22*, 413–451.
36. Tatar, D. (2014). Reflecting our better nature. *Interactions, 21*, 46–49.
37. Lee, J.-S., Branham, S., Tatar, D., & Harrison, S. (2012). Processlessness: Staying open to interactional possibilities. In *DIS'12* (pp. 78–81). ACM.
38. Pierce, J. (2014). Undesigning interaction. *Interactions, 21*, 36–39.
39. Dourish, P. (2004). What we talk about when we talk about context. *Personal and Ubiquitous Computing, 8*, 19–30.
40. Baumer, E. P. S., & Silberman, M. S. (2011). When the implication is not to design (Technology). In: *CHI'11* (pp. 2271–2274). New York, NY, USA: ACM.
41. Pierce, J. (2012). Undesigning technology: Considering the negation of design by Design. In *CHI'12* (pp. 957–966). New York, NY, USA: ACM.
42. Bednar, P. M., & Welch, C. (2012). Critical systemic thinking as a foundation for information systems research practice. *Journal of Information, Communication and Ethics in Society, 10*, 144–155.
43. Dunne, A., Raby, F. (2001). *Design noir: The secret life of electronic objects*. Springer.
44. Hollan, J., Hutchins, E., & Kirsh, D. (2000). Distributed cognition: Toward a new foundation for human-computer interaction research. *ACM Transactions on Computer-Human Interaction, 7*, 174–196.
45. Telier, A. (2011). *Design things*. The MIT Press.
46. Cabitza, F., & Simone, C. (2012). Affording Mechanisms: An integrated view of coordination and knowledge management. *Computer Supported Cooperative Work (CSCW), 21*, 227–260.

47. Carroll, J. M., Kellogg, W. A., & Rosson, M. B. (1991). The Task-artifact cycle. In J. M. Carroll (Ed.), *Designing Interaction: Psychology at the Human-Computer Interface* (pp. 74–102). New York, NY, USA: Cambridge University Press.

48. Orlikowski, W. J. (2006). Material knowing: The scaffolding of human knowledgeability. *European Journal of Information Systems, 15,* 460–466.

49. Buescher, M., Gill, S., Mogensen, P., & Shapiro, D. (2001). Landscapes of practice: Bricolage as a method for situated design. *Computer-supported Cooperative Work (CSCW), 10,* 1–28.

50. Fischer, G., Giaccardi, E., Ye, Y., Sutcliffe, A. G., & Mehandjiev, N. (2004). Meta-design: a manifesto for end-user development. *Communications of the ACM, 47,* 33–37.

51. Fischer, G., & Herrmann, T. (2011). Socio-technical systems: a meta-design perspective. *International Journal of Sociotechnology and Knowledge Development (IJSKD), 3,* 1–33.

52. Fischer, G. (2003). Meta—design: Beyond user-centered and participatory design. *Human-Computer Interaction. Theories Pract. 1,* 88.

53. Henderson, A., Kyng, M.: There's no place like home: Continuing design in use. In *Design at Work: Cooperative Design of Computer Systems* (pp. 219–240). Hillsdale, New Jersey, USA: Lawrence Erlbaum Associates (1991).

54. Buchanan, R. (1992). Wicked problems in design thinking. *Design Issues* 5–21.

55. Cabitza, F., & Simone, C. (2013). "Drops hollowing the Stone". Workarounds as resources for better task-artifact fit. In *ECSCW 2013* (pp. 103–122). Berlin, D: Springer.

56. Sambasivan, N., Ventä, L., Mäntyjärvi, J., Isomursu, M., & Häkkilä, J. (2009). Rhythms of Non-use of device ensembles. In: *CHI '09,* pp. 4531–4536. New York, NY, USA: ACM.

57. Fry, T. (2009). *Design Futuring: Sustainability.* Berg: Ethics New Pract. Oxf.

58. Avgerou, C., Lanzara, G. F., & Willcocks, L. (2009). *Bricolage, care and information: Claudio Ciborra's legacy in information systems research.* NY, USA: Palgrave Macmillan.

59. Kristoffersen, S. (2007). Designing a program. Programming the Design. In *ECIS 2007: Proceedings of the Fifteenth European Conference on Information Systems* (pp. 901–912), Switzerland: St. Gallen.

60. Mumford, E. (2006). The story of socio-technical design: reflections on its successes, failures and potential. *Information Systems Journal, 16,* 317–342.

61. Trist, E. (1981). The evolution of socio-technical systems—A conceptual framework and an action research program. *Occas Pap, 2,* 1–67.

62. Kallinikos, J., Aaltonen, A., & Marton, A. (2013). The ambivalent ontology of digital artifacts. *MIS Quarterly, 37*(2), 357–370.

63. Cabitza, F., & Simone, C. (2014). Building socially embedded technologies: Implications on design. In: D. Randall, K. Schmidt, & V. Wulf (Eds.), *Designing Socially Embedded Technologies in the Real-World.* Springer Berlin, D. https://doi.org/10.1007/978-1-4471-6720-4.

64. Mørch, A. I. (2003). Evolutionary growth and control in user tailorable systems. In: Adaptive evolutionary information Systems (pp. 30–58.). Hershey PA: Idea Group Publishing.

65. Barad, K. (2003). Posthumanist Performativity: Toward an Understanding of How Matter Comes to Matter. *Signs: Journal of Women in Culture and Society, 28,* 801–831.

66. Boell, S., & Cecez-Kecmanov, D. (2012) Conceptualizing information systems: from "input-processing-output" devices to sociomaterial apparatuses. In *ECIS 2012 Proceedings.*

67. Walsh, K., & Kieron, W. (1995). Public services and market mechanisms: competition, contracting and the new public management. *Macmillan Basingstoke.*

68. Lieberman, H., Paternò, F., & Wulf, V. (2006). *End User Development.* Netherlands: Springer.

69. Cabitza, F., & Simone, C. (2014). "Through the glassy box": Supporting appropriation in user communities. In *COOP 2014* (pp. 173–188). Springer.

70. Cabitza, F., Fogli, D., & Piccinno, A. (2014). "Each to His Own": distinguishing tasks, roles and artifacts in EUD practices. In L. Caporarello, B. Di Martino, & M. Martinez (Eds.), *Smart organizations and smart artifacts—fostering interaction between people, technologies and processes* (pp. 193–206). Berlin Heidelberg: Springer.

71. Storni, C. (2014). The problem of de-sign as conjuring: Empowerment-in-use and the Politics of Seams. In: *Proceedings of the 13th Participatory Design Conference: Research Papers* (vol. 1, pp. 161–170). New York, NY, USA: ACM.

72. Ciborra, C. U. (1992). From thinking to tinkering: the grassroots of strategic information systems. *The Information Society, 8,* 297–309.
73. DesAutels, P. (2011). UGIS: Understanding the nature of user-generated information systems. *Business Horizons, 54,* 185–192.
74. Alvesson, M., & Sandberg, J. (2011). Generating research questions through problematization. *Academy of Management Review, 36,* 247–271.
75. Spicer, A., Alvesson, M., & Karreman, D. (2009). Critical performativity: The unfinished business of critical management studies. *Human Relations, 62,* 537–560.
76. Carlsson, S. A., Henningsson, S., Hrastinski, S., & Keller, C. (2011). Socio-technical IS design science research: developing design theory for IS integration management. *Information Systems and e-Business Management, 9,* 109–131.

Digital Infrastructures for Patient Centered Care: Examining Two Strategies for Recombinability

Miria Grisot, Tomas Lindroth and Anna Sigridur Islind

Abstract This paper examines recombinability as a quality of digital infrastructures. The recombination of heterogeneous digital capabilities enables and increases the fit between the infrastructure and the practices it supports. However, there is yet limited understanding of how to design for recombinability in digital infrastructures. This issue is critical in the healthcare setting where information and data needs of patients and health personnel vary in scope and time. This study reports from a comparative case study on the design and use of two patient-centered digital infrastructures. We identify two design strategies for recombinability and analyze their rationales and challenges.

Keywords Digital infrastructure · Recombinability · Flexibility · Patient centeredness · Patient-generated health data

1 Introduction

Society and people are critically dependent, in increasing degree, upon digital infrastructures. Digital infrastructures enable filtering, sorting, and classifying vital information, and support decision making. The IS field has examined digital infrastructure with various focuses such as the emergence of digital infrastructures [1], their architecture and structure [2], evolution [3], economics [4], and service innovation

M. Grisot (✉)
Kristiania University College, Oslo, Norway
e-mail: miria.grisot@kristiania.no; miriag@ifi.uio.no

University of Oslo, Oslo, Norway

T. Lindroth
University of Gothenburg, Gothenburg, Sweden
e-mail: tomas.lindroth@gu.se

A. S. Islind
Reykjavík University, Reykjavík, Iceland
e-mail: annasi@ru.is

© Springer Nature Switzerland AG 2020
A. Lazazzara et al. (eds.), *Exploring Digital Ecosystems*,
Lecture Notes in Information Systems and Organisation 33,
https://doi.org/10.1007/978-3-030-23665-6_21

capabilities [5]. In this paper we focus on the flexibility of digital infrastructures, by which we mean their modularized capability and adaptability, which enables further changes and flexibility in the pattern of use [6]. More specifically, we examine *recombinability* as the quality of digital infrastructures which enables the recombination of heterogeneous modules to increase the fit between the infrastructure and the practice it supports. Recombinability is a core quality of digital infrastructures as it supports synergetic effects by allowing the combination of components to achieve specific infrastructural configuration [7]. In this paper, we are interested in understanding *how to design for recombinability in digital infrastructures.*

To address the research question, we have conducted two case studies of infrastructure development in the healthcare context. Healthcare is currently undergoing a fundamental digital transformation [8, 9]. Specifically, infrastructures in healthcare are increasingly designed according to a patient-centered logic [10, 11]. Patient-centeredness indicate a transformation both in the quality of the health provider-patient interaction and the entire organization of work and relationships related to the patient trajectory [11]. In this view, the patient is no longer just the passive recipient of diagnoses and treatment, but an active participant [12]. Digital infrastructures are seen as a central tool to achieve patient-centeredness, as they can provide patients with easy direct access to health information, and enable them to be active data providers. Recent advancements in personal computing technology have led to the generation of data by patients with potential health applications [13]. The use of patient-generated health data (PGHD) is seen as having the potential to drastically change the ways information is generated, collected and analyzed in healthcare practices, and used in clinical decision making [14, 15]. For instance, studies show that such solutions have can improve follow-ups and self-management by supporting a continuous patient-health provider interaction (rather than the traditional episodic logic of care delivery). In order to support patient-centeredness, digital infrastructures need to be designed to reach out to patients, outside of the traditional boundaries of healthcare organizations, such as hospitals.

However, to design digital infrastructures for patient-centeredness is challenging. Healthcare practices are complex and vary. The data needs of both patients and health professionals can be very different according to diseases, urgency, and complexity, and they change as patients' condition progress in time. Therefore, it is important that digital infrastructures are able to adapt and accommodate heterogeneous and changing data needs. In this effort, the recombinability of digital technologies plays a critical role.

In this paper, we identify two different design strategies for recombinability and analyze their rationales and challenges. The first strategy addresses the need for *generic* recombinability, the second one addresses the need for *tailored* recombinability. We examine these two approaches in two cases of digital infrastructures for remote patient care. In the first case, a digital infrastructure is designed for patients in cancer rehabilitation at a specialized cancer clinic in Sweden. In the second case, a digital infrastructure is designed for patients in chronic care management in municipal care in Norway. In both cases, the digital infrastructures are designed specifically to support the collection and analysis of PGHD which are then used in clinical decision making. Overall, the use of patient-centered digital infrastructures is expected to provide societal benefits by enabling patients to live longer in their homes, become active and empowered self-managers of their own conditions, and improve their health and quality of life. From the clinicians' perspective, the use of PGHD should support remote personalized and preventive care.

We discuss our findings in relation to the two bodies of literature. First, we contribute to understanding recombinability as a specific quality of digital infrastructures; second, we contribute to understanding the design of digital infrastructures for PGHD in healthcare. There are still many uncertainties and challenges related to the design, implementation, adoption, and use of telecare technologies in remote care [16, 17], and our intention is to contribute to an improved understanding of these novel services.

2 Theoretical Background

In this paper, we build on research on Information Infrastructure and Digital Infrastructures. Information Infrastructure research has specifically targeted the study of shared, evolving, heterogeneous, technological capabilities, and the interconnected institutional arrangements and practices [6, 18]. This stream of research investigates evolution trajectories, e.g., how the mobilization and coordination of various stakeholders in collective action of building and operating platforms are influenced by architectural form [e.g. 1, 2]. For instance, centralized, decentralized or federated architectures have different implications for the various stakeholders' autonomy in decision making regarding their applications [19]. The more recent research on digital infrastructures has further explored the role of architectures, most specifically in relation to digital platforms. One key finding of this research stream is that a modular architecture supports digital infrastructures' flexibility and adaptability. Modularity is an attribute of a complex system and a way to manage complexity based on the principle of decomposability and of loose coupling [7]. According to decomposability, complex systems perform better if they have hierarchical and 'near decomposable' structures [20]. Modularity allows for minimizing interdependence between modules and maximizing interdependence within them. Thus, modules can be mixed and matched in order to obtain new configurations without loss of the system's functionality or performance [21]. In digital infrastructure design, such architectural design translates into a quality of *recombinability* of heterogeneous modules which enables and increases the fit between the infrastructure and the supported practice. In this paper, we empirically examine how to design for recombinability.

3 Methodology

To investigate recombinability in digital infrastructures we conducted a comparative qualitative case study [22] of two digital infrastructures in the context of healthcare. We have selected two cases where two different approaches were implemented with the same aim: the use of PGHD for clinical decision making. These two cases were selected because they had different approaches to the design of the digital infrastructure and the logic of recombinability.

In the first case, the research started in 2015 (and it is still ongoing) as a project to improve the information and communication practices of nurses in their interaction with patients in cancer rehabilitation. To support patients, various digital technologies were implemented in the course of the project: an app for PGHD with a web interface for data visualization for nurses, a webpage with specialized information on cancer rehabilitation (e.g. radiation-induced diseases, treatment options), a Facebook page to rich out to patients not enrolled at the clinic. The focus of the case study has been on the design decisions in setting up the digital infrastructure, on the rationales to design each technological component in addition to a detailed analysis of the work practices and information needs of the nurses at the clinic before and after the implementation of the digital solutions, and of the practices of use of patients.

In the second case, the research was conducted from September 2016 to May 2018 and designed as an interpretive case study. The case study focused on how nurses interacted with remote patients for improving chronic care management. The remote care center where the nurses work is equipped with a decision support system, which is linked to patients' tablet and a set of personal digital devices (see case description for the details). We have focused on how their interaction took place, and which information they collected and analyzed in order to provide care. Specifically, we have considered how the design of the infrastructure accommodated the different needs of patients.

In both cases, data were collected with ethnographic observations of the nurses' work practices, interviews, and artifact analysis [23, 24]. In case 1 patients were also interviewed about their experience with the use of the app for data reporting. During observations, detailed notes were taken about how nurses use digital technologies to interact with patients, navigate the system and assess patients' conditions and take follow up actions. In both cases, we interviewed the nurses, the project managers, the IT developers, and the medical doctor involved in the projects.

The main data in case 1 come from 20 nonparticipant observation days at the clinic, four semi-structured interviews with the clinic's nurses, and seven individual interviews with patients. In addition, developers have been interviewed throughout the development process. In case 2 a total of 23 interviews and 27 h of observation were conducted. Interviews subjects included nurses, doctors, the project management team, and developers. All interviews were recorded and then fully transcribed. We also analyzed the digital technologies in use, their structure and data visualizations, as well as the paper-based artifact used by the nurses (e.g., checklists, guidelines).

4   Case Study Description

The first case is on a digital infrastructure in cancer rehabilitation (see [25, 26] for further details). The clinic receives patients who have been treated for cancer in the pelvic cavity and who suffers from chronic survivorship diseases, that is, diseases that are caused by the cancer treatment. The clinic treats around 200 patients per year, and the average patient has contact with the clinic from six months up to two years. The chronic survivorship diseases relate to intestinal health, fecal leakage, urinary incontinence, and impaired sexual function. There is a range of solutions for their symptoms, including diapers (for leakage), Imodium (for urgency and diarrhea), Inolaxol (for constipation, urgency and easier passing of stools), antibiotics (for bacterial overgrowth from the colon to the small bowel), and Dimor and muscular exercises (for gas and urgency).

When patients are enrolled to the clinic, information about them is gathered by using a patient survey (Clinical Trial Form) and information from their electronic patient record (EPR). The survey consists of 182 questions asking about demographic data, and a range of known side effects of cancer treatment (e.g. fecal and urinary leakage). The survey is extensive and provides nurses with rich data about the patients' problems during the last six months (see further e.g. [27] for publications based on the survey). The information in the EPR is used as a basis to assess the patients' condition and their specific problems. However, this information is not enough to provide efficient and good care. The clinic personnel faced a number of challenges that led to the design and implementation of a digital infrastructure in addition to the traditional hospital infrastructure (see Fig. 1: the hospital infrastructure is at the top of the figure). First, they needed more accurate patient data about the everyday experiences of living with the consequences of cancer treatments. Second, they wished to serve a larger population of patients and reach out to those patients who were not enrolled at the clinic. Cancer rehabilitation is a very specialized medical field, and this is one of the few clinics in Sweden offering specialized care and supports for patients. Third, the nurses working at the clinic felt that they were asked by patients to repeat the same information over and over again and thus wanted to make information easily available for patients in need.

To address these information and data needs, the project expanded the existing hospital information infrastructure with a loosely coupled set of digital technologies.

These included the following digital solutions: an information portal, a Facebook page, and an app. The *information portal* was set up as a webpage with information about diagnoses, symptoms, problems, and advice on how to address them. The portal was built on the Open Source, WordPress, Content Management System (CMS). This portal was linked to a *Facebook page*. The project participants argued that the Like and Share button on Facebook were critical features to reach out to new patients. However, it was decided not to use Facebook to generate content, but only for its capability to get in contact with patients. Nurses and the project's cancer communication expert posted links back to the portal. Between February 2016 and October 2017, this generated 2700 returning visitors out of 9000 total visits. Finally, an *app* for patients was designed. The purpose of the app was to obtain reports on symptoms and events as they were experienced by patients, and not as they were remembered. With the app, patients can report the number of toilet visits, level of pain, and use a standard scale which is a diagnostic medical tool (the Bristol scale) to classify the form of feces. The patient is expected to use the app and log measurements. The information is then accessible to the nurse as they are reported. In this way, nurses who no longer have to reconstruct the patient's experiences and symptoms by asking questions during the consultation, but have direct access to the reported patient data. This reduces the risk of memory bias and the uncertainty surrounding the quality of the data. The app is available in both the App Store and Google Play.

The second case is set in a private company offering remote care as a service to a small municipality. The company (which also develops the remote care system) run from October 2016 to April 2018 a remote care center, staffed with three nurses. Patients are assigned to the center by a nurse coordinator from the municipal care services. When patients are enrolled in the service, they receive a home visit from one of the nurses who deliver a set of personal digital devices (e.g. digital thermometer, scale, pulsometer) and explains how they should be used. After this visit, patients are remotely guided into using the devices, and they are expected to take measurements (e.g. temperature) at specific times (for instance every morning and every evening), attend to the directions given by the nurses and answer a set of personalized questions in the App.

The digital infrastructure is composed of personal digital devices, personal tablets, a cloud-based Remote Care System (RCS), the Electronic Patient Record (EPR), and their connections. Patients live at home and are equipped with a set of standard digital measuring devices that they use daily, and a tablet with the RCS app on which they read their data, access their record and communicate with the nurse via messages and questionnaires. The nurses are sitting in the remote care center and use the RCS.

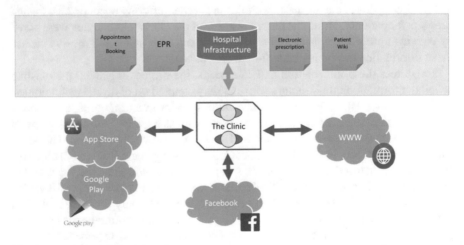

Fig. 1 The digital infrastructure in case 1

Figure 2 illustrates how the elements of the infrastructure are connected. The nurse in the care center uses the RCS. In this system, they receive the data from the measuring devices of the patients, they communicate with the patient through messages and questionnaires and document their interaction with the patient in the patient record of the RCS. The communication with the municipal care nurses is mainly done via phone calls, and the municipal care nurse also has access to the RMS through a web interface. The nurses at the care center are not employed by the municipal health services and do not have to document their work in the EPR of the municipality, to which they do not have access.

Patients receive a set of devices according to their diagnosis, for instance, a patient with diabetes would use a device for measuring blood glucose levels, and a digital scale for measuring body weight. Patients with COPD are equipped with a spirometer which measures the volume of air inspired and expired by the lungs (FEV 1 and PEF), a pulsometer which measures the pulse (frequency of heart beats per minute) and the oxygen saturation, a thermometer which measures body temperature, and a scale which measures body weight. The scale is given only to those patients for whom weight is a risk factor. The nurses in the center coordinate with the municipal services but do not have access to their electronic patient record system used in municipal health, including GPs.

The system supports nurses with various visualizations of the data from the digital devices of patients. Figure 3 provides an example of how data from blood pressure monitor are displayed, both as a graph and as a list. It is possible to zoom in and out of the graph, select and enlarge specific time periods, and calculate the average value per time period. Every time a patient takes a measurement, the system receives a message, which is displayed on a list and color coded. For each patient, a specific threshold per type of measurement can be set, thus the message could be green, yellow or red (if outside the acceptable range). Other functionality includes messages and questionnaire. The messages are text-based and unstructured. Both

Fig. 2 The digital
infrastructure in case 2

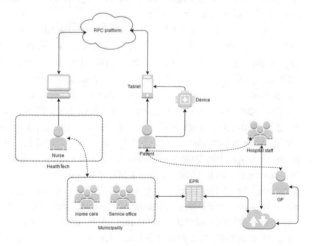

Fig. 3 The nurse's view on the patient data. The upper part shows the graph of the blood pressure measurements, the lower parts show the same measurements as a list

patients and nurses can send messages anytime. Patients are also asked a set of questions which should be answered daily. The questions are personalized and tailored to the patient-specific condition. For instance, for COPD patients the questionnaire covers a standard set of themes about COPD symptoms (e.g. cough, shortness of breath, fever, excess mucus) and activities that are important to follow (e.g. physical exercise, regular eating, and sleeping).

5 Analysis

Our analysis of the two cases focuses on the strategy for recombinability of digital technologies. In the following subsection, we identify and describe the two strategies, their rationales, and their challenges.

Strategy 1. In case 1, the digital infrastructure was designed to address an heterogeneous set of information and data needs. The nurses needed a more efficient way than making phone calls to communicate with patients, and needed to gather data of quality and reach out to new patients. To address these needs, the project team designed a digital infrastructure by combining different technologies which addressed these different needs. The app for PGHD was designed for patients to enable them to register and report data closer in time to their experience, for instance by logging toilet visits' frequency and stool quality. The website was designed to provide a specific information source for patients, thus avoiding nurses' repetitive information work. Finally, the Facebook page was created to reach out to patients not enrolled at the clinic. By utilizing the app stores to distribute the app through already well-established channels, by publishing specific health information online and using Facebook to spread the word about the clinic, three generic infrastructures/platforms were recombined. These infrastructural components are outside of the traditional boundaries of healthcare organizations but part of the everyday life of patients (for instance Facebook). The different types of selected technologies have generic functionality, directed at generic user groups, and could be combined.

The rationale with this strategy was based on two main arguments. First, the information needs of nurses and patients were heterogeneous. Nurses had a dual agenda, both to render more efficient their current communication and information practices, but also to scale up their service to a larger population of patients. Patients also had an additional need, that of providing accurate information nurses actually needed. The project team decided to design various loose coupled generic technology. Second, the project decided to use technologies patients would be familiar with. Thus, they selected digital components such as a website, a Facebook page, and an app, which patients could easily make sense of and use.

The challenge encountered in adopting this strategy (recombining generic digital technologies) was mainly related to the existing hospital infrastructure. While the project tried to gain support from the hospital IT department, they realized that the existing infrastructure was not made for gathering PGHD, reaching out to new patient groups or for loose couplings with external platforms. Thus, as depicted in Fig. 1, the novel infrastructure could not be integrated with the existing hospital infrastructure.

Strategy 2. In case 2, the digital infrastructure was built around a core system, the RCS. The system is designed to support two main activities: patient-nurses communication and the gathering of health data from the devices. The system is built around a set of flexible functions supporting patient-nurse communication. This core is generic and possible to recombine with a range of different devices in order to support different patient needs. Depending on where a certain patient is in her treatment trajectory or depending on the type of disease, the generic core is tailorable to enable the patient to collect data that supports her self-management as well as the nurses' clinical decision making. This combinatory strategy utilizes the generative flexibility between the core and different sets of devices enabling tailorability to many different diseases.

The rationale with this strategy was based on two main arguments. First, the nurses needed a system that allowed for two-way communication with patients. Thus, the RCS system is different from the app in case 1 since it does not only support the gathering of PGHD, but also a message functionality and a question-based functionality. These support nurses-patients communication in an open and flexible way. Open, as it is mainly text-based and both nurses and patients can tailor the messages for different purposes (e.g. notification, questions, reminders). Flexible, as the frequency of use is not pre-determined. Both patients and nurses can use the messages as they needed. Second, the patients enrolled in the remote monitoring service were suffering from different diseases (e.g. diabetes, heart failures, COPD). Thus, a variety of digital devices needed to be linked to the system for data generation. In addition, as the market for digital health devices is a fast-growing market, the designer wanted to maintain a flexibility that allowed them to 'pick and choose' more devices as they proved to be useful.

The main challenge faced in this second strategy related to the RCS becoming an additional system to be used. Thus, while in case 1 the app and the website serve a more specific purpose and a specific work practice (of the nurses in the specialized clinic), in case 2 the nurses had to learn to use a new system and develop new information practices accordingly.

6 Discussion

In this paper, we examine recombinability as a core quality of digital infrastructures. Recombinability supports synergetic effects by allowing the combination of components to achieve specific infrastructural configuration [7]. We have addressed the research question on how to design for recombinability in digital infrastructures. Our findings suggest that it is useful to distinguish between different design strategies for recombinability—generic and tailorable—and two phases where recombinability matters—during design and during use. We discuss these two distinctions in the following subsections.

6.1 Generic and Tailorable Recombinability

The recombinability of digital technologies is a core issue in the design of digital infrastructures as it allows for flexibility. In this study, we focus on recombinability as the quality of digital infrastructures which allows for the recombination of heterogeneous modules to enable and increase the fit between the infrastructure and the practice it is designed to support. Our findings show that recombinability can be aimed for with different strategies. This issue is critical in the healthcare setting where information and data needs of patients and health personnel are variable.

In case 1, the strategy for recombinability worked by building on generic, non-endemic digital technologies to expand the infrastructural reach with the aim to include new user groups and new situations of use beyond the traditional healthcare organizational context. These generic infrastructural components, such as Facebook, are non-endemic, as they emerge outside of the healthcare context. The strategy relies on *generic recombinability*. By recombining web, social media technologies and app delivery systems during the design phase, the case utilized a generic recombinatorial strategy.

In case 2, the strategy for recombinability worked by building a core system, and allowing for flexibility by providing a set of interchangeable standard devices such as the spirometer or a scale. These set of devices can then be combined in different ways and thus tailored according to the patients' particular disease pattern resulting in a *tailorable recombinability strategy*. This strategy requires recombinability in the design phase to allow for adding and removing standard devices to tailor for different diseases.

6.2 Design and Use Recombinability

Recombinability is not only a quality that is relevant during the design phase but also something enacted during use [28]. Since each patient situation is unique, in case 1 the patient has to adapt the infrastructure based on their own information and communication needs and usages. Thus, the generic recombinability strategy requires both recombinability during the design phase where the generic non-endemic infrastructural components are selected, and during the use phase where the patient makes use of the plasticity of the infrastructure by cherry-picking components based on her own needs.

In the second case, there was a design decision to build a service that would include a range of components, thus *design recombinability*. However, there was also a strategic design decision to allow for the recombination of a set of standard components (spirometer, thermometer etc.) and by doing so, enabling *use recombinability*. The use recombinability is the recombination of components which is enacted in the daily practice and not during the design phase.

7 Conclusion

In conclusion, this study aims to develop a better understanding of how recombinability can be supported, specifically in the context of digital infrastructures, to achieve patient-centeredness. As we have shown, infrastructure in healthcare is increasingly designed according to a patient-centered logic [10, 11]. From this perspective, one size does not fit all, but care needs to be tailored to each patient's needs, and it needs to allow for the patient to be an active participant in her own care [12]. Future work could take an actor-centric perspective and analyze who (and how) actually performs recombinability from a practice perspective, including designers, healthcare personnel, and patients.

References

1. Aanestad, M., & Jensen, T. B. (2011). Building nation-wide information infrastructures in healthcare through modular implementation strategies. *The Journal of Strategic Information Systems, 20*(2), 161–176.
2. Grisot, M., Hanseth, O., & Thorseng, A. A. (2014). Innovation of, in, on infrastructures: Articulating the role of architecture in information infrastructure evolution. *Journal of the Association for Information System, 15*(4), 197.
3. Henfridsson, O., & Bygstad, B. (2013). The generative mechanisms of digital infrastructure evolution. *Management Information Systems Quarterly, 37*(3), 907–931.
4. Ghazawneh, A., & Henfridsson, O. (2013). Balancing platform control and external contribution in third-party development: the boundary resources model. *Information Systems Frontiers, 23*(2), 173–192.

5. Barrett, M., Davidson, E., Prabhu, J., & Vargo, S. L. (2015). Service innovation in the digital age: Key contributions and future directions. *Management Information Systems Quarterly, 39*(1), 135–154.
6. Hanseth, O., Monteiro, E., & Hatling, M. (1996). Developing information infrastructure: The tension between standardization and flexibility. *Science, Technology, and Human Values, 21*(4), 407–426.
7. Garud, R., Kumaraswamy, A., & Langlois, R. (Eds.) (2009). *Managing in the modular age: Architectures, networks, and organizations.* Wiley.
8. Agarwal, R., Gao, G., DesRoches, C., & Jha, A. K. (2010). Research commentary—The digital transformation of healthcare: Current status and the road ahead. *Information Systems Research, 21*(4), 796–809.
9. Lupton, D. (2017). Digital health: Critical and cross-disciplinary perspectives. Routledge.
10. Klecun, E. (2011). Weaving discourses and changing organizations: The role of ICT in the transformation of healthcare towards patient-centered model.
11. Vikkelsø, S. (2010). Mobilizing information infrastructure, shaping patient-centred care. *International Journal of Public Sector Management, 23*(4), 340–352.
12. Lupton, D. (1997). Consumerism, reflexivity and the medical encounter. *Social Science and Medicine, 45*(3), 373–381.
13. Wood, W. A., Bennett, A. V., & Basch, E. (2015). Emerging uses of patient generated health data in clinical research. *Molecular Oncology, 9*(5), 1018–1024.
14. Swan, M. (2009). Emerging patient-driven health care models: An examination of health social networks, consumer personalized medicine and quantified self-tracking. *International Journal of Environmental Research and Public Health, 6*(2), 492–525.
15. Reading, M. J. (2018). *Optimizing the collection and use of patient-generated health data* (Doctoral dissertation, Columbia University).
16. May, C. R., Finch, T. L., Cornford, J., Exley, C., Gately, C., Kirk, S., et al. (2011). Integrating telecare for chronic disease management in the community: What needs to be done? *BMC Health Services Research, 11*(1), 131.
17. Pols, J., & Willems, D. (2011). Innovation and evaluation: Taming and unleashing telecare technology. *Sociology of Health and Illness, 33*(3), 484–498.
18. Hanseth, O., & Lyytinen, K. (2010). Design theory for dynamic complexity in information infrastructures: The case of building internet. *Journal of Information Technology, 25*(1), 1–19.
19. Aanestad, M., Grisot, M., Hanseth, O., & Vassilakopoulou, P. (Eds.) (2017). *Information infrastructures within european health care: Working with the installed base.* Springer.
20. Simon, H. A. (1965). The architecture of complexity. *Gen Sys, 10,* 63–76.
21. Baldwin, C. Y., & Clark, K. B. (2003). Managing in an age of modularity. *Managing in the modular age: Architectures, networks, and organizations, 149,* 84–93.
22. Stake, R. E. (1995). *The art of case study research.* Sage.
23. Silverman, D. (Ed.) (2016). *Qualitative research.* Sage.
24. Wolcott, H. F. (2005). *The art of fieldwork.* Rowman Altamira.
25. Lindroth, T., Islind, A. S., Steineck, G., & Lundin, J. (2018). From narratives to numbers: Data work and patient-generated health data in consultations. *St Health Technology Information, 247,* 491–495.
26. Islind, A. S., Lundh Snis, U., Lindroth, T., & Assmo, P. (2017). Taking care seriously: transforming practices by design. In *10th ICRWL 6–8 December 2017.* Grahamstown, South Africa: Rhodes University.
27. Dunberger, G., & Bergmark, K. (2012). Nurse-led care for the management of side effects of pelvic radiotherapy: What does it achieve? *Current Opinion in Supportive and Palliative Care, 6*(1), 60–68.
28. Henfridsson, O., Nandhakumar, J., Scarbrough, H., & Panourgias, N. (2018). Recombination in the open-ended value landscape of digital innovation. *Information and Organization, 28*(2), 89–100.

Time Accounting System: Measuring Usability for Validating the Socio-Technical Fit of E-service Exchange Solutions in Local Communities

Tunazzina Sultana

Abstract This paper reports the final validation step of the prototype of a Time Accounting System (TAS), which has been designed and developed to investigate the suitability and acceptability of a technology based service exchanges. TAS is able to facilitate service exchanges using local currency (i.e., time) in a developing country, namely in Bangladesh. The paper describes the results of usability tests, at the level of interface and user interaction. Heuristic evaluation was the method adopted for the usability testing. The results suggest addressing the following usability problems that occur in managing services: error prevention, aesthetic and minimalist design, user control and freedom.

Keywords Time accounting system · Usability testing · Heuristic evaluation method

1 Introduction

Uses of Information Communication Technology (ICT) around the globe differ significantly based on their impacts and benefits. The use of ICT in the developed world grows rapidly in the last five decades and its impacts and benefits are observed in administration, governance, education, business competitiveness and global operations [10]. Despite the fact that some developing countries have used ICT to enjoy the same benefits like developed world [3], a large number of developing countries failed in availing themselves of the benefits of ICT in many cases. The hope is that, an exceptional diffusion of network technologies into developing countries has been witnessed from the last decade [2]. This increasing diffusion of ICTs allows considering whether introduction of new technologies can have a positive impact on the socioeconomic development of these countries. With this consideration, we conducted a research to investigate whether a technology based service exchange

T. Sultana (✉)
Department of Marketing, University of Chittagong, Chattogram, Bangladesh
e-mail: t.sultana@campus.unimib.it; tunazzina@cu.ac.bd

© Springer Nature Switzerland AG 2020
A. Lazazzara et al. (eds.), *Exploring Digital Ecosystems*,
Lecture Notes in Information Systems and Organisation 33,
https://doi.org/10.1007/978-3-030-23665-6_22

system, known as Time Accounting System (TAS), would be useful and appropriate for Bangladesh and how this could be introduced in this country [29].

This paper reports the final validation step of the prototype of a TAS. The prototype has been designed and developed to investigate the above mentioned objectives i.e. suitability and acceptability of a technology able to facilitate service exchanges using local currency (i.e., time) in a developing country, namely in Bangladesh.

In what follows, we first give some brief introduction on the social context of Bangladesh and introduce the main motivations and background of this research considering the role of ICT and its impact and benefits particularly for TAS. We then describe the methodology adopted for the usability testing of the prototype of TAS and discuss the main findings from this usability testing. Finally, a short conclusion summarizes the contribution and the future direction of our research.

2 Social Context of Bangladesh

Bangladesh is one of the world's most densely populated countries with around 160 million people. According to the report of World Bank, 23% of this population lives below the national poverty line of US$2 per day. However, Bangladesh has undergone rapid socioeconomic and demographic changes. Its economic growth (an average of 5.5% a year during the past decade), coupled with investments in education, health, food security and disaster mitigation, has led to a rapid reduction in poverty. In the downside, about 40% of the population of this country is actually under-employed. Many persons counted as employed work only a few hours a week and at low wages which reduces the unemployment rate to 4.9%.[1] With regard to the labor force, 45% are engaged in agriculture, 30% are employed in industry and the rest in the service sector. The 78% of the total labor forces are males and only 22% are females, though women constitute about 50% of the total population. At present, around 48% of the total population consists of very young people who are below 25 years of age and 6% consists of the people more than 65 years.[2] Despite the fact that young people constitute a very large portion of the total population, population ageing is considered as one of the emerging problems in Bangladesh as this process of ageing is expected to accelerate in the near future and the country has a shorter time to adapt to the changes associated with population ageing [30]. Hence, it can be inferred that in near future Bangladesh is going to face the challenges that are associated with ageing population in parallel with its existing unemployment problem. Therefore, this problem is considered as one of the main barriers in its development.

---

[1] https://www.cia.gov/library/publications/the-world-factbook/geos/bg.html.
[2] https://www.cia.gov/library/publications/the-world-factbook/geos/bg.html.

3 Background and Motivation

A TAS is defined as "community based volunteer schemas whereby participants give and receive services in exchange of time credits" [22] and the main claimed aims are to foster "personal development, confidence-building, forging social networks and gaining skills for aiding job-readiness", as well as "building community capacity and self-help, as well as social inclusion" (ibid.). According to Marks, a TAS is based on the notion of co-production, as means to "value the work of everyone and to let people help others as well as themselves, in order to ameliorate the condition of each participant". Hence, a TAS focuses on the human aspect and the people orientation from the end-user perspective which is a contemporary sociotechnical agenda. Moreover, a TAS is a unique transaction based system for mutual aid and assistance that fosters economic opportunities, social inclusion, and community self-help and enhances civic engagement among often marginalized community members [15]. In many developed countries, TAS is considered as an alternative or complementary systems to the leading monetary-based system to overcome social exclusion among the elderly and low income groups [4, 15, 24, 23] which also connect underemployed people within the network of employed people [5, 9, 8, 12]. Considering the social context of Bangladesh and the benefits of TAS for the elderly people and unemployed people, we are motivated to investigate whether TAS could be a useful and suitable tool for the developing country in general, and for Bangladesh in particular. Our previous work have also showed the potentiality of a TAS as a supporting tool for different segments of people in the research area to address different problems like ageing, and unemployment [6, 27]. Moreover, the prototype of a TAS which was designed and developed taking into account the requirements that have been elicited through surveys and group discussions, and by involving potential users is also found a high level of acceptance in terms of simplicity and usefulness from the users [28].

The prototype of a TAS was designed for the Bangladeshi people for accomplishing a set of tasks, with the goal of creating a consistent and usable product for facilitating an online arrangement for service exchanges within the community. Hence, the prototype was subject to a usability study for evaluating user's experience (performance and satisfaction) when interacting with it. The usability study would be helpful in this case since it would focus on actual behavioral patterns and design solutions as opposed to solely relying on the assumptions and prescribed solutions by the participants at requirement elicitation phase. Hence, at this stage of our research, we are motivated to investigate the usability of the prototype to know how the users feel when they use the prototype of a TAS and to find where they encounter problems and experience confusion. For this purpose, we conducted the heuristic evaluation and usability testing among selected Bangladeshi people for two reasons: on one hand, three of them were usability experts due to their profession as software engineers and all of them are the potential user of a TAS; on the other hand, they also participated in the previous phases (requirement elicitation and design confirmation) of the design of the prototype. As a result, they were able to identify any heuristic violation (design problems) and to uncover usability problems, if any. As usability studies are fairly easy and inexpensive to conduct and one of the most commonly used usability inspection methods [11], it is probably a step worth taking during the design process of the TAS even if it results in only minor changes to the design.

4 Methodology

Different types of methods are used to evaluate the usability of an interface of a system or prototype. Usability evaluation or inspection is usually referred to as a method in which evaluators evaluate usability considering related aspects of an application and judge its usability based on their knowledge and expertise. Among many, the Heuristic Evaluation is considered as one of the most commonly used usability inspection methods [17–20] which is used for user evaluation and usability testing in many cases [1, 7, 13, 14, 31]. According to this method, a small set of experts inspect the system and evaluate its interface against the set principles for the usability. In this case, experts could be usability specialists, expert of the specific domain of the application which is going to be evaluated or expert of both usability and domain experience. This method is useful as a fast and easy method for usability testing. It usually does not require special equipment or lab facilities and require small number (3–5) of evaluators for the evaluation and takes 1 to 2 days to complete the procedure. Following are the Heuristics that have been suggested by Nielsen [19] for testing the usability of a system:

1. Visibility of system status (The system should always keep the user informed about what is going on through appropriate feedback within reasonable time).
2. Match between the system and the real world (The system should speak the user language with words and concepts that the users familiar with).
3. User control or freedom (The system should provide the user clearly marked "out" to leave an unwanted state without having to go through an extended dialogue in case he chooses system functions by mistake.
4. Consistency and standard (The system should follow the platform conventions so that the users should not have to wonder whether different words, situations, or actions mean the same thing).
5. Error prevention (The system should provide error message when needed).
6. Recognition rather recall (The objects, actions, and options should be visible so that the user should not have to remember information from one part of the dialogue to another and instructions for use of the system should be visible or easily retrievable whenever appropriate).
7. Flexibility and efficiency of use (The system should have accelerators which are unseen by the novice user and may often speed up the interaction for the expert user so that the system can cater to both inexperienced and experienced users).
8. Aesthetic and minimalist design (Dialogues should not contain information which is irrelevant or rarely needed since every extra unit of information in a

dialogue competes with the relevant units of information and diminishes their relative visibility).

9. Help users recognize, diagnose and recover from errors (Error should be expressed in plain language, precisely indicate the problem and constructive provide suggestions).

10. Help and documentation (Even though it is better if the system can be used without documentation, it may be necessary to provide help and documentation; help information should be easy to search, focused on the user's task, list concrete step to be carried out, and not be too large) (excerpted from [19].

Since, the Heuristic Evaluation method is considered as one of the best methods for usability testing that needs less time and few members for usability testing, we adopted this method for our research. As we have already mentioned that we involved five users (Bangladeshi people living in Milan) for this usability test who have some experience of usability testing. Three of them were software engineers and two were students in Information Systems. They were selected from the pool of the participants who participated in both exploratory and confirmatory focus group discussions which had been conducted in Milan to elicit requirements for designing the prototype and to confirm the design as well. For these reasons, they were considered as both experts and users for our study for evaluating the design and exploring any usability problems. They evaluated the interface independently and generated separate list of heuristic violations according to the ten standard heuristic principles mentioned above. At the beginning of the evaluation, we recall them how to consider each principle during the evaluation of the interface. This training session took around 1 h. Then we gave each user a template with the list of heuristics and asked them to identify at which point of the interface a heuristic is violated and to note it down. They were also asked to describe the reason why they considered that point as a problem. We also asked them to identify the phases where they encountered the problems and also to assess the severity of each usability problem. This also helped to uncover the usability problem. There was an observer who assisted the evaluators in operating the interface when they faced any problem. At the end of the interface evaluation, the evaluators" reports were collected and the descriptions of usability problems were synthesized. Each of the five evaluator provided individual severity ratings independently of the other four evaluators. When the independent analysis was completed, the results of the analyses were combined into the most complete set of interface problems. We completed the whole procedure in two days which took around 14 h.

Table 1 summarizes the severity of the usability problems found in the prototype of the TAS. We adopted a 5 point scale for severity ratings as suggested in [17]: a severity rating equals to 4 refers the severity of the problem as Usability Catastrophe (imperative to fix the problem before the product can be released); a severity rating equals to 3 is Major Usability Problem (important to fix, so high priority should be given); a severity rating equals to 2 is Minor Usability Problem (fixing this problem should be given low priority), a severity rating equals to 1 refers to cosmetic problem only (need not be fixed unless extra time is available on the project) and a severity rating equals to 0 means it is not a usability problem. Since the mean value of the set of ratings of the usability problems of the five evaluators ranges from 0.2 to 3.8, we divided the severity ratings into four scales: Catastrophe $> = 3.5$, Major $> = 2.5$, Minor $> = 1.5$ and Cosmetic <1.5.

5 Results and Discussions

5.1 Results

We found that heuristics were violated a total of 28 times. Recognition rather than recall (9) and Help and documentation (6) were the most frequently violated heuristics. The following table shows some examples of usability problems for the prototype along with their corresponding violation and the phases where the problems were found (Table 1). It was found that a single usability problem resulted in violation of multiple heuristics. For example, Option for Euro in case of acknowledgement violates „consistency and standards" as a TAS is all about time and no monetary transaction is there: so at first sight the evaluator got confused about it; and it also violates the heuristic of aesthetic and minimalist design because this additional information hampers the importance and visibility of the needed information.

5.2 Discussions

For the prototype, 3 catastrophes, 4 major, 5 minor and 7 cosmetic problems were identified by the evaluators. Some of these problems have been discussed below with some screenshots of the prototype of TAS.

   Catastrophes: For the prototype, there were 3 catastrophes of which problems should be fixed before the prototype is released. 3 areas that need to be fixed before releasing are as follows:

- There was an option for paying euro which was considered as a problem by the evaluator. Since TAS is a system based on exchange of time, which was explained to them at the beginning of the usability testing, the evaluator/users got confused when they saw 'euro' instead of community coins or Time as unit of exchange.

Table 1 Some usability problems out of twenty one and heuristic violation for a TAS

Phases	Usability problems	Heuristic violation	Severity rating
Home page	– There is no information about TAS; a visitor will not understand what TAS is about	– Match between the system and the real world, recognition rather than recall	3.10
	– It is not clear what does a group mean because there are zones under the group, the general perception of group is it is about people	– Match between the system and the real world, recognition rather than recall	3.00
	– Connect with Face book button is in between username and password and login button	– Error prevention	1.00
			1.00
	– Log in button is not closer to username and password	– Consistency and standards	0.80
	– 'Create new account' and 'request new password' fields are too close		
	– User may get confused with 'Request new password' , since 'forgot password?' is commonly used	– Help and recognition	1.25
Navigation	– After registration a novice user will not understand anything from add content menu	– Match between the system and the real world; Flexibility and efficiency of use	2.00
	– Selected field should appear with a different color or as highlighted one	– Recognition and recall; Help and Documentation	1.1
	– How to use TAS does not teach how to use, rather it teaches what an user can do	– Consistency and standards	3.69
Managing offer and want	– Past dates of the calendar is not blocked, no message has been shown in case of selecting past date for posting an offer	– Error prevention; Aesthetic and mi-nimalist design	3.75
	– There is no back option for any task	– Consistency and standards	2.35
	– In calendar, for posting any 'skill' (offer or need) true/false option is not clear	– User control and freedom	3.3

(continued)

Table 1 (continued)

Phases	Usability problems	Heuristic violation	Severity rating
	– Repetition in adding offer and want seems useless and trouble-some	– Error prevention	1.8
	– In case of judging capability (skill) of offers is not clear (who is judging this capability and how)	– Recognition and recall	1.76
	– 'Skill' can be a better descriptive term for the word capability	– Aesthetic and minimalistic design	1.75
	– A map appears when an Offer or Want is selected as additional information	– Match between system and the real world	1.00
Acknowledging the offer	– There is option for Euro	– Consistency and standard; Aesthetic and minimalist design;	3.8
	– 'Payment for receiving a service' may create some confusion, since the concept is non-monetary	– Error prevention	3.0
	– In case of acknowledging an offer, there should be 'Receiver' instead of 'other person'	– Aesthetic and minimalistic design	1.10
	– In case of completing a transaction, the watermark is inconsistent, though the transaction was signed by both users but it says it's still pending	– Consistency and standards	2.8

- In the prototype, 'how to use TAS' did not teach how to use the system, rather it provided information about what an user can do. A clear guide or a manual might be able to help the user to use the system.

Major: The users identified 4 problems that can be considered as 'major' according to Nielson's heuristic which should be given priority for fixing. These are:

- There is no information about TAS; a visitor will not understand what TAS is about. It would be better if there is adequate information regarding TAS in home page. Adequate information about TAS-what is it, how it works, who can be a member, what are the tasks of the member, how a transaction completes, how the accounts are kept-should be given in the home page. This information will help a visitor to get a comprehensive idea about TAS and to proceed with exchange of services.
- In Calendar, for posting any 'skill' (offer or need) true/false option is not clear. It is difficult to understand that true refers to an offer and false refers to a need. There is no reason for having an option for filtering.

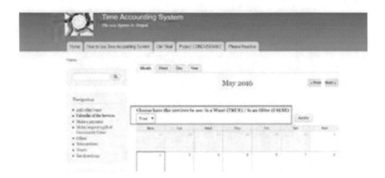

Minor: The users identified 5 problems that can be considered as 'minor' according to Nielson's heuristic which should be given low priority for fixing. Some of these problems have been discussed below:

- After registration, a user directs to a page where he or she gets different menus for navigations, like offers, wants, calendars, add menu etc. However, a novice user will not understand anything from 'Add content' menu. In order to make the design simpler, this menu can be deleted.
- The evaluators/users identified that there is no back option for any task which is a violation of the convention or standard. Users would feel better if there is a back option for the tasks so that they can reverse to any task if needed.

Cosmetic: The users also identified 7 usability problems that can be considered as cosmetic since these problems do not hamper the activities of the system; so the problems can be fixed later if there is enough/available time before the release of the final version of the software.

- Connect with Face book button is in between username and password and login button: It"s likely that a distract user will click the "connect with face book" button instead of the "log in" one, resulting in an error. So, the button should be positioned in a better place i.e. right next to the fields or right below them.
- User may get confused with 'Request new password': Since 'forgot password?' is commonly used in case of requesting new password, it would be better to comply with the standard.
- Selected field should appear with a different color or as highlighted one which could help the user to understand his present task and which is consistent with standard.

As we discussed before, for the prototype, there were 3 catastrophes, 4 major, 5 minor and 7 cosmetic problems (Fig. 1). There were 2 problems that violated heuristic, but in the aggregated result they were not considered as usability problems. For example, the option for logging out is placed at the bottom of the webpage which is usually placed at the top of the webpage; in this case, in terms of heuristic violation there is a mismatch between the system and real world as it did not follow the convention.

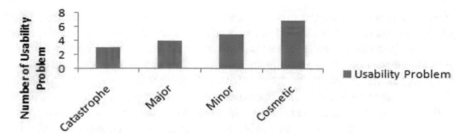

Fig. 1 Usability problems by severity rating

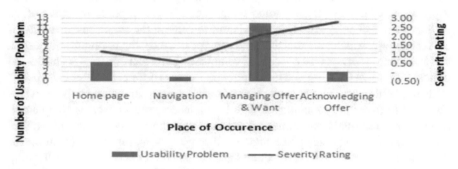

Fig. 2 Frequencies and severity rating by place of occurrences

Following figure (Fig. 2) shows the usability problems and the average severity rating in terms of place of occurrence.

The most numbers of usability problems occur in managing Offer and Want; though the number of usability problems in acknowledging Offer is very few (2) the severity rating is the highest in this case which 2.8 is. This could be explained in a way that since a TAS was described to the evaluators as s non-monetary system, the presence of 'Euro' in the system in case of payment for a service, instead of time, could make this highest severity in this case. The average severity ratings by place of occurrence for four places were in between 0.6 and 2.8.

Hence, we need to address the usability problems found in the process particularly the catastrophes and the major one. Since, there are very few catastrophes in the interface and severity rating is high for the usability problems for one particular case (acknowledging the Offer) with only usability problems, these problems could be fixed within a reasonable time.

6 Conclusions

The design and development of the prototype of the TAS were conceived as a continuous process involving both designers and users, and considering the requirements of the potential users in order to make it more effective and efficient; and, from this perspective, we argue that a TAS is as a sociotechnical solution that can make service exchanges possible through a system within a community. In other words, we comply with the idea of giving equal importance to technology and human needs while designing and developing the prototype of the TAS which was promoted by Mumford [16] as a sociotechnical solution. The objective of this paper is to test the usability of the prototype of a TAS to know how the users feel when they use the prototype and to find where they encounter problems and experience confusion. In order to reach the objectives of this research, we looked for a methodological approach that would help us from both social and technological perspectives. Basically, western experiences with TAS suggests some social [26, 25] challenges to be aware of, as well as some technological [4] lessons learnt to achieve the actual sustainability of the technology. Among the social challenges, for instance, the importance to keep a clear distinction between the concept of volunteering and that of a TAS is considered critical [25], as well as the need to "differentiate across different service categories" so as to possibly smooth the perception of unequal value in incomparable services [26], and to foster the commitment of full-time leaders or to conceive "help desk" services on a constant basis. Among the technological challenges, relevant requirements include the provision of intelligent and context-aware services [4] to allow for the matching between real-time requests and offers and for services of localization, online profiling updates, and the automatic recording of time balances just after the provision of a service, that is without the need to log into the system and manually adjust the provision or consumption of time. Moreover, capitalizing the opportunities of ICT depends not only on the existence and access to a suitable infrastructure also on the ICT related human capacities. Among these latter, the capacity to understand an application and to use an application by the users is a vital precondition [21]. Hence, in the light of these high level recommendations and design principles we use a sociotechnical approach for conceiving a prototype of a TAS. On the one hand, this approach involves the end users from the very beginning of development process for identifying their requirements for the system. On the other hand, the interactive nature of the method helped us to receive feedbacks from the end users in terms of usability.

At different phases of our whole research [6, 27, 28], we involved two groups of Bangladeshi people: those living in their country and those who in the recent years moved to Italy. These two groups share the same basic culture and the concerns that are motivated by their common experience to live in an urban area. This fact made it possible to consider them as homogeneous enough to guarantee the soundness of our research outcomes.

This study has addressed the limitation of our previous work [28] by testing the usability of the current prototype in order to assess the user experience with a TAS that helped us to identify usability issues with the prototype interface. The study has provided a unique contribution in addressing design issues in developing countries, particularly in Bangladesh, as it examined the usability of a TAS for a new context which has never been accomplished before. However, our future work directs to validate the prototype among the Bangladeshi people in Bangladesh, to unfold the functionalities of a TAS and help improve its design.

References

1. Agarwal, R., & Venkatesh, V. (2002). Assessing a firm's web presence: a heuristic evaluation procedure for the measurement of usability. *Information Systems Research, 13*(2), 168–186.
2. Albirini, A. (2008). The Internet in developing countries: A medium of economic, cultural and political domination. *International Journal of Education and Development using Information and Communication Technology, 4*(1), 49.
3. Avgerou, C. (1996). *How can IT enable developing countries to integrate into the global economy?* Ivy League Publishing.
4. Bellotti, V., Carroll, J. M., & Han, K. (2013). Random acts of kindness: The intelligent and context-aware future of reciprocal altruism and community collaboration. In *Collaboration Technologies and Systems (CTS), 2013 International Conference on* (pp. 1–12).
5. Boyle, D. (2014). The potential of Time Banks to support social inclusion and employability. *EC JRC Scientific and Policy Reports, Report ER 26346 EN.*
6. Cabitza, F., Locoro, A., Simone, C., & Sultana, T. (2016). Moving western neighbourliness to East? A study on local exchange in Bangladesh. In *Presented at the 19th ACM conference on Computer-Supported Cooperative Work and Social Computing*, USA: San Francisco.
7. Choi, J., & Bakken, S. (2010). Web-based education for low-literate parents in neonatal intensive care unit: Development of a website and heuristic evaluation and usability testing. *International Journal of Medical Informatics, 79*(8), 565–575.
8. Collom, E. (2008). Engagement of the elderly in time banking: The potential for social capital generation in an aging society. *Journal of Aging & Social Policy, 20*(4), 414–436.
9. Collom, E. (2008a). Banking time in an alternative market: A quantitative case study of a local currency system. In *103rd Annual Meeting of the American Sociological Association*, Boston.
10. Gunatunge, R., & Karunanayake, M. (2004). Information and communication technologies for enhancing socioeconomic development at the local level in Sri Lanka: Issues, challenges and strategies. *SAREC Research Cooperation Project on Overcoming Regional Im-balances and Poverty.*
11. Jimenez, C., Lozada, P., & Rosas, P. (2016, September). Usability heuristics: A systematic review. In *Computing Conference (CCC), 2016 IEEE 11th Colombian* (pp. 1–8). IEEE.
12. Lampinen, A., Lehtinen, V., Cheshire, C., & Suhonen, E. (2013). Indebtedness and reciprocity in local online exchange. In *Proceedings of the 2013 conference on Computer supported cooperative work* (pp. 661–672). ACM.
13. Lilholt, P. H., Jensen, M. H., & Hejlesen, O. K. (2015). Heuristic evaluation of a telehealth system from the Danish TeleCare North Trial. *International Journal of Medical Informatics, 84*(5), 319–326.
14. Mankoff, J., Dey, A. K., Hsieh, G., Kientz, J., Lederer, S., & Ames, M. (2003, April). Heuristic evaluation of ambient displays. In *Proceedings of the SIGCHI conference on Human factors in computing systems* (pp. 169–176). ACM.
15. Marks, M. B. (2012). Time banking service exchange systems: A review of the research and policy and practice implications in support of youth in transition. *Children and Youth Services Review, 34*(7), 1230–1236.
16. Mumford, E. (2006). The story of socio-technical design: Reflections on its successes, failures and potential. *Information Systems Journal, 16*(4), 317–342.
17. Nielsen, J. (1994b). *Usability Engineering*. San Francisco: Morgan Kaufmann.
18. Nielsen, J. (1992). Finding usability problems through heuristic evaluation. In *Proceedings of the SIGCHI conference on Human factors in computing systems* (pp. 373–380). ACM.
19. Nielsen, J. (1994a). Heuristic evaluation. *Usability Inspection Methods, 17*(1), 25–62.

20. Nielsen, J. (1994c). Usability inspection methods. In *Conference companion on Human factors in computing systems* (pp. 413–414). ACM.
21. Osterwalder, A. (2002). *ICT in developing countries* (1–13). Lausanne, Switzerland: University of Lausanne.
22. Seyfang, G. (2002). Tackling social exclusion with community currencies: Learning from LETS to Time Banks. *International Journal of Community Currency Research, 6*(1), 1–11.
23. Seyfang, G. (2004a). Time banks: Rewarding community self-help in the inner city? *Community Development Journal, 39*(1), 62–71.
24. Seyfang, G., & Smith, K. (2002). The time of our lives: Using time banking for neighbourhood renewal and community capacity building.
25. Seyfang, G., (2004b) Working outside the box: community currencies, time banks and social inclusion. *Journal of Social Policy, 33*(1), 49–71.
26. Shih, P. C., Bellotti, V., Han, K, & Carroll, J. M. (2015). *Unequal time for unequal value: implications of differing motivations for participation in timebanking.* Presented at the CH12015, Seoul Republic of Korea.
27. Sultana, T., & Locoro, A. (2016). No more throwaway 'elderly' people: Building a new image of ageing via a time accounting system. In M. Garschall, T. Hamm, D. Hornung, C. Müller, K. Neureiter, M. Schorch, & L. van Velsen (Eds.), *International Reports on Socio-Informatics (IRSI), Proceedings of the COOP 2016—Symposium on challenges and experiences in designing for an ageing society* (vol. 13, Iss. 3, pp. 35–42).
28. Sultana, T. & Locoro, A. & Da Silva, F. S. C. (2016). Time Accounting System: Validating a socio-technical solution for service exchange in local communities. In *the Procsof ItAIS2015: XIII Conference Of The Italian Chapter of AIS*. Verona, Italy.
29. Sultana, T., Locoro, A., & Cabitza, F. (2015) Investigating opportunities and obstacles for a community-oriented social media in Bangladesh. *International Reports on Socio-informatics* (vol. 12(1), pp. 15–24). Limerick: IISI—International Institute for Socio-Informatics. Limerick, Ireland.
30. United Nations. (2007). World population ageing. New York, USA: UN Department of Economic and Social Affairs.
31. Walsh, L., Hemsley, B., Allan, M., Adams, N., Balandin, S., Georgiou, A., … & Hill, S. (2017). The E-health literacy demands of australia's my health record: A heuristic evaluation of usability. *Perspectives in health information management, 14*(Fall).

Digital Identity: A Case Study of the ProCIDA Project

Francesco Bellini, Fabrizio D'Ascenzo, Iana Dulskaia and Marco Savastano

Abstract The role of cloud computing in today's world of globalization has seen as a major contribution for application development and deployment. Many enterprises see cloud computing as a platform for organizational and economic benefit. Managing digital identities and access control for cloud users and applications remains one of the greatest challenges facing cloud computing today. The aim of the paper is to summarise the results of the ProCIDA research project funded under Regional Operational Programme "Insieme x Vincere", co-financed by the European Regional Development Fund, where a digital platform has been developed in order to simplify access to different kind of digital services (public and private) using the digital identity.

Keywords Digital identity · Cloud computing · Digital identity management

1 Introduction

Cloud Computing is a network-based environment that focuses on sharing computing resource, storage space, data and other kinds of software services [1].

Digital identity is a keystone that can ensure that the Internet infrastructure is strong enough to meet basic expectations for not just service and functionality, but security, privacy, and reliability. It becomes a complex question when we think of

F. Bellini (✉) · F. D'Ascenzo · I. Dulskaia · M. Savastano
Department of Management, Sapienza University of Rome, Rome, Italy
e-mail: francesco.bellini@uniroma1.it

F. D'Ascenzo
e-mail: fabrizio.dascenzo@uniroma1.it

I. Dulskaia
e-mail: iana.dulskaia@uniroma1.it

M. Savastano
e-mail: marco.savastano@uniroma1.it

© Springer Nature Switzerland AG 2020
A. Lazazzara et al. (eds.), *Exploring Digital Ecosystems*,
Lecture Notes in Information Systems and Organisation 33,
https://doi.org/10.1007/978-3-030-23665-6_23

how to create, use, store and verify the identity in the context of Internet, especially when it refers to public and private sectors.

How much control individuals will be able to take—or will desire to take-over their digital identity is an issue of an intense debate [2].

The identity of a cloud user authorizes him to access data or resources from the cloud environment. When the users make requests to access the cloud resources and services, it is highly important that the digital identity and the access rights of the users are verified before granting the requested services. An effective digital identity management mechanism is required to make the cloud computing platform trusted, secure, reliable and scalable [3].

In this context, the main goal of this paper and also its novelty is to describe and propose a model through which new digital service platforms based on cloud computing permits users to obtain different digital services in a safe and reliable way using their Digital Identity. The authors also aim at contributing to scientific literature by providing a literature review on digital identity and digital identity management by given an example of digital identity management process through the analysis of case study of ProCIDA project.

The empirical analysis based on a case study was done by analysing ProCIDA project approved as part of the Regional Operational Programme "Insieme x Vincere", co-financed by the European Regional Development Fund (ERDF), under Axis I the "Research, Innovation and Strengthening of the productive base".

Project aims to replace the large number of services already presented in the network based on weak authentication systems (such as username/password, login credentials), making available a new generation of services based on innovative mechanisms to identify users and simplify access to services as well as promoting cooperation.

The work is structured as follows. The first part of the study presents a brief literature review in order to build a conceptual framework for analysing the ProCIDA.

In the second part of the paper are presented the ProCIDA case description, and its experimentation phase together with general results. The paper concludes highlighting the main findings, limitations and proposing some further research directions.

2 Background

2.1 Identity Management System

Identity is a core of any security aware system. It allows the users, services, servers, clouds, and any other entities to be recognized by systems and other parties. Identity consists of a set of information associated with a specific entity. This information is relevant based on context. Identity should not disclose user personal information "privacy" [4].

Access is one of serious issues in cloud computing. Access comprises the concern around cloud access (authentication, authorization and access control or AAA), encrypted data communication, and user identity management [5].

Having username/password is not sufficient for data protection on cloud. There is high need for using better protocols that do not increase the complexity of the system.

Identity Management can be taken as a service offered by cloud as an innovative opportunity of externalizing the workload of managing identity [6].

Digital Identity management is the process of representing and identifying individuals in computer networks [7].

Cloud platforms should deliver or support a robust and consistent identity management system. This system should cover all cloud objects and cloud users with corresponding identity context information. It should include: Identity Provisioning and de-provisioning, identity information privacy, identity linking, identity mapping, identity federation, identity attributes federation, single sign on, authentication and authorization [8].

According to Pato and Center [9] identity management solutions are modular and composed of multiple service and system components. This section outlines components of an example identity management architecture illustrated in Fig. 1.

- Repository—At the core of the system is the logical data storage facility and identity data model, which is often implemented as an LDAP accessible directory or meta-directory. Policy information governing access to and use of information in the repository is generally stored here as well.
- Authentication Provider—The authentication provider, sometimes referred to as the identity provider, is responsible for performing primary authentication of an individual, which will link them to a given identity.

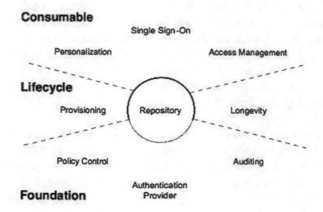

Fig. 1 Identity management system components

- Policy Control—Access to and use of identity information is governed by policy controls. Authorization policies determine how information is manipulated; privacy policies govern how identity information may be disclosed.
- Auditing—Secure auditing provides the mechanism to track how information in the repository is created, modified and used.
- Provisioning—Provisioning is the automation of all the procedures and tools to manage the lifecycle of an identity: creation of the identifier for the identity; linkage to the authentication providers; setting and changing attributes and privileges; and decommissioning the identity.
- Longevity—Longevity tools create the historical record of an identity. These tools allow the examination of the evolution of an identity over time.
- Single Sign-On—Single sign-on allows a user to perform primary authentication once and then access the set of applications and systems that are part of the identity management environment.
- Personalization—Personalization and preference management tools allow application specific as well as generic information to be associated with an identity. These tools allow applications to tailor the user experience for a given individual leading to a streamlined interface for the user and the ability to target information dissemination for a business.
- Access Management—Similar to the policy controls within the identity management system foundation components, access management components allow applications to make authorization and other policy decisions based on privilege and policy information stored in the repository.

3 Case Study: ProCIDA Project

ProCIDA—(**Project for Certified Identity in the Digital Agenda**)[1]—was created from the need to make available a new generation of services based on innovative mechanisms to identify users and their secure access to network services, with the aim of promoting digital cooperation including PA (Public Administration), businesses and citizens, organizations and individuals. The project was approved as part of the Regional Operational Programme "Insieme x Vincere", co-financed by the European Regional Development Fund (ERDF), under Axis I the "Research, Innovation and Strengthening of the productive base".

The ProCIDA project is carried out in coordination with a SPID project (Sistema Pubblico di Identità Digitale) (Public System of Digital Identity), coordinated by the Agency for l'Italia Digitale thanks to which citizens will have the ability to access governmental services using a single set of credentials, (the so-called "unique PIN").

The project aims to replace the large number of services already presented in the network based on weak authentication systems (such as username/password, login credentials), making available a new generation of services based on innovative

---

[1] (http://procida.directory/)—the website of Procida project.

mechanisms to identify users and simplify access to services as well as promoting cooperation.

Primary objectives of the ProCIDA project:

1. Define and implement an authentication system, Identity Access Management (IAM), universal, robust, multi-channel and federated with the main operators in the sector, to assign to each subject in the network secure digital credentials and allow it access to the available services.
2. Design a value-added service called Cassetto Informativo Personale (Personal Information Folder—PIF), which, according to the model of cloud computing, provides users with personal online data repository always accessible from anywhere, in full mobility and anytime.

Features and benefits

The PIF will implement in a complete way the concept of digital identity. In the folder it should be possible to collect in a more and more automatic way all user's digital documents, from different sources, and provide value-added services and information.

For example, instead of collecting paper clinical analysis reports that are unlikely to be consulted in the future, the testing laboratory will deliver these documents in digital format directly to the user's folder (automatically identified from its fiscal code or its digital ID).

The folder must be opened only by the owner, who will also be the only one who can activate it. The PIF is therefore proposed as the instrument for the widespread dematerialization, integrating the needs of public administrations and private companies with those of citizens.

The PIF is conceived by imagining that the user can independently organize or extend its information base by choosing the preferred taxonomy and making it evolve after the increase of the document sources.

As regards the authentication system, must be referring to the more modern cryptographic technologies, to provide highly reliable recognition services.

The service is offered in a transversal manner to all network service provider (Service Provider—SP). This makes it possible to decouple the phase of access to the service by the user recognition phase. As a positive side effect, the decrease of the number of credentials that the user has to handle in his/her digital life. In fact, numerous studies show how the management of the new login credentials can be an obstacle to the adoption of a new service, although useful or interesting.

There are many services that use the credentials of the major social network to assign an identity to their new users. A similar approach can make life easier for users, but it is considered weak and unreliable services that treat such sensitive data.

The system integrates a federated authentication system with CNS, by importing the registry index, temporarily or permanently depending on agreements with the Identity Provider stipulated from time to time. Each user is associated together with its own digital identity, also a result of reliability index of the authentication system used and the origin of the data. The advantage for the user is that with only one system (the CNS or the Digital Identity released from ProCIDA) has access to all services in the network.

The paradigm of cloud computing besides allowing user safe and multi-channel access to their digital archive ensures reliable retention over time of the documents and information. With PIF the user no longer has to worry about the age of their digital support, or data back up to multiple devices to reduce the risk of their loss. With the paradigm of cloud computing is adopted also the new generation of NoSQL database type, characterized by extreme flexibility (the least restrictive way of storing data than the relational model), being designed for a distributed management across the network and, also for this, allowing the storage of massive amounts of data/documents.

ProCIDA contributed to:

1. **Privacy and protection of personal data**

Social acceptance of the Internet of Things (IoT) will be strongly intertwined with respect for privacy and the protection of personal data, two fundamental rights of the EU.

2. **Trust, Acceptance and Security**

Information security is considered one of the main problems IoT. In the private sphere, information security is closely linked to the questions of trust and privacy mentioned above. It is crucial that IoT components are designed from the outset to ensure the security and protection of privacy and comprehensively include user requirements.

3. **Dematerialisation**

With reference to the processes of dematerialisation, ProCIDA within the project is addressed three components:

- Legislation component: currently we are facing a very structured and constantly changing system, to which the change of the legal frame of reference is one of the major risks in the implementation of dematerialization projects for verification demands arising for the purpose of identification of effective and timely adjustment mode and, above all, on the relative times and costs.
- Technological component: is determined by the difficulty of managing heterogeneous set of technologies involved (document management, digital signature, physical storage, etc.) and the need to overcome the technical obsolescence of the different infrastructure to ensure conservation of administrative documents for very long periods, some even indefinitely.
- Organizational component: the electronic document, rather than the paper, it is not self-consistent, and this entails the need to store in time and space, not only the document itself but also all the elements necessary to demonstrate their authenticity, for the purposes of its probative value and historic preservation: protocol identifier, classification archival, digital signature.

4. Innovative social networking models

ProCIDA project studied and specified some fundamental aspects in the approach to social networks. The project study evolution of social networks and their openness to businesses and other information on issues related to the federation of the person and the possibility of being able to access them with different profiles.

5. Change management

Italy has accumulated significant delays in the adoption of new technologies, especially digital ones. To retrieve and align Italy to the European Digital Agenda is necessary not only a significant effort to adapt infrastructure and services, but also to induce a deep cultural change, which puts digital services and the Internet in its various forms at the centre of the life of each of us. To ensure the success of the initiative, ProCIDA have studied and develop these new methods and new paradigms.

6. Innovative business models

The nature of services in the field of ProCIDA project, the particular mode of aggregation and demand (in the cloud), and the user environment and competitors, requires to rethink traditional models of intervention.

The business model underlying the ProCIDA project is following:

- financial and economic model (revenue model) on the identification of the target market and the penetration mode and market development;
- working model on the identification of the mode of remuneration of participants and, to stretch, the overall sustainability of the project.

7. Business intelligence

The development of communication technologies has led to a growing presence of information sources leading to a veritable explosion in the amount and variety of accessible data. Parallel to the growth of the sources of information it was possible to observe a degradation of the quality of the same.

Necessary to review the concept of "Information Integration" in a broader sense, developing it into one of "Intelligent Information Integration."

8. Business Process Management (BPM)

The PIF by its nature stands as an interchange of information between the parties on the network (individuals and organizations) mediated by the platform. The degree of interaction with external organizations can assume various degrees of complexity:

- The simple information store (e.g. The laboratory part of the PIF relative to a medical service document)
- The information store accompanied by a simple feedback (e.g. the owner of the PIF confirms that it has received or took the document view)
- Exchange of information with complex feedback
- Meta-information exchange (e.g. management of comments, annotations or requests for information related to documents in the PIF)

- The different levels of complexity, which may be provided in the use of the PIF, may have important functional impacts on the design of the overall platform.
- Business Process Management helps to improve functioning, better monitoring and traceability of events and information managed, and evaluate the performance of the platform.

3.1 ProCIDA Architecture

1. Personal Information Folder

Personal Information Folder (PIF) is a service module, which aims to provide a unified document management of the user's personal attributes. From the point of view of the previously described identity management service, it is a "client" service.

The system provides the capability for end users to create and safe use of documents and personal attributes (unskilled), according to the context model shown in the figure. The system provides a cloud infrastructure accessible from a PC via a special client or via the web, or from mobile devices via special apps for the various platforms.

The main implemented features are:

- Synchronization and backup of the contents of a replicated folder on different dispositive. The synchronization feature is available only through the service desktop client. Through the web, or through mobile device app, the service instead implements for users to upload and download functions of individual documents.
- Cross-platform functions for entering and editing personal information.

  - Encryption of a specific part of the data collection
  - Integrity check of the entire data collection
  - Client Management-related services and PIF (Fig. 2).

2. Identity Access Management

The ProCIDA Identity Access Management implements the functions that from the conceptual point of view it can be imagined as a nucleus (the identity store) surrounded by a set of functions, as in the underlying representation (see Fig. 3).

The identity store is powered by a set of logging services. The identities are then used for authentication services, which also make use of specific credential verification modules. The lifecycle management services are concerned about maintaining the archive consistency of identity over time. The administration services contain all the utilities necessary for the functioning of the system, including logging components, reporting, analytics, accounting. A set of services deals with the interaction with other identity provider.

In Fig. 2 it can be seen the requirements regarding the following services:

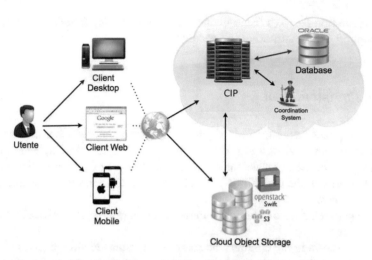

Fig. 2 Architecture of the PIF system

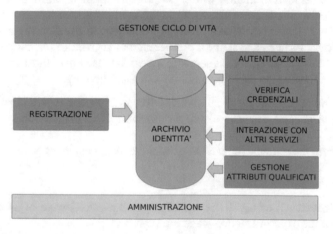

Fig. 3 Identity access management system

- Registration of the users of services (which mainly includes the enrolment functions and the delivery of the first set of credentials).
- Identity Life Cycle Management Services and Credentials (which includes the credential management functions).
- Authentication Services (which implements the entity authentication functions).
- Credentials Verification Services, which are an integral part of the authentication services but, for ease of description, it prefers to unbundle.

  The following services were also added:

- Management of the qualified attributes.
- Interaction with other services (other IdP InfoCert and other services).

- Administration Services (centralizing the record-keeping functions and provides the support of administration and support too.

3.2   Experimentation

The testing phase has a manifold significance, embracing different aspects of the project itself, the services and functions related to Digital Identity, which are the result and the reaction of stakeholders in this first phase of prototype development to take the pulse to the possibility of developing digital access to public and private services by citizens.

The experiments were held in two macro sectors (public and private) as well as with consumers.

Figure 4 shows in the columns the main macro areas identified as an object of experimentation that appear most appropriate in the assignment of pre-operating stage for assessments of interest within the project ProCIDA, while in the rows they are the main functional areas that verify in the field in various sectors.

The cells at the intersection of row and column are filled in the case that the functionality class indicated at line is of interest for the given sector, has possibility of application, is appropriate for the sector to assess the reaction of the users, and so on.

The objectives of the experimentation were the following:

- clarify and communicate to all stakeholders the functional requirements of the system; in general, analyse, identify, describe typical uses of the system by its users;
- consider all the possible logic arising from the management of errors, exceptions, alternate streams;
- validate the user requirements.

In order to reach this goals series of experimentations were organized. Some examples of the experimentation stage are represented below.

1. **Experimentation in Finance private sector**

The test meetings with various financial institutions in the banking and insurance have occurred, in order to explore the practical significance of the use of Identity Provider services by operators in view of the dematerialization and modernization of processes typical of the sector. The participants have expressed great interest in the initiative ProCIDA and SPID technical rules, which are a point of reference for operators, both public and private. After the participation in the test, banks have expressed an interest in the possibility of analysing the evolution of online services thanks to the simplification of the detection phases management and user authentication provided by the adoption of Digital Identity provided by SPID.

In particular, the banks have noticed the possibility of enlargement of the proposed digital services to its customers, current and potential, with the possibility of offering

Macro sector	Private			Public			Consumer
Sector / Functional areas	Finance	Telco	Health care	SPID	Health care	University	
Provisioning	✓	✓	✓	✓	✓	✓	✓✓
Access Management	✓	✓		✓		✓	✓
Personal Information Folder (PIF) (Documental)	✓		✓		✓	✓	✓
PWD Management				✓			
Attribute Management						✓	✓

Fig. 4 Experimentation matrix

simplified and remote control of the processes of interaction between customer and institution.

2. **Experimentation in the Telco private sector**

In the experiment were involved such operators as Vodafone, Wind, H3G, which, were certainly interested in the role of Mobile Identity and have expressed an evaluation attitude on the role of IdP or to focus on the role of Service primarily providers focusing on mobile payments with phone credit even for physical goods to "digital consumption" introduced by the recent Decree Digitalia, such as, for example, mobile ticketing services, which allow to purchase bus tickets via SMS.

3. **Experimentation in the Public Administration sector**

The main participants, who had already available digital services with secure access for citizens, have ventured in the execution of integration tests with digital identity factors specified by SPID.

The goal was to make available to SPID users all services currently provided by integrating the means of access to understand the use of Digital Identity SPID as a credential recognized worldwide.

The partners participating in the ProCIDA took part in the operational phases of experimentation with various administrations, constantly monitoring the alignment between technological implementation object of integration testing and formal and non-formal technical specifications that during the experimental period were refined according to the same feedback from experimental tests.

The work was performed in close contact with administrations, both in the laboratory environment, and at the headquarters of the administration.

The most involved in this activity have been Administrations: Tax Agency, INPS, INAIL, Tuscany Region, Region Friuli Venezia Giulia, Emilia Romagna, Piemonte, Liguria Region, Marche Region, the City of Florence, Milan City Council, the City of Lecce.

The participants remained satisfied by services proposed by SPID and ProCIDA and express the willingness to use them.

4 Conclusions, Limitations and Future Research

This research has demonstrated how digital service platform can provide a simplified way of using public and private digital services by using digital identity systems, supported by cloud computing technology.

ProCIDA proposes the wide adoption of this technological instrument that is in any case essential to enable the digitization process and strongly desired by all the latest standards.

Therefore, the result was to provide of a complete solution, widespread and independent from the available technologies, that can support multiple authentication systems, integrating with leading legacy systems.

At the same time the results of the project can be perceived as an accelerator for any company deemed to offer the online services market.

A single-case study was conducted with the representatives of different macro sectors (public and private) in order to evaluate the functionality and quality of the software system. The results of the feedback obtained from the participants have been perceived as very satisfactory and they have demonstrated the willingness to use it.

The main limitation of this study is that the ProCIDA platform has only been implemented in the pilot phase of the project. In this respect, only the design and functionality levels were taken into consideration.

The next step will be to conduct a research after the platform starts to function.

References

1. Goel, A., Gupta, G., Bhushan, M., & Nirwal, N. (2015). Identity management in hybrid cloud. In *International Conference Green Computing and Internet of Things (ICGCIoT)*, 2015, IEEE, pp. 1096–1100.
2. Windley, P. J. (2005). Digital identity, O'Reilly Media, Inc.
3. Thomas, M. V., & Chandrasekaran, K. (2016). Identity and access management in the cloud computing environments. *Developing Interoperable and Federated Cloud Architecture, 61.*
4. Raghavendra, K., & Ramesh, B. (2015). Managing the digital identity in the cloud: The current scenario. In *2015 IEEE International Conference Electrical, Computer and Communication Technologies (ICECCT)*, (pp. 1–4).
5. Shubhashis S., Vikrant K., & Vibhu S. S. (2011). Cloud computing security—trends and research directions. *IEEE world congress on services* (pp. 524–531).
6. Agudo D. N. I., & Lopez J. (2012). Integrating OpenID with proxy re-encryptionto enhance privacy in cloud-based identity services. In *Proceedings of IEEE Cloud Computing* (p. 241).
7. Halim, R., Shaharyar, S. A., & Vapen, A. (2009). *Digital identity management.*
8. Almorsy, M., Grundy, J., & Müller, I. (2010). An analysis of the cloud computing security problem. In *Proceedings of APSEC 2010 Cloud Workshop*, Sydney, Australia.
9. Pato, J., & Center, O. C. (2003). *Identity management: Setting context.* Cambridge, MA: Hewlett-Packard.

A Monte Carlo Method for the Diffusion of Information Between Mobile Agents

Alberto Berretti and Simone Ciccarone

Abstract A new model for the local spread of some token (e.g. malware between mobile computing devices, information in a mobile social network, rumors in a moving crowd) is introduced. The diffusion of the information is analyzed both empirically by a Monte Carlo method and analytically by mean field theory, revealing the existence of a phase transition. The results are compared and found in strong qualitative agreement.

Keywords Monte Carlo Simulation · Information Diffusion · Social Networks

1 Introduction

An interesting phenomenon is the spread of transmissible tokens in a network of agents structured in different ways. From traditional percolation problems on a lattice, used for example to model forest fires [1], to more advanced model using graphs of different kind to model e.g. the spread of news in a social network [2–4].

We consider here the problem of the spread of a token (e.g. a biological virus, malware, news and rumors, etc.) among a network of randomly connecting agents. Examples of this come out in several context: from mobile social networks [5], especially native ones where connections can be made on the basis of proximity, to malware spreading over bluetooth on mobile computing devices (e.g. smartphones [6]), to propagation of rumors in crowds.

The so called *virtual*, on line communities that aggregate around new digital services provide new ways for information propagation, which can be exploited for good and for bad: so the analysis of the dynamics of the diffusion of information

A. Berretti · S. Ciccarone (✉)
Dipartimento di Ingegneria Civile ed Ingegneria Informatica,
Università di Tor Vergata, Roma, Italy
e-mail: Simone.Ciccarone@uniroma2.it; simone@ciccarone.it

A. Berretti
e-mail: Alberto.Berretti@uniroma2.it

© Springer Nature Switzerland AG 2020
A. Lazazzara et al. (eds.), *Exploring Digital Ecosystems*,
Lecture Notes in Information Systems and Organisation 33,
https://doi.org/10.1007/978-3-030-23665-6_24

in such environments is essential to contain "bad" information (e.g. so-called *fake news*) and to help diffuse "good" information, such emergency communications in case of natural disasters.

Many such novel on line communities are based on mobile devices and services, and short range communications, as well as location-enabled services, are of fundamental importance. In these mobile social networks, users typically form small and dynamic local communities sparsely connected and without a fixed topology (e.g. a house, a company office, a residential neighborhood). Inside these local communities, based on location and proximity, mobile users can share information with other users in the same places whenever their devices are close enough. In this scenario the mobility of the agents can significantly affect the information spreading.

This is a first, necessarily rough, attempt at modeling the dynamics of the spread of information on random, rapidly changing networks. As such, it is not–yet–at the level of providing a realistic modeling of concrete and specific phenomena, but it provides a mechanism for the appearance of an interesting feature like a phase transition.

To account for this phenomenology, we develop a "microscopic", stochastic model for information spreading based on random walk processes, suitable for a simulation [7] using a dynamic Monte Carlo method [8]. We also develop a mean field theory for the model, in which a single mobile user is considered, interacting with an *average* number of other mobile users. The model depends on the probability p of transmission of the information in case of contact, the probability q of withdrawing, and the density d of the mobile users. We show the existence of a phase transition between a regime in which all tokens are lost (the malware is eradicated, the rumor stops, the information disappears) and one in which there is a steady fraction of agents holding the token (the malware still thrives, the rumor still spreads, the information diffuses). The critical values of the probabilities define a critical curve on the (p, q) plane, which is determined numerically by a Monte Carlo simulation and analytically by mean field theory, showing a strong qualitative agreement.

2 Definition of the Model

When modeling the spread of a token via proximity it is natural to consider percolation models, where susceptible objects (agents or users) occupy sites on a regular lattice – or are distributed with different topologies: for example a graph–and the token spreads from a site to neighbor sites. This approach doesn't take into account mobility, where neighbors change as agents moves around.

A simple and realistic way to take into account mobility is to make each agent perform a random walk in a regular lattice. As agents get to approach, a token can pass to each of its–temporary–neighbor, with a given probability.

To be definite, we assume that N mobile agents perform each a random walk on a square portion of a two-dimensional lattice $\mathcal{L} = \{0, \ldots, L-1\} \times \{0, \ldots, L-1\}$. The density of agents is therefore $d = N/L^2$. These agents are initially placed in some arbitrary way on the lattice, for example are uniformly distributed. Time is discrete, and each agent performs a random walk moving with equal probability in one of the four possible directions into one of the four nearest neighbor sites.

We have to deal somehow with the finite size of the box $\mathcal{L}$ in which the agents move. "Free" boundary conditions, in which each agent is free to leave the box $\mathcal{L}$, would deplete the box itself with probability one after a finite amount of time, so one would have to take into account the appearance of new agents which *move into* $\mathcal{L}$: this would give rise to a model with variable number of agents, something like a "grand canonical ensemble" in statistical mechanics. We prefer for the moment to avoid the complexity of dealing with disappearing and reappearing new agents, which we consider inessential to the problem, so we use periodic boundary conditions: as one agent moves out of $\mathcal{L}$ on one side, it reappears from the opposite side of the box; the random walk happens therefore on a torus. Another possibility would be to have agents bouncing when they reach the boundary: while this is relatively simple to take into account in the simulation, again it would add complexity to the model without really changing in any significant way the phenomenology of the model (as we tested).

Each agent can be in one of two states: in possession of a given information T or without (imagine infected or healthy in the case of computer malware, a member of a crowd under the influence of some rumor, or not in the case of rumor spreading in crowds). From now on, to make the language simpler, a mobile agent in possession of the information will be called *infected, healthy* otherwise.

As agents move into the same site the information can spread from one of the infected object to each one of the object which occupy the same site with a given probability p (probability of persuasion or infection). Of course, more than two mobile agents can be on the same site at a given time: in this case we consider separately all pairs as a possible source of infection (i.e. if we have three agents on a site, two infected and one healthy, then we test for a possible infection of the healthy agent *twice* independently, because of the two possible sources of infection).

As all mobile agents eventually intersect their trajectories, and eventually get the infection, all of them sooner or later would become infected. We therefore have to take into account also the chance that a given agent heals itself (perhaps because the infection has been detected and dealt with, in case of computer malware; or because the subject decided the rumor was false, in the case of a crowd). So at each (discrete) instant of time each infected agent has a probability q of *healing*.

We therefore have three parameters which determine the spread of the information on a given box $\mathcal{L}$ (besides the size of the box): the density of agents d, the *infection* probability p and the *healing* probability q.

We look at the case in which the box is large, i.e. what would be called an "infinite volume limit" or "thermodynamic limit" in statistical mechanics. This is basically a SIS (*Susceptible–Infected–Susceptible*) model, using standard epidemiological terminology: recovered objects can get infected again and don't get to be immune, as in so-called SIR (*Susceptible–Infected–Removed*) models. If, using our mobility model, we were to use a SIR model, all objects eventually would be infected, recover and never get infected again and the epidemics would stop with probability one in a finite amount of time, independently on the side of the box.

This model is, mathematically, a Markov chain with a huge state: if we have M agents in our box, the different possible configurations are 2^M. It is clearly possible to transition from any state to any state, with the exception of the state in which all objects are healthy and so there isn't anymore a way to get infected: this is an absorbing state that eventually the Markov chain will reach; for instance, if we have N infected objects, with probability q^N (extremely small but non-zero) they could get all healthy at the same time. We believe that the probability of reaching such a state in a given fixed amount of time, given some fixed values of p, $q > 0$ and d, is exponentially small in the volume of the box and so negligible in the "thermodynamic limit" that we are considering.

The choice of a square lattice and a simple random walk over it as a mobility model is somewhat arbitrary and motivated basically by mathematical simplicity. More complicated mobility models could be (and have been) devised. But as we are interested in *qualitative* features, and not in exact *quantitative* features of specific, realistic models, we concentrate our attention on a mathematically simple model which, while avoiding the complexities of a realistic one, keeps its qualitative features, much in the spirit of most statistical mechanical models commonly used in mathematical physics. As a byproduct, our simulation code is simpler, faster and more efficient. We also emphasize that our model, being based on a discrete random walk in a lattice, is a discrete time simulation.

3   Related Work

A few papers have studied simulations of SIS models via random walks. In [9] the spatial distribution of nodes in a random waypoint model is studied, and it is shown to be inhomogeneous. The authors only take into account the distribution of the agents, without ever considering propagation of infection or the transmission of some token between agents. They use physical units of measures in the simulation, taking into account an area of 1000×1000 m^2 divided into square cells whose side is 20 m, so they actually use 50×50 lattice (and so quite small).

In [10] the transmission of messages in a network of mobile nodes is studied. The authors again use physical units and so they consider an area of 1500×300 m where 50 agents move using a random waypoint model, with a transmission radius which varies between 10 and 2500 m (so again the effective size of the region is quite small). Using a simulation the authors study the mean time to deliver a message and the number of hops necessary to reach destination.

In [11] a SIR model with different mobility models is considered, with a populations of up to 1000 objects and a time of up to 1000 discrete units, and they look at the average number of immunized objects.

In [12] physical units are used again: they consider an area of dimension 200×200 m with an interaction radius of 5 m, so the model can be compared to a lattice model with dimension 40×40, that is rather small. Several mobility models are taken into account, suitable for a continuous space and time model. The authors compute an approximate formula for the epidemic threshold and shows that it depends only by the ratio of the probabilities of infection and disinfection. While similar in general conception, our model is rather different (and quite simpler to simulate: in fact we could handle a simulation with a much larger number of agents and area) as it is based on random walks on a lattice, and we found instead a more complex dependence of the epidemic threshold from infection and disinfection probabilities, even in the mean field theory approximation.

More recently, movement in epidemiological models has been considered in [13]. The spread of malware in mobile networks has been recently studied in a military context in [14].

4 The Simulation

The code for the simulation has been written in C language to achieve optimum performance. We ran it on a small cluster using at most eight computational cores (four Intel Xeon dual core processors at 3 GHz) and on a small personal workstation (with an Intel i3 processor at 3.1 GHz), all running Linux.

We used square lattices of sizes from 16×16 up to 512×512. The results from lattices of different size have been compared and we observed that they do not change significantly for lattices of size higher than 64×64, while they are more volatile for lattices of smaller sizes: so a kind of "thermodynamic limit" is practically achieved already for this size. So we settled for a size of 128×128.

The agents density was chosen between 0.1 and 1 in step of 0.1, and also a few run at higher densities have been performed (with densities equal to 2, 5 and 10). Note that densities higher than 1 imply that most sites are occupied by more than one agent, which is entirely possible within our model.

The built-in random number generator of the compiler has been used for the simulations.

As expected, the limit fraction of infected agents f_∞ doesn't depend on its initial value f_0, so we took $f_0 = 0.2$ in all production runs. We also took a uniform initial distribution of the agents, as we expect that at equilibrium the agents are uniformly distributed.

We performed an autocorrelation analysis of the data from each simulation, to compute its autocorrelation time τ. This is of course what must be done in any dynamic Monte Carlo simulation to make sure that data points are taken from an equilibrium distribution and that they are taken sufficiently far apart so that they can be considered independent. In our case, moreover, the time to reach the equilibrium is an interesting quantity *per se*. To compute autocorrelation times, we used a Python version of the `acor` package written by Jonathan Goodman [15].

5 Mean Field Theory

We can approximate our model using a "mean field theory" approach, which is expected to have a *qualitative* agreement with the exact model. In this approximation we consider *a single agent*, whose evolution is based on the average behavior of the rest of the system.

In average, each agent undergoes $\approx d$ intersections at each time, with each intersection giving a chance to get infected if it happens with an infected agent. As $f = N/M$ is the fraction of the infected agents, at each time each agent *approximately* intersects with an infected one "*fd* times".

Therefore approximately the probability that an agent gets infected is $p' = 1 - (1 - p)^{fd}$ (pretending that fd is an integer), that is 1 minus the probability of never getting infected in each of its intersections with an infected agent.

So let $X = H$ or I denote the status of an agent (H for healthy and I for infected). The following diagram shows the transition to the new state with each probability:

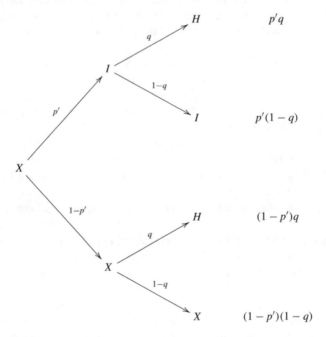

The dynamics of a single agent can therefore be approximated by a much simpler Markov chain, where the state space is just the set $\{H, I\}$ (being healthy or being infected) and the transition probabilities are given by:

State at t	State at $t+1$	Probability
H	H	$p'q + (1-p')q + (1-p')(1-q) = 1 - p' + p'q$
H	I	$p'(1-q) = p' - p'q$
I	H	$p'q + (1-p')q = q$
I	I	$p'(1-q) + (1-p')(1-q) = 1 - q$

The transition matrix is therefore:

$$M = \begin{bmatrix} 1 - p' + p'q & p' - p'q \\ q & 1 - q \end{bmatrix}.$$

This is an ergodic Markov chain whose invariant probability distribution is given by the normalized eigenvector of the eigenvalue 1, given by:

$$\begin{pmatrix} \dfrac{q}{p' + q - p'q} \\ \dfrac{p' - p'q}{p' + q - p'q} \end{pmatrix}.$$

This Markov chain therefore approach an equilibrium state with a probability of having an infected agent equal to $\dfrac{p' - p'q}{p' + q - p'q}$. We take this value as the mean-field approximation for the fraction of the infected agents:

$$f_{MF} = \frac{p' - p'q}{p' + q - p'q}.$$

As p' depends on the fraction of the infected agents itself, after a few elementary steps we obtain a transcendental equation for f_{MF}:

$$f_{MF} = 1 - \frac{q}{1 - (1-q)(1-p)^{f_{MF}d}}. \tag{1}$$

Please note that besides assuming a perfect uniform distribution of agents and also a perfect uniform distribution of *infected* agents, we also assumed fd to be an integer, which of course is another approximation. Moreover in mean field theory there is always a chance of getting infected (the Markov chain is actually really ergodic).

To compute the epidemic threshold in mean field theory, we start by observing that Eq. (1) always has a solution $f = 0$. So we are in the *epidemic regime* if there is *another* solution $f = f_{MF} > 0$, for given values of p, q and d. To study the existence of solutions to (1) we consider the intersection of the graph of:

$$\phi(f) = 1 - \frac{q}{1 - (1-q)(1-p)^{fd}}$$

with the bisectrix of the first quadrant with $0 \leq f \leq 1$. By trivial calculations, we have that for any physical values of p, q and d (that is for $0 \leq p \leq 1$, $0 \leq q \leq 1$, $d \geq 0$):

$$\phi'(f) > 0 \text{ and } \phi''(f) < 0$$

and of course $\phi(0) = 0$, $\phi(f) < 1$. Therefore if $\phi'(0) > 1$ we have another solution $f = f_{MF} \in (0, 1)$, while if $\phi'(0) \leq 1$ the only solution to (1) is $f = 0$. So the condition $\phi'(0) = 1$ determines the epidemic threshold in mean field; a trivial calculation gives:

$$q_0 = \frac{d \log \frac{1}{1-p}}{1 + d \log \frac{1}{1-p}},$$

with the epidemic thriving if $q < q_0$ and extinguishing if $q > q_0$.

Contrary to the findings of other authors, the data obtained by the simulation doesn't seem to show a dependence of the number of infected agents at equilibrium, or of the epidemic threshold, exclusively by the mere ratio p/q, as happens in different, typically continuous-time, models. The epidemic threshold $q_0(p, d)$ is only approximately linear for small values of p and d, which is what we expect to matter, heuristically, if we were to take a sort of continuum time limit of our model. In Fig. 1 we plotted the epidemic threshold $q_0(p, q)$ for selected values of d.

6   Results of the Simulation and Future Work

The observed fraction of infected agents at equilibrium f_∞ depends on all the three parameters: the infection probability p, the disinfection probability q and the density of agents d. There appear to be a value $q^*(p, d)$ such that if $q > q^*$ then $f_\infty = 0$ while if $q < q^*$ then $f_\infty \neq 0$, as the mean field theory predicts. q^* is increasing both in p and in d, as it can be easily expected. q^* is again, as predicted by mean field theory, *not linear* in p, and so there's no "epidemic threshold" *depending simply on the ratio p/q*. In Fig. 2 we see some plots of $q^*(p, d)$ for selected values of d.

The empirical results are qualitatively similar to the predictions of mean field theory, but there are some quantitative discrepancies which are stronger for small densities of infected agents. We believe that the discrepancies are mostly due to the fact that, ultimately, the mean field model is an ergodic Markov chain while the real model, which we simulate, is not actually ergodic as there is a state (no infected agents at all) which is attracting. Simply said, in mean field theory, where we consider only one agent, it can always get infected, while in the real model when there are no longer any infected agents the infections has no chance to reignite itself. Also, when in the real model the density of infected agents is small enough the chance to interact with one of the few remaining infected agents is practically negligible and unless q is extraordinarily small the infections dies out fast. Note also that in our model the probabilities of infection and disinfection p and q are actual probabilities of events

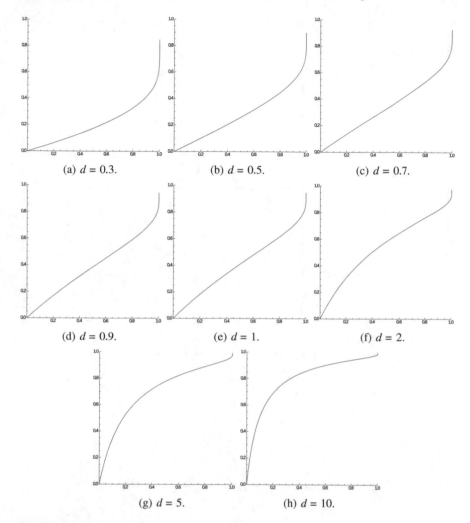

Fig. 1 Epidemic threshold given by mean field theory $q_0(p, q)$ for selected values of d. On the horizontal axis we have p and on the vertical axis q.

happening upon intersection of the trajectories of the agents, not the infection and disinfection frequencies (which are observable random variables and not parameters of the model).

Concluding, we proposed a model for the spread of tokens between mobile agents moving randomly on a plane, regular lattice, showing, both empirically and by an analytic calculation, the existence, for large populations, of a phase transition–i.e. a sharp threshold in the (p, q) plane above which the information diffusion stops and below which the information keeps diffusing. The main practical consequence is that, when the parameters are near the transition threshold, a very small variations of

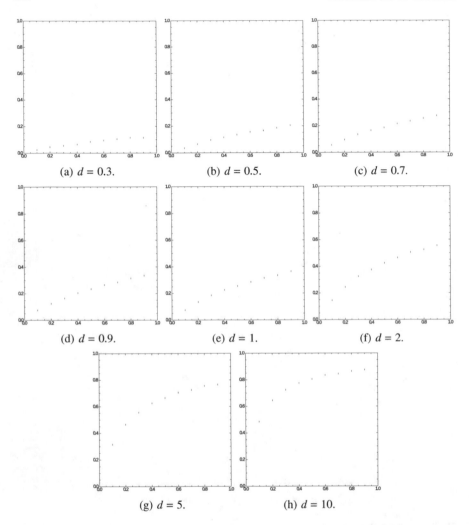

Fig. 2 Empirical epidemic threshold $q^*(p, q)$ for selected values of d. On the horizontal axis we have p and on the vertical axis q

the parameters can be quite significant for the final outcome of the epidemic spread. This is a kind of instability which is often observed in concrete systems.

Of course a possible extension of the results could be the analysis of a SIR, rather than SIS, model: we believe that the results wouldn't be very different qualitatively though.

From the purely mathematical point of view, changing the dimension of the lattice would probably instead mean a lot, since it would impact the probability of intersection of the random walks, but we fail to see a practical application for higher dimensional lattices. It would be very interesting anyway to change the topology of the environment in which the agent move: for example, the agents could be constrained to move along a graph of connections which is more general than a simple square lattice (see e.g. [16]).

This would rise the interesting problem of finding an optimal containment strategy (or even just a better one) by modulating the probabilities of infection and disinfection depending on the topological properties of the graph.

References

1. Beer, T., & Enting, I. G. (1990). Fire spread and percolation modelling. *Mathematical and Computer Modelling, 13*(11), 77–96.
2. Doerr, B., Fouz, M., & Friedrich, T. (2012). Why rumors spread so quickly in social networks. *Communications of the ACM, 55*(6), 70–75.
3. Vosoughi, S., Roy, D., & Aral, S. (2018). The spread of true and false news online. *Science, 359*(6380), 1146–1151.
4. Wen, S., Jiang, J., Liu, B., Xiang, Y., & Zhou, W. (2017). Using epidemic betweenness to measure the influence of users in complex networks. *Journal of Network and Computer Applications, 78*, 288–299.
5. Xu, Q., Su, Z., Zhang, K., Ren, P., & Shen, X. S. (2015). Epidemic information dissemination in mobile social networks with opportunistic links. *IEEE Transactions on Emerging Topics in Computing, 3*(3), 399–409.
6. Symantec. *SymbOS.Commwarrior.I.* https://www.symantec.com/security-center/writeup/2006-052510-4833-99. Retrieved May 15, 2018.
7. Za, S., Spagnoletti, P., Winter, R., & Mettler, T. (2018). Exploring foundations for using simulationsin IS research. *Communications of the Association for Information Systems, 42*, 10. https://doi.org/10.17705/1CAIS.04210. Available at http://aisel.aisnet.org/cais/vol42/iss1/10.
8. Sokal, A. (1996). *Monte Carlo methods in statistical mechanics: Foundations and new algorithms.* Lectures at the Cargèse Summer School on "Functional Integration: Basics and Applications", Sept 1996.
9. Bettstetter, C., & Wagner, C. (2002). *The spatial node distribution of the random waypoint mobility model.* Mobile Ad-Hoc Netzwerke, 1. deutscher Workshop über Mobile Ad-Hoc Netzwerke WMAN 2002.
10. Vahdat, A., & Becker, D. (2000). *Epidemic routing for partially connected Ad Hoc networks.* Duke University.
11. Jaffry, S. W., & Treur, J. (2008). Agent-based and population-based simulation: A comparative case study for epidemics. In *Proceedings of the 22th European Conference on Modelling and Simulation, ECMS'08.* European Council on Modeling and Simulation.
12. Valler, N. C., Prakash, B., Aditya, B., Tong, H., Faloutsos, M., & Faloutsos, C. (2011). Epidemic spread in mobile Ad Hoc networks: Determining the tipping point. In *NETWORKING'11 Proceedings of the 10th International IFIP TC 6 Conference on Networking - Volume Part I.*
13. Fofana, A., & Hurford A. (2017). Mechanistic movement models to understand epidemic spread. *Philosophical Transactions of the Royal Society B: Biological Sciences, 372.* https://doi.org/10.1098/rstb.2016.0086.
14. Thompson, B., & Morris-King, J. (2017). An agent-based modeling framework for cybersecurity in mobile tactical networks. *The Journal of Defense Modeling and Simulation: Applications, Methodology, Technology, 15*(2), 205–218.
15. http://www.math.nyu.edu/faculty/goodman/software/software.html.
16. Barrat, A., Barthelemy, M., & Vespignani, A. (2008). *Dynamical processes on complex networks* (Vol. 1). Cambridge University Press.

Part IV
Organizing in Digital Ecosystems

Understanding the Use of Smart Working in Public Administration: The Experience of the Presidency of the Council of Ministers

Maurizio Decastri, Francesca Gagliarducci, Pietro Previtali
and Danila Scarozza

Abstract While there is no consensus in terms of what "smart government" includes and how it is related to emergent technologies and innovation in the public sector, in this paper smart working (SW) is regarded as one of the most important initiatives for building smart government. In the Italian public sector—according to the Law n. 81/2017—SW has emerged as a "new" way to define what is considered as an innovative approach to work organisation and human resource management. Analysing the Presidency of the Council of Ministers case study the paper aims to investigate to answer to the following questions: (i) to what extent is the interface between organisational model for working and new technology contextually bound? (ii) what are the combination of the different elements affecting the configuration of SW? (iii) what are the outcomes of SW likely to be for smar-workers, organisations and society?

Keywords Smart working · Public administration · ICT · Organizational improvement · Work-life balance

1 Introduction

Smartness has been emerging worldwide as a keyword of government reform strategies. While there are many different perspectives on smart government, according to Gil-Garcia et al. [1] smart government can be used to characterize activities that cre-

M. Decastri
University of Rome "Tor Vergata", 00133 Rome, Italy

F. Gagliarducci
Presidency of the Council of Ministers, 00187 Rome, Italy

P. Previtali
University of Pavia, 27100 Pavia, Italy

D. Scarozza (✉)
University of Pavia, Via San Felice 5, 27100 Pavia, Italy
e-mail: danila.scarozza@unipv.it; danila.scarozza@uniroma2.it

© Springer Nature Switzerland AG 2020
A. Lazazzara et al. (eds.), *Exploring Digital Ecosystems*,
Lecture Notes in Information Systems and Organisation 33,
https://doi.org/10.1007/978-3-030-23665-6_25

atively invest in emergent technologies coupled with innovative strategies to achieve more agile and resilient government structures and governance infrastructures. However, there is no consensus in terms of what this term includes and how it is related to emergent technologies and innovation in the public sector. On the one hand, new and emergent technologies, over the last three decades, have continuously disrupted the administrative landscape of bureaucracies and the public sector around the world. Governments at different levels, and across different branches, are adopting tools and applications to reach out, to deliver, to function, and to organize themselves in ways that allow them to cope with rapid changes. The emergent technologies available offer both new possibilities to explore and new challenges to overcome, and require attention to evolving relationships, different processes, and changing structures, in order to attain a more efficient and smarter government [2]. As technology offers additional tools and options, more is expected and required from government not only in what it delivers but how and when [3]. On the other hand, it is generally accepted that today also governments operate in challenging and rapidly changing environments. The concept of innovation in the public sector has shifted from a value-based concept into a concrete goal with specific targets, including innovation as a specific performance objective for government administrators [4]. This shift requires that innovation be tied to specific goals and objectives within the organization and that the organizational structure supports the changes. Garicano and Heaton [5] found that while IT investments were not strongly associated with improvements in relevant productivity measures when examined in isolation, when combined with complimentary organizational changes IT investments were linked to increased productivity.

Starting from these premises and sharing the assumption that smart government is a central part of the government reform strategies, in this paper we assume SW as one of the most important initiatives for building smart government. SW, in fact, refers to an alternative means of organizing work deploying a creative mix of emerging technologies and innovation also in public sector organizations [1]. Therefore, SW can be seen as an internal working process or working environment of smart government, which contributes to achieve a more efficient government and helps government employees enjoy higher quality of life. Previous studies show that applying emerging technologies to existing administrative processes, even to a relatively small degree, can have a substantial impact [6]. As Morgan [7] notes, there are many fascinating things happening in the world of technology that are impacting on work. Today, successful organisations are increasingly characterized by the ability to abandon now inappropriate working configurations [8] to support new organisational principles, new methods and tools through which work practices are accomplished [9]. The use of ICT provides an opportunity to be innovative in when we work, where we work and the way we work [10]. Specifically, there has been a noticeable diffusion among organisations of innovative ways of working and growing opportunities for their employees to perform work activities remotely, let them generally free to choose where (places) and when (time) carry out the assigned activities (spatial-temporal flexibility). This resulted in an increasing interest showed by both academics and practitioners towards different typologies of remote work arrangements, including telework, home-based telework, mobile work, virtual teams and, more recently, smart work.

SW has the potential to offer a wide range of individuals an alternative to traditional work arrangements. SW succeeds in modifying traditional work conditions and their natural environment, searching different and (till now) not totally and uniquely defined solutions, essentially grounded on a greater discretion in work activities and on a larger responsibility towards results workers are requested to provide. These two elements together are indeed believed to favour better performances by workers [11, 12]. This connection explains the increasing interest for SW, favoring the promotion of projects in the field [13–15]. Furthermore, over the last few years managers have started to acknowledge the potential advantages offered to both employees and organisations by SW. Howcroft and Taylor [16] point out that society is seeing a new wave of revolutionary technology that provides the platform for significant change in the way people work. These changes are creating renewed interest in how work is conceptualized—what we describe as the 'smart-side' of technology.

Also in Italy—especially after the adoption of the Law n. 81/2017—Smart Working (SW) has emerged as a "new" way to define what is considered as an innovative approach to work organisation and human resource management. The phenomenon is on the up in Italy's small and medium-sized enterprises, although informal arrangements still tend to prevail: 22% of such enterprises have launched smart working projects, but only 7% have adopted regulated arrangements. But the news is that the phenomenon is taking hold in Public Administration. Smart working has trickled into the administrative offices of the Council of Ministers, into the Ministry of the Economy, and into major Italian city councils.

In this frame this paper proposes a conceptual models to better define and investigate SW practices. SW makes it possible the best use of both innovative technologies and traditional infrastructures; consequently, the definition of an integrated system of SW asks for the joint and coherent re-design of all the technological and organizational-managerial tools ("SW elements") and a lot of thought about important concepts such as "context" and "results". Furthermore, analysing the Presidency of the Council of Ministers case study the paper aims to investigate the nature and the dynamics of SW in order: (a) to offer a contribution to the debate on the workplaces' changes in response to increasingly sophisticated technology; (b) to understand the effects of SW in terms of both work-life balance, individual performance and external benefits.

2 Conceptualizing Smart Working: An Organizational Perspective

Technologies have changed (through enabling and/or constraining) HRM practices by introducing for example, e-recruitment, e-training, e-competence management or e-work [17]. These technologies have brought a new vocabulary to the HRM dis-

Fig. 1 The conceptual
framework

course as the conventional terminology is supplemented by new terms like electronic
HRM (e-HRM), HRM data mining, HRM cloud computing, application of HRM (for
mobile technologies) and HRM big data [18]. These technologies have altered the
HRM organisational communications [19], and enabled new means of employer
branding [20]. In particular, changes in HRM and technologies have modified the
geographical boundaries of HRM practices, distances in and between organisations
have become shortened. Due to diverse technological advancements, organisations
can offer their employees new ways of working by eliminating physical and time barriers and relying on such organisational forms as HRM shared services, virtual teams
or SW. In their turn, technology-enabled new organisational forms embrace new
stakeholders in HRM processes. Applying smart working—for example—workers,
first line supervisors, middle and top managers get directly involved in co-creation
of HRM.

Starting from these premises and focusing on SW in public sector, this paper was
inspired by following questions (Fig. 1): (i) to what extent is the interface between
organisational model for working and new technology contextually bound? (ii) what
are the combination of the different elements affecting the configuration of SW?
(iii) what are the outcomes of SW likely to be for smar-workers, organisations and
society?

2.1   The Context (of Public Organizations)

An important element for an effective SW implementation (not external to it, but
part of the SW itself) is the context within which SW is adopetd. SW could be
seen as a system consisting of people, technology, organisations, and management
practices related to human resource management [21]. According to the principle of
equifinality [22] the same final state may be reached from different initial conditions
and HRM antecedents, in different ways, through different mechanisms. In order to
better understand the relevance of SW and its functioning within public organisations,
the context can be defined as the HRM context as the relevant external and internal
conditions and elements [18]. The external elements include societal values, the laws,
the regulation and the labour market and the territorial level conditions within which
the public organisation has to work. There will be elements that are more directly
under the organisation's control but that are limited by previous managerial decisions

and history, including the workforce characteristics. There will also be elements that are directly related to the administrative activities but are outside the direct remit of HRM, such as the management philosophy and the territorial features.

Focusing on SW, probably location has a major effect on how SW is understood and implemented, what practices have legitimacy and what the effects of those practices are likely to be [23]. Countries have different SW regulations and practices because they are in different situations, have different cultures and different institutions. Specifically, government and regulations play an important role for changing HRM practices and—consequently—SW [24]. In particular, regulations for the Italian context was one of the most important elements. Starting from the Nineties, the telework was introduced in public administration as a form of distance work by Decree n. 70/1999 providing information on both the features and the criteria in order to realize and use the teleworking stations. In 2012 another step was moved in the perspective of public organizations' modernization: the enactment of the decree n. 221/2012 introduced the so called "Telelavoro by default" inspired by what was done by the Obama government in the USA. Following this decree public administrations were required to implement a plan for the telework adoption in which they had to specify "the modalities of realization and the possible activities for which the use of the telework was not possible". Despite these legislative interventions, Italy has not been able to make the best use of telework, which has been "trapped" by rigid rules. It has therefore become necessary to introduce new instruments of flexibility. In this direction, the Law for the Reform of the Public Administration (Madia Reform, law n. 124/2015) on the one hand, provided suggestions for the strengthening of the telework adoption; on the other hand, promoted the adoption of SW. In addition, the law stated that in 2018 (3 years later the enactment of the law) flexible work tools should be used at least by the 10% of public employees. The last step in the regulatory framework in Italy is represented by the adoption of the Law n. 81/2017, which marks the shift from a telework to a SW approach. The law defined SW as "a way to regulate the workers-organisation relationship, according to an agreement between the parties, also recurring to forms of organisation by stages, cycles and goals, without a defined timetable or place constraints working and the opportunity to use any technological tools to perform activities". Moreover, the Law (art. 18) stated that the main purpose of this new way to work is "both to increase competitiveness and to facilitate the balance of working and living times". The ratio of the Italian legislation is, on the one hand, to promote an improvement of the organisations' productivity and—on the other hand—to guarantee a better work life balance to workers involved in the SW adoption [25]. Creating new rules with lightweight characteristics and obligations (for the worker and the employer), the SW law aims to stimulate a deep cultural change in the concept of work: the shift from "stamping the time-card" to work for goals, where the worker have large freedom to self-organize job as long as they meet the goals set at the due dates. The innovative part of the law is to configure SW as an organizational tool and not as a contractual type, with the aim of making it workable by all employees who carry out tasks that are compatible with SW.

Also globalisation will apply to SW too, since universal 'good practice' will inevitably spread around the world [26], but there is little evidence that countries are becoming more alike in the way they conceive of and manage SW [27]. Some current problems characterizing Italian public administrations could impact the adoption of SW. One of the main issues of the Italian PA is the huge presence of elderly people working. Indeed, in 2015 less than 3 employees on 100 workers were younger than 30 years old and the average age was of 50.4 years [28]. One of the most important direct consequences is, for example, the closure towards innovation. Another critical aspect related to the Italian PA is the presence of corruption and the lack of transparency. In spite of the innovations introduced by the Madia Reform, such as the Freedom of Information Act (FOIA), the position covered by Italy in the international ranking of corruption is very disappointing. The causes of this positioning are that the FOIA needs time to be implemented properly and that the level of digitalization of Italian PA is still insufficient. Another problem is represented by the insufficient propensity to measure and evaluate the employees on their performances and by the inadequate planning: these are the bases of a culture that rewards the presence and not the actual effort destroying talents and productivity. Finally, due to the inadequate capability of Italian public administration to attract and retain valuable and highly qualified employees, it is more important than ever to understand what could attract people to the public service [29].

There may be debate about the balance between cultural differences and institutional differences [30], but together or independently culture and institutions will impact the SW/technology interface too.

2.2   The Smart-Working Elements

The development and diffusion of ICT, can support organisations in developing a SW system [31]. Previous literature has analysed how ICT has made work more portable and pervasive [32], there is not yet a comprehensive understanding the elements on which organisations should focus in case they want to adopt a SW organisational model.

According to the analysis developed by Mann [33], the three elements that can constitute a SW model are:

1. the ICT element: it is referred to the usage of ICT-based solutions. ICT solutions allow workers to share more easily files, information, data and ideas [34]. In such a way, all employees can interact in real time in a flexible and effective way by contributing to a SW environment (software collaboration);
2. the HR element: this includes the innovations in the HR practices and in the organisational model (HR element). Changes in the HR practices can be introduced when a new organisational model is chosen, as SW is. Specifically, change management actions for managing the organisational models chosen can be applied by the organisations [35], such as training programmes, new communication plans, projects of cultural change, processes reorganisation or a re-desing of job role profiles;

Table 1 Smart working elements

Elements	Dimension	References
ICT	Extent to which employees telework	Martínez-Sánchez et al. [73]
	Use of ICT personal devices and/or external ICT services	
HR	Extent to which employees can manage in a flexible way their working hours	Coenen and Kok [74]
	Change management actions implemented in the organisation and new HRM practices/tools developed	
Layout	Adoption of initiatives of redesigning of the physical workspace for creating environments more flexible and oriented to collaboration	Elsbach and Pratt [75]

3. the layout element: it is related to the reconfiguration of the workplace and of the office layout. According to some study, the strategy focused on the spatial reconfiguration of the office have an important role for the effectiveness of a SW system. The attention to the layout can increase individual and team productivity and can allow to workers to better their work-life balance. Therefore, particular office reconfigurations may lead to innovative ways of collaborating with others and thus simplifying the development of a SW model (Table 1).

2.3 Individual, Organisational and Societal Outcomes

SW has various impacts and consequences at different level: individual, organisational and societal. An understanding of these will help identify the values and motives that may support the promotion of this way of working.

At the individual level a potential benefit of SW is represented by the opportunity for individual workers to establish an arrangement that is very personal and conducive to a superior quality of domestic life. SW can offer opportunities for people to improve their worklife balance more so than under traditional work conditions [36]. As a result, smart workers are often more motivated and enjoy better job satisfaction than conventional workers [37–39]. The positive perception of an improved work/life balance is recognized as one of the most important outcome of SW adoption. Other studies, suggested that smart workers are more committed since they worked longer hours than traditional employees, often without additional payment or remuneration for these extra hours [40–44]. One of the more sufficient potential benefits is increasing worker productivity that accrues from the practice of SW [45]. Organisations and businesses that have embraced SW have been able to increase output with the same number of staff, or reduce headcount and still provide the same level of service to their clients and customers.

Looking at the organisational level, SW must not be considered in isolation but rather placed in the overall context of existing and continuous business reorganisation and change management environments. SW has the potential to become an integral, rather than an optional, way of working. Studies have shown SW can increase organisational productivity [46]. SW can reduce absenteeism and increases resilience, especially with decreased stress and anxiety levels and more control over working times and location [47, 48]. Another organisational impact of SW is the improvement it offers for services to citizens in a variety of ways. It can allow higher personalised responses to citizen demands without the need for a conventional base or office. This flexibility can fit into the ethos of how a PA operates and can lead to co-operative work across international boundaries and different time zones. SW implies also a rethiking of the control and supervision issues [46, 49]: the organisations need to difficult to trust unsupervised workers in a different manner. Moreover, the management of individual differences, and indeed similarities, between women and men and how they perceive their professional and domestic roles is an important issue when considering the adoption or development of SW. However, White et al. [50] maintained gender differences associated with frequency of working from home is insignificant, indicating a slightly lower proportion of females working from home at least once a week.

Finally, societal outcomes can be regarded also as the long-term outcomes [21]. PA need to create public value: since public organisations derive their legitimacy from society, HRM decisions and practices will have long-term benefits for the society.

In literature, there was a lack of interest in and evidence about the effects of SW adoption both on the community within which the organisation operates and— more in general—on the society. Nevertheless, with the more recent development of notions such as sustainable HRM [51, 52] and corporate social responsibility [53] this is beginning to change. From a societal point of view, in fact, the magnitude of the impact of SW on environment, mobility and socioeconomic aspects is therefore relevant in order to determine whether a further encouragement of SW is useful and sustainable for the society as a whole [54]. SW can be seen a way of offering environmental protection benefits by reducing, or eliminating, the commute to work leading to less fuel consumption and less CO_2 emissions, fewer traffic congestion problems and, savings in energy use in urban office spaces and buildings [55, 56]. Although these benefits are, to a certain extent, achievable with the correct understanding and strategies, the impact of SW on society continues to remain poorly understood [57]. SW also has the potential to bring about a more equitable distribution of economic activity throughout geographical areas and help redress the aggregation of economic activity in the main urban centres [58]. In addition, the spread of SW can assist in improving the economic and employment opportunities of underdeveloped areas [59].

3 Method

Since only limited empirical research on how PA deal with the adoption of SW [60] has been found an explorative approach has been chosen. Particularly, the research being reported in this paper involved the case study of Presidency of the Council of the Ministers (PCM) in the adoption of SW since 2017. Other scholars used the case study approach to examine SW [61]. In this study, a single case is used, which is an appropriate way of establishing the field at the early stages of an emerging topic [62]. Moreover, the single case study approach is normally preferred when an inductive approach can be adopted, using theory to explain empirical observations and also to inform refinements and extension of the theory [63–65].

The case study presented in this paper aims to explore and to understand the configuration of SW and its outcomes at the individual, organisational and societal level.

According to our exploratory approach, we selected PCM as an exemplar case study [65], with unique circumstances. In particular, in PCM, the group project on SW begun to define the call and the way to implement SW prior to the regulatory intervention by Italian legislation. In this setting, we analyzed five different building blocks in order to understand both why and how SW has been adopted and what the outcomes obtained by a SW organisational model: (a) context; (b) ICT element; (c) layout element; (d) HR element; (e) SW outcomes.

The information gathered during this research relates to the pilot phase, which began in December 2017 and it is still ongoing. The pilot phase was due to finish in April but PCM decide to extend the deadline to the end of September. From a methodological point of view, data and information collection period is particularly significant for our analysis, since it allows us to better define the nature and the relevance of the collected information. The longitudinal approach used in the observation of the project development led to the analysis of context, groups, and individuals dynamics, concerning the adoption of SW. To improve validity and reliability [65], of our finding and conclusions, we collected data from different sources. In relation to the four conceptual dimensions of analysis (ICT element, layout element, HR element and outcomes), a triangulation was carried out between documental information and interviews. The documents helped understanding the relevance given to the different phases and practices, the modes of interaction between actors and the technologies adopted for SW. Data have been collected by the "organisation co-author" also through interviews and continuous information flows. All information gathered provided also evidence on both the process of internal communication and the role of people involved in trialing and adopting SW. The interviews were conducted with some of the key organisational actors involved in the SW adoption process. The interviews were conducted to ensure that the case study is "bounded" [65] and to guarantee that the conclusions of this study are based upon specific observations [66]. Thanks to a collaborative writing and analysis process between academics and organisation coauthor, the case study description has improved and the construct validity has increased [65].

4   The Case Study of the Presidency of the Council of Ministers: Findings and Discussion

The Presidency of the Council of Ministers (PCM) is the administrative structure which supports the Prime Minister of Italy. It is thus the Italian equivalent of the Prime Minister's Office. It contains those departments which carry out duties invested in the office of the Prime Minister. Duties invested in the Italian executive government generally are not administered by the Presidency, but by the individual ministries. The creation of the Presidency of the Council of Ministers is comparatively recent: only in 1961 PCM began to take shape, although not in an organic manner, since it lacked a law which regulated its whole operation. In 1988, a new law (l. 400/1988) was approved, which regulated the Presidency. Finally, in 1999, the re-organisation of the PCM was carried out with Decree law no. 303 of 30 July 1999, that is a part of the Bassanini reforms.

The structure of the PCM consists in five different offices' type: (i) offices which work with the Prime Minister directly; (ii) general departments and offices which the Prime Minister employs for directing and co-ordinating specific political and institutional areas; (iii) general offices which support the Prime Minister in general co-ordination and general political direction; (iv) technical unities; (v) other committees and commissions.

In this setting, at the end of 2017, PCM launched a trial to prepare the context for the development of a new way of working: the project was presented and its objectives and phases shared. Only in January 2018 the pilot started and the SW model became a reality in the organization. During the pilot phase only four Department are involved in the SW project: Department of Public Function, Department for Equal Opportunities, Department for Family Policy, Department for Human Resources.

The project conducted by PCM represent not only one of the first SW initiative at the central level of Italian PA, but its experience and the SW model developed should become a guide for all the other Italian administrations.

4.1   The Context for the Adoption of SW in PCM

As stated before the context within the SW is adopted is one of the preliminary conditions to guarantee the effectiveness of the new working model. Looking at the internal context at the end of the 2017 (september) PCM launched a pilot phase in order to define a roadmap and to create the "right internal context" for the adoption of SW itself. Specifically, the pilot phase started with a public call aimed to collect (voluntary) applications by workers for the SW project.

The project was realized following—as conceptual and practical framework—the Directive published by the Council President and referred to the actuation of article 14 of the Law of the 7th august 2015, known as PA Reform of the Minister Madia. Firstly, the Directive recalls the point 48 of the European Parliament Resolution of the 13th september 2016 affirming that "the Parliament supports SW, a working approach based on combination of flexibility, autonomy and collaboration, which does not require the physical presence of the worker in the office and let him manage the working time, underlining its potentiality for a better work-life balance; [...]; the Parliament recommends to not assign additional obligations to employees, but simply focus on workers' welfare, pointing out the need of a "result-based" management to avoid abuse and promoting the utilization of digital technologies". About workers' eligibility, the Directive states that all the categories are suitable for SW initiatives. Moreover, each PA has the opportunity to develop and to implement a SW model according to its features and needs.

The qualitative objective defined in the Directive is to favour the adoption of SW and/or any other flexible initiatives/tools/instruments. The quantitative one is to ensure—by the 2018—the participation to SW projects at least to the 10% of workers in each public organization.

According to the general path designed by the Directive, PCM decided to develop a SW model following four different phases:

- *phase 1*: create an internal work group including administrative members to support the start of experimentation and monitoring. This group must analyse the macrostructure of the organization, map activities, processes, personnel and workers' needs (familiar or private);
- *phase 2*: define the main characteristics of the SW project through the draft of a plan (duration, days of remote working, technological devices, recruitment criteria, etc.). Therefore, define the activities that cannot be worked remotely, identify yearly targets to reach the final objective of 10% and discuss the plan with trade unions. In this phase, it should be taken in consideration the possibility of creating co-working areas;
- *phase 3*: select one (or more) department(s) for the SW pilot phase starting (identifying personnel, duration and starting date);
- *phase 4*: provide a monitoring system for both performance and productivity evaluation, identifying some relevant indicators based on features and functions of the selected department.

The process adopted in PCM reflects the model suggested by the Directive, identifying in detail all the elements involved and the objectives to be reached. Although the difficulties of generating a standard cycle to implement SW, the paradigm proposed by PCM aims to become a best practice for other Italian public organizations.

PCM workers involved in this experiment can choose to work from home or from various indoor/outdoor locations.

Figure 2 summarizes all the managerial and organizational elements characterizing the context in which the process of change have to be realized. Particularly, the first change concerns the shift from a focus on work process to a focus on results: following both the managerialization movement (called as New Public Management and started in 90s) and adopting a SW approach, the standardization of the processes, the definition of procedures are replaced by a bigger attention to results obtained by each process.

Fig. 2 The context of change

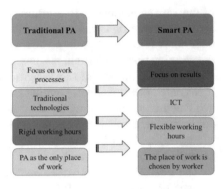

Table 2 Smartworkers involved in the project

Departments	Number	(%)
Public function	14	24.6
Equal opportunity	8	14
Family policy	3	5.3
Personnel	32	56.1

Table 3 Category of people involved in the SW project

Category	Number	(%)
Managers	8	14
Category A	38	66.7
Category B	11	19.3

4.2 The Smart Working Elements in PCM

From January 2018 the first pilot phase of SW started. Table 2 shows the percentage of workers who decided to take part to the SW project in the Departments involved in the project. The total amount of people (57 workers) involved in the SW project represent the 10% of all the human resources employed in these Departments.

However, at the beginning of the SW project, more than 57 workers applied to take part to the initiative but the top management—who is responsible for ensuring the normal functioning of the Department—preliminary evaluated each request and selected only those applications that did not compromise the activities and the achievement of the assigned objectives. The final selection of the applications was made by a Commission created specifically for the SW project.

In order to complete the analysis related to the extent to which employees adopt SW a focus can been made on the category level. Similarly, Table 3 shows the number and the percentage of both managers and workers contractualized as category A/B who decided to take part to the SW project along the experimentation period. The adoption trend of SW by managers in PCM seems to be very low.

Another important data is related to the level of education: more than 70% of the smart-workers have completed a bachelor or higher degree, the 20% a high school diploma and the 10% completed a grade school.

Considering the absence of a supportive and mature digital infrastructure, PCM invested in the ICT element developing a digital environment able to complete the HR strategy of letting people work whenever and wherever they wanted. Thus, in addition to some investments in unified communication and collaboration tools, a mobile workspace (constituted by a laptop, a smartphone and an internet connection) has been made available to all employees. In PCM worker indicated if he/she intend to use personal tools (laptop, smartphone, etc.) configured by the administration or tools directly provided by the administration. In both the cases PCM provided to every smart-worker an informative note indicating general and specific risks related to the particular mode of execution of the activities, providing useful indications for the worker to make a conscious choice of the place where carry out the work activity.

Moreover, a set of cloud-based solutions has been developed in order to improve the performance and to ensure to the smart-workers the access to the shared documents. In this way, the working place is highly simplified, and human resource can focus on one task at a time and boost both their efficiency and effectiveness. Moreover, the PCM ensured the access to several public platforms necessary to complete some activity (e.g. SIGOCE is the platform used by PA to complete payments). In addition, using the smartphone workers are able to connect to the intranet and to use the mail as well as if in the office. In order to guarantee an effective interaction with their offices and a good performance, non-managerial workers must ensure, during the SW day, the contactability for at least 3 h (or for at least 1.5 h in the case of half a day), according to the time slots identified in the individual project.

The analysis of the HR element revealed that some new features have been introduced. Before to start with the pilot phase, in fact, several requirements are identified: in order to take part to the SW pilot project, each workers have to respect the following requirements:

- the activities assigned to the employee can be relocated without the necessary physical presence in the workplace;
- the technological equipment used by the employee must be suitable for realize the work outside the workplace;
- the employee must enjoy operational autonomy and must be able to organize the execution of work outside the workplace respecting the assigned objectives;
- the results of the activities assigned to the employee must be able to be monitored and assessed;
- the activities assigned to the employee are not among those, for which it is not possible the SW, due to the specific nature and methods of carrying out the tasks.

In addition, each worker have to present its application for taking part to the SW project consisting in two documents: the individual project and the schedule of activities (see Table 4 for their contents). Both the documents must be shared between the worker and his hierarchical superior in order to understand the real opportunity to present the application. The Director of each Department approves the contents and

Table 4 The documents for the SW application in PCM

Individual project	Schedule of activities
Identification information of the employee	Duration of the project
Identification information of the office/service he/she belongs to	Aims of the project
Methods of implementation	Expected results
Timing of SW mode	Quantitative and/or qualitative indicators
Contactability hours	Target
Times for monitoring	Procedures for monitoring, verifying and evaluating the activity carried out

methods of implementation, ensuring the alignment with the organizational needs of the structure.

Aiming to analyse these documents, to define the selection criteria, to select the applications and to monitor the activities carried out adopting SW, other two "instruments" are introduced at the organizational level: the technical group and the monitoring group.

The first group consists of managers only and performs more operational activities; the second group consists of managers and labour unions, its main tasks consist in the supervision of the project and in the monitoring of the smartworkers. The adoption of SW, in fact, is subject to the assessment for both the organizational and individual performance evaluation. PCM progressively adjusts its internal monitoring and control systems, identifying suitable indicators in order to evaluate the efficiency, effectiveness and economy of the activities carried out using SW. However, SW does not vary the nature of the work agreement, the role of the employee in the administration and its workplace.

Another important innovation at the organizational level is represented by the mapping of the activities carried out by each Department in order to identify which activities had to be excluded. In general, almost all activities were included except for those that: (i) require the physical presence (ii) require a constant and continuous relationship with the management. Some examples of excluded activities are: secretariats, protocol and archive, warehouse management, library management, etc.

In addition, on HR element PCM realized several training initiatives for supporting the change management process started trough the adoption of a SW model. The general aim was to develop new compentencies and capabilities necessary to efficiently and effectively accomplishing the new tasks and activities connected to the new working model. Specifically, in terms of contents - two different training sessions are organized. The first one is focused on safety at work; the second session is focused on the use of technological tools.

Finally—at the moment—no significant interventions are started on layout element.

4.3   Individual, Organisational and Societal Outcomes for PCM

The pilot phase is still ongoing in PCM for this reason it is difficult to state the real outcomes of the SW project. However, it is possible to discuss about the expectations of the PCM working group on SW and to discuss some preliminary outcomes from personal, business and society perspectives.

At the *individual level*, perceived job flexibility, given a reasonable workweek, enables more employees to have work-family balance (personal and family benefit) and also enables employees to work longer hours before impacting work-family balance. Also in PCM perceived job flexibility should be significantly and positively related to work-family balance. Given a workweek of reasonable length, employees who perceive flexibility in the timing and location of work have less difficulty with work-family balance. In addition, employees with perceived flexibility in the timing and location of work can work longer hours before work-family balance becomes difficult. In particular, one possible benefit of SW has to do with a reduction in the stress associated with the daily commute. Flexplace also provides more options for where an employee might choose to live. Smartworkers in PCM, in fact, may choose to work from home or from other indoor/outdoor locations. In addition, the work in PCM is strongly influenced by the political moment. In a rigid work environment, during a political crisis, for example, could be extremely difficult simultaneously to meet the demands of work and family life because the work has to be done physically from the work location. By contrast, in a flexible work environment, an employee can work the same long number of hours, but intersperse several hours of quality family time each day. For this last reasons remains unclear the choice to use SW by PCM managers. Finally, our analysis reveals that, the vast majority of smartworkers (38%) are between 50 and 59, another group of smartworkers (35%) are between 40 and 49, while young people are almost absent, a phenomenon which can easily be explained by the high number of employees seeking SW for medical pathologies, of course more frequent as the age increases.

At the *organisational level* the technology and, more in general, the role of the SW is one of the element supporting the digital transformation in PCM and in the public sector organizations. Since PCM can be classified as a large organization, it may have greater resources to support the technology required for flexplace. Moreover, with the SW adoption people in PCM are more aware of the use of digital technologies and the SW itself has became an opportunity in terms of organisational learning. Furthermore, in PCM the SW adoption is requiring a different stratification processes and procedures in order to maintain the alignment among objectives, behaviours and tools. Another implication is related to the culture and the philosophy in PCM. The organization that adopts SW also should move away from a "process-oriented" culture to a "results-oriented" culture, and performance evaluation systems must adapt to include more specifically measured objectives. Additionally, implementing SW should be possible to change the object of the evaluation moving from the physical presence to the obtained results presence. This new culture could discourage

Fig. 3 SW and gender
differences in PCM

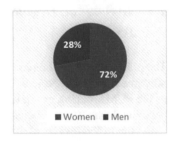

misbehaviours that are common in the public institutions. By betting on trust and giving more responsibility to workers, it would be possible to distinguish valuable and willing people from lazybones and give to everyone the rewards that deserves. Adopting a leaders' supportive behaviour based on trust has also a direct effect on feelings and emotions of employees and it is a way to create a work environment that enables employees to achieve organizational goals in public institutions [67].

The last, but not least, important aspect at the organisational level refers to the management of individual differences within PCM, especially the gender differences. As suggested from some scholars [68, 69], the analysis of the case study revealed that gender differences (Fig. 3) associated with adoption of SW could be significant, indicating a lower proportion of men adopting SW. In PCM, in fact, the 71.9% are women (41 workers) and only the 28.1% are men (16 workers).

Finally, outcomes at the societal level are not yet evaluated because of the pilot phase of the project is still ongoing. However, it is possible to discuss about the expectations of PCM on this level. Of course, looking at the environmental consequences and sustainability of SW, the experience conducted in PCM and its further extension to other Departments should moderate private car use reducing environmental and socio-economical impacts of mobility on society. Congestion, air pollution, noise, the increase in time loss due to traffic and externalities linked to up-and downstream processes are the most well known transport related externalities. Roma results, in fact, the city where the number of smarwokers is higher than in other cities. More in general, trough the adoption of SW, PCM could provide a significant externalities saving.

Furthermore, the introduction of SW in the public sector would imply an additional investment on the digitalization of processes and practices. It has been proven by several researches that the creation of an e-government reduces corruption and enhances transparency [70–72].

The adoption of SW would produce positive economic effects also on the national budget. The private companies that adopted these methodologies demonstrated how the application of SW enabled them to save money and to improve productivity. The savings deriving from only the reduction of the required spaces could be between 1 and 3 billion of Euro. Adopting SW, it is possible to increase efficiency without reducing the number of workers, to improve productivity and, consequently, the quality of the services. Furthermore, extending SW to public employees is a way to avoid creating a further discrimination and to improve the relationship between politics, public opinion and social parts.

5 Conclusions and Next Steps

SW represents a journey at both organisational and national level and this journey has only just begun. Starting from the assumption that there is not a unique path for developing a SW, but a set of potential paths that have to be designed taking into account the characteristics of the organisation investing in SW, this study highlights some considerations regarding the context, the elements and the outcomes characterising a SW model. In particular, the analized case study help to understand that there are a number of pre-requisites for SW adoption and implementation in an organisation. The main reasons for which an organisation invests in SW tend to shape and being shaped by the investments accomplished in SW elements [61]. However, SW is not only a way to reduce costs: there is the need to go beyond the SW elements (ICT, layout and HR) analyzed in this paper and to focus on the core beliefs and culture of the organisation as the underpinning factor that makes an organisation 'smart'. Moreover, PCM case study suggests it is better to proceed through a gradual developmental process in order to identify the most effective solutions for creating value both for people and the organisation. The adoption of SW can be seen as a change management process. For this reason the design and the implementation of a SW model should be followed by the monitoring activities.

In conclusion, despite SW was studied in literature from using different perspectives, this paper provides an important approach to how conceptualize and operationalize SW concept in public administration. The application of this conceptual framework, in fact, is important from a practical viewpoint when introducing SW in organisation as planners and implementers will consider the readiness to adopt, the SW options available and how their impact will be assessed before the implementation occurs.

Future research could better determine the nature of strategy, organisational structure and culture patterns during the adoption of a SW model. This case study showed that PCM begin implementing SW with a small group of smartworkers and anticipate scaling their efforts; future research could identify core factors that need to be considered during institutional scaling. Examples of such issues could include physical and technical infrastructure needs and the continued use of incentives to facilitate workers adoption. Moreover, the next phases of the study would like to investigate also the perceptions and the opinion about the SW project in PCM at different level (workers, managers, users, etc.).

Finally, as with many exploratory studies, several limitations should be taken into account. First, the results are derived from a single organisation operating in the public sector. It is thus not possible to predict the extent to which the results can be found in other public organizations adopting a SW model in Italy. No attempt are be made, in this research phase, to generalize the obtained results to the wider Italian public sector. On this point, a next step of the research is to increase the number of case in order to compare different approaches for adopting SW.

References

1. Gil-Garcia, J. C. R., Helbig, N., & Adegboyega, O. (2014). Being smart: Emerging technologies and innovation in the public sector. *Government Information Quarterly, 31,* 11–18.
2. Gil-Garcia, J. R. (2012). Towards a smart state? Inter-agency collaboration, information integration, and beyond. *Information Polity, 17,* 269–280.
3. Reddick, C. G. (2009). The adoption of centralized customer service systems: A survey of local governments. *Government Information Quarterly, 26,* 219–226.
4. Georges, G., Glynn-Burke, T., & McGrat, A. (2013). Improving the local landscape for innovation: Mechanics, partners, and clusters. Ash Center for Democratic Governance and Innovation, Harvard Kennedy School.
5. Garicano, L., & Heaton, P. (2010). Information technology, organization, and productivity in the public sector: Evidence from police departments. *Journal of Labor Economics, 28,* 167–201.
6. Jin, G. Z., & Lee, J. (2013). *Inspection technology, detection and compliance: Evidence from Florida restaurant inspections.* National Bureau of Economic Research, w18939.
7. Morgan, J. (2014). *The future of work: Attract new talent, build better leaders, and create a competitive organization.* Hoboken, NJ: Wiley.
8. Birkinshaw, J., Hamel, G., & Mol, M. (2008). Management innovation. *Academy of Management Review, 33,* 25–845.
9. Hamel, G. (2012). *What matters now: How to win in a world of relentless change, ferocious competition, and unstoppable innovation.* San Francisco: Jossey-Bass.
10. Harvey, D. (2010). *The enigma and capital: And the crises of capitalism.* London: Profile Books.
11. Haines, V. Y., III, & Stoge, S. (2012). Performance management effectiveness: Practices or context? *The International Journal of Human Resource Management, 2,* 1158–1175.
12. Wood, S., Van Veldhoven, M., Croon, M., & De Menezes, L. M. (2012). Enriched job design, high involvement management and organizational performance: The mediating roles of job satisfaction and well-being. *Human Relations, 65,* 419.
13. Clapperton, G., & Vanhoutte, P. (2014). *The smarter working manifesto.* Oxford: Sunmakers Eldamar.
14. Iacono, G. (2013). *Smart knowledge working.* Milan: Digitpub.
15. Hartog, K. L., Solimene, A., & Tufani, G. (2015). *The smart working book.* Rome: Seedble.
16. Howcroft, D., & Taylor, P. (2014). Plus ca change, plus la meme chose?—Researching and theorising 'new' new technologies. *New Technology, Work and Employment, 29,* 1–8.
17. Stone, D. L., Deadrick, D. L., Lukaszewski, K. M., & Johnson, R. (2015). The influence of technology on the future of human resource management. *Human Resource Management Review, 25,* 216–231.
18. Bondarouk, T., & Brewster, C. (2016). Conceptualising the future of HRM and technology research. *The International Journal of Human Resource Management, 27,* 2652–2671.
19. Kiesler, S., Siegel, J., & McGuire, T. W. (1984). Social psychological aspects of computer mediated communication. *American Psychologist, 39,* 1123–1134.
20. Martin, G., & Cerdin, J. L. (2014). Employer branding and career theory: New directions for research. In P. R. Sparrow, H. Scullion, & I. Tarique (Eds.), *Strategic talent management: Contemporary issues in international context* (pp. 151–176). Cambridge: Cambridge University Press.
21. Bondarouk, T. (2014). *Orchestrating electronic HRM.* Enschede: Twente University Press.
22. Von Bertalanffy, L. (1969). *General systems theory.* New York: George Braziller.

23. Brewster, C., & Mayrhofer, W. (2012). *Handbook of research on comparative HRM*. Cheltenham: Edward Elgar.
24. Jackson, S. E., Schuler, R. S., & Jiang, K. (2014). An aspirational framework for strategic human resource management. *The Academy of Management Annals, 8,* 1–56.
25. Capobianco, M. (2017). *Il lavoro agile tra proposte di legge e accordi di fatto*. Lo stato di attuazione dello smart working in Italia e nell'U.E. (forthcoming).
26. Cooke, W. N. (2003). *Multinational companies and global human resource management strategies*. Westport: Quorum Books.
27. Gooderham, P. N., & Nordhaug, O. (2011). One European model of HRM? Cranet empirical contributions. *Human Resource Management Review, 21,* 27–36.
28. Aran. (2015). *Dati statistici: Occupati nella PA per classi di anzianità e genere*.
29. Lewis, G. B., & Frank, S. A. (2002). Who wants to work for the government? *Public Administration Review, 62,* 395–404.
30. Aycan, Z., Kanungo, R., Mendonca, M., Yu, K., Deller, J., Stahl, G., et al. (2000). Impact of culture on human resource management practices: A 10-country comparison. *Applied Psychology, 49,* 192–221.
31. Ahuja, M. K., Chudoba, K. M., Kacmar, C. J., McKnight, D. H., & George, J. F. (2007). IT road warriors: Balancing work-family conflict, job autonomy, and work overload to mitigate turnover intentions. *MIS Quarterly, 31,* 1–17.
32. Yoo, Y., Henfridsson, O., & Lyytinen, K. (2010). Research commentary—The new organizing logic of digital innovation: An agenda for information systems research. *Information Systems Research, 21,* 724–735.
33. Mann, J. (2012). *Transform the workplace with focus on bricks, behaviors and bits*. Gartner report no. G0021229.
34. Chudoba, K. M., Wynn, E., Lu, M., & Watson-Manheim, M. B. (2005). How virtual are we? Measuring virtuality and understanding its impact on a global organisation. *Information Systems Journal, 15,* 279–306.
35. Cameron, E., & Green, M. (2012). *Making sense of change management: A complete guide to the models tools and techniques of organisational change*. London: Kogan Page Publishers.
36. Duxbury, L. E., Higgins, C. A. (2002). Telework: A primer for the millennium introduction. In C. L. Cooper, & J. R. Burke (Eds.), *The new world of work: Challenges and opportunities* (pp. 157–200). London: Sage Publications.
37. Spillman, R. D., & Markham, F. B. (1997). Telecommuting: Acceptance, adoption and application. *Journal of Computer Information Systems, 37,* 8–12.
38. Himmelsbach, V. (1998). Working at home given top marks by employees. *Computing Canada, 24,* 29.
39. James, P. (2004). *Is teleworking sustainable?—An analysis of its economic, environmental and social impacts*. SUSTEL, Sustainable Telework.
40. Huws, U., Robinson, W. B., & Robinson, S. (1990). *Telework towards the elusive office*. New York: Wiley.
41. Michelson, W. (2000). Home-based employment and quality of life: A time-use analysis. In E. Diener, & D. R. Rahtz (Eds.), *Advances in quality of life theory and research* (pp. 183–203). London: Kluwer.
42. Hill, E. J., Hawkins, A. J., Ferris, M., & Weitzman, M. (2001). Finding an extra day a week: The positive influence of perceived job flexibility on work and family life balance. *Family Relations, 50,* 49–58.
43. Duxbury, L. E., & Higgins, C. A. (2002). *Work-life balance in the new millennium: Where are we?: Where do we need to go?* Canadian Policy Research Networks.
44. Peters, P., Wetzels, C., & Tijdens, K. (2008). Telework: Timesaving or time-consuming? An investigation into actual working hours. *The Journal of Interdisciplinary Economics, 20,* 421–422.
45. Ruth, S., & Chaudhry, I. (2008). Telework: A productivity paradox? *IEEE Internet Computing, 12,* 87–90.

46. Baruch, Y. (2000). Teleworking: Benefits and pitfalls as perceived by professionals and managers, new technology. *Work and Employment, 15,* 34–49.
47. Costa, G., Åkerstedt, T., Nachreiner, F., Baltieri, F., Carvalhais, J., & Folkard, S. (2004). Flexible working hours, health, and well-being in Europe: Some considerations from a SALTSA project. *Chronobiology International, 21,* 831–844.
48. Olsen, K. M., & Dahl, S. Å. (2010). Working time: Implications for sickness absence and the work-family balance. *International Journal of Social Welfare, 19,* 45–53.
49. Flynn, G. (1995). Warning: Your best ideas may work against you. *Personnel Journal, 74,* 76–99.
50. White, P., Christodoulou, G., Mackett, R., Titheridge, H., Thoreau, R., & Polak, J. (2010). The impacts of teleworking on sustainability and travel. In T. Manzi, K. Lucas, T. L. Jones, & J. Allen (Eds.), *Social sustainability in urban areas: Communities, connectivity and the urban fabric* (pp. 141–154). London: Earthscan Publications Ltd.
51. Ehnert, I., & Harry, W. (2011). Recent developments and future prospects on sustainable human resource management: Introduction to the special issue. *Management Revue, 23,* 221–238.
52. Taylor, S., Osland, J., & Egri, C. P. (2012). Introduction to HRM's role in sustainability: Systems, strategies, and practices. *Human Resource Management, 51,* 789–798.
53. Lindgreen, A., & Swaen, V. (2012). Corporate social responsibility. *International Journal of Management Reviews, 12,* 1–7.
54. van Lier, T., De Witte, A., & Macharis, C. (2012). The impact of telework on transport externalities: The case of Brussels Capital Region. *Procedia—Social and Behavioral Sciences, 54,* 240–250.
55. Verbeke, A., Schulz, R., Greidanus, N., & Hambley, L. (2008). *Growing the virtual workplace: The integrative value proposition for telework*. Cheltenham: Edward Elgar Publishing.
56. Nidumolu, R., Prahalad, C. K., & Rangaswami, M. R. (2009). Why sustainability is now the key driver of innovation. *Harvard Business Review, 87,* 56–64.
57. Glaister, S. (2008). Alternative view: Homeworking won't stem rising car use. In T. Dwelly, & A. Lake (Eds.), *Can homeworking save the planet? How homes can become workspaces in a low carbon economy* (pp. 80–85). London: The Smith Institute.
58. Callanan, T. A. (1999). *New ways of living and working: Teleworking in Ireland*. Report of the National Advisory Council on Teleworking, Department of Enterprise Trade and Employment.
59. Forgács, T. (2010). Empirical research findings on telework: Management experiences and attitudes. *Business and Economic Horizons, 1,* 6–13.
60. Eom, S.-J., Choi, N., & Sung, W. (2016). The use of smart work in government: Empirical analysis of Korean experiences. *Government Information Quarterly, 33,* 562–571.
61. Gastaldi, L., Corso, M., Raguseo, E., Neirottic, P., Paolucci, E., & Martini, E. (2014). Smart working: Rethinking work practices to leverage employees' innovation potential. In *15th International CINet Conference, Operating Innovation—Innovating Operations*. Budapest.
62. Eisenhardt, K. M. (1989). Building theories from case study research. *Academy of Management Review, 14,* 532–550.
63. Berry, A., Loughton, E., & Otley, D. (1991). Control in a financial services company (RIF): A case study. *Management Accounting Research, 2,* 109–139.
64. Otley, D. T., & Berry, A. J. (1994). Case study research in management accounting and control. *Management Accounting Research, 5,* 45–65.
65. Yin, R. K. (1994). *Case study research–design and methods*. Thousand Oaks: Sage Publications.
66. Maxwell, J. A. (1996). *Qualitative research design: An interactive approach*. Thousand Oaks: Sage.
67. Wijewardena, N., Samaratunge, R., & Härtel, C. (2014). Creating better employees through positive leadership behavior in the public sector. *International Journal of Public Administration, 37,* 288–298.
68. Posig, M., & Kickul, J. (2004). Work-role expectations and work family conflict: Gender differences in emotional exhaustion. *Women in Management Review, 19,* 373–386.
69. Walker, E. A., & Webster, B. (2004). Gender issues in home-based businesses. *Women in Management Review, 19,* 404–412.

70. Zhao, X., & Xu, H. D. (2015). E-government and corruption: A longitudinal analysis of countries. *International Journal of Public Administration, 38,* 410–421.
71. Anderson, J. (2007). Solving China's rebalancing puzzle. *Finance and Development, 44,* 32–35.
72. Cho, Y. H., & Choi, B. D. (2004). E-government to combat corruption: The case of Seoul Metropolitan Government. *International Journal of Public Administration, 27,* 719–735.
73. Martínez-Sánchez, A., Pérez-Pérez, M., De Luis Carnicer, P., & Vela Jiménez, M. J. (2007). Telework, human resource flexibility and firm performance. *New Technology, Work and Employment, 22,* 208–223.
74. Coenen, M., & Kok, R. A. W. (2014). Workplace flexibility and new product development performance. *European Management Journal, 32,* 564–576.
75. Elsbach, K. D., & Pratt, M. G. (2007). The physical environment in organizations. *Academy of Management Annals, 1,* 181–224.

Decisions and Infrastructure (In)visibility: A Case Study

Roberta Cuel and Diego Ponte

Abstract This work focuses on how digital infrastructures of a complex inter-organizational system becomes visible and changes. While scientific research on infrastructures have addressed both theoretical and methodological issues, the way in which an inter-organizational and complex infrastructure is shaped and "cultivated" remains unexplored. The aim of this paper is to describe the most significant elements that characterize the interplay between human decisions and behaviors, infrastructure innovation and its visibility. These have been used as requirements to create a decision support system that could help experts to take decisions on an infrastructure for a planned change. In the paper, a longitudinal analysis is proposed with a focus on changes planned and implemented in the Air Traffic Management (a complex inter-organizational system adopted in all the European countries).

Keywords Digital infrastructure · Decisions · Socio-technical system · Air traffic management (ATM) · Longitudinal analysis

1 Introduction

A large body of literature on infrastructures has studied both theoretical and methodological issues of their visibility or invisibility and the role played by work practices, individual habits, and organizational cultures [20, 23]. The way in which an inter-organizational and complex infrastructure is shaped and "cultivated", however, remains unexplored. In this paper, authors analyze the changes implemented in a complex inter-organizational system and its (in)visible infrastructure unveiling different elements that may shape and modify the infrastructure itself. These

R. Cuel (✉) · D. Ponte
Department of Economics and Management, University of Trento, Via Inama, 5,
38122 Trento, Italy
e-mail: roberta.cuel@unitn.it

D. Ponte
e-mail: diego.ponte@unitn.it

© Springer Nature Switzerland AG 2020
A. Lazazzara et al. (eds.), *Exploring Digital Ecosystems*,
Lecture Notes in Information Systems and Organisation 33,
https://doi.org/10.1007/978-3-030-23665-6_26

are actors, organizational culture, processes, technology, and artefacts. In the case planned changes occur, a multitude of decisions and negotiations actions are taken on the interconnections and interdependencies of people, activities, structures and cognitive elements.

These changes are investigated in the case of European Air Traffic Management (thereafter ATM), the complex inter-organizational infrastructure, which assists the flight of an aircraft when departing, cruising, and landing at an airport. This is accomplished through distinct activities such as air traffic control and air traffic flow management. ATM services are complex systems because they exploit advanced technologies and require highly skilled human resources entailing significant investment in personnel, assets and training. Moreover, they are endow by different national and international organizations all over the Europe.

The analysis is carried out using qualitative research made up of semi-structured interviews, focus groups with experts from the sector and review of documents and reports [40]. The conclusion outlines the elements and categories of the decision processes that come into play when creating, maintaining or changing an infrastructure. These were used to create a decision support system that could help ATM experts to represent a domain and its underlying infrastructure (from the perspective of an organizational unit/function), simulate a change, reason on its consequences on other functional areas (other unit infrastructures), and finally take a decisions, namely plan a change of a global or inter-organizational infrastructure.

The following section introduces the literature review on infrastructure (in)visibility and its dynamics. The third and fourth sections present the case study and the research method. Thereafter the results are illustrated. The last section sketches out the theoretical implications of this research on software requirements for the development of a decision support system.

2   Infrastructures, (In)visibility and Decision Making

Among others, one common definition of sociotechnical infrastructure is that it is a robust network of people, artefacts, and institutions that generate, share and maintain specific knowledge about the human and natural worlds [14]. A large body of literature—from interactionism to the workplace studies about infrastructures, has stressed the important role played by the human elements of infrastructures such as work practices, individual habits, and the organizational culture [2, 7, 15, 18, 28, 35, 36].

Infrastructures shape what and how actors understand and interpret their world through practices, routines and organizational cultures, informational and knowledge infrastructures [9]. Infrastructures exist in the background, are invisible and are taken-for-granted by actors who perform routines and practices [7].

An infrastructure is generally invisible in daily life and operates below the surface but becomes visible in two main cases [23].

1. When it breaks down [7]. When a server goes down, a bridge is washed out, or when a power blackout occurs, the infrastructure becomes evident to the actors that use it. The safe management of such situations implies the creation and implementation of ex-ante and ex-post procedures such as back-up mechanisms or other emergency procedures, which should fix breakdowns and bugs.
2. When it is analyzed during meetings (as in a "sensemaking" process) that aim to create, maintain or change an infrastructure [7, 21, 24]. Visibility of an infrastructure is very much intertwined with the change of an infrastructure. When the infrastructure is complex, the changing process become an extremely complex venture. It is not an instantaneous process; it requires time and iterative development, involves multiple actors and implies various non-deterministic phases [1, 16, 19].

Since the infrastructure supports and is, in turn, inhabited by social, political and technical rudiments, its creation or change cannot be analyzed only from a techno-logical point of view but rather from the result of the actors' decisions, negotiations on practices, routines, assets and the sociotechnical elements that make up the infrastructure itself. Previous research [7, 29] has shown that two important characteristics are linked to the (in)visibility of infrastructures:

1. The infrastructure is the result of negotiation among heterogeneous actors.
2. People is connected to activities, structures and cognitive elements embedded in an infrastructure.

As such, decision processes in complex organizations represent one of the most important activities [39] for changing, cultivating, and making visible infrastructures.

According to Beersma and De Dreu [4, 11], group work involves negotiations, then negotiation dynamics have a prominent role in decision making, and finally decisions are closely linked to the knowledge of individuals, their ability to share and the common knowledge infrastructure they rely on.

Various elements are considered antecedents in negotiation and decision processes that shape infrastructures and may be used to make "visible" the infrastructures themselves. Among others: skills, knowledge and competencies [27]; procedures, routines and rules [3]; roles, power and social motives [17, 26]. The importance of these elements emerges even more forcefully when the organization is large and complex.

The goal of our work is to investigate how an inter-organizational and complex infrastructure is shaped and "cultivated" once a change is planned and implemented in a complex inter-organizational system. In the interplay between infrastructure and its (in)visibility decision an negotiation have an important role and an impact on actors perception, organizational and inter-organizational culture, processes, technology, artefacts, etc. (Fig. 1). These elements will be investigated in the following case study.

Fig. 1 The goal of the
research

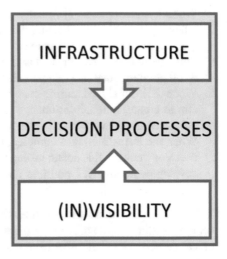

3 The Case Study

Air Traffic Management (thereafter ATM) is the entire ecology of systems that assist
the flight of an aircraft—departing, cruising, and landing at an airport [12]. The European Organisation for the Safety of Air Navigation (EUROCONTROL) manages and
controls—in cooperation with national bodies of EU Nations—the air traffic across
Europe. Two main elements make ATM a very complex infrastructure. First, ATM is
an inter-organizational system currently populated by a set of heterogeneous actors:

- air navigation service providers (e.g. DFS in Germany and ENAV in Italy)
- European Civil Aviation Conference member states
- civil and military experts in airspace design
- passengers and airspace users
- flight planner organisations
- relevant international bodies.

Second, since one of the main goals is the safety of flights, ATM and the interaction
among actors is driven by strict national and international regulation that formalise
the working procedures. Therefore, the ATM infrastructure is quite rigid and any
change is a complex endeavour that affects hundreds of national and international
organizations, actors, procedures, assets and is subject to many regulations aimed at
assuring flight safety and security.

Such complexity is particularly evident in the Single European Sky initiative, an
EU initiative that has the goal to design and manage the evolution of the airspace in
EU toward the creation of a unique regulator for ATM within EU. Such project, started
in 2001, is still running and its efforts to change the infrastructure are described in
the following section.

3.1 Background: Willingness to Make ATM More Efficient in Europe

The current configuration of European ATM is the result of the harmonization process in European countries implemented by the EU in the 1960s. The foundation of EUROCONTROL is the visible element of this effort.

Twenty years ago, the EU introduced the Single European Sky (SES) initiative with the goal of improving operational efficiency of ATM designing, managing and regulating a single coordinated airspace throughout the European Union. European airspace is one of the busiest in the world but the current system of ATM suffers from inefficiencies, such as the boundaries of air traffic control that follow national borders, and having large areas of European airspace reserved for military use. ATM relies on a number of new key features including better trajectory management, new aircraft separation modes and full integration of airport operations. The full initiative is an EU collaborative research programme called Single European Sky ATM Research (SESAR) and it is intended to last several decades through three phases [38]. Considering the complexity of the project and the numerous initiatives underway, this paper focuses on only one of these issues, namely Air Traffic Control (ATC) activity aimed at assisting aircraft in the upper airspace; one of the most critical activities, it is further described below.

3.2 The Starting Point: Sectored Air Traffic Control

The duty of ATC is to organize air traffic flow, to prevent collisions between aircraft and to provide pilots with information. Controllers apply separation rules to keep aircraft at a safe distance from each other to reduce the risk of collisions or other types of accidents (e.g. wake turbulence) and move all aircraft safely and efficiently through their assigned sector of airspace as well as on the ground. Managing the traffic flow, balancing the demand and capacity of the airspace, and preventing collisions is a complex service involving organizational, cognitive, structural and technological issues. One of the most important is the management of complexity. Diverse organizational, technological and structural solutions have been adopted to manage complexity when controlling aircraft. One solution adopted for ATC in Europe is the partitioning of the airspace into geographical sectors. Each airspace passing through a sector is controlled by a specific organization or Air Control Centre (ACC). In each sector, a pool of controllers perform different activities:

- Take care of and interact with pilots of the aircraft flying within the sector.
- Coordinate with controllers of other sectors to define the specific paths to bridge sectors (Fig. 2, left).

One of the main limitations of this type of work setting is that an increase in the air traffic flow means an increase on the workload for the air traffic controllers.

In particular, the coordination efforts between sectors increase significantly [5]. A common practice used to reduce this workload excess has been to decrease the size of the sectors thus creating more sectors. Unfortunately, such practice displays limitations:

1. A smaller sector means that controllers may exert less tactical and strategic control on aircraft.
2. Partitioning the airspace cannot be done indefinitely. Physical limitations do not allow partitioning the airspace indefinitely. This problem is already present in some European countries [6, 37].

Over the last two decades, different solutions have been proposed and scrutinized to overcome the limitations of the traditional sector-based control system; one of the most explored is the Sectorless scenario.

3.3 The Proposed Change: The Sectorless Scenario

For the last two decades, international bodies, practitioners and scholars in the sector have discussed an innovative approach to controlling airspace: the Sectorless scenario [5, 12, 13, 34]. The Sectorless scenario envisages air traffic control without the conventional geography-based sectors. This new approach means that several aircraft are assigned to a single controller regardless of their location. Each single controller guides the aircraft during its entire flight in upper airspace (Fig. 2, right).

The Sectorless scenario is said to offer significant improvements while addressing the main bottlenecks of the traditional sectored approach. The main foreseen improvements can be summarised as [6, 22, 37]:

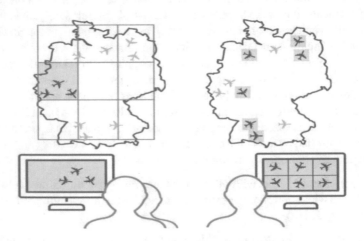

Fig. 2 Sectored versus Sectorless control scenario *Source* [13]

- A higher number of air traffic flights: the system is able to control a greater number of flights.
- Less workload: controllers face less workload and also less handovers.
- Efficiency in terms of costs and time: Sectorless allows for more linear trajectories meaning less fuel and less travel time for each flight.
- A single point of contact for pilots: when entering a Sectorless area pilots have a sole controller to talk to.

In order to assess the feasibility of this concept, over the last decade scholars have focused on several operative aspects of the Sectorless scenario including the change in controllers' tasks, the assignment procedures of aircraft, the priority rules and the safety assessment routines [6, 25]. Since the Sectorless scenario is a complex innovation, its implementation will last for several years to become gradually operational over the next ten years, more than a decade since the initial exploration of the concept. The technical, organizational, economic and procedural innovations of the scenario imply numerous changes within the sector as a result of decisions to plan and implement changes to the infrastructure and its interconnected practices.

3.4 Research Method

The work was organised in the following phases. First, the review of documents of official ATM reports and scientific papers describing innovation and changes in ATM and, more specifically, in air traffic control systems. Second phase, semi-structured interviews: 4 ATM experts were interviewed to identify the most important decision process categories that affect changes in ATM. Third phase, one-day focus groups took place in June 2016 and March 2017. Table 1 briefly describes the experts' roles and competences.

All the interviews and the focus groups were recorded and transcribed. The narrative data was organized into elements and analytical categories. In particular, the interviews were aimed at identifying the most significant antecedent elements and emerging categories in the decision processes on change and innovation of the ATM infrastructure and of flight control systems. The categories identified during the preliminary interviews, were verified with the discussion in the focus groups [40].

4 Data Analysis

In the analysis of all documents, interviews, and focus groups five of the most significant key elements that characterize decision processes within ATM systems and which may influence the infrastructure (in)visibility are uncovered. Each element (Table 2) was analysed in depth and various analytical categories emerged [33]. The

Table 1 Expertise of the experts participating in the focus groups

Role	Competences
ATM Security Expert	Supports national service providers, state authorities and the industry with respect to ATM security; works for an international organization providing ATM services
Senior Enterprise Architect	Supports the strategic development of Air Traffic Management; works for a European National Service Provider
ATM Safety Expert	Expert on human resource within ATM; works for a European National Service Provider
ATM Safety and Security Expert	Expert in security and safety; works for a European National Service Provider
Manager of an ATM R&D team	Expert in process reorganization and innovation in the ATM system; works for a European National Service Provider
Head of the research unit	Expert in innovative systems; works for a European National Service Provider
Senior researcher	Expert in communication, navigation and surveillance; works for a research unit of a European National Service Provider

Table 2 Expertise of the experts participating in the focus groups

Element	Categories
The actor involvement	Play a role; Actor engaging; Doing cultures
Dealing with the problem/issue	Objectifying the problem
Solving the conflicts	Acting on procedures and artefacts; Mastering in command
Driving the decision process	Motivating socially
The levels of decision process	Handling events; Changing procedures; Crossing the boundaries

following describes only the elements and then outlines whether and to what extent these elements are embedded in a decision making tool.

4.1 The Actors Involvement

As explicated during the interviews, actors play different roles while dealing with decision-making processes. Therefore, the "play a role" category has been unveiled. It identifies the position actors have within ATM and the situation they encounter while participating. The role played by each actor is inevitably influenced by individual motivation and level of engagement so "actor engaging" is another key category. The role played and the type of engagement are, however, closely related to the existing organizational culture within the ATM system. Thus, "doing culture" category explain how decisions affect other actors. This is evident when reading one of the interviewees' words: *"There must be a proactive debate among the various actors around the table and there must be no hypersensitivity. This is part of a culture, which means creating a solid organizational culture [...]"*.

4.2 Dealing with the Problem/Issue

The problem/issue or subject of the decision process often appears to be a set of unresolved secondary and often subjective issues that contaminate the real problem to be decided. For this reason, a decision process may be carried out over a very long term, and should involve various actors with different views and approaches.

The category "objectifying the problem" is represented by these words from an interviewee: *"[...] first of all the presentation of the problem. It must be presented in as objective a way as possible, because usually the problem comes contaminated. [...]"*.

Knowledge has to be cleaned to clearly represent a problem or an issue at stake. In other words, the problem is usually described from the expert's point of view, but in order to make a more objective decision involving various actors, the problem should be clearly described using common language and common values.

4.3 Solving the Conflicts

Conflicts may occur during decision processes for different reasons such as conflicting interests and motivations or gaps in the process. A common reason for conflicts is having "contaminated information" which may make actors bias in favour of a specific interest. In case of conflict, the decision makers must consider various elements in an attempt to reach a common decision: the actors themselves, the procedures and the artefacts involved. The category "mastering in command" can be represented by the following sentence provided by an interviewee: *"[...] There must be the master in command when an unforeseen problem occurs that has an effect on a decision [...]"*. In other words, when a dialectic process arises and the conflict cannot be solved, the presence of a master in command actor drives the whole decision process is required.

4.4 Driving the Decision Process

A decision may affect the balance within the system and favour the interests of one side or another. In this complex system, the above-mentioned elements are interwoven with power, interests and social motives, and drive decision processes. Another category identified is "motivating socially". Social motives seem to play a prominent role, especially if related to reputation, confidence and trust within any hierarchical structure.

4.5   The Levels of Decision Process

The analysis of the collected data allowed highlighting three levels at which decisions are made, namely operational, managerial and strategic.

The operational level deals with the daily management of any air traffic action, and decisions are made in real-time. The category identified is defined as "handling events". Event management should be proactive but in most cases, the management places the guilt on the single individual leader (the master in command).

The managerial level deals with any technical change that may occur during a revision of ATM procedures, such as the introduction of new technologies, protocols etc. The changes are usually planned and are based on in depth technical and specialized knowledge shared in national and multinational projects. Thus, the authors identified a category called "changing procedures".

Changes in complex inter-organizational systems must necessarily take into account a variety of aspects; those linked to the actors involved (particularly stakeholders), those related to the economics and, no less important, those linked to the political elements. The strategic practices deal with the adoption of policies, norms and regulations at national and international levels. The category identified in this level is "crossing the boundaries" as decisions must necessarily take into account different contexts across national and international boundaries.

5   Discussion on Infrastructure (In)visibility

From the collected data, five elements and ten analytical categories were identified (Table 2). The relationships that forms the sociotechnical infrastructure emerges as the result of negotiations between actors and the role they play (even in terms of power) in the decision processes. Actors involved in the decision processes attempt to "clean" the information from contamination in order to share the most objective and comprehensive information, thus making visible the infrastructure and introducing new changes. Often the negotiation is not an easy process because actors belong to different organizations that operate in a complex inter-organizational system and decisions are often taken "acting on" human actors, procedures and/or artefacts. Experts can play the role of masters in command because of their skill sets, expertise and reputation in the entire organizational system. Decision processes on infrastructures go through three levels, namely operational, managerial and strategic which all have different effects on the infrastructure (in)visibility (Fig. 3).

These results are used to develop a decision support system called PACAS Platform (Fig. 4). It enables ATM experts to: (i) represent a domain and its underlying

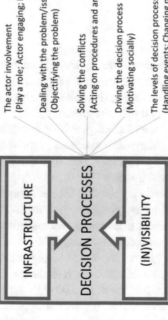

Fig. 3 Elements and categories that should be taken into account as requirements

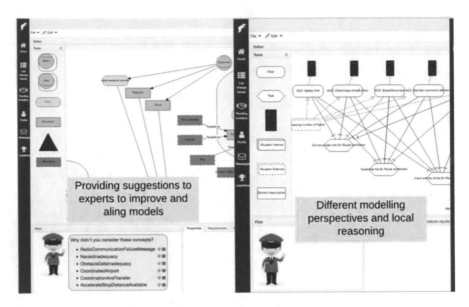

Fig. 4 1st release of the Pacas Platform

infrastructure (from the perspective of an organizational unit/function); (ii) simulate a change; (iii) reason on its consequences on the representation model of other functional areas (other unit infrastructures); (iv) take a decisions, namely plan a change of a global or inter-organizational infrastructure [30, 31].

In other words, the goal of the PACAS platform is to allow ATM domain stakeholders to take decisions for change management improving air transportation performance aspects such as safety, capacity, security, while ensuring cost efficiency and cutting down environmental impacts [8, 10].

The idea, is that actors, directly involved in the decision processes, play a specific role in both the real life and in the platform, and make the infrastructure visible because, through the negotiation of interests, power and strategies, they use and at the same time may influence the inter-organizational culture and reveal the infrastructure underlying the entire ATM system. The actor engagement is carried out through gamification processes and gamified roles (such as the game master) in which users are involved [32]. In order to allow users to deal with their issues in a proper way, a modelling language based tool and a multi-view approach have been developed allowing each user to focus on her own individual perspective, without the need of a holistic representation, and to negotiate with the others what really matters and what really should be objectified. Conflicts are solved acting on procedures, unveiling connection between different views (through automatic reasoning), or asking the master in command to take a decision. The control of the process and the action taken in the platform push actors to get socially motivated and to take a decision in a reasonable period. The different roles planned in the platform enable users to handle events, change procedure and cross boundaries acting at different levels of decision processes.

This paper has shown how the elements that characterize group decisions contribute to ATM infrastructures (in)visibility and how these can be embedded in a Decision Support System.

Acknowledgements This work has received funding from a grant agreement under European Union Horizon 2020 research and innovation programme.
The authors wish to thank Dr. Giusi Orabona for her contribution on a previous version of the paper.

References

1. Aanestad, M., et al. (2014). Infrastructuring work: Building a state-wide hospital information infrastructure in India. *Information Systems Research, 25*(4), 834–845.
2. Argyris, C. (1973). Personality and organization theory revisited. *Administrative Science Quarterly, 18*(2), 141.
3. Bazerman, M., et al. (1991). Negotiator rationality and negotiator cognition: The interactive roles of prescriptive and descriptive research. *Negotiation Analysis*, 109–130.
4. Beersma, B., & De Dreu, C. K. (2002). Integrative and distributive negotiation in small groups: Effects of task structure, decision rule, and social motive. *Organizational Behavior and Human Decision Processes, 87*(2), 227–252.
5. Birkmeier, B., et al. (2016). Controller team possibilities for sectorless air traffic management. In *Integrated Communications Navigation and Surveillance (ICNS)*, 6C3-1, IEEE.
6. Birkmeier, B., et al. (2014). Five transition strategies for sectorless ATM. In *Digital Avionics Systems Conference (DASC), 2014 IEEE/AIAA 33rd*. IEEE.
7. Bowker, G. C., Star, S. L. (1999). *Sorting things out: Classification and its consequences*. MIT Press.
8. Chopra, A. K., et al. (2011). Sociotechnical trust: An architectural approach. In *International Conference on Conceptual Modeling*. Heidelberg: Springer.
9. Constantinides, P., & Barrett, M. (2014). Information infrastructure development and governance as collective action. *Information Systems Research, 26*(1), 40–56.
10. Dalpiaz, F., et al. (2016). *Security requirements engineering: Designing secure socio-technical systems*. MIT Press.
11. De Dreu, C. K., et al. (2000). Influence of social motives on integrative negotiation: A meta-analytic review and test of two theories. *Journal of Personality and Social Psychology, 78*(5), 889.
12. Duong, V., et al. (2002). Sector-less air traffic management: Initial investigations. *Air Traffic Control Quarterly, 10*(4), 379–393.
13. Duong, V., et al. (2001). Sectorless air traffic management. In *4th USA/Europe Air Traffic Management R&D Seminar*.
14. Edwards, P. (2010). *A vast machine: Computer models, climate data, and the politics of global warming*. MIT Press.
15. Edwards, P. N. (2003). Infrastructure and modernity: Force, time, and social organization in the history of sociotechnical systems. *Modernity and Technology, 1*, 185–226.
16. Gasson, S. (2006). A genealogical study of boundary-spanning IS design. *European Journal of Information Systems, 15*(1), 26–41.
17. Giebels, E., et al. (2000). Interdependence in negotiation: Effects of exit options and social motive on distributive and integrative negotiation. *European Journal of Social Psychology, 30*(2), 255–272.
18. Heath, C., & Luff, P. (2000). *Technology in action*. Cambridge: Cambridge University Press.

19. Horton, K. S., & Wood-Harper, T. A. (2006). The shaping of I.T. trajectories: Evidence from the U.K. public sector. *European Journal of Information Systems, 15*(2), 214–224.
20. Iannacci, F. (2010). When is an information infrastructure? Investigating the emergence of public sector information infrastructures. *European Journal of Information Systems, 19*(1), 35–48.
21. Jackson, S. J. (2014). 11 rethinking repair. *Media technologies: Essays on communication, materiality, and society*, pp. 221–239.
22. Kaltenhaeuser, S., et al. (2017). A concept for improved integration of Space Vehicle Operation into ATM. In *33rd Space Symposium*.
23. Karasti, H., et al. (2010). Infrastructure time: Long-term matters in collaborative development. *Computer Supported Cooperative Work, 19*(3–4), 377–415.
24. Karasti, H., et al. (2016). Special issue on knowledge infrastructures. *Science & Technology Studies, 29*, 1–4.
25. Korn, B., et al. (2009). Sectorless ATM—A concept to increase en-route efficiency. In *DASC'09. IEEE/AIAA 28th*. IEEE.
26. Mannix, E. A. (1993). Organizations as resource dilemmas: The effects of power balance on coalition formation in small groups. *Organizational Behavior and Human Decision Process, 55*(1), 1–22.
27. Maznevski, M. L. (1994). Understanding our differences: Performance in decision-making groups with diverse members. *Human Relations, 47*(5), 531–552.
28. Mongili, A., & Pellegrino, G. (2014). *Information infrastructure(s): Boundaries, ecologies, multiplicity*. Cambridge: Cambridge Scholars Publishing.
29. Neumann, L., et al. (1996). *Making infrastructure: The dream of a common language*. PDC.
30. PACAS Consortium: D4.2 First Release of the Reasoning Proof-of-Concept. (2017).
31. PACAS Consortium: D5.2 Validation Report. (2018).
32. Piras, L., et al. (2017). Gamification solutions for software acceptance: A comparative study of Requirements Engineering and Organizational Behavior techniques. In *Proceedings - International Conference on Research Challenges in Information Science*.
33. Ponte, D., et al. (2018). Decision making processes and visibility of a global infrastructure: The air traffic management. In *Workshop di Organizzazione Aziendale*. Rome.
34. Riviere, T. (2004). Redesign of the European route network for sector-less. In *ICRAT 2004, 1st International Conference on Research in Air Transportation*.
35. Schein, E. H. (1980). *Organizational psychology* (pp. 177–178). Englewood Cliffs, NJ Repr. by Permis. Prentice-Hall., Inc., Englewood Cliffs, NJ.
36. Schmidt, K., & Bannon, L. (2013). Constructing CSCW: The first quarter century. *Computer Supported Cooperative Work, 22*(4–6), 345–372.
37. Schmitt, A. R., et al. (2011). Balancing controller workload within a sectorless ATM concept. *CEAS Aeronautical Journal, 2*(1–4), 35–41.
38. SESAR: SESAR Joint Undertaking. https://www.sesarju.eu/approach. Last accessed January 30, 2019.
39. Simon, H. (2000). Barriers and bounds to rationality. *Structural Change and Economic Dynamics, 11*(1–2), 243–253.
40. Yin, R. (2003). *Case study research, design and methods*. Thousand Oaks, California: Sage Publications Inc.

Unlocking the Value of Public Sector Personal Information Through Coproduction

Walter Castelnovo

Abstract In their day-to-day operations, public sector organizations collect and use huge amounts of information that if made available for re-use would contribute to economic growth. Much of this information directly or indirectly can lead to the identification of 'natural persons' and, as such, the personal data protection regulation applies to it. According to the General Data Protection Regulation (GDPR) issued by the EU in 2016, unless it is regulated by a specific legislation, personal information can be processed only based on the data subject's explicit consent. This raises the question of what strategies public organizations could implement to make the data subjects willing to allow the (possible) re-use of their personal information. By elaborating on evidences from the economics and the psychology of privacy literature, the paper suggests that public sector organizations can implement a coproduction strategy to unlock the value of public sector personal information in a user-centric personal information ecosystem. More specifically, the paper argues that the data subjects can be made more willing to consent to the processing (and possibly to the re-use) of personal information by involving them as coproducers in the processes through which public sector organizations can support economic growth in the digital society.

Keywords Coproduction · Public sector information · Privacy · Personal information

1 Introduction

Information is the fundamental resource in the Digital Society. The pervasive diffusion of devices with high information processing capacity and low cost allows producing huge amounts of information every day. People using personal information processing devices produce an ever-increasing share of this information. Spieker-

W. Castelnovo (✉)
University of Insubria, Varese, Italy
e-mail: walter.castelnovo@uninsubria.it

© Springer Nature Switzerland AG 2020
A. Lazazzara et al. (eds.), *Exploring Digital Ecosystems*,
Lecture Notes in Information Systems and Organisation 33,
https://doi.org/10.1007/978-3-030-23665-6_27

mann et al. [47] report that every day individuals send or receive 196 billion e-mails, submit over 500 million tweets and share 4.75 billion pieces of content on Facebook. This information is generated by individuals and (directly or indirectly) pertains to individuals; hence, it should be considered as personal information, according to the extended definition of Kang [22].

Acquisti et al. [2, p. 444] observe that "individuals' traits and attributes (such as a person's age, address, gender, income, preferences, and reservation prices—but also her clickthroughs, comments posted online, photos uploaded to social media, and so forth) are increasingly regarded as business assets that can be used to target services or offers, to provide relevant advertising, or to be traded with other parties". This explains why personal information is increasingly being considered as a fundamental economic asset, the new 'oil' of the 21st century [53], an important currency in the new millennium to which also a relevant monetary value can be associated [51].

While a remarkable value resides in personal information, it often remains untapped due to the quite stringent limitations the privacy preserving regulations impose on its use by both public and private subjects. According to the World Economic Forum, creating a user-centric personal information ecosystem in which "individuals can have greater control over their personal data, digital identity and online privacy" and where individuals "would be better compensated for providing others with access to their personal data" [53, p. 10], can represent a possible strategy for unlocking the value of personal information. If the control (if not legal ownership) over personal information is given back to them, the data subjects are allowed "to decide whether and with whom to share their personal information, for what purposes, for how long, and to keep track of them and decide to take them back when so wished" [16, p. 5].

This raises the research question the paper intends to address, i.e. what strategies can organizations implement to make the data subjects willing to share their personal information, once the control over that information is given back to them? This is a timely endeavor, since new regulations are being issued that grant to the data subjects more control over the use of their data. An example of such regulations is the General Data Protection Regulation (GDPR) issued by the European Parliament in 2016 that represents an important step toward the establishment of a user-centric personal information ecosystem [43].

The GDPR defines stricter obligations for the data controller (defined as the natural or legal person, public authority, agency or other body which determines the purposes and means of the processing of personal data) to ask for explicit consent to process personal information. Moreover, the new regulation establishes some new rights for the data-subjects: the right to obtain from the data controller access to and rectification or erasure of personal information; the right to restrict or object to the processing of personal information; and the right to data portability.

The GDPR provisions reinforce the data subjects' control over the processing of personal information, defined as collection, recording, organization, structuring, storage, adaptation or alteration, retrieval, consultation, use, disclosure by transmission, dissemination or otherwise making available, alignment or combination, restriction, erasure or destruction. This could limit the possibility of re-using personal information since according to the GDPR, unless a specific regulation applies to it, personal information can be processed only based on the data subjects' explicit consent (Article 6.1.a).

This qualitative paper, which is based on a conceptual research approach [31], tries to answer the research question above by considering the case of personal information collected and used by public sector organizations (PSOs) without being mandatory for the data subjects to provide them (for instance, information collected from sensor networks in smart cities). The case of the processing of personal information collected by public sector organizations is interesting since, different from non-public organizations, PSOs can offer the data subjects neither economic compensation nor non-monetary benefits specifically delivered to them in order to obtain the consent to process their personal information. However, evidences from the economics and psychology of privacy literature suggest that economic compensation is not the only reason that could motivate data subjects to disclose their personal information. Empirical researches found that psychological elements related to self-expression, self-efficacy and self-identity provide a better explanation of the individuals' online disclosure behaviors than motivations related to economic compensation or non-monetary benefits.

Interestingly, in the marketing literature these elements have been related to the benefits (potentially) deriving from the coproduction experience. Based on this observation, the paper suggests that PSOs could implement a coproduction strategy to unlock the value of public sector personal information (PSPI) in a user-centric personal information ecosystem. More specifically, the paper argues that, by assuming a concept of privacy as data control [6, 56], the data subjects' consent to allow PSOs to collect, use and (possibly) make available for re-use information pertaining to them can be considered as the individuals' contribution to the processes through which PSOs can support economic growth in the digital society. Such contribution amounts to the individuals' provision of a critical resource, which is what the coproduction of public services usually amounts to.

2 The Impact of the Data Protection Legislation on the Re-use of Public Sector Personal Information

The technological evolution makes available to individuals and to public and private organizations devices, tools and services that allow generating every day huge amounts of information. According to IDC's 2017 Digital Universe update, the number of connected devices is projected to expand to 30 billion by 2020 and to 80 billion by 2025 when the amount of data created and copied annually will reach 180 Zettabytes (180 trillion gigabytes). The dimension of the phenomenon supports the emerging of a new data-driven economy whose value in the EU was €285 billion in 2015 and that is expected to increase to €739 billion by 2020 if favorable policy and legislative conditions are put in place in time and investments in ICT are encouraged.

Fostering Open Data policies is among the strategic actions that could have high impact on the development of the EU data-driven economy. The implementation of the open data policies directly involves public sector organizations since the public sector is one of the most data-intensive sectors. In their day-to-day operations, PSOs process large amounts of information (including demographic, socio-economic, geographical, meteorological and municipal management data, as well as data from publicly funded research projects and digitized books from libraries) that if shared could be of great value for both people and firms. According to an EU Commission report, the total direct economic value of public sector information (PSI) is expected to increase from a baseline of €52 billion in 2018 for the EU28, to €194 billion in 2030, whereas the indirect economic value is estimated to be between 3.5 and 3.78 times as large as the direct economic value [1]. Due to this value of public sector information, many governments worldwide implemented policies to foster PSI re-use, also as open data, as a way to contribute to economic growth in the digital society. This is the principle at the basis of the EU Directive on the re-use of PSI, currently under revision, and the open data/open government policies implemented by many EU national governments [21, 37, 58].

Much of the public sector information contains personal information, both 'ordinary' and sensitive [41, 44], that can be qualified as public sector personal information (PSPI). To PSPI the data protection legislation applies, which could limit severely the possibility of re-using PSPI to contribute to value creation in the data-driven economy. This could be a problem since personal information is among the most valued information for companies operating in the sector. Liem and Petropoulos [26] estimate that applications built on personal information can provide quantifiable benefits of as much as €1 trillion annually by 2020, with a benefit of about € 330 billion annually accruing to private and public organizations. For this reason, besides policies to foster open data, also measures concerning personal data protection and consumer protection are among the strategic actions that are expected to have high impact on the development of the EU data-driven economy.

The General Data Protection Regulation (GDPR), issued by the European Parliament in 2016, is one such measure. By defining reinforced rules on use and consent, on profiling and on the obligations of companies when handling personal information, the GDPR is expected to reinforce trust of citizens resulting in a continuous sharing of personal information as an important input for value-added data services. Moreover, rules on consent of re-use of data for purposes different from the original purpose of collection, and data minimization will allow Big Data analytics to exploit more data with fewer restrictions.

The GDPR gives a quite extensive definition of personal information as any information relating to an identified or identifiable natural person. This definition of personal information as personally identifiable information is strictly related to the idea of privacy as 'the right to be let alone', as defined by Warren and Brandeis in 1890 [22, 45]. Based on this concept of privacy, the processing of personal information must be limited because it can lead to the identification of an individual, which could represent an intrusion in his private life.

Influential as it has been, the definition of personal information as personally identifiable information appears to be problematic in the highly interconnected world of today in which individuals are embedded in complex networks of relationships that make the distinction between the public sphere and the private sphere more and more blurred. Moreover, the technological evolution, the increasing amount of publicly available information, the diffusion of data analytics tools and the emergence of powerful re-identification algorithms have made the personally identifiable information concept critical since even anonymized data could have significant privacy consequences [39, 50]. This impacts also on open data initiatives: open data that do not seem to be personal data on first glance may become personal data by combining it with other publicly available information or when it is de-anonymized [24].

There are already plenty of examples of publicly available information released as open data that have been used to identify individuals [19, 20, 40, 49]. Aggregated or anonymized information contained in open data set that do not allow the identification of individuals when released, may become personally identifiable information as more and more powerful re-identification tools and auxiliary information become available [15].

The GDPR tries to avoid, or at least to reduce, these risks for privacy by assuming an extensive definition of 'identifiable':

> To determine whether a natural person is identifiable, account should be taken of all the means reasonably likely to be used, such as singling out, either by the controller or by another person to identify the natural person directly or indirectly. To ascertain whether means are reasonably likely to be used to identify the natural person, account should be taken of all objective factors, such as the costs of and the amount of time required for identification, taking into consideration the available technology at the time of the processing and technological developments. (Recital 26)

According to this definition, the concept of personal information should be considered as a dynamic concept since with the development of technology more and more information can fall under the characteristics of personal information and, consequently, should be treated according to the privacy protection rules [57]. This can determine critical consequences on the possibility to exploit the value of PSPI (and, more generally, of personal information) to create value within the emerging data-driven economy. In fact, any information that in the future might be linked to individuals, should be considered and treated *today* as personal information [24, 28]. Moreover, if information shared today as open data becomes personal information in the future simply because technological developments have made it possible to use it to identify individuals, how can privacy breaches be avoided, given that it is very difficult to effectively remove information once it has been published? According to the GDPR (article 6), in order to be lawful the processing of personal information must be based on the data subject's consent (as a general rule). How can the data subject's consent be obtained for the processing of information that has been published (possibly) a long time before?

If PSI containing personal information is made available for re-use, the application of the principles of data protection stated in the GDPR will create a tension, if not a contradiction, between two apparently conflicting principles. On the one hand, the need to contribute to economic growth through the sharing of PSPI, which can potentially lead to the (re)identification of individuals. On the other hand, the need to safeguard the individuals' privacy that, in the EU legislation, is considered a fundamental human right [20, 38]. This makes the re-use of PSPI a non-trivial matter, which makes the simplest choice to exclude as much PSI containing personal information as possible from the scope of PSI legislation [1, p. 137] thus leaving an huge amount of potential value untapped [21, 28, 59].

3 Privacy and Personal Information Protection in an Interconnected and Networked World

The notion of data protection originates from the individuals' right to privacy: how privacy is conceptualized influences the definition of personal information and, consequently, the scope of the data protection legislation as well. Depending on how extensive the definition of personal information is, the possibility of processing certain classes of information pertaining to individuals is limited or even excluded.

As observed by Erich Andersen, Deputy General Counsel of Microsoft's Windows Division, "in the digital era, privacy is no longer about being 'let alone'. Privacy is about knowing what data is being collected and what is happening to it, having choices about how it is collected and used, and being confident that it is secure" [7]. Westin [56, p. 7] defines privacy as "the claim of individuals, groups, or institutions to determine for themselves when, how, and to what extent information about them is communicated to others". Hence, privacy can also be defined in terms of the "control over transactions between person(s) and other(s), the ultimate aim of which is to enhance autonomy and/or to minimize vulnerability" [30, p. 10]. Based on this definition of privacy, an alternative definition of personal information emerges as "the information over which a person has some interest or control, in order to negotiate their environment or order their lives" [23, p. 8].

Although the data-control view of privacy is not immune of problems [6, 46], it makes obsolete the traditional distinction between personally identifiable and non-personally identifiable information that, as observed above, is blurring in the digital world of today. Moreover, it shifts the focus of the protection of privacy to the user-based understanding of the perceived risks associated with different types of personal information [32]. Giving individuals the control over the management of the information pertaining to them entails a shift from the traditional organization-centric personal information ecosystem to a user-centric personal information ecosystem. In the organization-centric ecosystem, the management of privacy is delegated to the organizations that process personal information. By agreeing on the terms and conditions defined by the data collectors, individuals delegate to them the protection of their data. On the contrary, in the emerging user-centric ecosystem, the data subjects are allowed to decide whether and with whom to share their personal information, for what purposes and in exchange for what. As Acquisti et al. [2, p. 445] point out, "privacy is not the opposite of sharing - rather, it is control over sharing".

The data-control view of privacy seems to better account for the individuals' behaviors in the digital society. Actually, even when they are made aware of the potential risks for privacy, individuals are likely to share their personal information (including also very sensitive data, such as their address, phone number, location data, or political preferences) quite easily with other individuals [29], and sometimes even with commercial organizations.

Many authors have observed the incongruence between the high levels of privacy concerns individuals declare and their online behaviors and refer to it as the 'privacy paradox' [8, 33]. Among the explanations of the paradox, the rational-choice argument is one of the most cited: even when they are aware of the risks for their privacy, individuals disclose personal information because the benefits of doing outweigh the cost or risks. This argument is the basis for the so-called 'privacy calculus' [14, 42] individuals are supposed to resort to when requested to provide personal information in exchange for some kind of compensation.

However, while there are evidences that a compensation based strategy can work in transactions between individuals and firms, it is highly disputable that public sector organizations can resort to it to obtain the data subjects' consent to collect their personal information, to use it and (possibly) to make it available for third parties' re-use. In fact, PSOs can offer neither economic compensation to the data subjects in order to make them willing to disclose their personal information in absence of legal obligations, nor non-monetary benefits specifically delivered to them (since this would contradict the principle of impartiality).

What strategies, then, could PSOs implement to make the data subjects willing to consent to the processing (including the possible re-use) of their personal information in the absence of a legal obligation to do that?

4 Unlocking the Value of PSPI

Economic compensation and benefits are not the only elements individuals can consider in deciding whether to disclose their personal information. Recent studies show that the sense of 'psychological ownership' [35, 34] represents an important driver, maybe the most important one, of the individuals' personal information valuation over and above information sensitivity and privacy concerns [48]. Based on an empirical research, Cichy et al. [12] found that the willingness to disclose personal information increases if individuals perceive this as a way to "express themselves, enhance their self-efficacy or contribute to their self-identity by supporting a greater good as a direct consequence of disclosing their personal data" (p. 5).

Psychological elements play a role also in motivating the individuals' disclosure behaviors on social media. Lee et al. [25] found that information disclosure on social media is related to self-clarification, social validation, relationship development, social control, and self-representation. Lutz and Strathoff [29] observe that the use of social networks represents a form of post-traditional community building individuals resort to foster their relationships and search for a feeling of belonging.

Quite interestingly, the determinants of psychological ownership that have been found to influence the individuals' disclosure behaviors on social media can also motivate the individuals' willingness to be involved as coproducers in the firms' value-producing processes. Starting from the seminal work of Prahalad and Ramaswamy [36], the individuals' involvement as coproducers in value-producing processes has been studied quite extensively within the marketing literature, also with respect to the psychological implications of coproduction for customers' satisfaction [9]. Fuchs et al. [18] found that customers involved as coproducers experience higher levels of psychological ownership than customers who do not participate in the production and delivery processes. Etgar [17] observes that the psychological benefits (potentially) deriving form coproduction include excellence, autonomy, self-expression and uniqueness, enjoyment and self-confidence, as well as status and social esteem (p. 102). These are the same psychological elements that have been found to motivate the individuals' online disclosure behavior. This suggests the possibility of considering coproduction as a possible strategy PSOs can implement to unlock the value of PSPI under the PSI-reuse principle.

The reuse principle makes PSI available to third parties (individuals and organizations) as a resource they could use in their value-producing processes. For PSOs, enabling the reuse of PSI is part of an administrative macro-process that aims at enabling the creation of social value (economic growth and community well-being) by supporting the value-producing processes of public and non-public subjects. When this administrative macro-process uses personal information as a resource, the individuals that information pertains to, and that consent to the use of that resource, should be considered as involved in the process as the providers of a critical resource. Within the public services literature, this is considered as a form of participation in which the users play an active role in the coproduction of value by contributing relevant resources [10] in terms of time, expertise and effort [27], but also compliance and information [4].

Alford [3] observes that the willingness to coproduce is difficult to foster through specific material rewards that are exchanged for the performance of specifically defined tasks. Non-material rewards such as sense of self-determination and competence, sense of belonging to a group (which can be related to some of the determinants of psychological ownership) appear to be more effective as motivators of coproduction behaviors. Besides these, the willingness to contribute to the well-being of other people and towards society at large is an important element of the concept of coproduction in the public sector [5]. Verschuere et al. [52] observe that in order to motivate an individual to engage in coproduction, the issue at hand needs to be of salience to him, where salience may be related also to a concern for community related benefits. Similarly, Bovaird and Löffler [11] observe that there is a huge latent willingness of citizens to act as public services coproducers, but only if they feel that a value for people is created through coproduction.

How can PSOs leverage the motivators of coproduction to unlock the value of PSPI?

The World Economic Forum [54, 55] identified three conditions that need to be satisfied to unlock the value of personal information in a user-centric personal information ecosystem: deliver meaningful transparency, strengthen accountability and empower individuals. Deliver meaningful transparency means to make transparency practices more meaningful, actionable and relevant for individuals by simplifying the ways in which organizations communicate their data practices and presenting individuals with understandable and relevant information on how their information is being used. Strengthen accountability means linking accountability to the impact of different data uses on individuals, and distributing risks equitably among all the stakeholders (not only on the individuals who give the consent to the collection of their data). Empower individuals means giving them a say in how their data is used and engaging them in understanding (and managing) the intended impact of data usage.

Quite interestingly, the three conditions above can be related to the conditions that according to Prahalad and Ramaswamy [36] could facilitate cocreation experiences, i.e. Dialogue, Access, Risk-benefits assessment, and Transparency (the so-called DART framework). Dialogue implies interaction, the willingness to avoid opportunistic behaviors and to recognize an active role to the consumers. Access, implies granting consumers the direct access to information relevant for informed decision-making. Transparency implies reducing the information asymmetry between consumers and firms through the sharing of information. Finally, dialogue, access and transparency make consumers aware of the potential risks of goods and services, so that they can assume more responsibility for dealing with them.

In a user-centric personal information ecosystem, open dialogue and interactivity allow data-subjects, conceptualized as coproducers, to get a clear understanding of how their personal information is collected, used and, possibly, made available for re-use. Giving individuals direct access to the information concerning the use of their data enables the empowerment of individuals and allows them to assume responsibility on the disclosure of personal information and to share with the data collectors the risks involved in the use of their information, as entailed by the same idea of user-centric personal information ecosystem. Pursuing transparency is a way to reduce the information asymmetry between individuals and the organizations that collect and use their personal information. Through transparency, individuals can be made aware of not only how and by whom their personal information is used, but also of what value has been generated by using that information.

Important as it is for reducing the information asymmetry, the control on how personal information is re-used by third parties is a critical activity that would require the data subjects to engage in complex and burdensome data tracking activities, which cannot be reasonably expected. A possible solution to this problem can be based on PSOs playing an information stewardship role within the personal data ecosystem, on behalf of the data subjects. As a component of data governance, information stewardship focuses on assuring accuracy, validity, security, management, and preservation of information holdings [13, p. 380]. Acting as information stewards, PSOs can define data governance policies and implement information management tools that allow them to monitor, and report to the data subjects, how third parties reuse their personal information. By integrating the data stewardship role within the open, transparent and interactive dialogue with the data subjects, PSOs can assure them that the third parties' reuse of PSPI complies with agreed upon rules, is fair and not purely opportunistic, which is a fundamental condition for the data subjects to consent to the reuse of their personal information.

Based on the observations above, it can be concluded that a possible strategy PSOs can resort to for unlocking the value of PSPI through the application of the PSI-reuse principle within a user-centric personal data ecosystem can be based on two pillars. On the one hand, the implementation of measures to foster transparency through open dialogue and information sharing, which includes undertaking the role of information steward. On the other hand, the involvement of the data subjects as coproducers in the decisions concerning whether and at what conditions to make PSPI available for reuse.

5 Conclusions, Limitations and Further Research Directions

In the paper it has been suggested a possible solution for extending the application of the PSI-reuse principle to PSPI in a user-centric personal data ecosystem. The suggested solution depends on two critical conditions PSOs must satisfy. On the one hand, they should involve the data subjects as coproducers in the process that allows the reuse of PSPI, which entails a continuous, open, transparent and interactive dialogue between the two parts. On the other hand, PSOs should act as information stewards on behalf of the data subjects, which entails implementing technological and organizational solutions to assure the data subjects that third parties will not use their personal information opportunistically.

Both conditions require PSOs to implement complex processes of organizational change. Coproduction entails re-balancing the power relationships between public officials and citizens, which affects responsibility and accountability. This explains why, as it is widely discussed within the marketing and the public management literature, there are still many resistances within public organizations toward coproduction. Such resistances can be even stronger if PSOs are required to play a stewardship role on behalf of the data subjects, which entails performing critical activities to monitor third parties' reuse of PSPI and assuming a new responsibility toward the data subjects for how their personal information will be reused by third parties.

The solution suggested in the paper rests critically on the assumption that the right to decide whether, under what conditions and in change for what to disclose personal information to trusted counterparts is actually granted to the data subjects. This principle, which is the foundation of the user-centric personal data ecosystem, has not been fully incorporated yet within the privacy preserving legislation, although the General Data Protection Regulation currently in force in the European Union represents an important step in that direction.

In the paper no distinction has been made among different types of personal information that, as argued in [32], can be associated to different types and levels of perceived risks. This represents a limitation of the present study that needs to be overcome to identify the incentive mechanisms that can be most effective in the different cases.

Finally, the paper has been based exclusively on a conceptual analysis and this is its main limitation. The literature discussed in the paper provides only indirect evidences supporting the hypothesis that a coproduction strategy could motivate the data subjects to consent to the reuse of their personal information. Hence, more research is needed to develop further and to test this hypothesis also based on empirical data.

However, preliminary as it is, the results of the discussion in this paper show that coproduction can play a relevant role to unlock the value of personal information in the emerging user-centric personal information ecosystem.

References

1. AA.VV. (2018). *Study to support the review of Directive 2003/98/EC on the re-use of public sector information—Final Report*, European Union, Brussels.
2. Acquisti, A., Taylor, C., & Wagman, L. (2016). The economics of privacy. *Journal of Economic Literature, 54*(2), 442–492.
3. Alford, J. (2002). Why do public-sector clients coproduce? Toward a contingency theory. *Administration & Society, 34*(1), 32–56.
4. Alford, J. (2009). *Public sector clients: From service-delivery to co-production*. Basingstoke: Palgrave Macmillan.
5. Alford, J. (2012). *The multiple facets of co-production*. Building on the work of Elinor Ostrom. Paper for the Seminar on 'Co-production: The State of the Art', Budapest.
6. Allen, A. L. (2000). Privacy as data control: conceptual, practical, and moral limits of the paradigm. *Connecticut Law Review, 32*, 861–875.
7. Andersen, E. (2011). *Prepared statement for the hearing before the committee on commerce, science, and transportation*, United State Senate, March 16, 2011.
8. Awad, N. F., & Krishnan, M. S. (2006). The personalization privacy paradox: An empirical evaluation of information transparency and the willingness to be profiled online for personalization. *MIS Quarterly, 30*(1), 13–28.
9. Bendapudi, N., & Leone, R. P. (2003). Psychological implications of customer participation in co-production. *Journal of Marketing, 67*, 14–28.
10. Bovaird, T. (2007). Beyond engagement and participation: User and community coproduction of public services. *Public Administration Review, 67*(5), 846–860.
11. Bovaird, T., & Löffler, E. (2012). From engagement to co-production: The contribution of users and communities to outcomes and public value. *VOLUNTAS: International Journal of Voluntary and Nonprofit Organizations, 23*, 1119–1138.
12. Cichy, P., Salge, T. O., & Kohli, R. (2014). Extending the privacy calculus: The role of psychological ownership. In *Proceedings of ICIS 2014* (pp. 1–19). AIS-ICIS, Atlanta.
13. Dawes, S. S. (2010). Stewardship and usefulness: Policy principles for information based transparency. *Government Information Quarterly, 27*(4), 377–383.
14. Dinev, T., & Hart, P. (2006). An extended privacy calculus model for E-Commerce transactions. *Information Systems Research, 17*(1), 61–80.
15. Dwork, C. (2006). Differential privacy. In *Proceedings of 3rd International Colloquium on Automata, Languages and Programming (ICALP)* (pp. 1–12). Berlin: Springer.

16. EDPS. (2016). *EDPS opinion on personal information management systems*. European Data Protection Supervisor, Opinion 9/2016. European Union, Brussels.
17. Etgar, M. (2008). A descriptive model of the consumer coproduction process. *Journal of the Academy of Marketing Science, 33,* 97–108.
18. Fuchs, C., Prandelli, E., & Schreier. M. (2010). The psychological effects of empowerment strategies on consumers' product demand. *Journal of Marketing, 74*(1), 65–79.
19. Golle, P. (2006). Revisiting the uniqueness of simple demographics in the US population. In *Proceedings of the 5th ACM Workshop on Privacy in Electronic Society (WPES'06)* (pp. 77–80). NY: ACM.
20. Graux, H. (2011). *Open government data: reconciling PSI re-use rights and privacy concerns*. European Public Sector Information Platform. Topic Report No. 2011/3.
21. Janssen, K. (2011). The influence of the PSI directive on open government data: An overview of recent developments. *Government Information Quarterly, 28*(4), 446–456.
22. Kang, J. (1998). Information privacy in cyberspace transactions. *Stanford Law Review, 50*(4), 1193–1294.
23. Van Kleek, M., & O'Hara, K. (2014). The future of social is personal: The potential of the personal data store. In D. Miorandi, V. Maltese, M. Rovatsos, A. Nijholt, & J. Stewart (Eds.), *Collective intelligence: Combining the powers of humans and machines to build a smarter society* (pp. 125–158). NY: Springer.
24. Kulk, A., & van Loenen, B. (2012). Brave new open data world? *International Journal of Spatial Data Infrastructures Research, 7*(2), 196–206.
25. Lee, H., Park, H., & Kim, J. (2013). Why do people share their context information on social network services? A qualitative study and an experimental study on users' behavior of balancing perceived benefit and risk. *International Journal of Human-Computer Studies, 71*(9), 862–877.
26. Liem, C., & Petropoulos, G. (2016). *The economic value of personal data for online platforms, firms and consumers*. LSE Business Review, January 19, 2016.
27. Linders, D. (2012). From e-government to we-government: Defining a typology for citizen coproduction in the age of social media. *Government Information Quarterly, 29,* 446–454.
28. van Loenen, B., Kulk, S., & Ploeger, H. (2016). Data protection legislation: A very hungry caterpillar: The case of mapping data in the European Union. *Government Information Quarterly, 33*(2), 338–345.
29. Lutz, C., & Strathoff, P. (2013). Privacy concerns and online behavior—Not so paradoxical after all? Viewing the privacy paradox through different theoretical lenses. In S. Brändli, R. Schister, & A. Tamò (Eds.), *Multinationale Unternehmen und Institutionen im Wandel –Herausforderungen für Wirtschaft, Recht und Gesellschaft* (pp. 81–99). Berne: Stämpfli.
30. Margulis, S. T. (1977). Conceptions of privacy: Current status and next steps. *Journal of Social Issues, 33*(3), 5–21.
31. Meredith, J. (1993). Theory building through conceptual methods. *International Journal of Operations and Production Management, 13*(5), 3–11.
32. Milne, G. R., Pettinico, G., Hajjat, F. M., & Markos, E. (2017). Information sensitivity typology: Mapping the degree and type of risk consumers perceive in personal data sharing. *Journal of Consumer Affairs, 51*(1), 133–161.
33. Norberg, P. A., Horne, D. R., & Horne, D. A. (2007). The privacy paradox: Personal information disclosure intentions versus behaviors. *Journal of Consumer Affairs, 41*(1), 100–126.
34. Pierce, J. L., & Jussila, I. (2011). *Psychological ownership and the organizational context*. Cheltenham, UK: Edward Elgar.
35. Pierce, J. L., Kostova, T., & Dirks, K. T. (2003). The state of psychological ownership: Integrating and extending a century of research. *Review of General Psychology, 7,* 84–107.
36. Prahalad, C. K., & Ramaswamy, V. (2004). Cocreation experiences: The next practice in value creation. *Journal of Interactive Marketing, 18*(3), 5–14.
37. Pyrozhenko, V. (2017). Open government: Missing questions. *Administration & Society, 49*(10), 1494–1515.
38. Scassa, T. (2014). Privacy and open government. *Future Internet, 6,* 397–413.

39. Shmatikov, V., & Narayanan, A. (2010). Myths and fallacies of 'personally identifiable information'. *Communications of the ACM, 53*(6), 24–26.
40. Simpson, A. C. (2011). On privacy and public data: A study of data.gov.uk. *Journal of Privacy and Confidentiality, 1*, 51–65.
41. Sloot, B. (2011). Public sector information & data protection: A plea for personal privacy settings for the re-use of PSI. *Informatica e Diritto, 1–2*, 219–236.
42. Smith, H. J., Dinev, T., & Xu, H. (2011). Information privacy research: An interdisciplinary review. *MIS Quarterly, 35*(4), 99–1015.
43. Sobolewski, M., Mazur, J., & Paliński, M. (2016). GDPR: A step towards a user-centric internet? *Intereconomics, 52*(4), 207–213.
44. Solove, D. J. (2002). Access and aggregation: Public records, privacy and the constitution. *Minnesota Law Review, 86*, 1137–1209.
45. Solove, D. J. (2006). A taxonomy of privacy. *University of Pennsylvania Law Review, 154*(3), 477–560.
46. Solove, D. J. (2013). Privacy self-management and the consent dilemma. *Harvard Law Review, 126*(7), 1880–1904.
47. Spiekermann, S., Acquisti, A., Böhme, R., & Hui, K. (2015). The challenges of personal data markets and privacy. *Electronic Markets, 25*, 161–167.
48. Spiekermann, S., & Korunovska, J. (2016). Towards a value theory for personal data. *Journal of Information Technology.* https://doi.org/10.1057/jit.2016.
49. Sweeney, L. (2006). *Uniqueness of simple demographics in the U.S. Population.* Carnegie Mellon University.
50. Tene, O. (2011). Privacy: The new generations. *International Data Privacy Law, 1*(1), 5–27.
51. Thaler, R. H., & Tucker, W. (2013). Smarter information, smarter consumers. *Harvard Business Review, 91*, 45–54.
52. Verschuere, B., Steen, T., Van Eijk, C., & Verhaeghe, T. (2014). *Motivations for coproduction of public services: Empirical evidence from a comparative case study.* Paper presented at the *IIAS* Study Group on Coproduction of Public Services Meeting. Bergamo, IT.
53. WEF. (2011). *Personal data: The emergence of a new asset class.* World Economic Forum, Geneva.
54. WEF. (2013). *Unlocking the value of personal data: From collection to usage.* World Economic Forum, Geneva.
55. WEF. (2014). *Rethinking personal data: A new lens for strengthening trust.* World Economic Forum, Geneva.
56. Westin, A. F. (1967). *Privacy and freedom.* NY: Athenum.
57. Wiebe, A., & Dietrich, N. (2017). *Open data protection study on legal barriers to open data sharing—Data protection and PSI.* Göttingen: Universitätsverlag Göttingen.
58. Zuiderwijk, A., & Janssen, M. (2014). Open data policies, their implementation and impact: A framework for comparison. *Government Information Quarterly, 31*(1), 17–29.
59. Zuiderwijk, A., & Janssen, M. (2014). The negative effects of open government data—Investigating the dark side of open data. In *Proceedings of the 15th Annual International Conference on Digital Government Research* (pp. 147–152). New York: ACM.

Social Media Communication Strategies in Fashion Industry

F. Cabiddu⊙, C. Dessì⊙ and M. Floris⊙

Abstract This study quasi-replicates a previous work based on social communication strategies in the insurance sector, analyzing what happens in the Italian fashion industry. Our sample yields findings dissimilar to the earlier research and suggests new insights.

Keywords Social media communication strategies · Reputation · Fashion industry

1 Introduction

In this article, we quasi-replicate and extend the research conducted by Floreddu and Cabiddu [1], which was the first empirical paper that jointly analyzed communication strategies and corporate reputation. It identified six social media communication strategies: egocentric, conversational, selective, openness, secretive, and supportive. It revealed the different ways these strategies can affect a company's reputation by giving it a good, average, or poor reputation.

Floreddu and Cabiddu [1] used a longitudinal explorative multiple case study and theoretical sampling that focused the analysis on Facebook, as it is the most common social media website used in the context of insurance sector. In their work, the authors found that corporate reputation is positively related to companies that are able to engage customers in online conversations, and it is reinforced through transparent online customer relationships. Additionally, repeated social media interactions and quick response to the questions by the companies to their customers appears to have a positive effect on their relationships and on the companies' reputations. Our con-

F. Cabiddu (✉) · C. Dessì · M. Floris
Department of Economics and Business, University of Cagliari, Cagliari, Italy
e-mail: fcabiddu@unica.it

C. Dessì
e-mail: cdessi@unica.it

M. Floris
e-mail: micfloris@unica.it

© Springer Nature Switzerland AG 2020
A. Lazazzara et al. (eds.), *Exploring Digital Ecosystems*,
Lecture Notes in Information Systems and Organisation 33,
https://doi.org/10.1007/978-3-030-23665-6_28

tribution is based on a quasi-replication [2] of the research but seeks to determine the validity of the results in different settings, and to see whether the research's prior findings can be generalized to a new population. In particular, we use a different context from that of Floreddu and Cabiddu's study but the same research design as theirs [3, 4]. This quasi-replication is based on a sample of seven of the major Italian fashion industry companies. The longitudinal data is drawn from an analysis of the respective companies' official Facebook pages for 2016–2017. The fashion sector was identified for the study due to increased scholarly focus on social media communication strategies in the fashion industry that focus on customer perception [5], customer engagement [6], and, more recently, adoption of customer relationship building practices on Facebook by major fashion retailers [7]. Recent research findings reveal that Facebook is very useful for both large and small fashion companies that aim to improve their communication. Customer engagement through Facebook is particularly positive for small firms due to audience engagement and participation [7].

Our results extend the work done by Floreddu and Cabiddu and reveal insights into social media communication strategies.

2   Corporate Reputation and Social Media Communication: A Literature Review

Floreddu and Cabiddu define corporate reputation as "an overall evaluation produced by its stakeholders and based on the stakeholders' direct experience. The corporate reputation that a firm has with its stakeholders must be regarded as a dynamic construct that influences, and is influenced by, different factors, such as product and service quality, relationship with stakeholders, financial performance, social and environmental responsibility" [1] (p. 491). Previous research asserts that a firm can manage its corporate reputation by using adequate communication strategies to mold the interpretations and perceptions of stakeholders and to build a trustworthy relationship [8]. In this vein, firms interact with a wide range of stakeholders by using communication processes designed to develop the firm's reputation [9–11]. In other words, corporate reputation is influenced by corporate communication because a firm, through its chosen messages, enables stakeholders to understand its operations, positively loading the perception of its activities, which can lead to an overall positive evaluation of the company [12, 13]. The widespread of social media has brought many new opportunities to the way an organization communicates [11, 14]. In this context, corporate reputation in social media is determined by "a complex narrative web of meaning" that is realized in active dialog between users and firms [15, 16]. Social media provide firms with the opportunity to extract unfiltered, unchanged opinions and thoughts from many people in real time and at low cost [17]. Furthermore, they allow an active relationship between firms and customers [18] and cooperation and dialog with stakeholders [19]. However, these alternative channels can also damage corporate reputation [11, 20]. In fact, online corporate reputation refers to reputation that is derived by Internet users' judgments [1] and the increasing use of social media forces firms to adapt traditional corporate communication methods to the complexity of the social media environment [18]. Hence, Floreddu and Cabiddu [1] state that firms need to participate in social media in order to observe, monitor, and co-ordinate conversations.

3 The Setting of the Quasi-replication

3.1 Methodology

Given that our contribution is based on a quasi-replication [2] of Floreddu and Cabiddu's work, to determine the validity of the results in different settings and to see whether the results can be generalized to a new population, we used the same methodology and research design by analyzing a different context [1, 3]. Consequently, we used a longitudinal explorative multiple case study [4] because the methodology allows researchers to develop a holistic understanding of real-life events [21], and we used a qualitative approach that lets us collect information about stakeholders' views that are difficult to quantify [22]. In addition, a qualitative methodology is preferred to investigate communicative processes among stakeholders, and qualitative methods collect information about stakeholders' views that are difficult to quantify [23]. The analysis covers the period from 2016 to 2017, and the sector is referred to as the Italian fashion industry.

3.2 Research Context

The Italian fashion industry is particularly suitable for the quasi-replication of Floreddu and Cabiddu's study because companies in this sector are very active on Facebook (each of them has more than 10 million followers) and the sector represents the spearhead of Italian economy [23]. Scholars are increasingly paying attention to the fashion context by mainly focusing on social media communication strategies and their influence on customer perception [24], customer engagement [5], and, more recently, customer relationship management through Facebook practices [6]. Recent research shows that although Facebook use is beneficial for both large and small fashion companies that want to improve customer communication, it is particularly positive for small firms in terms of audience engagement and participation. As mentioned above, the fashion industry is a strategic sector in the Italian economy. Recent Area Studi Mediobanca reports [25, 26] highlight the significance of the sector in the world economy. In 2016, the personal luxury goods market was valued at approximately EUR 250 billion. The leather goods segment is valued at EUR 75 billion and clothing is valued at EUR 58 billion. The other sectors comprise jewelry and cosmetic products. In the period 2012–2016, the Italian fashion industry had a 20% increase in the volume of sales, whereas the Italian manufacturing sector registered a 6.6% increase. It is evident that the sales growth in the fashion industry is significant, especially in the e-commerce sector, which is continuously growing and had sales of EUR 18 billion in 2016. Online sales are expected to grow by about 24% over the next few years. The relevance for academic studies and the abovementioned trends in e-commerce inspire the quasi-replication of Floreddu and Cabiddu's research to determine whether corporate reputation is affected by the use of social media communication strategies, by discussing specificities and also current usage, if it appears in line with income results and perspectives.

3.3 Sample Selection

A theoretical sampling procedure [27] allows selection of cases that appear particularly relevant and meaningful for the analysis. We started our case selection by constructing a data set containing information about the main characteristics of the Italian fashion companies, based on the last reports provided by Area Studi Mediobanca [25, 26]. In total, we identified 146 firms operating in the fashion industry; to determine which companies in our data set utilized Facebook, we conducted a web search. We confirmed that all the companies in our data set have a Facebook account. We narrowed our sample by including only those firms which fulfilled the following criteria: featuring in the list of top 15 fashion firms in Italy [25], belonging to the clothing and leather sector, and having at least one million followers. This reduced our sample to seven companies that actively managed Facebook. By "active," we mean that the media page/channel was regularly used by the company to publish posts or other content. The number of companies (seven) appears to be adequate and in line with Eisenhardt [21] who argued that "while there is no ideal number of cases, a number between 4 and 10 cases usually works well" (p. 545). The characteristics of the sample firms are summarized in Table 1 and the number of followers and likes on Facebook official pages are shown in Table 2. As Table 1 shows, six of the seven firms are luxury brands, which may imply that the non-luxury brands could be substantially different. We decided to consider this in order to understand different social media communication strategies adopted by the companies.

3.4 Data Source and Data Analysis

As per Floreddu and Cabiddu's research, we collected our data from three sources:

(1) Archival data including governmental and business publications
(2) Newspaper articles and companies' websites
(3) Content shared on Facebook pages.

Table 1 Sampled companies

#	Firm	Foundation	Sector	Brands	Revenue in euros (2016)
1	Prada	1913	Leather	Prada, Miu Miu, Church's, Car Shoe	3,184,069
2	Armani	1975	Clothing	Giorgio Armani, Giorgio Armani Privé, Emporio Armani, EA7, A|X Armani Exchange, Armani Junior, Giorgio Armani beauty	2,551,443
3	Calzedonia	1986	Clothing	Calzedonia, Intimissimi, Tezenis, Falconeri, Atelier Emé, Cash & Carry by Calzedonia Group	2,127,772
4	Salvatore Ferragamo	1927	Leather	Ferragamo, Salvatore Ferragamo, Emanuel Ungaro (in license)	1,424,969
5	Dolce & Gabbana	1985	Clothing	Dolce & Gabbana	1,258,962
6	Valentino	1960	Clothing	Valentino, Valentino Garavani, RED Valentino, M Missoni (in license)	1,154,060
7	Tod's	1920	Leather	Tod's, Hogan, Fay, Roger Vivier	1,004,021

Table 2 Social media content of the sampled companies

#	Firm	Followers	Likes	Number of published posts per day (2016)	Number of published posts per day (2017)
1	Prada	6,364,421	6,426,528	1 or more	1 or more
2	Armani	8,141,640	8,308,392	3 or more	3 or more
3	Calzedonia	3,376,098	3,403,209	1 or more	1 or more
4	Salvatore Ferragamo	1,744,110	1,764,242	1 or more	1 or more
5	Dolce & Gabbana	11,126,539	11,385,901	3 or more	3 or more
6	Valentino	2,788,209	2,817,215	1 ore more	1 ore more
7	Tod's	1,175,612	1,186,267	1 or more	1 or more

In the first phase, we constructed a data set containing information on the main characteristics of the fashion firms in our sample. In the second phase, we supplemented this data set by including information on corporate strategies gathered through the companies' websites and business publications. Using NVivo 10, we continued data collection by gathering content from Facebook pages of the fashion firms as well as fan posts. Finally, we collected information on the number of followers, likes, posts, and comments shared on Facebook pages for each company in our sample. We used cross-case analysis techniques [21] to look for patterns, and we revisited the data using charts and tables to facilitate comparisons between the cases [28]. The collected data amounted to over 3000 posts and comments. Content transcripts were coded following the Miles and Huberman's procedure [28]. Formal coding of the first transcription began with a "start list" of broad codes that was used as a method of breaking the large data sets into more manageable sizes. To analyze the social media communication strategies, we reviewed each post and extracted all quotations associated with the theme of communication. We coded quotations into strategy categories (egocentric, selective, etc.) using category definitions derived from the kind of action mentioned by our informants. Content was coded independently by the three authors of our study, and inconsistencies were resolved through discussions and by consensus. We focused on content posted by fans, which contained indicators of positive and negative emotions and perceptions [29] to measure the fashion companies' reputations [30]. To do this, we read each comment line by line and coded it as positive, neutral, or negative. Following what Inversini et al. [31] suggest, we coded the comments expressing admiration and trust that stakeholders felt with respect to a firm as positive; those that were not related to feelings, appreciation, or judgment as neutral; and those that contained negative emotions and perceptions about a firm as negative. Table 3 lists the number of times (references) each code (positive, neutral, and negative) was found in each instance and defines the reputation levels as good, average, and poor, respectively. Specifically, on the basis of the literature on online reputation mechanisms [17] and sentiment analysis

Table 3 Frequency of codes and reputation levels

#	Firm	Positive codes (%) 2016	Positive codes (%) 2017	Neutral codes (%) 2016	Neutral codes (%) 2017	Negative codes (%) 2016	Negative codes (%) 2017	Level of reputation
1	Prada	83.00	84.00	13.00	12.00	4.00	4.00	Good
2	Armani	84.00	84.00	15.00	15.00	1.00	1.00	Good
3	Calzedonia	59.00	60.00	26.00	25.00	15.00	15.00	Good
4	Salvatore Ferragamo	85.00	85.00	11.00	11.00	4.00	4.00	Good
5	Dolce & Gabbana	82.00	83.00	13.00	13.00	4.00	3.00	Good
6	Valentino	68.00	68.00	25.00	26.00	7.00	6.00	Good
7	Tod's	80.00	80.00	17.00	17.00	3.00	3.00	Good

[32], we classified a company as having a poor reputation when it had over 50% negative codes; average reputation when the companies had 20–40% negative codes; and good reputations for companies that had less than 20% negative codes.

3.5 Findings

The analysis of the firms' Facebook content showed that all the firms in the sample have a good reputation. However, they differ into three basic dimensions: 1. categories of communication strategies traced over two years (2016–2017), 2. the time of interaction, and 3. the kind of interaction.

Categories of communication strategies and evolution

Following Floreddu and Cabiddu's work, we proceed to encapsulate Facebook's contents into strategies that they have conceived. The labels that identify each strategy were defined in relation to the propensity of the insurance company of making information available online when a client made a claim or a request of information or clarification. Specifically, the authors [1] identified six strategies—egocentric, conversational, openness, secretive, supportive and selective—by considering two main aspects: the kind of the connection with customers or fans (merely informative/informative and relational) and the aim of the relationship (increasing of visibility/reinforcement of trustworthy ties). Hence, egocentric strategy establishes a. merely informative relations characterized by an absence of direct interaction between firm and customers or fans and b. aim of increasing firm visibility through social media. Conversational strategy provides a. informative and relational connections based on deep relationships with customers or fans and b. creation of trustworthy ties based on responses to every comment shared by customers. Openness

Table 4 Communication strategies (2016–2017)

#	Firm	Egocentric	Conversational	Openness	Secretive	Supportive
1	Prada	X				
2	Armani				X	X
3	Calzedonia		X	X		X
4	Salvatore Ferragamo				X	X
5	Dolce & Gabbana	X				
6	Valentino				X	X
7	Tod's				X	

strategy consists of a. informative and relational connections characterized by the improvement of transparency of firm–customer conversations and b. development of trustworthy relationships, thanks to public response to every remark shared with customers. Secretive strategy aims to a. inform and create relationships with customers and fans by managing potential conflicts through private channels (mail or private message on Facebook) and b. increasing visibility deleting unsuitable posts and using alternative channels to contact customers of fans. Supportive strategy provides a. information about offers and quotations and b. reinforce trustworthy relationships by supporting clients during all phases of the purchase process [33]. Selective strategy implies a. informative and relational connections only for what concerns positive feedbacks of clients (negative posts are ignored) and b. creation of trustworthy ties with customers that publish positive comments on the Facebook page. In this study, after many iterations of our data analysis, we identified five of the six complementary communication strategies: egocentric, conversational, openness, secretive, and supportive. As shown in Table 4, Prada and Dolce & Gabbana used social media to provide information about products and brand policy and completely ignored comments and posts irrespective of whether they were positive or negative. Armani, Ferragamo, and Valentino used secretive and supportive strategies, preferring to manage interaction with customers via private channels, such as mail or Messenger and supporting clients in the purchase process. In fact, they answered customer questions about stores, shops, offers, and other similar aspects, referring the customers to official websites. Tod's showed only secretive strategies: eliminating unwelcome comments and posting an email address for additional information. Moreover, Tod's did not engage in private or public customer interactions. Calzedonia was unique in that it used contemporarily conversational, openness, and supportive strategies. Specifically, Calzedonia engaged in efficacious customer social relations by answering customer questions publicly and/or privately.

The longitudinal analysis highlighted that communication strategies were not different during the analyzed period (2016–2017).

Table 5 Timing

#	Firm	Immediately	Within few hours	Within one day	Took more than a day or none response
1	Prada				X
2	Armani	X			
3	Calzedonia	X			
4	Salvatore Ferragamo			X	
5	Dolce & Gabbana				X
6	Valentino			X	
7	Tod's				X

Table 6 Kinds of interactions

#	Firm	Public	Private	Absent
1	Prada			X
2	Armani		X	
3	Calzedonia	X		
4	Salvatore Ferragamo		X	
5	Dolce & Gabbana			X
6	Valentino		X	
7	Tod's	X		

Time of interactions

To understand the different degrees of the firms' reactions to posts and comments, we analyzed the times of interactions as shown in Table 5.

Table 5 reveals that only two firms (Calzedonia and Armani) immediately reacted to customer questions or comments. Salvatore Ferragamo and Valentino answered within one day, Prada and Dolce & Gabbana did not answer, and Tod's took longer than a day to respond.

Kinds of interactions

The last difference among the firms' social media communication was related to the kinds of interactions with the customers. We identified three kinds of interactions: public, private, and absent. Public interaction means that firms answered fans and followers' comments giving visibility to their posts. Private interaction signifies that firms interact with customers via private channels. Absent interaction means that firms did not engage in customer relationships. Table 6 shows the different types of interactions of the sample firms.

As shown in Table 6, Calzedonia and Tod's had public interaction. However, only Calzedonia interacted publicly on both negative and positive comments. Armani,

Table 7 A summary

#	Firm	Reputation	Communication strategy	Time of interactions	Kind of interactions
1	Prada	Good	Egocentric	Undefined	Absent
2	Armani	Good	Secretive and supportive	Immediately	Private
3	Calzedonia	Good	Conversational	Within few hours	Public
4	Salvatore Ferragamo	Good	Secretive and supportive	Within one day	Private
5	Dolce & Gabbana	Good	Egocentric	Undefined	Absent
6	Valentino	Good	Secretive and supportive	Within one day	Private
7	Tod's	Good	Secretive	Undefined	Private

Salvatore Ferragamo, and Tod's used private interaction. Valentino preferred one-to-one relation. There was an absence of any form of interaction on the Prada and Dolce & Gabbana Facebook pages. Table 7 summarizes the results by comparing the firms' reputations with their communication strategies and the time and kind of interactions.

The results reveal that the sampled firms used social media as a way to publicize their activities and products, but only one of them (Calzedonia) showed any interaction with public and quickly responded to comments or posts. These results highlight that a good reputation is not directly related to the use of social media made to manage it. Prada and Dolce & Gabbana, for instance, have good reputation in terms of customers' feelings but are not engaged in improving social communication strategies. On the contrary, Calzedonia, as mentioned earlier, is the most active on Facebook. It aims to improve customer perception, by basing its communication on honesty and transparency, but has the highest number of negative codes and the lowest number of positive codes (see Table 3).

4 Discussion and Conclusion

In this research, we undertook a quasi-replication of Floreddu and Cabiddu's research [1] and changed the context to understand whether previous findings would be confirmed or not, by referencing another sample. Floreddu and Cabiddu, by using a qualitative approach, analyzed the Facebook official pages of a sample of seven insurance companies and found that firms with good reputations use six kinds of social communication strategies (egocentric, conversational, selective, openness, secretive, and supportive) that have evolved over time. Additionally, they found that repeated and transparent interactions between firms and customers strengthen their relationships, positively affecting the firm's reputation. Our findings are only partially consistent with the previous research. First, we identified only firms with good reputations. Hence, we could not identify, as Floreddu and Cabiddu did in their research, which social media communication strategy is more effective with differing levels of reputations, and for the same reason, we could not analyze the differences between companies with good and poor reputation with respect to their ability to use corporate communication. The social media communication strategies that we identified (egocentric, conversational, selective, openness, and supportive) differ from those identified by Floreddu and Cabiddu only in terms of the selective strategy, as none of the sampled firms used a selective strategy. The difference could be explained by the fact that insurance industry, handles confidential information, which includes a range of data, such as financial histories, personal assets, health conditions, and histories. It also requires taking the utmost care when answering customer requests. This aspect is not present in the fashion industry. Second, we extend the previous study by suggesting that social communication strategies affect corporate reputation [1, 14, 34] and we show that firms with a well-positioned brand, such as Prada and Dolce & Gabbana, are not directly related to social media communication strategies. Specifically, our findings showed that the firms with the highest reputation (Prada and Dolce & Gabbana) did not interact with their customers. In fact, they used an egocentric strategy, which focused on their offers and products, and avoided any meaningful interactions with their followers. Comments and posts were ignored and a possible response time was not defined. However, these firms have the highest number of followers and likes. In contrast, Calzedonia is unique in that it uses a conversational strategy, with a quick response time and public interactions. However, this firm received the lowest percentage of positive codes and the highest percentage of negative codes. Thus, our findings demonstrate that firms with a well-positioned brand, such as Prada and Dolce & Gabbana, do not show any interest in actively influencing consumers' positive perceptions through conversional strategy, while firms like Calzedonia that have a different target market, spend a lot of time on customer relationship management in order to enhance customer's positive perception and reinforce their reputation. The credibility and image of companies like Prada and Dolce & Gabbana are already confirmed by market share and brand image. But companies that aim to increase trustworthiness and reliability among customers and investors are committed to engaging customers in public conversation. From a managerial perspective, our findings suggest that firms with a good reputation, strong brand positioning, special purchase effort for their product, little comparison to other brands, and lower price sensitivity to customers do not need to invest resources in social communication strategies. For these companies, the use of Facebook could be considered as an additional way to promote products, new collections, special offers, but not for engaging in customer interactions. Conversely, firms that have a good reputation, lower brand positioning, mass promotion, frequent purchase of product, a lot of comparison with other brands, and higher price sensitivity to customers, need to strategically use social media to reinforce their reputation and increase customer loyalty. Our research shows two main limitations that future studies could contemplate. The first is that in further studies, the sample dimensions could be increased. The second is that future studies could refer to other social media to verify whether what happens on Facebook happens on other social media, as Facebook is the main social media used.

References

1. Floreddu, P. B., & Cabiddu, F. (2016). Social media communication strategies. *Journal of Service Marketing, 30*(5), 490–503.
2. Bettis, R. A., Helfat, C. E., & Shaver, J. M. (2016). The necessity, logic, and forms of replication. *Strategic Management Journal, 37*(11), 2193–2203.
3. Kurke, L. B., & Aldrich, H. E. (1983). Note—Mintzberg was right! A replication and extension of the nature of managerial work. *Management Science, 29*(8), 975–984.
4. Tsang, E. W. K., & Kwan, K.-M. (1999). Replication and theory development in organizational science: A critical realist perspective. *Academy of Management Review, 24*(4), 759–780.
5. Kim, A. J., & Ko, E. (2012). Do social media marketing activities enhance customer equity? An empirical study of luxury fashion brand. *Journal of Business Research, 65,* 1480–1486.
6. Nadeem, W., Andreini, D., Salo, J., & Laukkanen, T. (2015). Engaging consumers online through websites and social media: A gender study of Italian Generation Y clothing consumers. *International Journal of Information Management, 35*(4), 432–442.
7. Escobar-Rodríguez, T., & Bonsón-Fernández, R. (2017). Facebook practices for business communication among fashion retailers. *Journal of Fashion Marketing and Management: An International Journal, 21*(1), 33–50.
8. Rindova, V. P., & Fombrun, C. J. (1999). Constructing competitive advantage: The role of firm–constituent interactions. *Strategic Management Journal, 20*(8), 691–710.
9. Gotsi, M., & Wilson, A. M. (2001). Corporate reputation, seeking a definition. *Corporate Communications: An International Journal, 6*(1), 24–30.
10. Furman, D. M. (2010). The development of corporate image: A historiographic approach to a marketing concept. *Corporate Reputation Review, 13*(1), 63–75.
11. Otubanjo, O., Amujo, O. C., & Cornelius, N. (2010). The informal corporate identity communication process. *Corporate Reputation Review, 13*(3), 157–171.
12. Bunting, M., & Lipski, R. (2000). Drowned out? Rethinking corporate reputation management for the Internet. *Journal of Communication Management, 5*(2), 170–178.
13. Wiedmann, K., & Prauschke, C. (2006), How do stakeholder alignment concepts influence corporate reputation? The role of corporate communication in reputation building. In *Proceedings of the tenth RI Conference on Reputation, Image, Identity and Competitiveness, New York, NY, 25–28 May 2006.*
14. Aula, P. (2011). Meshworked reputation: Publicists' views on the reputational impacts of online communication. *Public Relations Review, 37*(1), 28–36.
15. Aula, P. (2010). Social media, reputation risk and ambient publicity management. *Strategy and Leadership, 38*(6), 43–49.
16. Weber, L. (2009). *Marketing to the social web: How digital customer communities build your business.* New York, NY: Wiley.
17. Dellarocas, C. (2003). The digitization of word of mouth: Promise and challenges of online feedback mechanisms. *Management Science, 49*(10), 1407–1424.
18. Hennig-Thurau, T., Malthouse, E. C., Friege, C., Gensler, S., Lobschat, L., Rangaswamy, A., et al. (2010). The impact of new media on customer relationships. *Journal of Service Research, 13*(3), 311–330.
19. Argenti, P., & Barnes, C. (2009). *Digital strategies for powerful corporate communications.* New York, NY: McGraw-Hill.

20. Chun, R., & Davies, G. (2001). E-reputation: The role of mission and vision statements in positioning strategy. *Journal of Brand Management, 8*(4/5), 315–333.
21. Eisenhardt, K. M. (1989). Building theories from case study research. *Academy of Management Review, 14*(4), 532–550.
22. Yin, R. K. (1994). *Case study research*. Thousand Oaks, CA: Sage Publications.
23. Horster, E., & Gottschalk, C. (2012). Computer-assisted webnography: A new approach to online reputation management in tourism. *Journal of Vacation Marketing, 18*(3), 229–238.
24. Turker, D., & Altuntas, C. (2014). Sustainable supply chain management in the fast fashion industry: An analysis of corporate reports. *European Management Journal, 32*(5), 837–849.
25. Area studi Mediobanca (2018). Focus "Aziende Moda Italia" (2012–2016). http://www.mbres.it/sites/default/files/resources/Aziende%20Moda%20Italia%20(2012-2016).pdf.
26. Area studi Mediobanca (2017). Top15 Moda Italia e Aziende Moda Italia: 2012–2016 e primi nove mesi 2017. http://www.mbres.it/sites/default/files/resources/rs_Focus-Moda-2017.pdf.
27. Eisenhardt, K. M., & Graebner, M. E. (2007). Theory building from cases: Opportunities and challenges. *Academy of Management Journal, 50*(1), 25–32.
28. Miles, M. B., & Huberman, A. M. (1994). *Qualitative data analysis: An expanded sourcebook*. Newbury Park, CA: Sage Publications.
29. Arvidsson, A. (2011). General sentiment: How value and affect converge in the information economy. *The Sociological Review, 59*(2), 39–59.
30. Walker, K. (2010). A systematic review of the corporate reputation literature: Definition, measurement, and theory. *Corporate Reputation Review, 12*(4), 357–387.
31. Inversini, A., Cantoni, L., & Buhalis, D. (2009). Destinations' information competition and web reputation. *Information Technology and Tourism, 11*(3), 221–234.
32. Seebach, C., Beck, R., & Denisova, O. (2013). Analyzing social media for corporate reputation management: How firms can improve business agility. *International Journal of Business Intelligence Research, 4*(3), 50–66.
33. Castriotta, M., Floreddu, P. B., Di Guardo, M. C., & Cabiddu, F. (2013). Disentangling the strategic use of social media in the insurance industry: A value co-creation perspective. In R. O.-L. Miguel, & B. Tanya (Eds.), *Social media in strategic management (advanced series in management)* (Vol. 11, pp. 63–86). Emerald Group Publishing Limited.
34. Balmer, J. M. T., & Gray, E. R. (1999). Corporate identity and corporate communications: Creating a competitive advantage. *Corporate Communications an International Journal, 4*(4), 171–177.

The Illusion of Routine as an Indicator for Job Automation with Artificial Intelligence

Jason Bissessur, Farzad Arabikhan and Peter Bednar

Abstract The resurgence of artificial intelligence (AI) has empowered organizations to concentrate their research efforts on enhancing decision-making and automation capabilities. This is being pursued with the goal of increasing productivity, whilst reducing costs. With this, it is perceived that the jobs within these organizations that are considered subject to 'routine', or repetitive and mundane tasks, are more likely to be automatable. However, it may be recognised that these jobs are more than a simple set of routine tasks. This study aims to address the concept of routineness from the perspective of the job occupants themselves. The findings reveal that jobs which are considered routine from an organizational perspective, realistically require a degree of human intervention. This suggests that the fear of mass unemployment at the hands of AI may be an unrealistic notion. Rather, the introduction of AI into jobs paves the way for collaborative methods of working which could augment current jobs and create new jobs. Furthermore, this paper accentuates that the acceptance of AI by stakeholders requires an alignment of the technology with their own unique contextual needs.

Keywords Artificial intelligence · Employment · Routine work activities · Job automation · Organizational perspective · Stakeholder perspective

J. Bissessur (✉) · F. Arabikhan · P. Bednar
Computing, University of Portsmouth, Portsmouth, UK
e-mail: JasonTBissessur@gmail.com; jasonbissessur94@gmail.com

F. Arabikhan
e-mail: Farzad.Arabikhan@port.ac.uk

P. Bednar
e-mail: Peter.Bednar@port.ac.uk

P. Bednar
Informatics, Lund University, Lund, Sweden

© Springer Nature Switzerland AG 2020
A. Lazazzara et al. (eds.), *Exploring Digital Ecosystems*,
Lecture Notes in Information Systems and Organisation 33,
https://doi.org/10.1007/978-3-030-23665-6_29

407

1 Introduction

This study was initiated with the purpose of understanding what role AI might play in the future working environment beyond those views conveyed in mainstream media and literature. It was recognised that many of these views are based upon the premise that 'routine' jobs are more likely to be subject to automation with AI. This study seeks to question the concept of routine by addressing the hypothesis: *The presence of routine tasks in a stakeholder's job alone, does not determine the possibility of overall job automation.* To this, a bottom up approach was required. It was recognised that those individuals who are doing a job in practice, labelled here as stakeholders, would be more suitable to consult with when trying to develop an understanding of the level of acceptance and extent to which AI integration within the working environment might be expected. This paper provides a comparison of the elements which are traditionally considered to constitute a 'routine' task with the perspectives of the stakeholders who are doing such jobs in practice. It also includes an appreciation of the realistic level of cognition required to do a job in practice and draws an understanding of the impact this may have on AI-integrated employment in the future. Furthermore, it provides a description of the precautions that could be taken to navigate some of the arising complexities which may be presented with the introduction of AI in the working environment. Finally, this paper attempts to forecast how AI might be received by employees in the working environment based the primary data that was collected in this study.

2 Background

Multiple areas of industry have and stand to reap the perceived benefits of applied AI in their respective domains. Such applications include automating manufacturing processes [8], ascertaining user sentiment from social media activity [6], assisting clinicians with patient diagnosis [10] and intrusion detection with cyber security systems [12]. The perceived benefits organizations stand to obtain from such applications include increased productivity, higher and more consistent product/service quality and reduced costs. These applications are by no means exhaustive, however, do highlight how AI automation and decision-making is/may be applied within different industries and the potential benefits organizations stand to gain. Rather than defining AI, which is a contentious area due to varying perspectives about how it is expected to behave, this article focuses on the qualities expressed by AI that might be beneficial in a working environment involving a human presence. Therefore, this paper refers to the purpose for which AI and other automated decision-making technologies, such as Virtual Personal Assistants [5], might be adopted in the working environment; that is the automation of human interactions.

The anticipated benefits of automated decision-making come with the looming belief that the need for humans, occupying jobs in the areas elected for AI automation,

	Routine tasks	Nonroutine tasks
	Analytic and interactive tasks	
Examples	• Record-keeping • Calculation • Repetitive customer service (e.g., bank teller)	• Forming/testing hypotheses • Medical diagnosis • Legal writing • Persuading/selling • Managing others
Computer impact	• Substantial substitution	• Strong complementarities
	Manual tasks	
Examples	• Picking or sorting • Repetitive assembly	• Janitorial services • Truck driving
Computer impact	• Substantial substitution	• Limited opportunities for substitution or complementarity

Fig. 1 The ALM predictions of task model for the impact of computerization on four categories of workplace tasks (*Source* Autor et al. [1, p. 1286])

will be reduced leading to mass unemployment. This view is expressed in the Autor, Levy and Murnane (ALM) model, which attempts to categorise workplace tasks into areas of routineness (see Fig. 1).

The model concludes that the rapidly declining price of computer capital will reduce the labour input for routine tasks and increase the demand for nonroutine cognitive tasks [1]. Furthermore, Goos and Manning suggest that such a phenomenon will lead to job polarisation. This entails a rise in the demand for jobs involving nonroutine cognitive tasks (e.g. professional and managerial jobs) and nonroutine manual tasks (e.g. cleaning), with a reduction in jobs involving middle-skilled tasks (e.g. clerical jobs) [4]. Such a disparity could entail income inequality and subsequently necessitate/extend the "sharp divisions between the geographic areas that benefit and those that don't" [11].

With the consequences of job polarisation potentially worsening income disparity in society, it is important to question the grounds upon which the argument is based. The argument is underpinned by assertions about job routineness. It is therefore important to question these assertions, particularly those pertaining to what constitutes a routine task; can a job simply be described in terms of the set of tasks which it consists of, or is there more to it? The ALM model considers routine tasks as those which can be accomplished by an explicit set of programmed rules [1]. Contrastingly, Autor et al. describe nonroutine tasks as those of which the "rules are not sufficiently well understood to be specified in computer code and executed by machines" [1]. These descriptions inform the ALM model from which the aforementioned conclusions are drawn. However, the model can be criticised in terms of the task-orientated approach it takes towards defining routine and nonroutine tasks. Such an approach takes a positivistic view of job tasks and overlooks the important humanistic factors required to do a job to the expected, equivocal standard of a human job occupant. This study recognises that in order to navigate the complexities presented in the real-world, human intervention is needed to conduct tasks in correspondence with human expectations of quality.

Given that this study is focused on the impact of AI implementation in the working environment on stakeholders, it is of a socio-technical nature. As Mumford elaborates, "a sociotechnical approach is one which recognises the interaction of technology and people and produces work systems which are both technically efficient and have social characteristics which lead to high job satisfaction" [9]. This study investigates the perceptions held by stakeholders about their jobs and the influence automation may have on this. Thus, the concern is with human activity systems, that is notional systems which express some purposeful activity. Such systems are notional as they are intellectual constructs used by individuals to "debate about possible changes which might be introduced in a real-world problem situation" [3]. In other words, this study involves the contribution of individuals' perspectives about the purposeful activities, boundaries, properties and relationships which they believe to constitute their jobs and considers the impact AI may have on this based on their views regarding automation in the working environment.

Towards answering the hypothesis of this study, the following research questions were defined:

- *To what degree do stakeholders consider their job to be subject to routine? How does this impact on job automation?*
- *To what extent might AI affect stakeholders' jobs?*
- *How might stakeholders react to the introduction of AI in their jobs?*
- *Will AI displace or assist stakeholders?*

3 Methodology

The nature of this study required a detailed description of the modus operandi of an individuals' job, thus, a stakeholder-centric approach was deemed appropriate. The authors aimed to avoid any positive or negative preconceptions, which participants may hold regarding 'AI', therefore the term was not explicitly used. Rather, when posing questions to participants, 'automation' was the language used. In this way, participants were able to provide responses in regard to the intended purpose of AI in the context of their own jobs. Using this term also helped convey the purpose of AI to those participants who were not familiar with the concept.

Two methods were employed to gather the necessary quantitative and qualitative data anonymously. Firstly, five 30-min interviews were carried out with individual participants in order to elicit rich responses about their jobs and views on automation. These were of a semi-structured nature, taking a conversational approach towards the enquiry, which allowed participants to express their own feelings and opinions [7]. Interviews were conducted face-to-face with participants aged 20–40 years old and over, who had two or more years of experience in their respective fields. The participants were selected for interviews based on the authors' initial perceptions of the level of routineness present in their jobs. In ascending degree of perceived job routineness, beginning with highly routine jobs, participant occupations included a retail sales assistant, a pensions administrator, an account strategist and two university professors. The assurance of anonymity aided in the detail respondents were able to provide. Participants were able to provide a critical account of the organizational areas, relational to their job, which they perceived as problematic and how these might be improved by automation. For example, it was discovered that some professors face issues balancing the research aspects of their jobs due to the demanding teaching requirements imposed by the universities' lecture schedule. Thus, it was suggested that teaching could be automated to some degree. Interviews consisted of open-ended questions pertaining to the context of participants' jobs in their respective organization, what tasks they carry out in their jobs, how they use technology to support these activities, how they collaborate and employ creativity to complete tasks and the role they believe automation could play in supporting their job tasks.

The key themes derived from the interviews were used to inform questionnaires which were distributed as part of the subsequent survey. It was understood that the survey could not thoroughly describe the true behaviour of participants. Rather, the questionnaires were used to capture the varying levels of agreement among participants. Thus, the purpose of the survey was to gather information, across a wider population, about how stakeholders view their jobs in the context of the organizational environment and their thoughts about how automation might impact this. Evaluation of the structured data synthesised from the survey responses against the rich detail captured in the interviews allowed the authors to identify the shared/divided views of participants and the understand the potential reasons behind these. Resultantly, 56 respondents from eleven industries in the UK responded. Participants held positions spanning 13 job functions and were aged between 18 and over 60 years old. Furthermore, participants provided responses about the types of skills they mostly employ in their role, which aided further in establishing a profile of their jobs.

4 Main Discussion

Upon analysis of the survey results, it was found that 94% of participants perform tasks outside of their role on a frequent basis. This figure and the interviews conducted both suggest that tasks considered as routine, realistically comprise of complex relationships with other tasks, which can be invoked in certain conditions or at the will of the job occupants themselves (Fig. 2). Such relationships became apparent during the interviews with participants as the majority divulged some additional responsibility that they themselves undertook towards better performing/aiding with their core job responsibilities. For example, an interview was conducted with a Sales

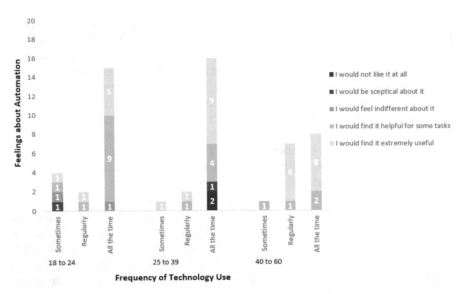

Fig. 2 Technology usage and age comparison chart

Assistant at a retail store, which is considered by the ALM model as routine and subject to 'substantial substitution'. The core job responsibilities of this individual involved processing sales transactions, maintaining the shop floor, providing customer service and managing stock, however, they also expressed that they undertook the non-routine responsibility of carrying out refunds. This allowed the participant to process refund transactions when the supervisor was elsewhere, thus easing queues and increasing customer satisfaction. Relationships like this may be difficult for organizations, who are looking to automate jobs, to perceive for a couple of reasons. Firstly, organizations may be tempted by the potential opportunity to reduce labour costs and increase productivity with the implementation of an autonomous system; this can be referred to as an organizational perspective. This can potentially cloud their understanding of the complexity of the job which they wish to automate as they may easily overlook the intricate relationships shared with other jobs and the contextual environment. Secondly, job occupants have difficulty expressing their tacit knowledge pertaining to the modus operandi with their job tasks. As such, they may not be consciously aware of the subtle interrelationships between the tasks within their jobs and those in other jobs, as well as the immediate environment. Therefore, they may be unable to articulate the tacit work practices which may be essential to overall organizational success. Attempts to understand the intricacies within an employees' job can be viewed as taking a stakeholders' perspective.

The difficulty shared from both an organizational and stakeholder perspective, when attempting to holistically understand a job, is a complicated gap to bridge. This is due to the varying conditions which influence job tasks, or exceptions. Where exceptions are presented, environments can be considered complex, requiring the individual to take alternative action to what they might usually; this action can be considered nonroutine. With the previously given example of the Sales Assistant interviewee, such an exception was that the employee took alternative action (i.e. conducting refunds) in order to ease customer queues. The presence of exceptions within work tasks was identified as a common theme across participants in the interviews. It can therefore be suggested that a task which might be considered routine, in practice, involves nonroutine elements. As Frey elaborates, nonroutine occupations involve "complex perception and manipulation tasks, creative intelligence tasks, and social intelligence" [2]. As such, the study confirmed that 87% of participants believe their jobs require them to work creatively and communicate with colleagues on a frequent basis. Such abilities are also used to overcome exceptions presented in practice, even where tasks are narrowly defined and subject to strict control. This was observed in an interview with a Pensions Administrator working within the financial services industry, whose main responsibilities involved dealing with customer queries. The participant acknowledged that his job required him to adhere to strict policies, thus did not allow much room for creative problem solving. However, upon further questioning it was found that when dealing with particularly complex client queries, the participant would proactively reach out to other members of the organization and third-party organizations in order to collaboratively develop a resolution. These new-founded relationships also allowed the participant to solve similar queries more quickly in the future.

One might question why the ability to conduct nonroutine tasks is important within a job. Given that an outcome of AI implementation is to reduce human labour input whilst increasing productivity, it can be observed that AI is expected to complete a task equivocally or to a higher standard than that of a human job occupant. Thus, the extent to which exceptions can be handled in a job is directly related to the level of quality observed in the output. To this, it might be suggested that organizations considering automating supposedly routine jobs, need to think carefully about the level of cognition realistically required to do such jobs in practice in relation to the output quality they desire/expect. Organizations might better understand the complexity present in tasks by considering them in terms of nonroutine requiring high cognition and nonroutine requiring low cognition from the stakeholders' perspective, rather than from an organizational perspective in terms of routine and nonroutine. With this, tasks are considered in terms of the extent to which they involve handling exceptions. For example, a nonroutine, high cognition task conducted by an Account Strategist, who was one of the interview participants in the study, would be that of understanding a client business problem as it involves a high degree of communication and reflection. Within the same profession, a nonroutine task requiring low cognition could include updating logs of conversations with a client onto a CRM system. Adopting the stakeholders' perspective may allow organizations to more accurately determine which job tasks are better left to a human workforce and to what degree some jobs could be automated without heavily sacrificing quality. In this way, an organization can work with stakeholders towards understanding which tasks might be automatable for the benefit of enhancing the worker's competency to do the job to an exceptional standard.

Having established an understanding of the difference between the perspectives taken when considering routineness in jobs, one can begin to think about the impact of AI implementation on employment within an organization. Specifically, the extent to which automation might impact on peoples' jobs and how they may welcome such change.

Towards developing an awareness of how stakeholders might react to the introduction of AI in their jobs, participants were asked how often they use technology in their jobs each day. This helped the investigation by developing an awareness of the importance of technology within stakeholders' jobs. Resultantly, 89% of survey respondents confirmed that they use technology within their jobs on a frequent basis. From this, it can be deduced that technology largely facilitates stakeholders in task completion, therefore people are already accustomed to using technology in their jobs. This suggests that the introduction of AI, as an entity which can beneficially aid stakeholders with task completion in some way, will be welcomed. Furthermore, participants were questioned as to how they would feel about a technology that could automate some of the repetitive tasks in their jobs. To this, 89% of survey participants agreed that they would find it useful. Exploring this further, the themes identified in the interviews with participants, who were posed the same question, illuminated the desire for automation with particular job tasks which are thought to impede progression with higher priority tasks. For example, an interview with a University Lecturer highlighted that automating the detection of minor errors (e.g. spelling, grammar, punctuation etc.) and the conducting of extensive plagiarism checks when marking student assignments, would allow them to focus more on assessing the meaning of the work. Similarly, the Pensions Administrator believed that a system which could automatically generate a document with the correct information, at the appropriate time for a client could save time and allow them to focus more on resolving queries. Such perceptions held by stakeholders about what could be automated in their jobs indicate the preference of automation with smaller tasks. It is perceived that such incremental automation would necessitate an overall augmentation of the stakeholders' competency to do their job. This also suggests that stakeholders may react positively to the introduction of AI as long as they can see the benefit of it to their jobs. As Mumford proposes, "people will actively welcome change if they believe that it brings with it personal benefits" [9].

Previous conclusions drawn about the nature of exceptions, which are present in any job task practically conducted, entails with it an appreciation of the relationships that exist between jobs in an organizational environment. Job tasks are not always conducted in isolation and often, in practice, involve some human interaction with other tasks. Thus, participants were asked how reliant they believe others (i.e. clients and colleagues) are on their job, to which 75% stated that others are highly reliant. This was also a common theme identified amongst interview participants, thus inferring that some change to the existing technology in an organization which supports stakeholders in their jobs, can affect multiple other jobs. Therefore, a technological change such as the introduction of AI, could necessitate either a positive or negative rippling affect throughout an organization pertaining to the ability of stakeholders to carry out jobs tasks effectively using technology. For AI to be considered a displacing phenomenon of human workers, it should be developed with a comprehensive understanding of the complex and subtle interrelationships between jobs in an organizational environment. As previously mentioned, this is a difficult task due to the mutual difficulty faced when attempting to conceive/express a holistic understanding of a job from both organizational and stakeholder perspectives.

The study also sought to determine how different age groups might react to AI. Initially, it was expected that those who are more acquainted with technology and use it often (i.e. younger generations) would be more welcoming of automation into their jobs. Contrastingly, it was thought that those in older generations, who were thought to be less familiar with technology, would be opposed to automation in their jobs. However, the results yielded suggest otherwise. All age groups questioned (classified into generations X, Y and Z), occupying a number of different jobs which entailed varying levels of technology use, agreed that they would find automation useful in their jobs. This, in combination with the previously drawn understanding that people desire automation with smaller tasks, could indicate that the adoption of AI by stakeholders, who wish to complete job tasks, cannot be reduced to a particular set of factors expressed in a given demographic. Rather, it may be considered that AI will be useful to a wide variety of stakeholders depending on their own unique needs. Such needs are influenced by the unique contextual situation associated with each stakeholder respectively. As an example of this, one of the interviewees, who can be classified into generation X, said they enjoy using technology on a frequent basis in both their personal time and in their working environment. In addition to this, they agreed that an automated entity could be useful in their jobs as long as it was not too intrusive.

5 Conclusion

When considering the likelihood of job automation at the hands of AI, two perspectives emerge. Those who take a task-based view of AI implementation, primarily with the aim of reducing costs and increasing productivity, tend to classify job tasks in terms of routine and nonroutine. This organizational perspective neglects to fully appreciate the exceptions present in a task which make an organizational environment complex and is conducive to the overall output quality desired or expected. Contrastingly, the stakeholder perspective can be adopted, whereby tasks are appreciated in terms of the unique complexity that they present. Such an outlook values the humanistic abilities employed to navigate complex environments, thus categorising jobs in terms of nonroutine tasks, requiring low cognition, and nonroutine tasks requiring high cognition. This will entail a shift in the focus of organizations considering AI implementation towards pursuing the augmentation of employee competencies with their jobs, so that they might perform to a higher standard. Organizations who take this perspective may benefit from increased productivity and quality of output through AI-augmented workers. This paper has also established that stakeholder acceptance of AI in the working environment may not be reduced to a number of particular factors. Rather it might be considered that AI should be developed to augment stakeholders in their jobs based on their own needs as influenced by their unique contextual situations. This would encourage the development of an AI system which stakeholders see the benefit of using.

It can be considered that those stakeholders who occupy positions in less complex environments may be displaced by AI. Such environments may exist where enough exceptions are known about a job to produce an output of a consistent and expected level quality. This could entail progressive change whereby these job occupants targeted for automation are displaced into consultative positions responsible for guiding the development of the system. It may also involve the elimination of some of these jobs, or marginal displacement, as productivity increases through AI-augmented workers thereby reducing the need for as many human workers. For these, advancements in AI-enabled education may be beneficial in effectively upskilling workers.

References

1. Autor, D. H., Levy, F., & Murnane, R. J. (2003). The skill content of recent technological change: An empirical exploration. *The Quarterly Journal of Economics, 118*(4), 1279–1333. https://doi.org/10.1162/003355303322552801.
2. Benedikt Frey, C., Osborne, M. A., Armstrong, S., Bostrom, N., Chinellato, E., Cummins, M., ... Shanahan, M. (2013). The future of employment: how susceptible are jobs to computerisation? 27. https://doi.org/10.1016/j.techfore.2016.08.019.
3. Checkland, P. (1999). *Systems thinking, systems practice*. Chichester: Wiley.
4. Goos, M., & Manning, A. (2007). Lousy and lovely jobs: The rising polarization of work in Britain. *Review of Economics and Statistics, 89*(1), 118–133. https://doi.org/10.1162/rest.89.1.118.
5. Imrie, P., & Bednar, P. (2013). Virtual Personal Assistant. Retrieved from https://www.researchgate.net/publication/264001644.
6. Kouloumpis, E., Wilson, T., & Moore, J. (2011). Twitter sentiment analysis : The good the bad and the OMG ! 538–541.
7. Matthews, B., & Ross, L. (2010). *Research methods*. Longman.
8. Mitra, S., & Gangadaran, M. (2016). Application of close loop expert system for heating control of rolling mill furnaces in a steel plant. In *2016 IEEE 1st International Conference on Control, Measurement and Instrumentation, CMI 2016 (CMI)* (pp. 290–294). https://doi.org/10.1109/CMI.2016.7413757.
9. Mumford, E. (2013). *Designing human systems: The ETHICS method* (1983) (pp. 3–4).
10. Ramesh, A. N., Kambhampati, C., Monson, J. R. T., & Drew, P. J. (2004). Artificial intelligence in medicine. *Annals of the Royal College of Surgeons of England, 86*(5), 334–338. https://doi.org/10.1308/147870804290.
11. Rotman, D. (2017). The relentless pace of automation. *MIT Technology Review, 120*(2 Mar/Apr 2017), 95. Retrieved from https://www.technologyreview.com/s/603465/the-relentless-pace-of-automation/#comments.
12. Sinclair, C., Pierce, L., & Matzner, S. (1999). An application of machine learning to network intrusion detection. In *Proceedings 15th Annual Computer Security Applications Conference (ACSAC'99)*, (Vol. 0293, pp. 1–7). https://doi.org/10.1109/CSAC.1999.816048.

IS in the Cloud and Organizational Benefits: An Exploratory Study

Emanuele Gabriel Margherita⊙ and Alessio Maria Braccini⊙

Abstract Several studies state information systems lead to organizational benefits improving organization efficiency and effectiveness. Cloud computing is nowadays an established strategy for adopting IS potentially providing many benefits. Among them IT costs savings are the most evident ones. However, literature remarks that the realisation of organizational benefits depends on contextual organizational factors and requires organizational change. Whether a cloud computing based strategy for IS delivers organizational benefits or just contributes to costs reduction can be disputed. Taking this point of view, the paper presents the results of an exploratory comparative study analysing 23 cases of different enterprises who run a cloud computing strategy. Using fs/QCA as a method of analysis in a multiple cases setting, the research paper explores the organizational benefits following cloud adoption other than cost savings.

Keywords Organizational benefits of ICT · IT value · Cloud computing · fs/QCA

1 Introduction

Recently several studies shed light on the relationship between information systems (IS) and organizational performance. These researches stated IT resources may play a strategic role when they are combined with organizational resources and integrated into the business value generation process [1, 2].

The information systems consist of resources sustaining organizational information processing [3–5]. ISs enable organizational benefits at every level of the organizational hierarchy in term of efficiency, effectiveness and reducing environmental

E. G. Margherita (✉) · A. M. Braccini
Department of Economics Engineering Society and Business Organization – DEIM,
University of Tuscia, Via del Paradiso, 47, 01100 Viterbo, Italy
e-mail: emargherita@unitus.it

A. M. Braccini
e-mail: abraccini@unitus.it

© Springer Nature Switzerland AG 2020
A. Lazazzara et al. (eds.), *Exploring Digital Ecosystems*,
Lecture Notes in Information Systems and Organisation 33,
https://doi.org/10.1007/978-3-030-23665-6_30

uncertainty [6, 7]. An on-premise strategy of IS ensures control, but opens for the issue of costs and specialisation of resources [8].

Cloud Computing is an emerging strategy for IS adoption, which exploits the advantages of outsourcing: in cloud computing IT resources are stored in massively scalable data centres, and provided as services to users through the Internet [9–11].

The adoption of cloud computing promises several organizational benefits in terms of operations, business continuity, and budget control: cloud computing user enjoys services with the same economies of scale that data centre provides [10, 12].

The literature points that the realization of organizational benefits of IS depends from contextual organizational factors, and requires organizational change [13]. Whether a cloud computing based strategy for IS delivers organizational benefits or just contributes to costs reduction can be disputed.

Taking this point of view, this paper presents the results of an exploratory comparative study analysing cases of different enterprises who run a cloud computing strategy. We focus on the organizational factors of size, type of IS cloud implementation, organizational level of adoption and depth of organizational change. The research paper aims at answering the following research questions:

- R1: Does cloud computing lead to organizational benefits in small, medium, and large enterprises other than just costs reduction?
- R2: Which cloud based IS strategies generate organizational benefits?

2 Theoretical Framework

2.1 Organizational Value of IT

Information technology (IT) has become an integral part of modern organizations [14]. IT resources—both human and technical ones—operate in a synergistic manner in ISs [5, 14, 15]. ISs aim at sustaining organizational information processing and leads to organizational benefits [3, 4]. Though disputed for a long time, the organizational benefits of ISs have been highlighted by several studies at every level of the organizational hierarchy [6, 7]. IS employs for improving decision making by reducing environmental uncertainty, to facilitate organizational knowledge management, to improve control by standardization and integration, and improving efficiency by reducing transaction costs facilitating information circulation [1, 3, 16–19]. Further studies points IS as a fundamental driver for obtaining competitive advantages over the competitors in the long-run, enabling organizational responsiveness to the market and organizational change [20–22].

Given these premises, organizations structure with internal IT departments in change of the technical, financial, and organizational management of IT resources. In a traditional IT environment, the department manages IT resources in-house. This strategy ensures control but IT costs tend to increase [8]. To deal with this disadvantage, organizations start by adopting cloud computing, which offers IT resources for achieving organization's goals at a convenient and affordable price [23, 24]. Besides costs reduction a cloud computing strategy promises other advantages as flexibility and scalability. In this scenario the department manages resources located outside organizational boundaries, accessible through the Internet.

2.2   Cloud Computing

Cloud computing is the successor of technologies for delivering utility computing, such as grid computing, virtualization, and application service provision hosting [24, 25]. For the purpose of this paper, and following the results of a literature review, we adopt the cloud computing definition provided by Mell & Grace for whom cloud computing is "*a model for enabling ubiquitous, convenient, on-demand network access to a shared pool of configurable computing resources (e.g., networks, servers, storage, applications, and services) that can be rapidly provisioned and released with minimal management effort or service provider interaction*" [9].

To furnish its services, cloud computing deploys different types of delivery models, that are distinguished by two building blocks: cloud computing architecture and infrastructure [26]. Cloud computing architecture is widely divided into three categories, namely infrastructure-as-a-service, platform-as-a-service and software-as-a-service [9, 12, 24, 27]. Infrastructure-as-a-service delivers a complete computer infrastructure (resources) as an outsourced service, including servers, software, data centre space, virtualization platforms and network equipment [9, 12, 23–25]. Platform-as-a-service delivers foundational elementals for developing new applications, including programming languages, libraries, services, and tools supported by the provider. The consumer does not manage the cloud infrastructure, albeit he has control on cloud environment configuration settings [9, 12, 23–25]. Software-as-a-service is the delivery of provider's applications on demand over a cloud infrastructure, that allows the consumer to obtain the same benefits of commercial licenses, without complexity of installation and management, as the consumer does not handle or control the cloud infrastructure [9, 10, 12, 23–25].

On the other hand, cloud computing infrastructures can be of different kinds: public, private, community, and hybrid. Public cloud refers to an infrastructure shared among different organizations. Private cloud refers to an infrastructure operated by a single organization. Community cloud is where the cloud infrastructure is provisioned for exclusive use by a specific community of consumers that have shared interests. Hybrid cloud is in the end a mix of two or more distinct cloud infrastructures (private, community, or public) that remain unique entities, but are linked together by standardized or proprietary technology [9, 12, 24, 26, 28].

The literature has extensively acknowledged that cloud computing generates several organizational benefits. Cloud computing is known for providing savings on IT related costs including lower implementation and maintenance costs; less hardware to purchase and support; energy consumption for power and cooling reduction, avoidance of floor space and storage [10, 12, 23, 25, 26]. Cloud computing enables organizations to be more competitive due to flexibility and agility of the computing platforms. Through cloud computing, IT departments save on application development, security, and maintenance time and costs [12, 24, 25]. Cloud computing users may access to specialized resources and applications at a lower cost. As such, license costs of application costs are included into annual fee, as well as Cloud computing users may use leading-edge on–demand applications, bypassing license costs (pay-for-use licenses) [12, 24]. Cloud computing users enjoy the benefits of scalability: the elimination of an up-front IT investment allows cloud computing users to start by a small amount of resources and increase hardware resources only when there is an increase in their needs ("pay as you go"). This peculiar feature is possible by elasticity, the Cloud ability to add or remove resources at a fine grain. It makes Cloud Computing suitable both for new and old organizations [10, 12, 24].

3   Research Design

Given our research questions we investigated potential cause/effect relationships between organizational factors and the quantitative benefits using fs/QCA for data analysis [29–31]. The fs/QCA is an extension of a Boolean data analysis technique called Qualitative Comparative Analysis (QCA), which allows to make casual statements on how multiple combinations of different factors are significant for the observation of a specific outcome [32–34]. fs/QCA allows to use fuzzy set scores to associate cases with factors, and allowing to include in the analysis different degrees of factors presence or absence [34]. fs/QCA is an efficient means for understanding causal complexity in small samples [34]. Given these considerations we retain fs/QCA a suitable method of analysis given our RQs.

3.1   Factors, Calibration and Analysis

The exploratory study is based on the analysis of a sample of 23 case units that have successfully implemented an ISs provide in cloud computing using a public infrastructure. The sample is composed by both profit oriented (12 units) and non-profit oriented (11 units) organizations. The case units are selected from a publicly available database of reports regarding enterprises adopting public cloud computing. These reports have been released by IS vendor describing the kind of cloud adoption, organization factors and the benefits achieved. In particular, we measured from each case unit the following organizational factors:

- Size: SMEs, and large enterprises;
- Value generation orientation: profit oriented, and non-profit oriented;

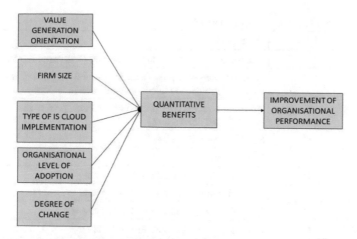

Fig. 1 Schematic representation of data analysis

- Type of IS cloud implementation: enterprise resource planning systems (ERP), customer relationship management systems (CRM), computer supported cooperative work systems (CSCW);
- Organizational level of adoption following the classification suggested by Anthony [35]: operational, middle, top-management [35];
- Depth of organizational change following the taxonomy provided by Venkatraman [21]: evolutionary change, and revolutionary change [21].

Furthermore, we employed the EBITDA index and the staff cost index in the three years following the cloud adoption as further factors. We use quantitative benefits as outcome to measure the impact of the cloud computing implementation. Quantitative benefits encompass both the described benefits of IS in Cloud, the EBITDA index, and the staff costs for the three years following the cloud adoption. Indeed, EBITDA index results from the subtraction between operational margin and staff cost. Accordingly, whether the two indexes increased in the studied period, we can prove the cloud computing leads to a positive organizational change due to improvement of organizational performance increasing the organizational margin rather than a cost reduction. Our research model aims at uncovering these benefits showing where these benefits are captured within the organizations. Our research model is summarized in Fig. 1.

These factors are measured in the fuzzy set interval [0, 1]: a membership score of 1 indicates full membership in the set, whereas a score of 0 indicates full non-membership in the set. Values between 0 and 1 indicate partial membership, with the score of 0.50 representing the threshold of uncertainty between membership and non-membership [36]. The factors used in the analysis are described in Table 1, and the calibration procedure we adopted is described in Table 2. We run the analysis combining the factors as described by the following equation:

Table 1 Description of the investigated variables

Factors	Type	Description
QUANT_BEN	O	Quantitative Benefits accomplished by IS in cloud implementation
PROFIT	C	Profit oriented enterprise (banks, insurances agencies, Italian industrial groups and telecommunication enterprise)
NOPROFIT	C	No-profit oriented enterprise (consortiums, public administrations, hospitals and universities)
SME	C	Small Media Enterprise (SME)
LARGE	C	Large enterprise
ERP	C	Enterprise implemented an ERP system
CRM	C	Enterprise implemented an CRM system
CSCW	C	Enterprise implemented an CSCW system
OPER-LEV	C	IS in cloud manages operational level
TACT-LEV	C	IS in cloud manages tactical level
EVL-BT	C	Evolutionary business transformation effectuated by IS in cloud (enterprises that effectuated a localized exploitation or an internal integration)
REV-BT	C	Revolutionary business transformation effectuated by IS in cloud (enterprises that effectuated a business process redesign or a business network redesign or a business scope redefinition)

$$QUANT\_BEN = f(SME, PROFIT, OPER - LEV,$$
$$EVL - BT, ERP, CRM, CSCW) \qquad (1)$$

Furthermore, we detail the results of the analysis in two groups: on one side SMEs, and large enterprises on the other.

4 Data Analysis and Discussion

We performed the analysis employing the Quine-McClusky algorithm to reproduce the most parsimonious solution. The fs/QCA produces three kinds of solution: complex, parsimonious, or intermediate. The complex solution is based on all the factors shown by all the case units that support the given solution, while the parsimonious solution is minimized through reducing the common factors present across different solutions [34]. The parsimonious solution is that with the greatest explanatory power, thence we relied on this one for answering our research question. The results of the analysis are in Table 3. The consistency and coverage indexes indicate: how closely the relation between the causal factors and the outcome is approximated (consistency), and the empirical relevance of a consistent subset across all the case units under analysis, similar to the R^2 of a linear regression analysis (coverage).

Table 2 Calibration of factors

Factor	Calibration
PROFIT	1: Profit-oriented enterprise 0: Non-profit oriented enterprise
NOPROFIT	1: Non-profit oriented enterprise 0: Profit-oriented enterprise
ERP	0.95: Enterprise implemented an ERP 0.05: Enterprise did not implement an ERP
CRM	0.95: Enterprise implemented a CRM 0.05: Enterprise did not implement a CRM
CSCW	0.95: Enterprise implemented a CSCW 0.05: Enterprise did not implement a CSCW
OPER-LEV	0.95: IS in Cloud manages Operational level 0.45: IS in Cloud manages Tactical level
EVL-BT	0.95: The IS adoption leaded to an evolution of the existing structure 0.05: The IS adoption leaded to a revolutionary business transformation
QUANT_BEN	0.95: IS in Cloud generates dramatic organizational benefits as well as EBITDA and number of employees increase successively IS implementation 0.65: IS in Cloud generated reasonable organizational benefits, as well as EBITDA and number of employees increase successively an IS in Cloud implementation 0.45: IS in Cloud generates sufficient organizational benefits, as well as EBITDA and number of employees decrease successively an IS in Cloud implementation 0.25: IS in Cloud does not generate tangible organizational benefits, EBITDA and number of employees decrease, as well as enterprise is winding up

Table 3 Results of the analysis

Equation	Solutions	Raw coverage	Unique coverage	Consistency
(1)	~OPER-LEV* ~PROFIT	0.08	0.00	1.00
	~OPER-LEV* ~SME	0.16	0.00	1.00
	~OPER-LEV* ~CSCW	0.18	0.00	0.96
	CRM*SME	0.21	0.00	1.00
	SME* ~PROFIT	0.19	0.00	1.00
	~CSCW * SME	0.35	0.00	0.92
	ERP * PROFIT	0.29	0.12	0.78
	EVL-BT* ~ERP* ~PROFIT	0.19	0.08	1.00
	Solution coverage: 0.62		Solution consistency: 0.88	

The symbol ~indicates absence of the factor, the symbol *reads "and"

According to our research model, we are expecting benefits following the cloud strategy to be captured among quantitative benefits. Therefore, the results of the analysis shown in Table 3, allow us to positively answer to the first half of our research question.

We can expect quantitative organizational benefits from a cloud computing strategy for IS management in the following situations:

- For SMEs: in the case of the adoption of CRM systems, for non-profit oriented organizations, and for the adoption of systems other than CSCW;
- For the application of the cloud strategy out of the operational level: not in the case of profit oriented organizations, not in the case of SMEs, and not in the case of CSCW adoption;
- For evolutionary approaches in non-profit oriented organizations targeted at the adoption of systems other than ERPs.
- For the adoption of an ERP system in profit-oriented organizations.

The obtained results so far are a consequence of both the minimization of the complex solution, and the capability of fs/QCA of formulating solutions based on what is stated and what is implied by the data provided. Considering that the sample of analysis mixes both small and large enterprises and given that some solutions specifically refer to one of the two groups, we analysed separately large and SMEs for sharpening the investigation and seek a more detailed relationship. The results of these two further analyses are shown in Table 4 (for large enterprises) and Table 5 (for SMEs).

The two analyses provide further information on the groups of large and small and medium enterprises. For large enterprises, the benefits produced by cloud strategies are only at levels other than the operational one. Likewise, the adoption of ERPs in cloud in profit-oriented enterprise delivers quantitative benefits. Finally, the cloud strategy is expected to deliver quantitative benefits when:

- The adoption does not tackle the operational level;

Table 4 Results of the analysis for large enterprises

Outcome	Solution	Raw coverage	Unique coverage	Consistency
Quantitative benefits	~OPER-LEV	0.19	0.04	1.00
	CSCW* ~PROFIT	0.10	0.00	1.00
	ERP * PROFIT	0.36	0.27	0.84
	EVL-BT* ~ERP* ~PROFIT	0.18	0.03	1.00
	Solution coverage: 0.58		Solution consistency: 0.89	

Table 5 Results of the analysis for SMEs

Outcome	Solution	Raw coverage	Unique coverage	Consistency
Quantitative benefits	CRM	0.46	0.46	1.00
	Solution coverage: 0.46		Solution consistency: 1.00	

- CSCW systems are adopted in organizations that do not have profit orientation;
- A profit-oriented organization implements an ERP;
- An evolutionary approach to IS implementation is adopted for systems other than ERPs, and for organizations that do not have a profit orientation.

The considerations on SMEs are instead simpler: SMEs accomplish quantitative benefits from cloud-based strategies when they implement CRM systems.

5 Discussion and Conclusion

This work is motivated by the identification of benefits other than costs reduction for cloud based IS implementation strategies. The analysis allows us to answer positively to R1 meaning that cloud computing can be used to reduce costs, but also to obtain other forms of organizational benefits. In relation to R2, the summary of the analysis shown in Tables 3, 4 and 5 present the strategies, which contribute to generate organizational benefits. Beyond reduction of IT costs, these case units described organizational benefits in the form of more flexible and agile infrastructure, since it increased the ISs uptime. This enables workforce to increase the productivity. However, these improvements have been captured by tactical level rather than the operational level.

On the other hand, most of the benefits are connected to ISs benefits [18]: our case units contained data related to three different IS implementations ERP, CRM, and CSCW. All the three ISs provided in cloud are enabler of improvements in the organizational processes for large enterprises. Non-profit oriented enterprise shall obtain a valuable improvement by using a CSCW that reduce time for communicating within the organizations, reallocating saved resources in different tasks. CRM suites is also eligible for large and no profit enterprise, that undertakes an evolutionary business transformation. This feature means CRM generates improvement simply modifying processes and not reengineering them. ERP is suitable for large and profit oriented enterprise. Concerning SMEs instead, organizational benefits are expected from the adoption of CRM systems.

This work suggests implications both for managers and for research.

5.1 Implications for Managers

Concerning managerial implications, the results contradicts the popular belief that cloud computing is just for large organizations. We clearly identify that SMEs achieve improvement of financial performance through the implementation of CRM systems. Likewise, Cloud computing is also a viable strategy for implementing ERP systems in large profit-oriented organizations. In those cases, the cost reduction is often coupled by improvement of business processes carried by the best practice of ISs.

This means that managers can opt for a cloud computing strategy not only for a direct cost reduction, but also as a means to realise organizational changes. Whereas, large non-profit organizations may achieve benefits through cloud based collaborative cooperative work systems.

Lastly, this work does not consider the organization life cycle, as well as the reliability of service provider both in terms of SLA agreement and ISs vendors implemented. However, examining the organization that obtained these benefits we discern that quantitative benefits are leaded by implementers that use first-class ISs rather than native and opensource ISs, therefore organization may increase the likelihood of a satisfactory implementation deploying implementers that use top-brand vendors. Regarding the organizational age, the analysis reveal that cloud computing strategies may be adopted both by young companies and by mature companies.

5.2 Implications for Researchers

Concerning instead the research implications, the results of our analysis stimulate two considerations. Firstly, concerning cloud strategies in SMEs, our cases show that the benefits can be expected only in the case of CRM systems without considering the remaining ISs. An implication for research would be to verify whether and when the reaming ISs—like ERS systems, CSCW, or SCM systems—lead to quantitative benefits. Furthermore, ERP remains a prerogative for large enterprise, since the quantitative benefits do not overpass the investment both in immediate and afterwards the three years period following the cloud investment. Therefore, an implication for researchers is to study which peculiar characteristics should have an ERP in order to carry quantitative benefits for SMEs.

Secondly, for large enterprises a result that caught our attention is the focus at levels other than the operational one. This seems to suggest that organizational benefits of cloud-based strategies shall be expected only at the managerial level. In this case an implication for research would be that of specifically studying whether cloud adoption at the operational level produce benefits, or whether forms of resistance to change due to the loss of control on IT resources could explain why the benefits are lost. In doing so, in-depth interview to workforce is a suitable way to shed light on this event.

Moreover, we adopted for distinguishing the depth of organizational change according to the taxonomy of Venkatraman [21], where revolutionary business transformation lead to higher and more consistent benefits than the evolutionary business transformation [21]. However, our analysis did not capture revolutionary approach as a necessary and sufficient factor neither in the results for SMEs nor in the results for large enterprise the revolutionary business transformation appears, whereas the evolutionary business transformation does in the large enterprise results conjointly to non-ERP systems. Therefore, the implication for researchers is to pinpoint a more adequate and today's taxonomy or typology in order to explain depth of organizational change.

5.3 Limitations

Concluding, we have to acknowledge a partial limitation of our study. Our dataset contains only case units of successful cloud strategies adoption. We were therefore not in the condition to observe failures, so we could not confront the results of our analysis with negative cases, which would have increased the validity of our results. This aspect will be targeted in a future research project.

References

1. Melville, N., & Kraemer, K. (2004). Information technology and organizational performance: An integrative model of it business value. *MIS Quarterly, 28*, 283–322.
2. Wade, M., & Hulland, J. (2004). The resource-based view and information systems research: Review, extension, and suggestions for future research. *MIS Quarterly, 28*, 107–142.
3. Martinez M. (2004). Organizzazione, informazione e tecnologie. Il mulino.
4. Piccoli, G. (2012). *Information systems for managers: Text and cases*, 2nd edn. Wiley, Hoboken.
5. Davis, G. B. (2000). Information systems conceptual foundations: looking backward and forward (pp. 61–82). Springer.
6. Grover, V., & Kohli, R. (2012). CoCreating IT value: New capabilities and metrics for multifirm environments. *MIS Quarterly, 36*, 225–232.
7. Kohli, R., & Devaraj, S. (2003). Measuring information technology payoff: A meta-analysis of structural variables in firm-level empirical research. *Inf Syst Res, 14*, 127–145.
8. Braccini, A. M. (2011). *Value generation in organisations*.
9. Mell, P., & Grance, T. (2011). The NIST Definition of cloud computing recommendations of the national institute of standards and technology. *NIST Special Publication, 145*, 7.
10. Erdogmus, H. (2008). Cloud computing: Does Nirvana hide behind the nebula? *IEEE Software, 26*, 4–6.
11. Sandholm, T., & Lee, D. (2014). Notes on cloud computing principles. *Journal of Cloud Computing: Advances, Systems and Applications, 3*, 1–10.
12. Carroll, M., van der Merwe, A., & Kotze, P. (2011). Secure cloud computing: Benefits, risks and controls. In 2011 *Information Security* for *South Africa* (pp. 1–9).
13. Scheepers, H., & Scheepers, R. (2008). A process-focused decision framework for analyzing the business value potential of IT investments. *Information Systems Frontiers, 10*, 321–330.
14. Kohli, R., & Grover, V. (2008). Business value of IT: An essay on expanding research directions to keep up with the times. *Journal of the Association for Information Systems, 9*, 23–39.
15. Bracchi, G., Francalanci, C., & Motta, G. (2010). Sistemi informativi d'impresa.
16. Acar, M. F., Zaim, S., Isik, M., Calisir, F. (2017). Relationships among ERP, supply chain orientation and operational performance.
17. Davenport, T. (1998). Putting the enterprise into the enterprise system. *Harvard Business Review, 76*, 113–121.
18. Zammuto, R. F., Griffith, T. L., Majchrzak, A., et al. (2007). Information technology and the changing fabric of organization. *Organization Science, 18*, 749–762.
19. Kohli, R., & Devaraj, S. (2004). Realizing the business value of information technology investments: An organizational process. *MIS Quarterly Executive, 3*, 53–68.
20. Nevo, S., & Wade, M. W. (2010). resources: antecedents and consequences of sinergistic relationship. *MIS Quarterly, 34*, 163–183.
21. Venkatraman, N. (1994). IT-enabled business transformation—from automation to business scope redefinition. *Sloan Management Review, 35*, 73–87.
22. Izza, S., Vincent, L., Imache, L., Lounis, Y. (2008). An approach for the evaluation of the agility in the context of enterprise interoperability (pp. 3–14). Springer.

23. Sultan, N. (2010). Cloud computing for education: A new dawn? *International Journal of Information Management, 30,* 109–116.
24. Armbrust, M., Stoica, I., Zaharia, M., et al. (2010). A view of cloud computing. *Communications of the ACM, 53,* 50.
25. Creeger, M. (2009). CTO roundtable: Cloud computing. *Communications of the ACM, 52,* 50–56.
26. Grossman, R. L. (2009). The case for cloud computing. IT Professional.
27. de Oliveira, D., Baião, F. A., Mattoso, M. (2010). Towards a taxonomy for cloud computing from an e-science perspective. In *Cloud computing* (pp 47–62). Springer.
28. Hofmann, P., & Woods, D. (2010). Cloud computing: The limits of public clouds for business applications. *IEEE Internet Computing, 14,* 90–93.
29. Ragin, C. C. (1987). *The comparative method: Moving beyond qualitative and quantitative strategies* (Vol. 185). Berkeley/Los Angeles/London: University of California Press. https://doi.org/10.1080/19439340903141415.
30. Ragin, C. C. (2000). *Fuzzy-set social science.* Chicago/London: University of Chicago Press.
31. Schneider, C. Q., Wagemann, C. (2012). Set-*theoretic methods for the social science. A guide to qualitative comparative analysis.*
32. Braumoeller, B. F., & Goertz, G. (2000). The Methodology of necessary conditions. *American Journal of Political Science, 44,* 844–858.
33. Fiss, P. (2007). A set-theoretical approach to organizational configurations. *Academy of Management Review, 32,* 1180–1198.
34. Ragin, C. C. (2006). Set relations in social research: Evaluating their consistency and coverage. *Political Analysis, 14,* 291–310.
35. Anthony, R. N. (1965). *Planning and control: A framework for analysis.* Cambridge MA: Harvard University Press.
36. Ragin, C. C. (2008). Qualitative comparative analysis using fuzzy sets (fsQCA). In C. Thousand Oaks & LSP (Eds.), *Configurational comparative analysis* (pp 87–121).

Organizational Change and Learning: An Explorative Bibliometric-Based Literature Analysis

Stefano Za, Cristiano Ghiringhelli and Francesco Virili

Abstract This paper offers a literature investigation on Organizational Learning processes stemming from Organizational Change initiatives, based on SNA analysis of bibliometric data. The intentionally open, incomplete and question-provoking research outcomes offered by this initial literature analysis represent form one hand a limit, from the other hand they may be seen as an opportunity to listen to the voice of the research community, to collect new ideas and suggestions before proceeding forward towards a better understanding of the fascinating phenomena at the intersection of organizational change and learning.

Keywords Organizational change · Organization learning · Change management · Bibliometric analysis · Keyword analysis · Citation analysis · Social network analysis

1 Introduction

This paper offers a literature investigation on Organizational Learning processes stemming from Organizational Change initiatives. This interest arose from a previous study [1] on the development of an automated parcel sorting system in a major company in the logistic and parcel delivery industry. In that study, the Industrial Engineering (IE) function emerged with a key role of change agent, by balancing several crucial tensions: manual versus automated; planned versus emergent; local versus

S. Za
LUISS University, Rome, Italy
e-mail: sza@luiss.it

C. Ghiringhelli (✉)
University of Milano-Bicocca, Milan, Italy
e-mail: cristiano.ghiringhelli@unimib.it

F. Virili
University of Sassari, Sassari, Italy
e-mail: fvirili@uniss.it

© Springer Nature Switzerland AG 2020
A. Lazazzara et al. (eds.), *Exploring Digital Ecosystems*,
Lecture Notes in Information Systems and Organisation 33,
https://doi.org/10.1007/978-3-030-23665-6_31

global; standard versus ad hoc. According to that study, effective tension management is required for effective organizational change, in presence of high uncertainty. For example, to what extent should a standard software for barcode identification developed in another country be adapted to local practices in different countries (tension standard/ad hoc and global/local)? According to this perspective, the effective resolution of continuous paradoxical dilemmas is not only a requirement for effective change. It is also a trigger of organizational learning. By managing tensions and finding new unexpected solutions (often with trial and error), the organization develops new knowledge and generates a need to codify and institutionalize it. To this regard, in the case under observation Industrial Engineering was tasked with the challenge of enabling this process, by creating a change environment in which learning opportunities can be identified, discussed, integrated and institutionalized. But how is organizational learning actually produced during organizational change? What are the most important enablers and blockers? From the theoretical point of view, answers to such questions have their roots in two research traditions: on the one hand, in the organizational change studies, particularly in presence of uncertainty and high complexity; on the other hand, in the organizational learning research stream, particularly when learning emerges from action and behaviors.

The analysis of the literature on organizational learning change is challenging, for two main reasons. First, the two phenomena are connected in complex ways. Second, the historical succession of schools of thought has produced several different views, determining both evolution and overlapping or contrasting frameworks.

The intimate connection of change and learning is nowadays very well recognized in literature. For example, Clegg and colleagues [2] suggest to "[...] rethink and reframe organizational learning in terms of organizational becoming" (page 147).

To take into account the different views and perspectives proposed by the literature to explain the relationship between change and learning, we decided to carry out a methodological analysis of the literature based on database retrieval of bibliographic information and social network analysis.

The analysis is aimed on the one side at identifying the main schools of thought, on the other side at uncovering their connections in a general network of relationships, as depicted by bibliometric analysis.

The basic research question of our investigation is therefore the following: what are the main studies investigating in the same time organizational change and organizational learning phenomena?

In order to identify the main perspectives adopted overtime, our social network analysis of bibliographic data is focused on two sources. First, a keyword analysis of the high-impact research papers, second an analysis of co-citations evidencing flagship contributions.

2 Research Protocol

In this phase of the research project, the main aim is to identify the relevant literature discussing the topics of interest, exploring their contents using bibliometric information. Following the guidelines provided by Za and Braccini [3] we firstly focus on the creation of the dataset (data setting) and afterwards perform the data analysis.

The first step concerns the data collection and involves the identification of a suitable source for literature search. We identified ISI (Institute for Scientific Information) Web of Science (ISI-WoS, http://apps.webofknowledge.com) as the platform to perform the literature search and selection, as already done by several authors in other IS studies [4–7]. We conducted the searches and retrieved publication data taking into account the main four citation databases: Science Citation Index Expanded (SCI-E), Social Sciences Citation Index (SSCI), Arts & Humanities Citation Index (A&HCI) and Emerging Sources Citation Index (ESCI). They fully cover over 12,000 journals.

In order to identify a proper set of keywords, we performed a preliminary query using just three basic keywords: "Change Management", "Organizational Change" and "Organizational Learning". The American English words "organiz-" were also coupled with their correspondent British English version "organis-". The scope of the query was not limited to the author-provided keyword list on each contribution, but also extended to titles and abstracts.

The query syntax is shown below:

```
TOPIC: ("organisational change" OR "organizational
change" OR "Change management") AND TOPIC:
("organisational learning" OR "organizational
learning")
Refined by: LANGUAGES: (ENGLISH)
```

This query returned a first set of 278 papers. The list produced by the database was ordered by total citations. Consistently with our research approach, we restricted our focus to the high-impact papers. The selection criterium was based on total number of citations: we therefore included only papers with more than 50 total citations, restricting the dataset from 278 to 35 high-impact papers.

In order to refine the keyword list, we carried out a quick examination of the 35 articles, the most cited first, starting from title and abstract and, if necessary, going through the article content. This content analysis, not required in several cases of widely known flagship contributions, evidenced that most of the high-impact papers were actually fitting our research theme. A few of them, instead, were "false-positives" jointly using our keywords for different reasons. For example, Davison et al., in "Principles of Canonical Action Research" (2004), discusses the application of the action-research methodology in IS field. In this false-positive, the presence of our keywords is not surprising, because the action-research approach is often relevant for both organizational change and organizational learning. But, given that this paper is focused on purely methodological issues, it cannot be considered as a study focused on organizational change and organizational learning and it should be discarded as a false positive; on the other hand, the term "action research" should instead be considered as a candidate additional keyword the next step of analysis.

Excluding all the false-positives, we reduced the number of high-impact articles from 35 to 20, enlisted here below in Table 1.

These 20 articles represent a group of studies not only well focused on the two subjects of our research. They are also outstanding quality contributions, characterized for both high rigor and relevance, and appeared in prestigious outlets. Overall, the spectrum of theoretical views, methodological choices and levels of analysis is very wide and rich. These outstanding studies on change and learning often cross other relevant subjects, pointing out other promising new keywords. Often, but not always, such keywords are explicitly reported in the keyword list by authors. The resulting additional keywords list is the following:

- Knowledge Acquisition
- Knowledge Development
- Capability Building
- Capability Development
- Action Research
- Exploration
- Identity
- Trial-And-Error
- Innovation.

In order to limit the number of keywords in the final list, we decided to exclude partially overlapping expressions (e.g.: learning and experiential learning). Furthermore, we excluded the conference proceedings focusing only on journal and book contributions. In this way, the following second query was performed at the end of May 2018:

```
TOPIC: ("organisational change" OR "organizational
change" OR "Change management") AND TOPIC:
("organisational learning" OR "organizational learning"
OR "Knowledge acquisition" OR "knowledge development"
OR "Capability building" OR "Capability development"
OR "Action research" OR "Exploration" OR "Identity" OR
"Trial-and-error" OR "Innovation")
Refined by: [excluding] DOCUMENT TYPES: (EDITORIAL
MATERIAL OR MEETING ABSTRACT OR PROCEEDINGS PAPER OR
BOOK REVIEW OR BOOK CHAPTER) AND LANGUAGES: (ENGLISH)
```

This time the query produced 1813 records corresponding to as many papers published from 1990 up to May 2018.

Following the further steps of the research protocol [3], we performed a descriptive analysis (Sect. 3.1) concerning the second dataset (1813 records), and the content analysis (Sect. 3.2) using SNA for exploring the main topics

Table 1 High-impact articles for refine the keyword list

Title	Authors	Source title	Year	Citations
Organizational learning: The contributing processes and the literatures	Huber, George P.	Organization Science	1991	2868
Capabilities, cognition, and inertia: Evidence from digital imaging	Tripsas, M; Gavetti, G	Strategic Management Journal	2000	782
Deliberate learning in corporate acquisitions: Post-acquisition strategies and integration capability in US bank mergers	Zollo, M; Singh, H	Strategic Management Journal	2004	367
Organizational transformation during institutional upheaval	Newman, KL	Academy of Management Review	2000	293
An organizational learning-model of convergence and reorientation	Lant, Tk; Mezias, Sj	Organization Science	1992	224
Adaptation as information restriction: The hot stove effect	Denrell, J; March, JG	Organization Science	2001	200
Organizational identity and learning: A psychodynamic perspective	Brown, AD; Starkey, K	Academy of Management Review	2000	198
Business Model Innovation through Trial-and-Error Learning. The Naturhouse Case	Sosna, M; Trevinyo-Rodriguez, RN; Velamuri, SR	Long Range Planning	2010	191
Creating a market orientation: A longitudinal, multifirm, grounded analysis of cultural transformation	Gebhardt, GF.; Carpenter, GS.; Sherry, John F., Jr.	Journal of Marketing	2006	172
Learning/becoming/organizing	Clegg, SR; Kornberger, M; Rhodes, C	Organization	2005	124
Organizational unlearning	Tsang, EWK.; Zahra, SA	Human Relations	2008	107

(continued)

Table 1 (continued)

Title	Authors	Source title	Year	Citations
Conditioned emergence: A dissipative structures approach to transformation	Macintosh, R; Maclean, D	Strategic Management Journal	1999	104
Organizational unlearning as changes in beliefs and routines in organizations	Akgun, AE.; Byrne, JC.; Lynn, GS.; Keskin	Journal of Organizational Change Management	2007	100
When problem solving prevents organizational learning	Tucker, AL; Edmondson, AC; Spear, S	Journal of Organizational Change Management	2002	97
Development of a measure for the organizational learning construct	Templeton, GF; Lewis, BR; Snyder, CA	Journal of Management Information Systems	2002	96
Transforming work through information technology: A comparative case study of geographic information systems in county government	Robey, D; Sahay, S	Information Systems Research	1996	92
Structural evolution through idiosyncratic jobs: The potential for unplanned learning	Miner, Anne S.	Organization Science	1990	68
A learning perspective on the offshoring of advanced services	Jensen, PD, Orberg	Journal Of International Management	2009	59
Situated learning and the situated knowledge web: Exploring the ground beneath knowledge management	Nidumolu, SR; Subramani, M; Aldrich, A	Journal of Management Information Systems	2001	59
Responding to hypercompetition: The structure and processes of a regional learning network organization	HanssenBauer, J; Snow, CC	Organization Science	1996	56

discussed by the corpus, proposing in this second section a comparison between the results produced by both queries.

3 Data Analysis

The examination of the 1813 publications was done following two steps: (i) a descriptive analysis of our sample providing information on the evolution of number of publications and citations over the year and an overview of the most productive journals, and (ii) the content analysis, considering the keywords defined by the authors in their contributions as well as the main references cited in the dataset. In order to recognize the relationships among the discussed topics, SNA tools are used for creating the co-occurrence graph for the keywords and the co-citation graph based on the most cited references.

3.1 Descriptive Analysis

Figure 1 depicts the publications and citations trends over the last three decades. In particular, the dark grey line portrays the distribution over the years of the 1813 publications of the dataset (left scale). The bright grey line displays the evolution of citations (right scale).

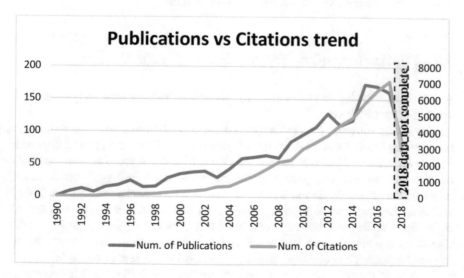

Fig. 1 The publications and citations trend over the years

Table 2 The most active journals (with more than 15 papers in the dataset)

Journals	N. papers	Journals	N. papers
Journal of Organizational Change Management	149(8%)	Organization Studies	26(1%)
Organization Science	43(2%)	Journal of Applied Behavioral Science	23(1%)
Academy of Management Journal	30(1%)	Organization	21(1%)
Strategic Management Journal	29(1%)	International Journal of Technology Management	19(1%)
Human Relations	27(1%)	Systemic Practice and Action Research	17(0%)

The two trends are not only clearly ascending, but with a growing inclination. This pattern evidences the ever-increasing popularity of the subject, particularly in the last ten years. The data obtained for the current year (2018) are not complete since we conducted the search on May 2018. In order to have an updated dataset on which performing our analysis, we decide to keep them in. For this reason, there is a misleading perception of decline of publication and citation trends concerning the last year.

The following table shows the journals with more than 15 papers in the dataset. Overall, these results suggest that the increasing interest on organizational change and learning is still confined to a relatively limited number of outlets. The top three journals in the table are Journal of Organizational Change Management, Organization Science and Academy of Management Journal (Table 2).

3.2 The Analysis of the Topics Discussed in the Dataset

We carried out the topics analysis in two ways. First, by keywords analysis, second, by co-citations analysis.

Keywords analysis. As a basis for a comparative analysis between the datasets produced by the first and the second query, we identified the most popular keywords in the two datasets (Tables 3 and 4). We also carried out a social network analysis of keywords occurrences, producing the graph displayed in Figs. 2 and 3. In the network, the keywords are the nodes and there is a tie between two of them if they are mentioned together in the same publication (co-occurrence). The thickness of each edge reflects the number of contributions in which the pair appears, while the size of each node is based on the number of papers in which the corresponding keyword is used. The node label size is proportional to the size of the node.

Looking at the information regarding the first dataset (278 papers) it is possible to observe that even though "organizational learning" (frequency: 114) is mentioned 33% more than "organizational change" (81), they are used together in almost 20%

Table 3 Most recurring keywords in the first dataset (mentioned at least in 6 papers)

Keywords	N. papers	Keywords	N. papers
Organizational learning	114	Action research	8
Organizational change	81	Organizational culture	7
Change management	32	Change	6
Organisational learning	20	Culture	6
Knowledge management	17	Information technology	6
Innovation	15	Organisational change	6
Learning	13	Organizational development	6

Table 4 Most recurring keywords in the second dataset (mentioned at least in 20 papers)

Keywords	N. papers	Keywords	N. papers
Organizational change	449	Knowledge management	29
Change management	190	Institutional theory	28
Innovation	173	Case study	27
Organizational learning	89	Learning	26
Action research	62	Sustainability	26
Leadership	55	Technological change	24
Organisational change	53	Information technology	23
Change	45	Organizational innovation	23
Identity	36	Sensemaking	23
Organizational culture	35	Management	22
Implementation	29	Organizational development	22

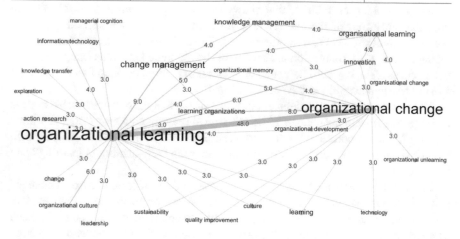

Fig. 2 Keywords co-occurrence graph for the first dataset (278)

Fig. 3 Keywords co-occurrence graph for the second dataset (1813)

of the papers in the dataset (48). It is the most relevant co-occurrence, since the other pairs occur in less than 10 papers. The following co-occurrence (9) is between "organizational change" and "change management", the third keyword by frequency (32). This situation, clearly due to the construction of the query, suggests the need of a further step of analysis.

The information regarding the second dataset (1813 papers) shows a different scenario. Looking at Table 4, that shows the occurrences more than 20, we can note that only four of the ten new keywords introduced in the second query are present: "innovation" (173), "action-research" (62), "identity" (36) and "knowledge management" (29). Innovation is also one of the top three keywords (more than 100 occurrences). The keyword "organizational learning" dropped from first (frequency: 114) to fourth place (89) in the second dataset.

The co-occurrence graph depicted in Fig. 3 shows that the most connected node is by large "organizational change". The other most relevant nodes are "organizational learning", "innovation" and "change management". All of them are connected, with the noticeable exception of the missing link between "organizational learning" and "innovation".

The different patterns of occurrences and connections of "organizational change" and "change management" may suggest that the two keywords are often used in different kinds of research. On the one hand, change management could be seen as a narrower field of investigation, usually focused on the management of change projects at the internal side of organization, with a level of analysis often restricted to individuals and groups. On the other hand, organizational change research has a much wider span, including not only change management subjects (sometimes the two keywords are used in conjunction, as testified by their direct connection),

Table 5 Mot cited references in the second dataset (receiving more than 100 citations)

References	No. of citations	Subgraph
Hannan and Freeman [8]	154	Green
March [9]	138	Green
DiMaggio and Powell [10]	136	Green
Nelson and Winter [11]	128	Green
Cyert and March [12]	122	Green
Weick [13]	116	Purple
Eisenhardt [14]	113	Purple
Cohen and Levinthal [15]	106	Green
Meyer and Rowan [16]	99	Green
Miles et al. [17]	91	Purple
Levitt and March [18]	90	Green

but also studies at the interorganizational level analysis, including for example the investigation on the effects of the technological change, institutional influences and ecological selection on evolution among groups of organizations.

Co-citation analysis. In order to further investigate the high impact studies extracted in the second dataset, we performed a citation and co-citation analysis. Table 5 shows, in descending order, the main references cited by at least 90 papers in the dataset. It is possible to observe that some highly cited references are representative of entire schools of thought, and they are often used as customary citations to identify the research framework/tradition, like for example Hannan and Freeman [8], a development of the Population Ecology of Organization, or DiMaggio and Powell [10], for the Neoinstitutionalism.

As a complement, we performed also the co-citation analysis creating the co-citation graph (Fig. 4), where each node represents a reference cited by a paper in the dataset. There is an arc between two nodes if both are cited together at least in 15 papers. The size of each node reflects the number of papers in the dataset citing the specific reference.

The co-citation graph gives us the possibility to recognize, also in this case, two main network clusters based on the references mentioned in two main subgraphs (the green and the purple one). The first group of studies (the green one, at the top of the figure), including flagship references of interorganizational relationship studies like the Neoinstitutionalism, the Population Ecology of Organization and the Innovation Theory [11] may be interpreted as representative of the larger, collective sense of organizational change, concerned with groups of organizations interacting and evolving together under the influence of the external environment.

The second group (the purple one, at the bottom of the figure) is smaller than the first and it includes, among others, several flagship methodological references (qualitative research methods: [17], case studies: [14], [19]; grounded theory: [20]). Among the most cited theoretical references, several studies with perspectives on

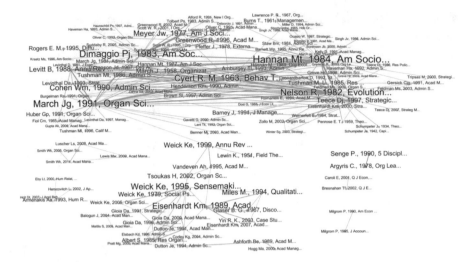

Fig. 4 Co-citation graph for the second dataset (1813)

change based on sensemaking and organizational identity are present here, with flagship scholars like Weick, Gioia, Tsoukas and Chia. In the upper part of the cluster, a classical, definitional theoretical analysis on change management by Van De Ven and Poole [21]. By large, this second group of studies may be seen as including perspectives focused on the psychological analysis of behavioral aspects, often at the individual and group level, looking at the social construction and the shaping of change from the internal side of organization.

It may be interesting to notice that the study by Van De Ven and Poole [21] connects the two clusters: on the one hand, change management analyses focused on the shaping of behaviors in the internal side of organizations (red cluster, below); on the other hand, studies on larger phenomena of evolutionary change at the interorganizational level as a reaction to environmental, technological or institutional discontinuities (green cluster, above).

In which of the two groups can we identify organizational learning flagship contributions? At a first view the answer is: in the upper cluster. The most evident highly cited organizational learning studies are Cohen and Levinthal [15] and Levitt and March [18]; we may also include Cyert and March [22], as a foundational contribution. We might see here organizations as learning in reaction to wider external phenomena, by generating organizational knowledge and institutionalized routines.

Another seminal contribution on organizational learning is the 1978 book from Argyris and Schon, absent in Table 5, but cited in four different version and editions in our data set. The cumulative count of citations, including the 1996 update of the book, is therefore over 100. It appears as a separate small red cluster, with a connection to the widely diffused, practice oriented popularization of the concept of "learning organization" by Senge [23].

4 Discussion and Conclusions

The literature exploration proposed here was originally motivated by the field observation of organizational learning processes stemming from complex change management projects. What do we already know about organizational learning processes originated by change management? Our exploration strategy is based on keyword extraction and bibliometric analysis of high-impact papers. A first stage with three basic keywords identified a core initial data set of 278 papers, including 20 high-impact core studies at the intersection of organizational change and learning. Ten additional keywords were identified and used in a second stage to extract a new data set of 1813 papers. The keyword, citation, and co-citation analysis of the two data sets, besides the identification of prominent high-impact studies and highly cited references, interesting indications and directions for further research.

The most relevant pattern discussed above include (1) the empirical identification of a small but ever growing stream of research on organizational learning, besides a much wider and mature research stream on organizational change; (2) the distinction of different sense and meaning in the use of the keywords "organizational change" and "change management", the second one often connected to a portion of organizational change studies focused on internal change projects; (3) the identification by co-citation analysis of two clusters of reference studies, connected on the one side with environmental, technological or institutional change at the interorganizational level, on the other side to behavioral studies on the social construction and shaping of change both at the individual and at the group level; (4) the presence of highly cited reference studies on learning in the first cluster (5) an interesting pattern of links and relationships between different schools of thought that certainly deserves a closer attention and further investigation, paving the way for further analysis.

The intentionally open, incomplete and question-provoking research outcomes offered here may be seen as a limit, but they are also an opportunity to listen to the voice of the research community, to collect new ideas and suggestions before proceeding forward towards a better understanding of the fascinating phenomena at the intersection of organizational change and learning.

References

1. Virili, F., & Ghiringhelli, C. (2019). Automation as Management of Paradoxical Tensions: The Role of Industrial Engineering. In F. Cabitza, C. Batini, & M. Magni (Eds.), *Organizing for the Digital World* (pp. 7–21). IT for Individuals: Communities and Societies, Springer International Publishing.
2. Clegg, S. R., Kornberger, M., & Rhodes, C. (2005). Learning/Becoming/Organizing. *Organization, 12*(2), 147–167.
3. Za, S., & Braccini, A. M. (2017). Tracing the Roots of the organizational benefits of IT services. In S. Za, M. Drăgoicea, & M. Cavallari (Eds.), *LNBIP—exploring services science* (pp. 3–11). Berlin, Heidelberg: Springer International Publishing.

4. Baskerville, R. L., & Myers, M. D. (2002). Information systems as a reference discipline. *Management Information Systems Quarterly, 26,* 1–14.
5. Clarke, R. (2008). An exploratory study of information systems researcher impact. *Communication of the Association for Information Systems, 22,* 1–32.
6. Za, S., & Spagnoletti, P., (2013). Knowledge creation processes in information systems and management: Lessons from simulation studies. In *Lecture Notes in Information Systems and Organisation.*
7. Ricciardi, F., & Za, S., (2015). Smart city research as an interdisciplinary crossroads: A challenge for management and organization studies. In Mola, L., Pennarola, F., Za, S. (Eds.), *From information to smart society* (vol. 5. pp 163–171), LNISO.
8. Hannan, M. T., & Freeman, J. (1984). Structural Inertia and organizational change. *American Sociological Review, 49*(2), 149–164.
9. March, J. G. (1991). Exploration and exploitation in organizational learning. *Organization science, 2*(1), 71–87.
10. Dimaggio, P. J., & Powell, W. W. (1983). The iron cage revisited: Institutional isomorphism and collective rationality in organizational fields. *American Sociological Review, 48,* 147–160.
11. Nelson, R., & Winter, S. (1982). *An evolutionary theory of economic change.* Cambridge, MA: Harvard University Press.
12. Cyert, R. M., & March, J. G. (1963). A behavioral theory of the firm. *Englewood Cliffs, NJ, 2,* 169–187.
13. Weick, K. E. (1995). *Sensemaking in organizations* (vol. 3). Sage.
14. Eisenhardt, K. M. (1989). Building theories from case study research. *Academy of Management Review, 14,* 532–550.
15. Cohen, W. M., & Levinthal, D. A. (1990). Absorptive capacity: A new perspective on learning and innovation. *Administrative Science Quarterly, 35,* 128–152.
16. Meyer, J. W., & Rowan, B. (1977). Institutionalized organizations: Formal structure as myth and ceremony. *American journal of sociology, 83*(2), 340–363.
17. Miles, M. B., Huberman, A. M., Huberman, M. A., & Huberman, M. (1994). *Qualitative data analysis: An expanded sourcebook,* Sage Publications.
18. Levitt, B., & March, J. G. (1988). Organizational learning. *Annual Review of Sociology, 14,* 319–338.
19. Yin, R. K. (2003). *Case study research : Design and methods,* Sage Publications.
20. Glaser, B. G., & Strauss, A. L. (1973). *The discovery of grounded theory : Strategies for qualitative research.* Aldine Pub.
21. Van de Ven, A. H., & Poole, M. S. (1995). Explaining development and change in organizations. *Academy of Management Review, 20*(3), 510–540.
22. Cyert, C., & March, J. G. (1963). *A behavioral theory of the firm.* New York: Prentice-Hall.
23. Senge, P. M. (1990). *The fifth discipline.* Doubleday/Currency: The Art and Practice of the Learning Organization.

Community-Oriented Motivations and Knowledge Sharing as Drivers of Success Within Food Assemblies

Paola De Bernardi⑩, Alberto Bertello⑩ and Francesco Venuti⑩

Abstract Despite the increased level of awareness and concern towards social and environmental issues, many consumers have not yet modified their consumption and lifestyle behaviour. In response to this trend, previous works have shown that social and collective actions among customers, enabled by certain food system networks, have the potential to transform passive consumers into active citizens. The aim of this paper is to analyse if community-oriented motivations and knowledge sharing within a network have a positive effect on customers' consumption in terms of purchase frequency and quantity. To do so we collected data from Italian Food Assemblies, a particular kind of alternative food network based on a digital platform enabling the direct trade between communities and local farmers and producers. The simultaneous coexistence of online and on-site elements characterizing Food Assemblies allowed us to individuate possible differences between knowledge sharing through online and onsite interactions. We developed a quantitative analysis based on a regression model, collecting data from a questionnaire submitted to 8497 Italian food assembly customers, finally receiving 2115 valid answers. The results show that community-oriented motivations and on-site knowledge sharing appear to be statistically significant for purchase frequency, while online knowledge sharing affects both frequency and quantity.

Keywords Alternative food network · Social capital · Digitalisation · Food assembly · Knowledge sharing · Community-oriented motivations

P. De Bernardi (✉) · A. Bertello
Department of Management, University of Turin, C.so Unione Sovietica,
218/bis, Turin, Italy
e-mail: paola.debernardi@unito.it

F. Venuti
ESCP EUROPE Turin Campus, C.so Unione Sovietica, 218/bis, Turin, Italy

© Springer Nature Switzerland AG 2020
A. Lazazzara et al. (eds.), *Exploring Digital Ecosystems*,
Lecture Notes in Information Systems and Organisation 33,
https://doi.org/10.1007/978-3-030-23665-6_32

1 Introduction

Over the last decades, concerns over sustainability issues have pushed the adoption of different approaches to consumption. Initiatives such as farmers' markets, box schemes, solidarity purchasing groups, and community supported agriculture have challenged conventional food systems by proposing a decentralized, community-focused, independent, and sustainable model, based on the concept of short food supply chain (SFSC) [1–4]. These new forms of food production, distribution, and consumption are also known within the academic world under the heading of Alternative Food Networks (AFNs) [5].

AFNs have given rise to cross-sectional research streams [1, 3, 6–11]; the novelty of this topic has led scholars to mainly focus on qualitative studies [9]. However, the adoption of quantitative approaches focusing on the complex system of relationships and knowledge sharing created throughout AFNs could help to extend the body of knowledge reached to date. For this reason, we carried out a regression analysis to deeply understand if knowledge sharing practices and community-oriented motivations affect the success of an AFN.

To do so we focused our analysis on a particular kind of AFN, the so-called Food Assembly (FA), a social and collaborative enterprise born in France in 2010 and spread to other European countries, characterized by a hybrid form where on-site (i.e., farmers' markets) and online elements (i.e., e-commerce) coexist simultaneously [2, 12]. Data were collected with a questionnaire submitted to 8497 Italian FA customers, receiving a total of 2115 valid responses.

The results show that both direct onsite contact with the local producers and with other buyers during the produce distribution significantly affect purchase frequency. While knowledge sharing through the FA digital platform positively affect both the frequency and the quantity. Customer's community-oriented motivations are instead significant for purchase frequency.

This paper contributes to the literature on social capital theory and knowledge-based view by applying these two well-known theories to a new field such as that of FA. The paper has also practical contributions since it aims to understand which consumer attitudes and practices, and which interaction channels represent a leverage to enhance customer participation in AFNs [13, 14].

2 Background Review and Hypothesis Development

2.1 Alternative Food Networks

The term AFN identifies a comprehensive body of practices characterised by short supply chains such as community supported agriculture [15, 16], box schemes [17, 18], farmers' markets [19], solidarity purchasing groups [20, 21], food cooperatives [22], farm stands [23], and food assemblies [2, 12, 24]. The AFN phenomenon is on the increase in Europe and North America [25], and is especially booming in Italy, both as a consequence of governmental strategies [1, 26, 27] and increased public sensitivity to transparency and safety issues regarding food [28, 29]. Food systems based on local networks have already begun to transform costumers from passive to active citizens [13], however, not every AFN can survive over time. Although AFNs' resilience depends on several factors [30, 31], it seems readily apparent that AFN's survival is directly related to the customers' purchase frequency and quantity within every AFN.

2.2 Community-Oriented Motivations

The SFSC characterizing AFNs has redesigned the way a variety of social and economic actors engage and coalesce together in order to create novel economic circuits ready to respond to community needs [32–35]. Many scholars have focused their attention on the new role played by the customer, and even more attracted by transparency and sustainable food systems [20, 21, 36]. The higher level of cooperation and co-participation between AFN's members is a direct consequence of the climate of trust and reciprocity characterizing this new form of food production, distribution, and consumption [2, 21]. Between the various factors that increase active participation in AFN, customer's community-oriented motivations play an important role that needs to be explored more in depth [37–40]. Community-oriented motivations have been defined as those aspects related to social relationships, sense of togetherness and solidarity between AFN actors [11]. According to their results, although self-oriented motives remain the main reason for AFN members from all models to engage, community-oriented motivations also play an important role; as a matter of fact, even those people who did not indicate community-oriented motivations as a first driver, acknowledged their importance stating that they have become an important driver during the network participation. According to [41], relationships based on trust among AFN members boost a sense of community aimed at achieving social, economic, and environmental goals. Thus, considering the importance of community-oriented motivations within AFNs, we can express our first two hypotheses as follows:

- H1a
  (COM → PF): The higher the customer's community-oriented motivations (COM), the higher the purchase frequency (PF) within the Food Assembly.
- H1b
  (COM → PQ): The higher the customer's community-oriented motivations (COM), the higher the purchase quantity (PQ) within the Food Assembly.

2.3 Knowledge Sharing Through Online and On-Site Channels

Social embeddedness has been evidenced as being one of the main features of AFNs [42]. Through its social dimension, in fact, AFNs enhance the development of personal relationships between members [13], and such relationships have been shown to increase social capital [43, 44]. According to [45], social capital attributes can be collected into three clusters, while [46] identified the main feature of each cluster: social trust, shared goals, and network ties. Trust is the most frequently mentioned facilitator of knowledge sharing [47–49], and more generally, a fundamental characteristic of networks that aim to facilitate interaction between its actors [50–54]. However, shared goals and network ties have been found to be relevant in knowledge integration and exchange as well [46, 55]. Knowledge has been widely recognized in the modern society as a strategic asset and a driver of success for many organisations from different points of view and different outcomes [56–59]. As argued by Inkpen and Tsang [60], networks provide members with access to knowledge, however, different types of network correspond to different ways of exchanging and sharing knowledge. While it is already established that relationships within AFNs boost knowledge sharing processes [41, 61], to date few studies have focused on opportunities enabled by online platform cooperatives as, in this case, FA. According to [12], a digital platform can enhance organisational cooperation among their members. Community-oriented platforms geared to achieving social and environmental goals, such as a FA, can benefit from online interactions since digital platforms develop some collective rules leading to knowledge sharing and self-management practices based on individuals' ability to manage trust within the network. At the same time, the mixture of online communications on digital platforms and on-site interactions in a decentralized-local physical network [62] can enable interaction and coordination across a network of actors [2, 36] who otherwise would remain separated or unable to contribute to the system. The spreading of the so called ROPO phenomenon ("research online, purchase offline") opened the doors to new behaviours from customers and new ways of information provision [63–65], making online and on-site interactions complementary and bearers of different contents and meanings [36, 66]. As pointed out by many scholars [67–69], knowledge exchange and sustainable value co-creation may be triggered by technological infrastructure allowing individuals to communicate and self-organise in a more transparent and less complex way. Based on these previous findings, we analysed both on-site and online knowledge sharing practices, positing that:

- H2a
  (CKS → PF): The higher the knowledge sharing among the customers during the produce distribution (CKS), the higher the purchase frequency (PF) within the Food Assembly.

- H2b

  (CKS → PQ): The higher the knowledge sharing among the customers during the produce distribution (CKS), the higher the purchase quantity (PQ) within the Food Assembly.

- H2c

  (PKS → PF): The higher the knowledge sharing through the direct contact with the producers (PKS), the higher the purchase frequency (PF) within the Food Assembly.

- H2d

  (PKS → PQ): The higher the knowledge sharing through the direct contact with the producers (PKS), the higher the purchase quantity (PQ) within the Food Assembly.

- H2e

  (OKS → PF): The higher the online knowledge sharing through the digital platform (OKS), the higher the purchase frequency (PF) within the Food Assembly.

- H2f

  (OKS → PQ): The higher the online knowledge sharing through the digital platform (OKS), the higher the purchase quantity (PQ) within the Food Assembly.

3 Research Design and Methodology

The research development was articulated in different steps. After the analysis of the existing literature on AFNs, FAs, social capital theory and knowledge-based view, and the development of the theoretical framework we carried out focus groups and in-depth interviews as preliminary study to find the questionnaire items. The next step was the questionnaire development, administration and the quantitative regression analysis based on data collected from questionnaires.

3.1 Data Collection

The emergence of AFNs has been drawing the attention of scholars from different fields, who have been trying to understand and explain these recent phenomena. In order to better understand the FA organisation, its value creation process and its critical success factors, a set of 6 face to face semi-structured interviews with FA managers have been conducted. They were followed by specific focus groups with FA customers (both active and non-active) in order to elicit more in-depth information through interactive discussions [70] about the community collaborative and participatory behaviours. Focus groups were found to be useful for the issue under investigation, as both active and non-active customers could have described, using their own words, their experiences, perceptions, motivations, attitudes, and habits [71, 72].

After the interviews and the focus groups, a detailed questionnaire was designed in order to collect specific information to test our hypothesis. On September 2017, there were 10194 active customers in the Italian FA. Clients that had made at least one purchase from the FA during the previous 12 months were considered "active customers". In this group, those who made at least one purchase per month in the last year could be considered "loyal customers" and they represented the specific target of our research. Those 8497 loyal customers of the FA received an invitation to answer an online questionnaire. The questionnaire was designed according to the literature [73, 74], the research hypotheses and all the elements emerged from the interviews and the focus groups. It was previously tested through a preliminary pilot survey involving a sample of 40 randomly selected customers from the total loyal customers in order to observe patterns, consistency, bias-free, and representative results [75]. No significant changes to the original questionnaire were made after this preliminary test.

The questionnaire was made up of 48 close-ended questions (simple factual questions, rating scale, and checklist type questions), grouped into four major areas. 2115 valid answers were received, with a 25% return rate (only 5 responses were not valid).

3.2   Research Model and Data Analysis

Given the existing literature background and the findings from the preliminary study, we empirically tested a simple model in order to investigate community-oriented motivations and knowledge sharing as key success factor for the FA business model (see Fig. 1).

The success of the business model had been measured by the survey responses on two different aspects: the purchase frequency from the FA (shortly, Frequency), and the change in the amount of products purchased from the FA (shortly, Quantity).

The independent variables were related to knowledge sharing processes and community-oriented motivations. Knowledge sharing has been measured with three variables: online communication flows on the digital platform, on-site interactions with producer, and on-site interactions among customers. All these variables caught the customer's perception about the effectiveness of each mean of communication with a Likert scale. The other independent variable—community-oriented motivations—was constructed on three levels (low, medium, and high). Customers were requested to indicate the most significant motivation(s) (from a list of items) that determine purchases in the FA. Among the possible answers to this question, there were two community-oriented motivations. We considered a "low level" of motivation if none of these options was selected, a "medium level" if only one was selected, and a "high level" if both these motivations were selected.

The regression model, according to the existing literature, was then controlled for some socio-demographic variables (age, gender, level of education, marital status, number of children, employment, and family income level) [76–78], and some sustainability factors (recycle, local production, awareness,

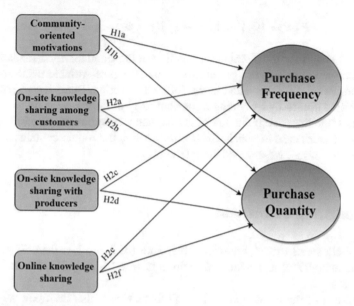

Fig. 1 The research model

label, environment protection, animal welfare, organic production, and climate change) [11, 37, 38, 41, 79].

3.3 The Regression Analysis

Formally, for each individual i in the sample of respondents, we collected the choices between $j = 1, \ldots, M$ alternatives ($M = 4$ for both *Frequency* and for *Quantity*). Since there is a logical ordering in these alternatives, a so-called ordered response model had been specified. This model is based on one underlying latent variable, say y_i^*, with a different match from y_i^* to the observed variable y_i ($i = 1, \ldots, N$); i.e.,

$$y_i^* = x_i^T \beta + \varepsilon_i, \quad y_i = j \;\; if \;\; \gamma_{j-1} < y_i^* \le \gamma_j,$$

for unknown "*cut points*" γ_j s with $\gamma_0 = -\infty$ and $\gamma_{M+1} = \infty$. Precisely, the research question here is whether it is reasonable to assume the existence of a single index $x_i^T \beta$ such that higher values for this index correspond to, on average, larger values for y_i. Assuming that ε_i is independent identically distributed (i.i.d.) standard normal (with constrained variance equal to one) results in the well-known ordered probit model. We remark that for $M = 2$ we are back at the binary probit model. As a consequence, the probability that alternative j is chosen is the probability that the latent variable y_i^* is between two boundaries γ_{j-1} and γ_j; i.e.,

$$P\{y_i = j|x_i\} = \Phi(\gamma_j - x_i^T \beta) - \Phi(\gamma_{j-1} - x_i^T \beta),$$

where $\Phi(\cdot)$ stands for the distribution function of the standard normal distribution.

We estimated one ordered probit model per response variable using maximum likelihood. Results are presented in the following section. Since the γ_j parameters can be shifted arbitrarily by adding a constant to $x_i^T \beta$, the model is under-identified if there is some linear combination of the explanatory variables, which is constant. The most obvious case in which this occurs is when the model contains a constant term: for this reason, we dropped the intercept.

4 Results and Discussions

The loyal clients of the FA are relatively young (65% are less than 50 years old), mainly female (77%) and with a bachelor's degree (47%). 57% do not have any children at all.

The results of the regression analysis (Table 1) show that the frequency of purchases significantly increases with customer's age, employment status, income, and organic production sensibility, while the quantity significantly increases with age and income. On the other hand, there is no statistical evidence of gender, education, marital status, and number of children effects on the two dependent variables.

Knowledge sharing between customers and with producers during the product distribution at the weekly market was found to be statistically significant in the regression model only for purchase frequency but not for purchase quantity. While online knowledge sharing affects both frequency and quantity of purchases within the FA.

Community-oriented motivations appear to be significantly related to purchase frequency while no statistical relationship emerged regarding the dependent variable quantity.

To summarize, besides the control variables, all the four key independent variables (community-oriented motivation, on-site knowledge sharing both among customers and with producers and online knowledge sharing) affect positively purchase frequency, whereas only online knowledge sharing is statistically significant for purchase quantity.

As in the binary probit model, the assumption of normality is crucial here for consistency of the estimators as well as the interpretation of the parameter estimates. A Chi-squared asymptotically distributed test for normality had been carried out within the Lagrange multiplier framework. The statistics in Table 1 do not lead to rejection of the model with individual characteristics.

A way to evaluate the goodness-of-fit of models consists of comparing correct and incorrect predictions. The overall proportion of correct predictions could be considered quite satisfactory for both the models, even though it is clearly much higher for the quantity (71%).

Table 1 Ordered probit regression results (***p < 0.001, **p < 0.01, *p < 0.05)

	Frequency	Quantity
Age	**0.11*** (0.03)**	**0.08* (0.04)**
Gender	−0.04 (0.06)	0.02 (0.06)
Education	−0.05 (0.04)	−0.03 (0.04)
Marital_status	0.08 (0.06)	0.04 (0.07)
Children	0.01 (0.03)	−0.00 (0.03)
Employment	**0.08** (0.03)**	−0.04 (0.03)
Income	**0.09** (0.03)**	**0.08* (0.04)**
Recycle	−0.02 (0.04)	−0.06 (0.04)
Local production	0.03 (0.04)	0.03 (0.05)
Awareness	0.05 (0.04)	−0.02 (0.05)
Label	0.01 (0.05)	0.10 (0.05)
Environmental protection	−0.05 (0.05)	−0.03 (0.06)
Animal welfare	0.06 (0.04)	0.02 (0.05)
Organic production	**0.11** (0.04)**	−0.02 (0.05)
Climate	−0.04 (0.04)	−0.01 (0.04)
Knowledge sharing among customers	**0.10*** (0.03)**	0.03 (0.03)
Knowledge sharing with producers	**0.19*** (0.04)**	0.05 (0.05)
Community-oriented motivations	**0.10* (0.04)**	0.05 (0.04)
Online knowledge sharing	**0.15** (0.05)**	**0.14** (0.05)**
Log Likelihood	−2812.60	−1667.53
Deviance	5625.20	3335.07
Normality test (22)	0.36	1.51
Number of cases "correctly predicted"	777 (36.8%)	1495 (70.7%)

The results of the regression analysis show that knowledge sharing through online and on-site interactions and community-oriented motivations affect the success of FA business model, especially in terms of customers' purchase frequency within the network. The higher is the level of knowledge sharing and the declared community-oriented attitude, the higher is the success of the business model, mainly in terms of higher purchase frequency. Table 2 contains results with reference to research hypotheses.

Our findings help to provide evidence that online knowledge sharing plays an important role, confirming that virtual interactions can have a practical impact, triggering physical relationships as well [36, 62]. Customer involvement on digital platforms—the main factor differentiating FA business model from the other more traditional AFNs—can therefore be considered a catalyst for more sustainable behaviour models.

Table 2 Synthesis of results with reference to research hypotheses

Hypothesis	Results
H1a (COM → PF)	Supported
H1b (COM → PQ)	Not supported
H2a (CKS → PF)	Supported
H2b (CKS → PQ	Not supported
H2c (PKS → PF)	Supported
H2d (PKS → PQ)	Not supported
H2e (OKS → PF)	Supported
H2f (OKS → PQ)	Supported

On the other hand, the success of the business model does not depend simply on the existence of a digital technical infrastructure; it also requires an effective mixture of online and on-site elements. As pointed out before, the co-existence of interactions through both online and on-site channels enable, within a FA, communication and coordination across a network of actors [2, 62] who otherwise would be separated and unable to contribute to system. These results have some similarities with the "ROPO" phenomenon already mentioned in the literature review [63–65].

Community-oriented motivations, already investigated in both quantitative and qualitative previous studies [11, 38, 41], are found to affect the purchase frequency. Customers show a higher sense of social commitment and this is reflected by an increased frequency in purchasing food from the FA. Probably, strong community-oriented motivations reinforce and increase knowledge sharing practices even if this relationship has not been tested within our model.

Regarding socio-demographic variables, income, and age are the only two that are significant for both purchase frequency and quantity. In the first case the relation is quite obvious and widely confirmed in the previous literature [76, 77]. Consumers with higher levels of income consume more from the FA in terms of both frequency and quantity. With respect to the age, the results suggest that older people purchase greater quantity and with higher frequency. Probably, if they feel themselves comfortable within the FA community, they will increase purchases (in terms of both quantity and frequency), consolidating their practices within that network. Employment level affects positively the success of the FA as well, but only in terms of purchase frequency.

Since AFNs aim to connect people who care about health, environment, and other sensitive issues [79], the model was also controlled by a list of eight sustainability factors. Among them, only organic production shows significance, while the other ones seem to not affect the two dependent variables (quantity and frequency). Reasonably, customers with a higher sensibility to these topics get more involved and participate more actively in the value sharing and knowledge creation processes that led to the success of the model [2, 13].

5 Conclusions, Limitations and Further Developments

This study aims to investigate, with a regression analysis, the relationship between some independent variables—community-oriented motivations and online and on-site knowledge sharing (among customers and with producers)—and the success of an AFN business model in terms of purchase frequency and quantity. To do so we recruited customers of the Italian FA customers as a sample and then we administered a questionnaire to them. According to the results, community-oriented motivations and knowledge sharing within the FA can be considered as drivers of success, especially with regards to the frequency of purchases. We demonstrate that higher level of community-oriented perception among customers as well as knowledge sharing led clearly to higher level of success of the FA business model. Moreover, we show also the effect of some additional factors such as age, income, employment on the performance of the FA in terms of purchasing quantities and frequencies.

These evidences can be useful not only to investigate deeper the success factors for the development of FA business model, but also for practitioner and FA managers in order to help them to highlight the drivers that could be useful to improve the performance and the growth of the FA itself.

This study has some limitations, since the dependent variables—purchase quantity and frequency—are based on customers' perception and they do not refer to the effective number of transactions. At the same time, the success of an AFN depends on several factors that reach beyond those related to customers' purchases.

As mentioned before, FAs are recently emerging initiatives, and further studies need to be carried out to deeply investigate both the customer and producer sides, especially with regard to the consequences resulting from the existence of a digital platform. Further research, for instance, could be conducted to understand which institutional pressures [80] hinder farmers' participation in FAs and what is the digital literacy degree [81] of those already involved in a FA.

References

1. Carzedda, M., Marangon, F., Nassivera, F., & Troiano, S. (2018). Consumer satisfaction in alternative food networks (AFNs): Evidence from Northern Italy. *Journal of Rural Studies, 64,* 73–79. https://doi.org/10.1016/j.jrurstud.2018.10.003.
2. De Bernardi, P., & Tirabeni, L. (2018). Alternative food networks: Sustainable business models for anti-consumption food cultures. *British Food Journal, 120,* 1776–1791. https://doi.org/10.1108/BFJ-12-2017-0731.
3. Hinrichs, C. C. (2000). Embeddedness and local food systems: Notes on two types of direct agricultural market. *Journal of Rural Studies, 16*(3), 295–303. https://doi.org/10.1016/S0743-0167(99)00063-7.
4. Ilbery, B., & Maye, D. (2005). Food supply chains and sustainability: Evidence from specialist food producers in the Scottish/English borders. *Land Use Policy, 22*(4), 331–344. https://doi.org/10.1016/j.landusepol.2004.06.002.

5. Corsi, A., Barbera, F., Dansero, E., & Peano, C. (2018). Introduction. In: A. Corsi, F. Barbera, E. Dansero, C. Peano (Eds.), *Alternative food networks* (pp. 57–86). Cham: Palgrave Macmillan. https://doi.org/10.1007/978-3-319-90409-2_1.

6. Murdoch, J., Marsden, T., & Banks, J. (2000). Quality, nature, and embeddedness: Some theoretical considerations in the context of the food sector. *Economic Geography, 76*(2), 107–125. https://doi.org/10.1111/j.1944-8287.2000.tb00136.x.

7. Charatsari, C., Kitsios, F., Stafyla, A., Aidonis, D., & Lioutas, E. (2018). Antecedents of farmers' willingness to participate in short food supply chains. *British Food Journal, 120*(10), 2317–2333. https://doi.org/10.1108/BFJ-09-2017-0537.

8. Holloway, L., & Kneafsey, M. (2000). Reading the Space of the framers' market: A case study from the United Kingdom. *Sociol Rural, 40,* 285–299. https://doi.org/10.1111/1467-9523.00149.

9. Tregear, A. (2011). Progressing knowledge in alternative and local food networks: Critical reflections and a research agenda. *Journal of Rural Studies, 27*(4), 419–430. https://doi.org/10.1016/j.jrurstud.2011.06.003.

10. Venn, L., Kneafsey, M., Holloway, L., Cox, R., Dowler, E., & Tuomainen, H. (2006). Researching European "alternative" food networks: Some methodological considerations. *Area, 38,* 248–258. https://doi.org/10.1111/j.1475-4762.2006.00694.x.

11. Zoll, F., Specht, K., Opitz, I., Siebert, R., Piorr, A., & Zasada, I. (2018). Individual choice or collective action? Exploring consumer motives for participating in alternative food networks. *International Journal of Consumer Studies, 42*(1), 101–110. https://doi.org/10.1111/ijcs.12405.

12. Rodrigo, R. E., Peña-López, I., Vega, N. (2017). Plataformas digitales: Grupos y cooperativas de consumo versus La Colmena que dice sí, el caso de Barcelona. *Revista de Estudios para el Desarrollo Social de la Comunicación, 144–174.* https://doi.org/10.15213/redes.n15.p145.

13. Lyson, T. A. (2005). Civic agriculture and community problem solving. *Culture & Agriculture, 27*(2), 63–79. https://doi.org/10.1525/cag.2005.27.2.92.

14. Renting, H., Schermer, M., & Rossi, A. (2012). Building food democracy: Exploring civic food networks and newly emerging forms of food citizenship. *The International Journal of Sociology of Agriculture and Food, 19*(3), 289–307.

15. Allen, J. E., Rossi, J., Woods, T. A., & Davis, A. F. (2017). Do Community Supported Agriculture programmes encourage change to food lifestyle behaviours and health outcomes? New evidence from shareholders. *International Journal of Agricultural Sustainability, 15*(1), 70–82. https://doi.org/10.1080/14735903.2016.1177866.

16. Brown, C., & Miller, S. (2008). The impacts of local markets: A review of research on farmers markets and community supported agriculture (CSA). *American Journal of Agricultural Economics, 90*(5), 1298–1302. https://doi.org/10.1111/j.1467-8276.2008.01220.x.

17. Bosona, T., Gebresenbet, G., Nordmark, I., & Ljungberg, D. (2011). Box-scheme based delivery system of locally produced organic food: Evaluation of logistics performance. *Journal of Service Science and Management, 4,* 357–367. https://doi.org/10.4236/jssm.2011.43042.

18. Hertz, F. D., & Halkier, B. (2017). Meal box schemes a convenient way to avoid convenience food? Uses and understandings of meal box schemes among Danish consumers. *Appetite, 114,* 232–239. https://doi.org/10.1016/j.appet.2017.03.016.

19. Lieff, S. A., Bangia, D., Baronberg, S., Burlett, A., & Chiasson, M. A. (2017). Evaluation of an educational initiative to promote shopping at Farmers' markets among the special supplemental nutrition program for women, infants, and children (WIC) participants in New York City. *Journal of Community Health, 42*(4), 701–706. https://doi.org/10.1007/s10900-016-0306-3.

20. Brunori, G., Rossi, A., Guidi, F. (2012). On the new social relations around and beyond food. Analysing consumers' role and action in Gruppi di Acquisto Solidale (Solidarity Purchasing Groups). *Sociol Ruralis, 52*(1), 1–30. https://doi.org/10.1111/j.1467-9523.2011.00552.x.

21. Migliore, G., Forno, F., Dara Guccione, G., & Schifani, G. (2014). Food community network as sustainable self-organized collective action: A case study of a solidarity purchasing group. *New Medit, 13*(4), 54–62.

22. Fonte, M., & Cucco, I. (2017). Cooperatives and alternative food networks in Italy. The long road towards a social economy in agriculture. *Journal of Rural Studies, 53,* 291–302. https://doi.org/10.1016/j.jrurstud.2017.01.019.

23. Evans, A. E., Jennings, R., Smiley, A. W., Medina, J. L., Sharma, S. V., Rutledge, R., et al. (2012). Introduction of farm stands in low-income communities increases fruit and vegetable among community residents. *Health Place, 18*(5), 1137–1143. https://doi.org/10.1016/j.healthplace.2012.04.007.

24. De Bernardi, P., Bertello, A., & Venuti, F. (2019). Online and On-Site Interactions within Alternative Food Networks: Sustainability Impact of Knowledge-Sharing Practices. *Sustainability, 11*(5), 1457. https://doi.org/10.3390/su11051457.

25. Morgan, K. (2015). Nourishing the city: The rise of the urban food question in the Global North. *Urban Studies, 52*(8), 1379–1394. https://doi.org/10.1177/0042098014534902.

26. Feola, G., & Butt, A. (2017). The diffusion of grassroots innovations for sustainability in Italy and Great Britain: an exploratory spatial data analysis. *Geographical Journal, 183*(1), 16–33. https://doi.org/10.1111/geoj.12153.

27. Migliore, G., Schifani, G., & Cembalo, L. (2015). Opening the black box of food quality in the short supply chain: Effects of conventions of quality on consumer choice. *Food Quality and Preference, 39,* 141–146. https://doi.org/10.1016/j.foodqual.2014.07.006.

28. Follett, J. R. (2009). Choosing a food future: Differentiating among alternative food options. *Journal of Agricultural and Environmental Ethics, 22*(1), 31–51. https://doi.org/10.1007/s10806-008-9125-6.

29. Sonnino, R., & Marsden, T. (2005). Beyond the divide: rethinking relationships between alternative and conventional food networks in Europe. *Economic Geography, 6*(2), 181–199.

30. Blay-Palmer, A., Landman, K., Knezevic, I., & Hayhurst, R. (2013). Constructing resilient, transformative communities through sustainable "food hubs". *Iternational Journal of Justice and Sustainability, 18*(5), 521–528. https://doi.org/10.1080/13549839.2013.797156.

31. King, C. A. (2008). Community resilience and contemporary agriecological systems: Reconnecting people and food, and people with people. *Systems Research and Behavioral Science, 25*(1), 111–124. https://doi.org/10.1002/sres.854.

32. Anderson, M. D. (2008). Rights-based food systems and the goals of food system reform. *Agriculture Human Values, 25*(4), 593–608. https://doi.org/10.1007/s10460-008-9151-z.

33. Goodman, D., DuPuis, E. M., & Goodman, M. K. (2012). *Alternative food networks: Knowledge, practice, and politics.* Routledge, London. https://doi.org/10.4324/9780203804520.

34. Marsden, T., Banks, J., & Bristow, G. (2002). The social management of rural nature: understanding agrarian-based rural development. *Environment and Planning A, 34*(5), 809–825. https://doi.org/10.1068/a3427.

35. Miralles, I., Dentoni, D., & Pascucci, S. (2017). Understanding the organization of sharing economy in agri-food systems: Evidence from alternative food networks in Valencia. *Agriculture Human Values, 34*(4), 833–854. https://doi.org/10.1007/s10460-017-9778-8.

36. Bos, E., & Owen, L. (2016). Virtual reconnection: The online spaces of alternative food networks in England. *J Rural Stud, 45,* 1–14. https://doi.org/10.1016/j.jrurstud.2016.02.016.

37. Brehm, J. M., & Eisenhauer, B. W. (2008). Motivations for participating in community-supported agriculture and their relationship with community attachment and social capital. *Southern Rural Sociological, 23*(1), 94–115.

38. Corsi, A., & Novelli, S. (2018). Determinants of participation in AFNs and its value for consumers. In: A. Corsi, F. Barbera, E. Dansero, & C. Peano, (Eds.), *Alternative Food Networks.* Cham: Palgrave Macmillan, pp. 57–86. https://doi.org/10.1007/978-3-319-90409-2_4.

39. Cox, R., Holloway, L., Venn, L., Dowler, L., Hein, J. R., Kneafsey, M., et al. (2008). Common ground? Motivations for participation in a community-supported agriculture scheme. *Local Environment, 13*(3), 203–218. https://doi.org/10.1080/13549830701669153.

40. Pascucci, S., Dentoni, D., Lombardi, A., & Cembalo, L. (2016). Sharing values or sharing costs? Understanding consumer participation in alternative food networks. *Njas-Wageningen Journal of Life Sciences Impact, 78,* 47–60. https://doi.org/10.1016/j.njas.2016.03.006.

41. Kneafsey, A. M., Venn, L., Schmutz, U., Balázs, B., Trenchard, L., Eyden-Wood, T., Sutton, G., Blackett, M., Santini, E. F., & Gomez, S. (2013). Short food supply chains and local food systems in the EU. A state of play of their socio-economic characteristics; EUR—Scientific and Technical Research Series. Publications Office of the European Union, Luxembourg.
42. Blay-Palmer, A., Santini, G., Dubbeling, M., Renting, H., Taguchi, M., & Giordano, T. (2018). Validating the city region food system approach: enacting inclusive, transformational city region food systems. *Sustainability, 10*(1680). https://doi.org/10.3390/su10051680.
43. Putnam, R. D. (1995). Tuning in, tuning out: The strange disappearance of social capital in America. *PS, Political Science & Politics, 28,* 664–683. https://doi.org/10.2307/420517.
44. Putnam, R. D. (1995). Bowling alone: America's declining social capital. *Journal of Democracy, 6*(1), 65–78. https://doi.org/10.1353/jod.1995.0002.
45. Nahapiet, J., & Ghoshal, S. (1998). Social capital, intellectual capital, and the organizational advantage. *Academy of Management Review, 23,* 242–266. https://doi.org/10.2307/259373.
46. Chow, W. S., & Chan, L. S. (2008). Social network, social trust and shared goals in organizational knowledge sharing. *Information and Management, 45*(7), 458–465.
47. Cheng, J., Yeh, C., & Tu, C. (2008). Trust and knowledge sharing in green supply chains. *Supply Chain Manag Journal, 13,* 283–295. https://doi.org/10.1108/13598540810882170.
48. Coleman, J. S. (1988). Social capital in the creation of human capital. *American Journal of Sociology, 94,* S95–S120. https://doi.org/10.1086/228943.
49. Hau, Y. S., Kim, B., Lee, H., & Kim, Y. G. (2013). The effects of individual motivations and social capital on employees' tacit and explicit knowledge sharing intentions. *International Journal of Information Management, 33,* 356–366. https://doi.org/10.1016/j.ijinfomgt.2012.10.009.
50. Besser, T. L., & Miller, N. (2011). The structural, social, and strategic factors associated with successful business networks. *Entrepreneurship and Regional Development, 23*(3–4), 113–133.
51. Jarratt, D., & Ceric, A. (2015). The complexity of trust in business collaborations. *Australasian Marketing Journal (AMJ), 23*(1), 2–12.
52. McKitterick, L., Quinn, B., & Tregear, A. (2018). Trust formation in agri-food institutional support networks. *Journal of Rural Studies, 65,* 53–64. https://doi.org/10.1016/j.jrurstud.2018.11.008.
53. Newbery, R., Gorton, M., Phillipson, J., & Atterton, J. (2016). Sustaining business networks: Understanding the benefit bundles sought by members of local business associations. *Environment and Planning C Government and Policy, 34*(7), 1267–1283.
54. Sökjer-Petersen, M. (2010). The role of Grassroot Leaders in building Networks and organizing Learning Groups. *Nordic Psychology, 62*(1), 4–23. https://doi.org/10.1027/1901-2276/a000002.
55. Chiu, C. M., Hsu, M. H., & Wang, E. T. G. (2006). Understanding knowledge sharing in virtual communities: An integration of social capital and social cognitive theories. *Decision Support Systems, 42,* 1872–1888. https://doi.org/10.1016/j.dss.2006.04.001.
56. Bollinger, A. S., & Smith, R. D. (2001). Managing organizational knowledge as a strategic asset. *Journal of Knowledge Management, 5*(1), 8–18. https://doi.org/10.1108/13673270110384365.
57. Civi, E. (2000). Knowledge management as a competitive asset: A review. *Marketing Intelligence & Planning, 18*(4), 166–174. https://doi.org/10.1108/02634500010333280.
58. Loebbecke, C., van Fenema, P. C., Powell, P., & Managing, (2016). Inter-organizational Knowledge Sharing. *The Journal of Strategic Information Systems, 25,* 4–14. https://doi.org/10.1016/j.jsis.2015.12.002.
59. Meso, P., & Smith, R. (2000). A resource-based view of organizational knowledge management systems. *Journal of Knowledge Management, 4,* 224–234. https://doi.org/10.1108/13673270010350020.
60. Inkpen, A. C., & Tsang, E. W. (2005). Social capital, networks, and knowledge transfer. *Academy of Management Review, 30*(1), 146–165. https://doi.org/10.2307/20159100.
61. Beckie, M. A., Kennedy, E. H., & Wittman, H. (2012). Scaling up alternative food networks: Farmers' markets and the role of clustering in western Canada. *Agriculture and Human Values, 29*(3), 333–345. https://doi.org/10.1007/s10460-012-9359-9.

62. The Food Assembly Team. (2017). Reinventing local food supply in connected cities: The example of The Food Assembly. *Field Actions Science Reports, 16,* 44–49.

63. Bell, D. R., Gallino, S., & Moreno, A. (2014). How to win in an omnichannel world. *MIT SMR, 56,* 45–53.

64. Brynjolfsson, E., Yu, J. H., & Rahman, M. S. (2013). Competing in the age of omnichannel re-tailing. *MIT SMR, 54,* 23–29.

65. Manser Payne, E., Peltier, J. W., & Barger, V. A. (2017). Omni-channel marketing, integrated marketing communications and consumer engagement: A research agenda. *Journal of Research in Interactive Marketing, 11,* 185–197. https://doi.org/10.1108/JRIM-08-2016-0091.

66. van Dijk, G., Minocha, S., & Laing, A. (2007). Consumers, channels and communication: Online and offline communication in service consumption. *Interacting with Computers, 19,* 7–19. https://doi.org/10.1016/j.intcom.2006.07.007.

67. Benkler, Y. (2006). *The wealth of networks: How social production transforms markets and freedom.* New Haven: Yale University Press.

68. Kostakis, V., Latoufis, K., Liarokapis, M., & Bauwens, M. (2018). The convergence of digital commons with local manufacturing from a degrowth perspective: Two illustrative cases. *Journal of Cleaner Production, 197,* 1684–1693. https://doi.org/10.1016/j.jclepro.2016.09.077.

69. Randelli, F., & Rocchi, B. (2017). Analysing the role of consumers within technological innovation systems: The case of alternative food networks. *Environmental Innovation and Societal Transitions, 25,* 94–106. https://doi.org/10.1016/j.eist.2017.01.001.

70. Goldman, A. E. (1962). The group depth interview. *Journal of marketing, 26,* 61–68. https://doi.org/10.2307/1248305.

71. Carey, M. A., & Smith, M. W. (1994). Capturing the group effect in focus groups: A special concern in analysis. *Qualitative Health Research, 4*(1), 123–127. https://doi.org/10.1177/104973239400400108.

72. Morgan, D. L., & Kreuger, R. A. (1993). When to use focus groups and why. In: D. L. Morgan (Ed.), *Sage focus editions. Successful focus groups: Advancing the state of the art* (vol. 156, pp 3–19). Thousand Oaks: Sage Publications. https://doi.org/10.4135/9781483349008.n1.

73. Aiken, L. (1996). *Rating scales and checklists: Evaluating behavior, personality, and attitudes.* New York: Wiley.

74. Aldridge, A., & Levine, K. (2001). *Surveying the social world: Principles and practice in survey research.* Buckingham, Philadelphia.

75. Rea, L. M., & Parker, R. A. (2014). *Designing and conducting survey research: A comprehensive guide.* Hoboken: Wiley.

76. Brown, E., Dury, S., & Holdsworth, M. (2009). Motivations of consumers that use local, organic fruit and vegetable box schemes in Central England and Southern France. *Appetite, 53*(2), 183–188. https://doi.org/10.1016/j.appet.2009.06.006.

77. Nie, C., & Zepeda, L. (2011). Lifestyle segmentation of US food shoppers to examine organic and local food consumption. *Appetite, 57*(1), 28–37. https://doi.org/10.1016/j.appet.2011.03.012.

78. Vasquez, A., Sherwood, N. E., Larson, N., & Story, M. (2017). Community-supported agriculture as a dietary and health improvement strategy: A narrative review. *Journal of the Academy of Nutrition and Dietetics, 117*(1), 83–94. https://doi.org/10.1016/j.jand.2016.09.029.

79. Tecco, N., & Peano, C. (2018). The environmental quality factors sought by consumers in alternative and conventional market channels. In: A. Corsi, F. Barbera, E., Dansero, C., Peano (Eds.), *Alternative Food Networks,* (pp 119–136). Palgrave Macmillan, Cham. https://doi.org/10.1007/978-3-319-90409-2_6.

80. De Bernardi, P., Bertello, A., & Shams, S. M. R. (2019). Logics hindering digital transformation in cultural heritage strategic management: Evidence from Turin museums. *Tourism Anal, 24.*

81. Alkali, Y. E., & Amichai-Hamburger, Y. (2004). Experiments in digital literacy. *Cyberpsychology Behavior, 7*(4), 421–429. https://doi.org/10.1089/cpb.2004.7.421.

Author Index

A

Agrifoglio, Rocco, 33
Amantea, Ilaria Angela, 211, 223
Antonelli, Gilda, 101
Arabikhan, Farzad, 407
Asmar, Michele Kosremelli, 195

B

Badr, Nabil Georges, 195
Bednar, Peter, 25, 407
Bellini, Francesco, 315
Berretti, Alberto, 329
Bertello, Alberto, 443
Bissessur, Jason, 407
Braccini, Alessio Maria, 85, 417
Briganti, Paola, 47

C

Cabiddu, F., 393
Cabitza, Federico, 273
Caporarello, Leonardo, 135, 179
Castelnovo, Walter, 379
Ciccarone, Simone, 329
Cuel, Roberta, 365

D

D'Ascenzo, Fabrizio, 315
De Angelis, Massimo, 67
De Bernardi, Paola, 443
Decastri, Maurizio, 343
De Lellis, Angela, 211
Dessì, C., 393
Di Lauro, Stefano, 101
Di Leva, Antonio, 211, 223
Dulskaia, Iana, 315

F

Floris, M., 393

G

Gagliarducci, Francesca, 343
Gatti, Mauro, 121
Gewald, Heiko, 237
Ghiringhelli, Cristiano, 429
Giacomelli, Desiree, 121
Grisot, Miria, 289
Guerrazzi, Emanuele, 251

H

Haug, Maximilian, 237

I

Iannotta, Michela, 121
Islind, Anna Sigridur, 289

J

Jones, Jonathan, 25

L

Lardo, Alessandra, 67
Lazazzara, Alessandra, 1, 151
Leon, Ramona-Diana, 11
Lindroth, Tomas, 289
Locoro, Angela, 261, 273

M

Mancini, Daniela, 67
Manzoni, Beatrice, 135, 179
Margherita, Emanuele Gabriel, 417
Martinez, Marcello, 101, 261
Mele, Stefania, 47

© Springer Nature Switzerland AG 2020
A. Lazazzara et al. (eds.), *Exploring Digital Ecosystems*,
Lecture Notes in Information Systems and Organisation 33,
https://doi.org/10.1007/978-3-030-23665-6

459

Menichelli, Michael, 85
Meret, Chiara, 121
Metallo, Concetta, 33
Moscardo, Chiara, 135

N
Nacamulli, Raoul C. D., 151

P
Pallud, Jessie, 33
Pirani, Elena, 165
Ponte, Diego, 365
Previtali, Pietro, 343

R
Ravarini, Aurelio, 261, 273
Ricciardi, Francesca, 1
Romanelli, Mauro, 11

S
Sarti, Daria, 165

Savastano, Marco, 315
Scarozza, Danila, 343
Sirolli, Ida, 121
Sulis, Emilio, 211, 223
Sultana, Tunazzina, 301

T
Torre, Edoardo Della, 151
Torre, Teresina, 165
Trabelsi, Lilach, 135, 179
Tursunbayeva, Aizhan, 101

V
Varriale, Luisa, 47
Venuti, Francesco, 443
Virili, Francesco, 429

Z
Za, Stefano, 1, 33, 429